Citizen E-Participation in Urban Governance:

Crowdsourcing and Collaborative Creativity

Carlos Nunes Silva
University of Lisbon, Portugal

A volume in the Advances in Electronic Government, Digital Divide, and Regional Development (AEGDDRD) Book Series

Managing Director:	Lindsay Johnston
Editorial Director:	Joel Gamon
Production Manager:	Jennifer Yoder
Publishing Systems Analyst:	Adrienne Freeland
Development Editor:	Myla Merkel
Assistant Acquisitions Editor:	Kayla Wolfe
Typesetter:	Lisandro Gonzalez
Cover Design:	Jason Mull

Published in the United States of America by
Information Science Reference (an imprint of IGI Global)
701 E. Chocolate Avenue
Hershey PA 17033
Tel: 717-533-8845
Fax: 717-533-8661
E-mail: cust@igi-global.com
Web site: http://www.igi-global.com

Library of Congress Cataloging-in-Publication Data

Citizen e-participation in urban governance : crowdsourcing and collaborative creativity / Carlos Nunes Silva, editor.
  pages cm
 Includes bibliographical references and index.
 Summary: "This book explores the nature of the new challenges confronting citizens and local governments in the field of urban governance, exploring the role that Web 2.0 technologies play to promote citizen participation and empowerment in the city government"--Provided by publisher.
  ISBN 978-1-4666-4169-3 (hardcover) -- ISBN 978-1-4666-4170-9 (ebook) -- ISBN 978-1-4666-4171-6 (print & perpetual access) 1. Internet in public administration. 2. Local government--Citizen participation. 3. Human computation. I. Silva, Carlos Nunes.
 JF1525.A8C56 2013
 351.0285'4678--dc23
                          2013009583

This book is published in the IGI Global book series Advances in Electronic Government, Digital Divide, and Regional Development (AEGDDRD) (ISSN: 2326-9103; eISSN: 2326-9111)

British Cataloguing in Publication Data
A Cataloguing in Publication record for this book is available from the British Library.

All work contributed to this book is new, previously-unpublished material. The views expressed in this book are those of the authors, but not necessarily of the publisher.

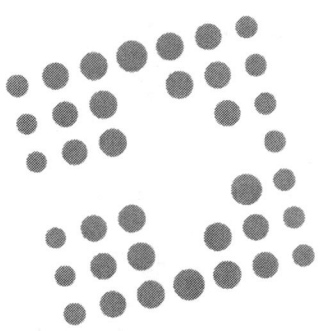

Advances in Electronic Government, Digital Divide, and Regional Development (AEGDDRD) Book Series

Zaigham Mahmood
University of Derby, UK & North West University, South Africa

ISSN: 2326-9103
EISSN: 2326-9111

MISSION

The successful use of digital technologies (including social media and mobile technologies) to provide public services and foster economic development has become an objective for governments around the world. The development towards electronic government (or e-government) not only affects the efficiency and effectiveness of public services, but also has the potential to transform the nature of government interactions with its citizens. Current research and practice on the adoption of electronic/digital government and the implementation in organizations around the world aims to emphasize the extensiveness of this growing field.

The **Advances in Electronic Government, Digital Divide & Regional Development (AEGDDRD)** book series aims to publish authored, edited and case books encompassing the current and innovative research and practice discussing all aspects of electronic government development, implementation and adoption as well the effective use of the emerging technologies (including social media and mobile technologies) for a more effective electronic governance (or e-governance).

COVERAGE

- Digital Democracy
- E-Citizenship
- Electronic & Digital Government
- ICT Adoption in Developing Countries
- ICT within Government & Public Sectors
- Knowledge Divide
- Public Information Management
- Regional Planning
- Urban & Rural Development
- Web 2.0 in Government

IGI Global is currently accepting manuscripts for publication within this series. To submit a proposal for a volume in this series, please contact our Acquisition Editors at Acquisitions@igi-global.com or visit: http://www.igi-global.com/publish/.

Titles in this Series

For a list of additional titles in this series, please visit: www.igi-global.com

Developing E-Government Projects Frameworks and Methodologies
Zaigham Mahmood (University of Derby, UK & North West University, South Africa)
Information Science Reference • copyright 2013 • 346pp • H/C (ISBN: 9781466642454) • US $180.00 (our price)

Citizen E-Participation in Urban Governance Crowdsourcing and Collaborative Creativity
Carlos Nunes Silva (University of Lisbon, Portugal)
Information Science Reference • copyright 2013 • 353pp • H/C (ISBN: 9781466641693) • US $180.00 (our price)

E-Government Success around the World Cases, Empirical Studies, and Practical Recommendations
J. Ramon Gil-Garcia (Centro de Investigación y Docencia Económicas (CIDE), Mexico)
Information Science Reference • copyright 2013 • 467pp • H/C (ISBN: 9781466641730) • US $180.00 (our price)

E-Government Success Factors and Measures Theories, Concepts, and Methodologies
J. Ramon Gil-Garcia (Centro de Investigación y Docencia Económicas (CIDE), Mexico)
Information Science Reference • copyright 2013 • 352pp • H/C (ISBN: 9781466640580) • US $180.00 (our price)

E-Government Implementation and Practice in Developing Countries
Zaigham Mahmood (University of Derby, UK & North West University, South Africa)
Information Science Reference • copyright 2013 • 348pp • H/C (ISBN: 9781466640900) • US $180.00 (our price)

Global Sustainable Development and Renewable Energy Systems
Phillip Olla (Madonna University, USA)
Information Science Reference • copyright 2012 • 354pp • H/C (ISBN: 9781466616257) • US $180.00 (our price)

City Competitiveness and Improving Urban Subsystems Technologies and Applications
Melih Bulu (Istanbul Sehir University, Turkey)
Information Science Reference • copyright 2012 • 322pp • H/C (ISBN: 9781613501740) • US $180.00 (our price)

International Exploration of Technology Equity and the Digital Divide Critical, Historical and Social Perspectives
Patricia Randolph Leigh (Iowa State University, USA)
Information Science Reference • copyright 2011 • 254pp • H/C (ISBN: 9781615207930) • US $180.00 (our price)

Regional Innovation Systems and Sustainable Development Emerging Technologies
Patricia Ordóñez de Pablos (Universidad de Oviedo, Spain) W.B. Lee (Polytechnic University of Hong Kong) and Jingyuan Zhao (Harbin Institute of Technology, China)
Information Science Reference • copyright 2011 • 276pp • H/C (ISBN: 9781616928469) • US $180.00 (our price)

www.igi-global.com

701 E. Chocolate Ave., Hershey, PA 17033
Order online at www.igi-global.com or call 717-533-8845 x100
To place a standing order for titles released in this series, contact: cust@igi-global.com
Mon-Fri 8:00 am - 5:00 pm (est) or fax 24 hours a day 717-533-8661

Table of Contents

Preface xvi

Acknowledgment xx

Section 1
Basic Concepts and Key Issues

Chapter 1
Open Source Urban Governance: Crowdsourcing, Neogeography, VGI, and Citizen Science.............. 1
    Carlos Nunes Silva, University of Lisbon, Portugal

Chapter 2
E-Democracy Systems and Participation Outcomes in Urban Governance 19
    Rajeev Sharma, University of Wollongong, Australia
    Atreyi Kankanhalli, National University of Singapore, Singapore
    Mahdieh Taher, National University of Singapore, Singapore

Chapter 3
Public Participation, Social Equity, and Technology in Urban Governance 35
    Thomas W. Sanchez, Virginia Tech, USA
    Marc Brenman, Social Justice Consultancy, USA

Section 2
Mass Collaboration in Urban Governance

Chapter 4
The Four Urban Governance Problem Types Suitable for Crowdsourcing Citizen Participation 50
    Daren C. Brabham, University of North Carolina at Chapel Hill, USA

Chapter 5
Web 2.0, Neogeography, and Urban E-Governance 69
    Barney Warf, University of Kansas, USA

Chapter 6

Tracking Public Participation in Urban Governance: Democracy and Data Privacy 80
        Nancy J. Obermeyer, Indiana State University, USA

Chapter 7

Volunteered Geographic Information for Disaster Management 98
        Doris Dransch, GFZ German Research Centre for Geosciences, Germany
        Kathrin Poser, Water Insight BV, The Netherlands
        Joachim Fohringer, GFZ German Research Centre for Geosciences, Germany
        Christian Lucas, Karlsruhe Institute of Technology (KIT), Germany

Chapter 8

Urban Geo-Wiki: A Crowdsourcing Tool to Improve Urban Land Cover.. 119
        Linda See, International Institute for Applied Systems Analysis (IIASA), Austria
        Steffen Fritz, International Institute for Applied Systems Analysis (IIASA), Austria
        Christoph Perger, International Institute for Applied Systems Analysis (IIASA), Austria
        Marijn Van der Velde, International Institute for Applied Systems Analysis (IIASA), Austria
        Franziska Albrecht, International Institute for Applied Systems Analysis (IIASA), Austria
        Ian McCallum, International Institute for Applied Systems Analysis (IIASA), Austria
        Dmitry Schepaschenko, International Institute for Applied Systems Analysis (IIASA), Austria
        Michael Obersteiner, International Institute for Applied Systems Analysis (IIASA), Austria
        Christian Schill, University of Freiburg, Germany

Chapter 9

The Geospatial Web: A Tool to Support the Empowerment of Citizens through E-Participation? 144
        Karl Atzmanstorfer, Paris-Lodron University Salzburg, Austria
        Thomas Blaschke, Paris-Lodron University Salzburg, Austria

Chapter 10

Citizen Science Perspectives on E-Participation in Urban Planning 172
        Caren Cooper, Cornell Lab of Ornithology, USA
        Ashwin Balakrishnan, Southern Bronx River Watershed Alliance, USA

**Section 3
Citizen E-Participation**

Chapter 11

Mobile Participation: Citizen Engagement in Urban Planning via Smartphones............................. 199
        Stefan Höffken, University of Technology Kaiserslautern, Germany
        Bernd Streich, University of Technology Kaiserslautern, Germany

Chapter 12

Social Media for Civic Engagement: An Exploration of Urban Governments 226
        Thomas A. Bryer, University of Central Florida, USA
        Kimberly L. Nelson, Northern Illinois University, USA

Chapter 13

E-Participation and Citizen Relationship Management in Urban Governance: Tools
and Methods.. 247
> *Jim P. Huebner, University of Waterloo, Canada*

Chapter 14

Citizen Web Empowerment across Italian Cities: A Benchmarking Approach 284
> *Elena Bellio, CERMES - Bocconi University, Italy*
> *Luca Buccoliero, CERMES - Bocconi University, Italy*

Chapter 15

Policy Gadgets for Urban Governance in the Era of Social Computing: An Italian Pilot
on Telemedicine 303
> *Enrico Ferro, Istituto Superiore Mario Boella, Italy*
> *Michele Osella, Istituto Superiore Mario Boella, Italy*
> *Yannis Charalabidis, University of the Aegean, Greece*
> *Euripides Loukis, University of the Aegean, Greece*

Compilation of References 319

About the Contributors 359

Index 368

Detailed Table of Contents ·

Preface xvi

Acknowledgment xx

Section 1
Basic Concepts and Key Issues

Chapter 1
Open Source Urban Governance: Crowdsourcing, Neogeography, VGI, and Citizen Science 1
    Carlos Nunes Silva, University of Lisbon, Portugal

The chapter explores the emerging paradigm of Open Source Urban Governance, a new urban policy model associated with the extensive use of computer-mediated communication and with the use of different modes of citizen mass collaboration – Crowdsourcing, Neogeography, Volunteered Geographic Information (VGI), and Citizen Science. The chapter is organized into five main sections. The first section discusses the concept of e-participation. The next two sections address the objectives, context, determinants, and ethical issues in e-participation, and the different levels of e-participation in each policy stage and by stakeholder. The last two sections explore the e-tools available for citizen participation in urban governance and the impacts and benefits of e-participation. The chapter ends with a reference to future research directions in this field.

Chapter 2
E-Democracy Systems and Participation Outcomes in Urban Governance 19
    Rajeev Sharma, University of Wollongong, Australia
    Atreyi Kankanhalli, National University of Singapore, Singapore
    Mahdieh Taher, National University of Singapore, Singapore

The concept of democracy has a long tradition of research in the political science domain. In recent years, advances in Information and Communication Technologies (ICT) have provided opportunities for governments to deploy systems to actively engage citizens in the agenda-setting and decision-making processes for urban governance. Consequently, e-democracy and e-participation efforts have emerged and attracted researchers' attention in the Information Systems (IS) field. Information systems lay the foundations of active citizenry, which may impact on the participation outcome. However, in order to maximize the potential of this evolving form of democracy, researchers and practitioners need to address a number of challenges in the design of participation structures for city governance. This chapter sets out to explore e-democracy systems and their impact on a number of e-participation outcomes. Outlining both promoters and barriers of ICT use for e-democracy, the authors also uncover gaps in the previous literature and identify an agenda for future research.

Chapter 3

Public Participation, Social Equity, and Technology in Urban Governance 35

Thomas W. Sanchez, Virginia Tech, USA
Marc Brenman, Social Justice Consultancy, USA

Social equity commonly refers to fairness or impartiality, usually in terms of inputs or outcomes related to social and economic opportunity. In the case of urban planning, social equity can take the form of participation in decision-making activities, especially those that involve allocating public resources. An assumption (and hope) is that through participation, stakeholders have greater influence on outcomes that are in their collective interest. Opportunities to participate are rapidly expanding along with rapid technological innovation. Therefore, the authors argue that there is a connection among participation, equity, and technology in creating more equitable governance structures. In particular, the authors discuss how information and communications technologies can serve to reduce barriers to information exchange and thereby generate stronger bonds and quicker formation of partnerships and connections within the public realm. This chapter explores these issues through the lens of e-government, e-democracy, and the digital divide in a U.S. context.

Section 2
Mass Collaboration in Urban Governance

Chapter 4

The Four Urban Governance Problem Types Suitable for Crowdsourcing Citizen Participation 50

Daren C. Brabham, University of North Carolina at Chapel Hill, USA

Crowdsourcing is a method for harnessing the collective intelligence of online communities to solve specific problems or produce goods. Largely known as a business model, crowdsourcing has begun to make inroads as a supplemental public participation tool for governance, as a way to engage citizens in the business of government functions. Validating a new typology of crowdsourcing cases, this chapter outlines the four urban governance problem types that the crowdsourcing model can successfully address. This chapter also discusses the right of free speech in online crowdsourcing communities and its relevance for urban governance crowdsourcing applications in free societies. Concluding the chapter is an examination of crowdsourcing's place in the policy-advisory spectrum and the risks associated with bringing crowdsourcing applications into public participation programs.

Chapter 5

Web 2.0, Neogeography, and Urban E-Governance 69

Barney Warf, University of Kansas, USA

Web 2.0 technologies, which allow interactions between the producers and consumers of information, have important implications for how urban spaces are designed and governed. Spatial information on the web has become increasingly wikified, so that non-planners may contribute data, photos, and opinions in a variety of ways, a process that labeled neogeography (and which is closely related to participatory GIS). For example, websites such as GoogleMaps have greatly democratized the process of constructing and using spatial data. This process implies that planners are no longer the privileged producers of information about urban space. A case study of Brión, Galicia, is offered to illustrate this process in practice. Web 2.0 and neogeography have greatly elevated the philosophical significance of planning information: rather than received wisdom, users may construct their own communities of truth. The chapter argues this process resembles Habermas's notion of an ideal speech situation. The conclusion argues that Web 2.0 and the growth of neogeography imply that planning must be more inclusive and democratic in nature.

Chapter 6

Tracking Public Participation in Urban Governance: Democracy and Data Privacy 80
Nancy J. Obermeyer, Indiana State University, USA

This chapter examines the use of GIS, geovisualization, and other geo-locational technologies and applications, including social networking websites and mobile phones associated with Web 2.0, as a tool kit for promoting democratization or leading to loss of data privacy and freedom, focusing on the relevant historical events in 2011 and the first half of 2012. The chapter begins by presenting a brief history of the GIS and society literature, including public participation GIS, volunteered geographic information, and geoslavery. The discussion covers both the rosy view (geospatial and Web 2.0 technologies as a democratizing force) and the gloomy perspective (these same technologies as tools of control based on data capture and loss of privacy). Underlying both of these views are scale and the ability to jump scales, which are examined through the lens of Kevin Cox's (1998) "spaces of dependence and engagement." Having laid this groundwork, the chapter considers events in the recent past, focusing first on the Arab Spring movements in Tunisia and Egypt and the Occupy movement in the U.S. as examples of the optimistic perspective. It then proceeds to discuss data capture from smart phones and cell phones as examples of the pessimistic view. The chapter concludes with a discussion of how individuals may enhance the democratization potential of geotechnologies and Web 2.0 while minimizing data capture, loss of spatial data privacy, and the harm that these can bring.

Chapter 7

Volunteered Geographic Information for Disaster Management 98
Doris Dransch, GFZ German Research Centre for Geosciences, Germany
Kathrin Poser, Water Insight BV, The Netherlands
Joachim Fohringer, GFZ German Research Centre for Geosciences, Germany
Christian Lucas, Karlsruhe Institute of Technology (KIT), Germany

The amount of information generated and provided by citizens via the World Wide Web is constantly growing. Citizens share information, thoughts, and experiences in blogs and contribute information to web-based content sharing platforms, collaboratively created data bases that are freely usable by everybody. Disaster management as one component of urban planning to decrease a society's vulnerability can benefit from information provided by citizens. This chapter gives an overview of the application of information provided by citizens in disaster management. It points out the potential of using such information for the various phases of disaster management. Three main challenges, which affect the usefulness of information supplied by citizens, are presented in more detail: data collection, localization and quality assessment. For each of these challenges, various approaches to address them are discussed.

Chapter 8
Urban Geo-Wiki: A Crowdsourcing Tool to Improve Urban Land Cover..................................... 119
Linda See, International Institute for Applied Systems Analysis (IIASA), Austria

Steffen Fritz, International Institute for Applied Systems Analysis (IIASA), Austria

Christoph Perger, International Institute for Applied Systems Analysis (IIASA), Austria

Marijn Van der Velde, International Institute for Applied Systems Analysis (IIASA), Austria

Franziska Albrecht, International Institute for Applied Systems Analysis (IIASA), Austria

Ian McCallum, International Institute for Applied Systems Analysis (IIASA), Austria

Dmitry Schepaschenko, International Institute for Applied Systems Analysis (IIASA), Austria

Michael Obersteiner, International Institute for Applied Systems Analysis (IIASA), Austria

Christian Schill, University of Freiburg, Germany

Crowdsourcing is one mechanism for undertaking e-participation. This chapter considers the broader issues of crowdsourcing in the context of citizen participation and governance, illustrated with a case study in which citizens are used to validate global maps of urban extent. Urban extent is an important source of information for a range of applications related to urban planning and governance such as hazard management, food security, health and climate change. Although different products are available that map urban areas or human settlements at a global scale, they disagree in terms of both total urban extent and the spatial distribution of urban areas. Samples of the urban extent from three major cities (London, Beijing and São Paulo), in areas where three recent global land cover maps disagree, are validated using data from a crowdsourcing campaign undertaken with the Geo-Wiki crowdsourcing tool. The results show that crowdsourcing has the potential to contribute to the validation of existing products of urban extent and could help users of these products to determine which map to use in a given location. More accurate information on urban extent will lead to better urban models and improved decision making, which will ultimately affect the future of a growing urban population. However, issues of sustainability, crowd retention and data quality remain challenging areas that require further research in the field of crowdsourcing.

Chapter 9
The Geospatial Web: A Tool to Support the Empowerment of Citizens through E-Participation? 144
Karl Atzmanstorfer, Paris-Lodron University Salzburg, Austria

Thomas Blaschke, Paris-Lodron University Salzburg, Austria

This chapter introduces a spatial view to e-participation in urban governance which is based on the technological core of Geographical Information Systems (GIS) and their more recent transformation into service architectures. The chapter begins with the premise that the technological realms are available today in professional software packages and in open source software environments. It focuses on the utilization of GIS and various methodologies in participatory planning projects. The technical descriptions are limited to a degree that the reader can understand the applications envisaged. The chapter describes developments in the GIS domain which are summarized under the term 'Public Participation GIS' (PP-GIS) since the 1990s. In 2005 however, the launch of Google Earth changed the situation significantly: such mapping platforms—including Microsoft Bing and others—brought mapping functionality to the computers of hundreds of millions of internet users and soon after, the term "volunteered geographic information" was created. It refers to the two-way communication possibilities using geospatial tools and to the participation of citizens in planning initiatives. The chapter highlights a few of such applications in urban planning and administration and discusses the situation in developing and emerging countries, while posing the question of whether or not such options may lead to an empowerment of citizens.

Chapter 10
Citizen Science Perspectives on E-Participation in Urban Planning 172
Caren Cooper, Cornell Lab of Ornithology, USA
Ashwin Balakrishnan, Southern Bronx River Watershed Alliance, USA

Citizen science is a method for an interested public to share information in order to co-create scientific knowledge, typically drawing on games and hobbies and employing electronic media such as web-based data-entry forms and online social networks. Citizen science has emerged in many fields of science (e.g., ecology, astronomy, atmospheric studies, anthropology) and advanced to produce important research findings based on high-quality, reliable data collected, and/or processed, by the public. In turn, participants have increased their interest in, and understanding of, topics related to citizen science projects, and experienced greater civic engagement and social capital. Urban planning initiatives seek to engage people in activities from data gathering to community discussions. The authors review the history of urban planning models and highlight how e-participation can overcome some of the limitations in traditional planning. The authors review how information and communication technologies (ICT) for Citizen Science methods can facilitate public participation in data collection and co-creating knowledge useful to planning decisions. The authors suggest that such efforts can ensure a collaborative rather than adversarial type of public participation and have added outcomes of increasing involvement of an informed public in other aspects of the planning process.

Section 3
Citizen E-Participation

Chapter 11
Mobile Participation: Citizen Engagement in Urban Planning via Smartphones 199
Stefan Höffken, University of Technology Kaiserslautern, Germany
Bernd Streich, University of Technology Kaiserslautern, Germany

Smartphones and tablet computers are becoming essential in everyday life, connecting us in a powerful network through mobile web services. They open new channels of communication between citizens, institutions and administrations, offer greater access to public information, and facilitate increased participation. These new forms of collaborative social interaction revolutionize our information and knowledge society. The chapter examines the new opportunities opened up by mobile phones for mParticipation in the context of urban planning processes. After beginning with a theoretical overview about technical developments, eParticipation and the changes in communication in a networked society, it defines the concept of mParticipation. This is followed by an examination of six real-world projects. These examples are then used for the identification of best practices and for the analysis of the usefulness and effectiveness of these new participatory tools. In addition, the chapter discusses the possibilities as well as the barriers to mobile participation, and makes recommendations for the use of smartphones in urban planning. mParticipation opens new channels of communication, creates new ways of gathering local information and has the chance for creating a low-threshold gateway for citizen participation in urban planning, by improving databases and giving instant feedback.

Chapter 12

Social Media for Civic Engagement: An Exploration of Urban Governments 226

    Thomas A. Bryer, University of Central Florida, USA

    Kimberly L. Nelson, Northern Illinois University, USA

To explore the relationship between form of municipal government and deployment of social media tools for civic engagement, the authors conduct an analysis of a random set of purposively selected cities for content analysis of their social media tools. The authors use the seven forms of government identified by Nelson and Svara (2012) as the basis by which to select the sample cities. Across forms of government, there is no apparent pattern on deployment of social media tools for civic engagement. Municipalities of every form are using the tools, primarily Facebook and Twitter, and most, regardless of form, are not using the tools in a social manner. This finding is consistent with previous work by the authors and others. Important areas for future research are identified in a closing discussion.

Chapter 13

E-Participation and Citizen Relationship Management in Urban Governance: Tools

and Methods 247

    Jim P. Huebner, University of Waterloo, Canada

Citizen relationship management (CiRM) is a combination of management approaches and information technologies for improving citizen services and citizen participation used at all levels of government. As an adaptation of private sector customer relationship management (CRM), CiRM is experiencing significant public sector adoption rates globally. However, while private sector CRM has demonstrated significant impact in the private sector, CiRM benefits are limited, and particularly lagging in the area of citizen e-participation in urban governance. This chapter provides an overview of the scope of CiRM functionality, with particular regard to the CRM origins and CiRM extensibilities, to develop a broader perspective of CiRM's capacity for addressing e-participation. Developing this perspective further, theoretical and methodological approaches to e-participation are presented and evaluated in four categories: generic CiRM participation models, e-government CiRM, democratic CiRM, and strategic CiRM. Further research opportunities are highlighted within the context of emerging organizational, technological, and societal trends.

Chapter 14

Citizen Web Empowerment across Italian Cities: A Benchmarking Approach 284

    Elena Bellio, CERMES - Bocconi University, Italy

    Luca Buccoliero, CERMES - Bocconi University, Italy

This chapter summarizes the results of a research project aimed to enlighten the issue of citizens' empowerment through municipalities' Web portals. The study was designed in order to: (a) provide some key-elements to define the content of an efficient Web strategy for municipalities, with specific focus on the issue of citizens empowerment, (b) benchmark the degree of citizen empowerment of public administrations' Websites across Italian Municipalities through the adoption of a revised version of Citizens Web Empowerment Index (CWEI) for the assessment of the official Web portals of the 104 Italian cities with over 60,000 inhabitants.

Chapter 15
Policy Gadgets for Urban Governance in the Era of Social Computing: An Italian Pilot
on Telemedicine 303

   Enrico Ferro, Istituto Superiore Mario Boella, Italy
   Michele Osella, Istituto Superiore Mario Boella, Italy
   Yannis Charalabidis, University of the Aegean, Greece
   Euripides Loukis, University of the Aegean, Greece

The chapter introduces the concept of policy gadgets that may be expressed as the combined use of computer simulations and social media in policymaking. Such a concept is exemplified by providing the description of an Italian campaign on telemedicine, launched by the regional government of Piedmont (IT) in the context of an international research project named PADGETS (www.padgets.eu). In addition, some preliminary results are presented, which are very encouraging. The use of such instruments in urban and regional policymaking may generate significant advantages in terms of conveying society's inputs to policy makers, by providing them with a set of concise, fresh, and relevant data in a cost effective and easily understandable way.

Compilation of References 319

About the Contributors 359

Index 368

Preface

As local governments across the world increasingly employ advanced information and communication technologies to inform, consult, and engage citizens in urban governance, they are gradually transforming the relationship between citizens and city governments. *Citizen E-Participation in Urban Governance: Crowdsourcing and Collaborative Creativity* explores the nature of these changes and the new challenges confronting citizens and local governments in the field of urban governance. In particular, the book explores the role Web 2.0 technologies can play to promote citizen participation and empowerment in the governance of cities. These online digital technologies provide new opportunities for citizen e-participation in the policy-making process and can have significant repercussions on how urban spaces are planned and governed. The book, the result of the collective effort of 37 researchers from different academic backgrounds working in different parts of the world, offers a comprehensive, updated, and critical overview of innovative Web-based technologies that can be used to enhance citizen e-participation in urban governance. Its main goal is to provide a better understanding of how computer-mediated communication can create new opportunities for citizen participation in urban governance and for the development of e-democracy.

The book is intended for scholars, researchers, students, and practitioners in the field of Urban Studies, broadly defined, and in Urban Planning, Political Science, Public Administration, and Information Science, and is particularly directed to those looking for new methods and tools to advance citizen participation in urban governance. We trust it will contribute to clarify the role of these e-tools and Web-based technologies in urban governance and how these technologies can be successfully applied for the benefit of citizens.

In the book, we seek to answer the following research questions:

1. How can local government use the new Web-based technologies to involve citizens and other stakeholders in the urban governance process?
2. How are local governments and citizens employing these new e-tools?
3. To what extent is the widespread use of these new modes of citizen e-participation responsible for the emergence of a new urban governance paradigm?

The book is organized into three main sections and has fifteen chapters.

The first section, with three chapters, provides an outline of the basic concepts in the field of e-participation and the key issues confronting citizen e-participation in urban governance. The first chapter, "Open Source Urban Governance: Crowdsourcing, Neogeography, VGI, and Citizen Science," offers an overview of the meaning and attributes of what appears to be the emergence of a new policy model—Open Source Urban Governance—seen as an outcome of the increasing and widespread use of new modes of citizen e-participation. The key concepts related to e-participation, some of which with overlap meanings, as is the case of Crowdsourcing, Neogeography, Volunteered Geographic Information, and Citizen Science, are discussed in the chapter, setting the scene for a more detailed analysis of each of these modes of citizen e-participation in the following chapters. E-democracy systems and their impact on a number of e-participation outcomes are explored by Rajeev Sharma, Atreyi Kankanhalli, and Mahdieh Taher in the following chapter, "E-Democracy Systems and Participation Outcomes in Urban Governance." The authors describe the relevant theories to investigate citizen e-participation, identify an agenda for future research, and argue that e-participation has an enormous potential to transform both government and society. Finally, in the third and last chapter of this section, "Public Participation, Social Equity, and Technology in Urban Governance," Thomas W. Sanchez and Marc Brenman examine and discuss, in a U.S. context, the connections between citizen participation in the policy process and equity, and the role technology can play to enhance participation and equity in the outcomes of (urban) public policy. The authors discuss how information and communications technologies can be used to reduce barriers to information exchange and how can it produce stronger bonds and connections within the public sphere.

The second section of the book documents and carefully analyzes different modes of citizen mass collaboration in urban governance, and offers interesting insights on this new frontier in citizen-government relationship in urban governance: Crowdsourcing, Neogeography, Volunteered Geographic Information, and Citizen Science.

In the first of the seven chapters included in this section, "The Four Urban Governance Problem Types Suitable for Crowdsourcing Citizen Participation," by Daren C. Brabham, identifies and examines the main urban governance problems and public goods that can be addressed through the collective intelligence of online communities, although seen as a supplement to other forms of citizen participation in urban governance, a point of view shared by other authors in the book. The chapter includes an examination of the place of crowdsourcing in the public policy process and the risks associated with its use in that context.

Barney Warf, in chapter 5, "Web 2.0, Neogeography, and Urban E-Governance," brings this discussion on crowdsourcing to a broader context. Barney Warf shows and discusses how spatial information on the Web has become increasingly Wikified, in the sense that non-geographers and non-planners may contribute data in a multiplicity of forms, a process that has been named Neogeography, and which, as several authors in the book claim, has close relation to participatory GIS or Public Participation Geographical Information System (PPGIS). In other words, planners and policy-makers are no longer the sole producers of geographical information, as Barney Warf shows in the case study he uses to illustrate his main arguments, a condition that requires and facilitates a more inclusive and democratic urban governance.

In the next chapter, "Tracking Public Participation in Urban Governance: Democracy and Data Privacy," Nancy J. Obermeyer examines and discusses the use of GIS, geo-visualization, and other geo-locational technologies and applications, including social networking Websites and mobile phones associated with Web 2.0 to enhance citizen e-participation. Nancy Obermeyer examines and discusses if these e-tools are mainly employed for the promotion of democratization (optimist perspective) or for the control of citizens (pessimist perspective). This discussion follows a brief introduction to the history of the GIS and society literature, including public participation GIS and volunteered geographic information. In her discussion, Nancy J. Obermeyer uses the events on the Arab Spring and the Occupy movement in the U.S. as examples of the optimist view and the data captured from smartphones and cell phones and the loss of spatial data privacy as examples of the pessimist view. The chapter ends with a discussion of how to enhance the democratization potential of Web 2.0 technologies and geo-location technologies applied in e-participation while minimizing the loss of spatial data privacy, and the harm that this loss of privacy can bring to common citizens.

Doris Dransch, Kathrin Poser, Joachim Fohringer, and Christian Lucas, in chapter 7, "Volunteered Geographic Information for Disaster Management," offer an overview of the application of information provided by citizens in disaster management, the interest to use that sort of information in the various stages of disaster management, and examine the main challenges that are likely to affect the usefulness of the information crowdsourced by citizens, namely issues related to data collection, data localization, and data quality assessment.

In chapter 8, "Urban Geo-Wiki: A Crowdsourcing Tool to Improve Urban Land Cover," Linda See, Steffen Fritz, Christoph Perger, Marijn Van der Velde, Franziska Albrecht, Christian Schill, Ian McCallum, Dmitry Schepaschenko, and Michael Obersteiner show that crowdsourced information on urban land cover, in sample areas taken in three cities (London, Beijing, and São Paulo), in which three recent global cover maps disagree, has the potential to contribute to the validation of existing cartographic data and to determine which map to use in a given location. As the authors argue, this sort of data allows policy makers to develop better and more accurate urban models, and allows decision-makers to reach better decisions. Despite this overall positive view of crowdsourcing, the authors point to some of the challenges that confront it, such as crowd retention or sustainability of crowdsourcing processes, and the quality and reliability of crowdsourced data, issues also raised in other chapters.

Karl Atzmanstorfer and Thomas Blaschke, in chapter 9, "The Geospatial Web: A Tool to Support the Empowerment of Citizens through E-Participation?" describe developments, since the 1990s, in the field of Public Participation Geographical Information Systems (PPGIS) and the impact Google Earth had on the mapping functionalities available to the common citizen in the Internet, a change that led to the adoption of the term Volunteered Geographic Information (VGI). In other words, the chapter explores the use of geospatial tools for citizen e-participation in urban planning, and discusses the use of VGI in developing and in emerging countries, questioning the relevance of VGI for citizen empowerment.

Citizen Science, as a particular form of crowdsourcing, is addressed by Caren Cooper and Ashwin Balakrishnan, in chapter 10, "Citizen Science Perspectives on E-Participation in Urban Planning." The authors review the history of urban planning paradigms, discuss how e-participation can overcome some of the problems confronted by urban planning, and examine how ICT for Citizen Science can facilitate public participation in data collection and in the co-creation of knowledge useful for policy makers in the different stages of the urban planning process.

Section three explores specific modes of citizen e-participation that do not fall directly within the previous categories: participation through social media, smartphones and mobile applications, Website-based e-participation, or the use of management approaches to improve citizen participation.

Stefan Höffken and Bernd Streich, in chapter 11, "Mobile Participation: Citizen Engagement in Urban Planning via Smartphones," examine the new channels of communication between citizens, institutions, and administrations based on smartphones and tablet computers, and the opportunities for citizen e-participation in urban governance opened up by mobile phones and mobile applications (m-Participation). As the authors argue, based on six real-world projects, these new forms of collaborative social interaction have the potential to radically change the relationship between citizens and policy makers in the field of urban governance.

In the following chapter, "Social Media for Civic Engagement: An Exploration of Urban Governments," Thomas A. Bryer and Kimberly L. Nelson explore the relationship between forms of municipal government and the deployment of social media tools for citizen e-participation in urban governance. Based on empirical studies of different U.S. local governments, the authors conclude that municipalities, independently of the respective type, make use of social media tools, mainly Facebook and Twitter.

In chapter 13, "E-Participation and Citizen Relationship Management in Urban Governance: Tools and Methods," Jim P. Huebner provides an overview of Citizens Relationship Management (CiRM), with a particular focus on CiRM origins and functionalities. CiRM is a combination of management approaches and information technologies for improving citizen services and citizen participation and is used in all tiers of government. This use of private sector Customer Relationship Management (CRM) is experiencing high rates of public sector adoption, a facet Jim Huebner explores in the chapter, considering four categories in this approach: generic CiRM participation models, e-government CiRM, democratic CiRM, and strategic CiRM.

In chapter 14, "Citizen Web Empowerment across Italian Cities: A Benchmarking Approach," Elena Bellio and Luca Buccoliero explore the role of Web 2.0 tools for citizen empowerment and offer a benchmarking study of Italian cities. The authors argue that under the current circumstances, urban government has to offer access, through the Internet, to official, customized, and on demand information and services, and to provide new opportunities for direct and informal relationships between citizens, policy makers, and civil servants, as well as conditions for the development of a proactive role by interested citizen.

Lastly, in chapter 15, "Policy Gadgets for Urban Governance in the Era of Social Computing: An Italian Pilot on Telemedicine," Enrico Ferro, Michele Osella, Yannis Charalabidis, and Euripides Loukis present and discuss the concept of policy gadgets, a combined use of computer simulations and social media in policy making. The authors provide, as an example of this concept, the description of an Italian campaign on telemedicine, launched by the regional government of Piedmont, in the context of an international research project, whose preliminary results seem highly positive.

In sum, this collection of essays illustrates the diversity of approaches and Web technologies available for citizen e-participation in urban governance, and we trust the book makes clear the potential of these digital technologies to transform citizen-local government relationships. For that reason, we hope readers will find these essays inspirational for the development of new forms of citizen responsive urban governance more transparent and just.

Carlos Nunes Silva
University of Lisbon, Portugal

Acknowledgment

I'd like to acknowledge my gratitude to all colleagues that accepted my invitation to take part in the exploration of the new frontier of citizen e-participation in urban governance, in what appears to configure the emergence of a new policy model in different parts of the world: the Open Source Urban Governance paradigm. I'm also grateful to the colleagues that accepted my invitation to collaborate in the review process. The book benefited from the valuable insights, constructive comments, and thoughtful guidance so generously offered by them. Finally, my thanks go to the editorial staff at IGI Global, in particular to Myla R. Merkel with whom I worked closely during this project, for the continuous support, follow-up, and attention to detail.

Carlos Nunes Silva
University of Lisbon, Portugal

Section 1
Basic Concepts and Key Issues

Chapter 1

Open Source Urban Governance:
Crowdsourcing, Neogeography, VGI, and Citizen Science

Carlos Nunes Silva
University of Lisbon, Portugal

ABSTRACT

The chapter explores the emerging paradigm of Open Source Urban Governance, a new urban policy model associated with the extensive use of computer-mediated communication and with the use of different modes of citizen mass collaboration – Crowdsourcing, Neogeography, Volunteered Geographic Information (VGI), and Citizen Science. The chapter is organized into five main sections. The first section discusses the concept of e-participation. The next two sections address the objectives, context, determinants, and ethical issues in e-participation, and the different levels of e-participation in each policy stage and by stakeholder. The last two sections explore the e-tools available for citizen participation in urban governance and the impacts and benefits of e-participation. The chapter ends with a reference to future research directions in this field.

INTRODUCTION

Municipal governments' use of advanced information and communication technologies – the Internet, geographical information systems, and virtual reality – to inform, consult and actively engage citizens in the urban policy process is expected to revolutionize the reach and scope of collaboration between local government and citizens as well as the effectiveness of local public service delivery, now that around one third of the world population is connected to the Internet. These changes in the last decades are closely related to local e-democracy initiatives, in all regions of the world, with the implementation of local e-government, e-planning, and with the growing amount of information generated by citizens in the Internet (OECD, 2003; Gascó, 2003; UN, 2006; 2009; Peart & Diaz, 2007; Schatteman et al., 2012; Klosterman, 2012). These e-participation initiatives include a variety of methods, applications

DOI: 10.4018/978-1-4666-4169-3.ch001

and tools that can be used in highly innovative ways to involve citizens in the urban governance process, at any time and from any place, if necessary in an asynchronous mode.

These overall changes in citizen-government relationship seems to configure the emergence of a new policy model based on the idea that citizens can be empowered in order to have a more active role in the (urban) governance process through an ubiquitous use of Web-based collaborative tools. This new urban governance paradigm sees the policy process as a large Wiki built continuously by all interested citizens within the community. In this concept is embedded the idea that citizen e-participation aims to shape the content of urban policies, monitor and evaluate the implementation of these policies. Local/urban government acts as a networked organization, uses citizen mass-collaboration in different stages of the policy process, co-innovates with citizens and other local stakeholders, and shares resources. Different terms have been used, by different authors, to describe similar forms of citizen-government relationships, as is the case of Open Source Politics (Sifry, 2004) or Wiki Government (Noveck, 2009), or the notion of Open Source Urbanism that has been used, among others, by Saskia Sassen. Inspired by the 'Open Source' and the 'Wiki' metaphors, employed by these and other authors, this emerging paradigm in urban governance will be referred in this chapter as Open Source Urban Governance.

BACKGROUND: THE CONCEPT OF E-PARTICIPATION

E-participation is taken by some authors as synonymous of e-voting, while for others it has a broader meaning, being synonymous of e-democracy or digital democracy (Macintosh & Whyte, 2006). For this perspective, citizen e-participation includes e-voting but also innumerable other modes of citizen involvement in the policy making process. It is the case of Ann Macintosh (2004, p. 2), for whom "e-democracy is concerned with the use of information and communication technologies to engage citizens, to support the democratic decision-making processes and strengthen representative democracy." It is also the case of Albrecht et al. (2008, p. 4), for whom e-Participation is "the participation of individuals and legal entities (including groups thereof) in political and administrative decision-making processes by means of information and communication technology."

Therefore, in this broader perspective of e-democracy, the term e-Participation refers new modes of citizen involvement in the public policy process. It is an addition to conventional forms of citizen participation, more than a replacement for it. E-participation usually refers participatory initiatives within an institutional context, but can also be used to refer other modes of participation that emerge from the practices associated with the co-creation of digital content through the use of digital media technologies, as Saad-Sulonen (2012) shows in her study of Helsinki.

E-participation is confronted with numerous challenges and barriers, in particular when there is a declining participation in formal political processes, in elections, in political parties and trade union affiliations, and a growing disconnect and distrust between citizens and politicians (Coleman & Gotze, n.d.; Irvin & Stansbury, 2004), or between youth and politics (Macintosh et al., 2003; Lara & Naval, 2012). And all this when the number and importance of social movements, focused on single and temporary issues, tend to increase (Van Laer & Van Aelst, 2010), and when the incorporation of these online participatory tools and practices in the structures and processes of conventional urban governance seems to face, in some cases, significant resistance from the most conservative sections within municipal administration.

E-participation is referred under different names: tele-democracy, IT-democracy, e-consultation, Web-based citizen input, e-government

2.0, online public engagement (Coleman & Gotze, n.d.; Gronlund, 2003; Albrecht et al., 2008, among others). The terms Crowdsourcing, Neogeography, Volunteered Geographic Information and Citizen Science have also been used to refer specific modes of e-participation through mass collaboration or collective intelligence.

Crowdsourcing, a term coined by Howe (2006), refers the process of outsourcing a task to an unknown group of individuals, non-experts or experts, acting as volunteers, the crowd. Despite being a concept and a model developed in the business field, crowdsourcing can be used as a particular form of citizen participation in the public policy process (Brabham, 2008, 2009). If properly designed, and if ethical issues are adequately addressed (e.g., cheap source of labor), crowdsourcing can be used as an additional model for citizen participation in urban governance, as Brabham (2009) proposes for urban projects.

For Enrique Estellés-Arolas and Fernando González-Ladrón-de-Guevara (2012, p. 197):

Crowdsourcing is a type of participative online activity in which an individual, an institution, a non-profit organization, or company proposes to a group of individuals of varying knowledge, heterogeneity, and number, via a flexible open call, the voluntary undertaking of a task. The undertaking of the task, of variable complexity and modularity, and in which the crowd should participate bringing their work, money, knowledge and/or experience, always entails mutual benefit. The user will receive the satisfaction of a given type of need, be it economic, social recognition, self-esteem, or the development of individual skills, while the crowdsourcer will obtain and utilize to their advantage what the user has brought to the venture, whose form will depend on the type of activity undertaken.

Neogeography and Volunteered Geographic Information (VGI) refer a specific form of citizen mass collaboration or crowdsourcing for the production of geographic information, in text, image or video (Haklay et al., 2008; Hudson-Smith et al., 2009; Foth et al., 2009; Rana et al., 2009; Goodchild, 2007; 2009; Goodchild & Glennon, 2010; Warf & Sui, 2010). Crowdsourcing information aggregation during disasters and mass emergencies (Starbird, 2011) or in emergency planning (Chun & Artigas, 2012) is an example of the role crowdsourcing can play in urban governance. However, this form of citizen mass collaboration in urban governance, seen as a development of the concept of Public Participation Geographic Information System (Ghose, 2001), is also confronted with a number of challenges: the quality of the data collected in VGI, in particular if it is to be used in further research, and the sustainability or durability of the participation process and ethical issues (Flanagin & Metzger, 2008; Elwood, 2006, 2008).

Another approach, which also makes use of a large pool of participants to collect information, citizen science or crowdsourcing applied to science (Cooper et al., 2007; Wiggins & Crowston, 2010, 2011), can be used in the context of urban policy processes to collect information about wildlife and other environmental aspects. While current examples of citizen science are mainly concerned with data collection, more advanced forms of this specific type of crowdsourcing can include the formulation of research questions and the analysis of results.

Crowdsourcing information for monitoring environmental issues by citizens and civil society organizations is a positive example of how citizens' participation can influence the policy process. Cases reported in the literature show that citizen science has contributed to the production of important research findings based on data collected by common citizens. It is the case examined by Overdevest and Mayer (2008), in which local antitoxic organizations, through crowdsourced data, were able to influence the responsiveness and accountability of regulators and firms. Two other examples are urban bird research (McCaffrey, 2005) and global land cover studies (Fritz et al., 2012).

In this chapter, citizen e-participation in urban governance, in its broadest sense, is defined as the ubiquitous use of information and communication technologies to support citizen involvement in the urban policy process, in its different stages, without limits of time and space, through processes of information, consultation or active participation, being crowdsourcing in urban governance, or any of the other related concepts—Neogeography, Volunteered Geographic Information (VGI) and Citizen Science—a specific mode of active e-participation. It is taken as including also the use of mobile devices for citizen participation, or m-participation, as well as Neogeography and VGI tools and services that allow non-geographers to use the functionalities of advanced geographical information systems.

E-PARTICIPATION: OBJECTIVES, CONTEXT, DETERMINANTS, AND ETHICAL ISSUES

As reported extensively in the literature (for instance, in OECD, 2001, 2003; Macintosh, 2004; Albrecht et al., 2008; Coleman & Gotze, n.d.), e-Participation has, among others, the following objectives: to enable the participation of a broader range of interests and perspectives; to make access to urban planning information easier and more understandable for all citizens; to enhance equity in the access to decision-making within urban governance processes; to provide the relevant information that supports planning decisions; to provide opportunities for negotiation between different perspectives; to help consensus building where appropriate; to increase transparency in public decision-making; to increase and improve citizens inputs for the policy process; to influence the content of policies, through mass collaboration; to help citizens to set up their own policy agendas; to provide adequate, timely and useful feedback on issues related to urban governance

decisions; to reinforce local identity through citizens engagement in community affairs; to improve the efficiency of local public services.

It is sometimes referred that the Internet disconnects citizens from public policy and contributes for the decline of civic life. However, the majority of the research findings available seem to suggest that collective intelligence, or wisdom of crowds, have a positive effect on civic and political participation (Surowiecki, 2004; Norris, 2004; Noveck, 2009; Smith et al., 2009). For this perspective, the Internet increases and improves citizen participation in urban governance (Weber et al., 2003; Gibson et al., 2005; Boulianne, 2009). Internet mobilizes more than it demobilizes citizens for political participation, although along similar social divides as before (Lara & Naval, 2012). Other authors claim that it is necessary more research before conclusions can be taken (French et al., 2007; Tait, 2012).

These reports also provide ample evidence on the importance of context for the differences found in urban e-governance sophistication, which is directly reflected in the level and sophistication of e-participation (Holzer & Kim, 2008; Albrecht et al., 2008; Holzer et al., 2010). In the three cases reported by Mackintosh (2004) – City of Edinburgh Council, Scottish Executive, and Scottish Parliament -, or in the cases examined in Albrecht et al. (2008), different conditions were referred as critical factors for success. In all these studies, citizen e-participation in urban governance appears to be affected by internal factors and external conditions as well.

Overall, the evidence points a number of key internal determinants—political, legal, cultural, economic, and technological conditions (Gronlund, 2003; EC, 2009)—that have an influence on the level of success of citizen e-participation processes and in the quality of e-democracy. For example, the evidence available suggests that to include e-participation procedures in the normal activities of the institution, avoiding the use of additional resources, improves the outcomes of these participatory processes. The use of different e-participation tools for different targets and the political commitment by those responsible for the e-participation process within the institution has also a positive effect. To provide clear evidence that the contribution offered by participants, citizens and other stakeholders, is indeed taken into consideration in the formulation of urban policies and in its implementation is also seen as an important factor for the sustainability of the participatory process. Besides technological, social, and financial external conditions, frequently referred in the literature as factors that influence the success of e-participation, James et al. (2004) refer as external determinants of e-participation in urban governance, for example, the political culture and the culture of the organization.

The design of e-tools, the accessibility for users with disabilities, is a critical factor for the success of e-participation, as well as the clarity of the policy content available online. The entire participatory process has to be perceived as relevant and legitimate before citizens can be involved in any significant way. Issues of privacy (Höffken & Streich, 2011), trust and security are critical. Information provided needs to be accurate and reliable, and perceived by participants as safe. Expectations that the participation will have impact on decision-making is crucial for the durability or sustainability of the e-participation process and, for that reason, success depends also on the feedback to participants.

The mode of governing, or the prevailing model of public service provision, is another factor that affects the level of citizen participation. The role and the importance assigned to citizen e-participation vary according to the mode of urban governance. Its importance is higher in networked urban governance and tends to be less important in hierarchical modes of urban governance. In networked urban governance, e-participation goes beyond information and consultation and comprises forms of active participation, including

direct inputs for the definition of policy content. In hierarchical and in market based modes of urban governance, e-participation tends to be mainly for information and consultation, with fewer opportunities for active participation. This different role assigned to citizen e-participation is reflected in the type of e-tools employed. However, as Mossberger and Wu (2012) point out, municipal governments, independently of the prevailing governance model, tend to adopt new and more diversified tools including, increasingly, the use of social media and social networks to involve citizens in the urban governance process.

E-participation is also confronted with several ethical challenges that need to be addressed, namely issues of trust, privacy, and the protection of identity of participants, in particular when citizens are required to provide personal data. Concerns related to social exclusion due to the elitist character of some of these technologies have also been raised and need to be considered in the design of participatory processes (Kingston, 2002, quoting Pickles, 1995; Sieber, 2006; Elwood, 2006). And as Buchanan (2012) argues, research in these new digital online environments raises additional ethical dilemmas. Security is another important dimension that urban policy makers have to consider in the design of e-participation processes.

E-PARTICIPATION: LEVEL OF PARTICIPATION, POLICY STAGE, STAKEHOLDERS

The value of e-participation is closely linked to the level of citizen engagement. This is commonly referred as the level of participation (OECD, 2001; 2003; Macintosh, 2004; Coleman & Gotze, n.d.; Ahmed, 2006; Fung, 2006; Albrecht et al., 2008). The influential article of Arnstein (1969), quoted in almost every work on citizen participation published since then, and a reference for other proposals, considers eight levels or gradations, according to the efficacy of citizen participation: manipulation, therapy, informing, consultation, placation, partnership, delegated power, citizen control. Simplified versions of this typology have been proposed by other authors and organizations. The International Association for Public Participation considers five levels in its spectrum of public participation (e.g., inform, consult, involve, collaborate, empower), and the OECD three main levels (e.g., information, consultation and active participation).

The OECD approach, although not focused specifically in urban governance or in urban planning, is a useful reference. According to the level of citizen engagement in the policy process, the OECD considers three main levels of citizen participation: Information, Consultation, and Active Participation. In the first level—Information—there is only a one way relationship, from government to citizens, mainly for the provision of information. In the second level—Consultation—there is a two-way relationship between government and citizens, a situation in which citizens have the possibility to react and provide feedback to government. In the third and upper level—Active Participation—there is a deeper citizen involvement, in the sense that they jointly participate in the formulation of policy content, and in the implementation, monitoring and evaluation of policies. Although the final decision rests with government officials, citizens have the possibility to influence considerably the policy process and policy outcomes. The different degrees of citizen participation, in the three levels of participation considered in the OECD report, may require the use of different information and communication technologies, although part of them may be common to all levels.

In the lower level of participation (information), ICT are used mainly to enable the spread of information produced by government to a larger number of citizens than would be the case with off-line analogical conventional procedures (e.g., Website postings – text, audio and video; e-newsletter; e-leaflets; community e-profiles; feedback on e-surveys; e-reports, etc.). However, due to the uneven informational literacy and the digital divide, the choice of these technologies needs to take these conditions into account when devising the information plan. In other words, in this level of participation, urban policy makers will have to choose ICT tools that are at the same time accessible and easily understandable even for those citizens within the local community with little or no familiarity with them.

In the second level of participation (consultation), the challenge is to select those ICT tools that allow local policy-makers or urban planners to consult and to engage larger audiences than would be possible with conventional off-line consultation procedures (e.g., e-surveys; e-focus group; e-forums; e-panels).

In the third level—active participation—citizens provide direct inputs for policy content, which requires e-tools that make easier the communication between citizens and urban decision-makers (e.g., e-petitions; e-referendum; e-panels; deliberative e-polls; citizen e-juries; consensus e-conferences; participatory GIS).

While in the first and second levels, citizens are mere consumers of information produced by urban government, with the possibility to react and comment on that information, in the third level citizens are direct producers of ideas and providers of policy content that urban policy makers have to incorporate in the final design of a specific policy or urban plan.

The policy stage in which citizen e-participation takes place can also have an influence on the type of e-tool used (Macintosh, 2004). By increasing the number and diversity of actors or stakeholders in the policy process and in the decision-making process e-participation makes accountability more complex.

E-PARTICIPATION TOOLS

The move from off-line and paper-based urban governance to a mode based largely on digital and online environments requires new working methods and new tools for administrative and technical activities as well as for research on urban and planning issues (Silva, 2012a, 2012b). For that reason, another critical dimension of open source urban governance is the technology used to engage citizens. Kingston (2002) argues that citizen e-participation tools, in all its multiple forms, including the use of GIS (Obermeyer, 1998; Sieber, 2006; Moody, 2007) should not be seen as a replacement of conventional modes of citizen participation in urban governance, but should be seen as a complement to the traditional participatory methods and tools. However, it is increasingly recognized that this is not just a new technology that replaces previous technologies without changing the essence of structures and processes. These technologies transform how municipal government works and cooperates with citizens, and make easier the redesign of structures and processes, and influence the development of new perspectives about the role of citizens in urban governance.

Although in most cases e-participation is part of a wider participatory process that also includes non-virtual and off-line activities (e.g., community meetings; personal consultations; mail; telephone info-line, etc.), the tendency seems to be for urban policy makers and urban planners to use little by little the new e-participation tools that are now available. These tools include, for example, user generate content applications, citizen consultation platforms, central portals for applications and petitions, social computing platforms, geo-visualization and other geo-locational technologies (Parameswaran & Whinston, 2007; Rosa & Pereira, 2008; Silva, 2010a, 2010b; Anttiroiko, 2012). In addition, there is an ever increasing use of innovative Web 2.0 applications (Osimo, 2008; Coleman & Gotze, n.d.; Albrecht et al., 2008; Casey & Li, 2012), social networks (e.g., Facebook), virtual worlds (e.g., Second Life) as described by Evans-Cowley and Hollander (2010), virtual globes, and public participation GIS (Obermeyer, 1998; Peng, 2001; Kingston, 2002; Elwood, 2006; Dunn, 2007). Mobile applications, smartphones and tablet computers (Höffken & Streich, 2011; Evans-Cowley, 2012; Sandstrom, 2012) are now opening new channels and possibilities for communication between citizens and government (m-participation), offering new possibilities for data collection, information and consultation in urban governance.

Although still mainly used for information and consultation (Holzer & Kim, 2008), most of these tools are also appropriate for advanced modes of citizen participation, as they allow an active engagement in the formulation of policy content, and in its implementation, monitoring and evaluation.

Each level of participation requires specific e-tools although some of them are common to more than one level of participation (Macintosh, 2004; Ahmed, 2006; Albrecht et al., 2008). In the first level of participation (information), the provision of text-based information in a Website, in a digital TV channel, in info-kiosks, mailing lists, RSS feeds, e-mail, SMS, and micro-blogging are examples of e-tools that can be used. In the second level of participation—consultation—there is interaction and feedback between policy-makers and citizens. This can be done with the e-tools already mentioned and with call centers, online input forms, online polls, online questionnaires, online e-surveys, e-petitions, online video conference, moderated chat rooms, interactive maps, online discussion forum, specialized e-panels, Wikis, Mash-ups, and other Web 2.0 applications. In the third level of e-participation—active participation—besides all e-tools and applications already mentioned, citizens need to have access to Internet-based applications that allow user generate content (Osimo, 2008; Ayanso & Moyers, 2012). Social networks, virtual worlds, video communities, and e-participatory municipal budgets are some of the additional e-tools available for e-participation in urban governance.

The choice of e-tools is also affected by a number of external conditions, such as the prevailing political culture (Albrecht et al., 2008; EC, 2009; Damurski, 2012). In cultural contexts where policy deliberation is valued, e-participation tools will tend to favor online forum, virtual communities, blogs, micro blogging, e-mail and other consultation tools that allow a continuous deliberative process. On the contrary, in political cultures that favor accountability and transparency, e-participation will tend to favor tools such as Webcasting, podcasting, video sharing, RSS feeds, and other Web 2.0 tools (e.g., dedicated and specific channels in YouTube or in similar platforms, blogs and micro-blogs, etc.). The evidence available from numerous evaluations of local e-democracy initiatives and e-participation in local governance suggests that some of these tools are more frequently used than others, being online forum one of the most popular e-tools applied by local government (Macintosh et al., 2005; Peart & Diaz, 2007; Kubicek, 2010).

E-participation tools differ, not only according to the objectives assigned to each specific participatory process, but also according to the context in which it takes place. Participants may use e-mails, online forums, mailing lists, chat rooms, surveys and polls, to promote discussion or to advise local policy makers but, for a different purpose, they may prefer to use e-petitions, e-surveys, Citizens e-Juries, Innovations Jams, and CiRM (Coleman & Gotze, n.d.; Macintosh, 2004; Albrecht et al., 2008; EC, 2009).

E-PARTICIPATION: IMPACTS, BENEFITS, AND RISKS

E-Participation in urban governance is generally seen as an activity with significant societal impacts and benefits for citizens, government, and other urban stakeholders, although risks such as loss of data privacy may also occur (Macintosh, 2004; Sieber, 2006; Albrecht et al., 2008; EC, 2009; Kubicek, 2010). E-participation increases the overall level of citizen involvement in urban governance, expands the number and type of stakeholders that take part in planning decisions, despite the digital divide, stimulates a more active citizenship, leads to a more open and transparent public administration, at the urban or local level, creates or reinforces a culture of dialogue between government and citizens, and a culture of information, consultation and active production of policy contents, empowers individuals and local communities, enhances collective intelligence and collaborative creativity, and finally can lead to a more inclusive society. In sum, e-participation helps the mobilization of knowledge for the formulation of better decisions in the field of urban governance. However, since e-participation addresses different governance issues, the impacts and the benefits that the different stakeholders can expect from it differ.

For citizens, when compared to off-line modes of citizen participation, e-participation provides better information on urban issues, is a more convenient form of participation, and an easy way to access the decision-making process. It is more transparent and improves accountability. E-participation increases the perception that citizens can influence not only the content of the policy but also its implementation, monitoring and evaluation. The complexity of the policy issues addressed by urban governments and the levels of expertise required to fully understand some of these issues limit the number of participants and the quality of their input to the policy process (Albrecht et al., 2008; EC, 2009; Kubicek, 2010). The visibility and accessibility of this participatory process is another factor that affects the number of potential participants. The entire process must be clear from the start, in terms of objectives, procedures (e.g., data collection, data analysis, publication, input for the policy process, ethical issues, etc.)

and outcomes. In order to maintain the interest of local citizens in the urban governance process it is important to provide feedback including, when appropriate, the explanation of the reasons for not considering the suggestions or proposals submitted by citizens.

For local (urban) government, increased citizen e-participation can lead to greater attention to their internal working procedures, and to improved efficiency and effectiveness, with more and better policy outputs, outcomes and impacts (Albrecht et al., 2008). Urban government can also benefit by raising the level of citizen support to key policy options. For policy makers, e-participation can improve the legitimacy of their decisions and the quality of the overall urban governance system, increase the level of decentralization from local government to the community, empowering the community and increasing its social capital.

Despite this overall positive view of e-participation, concerns have also been raised, in particular regarding the distrust between citizens and policy makers, as referred, among others, by Coleman and Gotze (n.d.), and by Irvin and Stansbury (2004). Concerns have also been raised about the social, political, and epistemological implications of GIS (Elwood, 2006), or regarding the perception of transparency in the policy making process (Kim & Lee, 2012). The use of social media as tools for citizen e-participation in urban governance also raises challenges (Cammaerts, 2008; Ayanso & Moyers, 2012; Zavattaro, 2012): the transmission of inappropriate messages or messages that may be misinterpreted due to cultural differences; data leaks from within the organization due to the misuse of these Web tools; the reliability and quality of the information; the legality of certain uses and contents; equity in the access to these tools; privacy protection in social media platforms; fraud, irregularities and technical problems in the organization of these processes. There is also the risk of personal data, including spatial data, being inappropriately used to control citizens.

CONCLUSION AND FUTURE RESEARCH DIRECTIONS

Despite declining levels of citizen participation in conventional political practices, participation in urban governance processes tend to grow in numerous places, in part associated with the increasing use of information and communication technologies. Similar findings have been found in political and administrative tiers other than local government. However, the potential of e-participation is far from being fully developed in the field of urban governance, as it continues to be used mainly for information and consultation purposes and less for the active participation of citizens in policy formation, monitoring, and evaluation.

The possibilities for a new policy model – open source inspired urban governance – are now, with the expansion of Web 2.0, much more feasible than few years ago. Mobile Internet access will increase the role of Crowdsourcing, Neogeography, Volunteered Geographic Information, and Citizen Science, as it will be easier for large groups of people to contribute to the policy process.

The use of these Web tools in citizen e-participation processes can have both positive and negative consequences, in the sense that the use of these tools can be a democratizing force but also an instrument of control by those in power. E-participation can help common citizens to acquire data they can use to influence urban public policy. However, in extreme cases, data collected can be used against the interests of these citizens. The decision process may be captured by social and economic elites. E-participation may also imply a diffusion of responsibilities, increasing the risk of unaccountability. Issues of data reliability and valid knowledge need also to be considered. Digital exclusion due to social and economic barriers is another dimension that requires further research.

While the use of ICT seems to bring to the policy making process individuals that otherwise would not participate and would not have the opportunity to contribute for the policy process, the existence of a digital divide seems to recommend a combination of both on-line and off-line forms of citizen participation in Open Source Urban Governance. For that reason, one of the challenges confronting urban policy-makers is to find the appropriate mix of participatory tools, both off- and on-line, to enhance citizen's involvement in urban affairs.

As we move to an increasingly mobile society, in particular in urban and metropolitan areas, the importance of ubiquitous mobile technologies will increase, which will certainly have an impact in the way citizen e-participation is organized, and in the overall level of citizen participation in urban governance. A systematic comparative analysis of e-participation in urban governance, in developed and in developing countries, is a line of research that needs to be expanded, in order to appraise how the use of information and communication technologies improve the role played by citizens in the urban policy process, what are the conditions that allow the development of best practices in this field, and how far have cities moved towards Open Source Urban Governance.

REFERENCES

Ahmed, N. (2006). *An overview of e-participation models*. New York: United Nations.

Albrecht, S., Kohlrausch, N., Kubicek, H., Lippa, B., Marker, O., Trénel, M., Vorwek, V.,…, Wiedwald, C. (2008). *E-participation. electronic participation of citizens and the business community on egovernment*. Bremen, Germany: Institut fur Informations management.

Anttiroiko, A.-V. (2012). Urban planning 2.0. *International Journal of E-Planning Research*, *1*(1), 16–30. doi:10.4018/ijepr.2012010103.

Arnstein, S. R. (1969). A ladder of citizen participation. *Journal of the American Institute of Planners*, *35*(4), 216–224. doi:10.1080/01944366908977225.

Ayanso, A., & Moyers, D. (2012). The role of social media in the public sector: Opportunities and challenges. In Kloby, K., & D'Agostinho, M. J. (Eds.), *Citizen 2.0: Public and governmental interaction through Web 2.0 technologies* (pp. 1–22). Hershey: IGI-Global. doi:10.4018/978-1-4666-0318-9.ch001.

Boulianne, S. (2009). Does Internet use affect engagement? A meta-analysis of research. *Political Communication*, *26*(2), 193–211. doi:10.1080/10584600902854363.

Brabham, D. C. (2008). Crowdsourcing as a model for problem solving: An introduction and cases. *Convergence. The International Journal of Research into New Media Technologies*, *14*(1). doi:10.1177/1354856507084420.

Brabham, D. C. (2009). Crowdsourcing the public participation process for planning projects. *Planning Theory*, *8*(3), 242–262. doi:10.1177/1473095209104824.

Buchanan, E. A. (2012). E-research ethics and e-planning: Emerging considerations for transformative research. *International Journal of E-Planning Research*, *1*(1), 5–15. doi:10.4018/ijepr.2012010102.

Cammaerts, B. (2008). Critiques on the participatory potentials of Web 2.0. *Communication, Culture & Critique*, *1*(4), 358–377. doi:10.1111/j.1753-9137.2008.00028.x.

Casey, C., & Li, J. (2012). Web 2.0 technologies and authentic public participation: Engaging citizens in decision making processes. In Kloby, K., & D'Agostinho, M. J. (Eds.), *Citizen 2.0: Public and governmental interaction through Web 2.0 technologies* (pp. 197–223). Hershey: IGI-Global. doi:10.4018/978-1-4666-0318-9.ch011.

Chun, S. A., & Artigas, F. (2012). Sensors and crowdsourcing for environmental awareness and emergency planning. *International Journal of E-Planning Research*, *1*(1), 56–74. doi:10.4018/ijepr.2012010106.

Coleman, S., & Gotze, J. (n.d.). *Bowling together: Online public engagement in policy deliberation.* London: Hansard Society – London School of Economics.

Cooper, C. B., Dickinson, J., Phillips, T., & Bonney, R. (2007). Citizen science as a tool for conservation in residential ecosystems. *Ecology and Society*, *12*(2), 11.

Damurski, Ł. (2012). E-participation in urban planning: Online tools for citizen engagement in Poland and in Germany. *International Journal of E-Planning Research*, *1*(3), 40–67. doi:10.4018/ijepr.2012070103.

Dunn, C. E. (2007). Participatory GIS – A people's GIS? *Progress in Human Geography*, *31*(5), 616–637. doi:10.1177/0309132507081493.

EC. (2009). *European e-participation. Summary Report.* Brussels: European Commission.

Elwood, S. (2006). Critical issues in participatory GIS: Deconstructions, reconstructions, and new research directions. *Transactions in GIS*, *10*(5), 693–708. doi:10.1111/j.1467-9671.2006.01023.x.

Elwood, S. (2008). Volunteered geographic information: Future research directions motivated by critical, participatory, and feminist GIS. *GeoJournal*, *72*, 173–183. doi:10.1007/s10708-008-9186-0.

Estellés-Arolas, E., & González-Ladrón-de-Guevara, F. (2012). Towards an integrated crowdsourcing definition. *Journal of Information Science*, *38*(2). doi:10.1177/0165551512437638.

Evans-Cowley, J., & Hollander, J. (2010). The new generation of public participation: Internet-based participation tools. *Planning Practice and Research*, *25*(3), 397–408. doi:10.1080/02697459.2010.503432.

Evans-Cowley, J. S. (2012). There's an app for that: Mobile applications for urban planning. *International Journal of E-Planning Research*, *1*(2), 79–87. doi:10.4018/ijepr.2012040105.

Flanagin, A. J., & Metzger, M. J. (2008). The credibility of volunteered geographic information. *GeoJournal*, *72*, 137–148. doi:10.1007/s10708-008-9188-y.

Foth, M., Bajracharya, B., Brown, R. A., & Hearn, G. N. (2009). The second life of urban planning? Using neogeography tools for community engagement. *Journal of Location Based Services*, *3*(2), 97–117. doi:10.1080/17489720903150016.

French, S., Insua, D. R., & Ruggeri, F. (2007). E-participation and decision analysis. *Decision Analysis*, *4*(4), 211–226. doi:10.1287/deca.1070.0098.

Fritz, S., McCallum, I., Schill, C., Perger, C., Seem, L., & Schepaschenko, D. et al. (2012). Geo-wiki: An online platform for improving global land cover. *Environmental Modelling & Software*, *31*, 110–123. doi:10.1016/j.envsoft.2011.11.015.

Fung, A. (2006). Varieties of participation in complex governance. Public Administration Review, Vol. 66, suplement: 66-75.

Gascó, M. (2003). New technologies and institutional change in public administration. *Social Science Computer Review*, *21*(1), 6–14. doi:10.1177/0894439302238967.

Ghose, R. (2001). Use of information technology for community empowerment: Transforming geographic information systems into community information systems. *Transactions in GIS, 5*(2), 141–163. doi:10.1111/1467-9671.00073.

Gibson, R. K., Lusoli, W., & Ward, S. (2005). Online participation in the UK: Testing a 'Contextualised' model of Internet effects. *British Journal of Politics and International Relations, 7*(4), 561–583. doi:10.1111/j.1467-856X.2005.00209.x.

Goodchild, M. F. (2007). Citizens as sensors: The world of volunteered geography. *GeoJournal, 69*, 211–221. doi:10.1007/s10708-007-9111-y.

Goodchild, M. F. (2009). NeoGeography and the nature of geographic expertise. *Journal of Location Based Services, 3*(2), 82–96. doi:10.1080/17489720902950374.

Goodchild, M. F., & Glennon, J. A. (2010). Crowdsourcing geographic information for disaster response: A research frontier. *International Journal of Digital Earth, 3*(3), 231–241. doi:10.1080/17538941003759255.

Gronlund, Å. (2003). Emerging electronic infrastructures: Exploring democratic components. *Social Science Computer Review, 21*(1), 55–72. doi:10.1177/0894439302238971.

Haklay, M., Singleton, A., & Parker, C. (2008). Web mapping 2.0: The neogeography of the GeoWeb. *Geography Compass, 2*(6), 2011–2039. doi:10.1111/j.1749-8198.2008.00167.x.

Höffken, S., & Streich, B. (2011). Engaging the mobile citizens – How mobile devices offer new ways of civil engagement. In M. Schrenk, V. V. Popovich, and P. Zeile (Eds.), *Proceedings REAL CORP 2011.* 18-20 May.

Holzer, M., & Kim, S.-T. (2008). *Digital governance in municipalities worldwide. A longitudinal assessment of municipal Websites throughout the world.* Newark: National Center for Public Performance, Rutgers University.

Holzer, M., Manoharan, A., & Ryzin, G. V. (2010). Global cities on the Web: An empirical typology of municipal Websites. *International Public Management Review, 11*(3), 104–121.

Howe, J. (2006). The rise of crowdsourcing. *Wired Magazine*, Issue 14/6.

Hudson-Smith, A., Crooks, A., Gibin, M., Milton, R., & Batty, M. (2009). NeoGeography and Web 2.0: Concepts, tools and applications. *Journal of Location Based Services, 3*(2), 118–145. doi:10.1080/17489720902950366.

Irvin, R. A., & Stansbury, J. (2004). Citizen participation in decision making: Is it worth the effort? *Public Administration Review, 64*(1), 55–65. doi:10.1111/j.1540-6210.2004.00346.x.

James, P., Fernando, T., Hamilton, A., & Curwell, S. (2004). *Enhancing the decision-making process in urban spatial planning using advanced ICT.* University of Salford, Issues Paper, April 2004.

Kim, S., & Lee, J. (2012). Citizen participation and transparency in local government: An empirical analysis. *2nd Global Conference on Transparency.* Utrecht University, Netherlands.

Kingston, R. (2002). *The role of e-government and public participation in the planning process XVI AESOP Congress.* Volos, Greece, July 10th –14th 2002.

Klosterman, R. E. (2012). E-planning in retrospect and prospect. *International Journal of E-Planning Research, 1*(1), 1–4. doi:10.4018/ijepr.2012010101.

Kubicek, H. (2010). The potential of e-participation in urban planning: A European perspective. In Silva, C. N. (Ed.), *Handbook of research on e-planning: ICTs for urban development and monitoring*. Hershey: IGI-Global. doi:10.4018/978-1-61520-929-3.ch009.

Lara, S., & Naval, C. (2012). Social networks, civic engagement, and young people. In Manoharan, A., & Holzer, M. (Eds.), *Active citizen participation in e-government. A global perspective* (pp. 187–205). Hershey: IGI-Global. doi:10.4018/978-1-4666-0116-1.ch010.

Macintosh, A. (2004). Characterizing e-participation in policy-making. *Proceedings of the 37th Hawaii International Conference on System Sciences*.

Macintosh, A., Robson, E., Smith, E., & Whyte, A. (2003). Electronic democracy and young people. *Social Science Computer Review, 21*(1), 43–54. doi:10.1177/0894439302238970.

Macintosh, A., & Whyte, A. (2006). *Evaluating how e-participation changes local democracy. E-Government Workshop '06 (eGov 06)*. London: Brunel University.

Macintosh, A., Whyte, A., & Renton, A. (2005). *From the top down. An evaluation of e-Democracy activities initiated by councils and governments*. Bristol: Bristol City Council.

McCaffrey, R. E. (2005). Using citizen science in urban bird studies. *Urban Habitats, 3*(1).

Moody, R. (2007). Assessing the role of GIS in e-government: A tale of e-participation in two cities. In Wimmer, M. A., Scholl, H. J., & Grönlund, A. (Eds.), *EGOV 2007, LNCS 4656* (pp. 354–365). doi:10.1007/978-3-540-74444-3_30.

Mossberger, K., & Wu, Y. (2012). *Civic engagement and local e-government: Social networking comes of age*. Chicago: Institute for Policy and Civic Engagement – University of Chicago.

Norris, P. (2004). *Deepening democracy via e-governance (Draft chapter for the UN World Public Sector Report)*. Retrieved from http://www.hks.harvard.edu/fs/pnorris/Acrobat/World%20Public%20Sector%20Report.pdf

Noveck, B. S. (2009). *Wiki government. How technology can make government better, democracy stronger, and citizens more powerful*. Washington: Brookings Institution Press.

Obermeyer, N. J. (1998). The evolution of public participation GIS. *Cartography and GIS, special issue on Public Participation GIS, 25*(2), 65-66.

OECD. (2001). *Citizens as partners: Information, consultation and public participation in policy-making*. Paris: OECD.

OECD. (2003). *Promises and problems of e-democracy: Challenges of citizen on-line engagement*. Paris: OECD.

Osimo, D. (2008). *Web 2.0 in government: Why and how?* Luxembourg: JRC Scientific and Technical Reports. Office of Official Publications of the European Communities, European Communities.

Overdevest, C., & Mayer, B. (2008). Harnessing the power of information through community monitoring: Insights from social science. *Texas Law Review, 86*(7), 1493–1526.

Parameswaran, M., & Whinston, A. B. (2007). Social computing: An overview. *Communications of the Association for Information Systems, 19*, 762–780.

Peart, M. N., & Diaz, J. R. (2007). *Comparative project on local e-democracy initiatives in Europe and North America*. Geneve: University of Geneve and European Science Foundation.

Peng, Z.-R. (2001). Internet GIS for public participation. *Environment and Planning. B, Planning & Design, 28*, 889–905. doi:10.1068/b2750t.

Rana, S., & Joliveau, T. (2009). Neogeography: An extension of mainstream geography for everyone made by everyone? *Journal of Location Based Services*, *3*, 75–81. doi:10.1080/17489720903146824.

Rosa, P., & Pereira, Â. G. (2008). *E-participation. Promoting dialog and deliberation between institutions and civil society*. Luxembourg: European Commission Joint Research Center.

Saad-Sulonen, J. (2012). The role of the creation and sharing of digital media content in participatory e-planning. *International Journal of E-Planning Research*, *1*(2), 1–22. doi:10.4018/ijepr.2012040101.

Schatteman, A., Mohammed-Spigner, D., & Poluse, G. (2012). Citizen participation through municipal Websites: A global scorecard. In Manoharan, A., & Holzer, M. (Eds.), *Active citizen participation in e-government. A global perspective* (pp. 403–414). Hershey: IGI-Global. doi:10.4018/978-1-4666-0116-1.ch020.

Sieber, R. (2006). Public participation geographic information systems: A literature review and framework. *Annals of the Association of American Geographers. Association of American Geographers*, *96*(3), 491–507. doi:10.1111/j.1467-8306.2006.00702.x.

Sifry, M. (2004). The rise of open-source politics. *Nation (New York, N.Y.)*, 4.

Silva, C. N. (2010). *Handbook of research on e-planning: ICTs for urban development and monitoring*. Hershey: IGI-Global. doi:10.4018/978-1-61520-929-3.

Silva, C. N. (2010a). The e-planning paradigm. Theory, Methods and Tools: An overview. In Silva, C. N. (Ed.), *Handbook of research on e-planning: ICTs for urban development and monitoring*. Hershey: IGI-Global. doi:10.4018/978-1-61520-929-3.ch001.

Silva, C. N. (2012). *Online research methods in urban and planning studies: Design and outcomes*. Hershey: IGI-Global.

Silva, C. N. (2012a). Research methods for urban planning in the digital age. In Silva, C. N. (Ed.), *Online research methods in urban and planning studies: Design and outcomes* (pp. 1–16). Hershey: IGI-Global. doi:10.4018/978-1-4666-0074-4.ch001.

Smith, A., Schlozman, K. L., Verba, S., & Brady, H. (2009). *The Internet and civic engagement*. Washington: Pew Internet & American Life Project.

Starbird, K. (2011). Digital volunteerism during disaster: Crowdsourcing information processing. CHI 2011. May 7-12. Vancouver, BC, Canada.

Sundstrom, L.-M. (2012). I-Government: Interactive government enabling civic engagement and a new volunteerism. In Kloby, K., & D'Agostinho, M. J. (Eds.), *Citizen 2.0: Public and governmental interaction through Web 2.0 technologies* (pp. 297–308). Hershey, PA: IGI-Global. doi:10.4018/978-1-4666-0318-9.ch015.

Surowiecki, J. (2004). *The wisdom of crowds*. New York: Anchor /Random House.

Tait, E. (2012). Web 2.0 for eParticipation: Transformational Tweeting or devaluation of democracy? In Kloby, K., & D'Agostinho, M. J. (Eds.), *Citizen 2.0: Public and governmental interaction through Web 2.0 technologies* (pp. 224–249). Hershey: IGI-Global. doi:10.4018/978-1-4666-0318-9.ch012.

UN. (2006). *Compendium of innovative e-government practices (Vol. II)*. New York: United Nations, Department of Economic and Social Affairs.

UN. (2009). *Compendium of innovative e-government practices (Vol. III)*. New York: United Nations, Department of Economic and Social Affairs.

Van Laer, J., & Van Aelst, P. (2010). Internet and social movement action repertoires. Opportunities and limitations. *Information Communication and Society, 2010*, 1–26.

Warf, B., & Sui, D. (2010). From GIS to neogeography: Ontological implications and theories of truth. *Annals of GIScience, 26*(4), 197–209.

Weber, L., Loumakis, A., & Bergman, J. (2003). Who participates and why? An analysis of citizens on the Internet and the mass public. *Social Science Computer Review, 21*(1), 25–32. doi:10.1177/0894439302238969.

Wiggins, A., & Crowston, K. (2010). Distributed scientific collaboration: Research opportunities in citizen science. In *The Changing Dynamics of Scientific Collaboration, CSCW 2010 Workshop*. Savannah, GA.

Wiggins, A., & Crowston, K. (2011). From conservation to crowdsourcing: A typology of citizen science. *44th Hawai International Conference on system Sciences (HICSS)*.

Zavattaro, S. M. (2012). Records management, privacy, and social media: An overview. In Kloby, K., & D'Agostinho, M. J. (Eds.), *Citizen 2.0: Public and governmental interaction through Web 2.0 technologies* (pp. 41–64). Hershey: IGI-Global. doi:10.4018/978-1-4666-0318-9.ch003.

ADDITIONAL READING

Al-Kodmany, K., Betancur, J., & Vidyarthi, S. (2012). E-civic engagement and the youth: New frontiers and challenges for urban planning. *International Journal of E-Planning Research, 1*(3), 87–104. doi:10.4018/ijepr.2012070105.

Anttiroiko, A.-V., & Malkia, M. (Eds.). (2006). *Encyclopedia of digital government*. Hershey: Information Science Reference. doi:10.4018/978-1-59140-789-8.

Batty, M., Hudson-Smith, A., Milton, R., & Crooks, A. (2010). Map mashups, Web 2.0 and the GIS revolution. *Annals of GIS, 16*(1), 1–13. doi:10.1080/19475681003700831.

Bishop, I. D. (2012). On-line approaches to data delivery and visualisation in landscape planning and management. *International Journal of E-Planning Research, 1*(1), 31–41. doi:10.4018/ijepr.2012010104.

Bricout, J., & Baker, P. (2010). Deploying information and communication technologies to enhance participation in local governance for citizens with disabilities. *International Journal of Information Communication Technologies and Human Development, 2*(2), 34–51. doi:10.4018/jicthd.2010040103.

Budthimedhee, K., Li, J., & George, R. V. (2002). e-Planning: A snapshot of the literature on using the World Wide Web in urban planning. *Journal of Planning Literature, 17*(2), 227–246. doi:10.1177/088541202762475964.

Carver, S., Evans, A., Kingston, R., & Turton, I. (2001). Public participation, GIS, and cyber democracy: Evaluating on-line spatial decision support systems. *Environment and Planning. B, Planning & Design, 28*, 907–921. doi:10.1068/b2751t.

Castells, M. (2010). The information age: Economy, society and culture (Vol. I-The Rise of the Network Society; Vol. II-The Power of Identity; Vol. III-End of Millennium). Oxford: Wiley-Blackwell.

Charlesworth, A. (2012). Addressing legal issues in online research, publication and archiving: A UK perspective. In Silva, C. N. (Ed.), *Online research methods in urban and planning studies: Design and outcomes* (pp. 368–393). Hershey: IGI-Global. doi:10.4018/978-1-4666-0074-4.ch022.

Chen, Y., Song, Y., Bowker, S., & Hamilton, A. (2012). The SURegen workbench: A Web-based collaborative regeneration tool. *International Journal of E-Planning Research*, *1*(2), 44–64. doi:10.4018/ijepr.2012040103.

Conroy, M. M., & Evans-Cowley, J. (2010). The e-citizen in planning: U.S. municipalities' views of who participates online. In Silva, C. N. (Ed.), *Handbook of Research on E-Planning: ICTs for Urban Development and Monitoring* (pp. 218–236). Hershey: IGI-Global. doi:10.4018/978-1-61520-929-3.ch011.

Falch, M. (2006). ICT and the future conditions for democratic governance. *Telematics and Informatics*, *23*, 134–156. doi:10.1016/j.tele.2005.06.001.

Fritz, S., McCallum, I., Schill, C., Perger, C., Grillmayer, R., & Achard, F. et al. (2009). Geo-Wiki.Org: The use of crowdsourcing to improve global land cover. *Remote Sensing*, *1*, 345–354. doi:10.3390/rs1030345.

Ganapati, S. (2010). *Using geographic information systems to increase citizen engagement*. Washington: IBM Center for the Business of Government.

Garson, G. D., & Khostow-Pour, M. (Eds.). (2008). *Handbook of research on public information technology*. Hershey: Information Science Reference. doi:10.4018/978-1-59904-857-4.

Goodchild, M. F. (2012). The future of digital earth. *Annals of GIS*, *18*(2), 93–98. doi:10.1080/19475683.2012.668561.

Graham, S. (2002). Bridging urban digital divides? Urban polarization and information and communications technologies. *Urban Studies (Edinburgh, Scotland)*, *39*(1), 33–56. doi:10.1080/00420980220099050.

Granberg, M., & Astrom, J. (2010). Planners support of e-participation in the field of urban planning. In Silva, C. N. (Ed.), *Handbook of research on e-planning: ICTs for urban development and monitoring* (pp. 237–251). Hershey: IGI-Global. doi:10.4018/978-1-61520-929-3.ch012.

Harrison, C., & Haklay, M. (2002). The potential of public participation geographic information systems in UK environmental planning: Appraisals by active publics. *Journal of Environmental Planning and Management*, *45*(6), 841–863. doi:10.1080/0964056022000024370.

Haubrock, S., Wittkopf, T., Grünthal, G., & Dransch, D. (2007). Community-made earthquake intensity maps using Google's API. *10th AGILE International Conference on Geographic Information Science*. Aalborg University, Denmark.

Heipke, C. (2010). Crowdsourcing geospatial data. *ISPRS Journal of Photogrammetry and Remote Sensing*, *65*, 550–557. doi:10.1016/j.isprsjprs.2010.06.005.

Hudson-Smith, A., Evans, S., & Batty, M. (2005). Building the virtual city: Public participation through e-democracy. *Knowledge, Technology & Policy*, *18*(1), 62–85. doi:10.1007/s12130-005-1016-9.

Hurworth, R. (2012). Search conferences and future search conferences: Potential tools for urban planning in an on-line environment. In Silva, C. N. (Ed.), *Online research methods in urban and planning studies: Design and outcomes* (pp. 216–222). Hershey: IGI-Global. doi:10.4018/978-1-4666-0074-4.ch013.

Jankowski, P. (2009). Towards participatory geographic information systems for community based environmental decision making. *Journal of Environmental Management*, *90*(6), 1966–1971. doi:10.1016/j.jenvman.2007.08.028 PMID:18550264.

Klosterman, R. E. (1997). Planning support systems: A new perspective on computer-aided planning. *Journal of Planning Education and Research, 17*(1), 45–54. doi:10.1177/0739456X9701700105.

Madon, S., Reinhard, N., Roode, D., & Walsham, G. (2009). Digital inclusion projects in developing countries: Processes of institutionalization. *Information Technology for Development, 15*(2), 95–107. doi:10.1002/itdj.20108.

Mossberger, K., Tolbert, C., & McNeal, R. (Eds.). (2008). *Digital citizenship. The Internet, Society, and Participation.* Cambridge, MA: The MIT Press.

Nedovic-Budic, Z. (2000). Geographic information science implications for urban and regional planning. *URISA Journal, 12*(2), 81–93.

Nordin, K., & Berglund, U. (2010). Children's maps in GIS: A tool for communicating outdoor experiences in urban planning. *International Journal of Information Communication Technologies and Human Development, 2*(2), 1–16. doi:10.4018/jicthd.2010040101.

Nyerges, T. L., & Jankowski, P. (2007). Participatory geographic information science. In Anttiroiko, A. V., & Malkia, M. (Eds.), *Encyclopedia of digital government* (pp. 1314–1318). Hershey: IGI-Global.

Poser, K., & Dransch, D. (2010). Volunteered geographic information for disaster management with application to rapid flood damage estimation. *Geomatica, 64*(1), 89–98.

Rinner, C. (2001). Argumentation maps: GIS-based discussion support for on-line planning. *Environment and Planning. B, Planning & Design, 28*, 847–863. doi:10.1068/b2748t.

Rinner, C., Keßler, C., & Andrulis, S. (2008). The use of Web 2.0 concepts to support deliberation in spatial decision-making. *Computers, Environment and Urban Systems, 32*(5), 386–395. doi:10.1016/j.compenvurbsys.2008.08.004.

Rowland, D., Kohl, U., & Charlesworth, A. (2012). *Information technology law* (4th ed.). London: Routledge.

Sheppard, S. R. J., & Cizek, P. (2009). The ethics of Google Earth: Crossing thresholds from spatial data to landscape visualisation. *Journal of Environmental Management, 90*, 2102–2117. doi:10.1016/j.jenvman.2007.09.012 PMID:18599184.

Silva, C. N. (Ed.). (2010). Special issue "Local governance in the digital age: e-Participation of children and citizens with disabilities.". *International Journal of Information and Communication Technologies, 2*(2).

Silva, C. N. (Ed.). (2010). Special issue "Local governance in the digital age: Citizen e-participation in rural areas and in displaced aboriginal communities.". *International Journal of Information and Communication Technologies, 2*(3).

Staffans, A., Rantanen, H., & Nummi, P. (2010). Local Internet forums. Interactive land use planning and urban development neighborhoods. In Silva, C. N. (Ed.), *Handbook of research on e-planning: ICTs for urban development and monitoring* (pp. 80–102). Hershey: IGI Global. doi:10.4018/978-1-61520-929-3.ch005.

Steinmann, R., Krek, A., & Blaschke, T. (2004). *Analysis of online public participatory GIS applications with respect to the differences between the US and Europe. Paper published in the Proceedings of Urban Data Management Symposium '04.* Italy: Chioggia.

Steinmann, R., Krek, A., & Blaschke, T. (2005). Can online map-based applications improve citizen participation? In Böhlen, M. et al. (Eds.), *TCGOV 2005, LNAI 3416* (pp. 25–35). doi:10.1007/978-3-540-32257-3_3.

Suri, H., & Patel, F. (2012). Ethical considerations in online research methods. In Silva, C. N. (Ed.), *Online research methods in urban and planning studies: Design and outcomes* (pp. 394–408). Hershey: IGI-Global. doi:10.4018/978-1-4666-0074-4.ch023.

Wallin, S., Horelli, L., & Saad-Sulonen, J. (Eds.). (2010). *Digital tools in participatory planning. Aalto.* Aalto University, School of Science and Technology, Centre for Urban and Regional Studies.

Wesolowski, A., & Eagle, N. (2012). Mobile phones as a lens into slum dynamics. In Silva, C. N. (Ed.), *Online research methods in urban and planning studies: Design and outcomes* (pp. 334–352). Hershey: IGI-Global. doi:10.4018/978-1-4666-0074-4.ch020.

Wessels, B., Dittrich, Y., Ekelin, A., & Eriksén, S. (2012). Creating synergies between participatory design of e-services and collaborative planning. *International Journal of E-Planning Research, 1*(3), 1–16. doi:10.4018/ijepr.2012070101.

Wyld, D. C. (2008). Blogging. In Garson, G. D., & Khosrow-Pour, M. (Eds.), *Handbook of research on public information technology* (pp. 81–93). Hershey, PA: IGI-Global. doi:10.4018/978-1-59904-857-4.ch009.

Chapter 2
E–Democracy Systems and Participation Outcomes in Urban Governance

Rajeev Sharma
University of Wollongong, Australia

Atreyi Kankanhalli
National University of Singapore, Singapore

Mahdieh Taher
National University of Singapore, Singapore

ABSTRACT

The concept of democracy has a long tradition of research in the political science domain. In recent years, advances in Information and Communication Technologies (ICT) have provided opportunities for governments to deploy systems to actively engage citizens in the agenda-setting and decision-making processes for urban governance. Consequently, e-democracy and e-participation efforts have emerged and attracted researchers' attention in the Information Systems (IS) field. Information systems lay the foundations of active citizenry, which may impact on the participation outcome. However, in order to maximize the potential of this evolving form of democracy, researchers and practitioners need to address a number of challenges in the design of participation structures for city governance. This chapter sets out to explore e-democracy systems and their impact on a number of e-participation outcomes. Outlining both promoters and barriers of ICT use for e-democracy, the authors also uncover gaps in the previous literature and identify an agenda for future research.

INTRODUCTION

Democratic processes can be enabled by information systems (IS) to provide communication and coordination means for governments to involve multiple participants. These capabilities attract

DOI: 10.4018/978-1-4666-4169-3.ch002

scholars to study the impact of IS on government. One stream of such research has focused on the capabilities of IS to improve the efficiency and effectiveness with which state-provided services, such as social security, housing and health care, are delivered to citizens. Generally referred to as e-government research, this stream has focused on e-government as a platform for exchanging information, providing services, and transacting with citizens, businesses, and other arms of government (Sahu, Dwivedi, & Weerakkody, 2009) and on integrated platforms enabling citizen-centric services (Weerakkody, Janssen, & Dwivedi, 2009). The issues investigated in this stream of research and the theoretical frameworks employed closely parallel those investigated in the research on the impact of IS on organizational effectiveness and the adoption and implementation of IS applications.

Another stream of research has focused on the impact of IS on the relationship between the citizen and state. Many scholars have long speculated on the possibility of employing IS to transform the functioning and governance of democratic governments (Behrouzi, 2005; Macpherson, 1977; Päivärinta & Sæbø, 2006). In particular, the capabilities of modern IS enable a much higher level of citizen participation in the agenda-setting and decision-making processes of government than are currently evident in even the most liberal western democracies operating today. This has important implications for the governance of urban areas, which has become a key issue for governments as half of the world population now lives in cities (UN, 2011).

The outcomes of the e-democratization process are closely linked to the design, development, and implementation of IS underpinning e-democracy. E-democracy initiatives can serve as two-way communication between government and citizens, educate citizens about the rationale and complexity of policy-making, legitimize government decisions, and provide opportunities for mutual learning (Coleman & Gøtze, 2001). Furthermore, they can enhance accessibility by overcoming the offline physical constraints of time and space (Phang & Kankanhalli, 2008).

While IS provides the capabilities to introduce more participatory forms of democracy and high levels of citizen engagement (Habermas, 1999), practical considerations suggest the need for participation limits in the interest of achieving closure

on decisions. Thus, a number of participation-limiting structures may require to be imposed e.g., limit discussion on an issue to a certain time frame and mandate voting on an issue on a certain date.

E-democracy raises important issues for IS researchers as the information systems created for transforming political and urban governance will both be shaped by such considerations and will, in turn, shape the processes and outcomes of those transformations. These issues are at the intersection of IS and political science research.

This chapter describes democracy concepts, e-democracy systems and tools, theoretical lenses to study e-democracy phenomenon, and e-democracy outcomes. Furthermore, it outlines challenges and provides directions for future research.

DEMOCRACY CONCEPTS

E-Democracy

The rapid development of new technologies, particularly networks and the WWW has impacted on the traditional means of government communication with citizens and increased the interest in IS for participation in political processes (Dijk, 2000). The exploitation of information and communication technology (ICT) is being extended to the democracy sphere, such as in increasing citizen involvement in policy-making and soliciting citizens' inputs in planning (Moon, 2000). Consequently, the concept of e-democracy emerged as the employment of ICT in political debates and decision-making processes, whether complementing or contrasting to the previous and traditional ways of communication, e.g., face-to-face interaction or one-way mass media (Sæbø, 2006). Here, in this chapter, e-democracy is defined as a form of government in which the technological capabilities of modern IS is employed to support citizen participation in the agenda-setting and decision-making processes of government. Similarly, it defines e-democratization as the process of moving towards more participatory forms of democracy employing the technological capabilities of modern IS. E-democratization initiatives are being reported at local, district, state and national levels of government, and also in other collectives such as workers unions, student unions and virtual communities (Hercheui, 2009).

One of the impetuses for e-democracy initiatives can be attributed to governments' growing recognition of the need to work toward more democratic governance (Coleman & Gøtze, 2001). In fact, as citizens have become less dependent and their demands more volatile, traditional representation is more under pressure to change. Another motivator of e-democracy is governments' response to a widespread public interest in the potential of ICT to empower citizens (Jain & Patnayakuni, 2003). Several e-democracy initiatives at the local municipality level (Grönlund, 2003; Sæbø & Päivärinta, 2005) as well as international programs (European Commission, 2007), are indicators that ICT can contribute to increased democratization. A number of e-democracy initiatives are under way around the world. For instance, regulations.gov is a United States initiative to provide citizens an online way to participate in and impact federal rules and regulations. The portal has

several features including search, view, and input comments for issued regulations. Thus, citizens can conveniently provide their comments online instead of visiting a government reading room to comment on proposed legislation. Similarly, in Asia, the Singapore government launched a portal called REACH to reach out to and engage citizens in the policy making process, gather ground sentiments and promote active citizenry. Table 1 summarizes various examples of e-democracy from around the globe.

The exploitation of IS in these existing initiatives is primarily as a complementary means of communication between citizens, elected representatives, and governments. In fact, through e-democracy governments have created a public sphere for deliberation (Habermas, 1985; 1999). However, these initiatives are still in their initial stage of changing the relationship between citizens and governments. In the future, they are likely to provide more IS-enabled initiatives for citizen participation in governance. Given continuing pressure for citizen participation in governance, the next generation of e-democracy initiatives is likely to offer more governance options to citizens, such as agenda-setting. For instance, the government of the Canadian province of British Colum-

Table 1. Examples of e-democracy initiatives

Country	E-democracy Initiative	Description
Australia	Community Builders (http://communitybuilders.nsw.gov.au)	A portal to enable online community consultation, e-petition, and broadcasting parliament activities
Denmark	Nordpol.dk (http://www.rn.dk/)	To enhance citizens' interest of politics and strengthen the dialogue among citizens and politicians
Israel	SHIL (http://www.shil.shil.info/)	To provide a new channel to communicate with decision makers, and improve public information flow
Singapore	REACH (http://www.reach.gov.sg)	A national-level portal to encourage policy information exchange and to better connect with citizens
Sweden	Kalix Annual consultation (http://www.kalix.se)	To engage citizens in a series of efforts to renew town policies, e.g., tax issues
UK	UK Government Consultations (https://www.gov.uk/government/consultations)	To provide a platform for citizen feedback on policy issues, and to offer political and civic information to citizens
US	Regulations.gov (http://www.regulations.gov)	A cross-agency effort to enhance public's ability to participate in regulatory decision-making

bia created a citizens' assembly of 160 near-randomly chosen citizens to deliberate on and design a proposal for electoral reform which was put to referendum in 2005 (Warren & Pearse, 2008). This example underscores the value of IS in agenda-setting and decision-making processes as governments respond to citizen demands for greater participation.

Representative Democracy

One of the leading models of democracy is representative democracy which is practiced in western countries like the U.S, Australia, and Western European countries. In this model, officials are selected by citizens through elections to run the government, and exercise government control over the agenda. However, the participation of citizens in the decision-making processes of government is only implicit (Hirst, 1990; Päivärinta & Sæbø, 2006). After elections, there is no direct control of citizens on the agenda and decisions; only the elected representatives are directly involved in decision-making processes. However, limited influence is retained by citizens through the forum of robust public debate. It is believed that periodic election and re-election can assure that elected representatives follow the will of citizens and citizens can impact on governments through robust public debate, thus protecting citizens against the tyranny of the state (Sartori, 1987; Sen, 1999).

Most scholars consider representative democracy as a practical model of democracy, though not an ideal one. An ideal form of democracy often described in the literature is one in which citizens have an explicit role in the decision-making processes and control over the agenda (Päivärinta & Sæbø, 2006). This model is similar to the descriptions of ancient Greek democracy where agenda-setting and decision-making were done directly and publicly by citizens (Mill, 2006). This ideal model of democracy is referred to as direct democracy; the main characteristic being that citizens directly run the government (Päivärinta & Sæbø, 2006; Warren & Pearse, 2008).

A challenging problem with representative democracies is how to resolve the conflict between the interests of the citizens and their representatives. Elected officials are the agents of the citizens, which imply that they should act in the interests of the people they represent. However, the interests of the representatives and the people they represent may not be aligned in all cases; in some cases they can even be opposed. Consequently, representative democracy is subject to the agency problem. In this case, opportunistic behaviors on the part of elected representatives can occur. There are ample examples in the popular press of elected representatives not acting in the interests of the people they represent but in their own interests, for instance frequent reports of corruption by elected officials.

Representative democracy has also been implicated in the rise of party politics, ideological rigidity and the power of special interest groups to thwart the will of the citizens. It also results in people being forced to accept trade-offs that they would not personally make but have to accept them as *fait accompli* when they are made by their elected representatives. It is questionable if elected representatives actually represent the will of the people in the decisions they take during their elected tenure (Macpherson, 1977). It is even arguable that people who support such decisions in public polls would actually choose these options if they were making those decisions. The estrangement between representatives and the citizens who they represent is manifested in many western countries by "falling voter turnout; lower levels of public participation in civic life; public cynicism towards political institutions and parties; and a collapse in once-strong political loyalties and attachments" (Coleman & Gøtze, 2001, p. 4).

In direct democracy, a large number of people need to negotiate and agree upon an agenda, making the processes of decision-making very complex and time-consuming. As a result, the process of governance slows down and comes to a standstill. As the number of participants increases, direct democracy becomes infeasible. Therefore, any alternative models that can fulfill the benefits of a democratic form of governance are far superior to the direct democracy model, which inevitably lead to a situation of collective paralysis of decision-making. One such alternative model is representative democracy. In this form, citizens preserve their rights to influence the agenda and decisions, though not directly.

E-DEMOCRACY SYSTEMS

E-Democracy Systems and Tools

A variety of tools and IS can be employed in e-democracy initiatives such as web comment forms, online discussion forums, online survey, e-vote, e-mail, online survey, and group support system. One of the emerging technologies is Web 2.0 which is being increasingly used by candidates, politicians, political parties, and interest groups to campaign online and engage citizens in the election process (Dai & Norton, 2008; Kang & Dyson, 2007). However, the selection of appropriate systems and tools should be considered important as well to better attain e-democracy objectives. It is suggested that e-democracy can have different objectives such as informing citizens, generating support among citizens, utilizing citizens' input in decision making, and probing for citizens' needs (Phang

& Kankanhalli, 2008). Thus, the ad-hoc utilization of ICT systems and tools may weaken participation outcomes and jeopardize resource investment and efforts. Table 2 illustrates the various tools and systems for different objectives. Depending on the purpose of e-democracy initiative and features desired, appropriate ICT tools and systems can be employed.

Participation-Limiting Structures

While efforts are being made to increase e-participation, it is believed that democratic ideals have been thwarted by the limitations of representative democracy (Behrouzi, 2005; Dai & Norton, 2008; Hercheui, 2009). Particularly, one of the characteristics of representative democracy is participation-limiting structures. This characteristic has some inherent limitations which may lead to expected adverse outcomes. For example, the rise of party politics, ideological rigidity of political parties, political corruption, and the power of special interest groups can thwart the will and interest of citizens (Hirst, 1990; Macpherson, 1977). Consequently, representative democracy may cause general disaffection of citizens with politicians, political parties, and the political process which, as a result, lower the levels of citizen engagement and question the legitimacy of democratic governments (Hirst, 1990; Mill, 2006; Warren & Pearse, 2008).

Table 2. ICT tools and systems for e-democracy (adapted from Phang & Kankanhalli, 2008)

E-Democracy Objectives and Support Systems				
Objective	Information Exchange	Education & Support-building	Decision-making Supplement	Input Probing
Features Desired	Open exchange of information	Formal selection of participants Maintenance of contact	Control of participation processes	Systematic collection and analysis of input
Best-fitting Techniques	Drop-in center, Public meeting	Citizen advisory committee, Citizen panel	Nominal Group Process, Value analysis	Citizen survey
ICT Tools and Systems to Support E-democracy	Web portal with Online bulletin boards, Online chats	Electronic profiling, Tele- & video-conferencing, E-mail	GSS, Structured surveys, Visualization tools	Online surveys, Web comment form, Data analysis tools

On the other hand, it is argued that e-democracy brings improved social and individual outcomes and can be closer to the idealized democracy form (Behrouzi, 2005; Locke, 2005). In fact, e-democracy has the potential of less restrictive participation-limiting structures than representative democracy. Thus, it is possible that a number of structures can emerge in the design of systems underpinning e-democracy. These structures can provide the broader social context within which e-democracy is enacted. In the design and successful implementation of e-democracy systems, an understanding of the emergence and effects of participation-limiting structures on social choice and citizen welfare are important issues.

Researchers have investigated the effect of participation-limiting structures for a smaller number of participants compared to the population of a state or a country such as online communities. One of the exemplary studies by Hercheui (2009) illustrates the effects of decision-making and participation-limitation structures on the legitimacy and transparency of community decisions as well as on the welfare and e-democratic process outcomes for citizens. Interviews were conducted with 58 members of four online communities to understand factors that foster and constrain democratic debate among participants. Online communities have some similar features to e-democracy systems such as discussions and debates among members through the Internet. In this study, democratic debates in online communities were studied and the impacts of participation-limiting structures in an e-democracy setting were examined: "These communities present themselves as informal collectives ... which have the aim of discussing environmental education mainly through discussion lists, and of mobilizing political efforts to influence the government and private organizations in their policies related to the theme" (Hercheui, 2009 p. 3).

Although, online communities promote freedom of speech and democratic debate, Hercheui's findings show that participation-limiting struc-tures emerged to limit and compromise democratic debate in a number of ways. For example, members with minority opinions or divergent view points from group leaders were suppressed and/or publicly shamed. The power of actors directed and could shape the debate. Accordingly, rewards and sanctions to the proponents and opposition, respectively, could be found. He highlights that the aim of these communities is to democratise discussion, however, "community members feel constrained in these very same virtual spaces as they understand they do not have freedom of opinion, especially in situations in which they would like to criticize the mainstream ideas and oppose the interests of powerful social actors" (Hercheui, 2009 p. 8). Hercheui concludes that the space for idealized democratic debate is limited even in these supposedly democratic communities: "on the one hand the communities appear as spaces for the democratization of the discussion ... and on the other hand members constrain their opinions, respecting established structures of authority and fearing the surveillance of more powerful members" (p. 3). This study emphasizes the importance of democratic processes themselves, separated from the democratic settings. The design of e-democracy systems needs to be shaped by the understanding of the effect of democratic processes on the outcomes that a country is expected to deliver for citizens. We describe below various theories which can help to investigate these issues.

THEORETICAL LENSES

Democracy and citizen participation have long been one of the main research themes in political science. A number of theoretical perspectives have been devised to study e-democracy and antecedents of it. The widely employed theoretical perspectives on participation limitation and enhancement are social choice theories, discourse theories (Sharma, 2011), socio-economic theories, and rational choice theories (Phang & Kankanhalli, 2005). We will provide a brief description of each theory and attempt to illuminate the links between the theory and e-democracy systems.

Social Choice Theories

One of the main purposes of democracy is aggregating the various preferences of participants in deciding on collective actions. Social choice theories contribute to identify the multiple social mechanisms for combining preferences (Arrow, 1951; Suzumura, 2005). For example, voting rule is one of these mechanisms commonly employed in a direct democracy, which proposes one-vote for one-person. As a result, a collective decision is the option favored by the majority of participants. Similarly, representative democracy is another more complex version of this rule. Depending on the various levels of democratic values, the underpinning social mechanisms can be different indicating multiple models of democracy. It is observed that all voting rules can have conflicts with some basic democratic norms, e.g., non-imposition and non-dictatorship (Arrow, 1951). However, a democracy form is far more acceptable than other governance forms (Sen, 1999). Furthermore, there is no one best forms of democracy; it may even be difficult to provide enough support for the proposition that direct democracy is "more democratic" than representative democracy.

Discourse Theories

An ongoing debate regarding democratic governance and the rationality of outcomes exists in the political science literature. In this stream of research, discourse theories provide a perspective on the democratic process which is focused on the legitimacy of selected decisions and actions. Unlike social choice theorist who believe that the outcomes of democratic processes are unstable and irrational (Mill, 2006), it is argued that the long, equal, and open collective deliberation in

democratic form could deliver valid and legitimate outcomes (Habermas, 1999; Mill, 2006). In order to gain more stable and rational social outcomes, it is claimed that it is necessary to limit participation and impose justifiable limits on freedom (Hercheui, 2009; Mill, 2006). Consequently, representative democracy can be considered as a viable option that fulfills this objective by participation-limiting structures designed to improve the collective decision-making processes.

Socio-Economic Theories

The basis of socio-economic theories is in the sociology of citizen participation (Parry, Moyser, & Day, 1992) where this theoretical strand can explain the attitude of an individual behind participation in terms of social circumstances. The social circumstances include education level, age, and financial status. These theories argue that older, better educated, and wealthier citizens probably have higher participation rate than younger, less educated, and poorer people (e.g., Verba & Nie, 1972). While, their proposition is that individuals with advantaged social circumstances are more likely to participate in democratic debates, there are a number of scholars who questioned such propositions and showed that a higher education level does not necessarily lead to higher electoral participation (e.g., Lyons & Alexander, 2000; Verba, Schlozman, & Brady, 1995). Thus, a refinement and more comprehensive list of factors and mechanisms are required to link social circumstances to participation.

Rational Choice Theories

Citizen participation can also be studied by rational choice theories (Phang & Kankanhalli, 2005). The theories explain participation as a rational activity to maximize benefits and minimize costs (e.g., Olson, 1965). In this regard, citizens are considered as economically rational and decide to participate based on benefit-cost analysis. Benefits can include the ability to influence the outcome and cost is their time and resources that they expend in order to participate. Moreover, there is a positive link between one's perceived benefits and political efficacy. Unlike the socio-economic theories, rational choice theories consider social circumstances as having lower importance as compared to benefit-cost analysis of participation.

E-DEMOCRACY AND PARTICIPATION OUTCOMES

The normative expectation is that e-democracy would lead to better social and individual outcomes and enable the realization of democratic ideals. Modern IS, in particular, their capabilities to support communication, coordination and multi-participant decision-making provide a technological solution to the bottleneck problem. In theory, this makes e-democracy feasible, at least technically. Just as IS-enabled transformation has had a major impact on the structure and functioning of organizations, e-democratization is also likely to have a major impact on the structure and functioning of government and society, as well as of institutions, such as the legislature, the executive and the judiciary, that underpin democratic governance. As these initiatives unfold, the relationship between citizens and government is likely to be fundamentally transformed. For instance, we, as citizens, could have a direct say in policy, such as deciding whether our tax dollars go to fund education and healthcare, or to other activities. In this section, we will review a number of e-democracy outcomes for citizens and processes.

Citizen Outcomes

In addition to democratic values, democratic governments are also more likely to deliver positive social benefits as compared to autocratic alternatives (Locke, 2005). E-democratization research will thus need to address a new set of outcome variables not normally considered in IS research. In addition to the emancipatory outcomes expected of democracies, states are also expected to deliver certain social outcomes and 'common goods', such as economic prosperity, individual rights, property rights, law and order and national security (Locke, 2005; Rousseau, 2005; Sartori, 1987). While there has been considerable discussion in the literature on fair voting schemes and closer proximity of e-democracy to the democratic ideal (Behrouzi, 2005), there has been less discussion on the outcomes for citizens and nations. Will an e-democracy deliver, for instance, greater economic prosperity, less crime, more egalitarian income distribution, and greater national security?

Minority Rights

There is a distinct possibility that direct democracy can quickly translate to tyranny of the majority. Such outcomes have been observed in virtual communities and other collectives (Hercheui, 2009). In which case, there is a real concern about the ability of an e-democracy to ensure minority rights and to prevent state-sanctioned abuse of human rights. Similar situations have prevailed even in liberal western democracies, for instance, the denial of civil rights and the segregation of minorities in the USA, as well as the failure of law enforcement to prosecute crimes against minorities. For IS researchers, the issue will be the design of e-democracy artifacts to prevent such outcomes.

Quality of Decisions

There is an inherent conflict between the majority-rule principle underpinning direct democracy and the role of expertise in delivering task outcomes. Groups, including virtual teams, deliver best performance on tasks when the influence of group members on outcomes is in direct proportion to the expertise of group members (Bottger & Yetton, 1988). Current representative democracies rely on expert cadres of civil servants in the executive branch to carry out the tasks of the state. The experts, or technocrats, enjoy a fair degree of autonomy and latitude in carrying out their roles. However, if the decision-making process of an e-democracy is subject to the majority-rule criterion in its decision-making, task performance is likely to suffer due to the diminished role of expertise in informing decisions. Further, research into decision-making finds that democratic decision-making processes are likely to deliver desirable outcomes under certain task contexts, while more autocratic, expert-led decision-making processes might be more appropriate in other task contexts (Yetton & Vroom, 1973).

Political Transformation Process

Representative democracies, as any other governance structure, rely on the interdependent behaviors of a number of large and complex institutions. For instance, the executive, legislative and the judicial branches of democratic governments are critical for delivering democratic values, social welfare and other functions of the state. In democracies around the world, these institutions and their roles have evolved over time and are constitutionally guaranteed. Effective functioning of the state subsequent to an attempted transition to an e-democracy would require interdependent changes to the roles and functioning of the executive, legislative and judicial branches of government. However, the three branches of government usually possess a high degree of autonomy in most well functioning representative democracies. Indeed, the autonomy of these three institutions is critical for delivering effective democratic governance. The political processes involved in making the political transformation from representative democracies to e-democracies will be very complex and challenging. Such institutional complexity gives rise to a high level of inertia,

making change difficult. For instance, the Canadian referendum for electoral reform mentioned earlier did not succeed (Warren & Pearse, 2008).

Further, it is not clear if the interests of top political leaderships in representative democracies are aligned with the successful implementation of e-democracy. Moving from representative democracy to e-democracy involves devolution of powers from incumbent political leaderships to citizens. History provides few instances of voluntary devolution of power by political leaderships. On the contrary, there are many instances of strong resistance by political leaderships to citizens' demands for devolution of power. Often, the struggle could be brutal and violent, involving bloodshed and tragic loss of life. The examples of the English, French, American and Russian revolutions come readily to mind.

This is an important issue for IS researchers as projects for developing e-democracy applications are likely to be sponsored, managed and implemented by political leaders. The motivations of political leaders are likely to have an important bearing on the design and success of e-democracy projects.

E-DEMOCRACY RESEARCH CHALLENGES AND FUTURE DIRECTIONS

The above section highlighted several important themes for IS researchers to contribute to e-democracy research. While this research will need to be grounded in theories drawn from political science, it will necessarily be multi-disciplinary in character. IS research has strong intellectual traditions in many of the theoretical domains that will inform e-democracy research. IS researchers have made important intellectual contributions in investigating decision-making in groups, as also in investigating the effect of participation structures on the outcomes of group processes (e.g., Dennis

& Reinicke, 2004). Moreover, IS researchers bring their own core intellectual traditions of research in the design, development and management of IS projects, which will be important in researching issues related to e-democracy (Beath & Orlikowski, 1994; Hirschheim, Klein, & Lyytinen, 1995). In addition, IS researchers have made important contributions to understanding the transformation of large and complex social systems in response to the introduction of technology (Markus, 2004; Markus & Robey, 1988).

We believe that neither discourse theory, nor social choice theory, have been the subject of rigorous empirical examination (Mill, 2006). Thus, we identify two IS research traditions that can contribute to research on e-democracy. The first is the laboratory- and field-based research on group decision support systems, or GDSS research (Dennis, Tyran, Vogel, & Nunamaker, 1997; Dennis, Wixom, & Vandenberg, 2001). This stream of research has well-developed protocols, instruments and artifacts for investigating the effects of group decision-making. This genre of research can be easily extended to understand the effects of various decision-making and participating limiting strategies on group decisions. Of course, the decision-making and participation-limiting strategies to be investigated in e-democracy research will be different from those employed in traditional GDSS research in organizational settings. Specifically, such strategies will need to be grounded in political science theories (Phang & Kankanhalli, 2005).

To effectively contribute to e-democracy research, the GDSS genre of research will also need to focus on a different set of outcome variables than it has traditionally focused on. Dennis and Reinicke (2004) argue that this stream of research has been somewhat myopic, focusing on a limited number of outcome variables, such as the number of ideas generated in brainstorming, which may not even be of much practical relevance. The previous section has identified a number of new outcome variables that can be employed by the GDSS tra-

dition of research to contribute to e-democracy research, such as the legitimacy and transparency of decisions and the welfare and political identities of participants. The second IS research tradition that can contribute to e-democracy research is the tradition of field-based research investigating the effects of IS on decision-making processes and outcomes in organizations.

While it is difficult to imagine a full-scale implementation of e-democracy within which the above research questions can be investigated, many decision-making processes at different levels of government can be investigated to address the above questions. For instance, many local governments have decision-making processes that require citizen input as part of the decision-making process. As an example, local governments often invite comments from interested citizens on development applications before they can be considered for approval. However, the level of citizen involvement and control over the process vary across local governments. Such variations offer an interesting avenue for researching the above questions. In addition, other collectives, such as unions, that are based on collective decision-making processes also offer opportunities for conducting field-based research on e-democracy. Field-based experiments involving the use of IS for participant input may also be possible in some settings. An example of field-based research in the e-democracy genre is Hercheui's (2009) study of democratic debates in virtual communities, and Phang et al.'s (2007) investigation of participation in online communities.

In contrast, the emerging field of e-government research addresses a different research agenda. For instance, Srivastava and Teo (2009) define e-government in terms of access to and delivery of government services and explore the role of citizen trust in government in the use of e-government services by citizens. Similarly, Phang et al. (2006) employ an individual-level perspective to identify the significance of factors such as perceived usefulness and ease of use on the intentions of citizens to use e-government services, such as executing government transactions electronically. Issues of transforming the relationship between citizen and state are not on the agenda for research in the e-government stream.

However, the extent to which expectations of transformation in the relationship between citizen and state will be realized are important research questions for both political scientists and IS researchers. Equally important are questions pertaining to the social and political processes through which the transformations will be realized. E-democratization is a significant phenomena for IS researchers on account of a new research agenda that it opens up. While prior IS research on group support systems, IS implementation and IS-enabled transformation can usefully inform e-democratization research, it will also need to be grounded in relevant political science theory. For instance, the theoretical foundations of e-democracy have unresolved tensions that will need to be resolved in the processes of design, development and implementation of IS artifacts required for realizing e-democracy.

CONCLUSION

Democracy and the formal political process are fundamentally dependent on informed decision-making and effective communication about public issues between citizens and governments. Governments may seek to promote participation in order to improve the efficiency, acceptance, and legitimacy of political processes. At the same time, citizens may demand participation to promote their own interests and serve their needs. Various forms of ICT with the potential to support participation are available or being developed. As a result, e-democracy and e-participation efforts have attracted research attention in the Information Systems (IS) field. However, in order to realize the potential of such efforts, researchers and practitioners need to address a number of challenges in the design of participation structures for political and urban governance. This chapter has explored e-democracy systems and their impact on a number of e-participation outcomes. After uncovering gaps in the previous literature, it describes the relevant theories to investigate the phenomenon and identifies an agenda for future research.

Overall, e-democratization is an important emerging phenomenon that has the potential to transform both government and society. The intersection of political science and IS research opens up this new area for investigation. Such research will contribute to both IS and political science theory, as well as to shaping the future of government-citizen interaction. IS researchers are well positioned to extend their existing research traditions to contribute to e-democracy research.

REFERENCES

Arrow, K. J. (1951). *Social choice and individual values*. New York: Wiley.

Beath, C. M., & Orlikowski, W. J. (1994). The contradictory structure of systems development methodologies: Deconstructing the IS-user relationship in information engineering. *Information Systems Research*, 5(4), 350–377. doi:10.1287/isre.5.4.350.

Behrouzi, M. (2005). *Democracy as the political empowerment of the citizen: Direct - deliberative e-democracy*. Lanham, MD: Lexington Books.

Bottger, P. C., & Yetton, P. W. (1988). An integration of process and decision scheme explanations of group problem solving performance. *Organizational Behavior and Human Decision Processes*, 42(2), 234–249. doi:10.1016/0749-5978(88)90014-3.

Coleman, S., & Gøtze, J. (2001). *Bowling together: Online public engagement in policy deliberation online public engagement in policy deliberation*. London, UK: Hansard Society.

Dai, X., & Norton, P. (2008). *The Internet and parliamentary democracy in Europe: A comparative study of the ethics of political communication in the digital age.* New York, NY: Routledge.

Dennis, A. R., & Reinicke, B. A. (2004). BETA versus VHS and the acceptance of electronic brainstorming technology. *Management Information Systems Quarterly, 28*(1), 1–20.

Dennis, A. R., Tyran, C. K., Vogel, D. R., & Nunamaker, J. F. (1997). Group support systems planning strategic. *Journal of Management Information Systems, 14*(1), 155–184.

Dennis, A. R., Wixom, B. H., & Vandenberg, R. J. (2001). Understanding fit and appropriation effects in group support systems via meta-analysis. *Management Information Systems Quarterly, 25*(2), 167–193. doi:10.2307/3250928.

Dijk, J. (2000). Models of democracy and concepts of communication. In Hacker, K., & van Dijk, J. (Eds.), *Digital democracy, issues of theory and practice.* London: Sage.

European Commission. (2007). *Communicating about Europe via the Internet - engaging the citizens.* Retrieved from http://ec.europa.eu/dgs/communication/pdf/internet-strategy_en.pdf

Grönlund, Å. (2003). Emerging electronic infrastructures: Exploring democratic components. *Social Science Computer Review, 21*(1), 55–72. doi:10.1177/0894439302238971.

Habermas, J. (1985). *The theory of communicative action (Vol. 1).* Boston: Beacon Press.

Habermas, J. (1999). Three normative models of democracy: Liberal, republican, procedural. In Kearney, R., & Dooley, M. (Eds.), *Questioning ethics: Contemporary debates in philosophy.* New York, NY: Routledge.

Hercheui, M. D. (2009). Virtual communities and democratic debates: A case study on institutional influences. *International Conference on Information Systems (ICIS) Proceedings.* Phoenix.

Hirschheim, R. A., Klein, H. K., & Lyytinen, K. (1995). *Information systems development and data modeling: Conceptual and philosophical foundations.* Cambridge University Press. doi:10.1017/CBO9780511895425.

Hirst, P. (1990). *Representative democracy and its limits.* Cambridge: Polity Press.

Jain, A., & Patnayakuni, R. (2003). Public expectations and public scrutiny: An agenda for research in the context of e-government. *American Conference on Information Systems (AMCIS) Proceedings.* Tampa.

Kang, D. J., & Dyson, L. E. (2007). Internet politics in South Korea: The case of Rohsamo and Ohmynews Internet politics in South Korea. *18th Australasian Conference on Information Systems Proceedings* (pp. 1027-1034). Toowoomba.

Locke, J. (2005). *The second treatise of government. Keystones of democracy.* New York, NY: Barnes and Noble.

Lyons, W., & Alexander, R. (2000). A tale of two electorates: Generational replacement and the decline of voting in presidential elections. *The Journal of Politics, 26*(4), 1014–1034.

Macpherson, C. B. (1977). *The life and times of liberal democracy.* Oxford: Oxford University Press.

Markus, M. L. (2004). Technochange management: Using IT to drive organizational change. *Journal of Information Technology, 19*(1), 4–20. doi:10.1057/palgrave.jit.2000002.

Markus, M. L., & Robey, D. (1988). Information technology and organizational change: Causal structure in theory and research. *Management Science, 34*(5), 583–598. doi:10.1287/mnsc.34.5.583.

Moon, M. J. (2000). The evolution of e-government among municipalities: Rhetoric or reality? *Public Administration Review, 62*(4), 424–433. doi:10.1111/0033-3352.00196.

Olson, M. (1965). *The logic of collective action: Public goods and the theory of groups.* Cambridge, MA: Harvard University Press.

Päivärinta, T., & Sæbø, Ø. (2006). Models of e-democracy. *Communications of the Association for Information Systems, 17*(1), 818–840.

Parry, G., Moyser, G., & Day, N. (1992). *Political participation and democracy in Britain.* New York, NY: Cambridge University Press. doi:10.1017/CBO9780511558726.

Phang, C. W., & Kankanhalli, A. (2005). A research framework for citizen participation via eConsultation. *Americas Conference on Information Systems (AMCIS) Proceedings.* Omaha, NE.

Phang, C. W., & Kankanhalli, A. (2008). A framework of ICT exploitation for e-participation initiatives. *Communications of the ACM, 51*(12), 128–132. doi:10.1145/1409360.1409385.

Phang, C. W., Kankanhalli, A., Chua, Z., & Goh, K.-Y. (2007). Investigating participation in online policy discussion forums over time: Does network structure matter? *International Conference on Information Systems (ICIS) Proceedings.* Montreal, Canada.

Phang, C. W., Sutanto, J., Kankanhalli, A., Li, Y., Tan, B. C. Y., & Teo, H.-H. (2006). Senior citizens' acceptance of information systems: A study in the context of e-government services. *IEEE Transactions on Engineering Management, 53*(4), 555–569. doi:10.1109/TEM.2006.883710.

Rousseau, J.-J. (2005). *The social contract. Keystones of democracy.* New York, NY: Barnes and Noble.

Sæbø, Ø. (2006). A process for identifying objectives and technological forms in e-democracy initiatives. *Americas Conference on Information Systems (AMCIS) Proceedings.* Acapulco.

Sæbø, Ø., & Päivärinta, T. (2005). Autopoietic cybergenres for e-democracy? Genre analysis of a web-based discussion board. *Proceedings of the 38th Hawaii International Conference on System Sciences.*

Sahu, G. P., Dwivedi, Y. K., & Weerakkody, V. (2009). *E-Government development and diffusion: Inhibitors and facilitators of digital democracy.* Hershey, PA: IGI Global. doi:10.4018/978-1-60566-713-3.

Sartori, G. (1987). *The theory of democracy revisited.* Chatham, NJ: Chatham House.

Sen, A. K. (1999). Democracy as a universal value. *Journal of Democracy, 10*(3), 3–17. doi:10.1353/jod.1999.0055.

Sharma, R. (2011). Investigating the effect of participation-limiting structures on outcomes of e-democracy systems. *Pacific Asia Conference on Information Systems (PACIS) Proceedings.* Brisbane, Paper 174.

Srivastava, S. C., & Teo, T. S. H. (2009). Citizen trust development for e-government adoption and usage: Insights from young adults in Singapore. *Communications of the Association for Information Systems, 25*(1), 359–378.

Suzumura, K. (2005). An interview with Paul Samuelson: Welfare economics, "old" and "new," and social choice theory. *Social Choice and Welfare, 25*, 327–356. doi:10.1007/s00355-005-0007-9.

UN. (2011). *World urbanization prospects, the 2011 revision.* Retrieved from http://esa.un.org/unup/Documentation/final-report.htm

van Mill, D. (2006). *Deliberation, social choice and absolutist democracy.* New York, NY: Routledge.

Verba, S., & Nie, N. (1972). *Participation in America: Political democracy and social equality.* New York, NY: Harper and Row.

Verba, S., Schlozman, K., & Brady, H. (1995). *Voice and equality: Civic voluntarism in American politics.* Cambridge, MA: Harvard University Press.

Warren, M. E., & Pearse, H. (2008). *Designing deliberative democracy: The British Columbia citizens' assembly.* Cambridge, UK: Cambridge University Press. doi:10.1017/CBO9780511491177.

Weerakkody, V., Janssen, M., & Dwivedi, Y. K. (2009). *Handbook of research on ICT-enabled transformational government: A global perspective.* IGI Global. doi:10.4018/978-1-60566-390-6.

Yetton, P. W., & Vroom, V. H. (1973). *Leadership and decision-making.* University of Pittsburgh Press.

ADDITIONAL READING

Adams, B. (2004). Public meetings and the democratic process. *Public Administration Review, 64*(1), 43–54. doi:10.1111/j.1540-6210.2004.00345.x.

Åström, J., Karlsson, M., Linde, J., & Pirannejad, A. (2012). Understanding the rise of e-participation in non-democracies: Domestic and international factors. *Government Information Quarterly.*

Barber, B. (1998). *A place for us: How to make society civil and democracy strong.* New York: Hill and Wang.

Bishop, P., & Anderson, L. (2011). Communicative mechanisms of governance: E-democracy and the architecture of the public sphere. In *Information communication technologies and the virtual public sphere* (pp. 52–71). Hershey, PA: IGI Global.

Chadwick, A. (2003). Bringing e-democracy back in: Why it matters for future research on e-governance. *Social Science Computer Review, 21*(4), 443–455. doi:10.1177/0894439303256372.

Cullen, R., & Sommer, L. (2011). Participatory democracy and the value of online community networks: An exploration of online and offline communities engaged in civil society and political activity. *Government Information Quarterly, 28*(2), 148–154. doi:10.1016/j.giq.2010.04.008.

Dahlberg, L. (2001). The internet and democratic discourse: Exploring the prospects of online deliberative forums extending the public sphere. *Information Communication and Society, 4*(4), 615–633. doi:10.1080/13691180110097030.

Efremov, R., & Insua, D. R. (2010). Collaborative decision analysis and e-democracy. In D. Rios Insua, S. French, M. F. Shakun, T. Bui, G. O. Faure, G. Kersten, D. M. Kilgour, et al. (Eds.), e-Democracy, 5, 83-99. Springer.

Gross, T. (2002). E-democracy and community networks: Political visions, technological opportunities, and social reality. In Gronlund, A. (Ed.), *Electronic government: Design, applications, and management* (pp. 249–266). London: Idea Group Publishing.

Hague, B. N., & Loader, B. (1999). *Digital democracy: Discourse and decision making in the information age.* New York, NY: Routledge.

Insua, D. R., & French, S. (2010). *E-democracy: A group decision and negotiation perspective. Advances in group decision and negotiation, 5.* London: Springer.

Jensen, J. L. (2003). Virtual democratic dialogue? Bringing together citizens and politicians. *Information Polity, 8,* 29–47.

Kumar, N., & Vragov, R. (2005). The citizen participation continuum: Where does the US stand? *Proceedings of Americas Conference on Information Systems*. Omaha, USA.

Lee, C., Chang, K., & Berry, F. S. (2011). Testing the development and diffusion of e-government and e-democracy: A global perspective. *Public Administration Review*, *71*(3), 444–454. doi:10.1111/j.1540-6210.2011.02228.x.

Macintosh, A. (2004). Characterizing e-participation in policy-making. *Proceedings of the 37th Hawaii International Conference on System Sciences (HICSS)*.

Mahrer, H., & Krimmer, R. (2005). Towards the enhancement of e-democracy: Identifying the notion of the "middleman paradox.". *Information Systems Journal*, *15*(1), 27–42. doi:10.1111/j.1365-2575.2005.00184.x.

Mathews, D. (1994). *Politics for people: Finding a responsible public voice*. Chicago: University of Illinois Press.

Meier, A. (2012). eDemocracy & eGovernment: Stages of a democratic knowledge society. Verlang Berlin Heidelburg: Springer.

Milner, H. (2002). *Civic literacy: How informed citizens make democracy work*. Hanover: University of New England Press.

OECD. (2003). *Promise and problems of e-democracy: Challenges of online citizen engagement*. Paris, France: OECD Publishing.

Phang, C. W., & Kankanhalli, A. (2006). Promoting citizen participation via digital government. In Anttiroiko, A., & Mälkiä, M. (Eds.), *Encyclopedia of digital government*. Hershey, PA: Idea Group. doi:10.4018/978-1-59140-789-8.ch206.

Phang, C. W., & Kankanhalli, A. (2008). Current state and future of e-participation research. In Garson, G. D., & Khosrow-Pour, M. (Eds.), *Handbook of research on public information technology*. Hershey, PA: Idea Group. doi:10.4018/978-1-59904-857-4.ch008.

Tambouris, E., & Gorilas, S. (2003). Evaluation of an e-democracy platform for European cities. In R. Traunmuller (Ed.), Electronic government 2003, 43-48.

Thrane, L. E., Shelley, M. C. II, Shulman, S. W., Beisser, S. R., & Larson, T. B. (2004). E-political involvement: Age effects or attitudinal barriers? *Journal of E-Government*, *1*(4), 21–37. doi:10.1300/J399v01n04_03.

Watson, R.T., & Mundy. (2001). A strategic perspective of electronic democracy. *Communications of the ACM*, *44*(1), 27–30. doi:10.1145/357489.357499.

KEY TERMS AND DEFINITIONS

Citizen Outcomes: The outputs of citizen participation in democratic government, e.g., positive social benefits such as economic prosperity and individual rights.

Direct Democracy: Direct democracy is a form of government in which people vote on policy initiatives directly, as opposed to a representative democracy in which people vote for representatives who then vote on policy initiatives.

Discourse Theories: Theories focusing on discourse in political forums (such as debates, speeches, and hearings) as the phenomenon of interest. Political discourse is the informal exchange of reasoned views as to which of several alternative courses of action should be taken to solve societal problems.

E-Democracy: Refers to the use of information and communication technologies and strategies in political and governance processes.

Minority Rights: Rights of individuals who are not a part of the majority group.

Political Transformation Process: Refers to interdependent changes that transform the roles and functioning of the executive, legislative and judicial branches of government.

Rational Choice Theories: Theories that explain political participation as a rational activity to maximize benefits and minimize costs.

Representative Democracy: A form of democracy in which citizens elect officials to be their representative to run the government.

Social Choice Theories: Theories that explain multiple social mechanisms for combining preferences of people towards decision-making.

Socio-Economic Theories: Theoretical strands that can explain the attitude of an individual towards political participation in terms of social circumstances.

Chapter 3
Public Participation, Social Equity, and Technology in Urban Governance

Thomas W. Sanchez
Virginia Tech, USA

Marc Brenman
Social Justice Consultancy, USA

ABSTRACT

Social equity commonly refers to fairness or impartiality, usually in terms of inputs or outcomes related to social and economic opportunity. In the case of urban planning, social equity can take the form of participation in decision-making activities, especially those that involve allocating public resources. An assumption (and hope) is that through participation, stakeholders have greater influence on outcomes that are in their collective interest. Opportunities to participate are rapidly expanding along with rapid technological innovation. Therefore, the authors argue that there is a connection among participation, equity, and technology in creating more equitable governance structures. In particular, the authors discuss how information and communications technologies can serve to reduce barriers to information exchange and thereby generate stronger bonds and quicker formation of partnerships and connections within the public realm. This chapter explores these issues through the lens of e-government, e-democracy, and the digital divide in a U.S. context.

INTRODUCTION

Urban planners have long recognized that plan making and decisions about community and regional development are most successful within a democratic framework. Involving the public

DOI: 10.4018/978-1-4666-4169-3.ch003

in planning processes not only improves communications but also redistributes authority and responsibility (Hoch, Dalton, & So, 2000). In addition, planners expect that effective outcomes are achieved when those participating are well informed and can in fact influence the fairness of outcomes (Kaiser, Godschalk, & Chapin, 1995). The public is best served when its desires and preferences are known and incorporated into plans. Therefore, a democratized planning process that gathers input from nonprofessionals should also demystify the decision-making process and make the consequences and alternatives of proposed policies as transparent as possible. Transparency is linked to accountability, with both being part of a foundation on which democratic planning processes can be built. New information and communication technologies (ICTs) have and will continue to facilitate how the public can make meaningful contributions to local and regional governance.

For organizations and individuals, the rapid rate of technological innovation makes planning and adapting to change an ongoing challenge. Democratic systems rely on representative modes because full and individual-level participation of all members of the society would be unwieldy and inefficient. Direct democracy approaches are an alternative that has particular technology applications, as will be discussed. ICTs seek to reduce barriers to information exchange, thereby generating stronger bonds and a quicker formation of partnerships and connections. For the purposes of understanding different viewpoints, it is important to distinguish the activities of the public (i.e., citizens, although there are also many non-citizens) and governing institutions. While this is a simplified view, it serves to highlight differences in how technology is used by those governed and by those governing, and their intermediaries. Social equity can be expressed by reducing the distances between the public and institutions as well as among members of the public across race, ethnicity, class, gender, disabilities, religion, and other dividing factors. In this case, *distance* refers to levels of transparency, accountability, and inclusiveness that connect (or separate) the public from governmental institutions. The application of technology occurs among citizens and within institutions in an attempt to narrow existing gaps, more commonly referred to as e-democracy (e-dem) and e-government (e-gov), respectively.

E-DEMOCRACY AND E-GOVERNMENT

The terms *e-gov* and *e-dem* have a variety of analogs. E-gov, which is also referred to as digital government, online government, or connected government, is the effort to digitally provide better and quicker access to government services, information, and communications; to provide information to constituents; and to provide better accountability (Evans-Cowley & Hollander, 2010). The objective is to substitute ICTs for manual, in-person, hard copy, or previously unavailable public services. The application of ICTs to government operations is intended to provide a virtual presence of government. For example, the functionality of a government Web site should be comparable to or more useful than an actual visit to the agency in terms of the services and information available. Not only can more information be made available, but also being electronically indexed allows for easier access and the targeting of specific information. Constituents can also sometimes manipulate information to provide new connections that they had previously not been aware of, as well as spatial images through mapping and geographic information systems (GIS).

E-Government

In e-gov, the primary channels are those between the government as an organization and service provider, and the public as constituents and customers. Less attention is placed on how the constituents or customers communicate with one another, or how (or if) they organize themselves. Exceptions may be neighborhood- or community-level activities, where the services provided are based on geographic parameters that affect groups of residents or businesses. In these cases, communications can be more efficient if directed toward or coordinated with local councils or boards rather than individual residents. However, others have recognized the significant role that social media technology can play in engaging the public in open government (Bertot, Jaeger, Munson, & Glaisyer, 2010).

Because social media is fundamentally a form of communications based on networks of associated individuals, organizations, or interest groups, it can represent common ground and a forum in which the public and government representatives/personnel can interact. For example, relative to urban and regional planning, Lanza and Prosperi (2009) refer to this as collaborative e-governance, which is a strong base for bringing e-gov and e-dem together. Yet, there are particular bureaucratic obstacles that stand in the way of implementation. There were initial fears that allowing public-sector government employees access to social media tools, such as Facebook, Twitter, YouTube, and Flickr, would decrease worker productivity (NAS-CIO, 2010). This has not proven to be the case. Many governmental levels restrict the access of their staff to these applications and the Internet, feeling that time, energy, and resources will be wasted. Firms should recognize the benefits of these technologies in terms of interaction with the public and information sharing with other governmental units. As these benefits become more tangible, the hope is that workplace restrictions on using these technologies will decrease.

By some accounts, the four primary purposes of e-gov are electronic information access (to previously print-only materials), communications with government agency personnel (e.g., questions, requests, complaints), transactions (e.g., bill pay, application for services, registrations), and governance (e.g., voting, public participation). GIS and satellite imagery should also be included in this list. While the current focus of e-gov activities is Internet based, there are non-Internet technologies used for similar purposes, including phone, fax, television, radio, and other traditional electronic means for dissemination and direct communications. Another example is the very successful 311 line that Mayor Michael Bloomberg started in New York City. The 311 phone number is a source of government information and nonemergency services. Not all citizens and other residents have access to the Internet or Web-based e-gov resources or are able to read or understand the resources when they can access them. For example, approximately 70% of the Navajo Nation does not have access to telecommunications (Wilson, 2009). Known as the digital divide (discussed later), digital and media literacy continues to be an issue for traditionally underserved populations, primarily those with low incomes, racial and ethnic minorities, people with disabilities, those with low literacy, and the elderly. Having a computer and access to the Internet is quite different from being able to effectively use computer hardware and software tools, applications, and features. The use of particular forms of telecommunications varies among racial and ethnic groups as will be discussed later.

Rapidly changing technologies requiring additional education or training represent further challenges. However, these technical needs can in fact provide the motivation to build community networks for cooperative assistance. This has multiple purposes. Not only can technically challenged individuals find assistance, but this also provides them the opportunity to extend their social networks. Whereas this seems like an unalloyed good, an extended social network in which the members share disadvantaged characteristics may not reduce social inequity, but rather perpetuate an inward-looking self-segregation. Even among those in positions of privilege, this self-segregation is already seen in how many advertisements and much of the news on the Web are directed to the individual user. Self-segregation and opportunities for unity of organization and thought can also be used by those opposed to greater democracy, such as hate groups.

Bélanger and Carter (2009) suggest that current e-gov activities further separate the information haves and have-nots because certain groups lack the skills necessary to effectively interact with the government online. Other research suggests that despite substantial and increasing spending on e-gov initiatives, usage of such services has plateaued (Baumgarten & Chui, 2009). One explanation is that the public is not intimately involved in system design, and therefore e-gov services do not meet the evolving demand for government services. Another possibility is that electronic technology is evolving faster than government can keep up with. A third possibility is that the current recession has stripped government of resources, so although there is more information online, there are fewer services overall. Some people are simply overwhelmed by the amount and type of information available. Others lack the ability to filter erroneous information. The Internet is often used to perpetuate and distribute false information. Even the most advanced technology still requires human beings to procure it, implement it, make it work, and maintain it. The government may also have concerns that too much access to high technology and telecommunications may put too much power into the hands of ordinary people, who then use that power to resist government. For example, in August 2011, Bay Area Rapid Transit, a public transit rail system in the San Francisco Bay Area, shut down cell phone access within its system for hours at a time because it feared that protestors against its police actions would use cell phones to coordinate their demonstrations. National governments such as those in the People's Republic of China, Iran, and Egypt make conscious and somewhat effective efforts to censor and jam the flow of information.

In theory, the adoption of social media should leverage the creativity of the public while increasing their level of interest and participation and reducing their level of dissatisfaction with unresponsive government services. Also, given the trends in youths' Internet and mobile communications activities, the hope is that e-gov and e-dem (or collaborative e-gov) will see higher levels of involvement as a consequence. As they become politically aware and active, the generation of Web 2.0 and social media will come to expect

these kinds of technologies. The challenge will not be due to technical barriers as much as they dealing with the barriers resulting from years of political disenfranchisement and disinterest. Members of political movements such as the Tea Party feel deep anger that their government has disenfranchised and restricted them, even though they are largely middle and upper class and have been the beneficiaries of a wide range of government programs. The availability of information does not lower their state of denial in obtaining and using such benefits to a larger extent than they have contributed. This may be an example of how ICTs do not necessarily foster a reality-based view of government services and privilege. In fact, ICTs have already been used for hateful purposes. Members of hate groups are able to find like-minded souls, such as the Norwegian domestic terrorist who bombed and shot more than 60 people in August 2011 after publishing a 1,500-page screed online, laying out his hate for Muslims in northern Europe. His clear warnings, like many others, were not taken seriously by the public or the law enforcement authorities. It may be that they were lost in a tsunami of unfiltered information.

E-Democracy

While e-dem includes ICT governance applications (i.e., e-gov), its reach extends to areas including media, political organizing, and voting. Activities surrounding public participation and direct forms of citizen involvement have greatly benefited from Internet and mobile communications technologies. The democratic process relies on interaction between citizens and government institutions, and digital technologies are rapidly changing the extent and nature of those interactions. The rapid rise of social media has played a significant role in electoral politics and campaigning, as has been widely reported concerning the U.S. Presidential campaign of Barack Obama in 2008. Many-to-many communications created the capacity for far-reaching, real-time organizing and mobilization. Supporters can be updated on gatherings (physical or virtual), fund-raising activities, canvassing, and general communications. In addition, grassroots-initiated organizing and public protests have witnessed a sea change in speed and global reach, as evidenced by uprisings in Tunisia, Egypt, and Libya during the so-called Arab Spring. As in the Bay Area Rapid Transit example noted earlier, the government of Egypt attempted to cut off and seize control of telecommunications. However, it is very difficult to put the genie back in the bottle. Some grassroots activists are developing portable Internet nodes to work around government-controlled networks, but the People's Republic of China has proved singularly resourceful in controlling telecommunications in the interests of suppressing democracy. In the United States, in response to anti-union state legislation, protests in Madison, Wisconsin, benefited not only from traditional electronic modes of communications such as television and radio but also from social media tools such as Facebook and Twitter (Maher & Belkin, 2011).

Much of the discussion around technology, especially as related to e-gov, is focused on a supply-side approach. Government and planning agencies dictate the technology platforms and parameters for engagement, as opposed to those being designed by the public themselves (the demand side). One example is when governmental organizations engage in listening sessions to ostensibly allow the public to set the agenda. Many of these activities are opportunities to give the appearance of an open dialogue and power being placed in the hands of the public (Felt & Fochler, 2008). Because these events are staged by government agencies, they impose the framework by which input is presented by the public, and they rarely evaluate the value or benefits of technology, including microphones, amplification, interactive whiteboards, television monitors, PowerPoint, and handheld polling devices used to obtain input, in these situations. The technology can give the

illusion of sensible and fruitful participation, but if the surveys and questions are badly designed, good data cannot result, except by accident. The governmental entity is ultimately responsible for action on any of the comments, suggestions, or ideas received, and the empowerment of public participants is temporary and not often integrated into decision-making or policy-making processes in a transparent way. Technologies facilitating input from the public are being tested and have seen rapid adoption among community planners and organizers. However, even with the best input, if the government chooses not to take action based on it, the efforts have no value. These efforts give the pretense of engaged participation while differing little from nontechnological interventions (Cooke & Kothari, 2001). A subset of the public may self-select for participation, thus moving away from democratic process.

GETTING THE TECHNOLOGY INTO THE HANDS OF THE PUBLIC

Other efforts focused on demand-side technologies have been put into innovation dissemination to make ICTs more widespread. These include some work done in the areas of e-gov and e-dem and facilitated through projects like the community technology centers through examples of nonprofit participation (Servon & Nelson, 2001). The objective of community technology centers was to increase access to computers and the Internet in neighborhoods and communities that were typically populated by low-income households. Individually, these represent technology applications by members of the public who seek to more effectively engage in the democratic decision-making process (e-dem), technology applications by government-sector agencies to more efficiently carry out their functions (e-gov), and coordinated efforts to increase levels of computer literacy and address the digital divide (collaborative e-gov). An idealized approach would consist of coordinating these efforts so they mutually reinforce objectives (i.e., nonprofits to help organize and support citizen groups). In these cases, there is some overlap between e-gov and e-dem efforts, especially in the areas of public information and public involvement; however, e-gov includes technology activities for primarily business-related functions such as payroll, human resources, and administrative operations.

Conversely, e-dem efforts include organizing and campaigning, and advocacy, which are not (and should not) be a responsibility of governmental institutions. At the community level, technology assistance and local organizations (social networks) could logically link with K–12 schools, community colleges, and perhaps universities to provide physical infrastructure, instructional support, linkages, articulation, and synergistic network-building activities. Universities could also see these relationships as opportunities for outreach, research, and instruction, which are commonly part of their primary mission. The following is a brief discussion of each of these as they relate to equity in governance. Further discussion touches on the feasibility of a coordinated effort to link government and people to technological advances more effectively. Sufficiently pervasive technology, broader availability of computers, and training for all users could even result in the rescission of government from some activities, and even autonomous, self-governing systems. Such spontaneous privatization of infrastructure effort and service provision has already occurred in such areas as intercity bus transportation.

Warschauer and Matuchniak (2010) describe how community technology centers can assist public groups with not only access to computer technology but also programs to improve technological literacy. Other forms of training and access have arisen in public libraries, schools, and other community centers. The near ubiquity of wired or wireless access to the Internet, especially with mobile devices (e.g., smartphones), is showing promise for increasing the communications and content availability among not only youths but also minority youths, as reported by the Pew Internet & American Life Project (see http://www.pewinternet.org/).

A significant portion of the literature on e-gov and e-dem assumes that technology can be used to make current approaches and operations more effective and efficient. As discussed earlier, traditional models of governance involve top-down, institutional-led efforts. The likelihood for innovation is limited through this model, however, because it uses technology to facilitate existing operations instead of generating new practices, processes, or methods. Using new technologies to enhance equity in planning and governance can be an opportunity to innovate on a larger scale—moving from task-level innovation to structural innovation that may result in fewer government-led initiatives.

Efforts to connect government more effectively could be placed directly in the hands of the public. While this could still constitute a partnership, the initiative could be driven from the public side, where constituencies can articulate needs and preferences. This was unfeasible previously because of resources that the public lacked to coordinate efforts and design processes and linkages to the governmental functions of interest. Instead, governmental units provided access to functions that were readily available and accessible, regardless of whether they were in fact what the public wanted. A significant amount of money has been spent on isolated projects to connect to the public rather than taking a more comprehensive approach to such endeavors.

As face-to-face human interactions decline because of innovations such as radio, television, e-mail, and social media, organizing becomes much easier and provides a forum through which the public and private sectors can exchange information. Operating in micro-crowdsourcing modes can be used to identify how and where they prefer to engage with government activities and services. This takes initiative on the part of public groups, but ultimately it provides direct benefits. This would also involve a shift of some resources from governmental entities to public groups as needed. However, as experienced from 2007 to 2009 during the worst part of the Great Recession, there was a drastic shift of government resources from taxpayers' coffers to businesses deemed too big to fail. At the same time, few resources were directed to public groups. The devolution of government has occurred up to those with more power and money rather than down to traditionally and newly disadvantaged groups.

DIGITAL DIVIDE

Although the availability of electronic information is nearly universal, the ability to consume, digest, and process the information for equal gains across socioeconomic groups is not uniform. Servon (2002) and Mehra, Merkel, and Bishop (2004) point to underlying and persistent inequalities within our society that maintain the current divide. The question then becomes whether ICTs will help alleviate exclusionary practices that have historically plagued public, private, and governmental sectors and allow more full and meaningful participation by oth-

erwise underrepresented groups. Alternatively, will technology adoption and knowledge gains translate into elevated social status for the previously excluded? It is difficult to predict how the equity-enhancing attributes of ICTs will evolve and whether current social and economic gaps between haves and have-nots will decline. Another scenario is that the traditionally privileged will gain even more power through their technological advantages and through the unproductive use of those same tools by others. Appreciating the dimensions of this digital divide—how users vary across the Internet—is important because it is increasingly recognized that poor access can lead to disadvantages in receiving vital information for education, health, and job opportunities.

As Internet access and use continues to increase dramatically, the ways we communicate with family, friends, employers, commerce, and other institutions continues to change on all levels. Overall, U.S. Internet usage rates have increased from 44% in 2000 to nearly 80% in 2010, according to recent surveys. Usage rates may be nearly 100% in the next few years, according to some analysts, given the expansion of residential broadband service, Wi-Fi, and cell phone–based Internet technologies (see Figure 1).

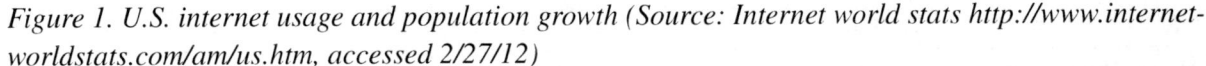

Figure 1. U.S. internet usage and population growth (Source: Internet world stats http://www.internetworldstats.com/am/us.htm, accessed 2/27/12)

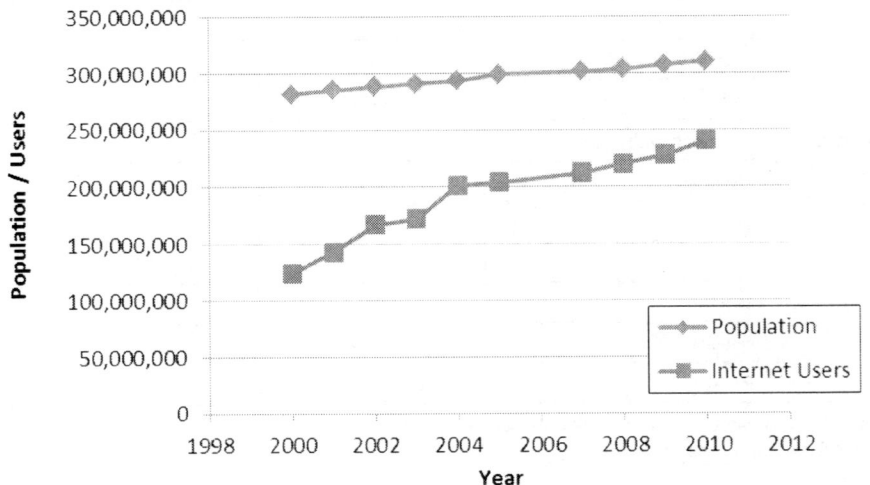

According to the research of the Pew Internet & American Life Project, over the last decade, the population of Internet users has begun to resemble more closely the racial and ethnic composition of the population as a whole. Between 2000 and 2010, the percentage of black and Latino Internet users has almost doubled, from 11% to 21% of all users, but whites continue to exhibit higher participation rates than do African Americans and Hispanics. Similarly, African Americans have also begun to use broadband at home, but their gains are still outpaced by whites. The broadband participation rate is still highest among whites (see Table1). African American adults (51%) are also less likely than white adults (65%) to own a personal computer (Rainie, 2010).

English-speaking Latinos are nearly identical to whites in their use of the Internet and home broadband. However, foreign-born, Spanish-dominant Latinos and English-speaking, native-born Latinos trail whites on both Internet and home broadband use (Rainie, 2010). Thus, controlling for other demographic factors, language proficiency is one of the most important predictors of Internet use in the United States. Additionally, as expected, younger persons are more rapidly adopting online technologies than seniors are. Low-income households, less-educated individuals, and rural residents also show significantly lower rates of Internet usage. The current divide in usage appears to be strongly associated with economic standing, which may prove to be of

Table 1. Internet, broadband, and wireless Internet users by select demographic segments.

Internet users	Category	Internet users	Broadband users	Wireless users
Total adults		74%	60%	55%
	Men	74%	61%	59%
	Women	74%	58%	51%
Race/ethnicity	White, non-Hispanic	76%	63%	52%
	Black, non-Hispanic	70%	52%	59%
	Hispanic	64%	47%	62%
Age	18–29	93%	76%	80%
	30–49	81%	67%	66%
	50–64	70%	56%	42%
	65+	38%	26%	16%
Household income per year	Less than $30,000	60%	42%	46%
	$30,000–$49,999	76%	62%	55%
	$50,000–$74,999	83%	73%	61%
	$75,000+	94%	83%	76%
Educational attainment	Less than high school	39%	24%	41%
	High school	63%	46%	42%
	Some college	87%	73%	63%
	College+	94%	83%	69%
Community type	Urban	74%	61%	57%
	Suburban	77%	64%	56%
	Rural	70%	47%	45%

Source: Pew Internet & American Life Project, August 9–September 10, 2010 Tracking Project. http://pewinternet.org/Static-Pages/About-Us/Our-Research/Use-Policy.aspx

greater relevance than racial/ethnic categories. Figure 2 presents the findings reported by the Pew Internet & American Life Project in recent studies in 2009 and 2010, illustrating the gap in participation rates among users of broadband, cell phones, and the Internet in general, between those earning $75,000 or more per year and those earning less than $30,000. This pattern differs from findings often reported by many studies that explore socioeconomic impacts such as housing discrimination and find correlations between race/ethnicity and income.

Looking ahead, usage rates for most groups will likely rise over time; however, the mode of access will play an important role in closing this gap. The evidence suggests that the divide is less pronounced in terms of cell phone and wireless Internet access compared to residential broadband service. For example, the Pew Internet & American Life Project has found that African Americans and Latinos show the highest rates of mobile Internet access and usage (see Table 1).

The digital divide is typically associated with race and economic class, although persons with physical disabilities can benefit greatly from access to the Internet for services and communications as well (Vicente & Lopez, 2010). A national survey conducted in 2010 found that 54% of adults living with a disability use the Internet, compared with 81% of adults who report none of the disabilities listed in the survey. For those with disabilities who use the Internet, they are less likely to have high-speed or wireless access than are those without disabilities. For example, 41% of adults living with a disability have broadband at home, compared with 69% of those without a disability (Rainie, 2010).

As discussed earlier, ICTs are closely allied with new media, social networking, and social media—tools and methods to increase social interaction among persons with common interests. Youths have been at the forefront of exploring video, instant messaging, social media, and other social-networking applications and have also been

Figure 2. At-home broadband, internet, and cellphone use by income segments, 2010 (Source: Pew Research Center's Internet & American Life Project, August 9 – September 10, 2010 tracking project)

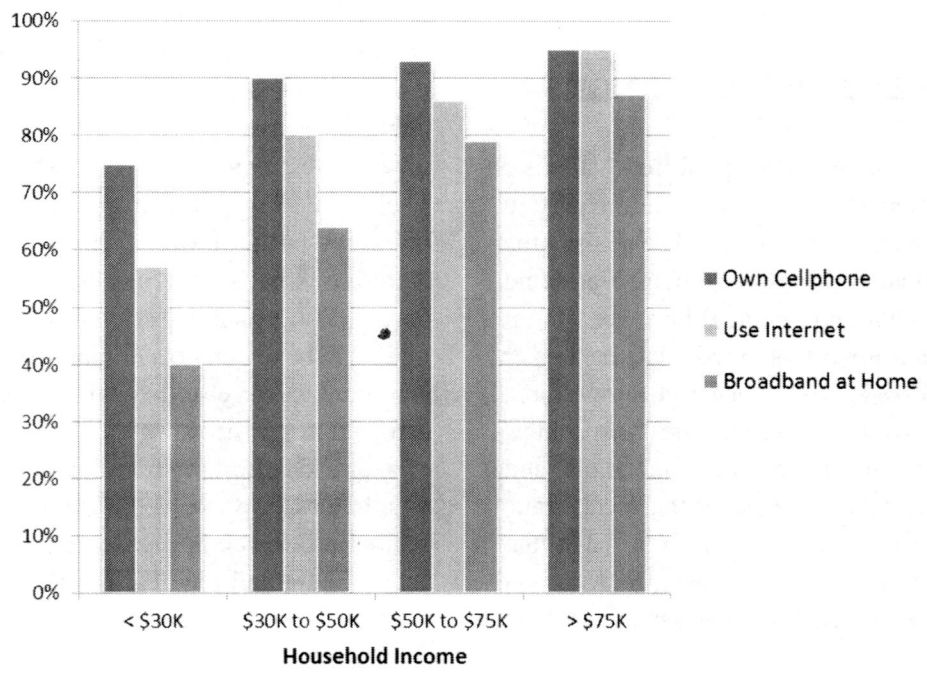

active, although not alone, in trying to explore their applications for transportation and public engagement. Some argue that ICTs have the potential to build social capital by strengthening connections and increasing the flow of information (Hargittai, 2003). ICTs are also closely associated with Web 2.0, an umbrella term for a new era of Web-enabled applications that are built around user-generated or user-manipulated content, such as wikis, blogs, podcasts, and social-networking sites. Although these technologies can be used to bridge the divide, they can also further divide us, straining our capacity to find workable solutions to our coming challenges. As we join together online, into networks of often like-minded individuals, the digital platform can fortify our most deeply held convictions and inflame our passions. It can potentially enforce greater allegiance to ideology among affiliated members, which can limit our tolerance for compromise—an often essential but underestimated element of effective government. Ultimately, we are responsible, as individuals, factional groups, and governing institutions, for using the tools to promote civil discourse and defend equitable values and just outcomes as we develop implementable solutions.

FUTURE RESEARCH DIRECTIONS

What are the anticipated or preferred outcomes for effective technology application to equity in urban planning and governance? The goals of the three general areas discussed (e-dem, e-gov, and increasing technology literacy) have been highlighted, but it is important to articulate the longer term, broad-based goals derived from these efforts. Five particularly important goals are transparency, accountability, inclusion, communication, and innovation. Enhancing these at the local, state, regional, and federal levels does not mean that separate initiatives are undertaken to focus on each, but rather that each approach should include these elements where applicable. For instance, improving accountability or transparency has positive implications for communications. Improving the reach and quality of communications will in turn generate positive effects on transparency and accountability. However, because each of these dimensions is multifaceted and complex, we cannot expect that improving any one of these will be sufficient on its own.

Nonetheless, as we learn to adapt to this new world, the emerging ICTs will present opportunities for future civic engagement, public involvement, and even future employment, including for traditionally underserved groups. This is particularly important for reaching youths who may be highly conversant with the technologies and interested in becoming more active in their communities. Public involvement efforts can and should target these youths to build a culture of participation.

Still, it is an open question as to whether the signs of technology adoption will actually result in better civic engagement extending across various segments of the traditionally underserved populations. These efforts typically have been resource intensive and have suffered from issues that have plagued public participation for many years. Because traditionally underserved groups have not realized a fair share of societal benefits from public investments, their expectations are notably lower as compared with those of other groups. Exclusion from political and decision-making processes further lowers their expectations, and therefore there is little incentive to participate. Participants in planning efforts must see how their input will be directly beneficial to them and their communities, or else they will choose not to be involved in a positive way.

Outreach efforts to traditionally underserved populations have achieved some success in health promotion, especially more recently in relation to active living and physical health (Yancey, Ory, & Davis, 2006). It can be argued that these successes, such as increased awareness and changes in behavior, have resulted because there are tangible benefits involved (in the form of improved health outcomes). Outreach to traditionally underserved groups in the context of transportation and other infrastructure decision-making processes, either with or without ICTs, will need to be appropriately structured to achieve similar successes.

For example, an estimated 45 million Americans do not speak English at home, and many want information in a language other than English (Lazarus & Mora, 2000). An estimated 8.5% of Americans have at least one disability that requires special features on computers and the Internet to make these resources accessible. An increasing number and a broader cross section of Americans are using the Internet, which creates a greater necessity for digital material to be created in multiple languages, information to be disseminated at a basic literacy level, the development of interfaces and content accessible to people with disabilities, and guidance on how to use online resources.

CONCLUSION

Most of the applications for technology related to social equity and governance are being developed in the areas of communications and civic engagement. Access to information such as government records, plans, regulations, and proceedings are gradually gaining attention from the public. Although previously available, it was difficult and time-consuming to obtain these types of information, especially if they were only in printed form. E-gov efforts have increased access, but it is not clear whether this in itself leads to a better informed citizenry. Having the information without knowing how to make meaning of it can be almost the same as not having the information in the first place. Even the Federal Communications Commission's Fairness Doctrine, which covers the transmission

of political views by television and radio stations, has disappeared in favor of more concern about curse words (Gill, n.d.). Conversely, e-dem efforts have attempted to increase participation and access to governmental affairs and democratize processes that have not evolved or kept pace with technological advancements. Voter registration, elections, petitioning, and deliberation are some notable areas with great potential.

As mentioned earlier, concerns about social equity and technology (i.e., digital divide) have shifted in meaning and context. When ICTs first become broadly available to the public, they are expensive, which excludes certain income groups from purchasing or accessing them. Although the costs for many of these technologies and services (e.g., personal computers, smartphones, broadband, Wi-Fi) have become increasingly affordable, the wealth of U.S. families, especially among African Americans and Latinos, has declined greatly. As a conglomeration, US families spend much more than they think on telecommunications. The divide is not necessarily a function of having these technologies but rather the ability and desire to use them in ways that have positive social and economic benefits. Technology training and education in schools and neighborhoods has shown promise in decreasing the technology gap, and recent statistics show that racial and national origin minorities are quick and sophisticated adopters. The hope is that these technological skills will translate over time into opportunities that increase fairness and mobility.

REFERENCES

Baumgarten, J., & Chui, M. (2009). E-government 2.0. *McKinsey Quarterly*. Retrieved from http://www.mckinseyquarterly.com/E-government_20_2408

Bélanger, F., & Carter, L. (2009). The impact of the digital divide on e-government use. *Communications of the ACM, 52*(4), 132–135. doi:10.1145/1498765.1498801.

Bertot, J. C., Jaeger, P. T., Munson, S., & Glaisyer, T. (2010). Engaging the public in open government: Social media technology and policy for government transparency. *IEEE Computer, 43*(11), 60–67. doi:10.1109/MC.2010.325.

Cooke, B., & Kothari, U. (2001). *Participation: The new tyranny?* London, UK: Zed Books.

Evans-Cowley, J., & Hollander, J. (2010). The new generation of public participation: Internet-based participation tools. *Planning Practice and Research, 25*(3), 397–408. doi:10.1080/026974 59.2010.503432.

Felt, U., & Fochler, M. (2008). The bottom-up meanings of the concept of public participation in science and technology. *Science & Public Policy, 35*(7), 489–499. doi:10.3152/030234208X329086.

Fisher, E. (1999). Low literacy levels in adults: Implications for patient education. *Journal of Continuing Education in Nursing, 30*(2), 56–61. PMID:10382455.

Gill, K. (n.d.). *What is the fairness doctrine?* Retrieved from http://uspolitics.about.com/od/electionissues/a/fcc_fairness.htm

Hargittai, E. (2003). The digital divide and what to do about it. In Jones, D. C. (Ed.), *New economy handbook* (pp. 821–839). San Diego, CA: Academic Press.

Hoch, C., Dalton, L. C., & So, F. S. (2000). *The practice of local government planning*. Washington, DC: International City/County Management Association.

Kaiser, E. J., Godschalk, D. R., & Chapin, F. S. Jr. (1995). *Urban land use planning* (4th ed.). Urbana: University of Illinois Press.

Lanza, V., & Prosperi, D. C. (2009). Collaborative e-governance: Describing and pre-calibrating the digital milieu in urban and regional planning. In Krek, A., Rumor, M., Zlatanova, S., & Fendel, E. M. (Eds.), *Urban and regional data management: UDMS annual 2009* (pp. 373–383). Leiden, The Netherlands: CRC Press/Balkema.

Lazarus, W., & Mora, F. (2000). *Online content for low-income and underserved Americans: The digital divide's new frontier*. Santa Monica, CA: The Children's Partnership. Retrieved from http://www.policyarchive.org/handle/10207/bitstreams/6881.pdf

Maher, K., & Belkin, D. (2011, February 16). State plans anger unions. *The Wall Street Journal*. Retrieved from http://online.wsj.com/article/SB 100014240527487033129045761465542635 30400.html

Mehra, B., Merkel, C., & Bishop, A. P. (2004). The Internet for empowerment of minority and marginalized users. *New Media & Society, 6*(6), 781–802. doi:10.1177/146144804047513.

NASCIO. (2010). *Friends, followers, and feeds: A national survey of social media use in state government*. Lexington, KY: Author. Retrieved from http://www.nascio.org/publications/documents/NASCIO-SocialMedia.pdf

Rainie, L. (2010). *Internet, broadband, and cell phone statistics*. Washington, DC: Pew Internet & American Life Project.

Servon, L. J. (2002). *Bridging the digital divide: Technology, community, and public policy*. Malden, MA: Blackwell. doi:10.1002/9780470773529.

Servon, L. J., & Nelson, M. K. (2001). Community technology centers: Narrowing the digital divide in low-income, urban communities. *Journal of Urban Affairs, 23*(3/4), 279–290. doi:10.1111/0735-2166.00089.

Vicente, M. R., & López, A. J. (2010). A multidimensional analysis of the disability digital divide: Some evidence for internet use. *The Information Society, 26*(1), 48–64. doi:10.1080/01615440903423245.

Warschauer, M., & Matuchniak, T. (2010). New technology and digital worlds: Analyzing evidence of equity in access, use, and outcomes. *Review of Research in Education, 34*(1), 179–225. doi:10.3102/0091732X09349791.

Wilson, D. B. (2009). Weaving the Navajo.Net. *Journal on Telecommunications & High Technology Law, 7*(2), 425–461.

Yancey, A. K., Ory, M. G., & Davis, S. M. (2006). Dissemination of physical activity promotion interventions in underserved populations. *American Journal of Preventive Medicine, 31*(4), 82–91. doi:10.1016/j.amepre.2006.06.020 PMID:16979472.

ADDITIONAL READING

Evans-Cowley, J. S., & Kitchen, J. (2011). *E-government* (American Planning Association PAS Report No. 564, rev. ed.). Chicago, IL: American Planning Association.

Silva, C. N. (Ed.). (2010). *Handbook of research on e-planning: ICTs for urban development and monitoring*. Hershey, PA: Information Science Reference. doi:10.4018/978-1-61520-929-3.

KEY TERMS AND DEFINITIONS

Crowdsourcing: Traditionally, government agencies ask for public input on planning projects by holding open meetings and workshops. Crowdsourcing seeks this public input from people online. The "crowd" is the public or some subset of it, often self-selected. A large group of people acting independently provide input to solve a problem or answer a question. The diversity of the group may provide better answers more quickly than a smaller group of experts.

Digital Divide: A substantial asymmetry in the distribution and effective use of information and communication resources between two or more populations. This results in differential access to information and communications services. Often used to refer to gaps between computer and Internet availability and use between minority and non-minority, or higher and lower income groups. Typically, the lower the income and more African-American, Hispanic, and Native American, the lower the availability and use.

Equity: Equity means that access to all aspects of a community (including health, housing, education, safety, open space, transport and economic development) are fair to all residents regardless of socioeconomic status, race, cultural background, national origin, gender, age and disability. The aim of equity-focused policies is to eliminate the unfair and avoidable circumstances that deprive people of their rights. Therefore, inequities generally arise when certain population groups are unfairly deprived of basic resources that are available to other groups.

Governance: Setting public policy as a societal or political group to guide an activity or constellation of activities toward the public good or public interest, and then making sure that the money, resources, people, energy, and institutions to do the work are in place, available, willing, and directed. It also means making sure that people and groups are accountable for the public work they do, measuring, evaluating, analyzing, and monitoring what happens and making and carrying out plans to carry the work forward.

Information and Communications Technologies (ICT): The use of technological devices, systems, and means by users for the purpose of communication or representation of knowledge such as facts, data, or opinions, in any medium or form, including textual, numerical, graphic, cartographic, narrative, and audiovisual forms. ICT includes networks such as the Internet, devices such as smartphones, software, and hardware. ICT has characteristics such as real-time, virtual, and time and geography shifting.

Participation: Participation is involvement by people in processes, systems, or structures. The involvement can be virtual or real. Participation normally involves or includes the concept of having some "say" or approval in the process and outcome. One form of participation is democratic or representational. Participation can include crafting or making the process, as well as judging it. Alienation or disinterest is the opposition of participation.

Planning: The term planning is used in the sense of urban, metropolitan, and rural. It is also a profession. It comes before building, and involves design and organization of the physical arrangement, built environment, and land use of a given area or place. It involves consideration of infrastructure, needs, and resources. Planning is working toward the deliberate improvement of the spatial organization and design of human settlement and human movement. It has to do with improving and making things better on the ground.

Technology: The scientific method and material used to achieve a commercial or industrial objective. Jargon for software, hardware, protocol, or something technical in nature. In his classic work on innovation, [Rogers (1995). *Diffusion of Innovations* (4th ed.). The Free Press.] suggests that "Technology is a design for instrumental action that reduces the uncertainty in the cause/effect relationships involved in achieving a desired outcome" that is, technology is a solution to an existing problem or suboptimal situation.

Section 2
Mass Collaboration in Urban Governance

Chapter 4

The Four Urban Governance Problem Types Suitable for Crowdsourcing Citizen Participation

Daren C. Brabham
University of North Carolina at Chapel Hill, USA

ABSTRACT

Crowdsourcing is a method for harnessing the collective intelligence of online communities to solve specific problems or produce goods. Largely known as a business model, crowdsourcing has begun to make inroads as a supplemental public participation tool for governance, as a way to engage citizens in the business of government functions. Validating a new typology of crowdsourcing cases, this chapter outlines the four urban governance problem types that the crowdsourcing model can successfully address. This chapter also discusses the right of free speech in online crowdsourcing communities and its relevance for urban governance crowdsourcing applications in free societies. Concluding the chapter is an examination of crowdsourcing's place in the policy-advisory spectrum and the risks associated with bringing crowdsourcing applications into public participation programs.

INTRODUCTION

In the past decade, crowdsourcing has emerged as an alternative public participation method for governance and planning projects that may complement traditional face-to-face methods for gathering citizen input. Crowdsourcing is an on-line, distributed problem solving and production model that leverages the collective intelligence of online communities for specific managed tasks

DOI: 10.4018/978-1-4666-4169-3.ch004

(Brabham, 2008a; Howe, 2006a). The process of crowdsourcing to harness citizen input on governance and planning decisions is another application of deliberative democratic principles which drive traditional, face-to-face participation methods, such as workshops and hearings (Brabham, 2009a).

This potential for crowdsourcing in governance is now being realized, thanks in part to pushes by politicians, citizen groups, and actions in the U.S. by the Obama Administration (Obama, n.d.). Crowdsourcing and other participatory online methods may drive e-governance finally beyond merely providing information, forms, and online transactions (McDonough, as cited in Noveck, 2003) to more radical, active forms of engagement. Recent government crowdsourcing projects include the U.S. Office of Management and Budget's SAVE Award (Long, 2009), the U.S. Patent and Trademark Office's Peer-to-Patent project (Noveck, 2006), the U.S. Federal Transit Administration's Next Stop Design project (Brabham, Sanchez, & Bartholomew, 2010), and many others.

In this chapter, I offer a typology of urban governance problem types suitable for crowdsourcing, validating and extending previous work in this area (Brabham, 2012). This examination includes analysis of actual cases of crowdsourcing in governance, as well as speculation on future applications of crowdsourcing to improve city administration through citizen participation. Understanding the kinds of problems that can be addressed by governments using the crowdsourcing model is a first step in the development of applications to improve public engagement in government work.

Also in the chapter I explore two important issues relating to the use of crowdsourcing in governance: moderation and free speech rights in managing disruptive and destructive online communities, and the government's commitment to use the crowd's input on a policy-advisory spectrum.

BACKGROUND

The concept of crowdsourcing is underpinned by a larger, older academic discourse on collective intelligence and open innovation (Chesbrough, 2003; Lévy, 1995; 1997; Von Hippel, 2005), but it was not until Jeff Howe (2006a) coined the term "crowdsourcing" in a June 2006 *Wired* magazine article that scholars and practitioners beyond the disciplines of computing and business took note. Howe (2006a, 2008), Brabham (2008a),

and others (e.g., Kleeman, Voss, & Rieder, 2008; Vukovic & Bartolini, 2010; Whitla, 2009) have each provided varying definitions for crowdsourcing, but in a recent article Estellés-Arolas and González-Ladrón-de-Guevara (2012) synthesized these many interpretations into a single integrated definition:

Crowdsourcing is a type of participative online activity in which an individual, an institution, a non-profit organization, or company proposes to a group of individuals of varying knowledge, heterogeneity, and number, via a flexible open call, the voluntary undertaking of a task. The undertaking of the task, of variable complexity and modularity, and in which the crowd should participate bringing their work, money, knowledge and/or experience, always entails mutual benefit. The user will receive the satisfaction of a given type of need, be it economic, social recognition, self-esteem, or the development of individual skills, while the crowdsourcer will obtain and utilize to their advantage what the user has brought to the venture, whose form will depend on the type of activity undertaken. (p. 197)

In plain terms, crowdsourcing involves an organization opening a challenge or a problem up to an online community and that online community—the "crowd"—providing solutions, all in a mutually beneficial arrangement.

Crowdsourcing must always involve a mix of bottom-up, open, creative input from an online community and top-down, hierarchical management from an organization. Cases such as Wikipedia, YouTube, and open source software are commonly conflated with crowdsourcing, but I have argued (Brabham, 2008a; 2012) that these instances do not count as true crowdsourcing because there is no entity directing the creative activities of online community members in a managed way for a specific purpose. Rather, these instances resemble "commons-based peer production" (Benkler, 2002), where an organization provides a sandbox or a set of tools for users to explore but no specific direction for what users must accomplish with those tools. On the other end of the spectrum, cases such as Pepsi's "DEW-mocracy" campaign in 2007 and 2009 to select a new flavor (Zmuda, 2009), M&M's 1995 and 2002 campaigns to add new colors for the candy ("M&M lovers pick purple," 2002), and similar marketing contests do not count as crowdsourcing either, because the organizations have predetermined a set of possibilities and merely ask consumers for preferences. This form is no more than marketing research or ad copy testing, and consumers do not have meaningful open, creative input. Only a blend of top-down and bottom-up efforts qualify as crowdsourcing.

CROWDSOURCING PROBLEM TYPES FOR URBAN GOVERNANCE

Crowdsourcing is perhaps best illustrated through case examples, and some of the business exemplars that have received thoroughly scholarly treatment include Threadless (Brabham, 2010; Fletcher,

2006; Lakhani & Kanji, 2008), InnoCentive (Brabham, 2008a; Jeppesen & Lakhani, 2010; Lakhani, 2008), iStockphoto (Brabham, 2008b; Grant & Stothers, 2007), Amazon's Mechanical Turk (Barr & Cabrera, 2006; Buhrmester, Kwang, & Gosling, 2011; Ipeirotis, 2010; Ipeirotis, Provost, & Wang, 2010), Doritos' Crash the Super Bowl contest (Brabham, 2009b; Urquhart, 2012), and the film *Star Wreck: In the Pirkinning* (Joutsen, Nieminen, Vuorensola, & Lekman, 2008; Lietsala & Joutsen, 2007). Organizing these cases according to their functional structures, the motivations of their participants, or their various outcomes presents a challenge, but I argue that these many cases can be understood according to the kinds of problems they attempt to solve. Four types of problems are suitable for crowdsourcing (see Table 1), and crowdsourcing applications approach these problems in the following ways: 1) the knowledge discovery and management approach; 2) the broadcast search approach; 3) the peer-vetted creative production approach; and 4) the distributed human intelligence tasking approach (Brabham, 2012).

Table 1. A typology of crowdsourcing problem types for urban governance (adapted from Brabham, 2012)

Type	How it Works	Kinds of Problems	Current and Potential Uses in Urban Governance
Knowledge Discovery and Management	Organization tasks crowd with finding and collecting information into a common location and format	Ideal for information gathering, organization, and reporting problems, such as the creation of collective resources	Patent application review; reporting non-emergency issues and repairs; reporting earthquake tremors; reporting use and state of repair of parks; reporting public transit use; cataloguing public art projects and murals
Broadcast Search	Organization tasks crowd with solving empirical problems	Ideal for ideation problems with empirically provable solutions, such as scientific problems	Proposing cost-saving solutions; developing formulas for predicting solar flares; finding better algorithms for timing traffic signals; improving actuarial formulas for social security
Peer-Vetted Creative Production	Organization tasks crowd with creating and selecting creative ideas	Ideal for ideation problems where solutions are matters of taste or market support, such as design or aesthetic problems	Designs for public structures and art projects; urban plans; transit plans; policy proposals; school redistricting plans
Distributed Human Intelligence Tasking	Organization tasks crowd with analyzing large amounts of information	Ideal for large-scale data analysis where human intelligence is more efficient or effective than computer analysis	Historical document analysis; language translation for documents and websites; data entry; cataloguing and organizing; behavioral modeling

The same typology that applies to for-profit business cases of crowdsourcing can be used to make sense of urban governance cases. What follows is an examination of this crowdsourcing typology with an eye toward existing and potential urban governance applications.

The Knowledge Discovery and Management Approach (KDM)

When the U.S. Patent and Trademark Office (USPTO) was faced with a backlog of patent applications and a staff that lacked the time and resources necessarily to properly assess whether technologies proposed for patent coverage were truly novel, it decided to open up the process online (Noveck, 2006). In a project called "Peer-to-Patent," the USPTO posted a small pilot sample of patent applications on the Internet and invited anyone willing to examine the applications to search for evidence of "prior art," or evidence whether a technology already existed in a similar form. The individuals in this online community who volunteered their time to track down evidence of prior art submitted their notes in a specified format, and the patent examiners used these notes to aid in their own formal investigations. By crowdsourcing the review of patent applications online, the USPTO was able to improve its process and detect instances of prior art, ultimately preventing the awarding of multiple patents for a single technology and keeping inventors out of the courts.

The Peer-to-Patent case is a fine example of the KDM approach to crowdsourcing, because it involved an organization confronted with the challenge of finding and assembling information into a common format. In this particular case, too, Peer-to-Patent was a way to bring citizens into the process of governance, engaging the intellectual abilities of ordinary volunteers to make a govern-ment agency more effective and efficient in its work and prevent unnecessary lawsuits later on.

Another example of the KDM approach in use for urban governance is SeeClickFix. SeeClickFix is a platform for citizens to report non-emergency issues in their community (A. Johnson, 2011; Smith, 2010). These non-emergency issues range from potholes in the road and graffiti on buildings to malfunctioning traffic signals and clogged storm drains. Citizens can report these issues on the Internet or through mobile phones, and city governments can subscribe to the service to see what issues are emerging in the community. Government agencies, especially local public works offices, can use the information to better allocate resources to address these small urban problems before they develop into large-scale urban decay. SeeClickFix is another example of the KDM approach to crowdsourcing, as city administrators gather information from citizens in a common location and format in order to improve the efficiency and effectiveness of government.

Yet another example of the KDM approach is the U.S. Geological Survey's (USGS) Community Internet Intensity Map, more commonly referred to as "Did You Feel It?" (Atkinson & Wald, 2007; Wald, Quitoriano, & Dewey, 2006). "Did You Feel It?" is an automatic mapping interface to plot reports of seismic activity submitted by everyday citizens. When an earthquake hits, citizens report feeling the tremors to the "Did You Feel It?" website, and the USGS assembles a map of the intensity of the earthquake activity. This kind of citizen-reported data allows the USGS to understand the patterns of earthquakes and their reach and informs emergency response planning and budgeting.

In each of these instances, government agencies utilize the KDM approach to crowdsourcing in order to charge online communities with locating and reporting specific kinds of information in specific formats that benefit governance. In essence, a government leverages the "eyes and ears" of its many stakeholders out in the community in order to make more informed policy decisions.

What other potential KDM applications exist for urban governance? Cities may find the KDM approach a cheaper and faster way to gather traffic data, perhaps. Regional transit authorities might ask citizens to report wait times for buses and trains or count the number of cars waiting at stop lights. Meters and sensors exist to automate this kind of data collection, but these methods are costly and not without their flaws. Mobilizing citizens to find and report these basic transportation data could turn up data of similar quality in more affordable ways, all the while engaging citizens and educating them about the complexities of transit planning, traffic systems, and transportation funding.

Similarly, city and county parks departments could use the KDM approach to gather data and input on its many park systems. A parks department may ask citizens to report the quality of walking and bicycle trails, the quality of lighting in parks at night, sightings of undesirable wildlife and insects, quality of sports fields, cleanliness and function of bathrooms, usage and popularity of playground equipment, and so on. All of these activities would help parks departments, which are frequently underfunded, perform basic assessments of facilities and allocate resources efficiently. Applied to other government agencies—water and sewer authorities, wildlife preservation boards, public arts departments, etc.—the KDM approach is a simple solution for information gathering and reporting that could greatly improve urban governance with relatively little effort and technological expense. And while KDM crowdsourcing efforts improve effectiveness and efficiency of governments, these efforts also engage citizens in the day-to-day activities of their government, educate them about important public issues, and motivate them to act, all benefits of effective deliberative democratic process.

The Broadcast Search Approach (BS)

An organization faced with a problem that requires a precise, empirically provable answer can use the BS approach to crowdsourcing to help its cause. While the KDM approach addresses problems of relatively simple information-gathering, the BS approach addresses difficult scientific problems that rely on novel solutions. With the U.S. Office of Management and Budget, President Obama started the Securing Americans' Value and Efficiency (SAVE) Award with an eye toward identifying novel solutions for reducing wasteful government spending. Federal employees were given the opportunity to submit cost-cutting ideas, and the best idea was awarded a prize. In the past two years, more than 56,000 ideas have been submitted by federal employees, and the winning ideas are projected to save the government millions of dollars long-term ("About the Government Reform," n.d.; "About the SAVE award," n.d.; Chopra & Metzenbaum, 2010; Long, 2009). In this situation, the U.S. government sought novel, provable solutions from its employees by broadcasting a call for ideas to reduce costs.

In some cases, government agencies use existing for-profit platforms, piggybacking on the success of companies such as InnoCentive. InnoCentive is a platform for companies to post difficult scientific research and development problems, and an online community is able to respond with solutions to those problems in pursuit of cash prizes provided by the companies. In 2009-2010, NASA posted a challenge to InnoCentive asking its online community for formulas to predict solar flares, offering a US $30,000 prize to a successful solution (N. B. Johnson, 2010). Only five people submitted a solution, and a retired radio engineer solved the problem successfully, but in the case of BS challenges, one correct solution is all that is needed.

The potential for urban governance applications of BS types of crowdsourcing is enormous. Any segment of the government that contains scientific professionals could potentially crowdsource difficult scientific problems using the BS approach. These could include environmental protection offices, space exploration agencies, mining safety organizations, actuarial and social security offices, traffic engineering offices, and other government entities.

The savings for a government agency in using a BS crowdsourcing approach, even with substantial cash prizes to winning solutions from citizens, are calculated by the amount of in-house staff hours and resources that would have otherwise been spent solving the problem. A cash prize of tens of thousands of dollars offered to the crowd in a BS crowdsourcing application is often far lower than the overhead and staffing costs of running a lab of government scientists in-house, and solutions can come quickly when a problem is opened up online. Opening up a tough problem to outsiders or those "on the margins" also has a significant bearing on if, how, or how fast those difficult problems are solved. This phenomenon of outsiders sometimes solving problems better than insiders is called marginality in problem solving. Technical marginality can occur when those on the margins of a technical domain of expertise bring unique ways of thinking about a problem to bear on the problem, such as when a biologist outperforms a chemist on a chemical engineering problem (Jeppesen & Lakhani, 2010). Marginality can also take place along lines of rank, when those in lower positions in a corporate hierarchy solve problems meant for managers and professionals with certain expertise (Villarroel & Reis, 2010). Thus, in an urban governance context, opening a scientific problem up to a crowd through a BS crowdsourcing application may not only save time and money, but it may also mean the difference between a problem getting solved or not.

The Peer-Vetted Creative Production Approach (PVCP)

Governments facing complex design, aesthetic, or policy problems, or problems of subjective taste or public support, seek yet a different form of crowdsourcing, the PVCP approach. In the PVCP approach, the organization asks the crowd not only to come up with complete design or policy ideas, but it also empowers the crowd to determine which design or policy is best. This peer-vetting process is crucial for gaining public support. Cases of urban planning, public art projects, or complex social and economic policy are matters requiring buy-in from citizen stakeholders, as public participation in these activities ensure plans, designs, and policies are more widely accepted by future users (Burby, 2003).

In 2009-2010, the Next Stop Design project was an attempt to test the PVCP approach to design better bus stop shelters for the Utah Transit Authority (UTA) transit system. In the project, individuals in the crowd submitted bus stop shelter designs to an online gallery. Once in the gallery, the crowd then rated each design and the design with the highest average score was declared the winner. This method generated 260 high-quality architectural renderings for bus stop shelters from nearly 3,200 registered users on the site, all while offering no monetary reward or promise to construct the winning design (Brabham et al., 2010). The Next Stop Design project demonstrated that, if given the tools to submit and rate the ideas of their peers, a crowd can come up with many usable, high-quality ideas for governance. Some of the ideas from Next Stop Design were expanded upon in a similar transit planning project in Somerville, Massachusetts, called inTeractive Somerville, and this project was also quite successful (Messina, 2012).

When it comes to policy, the same principles of the PVCP approach apply, except the track record for these kinds of policy experiments have been less successful. Between President Obama's election in 2008 and his inauguration in early 2009, his administration launched the "Citizen's Briefing Book," where citizens could submit policy ideas and vote on the ideas of peers. With 44,000 proposals and 1.4 million votes cast for these ideas, the most supported idea was to legalize marijuana, and some of the other most popular ideas included legalizing online poker and other causes supporting so-called vices (Giridharadas, 2009). The use of wikis and commenting functions on social media sites, rather than PVCP crowdsourcing applications, so far have better track records in collaborative online policymaking, as New Zealand and Iceland have found in recent years (Lips & Rapson, 2010; Siddique, 2011).

This does not mean the PVCP approach to crowdsourcing may be lost on policymaking. Rather, it may not be effective for crowdsourcing policymaking in diverse, populous countries such as the U.S. Local governance—at the city, county, and regional level—may find this approach particularly useful for smaller scale policy matters, such as school redistricting, the design of new community centers, community activity schedules, and the planning and budgeting for local parades and festivals. Strategies for guiding or moderating discussion in crowdsourced policymaking activities may also keep citizens focused on more pressing political issues at hand. I discuss these strategies under the topic of free speech rights in crowdsourcing communities below.

The Distributed Human Intelligence Tasking Approach (DHIT)

The DHIT approach is the most unlike of the other three types. Whereas KDM, BS, and PVCP approaches to crowdsourcing demand significant intellectual resources from individuals in the crowd, DHIT crowdsourcing activities are typically the least intellectually demanding. Organizations use the DHIT approach when they have large data sets that they need analyzed

quickly and cheaply, but processing those data through computer algorithms is not feasible. In these instances, individual data analysis tasks are distributed in small batches to individuals in the crowd, who apply human intelligence to relatively simple tasks, such as image tagging, for small monetary rewards in order to process the data quickly and cheaply.

In April 2012, the U.S. Census Bureau released the raw images of census records from 1940 in digitized form and made them available to the public for the first time. Transcribing these scans of microfilm of handwritten ledgers from more than 70 years ago is no easy task, and it requires human intelligence. McHenry, Marini, Kejriwal, Kooper, and Bajcsy (2011) propose that the government utilize a DHIT crowdsourcing approach, modeled on the reCAPTCHA system (von Ahn, Maurer, McMillen, Abraham, & Blum, 2008), to quickly, accurately, and inexpensively transcribe these data. Lang and Rio-Ross (2011) propose a similar approach to transcribing historical document images using instead the Amazon Mechanical Turk platform. Both approaches would make easy work of this kind of complicated transcription for any number of historical documents governments need analyzed and digitally archived.

Crowdsourced language translation is another important task for which the DHIT approach is well suited. Amazon Mechanical Turk, for instance, has been proven to facilitate successful, accurate language translation inexpensively (Callison-Burch, 2009). Many urban areas and agricultural areas with migrant workers are home to many people who do not speak the native language in a given country. Reaching these citizens is a difficult task for governments, and making even the most basic government information about taxes, school enrollment, immunizations, driver's licenses, and other topics available in a wide variety of languages is cost-prohibitive for many governments. For pennies on the dollar, however, services like Mechanical Turk enable crowdsourced translation of government documents and websites possible.

The same can be said of any tedious, simple, costly task a government agency faces, including data entry, transcription, cataloguing, captioning video, editing and proofreading, and data analysis.

Moving a step further, governments may find value in the DHIT crowdsourcing approach for modeling citizens' behaviors, such as predicting how and how often they utilize public transit, public parks, attend public meetings, or access government information. Bongard, Hines, Conger, Hurd, and Lu (in press) tested a system whereby users answered questions about obesity and electricity use, which included entering their body mass index numbers and their electricity usage as well as answering questions about their behaviors associated with these two facets of their lives. Users in turn were able to propose new questions about behaviors in the system for future users to answer. Over time, the sophistication of the system was improved with greater participation, and users essentially proposed new behaviors to model against their actual body mass index numbers and electricity usage. By crowdsourcing the generation of variables for behavioral modeling in conjunction with gathering data for these models, the users were contributing to the refinement of behavioral modeling that could be useful for public health practitioners and environmental policymakers. Taking these findings to the realm of urban governance could provide a wealth of information and sophisticated behavioral models for public administrators to use in the course of their work.

THE QUESTION OF FREE SPEECH

Free societies have the principle of free speech "not just because it is the law, but also because it is a really great idea. A strongly protected tradition of free speech is likely to encourage a wide range of criticism. That criticism is likely, in turn, to improve the systems or people or ideas criticized" (Lessig, 2004, p. 156). Free speech is not only a democratic value (Noveck, 2003), but it is also an

important value within organizations in order to foster innovation and problem solving (Amabile, 1998; Von Hippel, 2005). Surely, then, free speech is crucial to the success of any crowdsourcing application, but what happens when crowds protest and threaten to destroy the very platform? A government-sponsored crowdsourcing application faces the challenge of managing these protests without infringing on citizens' rights to speak out about and against the government. This section explores some of these instances of crowd unrest, which Howe (2006b) calls "crowdslapping," and what may be done to keep a crowdsourcing application on track without censorship.

To begin, it is helpful to consider a spectrum of potential crowdslapping strategies that may arise from a disgruntled crowd. I posit a distinction between disruptive crowdslapping, destructive crowdslapping, and other modes of crowd resistance. In all cases, though, I favor the power of community norms and software code as mechanisms for regulating this speech, rather than overt forms of government censorship.

Disruptive and Destructive Crowdslapping

Disruptive crowdslapping resembles protest in physical public spaces. That is, disruptive crowdslapping seeks to disrupt the smooth operation of a crowdsourcing venture through complaints posted in online forums, criticisms of the government which do not impede the abilities for others to be heard, and so on. This could take the form of a reasoned argument articulated by an individual in the crowd and posted to a crowdsourcing site, or it could take the form of a "peaceful" virtual petition against the government (or the specific government function under scrutiny in the crowdsourcing application).

Destructive crowdslapping, on the other hand, would entail interrupting the abilities for other citizens to participate on the site through overly obnoxious displays, such as "flaming"

(Lange, 2006). Suler (2004) has studied an "on-line disinhibition effect" where "dissociative anonymity" on the Web is a "principle factor" (p. 322). He finds that "[w]hen people have the opportunity to separate their actions online from their in-person lifestyle and identity, they feel less vulnerable about self-disclosing and acting out" (Suler, 2004, p. 322). In the adolescence of the Web in the 1990s, this "disinhibition effect was [evidenced] by the frequency of 'flaming'—the rapid escalation of terse remarks or insults in an electronic interchange—a phenomenon which is more often suppressed or avoided in face-to-face conversations" (Dutton, 1996, p. 270). Flaming, or its cousin "flooding," are tactics for destructive dialogue by users to lob insults (or cram an online bulletin board or chat space with junk text in the case of flooding) as a way to turn people off to the site and destroy the potential for meaningful, rational online conversation. Indeed, online crowds can become quite unruly, despite the stilted visions of rational debate hoped for by online deliberative democracy's proponents. Still, in this range of expression, from destructive flaming to disruptive criticism, these "slaps" from the crowd should be celebrated as moments of democratic engagement where even the most unpopular sentiments are valued as possible truths (Mill, 1859; 1985).

Cracking and Ignoring

Two other forms of crowd reaction beyond the bounds of disruptive and destructive crowdslapping hold more promise for actual destruction of a government crowdsourcing venture. These forms are cracking and ignoring. Cracking, the accurate term for malicious hacking, would be an instance where an individual in the crowd would take action to destroy the mechanisms of the site, probably through unlawful access to and manipulation of the site's code. Where destructive crowdslapping *deters* productive dialogue in a crowdsourcing application, cracking outright *prevents* individuals from engaging the crowdsourcing project. This

could come in the form of shutting down chat and bulletin board spaces, corrupting data files, and otherwise "breaking" the site. This form of malicious activity on a crowdsourcing site should be acted upon by government because it is akin to someone threatening a public forum and preventing people from engaging in expression for the sake of self-governance.

The final form of crowd resistance is the most peaceful—and probably would be the most effective—of all: ignoring. Crowdsourcing ventures are predicated on a sizable crowd of individuals each trying their hand at solving a given problem. Without enough minds to tackle the problem, the process fails. Noveck (2003) has explored these possibilities for online government ventures struggling to attract a critical mass of users.

Put simply, the four forms of crowd resistance—disruptive crowdslapping, destructive crowdslapping, cracking, and ignoring—are akin to traditional ranges of protest, respectively: lobbying and rational debate; annoying chants and image events; destruction of a public forum through a bomb threat; and boycotting.

Preserving Free Speech in Crowdsourcing Applications

In the U.S., public participation activities are a matter of public record (Bluestein, 2010b), and online public participation activities, such as government crowdsourcing applications, occupy a complicated place in the legal terrain. It is not surprising that outdated metaphors and ways of understanding the law have caused the law to lag behind the pace of technology (Drucker & Gumpert, 1995), and in the case of speech in online public participation applications the concept of the physical forum comes into play. In U.S. law, there are three different kinds of forums: the traditional forum, the limited public forum, and the non-public forum (Bluestein, 2009). Streets and parks, where citizens enjoy the freest of free speech rights, are examples of traditional public forums. Public meetings at city council are examples of limited public forums, where government can control the topics and time allotted to speakers. Non-public forums are spaces where government has the greatest control over speech, such as jails and schools. Generally, in limited public forums governments may control the time, place, and manner (e.g., prohibiting profanity) of speech in content-neutral ways for the sake of civil discourse, while in non-public forums governments may censor speech based on content as well.

A government crowdsourcing application may be considered more like a traditional public participation activity, such as a workshop or hearing, and thus is more like a limited public forum in legal terms. If a crowdsourcing application makes use of third-party platforms, such as Facebook or Twitter, the terms of use for those sites, which include provisions against threatening and hateful content, govern the application. Administrators may also impose restrictions on discussion topics beyond the narrow scope of a crowdsourcing project, too, however "it may be difficult…to reap the benefits of public participation in social media if there are too many limitations on what may be posted" (Bluestein, 2010a, para. 9). At a certain point, too many government restrictions on speech may turn participants away from a crowdsourcing project, which could cause the project to collapse for lack of input or interest.

I believe governments should impose only minimal restrictions on speech in crowdsourcing applications and instead should empower the crowd with the tools—code—necessary to self-govern through community standards.

Post (1995) makes the case for community standards as an effective way to resolve legal disputes, noting that communities have a good understanding for what is effective and appropriate for themselves. Applied online, the heuristic of community norms and standards is evident in some of the most robust, long-lasting communities. In these successful online communities, newcomers are treated with caution and the established communities work collectively to ignore or productively engage dissent from outsiders in ways which protect the values of the community. Examples of this kind of community action online occur in, for instance, pacts between women in online message board communities who agree not to respond to sexually harassing emails from men who "troll" the message board to meet women (Noveck, 2003, pp. 29–30). Yet, as Lessig (1999) points out, this vision of community policing only goes so far. Without technological measures, for instance, any outsider may insert themselves into an online community forum and rant all they want. Existing community members may ignore or productively engage the outsider, but the fact remains that they can do little to actually prevent the annoying posts from happening. Eventually, then, if the outsider is persistent enough, existing community members will grow tired of the rants and will exit the community, which may lead to the community's ultimate collapse.

Thus, the most effective online communities are equipped with lines of software code that enable the community to deal effectively with others and help to enforce community standards. For example, a simple code-based regulation in an online forum might be a limiting of message length or a mechanism which prevents someone from posting the same exact message multiple times in a row (e.g., in the instance of spam advertising posting in chat rooms). Constitutions might be set up in online communities with the senior-most members empowered to block users who violate those terms, though this is a problematic solution because the power to censor is merely shifted from government to a select few citizens, and this also departs from the ideal of the marketplace of ideas. Alternatively, communities may vote to suppress—but not entirely delete—some postings to the bottom of the heap or discussion thread. Still other code-based tools enable communities to assign reputational rankings to their peers, providing a kind of shorthand clue (usually through an icon) to others testifying to the quality of that member. eBay's reputation icons are a well-known instance of this. As buyers and sellers amass more successful transactions and provide good customer service to each other at eBay, members have the opportunity to leave feedback for each other and affect each other's reputation and status as trusted buyers and sellers. Lessig (1999) argues that this kind of information architecture through software code technology empowers communities to live out their desires to self-govern through community norms.

A crowdsourcing application with the right software tools can empower citizens to regulate themselves, by and large. And when citizens do get out of hand and threaten to destroy civil dialogue, governments have the ability to restrict speech in the spirit of the limited public forum.

THE POLICY-ADVISORY SPECTRUM

In any crowdsourcing application, the organization needs to communicate to the crowd exactly how much impact their ideas will have on the business of the organization going forward. Organizations should make a commitment to use the crowd's input in a policy or an advisory capacity—or somewhere in between—before the launch of any crowdsourcing venture.

On the policy end of the policy-advisory spectrum, the organization launches a crowd-sourcing application with the commitment to use the crowd's input in a direct, actionable way. The benefit of a government agency embracing a pure policy commitment is that the crowd knows they are being trusted with a serious public participation activity and may be more motivated to participate in the crowdsourcing application. The disadvantage to this kind of policy commitment,

however, is that if the government is not pleased with the outcome of a crowdsourcing venture— e.g., the people want a marijuana legalization policy—they must backpedal and disappoint the crowd by reneging on their commitment to enact crowdsourced policy.

On the advisory end of the policy-advisory spectrum, the organization makes no promises to the crowd to use any of their ideas. Rather, the organization states that the results of the crowdsourcing activity may or may not find their way into actual policy or government affairs. The advantage here is that the government can solicit ideas from the crowd with the risk of having to commit to anything, but the obvious disadvantage is that people may not participate if they do not feel their government will take their ideas seriously.

A point in the middle of the policy-advisory spectrum seems more reasonable for a government crowdsourcing venture. In a PVCP bus stop shelter design competition, for instance, this might involve the government committing to the top five rated designs from the public, but then the government reserves the right to choose which of those five bus stop shelters will be built. Or the inverse might be true, with the government choosing its top five designs and agreeing to build the top rated one as voted on by the crowd. Another middle-of-the-road position is for the government to use a panel to choose a winning design, and this panel could consist of a mix of everyday citizens, government officials, and design experts. Or perhaps it is a mix of these methods, with the crowd selecting the top five and a mixed panel of representatives selects the winner. No matter the level of commitment on the policy-advisory spectrum, it is important for the crowdsourcing organization to truly commit to the terms put forth at the outset of a crowdsourcing venture so that the public is not betrayed and discouraged from participating in government affairs in the future.

CONCLUSION

We are moving into an era in urban governance where citizens will be more connected to government than ever before. New media technologies, such as social media and mobile phones, enable increasingly sophisticated levels of engagement in fast and convenient ways. Governments should embrace these technological shifts by innovating new methods for citizen participation in urban governance, and I believe crowdsourcing is one such model that can facilitate engagement to address four different kinds of problems. Each of the crowdsourcing problem types discussed in this chapter—the knowledge discovery and management approach, the broadcast search approach, the peer-vetted creative production approach, and the distributed human intelligence tasking approach—turn up in any government agency, and it is up to leading public administrators to test the crowdsourcing model in their cities and states. In deploying these crowdsourcing experiments, it is important also to remember one's level of commitment to the outcomes on a policy-advisory spectrum and it is just as important to uphold the free speech rights of the crowd for democracy's and innovation's sake.

REFERENCES

About the Government Reform for Competitiveness and Innovation Initiative. (n.d.). *U.S. White House*. Retrieved September 15, 2012, from http://www.whitehouse.gov/federalvoices/about

About the SAVE award. (n.d.). *U.S. White House*. Retrieved September 15, 2012, from http://www.whitehouse.gov/save-award/about

Amabile, T. M. (1998). How to kill creativity. *Harvard Business Review*, 77–87. PMID:10187248.

Atkinson, G. M., & Wald, D. J. (2007). "Did You Feel It?" intensity data: A surprisingly good measure of earthquake ground motion. *Seismological Research Letters*, 78(3), 362–368. doi:10.1785/gssrl.78.3.362.

Barr, J., & Cabrera, L. F. (2006). AI gets a brain: New technology allows software to tap real human intelligence. *ACM Queue; Tomorrow's Computing Today*, 4(4), 24–29. doi:10.1145/1142055.1142067.

Benkler, Y. (2002). Coase's penguin, or, Linux and The nature of the firm. *The Yale Law Journal*, 112(3), 369–446. doi:10.2307/1562247.

Bluestein, F. (2009, August 5). Limited public forum analysis revisited. *Coates' canons: NC local government law blog* [Weblog]. Retrieved September 15, 2012, from http://canons.sog.unc.edu/?p=139

Bluestein, F. (2010a, March 3). Free speech rights in government social media sites. *Coates' canons: NC local government law blog* [Weblog]. Retrieved September 15, 2012, from http://canons.sog.unc.edu/?p=1970

Bluestein, F. (2010b, April 14). Citizen participation information as public record. *Coates' canons: NC local government law blog* [Weblog]. Retrieved September 15, 2012, from http://canons.sog.unc.edu/?p=2238

Bongard, J. C., Hines, P. D. H., Conger, D., Hurd, P., & Lu, Z. (in press). Crowdsourcing predictors of behavioral outcomes. *IEEE Transactions on Systems, Man, and Cybernetics. Part A, Systems and Humans*.

Brabham, D. C. (2008a). Crowdsourcing as a model for problem solving: An introduction and cases. *Convergence: The International Journal of Research into New Media Technologies*, 14(1), 75–90. doi:10.1177/1354856507084420.

Brabham, D. C. (2008b). Moving the crowd at iStockphoto: The composition of the crowd and motivations for participation in a crowdsourcing application. *First Monday, 13*(6). Retrieved September 15, 2012, from http://firstmonday.org/htbin/cgiwrap/bin/ojs/index.php/fm/article/view/2159/1969

Brabham, D. C. (2009a). Crowdsourcing the public participation process for planning projects. *Planning Theory, 8*(3), 242–262. doi:10.1177/1473095209104824.

Brabham, D. C. (2009b). Crowdsourced advertising: How we outperform Madison Avenue. *Flow: A Critical Forum on Television and Media Culture, 9*(10). Retrieved September 15, 2012, from http://flowtv.org/?p=3221

Brabham, D. C. (2010). Moving the crowd at Threadless: Motivations for participation in a crowdsourcing application. *Information Communication and Society, 13*(8), 1122–1145. doi:10.1080/13691181003624090.

Brabham, D. C. (2012). Crowdsourcing: A model for leveraging online communities. In Delwiche, A., & Henderson, J. J. (Eds.), *The participatory cultures handbook* (pp. 120–129). New York: Routledge.

Brabham, D. C., Sanchez, T. W., & Bartholomew, K. (2010). *Crowdsourcing public participation in transit planning: Preliminary results from the Next Stop Design case.* Presented at the annual meeting of the Transportation Research Board of the National Academies, Washington, DC.

Buhrmester, M., Kwang, T., & Gosling, S. D. (2011). Amazon's mechanical Turk: A new source of inexpensive, yet high-quality, data? *Perspectives on Psychological Science, 6*(1), 3–5. doi:10.1177/1745691610393980.

Burby, R. J. (2003). Making plans that matter: Citizen involvement and government action. *Journal of the American Planning Association. American Planning Association, 69*(1), 33–49. doi:10.1080/01944360308976292.

Callison-Burch, C. (2009). Fast, cheap, and creative: Evaluating translation quality using Amazon's mechanical Turk. *Proceedings of the 2009 conference on empirical methods in natural language processing* (pp. 286–295). Stroudsburg, PA: Association for Computational Linguistics.

Chesbrough, H. (2003). *Open innovation: The new imperative for creating and profiting from technology.* Boston, MA: Harvard Business Press.

Chopra, A., & Metzenbaum, S. (2010, December 8). Designing for democracy. *U.S. White House Open Government Initiative* [Weblog]. Retrieved September 15, 2012, from http://www.whitehouse.gov/blog/2010/12/08/designing-democracy-0

Drucker, S., & Gumpert, G. (1995). Freedom and liability in cyberspace: Media, metaphors and paths of regulation. *Free Speech Yearbook, 33*, 49–64. doi:10.1080/08997225.1995.10556182.

Dutton, W. H. (1996). Network rules of order: Regulating speech in public electronic fora. *Media Culture & Society, 18*(2), 269–290. doi:10.1177/016344396018002006.

Estellés-Arolas, E., & González-Ladrón-de-Guevara, F. (2012). Towards and integrated crowdsourcing definition. *Journal of Information Science, 38*(2), 189–200. doi:10.1177/0165551512437638.

Fletcher, A. (2006). *Do consumers want to design unique products on the Internet?: A study of the online virtual community of Threadless.com and their attitudes to mass customisation, mass production and collaborative design.* (Unpublished bachelor's thesis). Nottingham Trent University.

Giridharadas, A. (2009, September 12). "Athens" on the net. *New York Times*. Retrieved September 15, 2012, from http://www.nytimes.com/2009/09/13/weekinreview/13giridharadas.html?_r=3

Grant, R. A., & Stothers, M. (2007). iStockphoto.com: Turning community in commerce (Harvard Business School Case No. 907-E13). Cambridge, MA: Harvard Business School.

Howe, J. (2006a, June). The rise of crowdsourcing. *Wired, 14*(6). Retrieved September 15, 2012, from http://www.wired.com/wired/archive/14.06/crowds.html

Howe, J. (2006b, June 16). Neo neologisms. *Crowdsourcing: Tracking the rise of the amateur* [Weblog]. Retrieved September 15, 2012, from http://www.crowdsourcing.com/cs/2006/06/neo_neologisms.html

Howe, J. (2008). *Crowdsourcing: Why the power of the crowd is driving the future of business*. New York: Crown.

http://adage.com/article/agency-news/pepsi-dew-mocracy-push-threatens-crowd-shops/140120/

iceland-crowdsourcing-constitution-facebook?CMP=twt_gu

Ipeirotis, P. G. (2010). Analyzing the Amazon mechanical Turk marketplace. *XRDS: Crossroads. The ACM Magazine for Students, 17*(2), 16–21. doi:10.1145/1869086.1869094.

Ipeirotis, P. G., Provost, F., & Wang, J. (2010). Quality management on Amazon mechanical Turk. In R. Chandrasekar, E. Chi, M. Chickering, P. G. Ipeirotis, W. Mason, F. Provost, J. Tam et al. (Eds.), *Proceedings of the ACM SIGKDD Workshop on Human Computation* (pp. 64–67). New York: Association for Computing Machinery.

Jeppesen, L. B., & Lakhani, K. R. (2010). Marginality and problem-solving effectiveness in broadcast search. *Organization Science, 21*(5), 1016–1033. doi:10.1287/orsc.1090.0491.

Johnson, A. (2011, February 17). City: SeeClickFix has good first month. *WRAL.com*. Retrieved September 15, 2012, from http://www.wral.com/news/news_briefs/story/9128944

Johnson, N. B. (2010, August 30). How agencies are crowd-sourcing their way out of problems. *Federal Times*. Retrieved September 15, 2012, from http://www.federaltimes.com/article/20100830/AGENCY03/8300301/1001

Joutsen, A., Nieminen, V., Vuorensola, T., & Lekman, L. (2008). Wreck a movie: Empowering the masses for film productions. In A. Lugmayr, F. Mäyrä, H. Franssila, & K. Lietsala (Eds.), *12th international MindTrek conference: Entertainment and media in the ubiquitous era* (pp. 141–144). New York: Association for Computing Machinery.

Kleeman, F., Voss, G. G., & Rieder, K. (2008). Un(der)paid innovators: The commercial utilization of consumer work through crowdsourcing. *Science. Technology and Innovation Studies, 4*(1), 5–26.

Lakhani, K. R. (2008). *InnoCentive.com (A) (Harvard Business School Case No. 608-170)*. Cambridge, MA: Harvard Business School.

Lakhani, K. R., & Kanji, Z. (2008). Threadless: The business of community (Harvard Business School Multimedia/Video Case No. 608-707). Cambridge, MA: Harvard Business School.

Lang, A. S. I. D., & Rio-Ross, J. (2011). Using Amazon mechanical Turk to transcribe historical handwritten documents. *Code4Lib Journal, 15*. Retrieved September 15, 2012, from http://journal.code4lib.org/articles/6004

Lange, P. G. (2006). What is your claim to flame? *First Monday, 11*(9). Retrieved September 15, 2012, from http://firstmonday.org/htbin/cgiwrap/bin/ojs/index.php/fm/article/view/1393/1311

Lessig, L. (1999). *Code: And other laws of cyberspace*. New York: Basic Books.

Lessig, L. (2004). *Free culture: How big media uses technology and the law to lock down culture and control creativity*. New York: Penguin Press.

Lévy, P. (1997). *Collective intelligence: Mankind's emerging world in cyberspace* (Bononno, R., Trans.). New York: Plenum.

Lietsala, K., & Joutsen, A. (2007). Hang-a-rounds and true believers: A case analysis of the roles and motivational factors of the Star Wreck fans. In A. Lugmayr, K. Lietsala, & J. Kallenbach (Eds.), *MindTrek 2007 Conference Proceedings* (pp. 25–30). Tampere, Finland: Tampere University of Technology.

Lips, M., & Rapson, A. (2010). Exploring public recordkeeping behaviors in wiki-supported public consultation activities in the New Zealand public sector. In R. H. Sprague Jr. (Ed.), *Proceedings of the 43rd Hawaii International Conference on System Sciences*. Los Alamitos, CA: IEEE Computer Society.

Long, E. (2009, December 7). Administration announces finalists in cost-cutting contest. *GovernmentExecutive.com*. Retrieved September 15, 2012, from http://www.govexec.com/story_page.cfm?filepath=/dailyfed/1209/12070911.htm

McHenry, K., Marini, L., Kejriwal, M., Kooper, R., & Bajcsy, P. (2011, September 22). Toward free and searchable historical census images. *SPIE Newsroom*. Retrieved September 15, 2012, from http://spie.org/x57241.xml

Messina, M. J. (2012). *Crowdsourcing for transit-oriented planning projects: A case study of "inTeractive Somerville."* (Unpublished M.A. thesis). Tufts University.

Mill, J. S. (1985). *On liberty*. New York: Penguin Press.

M&M lovers pick purple. (2002, June 20). *CNN Money*. Retrieved September 15, 2012, from http://money.cnn.com/2002/06/20/news/companies/mandms/

Noveck, B. S. (2003). Designing deliberative democracy in cyberspace: The role of the cyberlawyer. *Boston University Journal of Science and Technology Law, 9*(1), 1–91.

Noveck, B. S. (2006). "Peer to Patent": Collective intelligence, open review, and patent reform. *Harvard Journal of Law & Technology, 20*(1), 123–262.

Obama, B. (n.d.). *Transparency and open government* [Presidential memorandum]. Retrieved September 15, 2012, from http://www.whitehouse.gov/the_press_office/Transparency_and_Open_Government

Post, R. C. (1995). *Constitutional domains: Democracy, community, management*. Cambridge, MA: Harvard University Press.

prodandref/WaldEtAlECEESDYFI.pdf

Siddique, H. (2011, June 9). Mob rule: Iceland crowdsources its next constitution: Country recovering from collapse of its banks and government is using social media to get citizens to share their ideas. *The Guardian*. Retrieved September 15, 2012, from http://www.guardian.co.uk/world/2011/jun/09/

Smith, A. (2010, August 7). SeeClickFix celebrates 50G issues reported. *New Haven Register.* Retrieved September 15, 2012, from http://www.nhregister.com/articles/2010/08/07/news/aa3_neseeclickfix080710.txt

Suler, J. R. (2004). The online disinhibition effect. *Cyberpsychology & Behavior, 7,* 321–326. doi:10.1089/1094931041291295 PMID:15257832.

Urquhart, E. S. (2012). *Listening to the crowd: A content analysis of social media chatter about a crowdsourcing contest.* (Unpublished B.A. Honors thesis). University of North Carolina at Chapel Hill.

Villarroel, J. A., & Reis, F. (2010). *Intra-corporate crowdsourcing (ICC): Leveraging upon rank and site marginality for innovation.* Presented at the CrowdConf2010, San Francisco, CA. Retrieved September 15, 2012, from http://www.crowdconf2010.com/images/finalpapers/villarroel.pdf

von Ahn, L., Maurer, B., McMillen, C., Abraham, D., & Blum, M. (2008). reCAPTCHA: Human-based character recognition via Web security measures. *Science, 321*(5895), 1465–1468. doi:10.1126/science.1160379 PMID:18703711.

Von Hippel, E. (2005). *Democratizing innovation.* Cambridge, MA: MIT Press.

Vukovic, M., & Bartolini, C. (2010). Towards a research agenda for enterprise crowdsourcing. *Lecture Notes in Computer Science, 6415,* 425–434. doi:10.1007/978-3-642-16558-0_36.

Wald, D. J., Quitoriano, V., & Dewey, J. W. (2006). *USGS "Did You Feel It?" community Internet intensity maps: Macroseismic data collection via the Internet.* Presented at the First European conference on earthquake engineering and seismology, Geneva, Switzerland. Retrieved September 15, 2012, from http://ehp2-earthquake.wr.usgs.gov/earthquakes/pager/

Whitla, P. (2009). Crowdsourcing and its application in marketing activities. *Contemporary Management Research, 5*(1), 15–28.

Zmuda, N. (2009, November 2). New Pepsi "Dewmocracy" push threatens to crowd out shops. *AdAge.com.* Retrieved September 15, 2012, from

ADDITIONAL READING

Alt, F., Shirazi, A. S., Schmidt, A., Kramer, U., & Nawaz, Z. (2010). Location-based crowdsourcing: Extending crowdsourcing to the real world. In *NordiCHI 2010 Proceedings.* New York: Association for Computing Machinery. doi:10.1145/1868914.1868921.

Barr, J., & Cabrera, L. F. (2006). AI gets a brain: New technology allows software to tap real human intelligence. *ACM Queue; Tomorrow's Computing Today, 4*(4), 24–29. doi:10.1145/1142055.1142067.

Bongard, J. C., Hines, P. D. H., Conger, D., Hurd, P., & Lu, Z. (in press). Crowdsourcing predictors of behavioral outcomes. *IEEE Transactions on Systems, Man, and Cybernetics. Part A, Systems and Humans.*

Brabham, D. C. (2009). Crowdsourcing the public participation process for planning projects. *Planning Theory, 8*(3), 242–262. doi:10.1177/1473095209104824.

Brabham, D. C. (2010). *Crowdsourcing as a model for problem solving: Leveraging the collective intelligence of online communities for public good.* (Unpublished Ph.D. dissertation). University of Utah.

Brabham, D. C. (2012). Crowdsourcing: A model for leveraging online communities. In Delwiche, A., & Henderson, J. J. (Eds.), *The participatory cultures handbook* (pp. 120–129). New York: Routledge.

Brabham, D. C. (2012). Managing unexpected publics online: The challenge of targeting specific groups with the wide-reaching tool of the Internet. *International Journal of Communication, 6*, 1139–1158. Retrieved September 15, 2012, from http://ijoc.org/ojs/index.php/ijoc/article/view/1542/751

Brito, J. (2008). Hack, mash, & peer: Crowdsourcing government transparency. *The Columbia Science and Technology Law Review, 9*, 119–157.

Burger-Helmchen, T., & Penin, J. (2010). *The limits of crowdsourcing inventive activities: What do transaction cost theory and the evolutionary theories of the firm teach us?* Paper presented at the Workshop on Open Source Innovation, Strasbourg, France.

Campbell, L. (2009). *Dotmocracy: Crowdsourcing, mashups, and social change*. Retrieved September 15, 2012, from http://www.mobiler-evolutions.org/Dotmocracy.pdf

Eagle, N. (2009). txteagle: Mobile crowdsourcing. *Lecture Notes in Computer Science, 5623*, 447–456. doi:10.1007/978-3-642-02767-3_50.

Estellés-Arolas, E., & González-Ladrón-de-Guevara, F. (2012). Towards and integrated crowdsourcing definition. *Journal of Information Science, 38*(2), 189–200. doi:10.1177/0165551512437638.

Fritz, S., McCallum, I., Schill, C., Perher, C., Grillmayer, R., & Achard, F. et al. (2009). Geo-Wiki.org: The use of crowdsourcing to improve global land cover. *Remote Sensing, 1*(3), 345–354. doi:10.3390/rs1030345.

Howe, J. (2006, June). The rise of crowdsourcing. *Wired, 14*(6). Retrieved September 15, 2012, from http://www.wired.com/wired/archive/14.06/crowds.html

Howe, J. (2008). *Crowdsourcing: Why the power of the crowd is driving the future of business*. New York: Crown.

Huberman, B. A., Romero, D. M., & Wu, F. (2009). Crowdsourcing, attention and productivity. *Journal of Information Science, 35*(6), 758–765. doi:10.1177/0165551509346786.

Ipeirotis, P. G., Provost, F., & Wang, J. (2010). Quality management on Amazon mechanical Turk. In R. Chandrasekar, E. Chi, M. Chickering, P. G. Ipeirotis, W. Mason, F. Provost, J. Tam et al. (Eds.), *Proceedings of the ACM SIGKDD Workshop on Human Computation* (pp. 64–67). New York: Association for Computing Machinery.

Jeppesen, L. B., & Lakhani, K. R. (2010). Marginality and problem-solving effectiveness in broadcast search. *Organization Science, 21*(5), 1016–1033. doi:10.1287/orsc.1090.0491.

Kamensky, J. (2009, September 16). Using crowdsourcing in government. *IBM Center for the Business of Government Blog* [Weblog]. Retrieved September 15, 2012, from http://bizgov.wordpress.com/2009/09/16/using-crowdsourcing-in-government/

Kaufmann, N., Schulze, T., & Veit, D. (2011). More than fun and money: Worker motivation in crowdsourcing--A study on mechanical Turk. In *Proceedings of the Seventeenth Americas Conference on Information Systems* (paper #340). Berkeley, CA: Digital Commons, Berkeley Electronic Press. Retrieved September 15, 2012, from http://aisel.aisnet.org/amcis2011_submissions/340/

Kessler, S. (2011, March 23). Crowdsourcing helps Holocaust survivors find answers. *Mashable* [Weblog]. Retrieved September 15, 2012, from http://mashable.com/2011/05/23/holocaust-museum-crowdsourcing/

Kleeman, F., Voss, G. G., & Rieder, K. (2008). Un(der)paid innovators: The commercial utilization of consumer work through crowdsourcing. *Science. Technology and Innovation Studies, 4*(1), 5–26.

La Vecchia, G., & Cisternino, A. (2010). Collaborative workforce, business process crowdsourcing as an alternative of BPO. *Lecture Notes in Computer Science, 6385*, 425–430. doi:10.1007/978-3-642-16985-4_40.

Lakhani, K. R., Jeppesen, L. B., Lohse, P. A., & Panetta, J. A. (2007). *The value of openness in scientific problem solving* (Harvard Business School Working Paper No. 07-050). Retrieved September 15, 2012, from http://www.hbs.edu/research/pdf/07-050.pdf

Lietsala, K., & Joutsen, A. (2007). Hang-a-rounds and true believers: A case analysis of the roles and motivational factors of the Star Wreck fans. In A. Lugmayr, K. Lietsala, & J. Kallenbach (Eds.), *MindTrek 2007 Conference Proceedings* (pp. 25–30). Tampere, Finland: Tampere University of Technology.

Messina, M. J. (2012). *Crowdsourcing for transit-oriented planning projects: A case study of "inTeractive Somerville."* (Unpublished M.A. thesis). Tufts University.

Muthukumaraswamy, K. (2010). When the media meet crowds of wisdom: How journalists are tapping into audience expertise and manpower for the processes of newsgathering. *Journalism Practice, 4*(1), 48–65. doi:10.1080/17512780903068874.

Noveck, B. S. (2009). *Wiki government: How technology can make government better, democracy stronger, and citizens more powerful.* Washington, DC: Brookings Institution Press.

Okolloh, O. (2009). Ushahidi, or "testimony": Web 2.0 tools for crowdsourcing crisis information. *Participatory Learning and Action, 59*(1), 65–70.

Page, S. E. (2007). *The difference: How the power of diversity creates better groups, firms, schools, and societies.* Princeton, NJ: Princeton University Press.

Siddique, H. (2011, June 9). Mob rule: Iceland crowdsources its next constitution: Country recovering from collapse of its banks and government is using social media to get citizens to share their ideas. *The Guardian.* Retrieved September 15, 2012, from http://www.guardian.co.uk/world/ 2011/jun/09/iceland-crowdsourcing-constitution-facebook?CMP=twt_gu

Stewart, O., Huerta, J. M., & Sader, M. (2009). Designing crowdsourcing community for the enterprise. In P. Bennett, R. Chandrasekar, M. Chickering, P. Ipeirotis, E. Law, A. Mityagin, F. Provost et al. (Eds.), *Proceedings of the ACM SIGKDD Workshop on Human Computation* (pp. 50–53). New York: Association for Computing Machinery.

Trompette, P., Chanal, V., & Pelissier, C. (2008). *Crowdsourcing as a way to access external knowledge for innovation: Control, incentive and coordination in hybrid forms of innovation.* Paper presented at the 24th EGOS Colloquium, Amsterdam.

Urquhart, E. S. (2012). *Listening to the crowd: A content analysis of social media chatter about a crowdsourcing contest.* (Unpublished B.A. Honors thesis). University of North Carolina at Chapel Hill.

Villarroel, J. A., & Reis, F. (2010). *Intra-corporate crowdsourcing (ICC): Leveraging upon rank and site marginality for innovation.* Presented at CrowdConf2010, San Francisco. Retrieved September 15, 2012, from http://www.crowd-conf2010.com/images/finalpapers/villarroel.pdf

von Ahn, L., Maurer, B., McMillen, C., Abraham, D., & Blum, M. (2008). reCAPTCHA: Human-based character recognition via Web security measures. *Science, 321*(5895), 1465–1468. doi:10.1126/science.1160379 PMID:18703711.

Vukovic, M., & Bartolini, C. (2010). Towards a research agenda for enterprise crowdsourcing. *Lecture Notes in Computer Science, 6415*, 425–434. doi:10.1007/978-3-642-16558-0_36.

Vukovic, M., Laredo, J., & Rajagopal, S. (2010). Challenges and experiences in deploying enterprise crowdsourcing service. *Lecture Notes in Computer Science, 6189*, 460–467. doi:10.1007/978-3-642-13911-6_31.

Whitla, P. (2009). Crowdsourcing and its application in marketing activities. *Contemporary Management Research, 5*(1), 15–28.

Wu, F., Wilkinson, D. M., & Huberman, B. (2009). Feedback loops of attention in peer production. *Proceedings of the 2009 IEEE international conference on social computing* (pp. 409–415). Los Alamitos, CA: IEEE Computer Society.

KEY TERMS AND DEFINITIONS

Collective Intelligence: The phenomenon whereby groups of individuals become collectively more intelligent than single individuals or even panels of experts.

Commons-Based Peer Production: A form of online participatory culture where users grow and maintain a set of resources in a sustainable and self-governing way.

Crowd: A group of individuals in an online community engaged in a crowdsourcing application.

Crowdslapping: When a crowd protests and disrupts a crowdsourcing application.

Crowdsourcing: An online, distributed problem solving and production process whereby organizations leverage the collective intelligence of online communities to address specific organizational needs.

Marginality in Problem Solving: The phenomenon whereby outsiders or those on the margins of a problem solving domain perform as well as, or better than, those at the core of the problem solving domain.

Open Innovation: The practice of opening the in-house innovation process, be it idea-generation or product research and development, to a community outside the organization.

Chapter 5
Web 2.0, Neogeography, and Urban E–Governance

Barney Warf
University of Kansas, USA

ABSTRACT

Web 2.0 technologies, which allow interactions between the producers and consumers of information, have important implications for how urban spaces are designed and governed. Spatial information on the web has become increasingly wikified, so that non-planners may contribute data, photos, and opinions in a variety of ways, a process that labeled neogeography (and which is closely related to participatory GIS). For example, websites such as GoogleMaps have greatly democratized the process of constructing and using spatial data. This process implies that planners are no longer the privileged producers of information about urban space. A case study of Brión, Galicia, is offered to illustrate this process in practice. Web 2.0 and neogeography have greatly elevated the philosophical significance of planning information: rather than received wisdom, users may construct their own communities of truth. The chapter argues this process resembles Habermas's notion of an ideal speech situation. The conclusion argues that Web 2.0 and the growth of neogeography imply that planning must be more inclusive and democratic in nature.

INTRODUCTION

As the internet has spread rapidly to encompass more than 32% of the planet's population at the end of 2012, its applications have multiplied accordingly, including an ongoing reshaping of the interactions between many urban governments and their citizens. This process has been greatly accelerated by the introduction of Web 2.0 technologies. Whereas most governance applications of the internet have allowed only a one-way flow of information, i.e., from the state to users (e.g., downloading documents), Web 2.0 technology allows users to upload information and engage in interaction with web sites. This process has important repercussions for urban planning, including the critical philosophical question as to whose information is deemed valid in the design

DOI: 10.4018/978-1-4666-4169-3.ch005

of urban spaces. One particularly important type of knowledge, spatial information, including that used in e-governance, has become increasingly "wikified," created in a "bottom-up" fashion rather than the traditional "top-down" form, a process commonly known as neogeography. In adopting geospatial tools via the web, citizens can produce information about places that is meaningful to them within specific "neighborhoods of truth" rather than on the terms dictated by urban planners.

This chapter explores the linkages between neogeography and urban e-governance in several respects. First, it summarizes the complex relations between Web 2.0 and urban planning. Rather than using data designed for, and usually by, experts in a top-down fashion, Web 2.0 applications have allowed users to access census data, and construct their own maps of electoral outcomes, access to health care, transportation routes, and responses to disasters. Second, it explores an example of how Web 2.0 fostered a series of changes in the community of Brión, Galicia. Third, it offers a philosophical critique of Web 2.0's implications for e-governance by invoking the works of Jürgen Habermas and the notion of the ideal speech situation. In democratizing access to information, neogeography is changing the nature of e-governance. These lines of thought indicate that urban planners must take citizen participation in e-governance far more seriously than they have hitherto. In short, the Web 2.0 reflects and contributes to the democratization of urban e-governance.

WEB 2.0, NEOGEOGRAPHY, AND URBAN PLANNING

Web 2.0 is a diverse set of software applications that have revolutionized usage of the Web. Key components of this technology are Asynchronous Javascript and XML (AJAX) and Application Programming Interfaces (API), which facilitate the creation of websites that allow instantaneous user interactions. The functionality offered by Web 2.0 has precipitated significant changes from traditional approaches to internet usage, making the web markedly more user-centric. In this sense, it has fostered an unprecedented democratization of knowledge. Goodchild (2007, p. 27), focusing on "citizen sensors," maintains that whereas "the early Web was primarily one-directional, allowing a large number of users to view the contents of a comparatively small number of sites, the new Web 2.0 is a bi-directional collaboration in which users are able to interact with and provide information to central sites, and to see that information collated and made available to others."

One dimension of e-governance is the production and consumption of spatial information. The term neogeography, which has been used in several ways with varying meanings (Vander Wal, 2005), points to the process by which people use on-line geospatial tools to describe and document aspects of their lives and environment in terms that are meaningful to them (Hudson-Smith et al., 2009). Web 2.0 is vital to the production and consumption of this volunteered geographic information, which is closely linked to neogeography and participatory GIS (Dunn, 2007). This approach lies at the heart of services such as GoogleMaps or OpenStreetMaps, in which users can upload location-based, geocoded information from a GPS and engage in a bi-directional process of cartographic design and production. The interactive websites characteristic of Web 2.0 allow users to upload information about locations into online content and apply their data in diverse ways, including, for example, simple displays of locations (e.g., favored routes for a proposed bike trail) or lists of attributes of a place near a user equipped with a GPS. This approach lies at the heart of mapping websites such as Google Maps, Yahoo!Maps, OpenStreetMap, and Bing Live Maps. Google Maps is used by more than 71 million people annually and Google Earth by 22.7 million (Haklay, Singleton, & Parker, 2008).

As Web 2.0 has enabled growing legions of people to interact with one another, and with government agencies, neogeography has enjoyed explosive growth (Turner & Forest, 2008). As a consequence, geographic knowledge has increasingly escaped the confines of academia or urban planning professionals and has been embraced by an enthusiastic and rapidly growing public of amateurs and hobbyists. Rather than rely on state or corporate-produced data, neogeography generates volunteered data/content, relocating the center of knowledge production from a handful of self-appointed experts to large numbers of people with limited formal geographic training. Sui (2008) labels these changes the "wikification of GIS," after Wikipedia, the famously popular, user-generated, online encyclopedia. User-generated maps of endangered bird species, handicapped-accessible restrooms, ideal camping locations, accident-prone roads, green buildings may not pass the standards of academics and professionals, but their efforts yield results that are important and meaningful to their respective groups of contributors, creating a "people's geography" quite distanced from the rarified world of academia.

Because Web 2.0 sites draw self-selected audiences, neogeographic media have enabled large numbers of people to choose those sources of information that mesh conveniently with their ideological presuppositions. There are obviously both advantages and disadvantages to this approach. Most obviously, it is not always the case that the "wisdom of the crowd" is superior to that of a few experienced individuals. By utilizing data that only confirm their beliefs, users may never be confronted with disturbing or contradictory sources of information. However, by putting the sources of data and the means to visualize it firmly in the hands of users and consumers rather than an elite group of expert producers, neogeography forces a broader recognition of the degree to which truth values reflect broader social concerns such as trust, reputation, and credibility (Bishr & Mantelas,

2008; Bishr & Kuhn, 2007; Flanagin & Metzger, 2008). Accuracy, in this context, is largely a matter of ideology and preference, contingent upon context and purpose, and tailored to the specific interests of communities of interest. In facilitating the emergence of numerous "neighborhoods of truth," neogeography encourages us to abandon universal generalizations and come to terms with the place-bound nature of geographic knowledge. In its stead, it opens up venues for viewing the world through the eyes of particular groups bound together by lifestyle, political values, recreational habits, and other dimensions of social life.

A sizable body of literature has demonstrated that information technologies are central to successful urban areas, including global cities and "learning regions" (Gurstein, 2000; Graham & Marvin, 2001). Ubiquitous computing has greatly enhanced the availability of real-time information about environments. As more cities become increasingly "wired," that is, as digital technologies become pervasive in their accessibility and usage, neogeographic data has multiplied in quantity and utility. There is, of course, a vast literature on urban information networks, which need not be recapitulated here. Computer code has become so woven into the fabric of urban space as to be indispensable, profoundly shaping the contours of everyday life (Dodge & Kitchin, 2005). Hudson-Smith et al. (2009, p. 271) argue that "computers in cities exist in abundance, of course, but it is cities inside of computers that now define the digital frontier." Neogeography implies that the real world and the world inside the wires are locked in a mutually transformative relationship, i.e., virtual space and physical space co-evolve (Hudson-Smith et al., 2009).

Mobile internet access, still largely in its infancy, is accentuating the growth of neogeography (Wareham, Levy, & Shi, 2004). Mobile phones have been key instruments in the "wikification" or bottom-up reconfiguration and utilization of many services, such as MapQuest or Google Earth, or, more broadly, "crowd sourcing," which allows large groups of people to work together toward a common goal (Sui, 2008). Indeed, the growth of mobile broadband services in many respects is folding real and virtual space into one another (Kellerman, 2010).

Inevitably, the popularity of Web 2.0 has had important effects on urban planning and governance. Malczewski (2004) suggests that GIS, for example, has moved from a scarce, specialized commodity operating on mainframe computers to a common tool of planners, in the forms of simple desktop programs such as MapInfo GIS and ArcView, and in the process facilitated collaborative decision making in planning circles. Analogously, Sieber (2006) argues that Public Participation GIS has markedly expanded the circle of stakeholders involved in planning decisions. As a consequence, GIS has been embraced by an enthusiastic and rapidly growing public of nonprofessional users, with results that have yet to be well understood. Kolbitsch and Maurer (2006) hold that the participatory qualities of Web 2.0 allow ordinary users to forge a collective intelligence, so that planning outcomes are "emergent" properties of multiple actors. Similarly, Foth et al. (2009) argue that neogeography may usher in a neo-planning paradigm, in which planning activities are carried out through active civic engagement aided by Web 2.0. In this view, virtual realities such as Second Life offer urban residents the chance to visualize how their worlds would be affected by urban planning designs. Adopted on a large scale, Web 2.0 and neogeography may encourage public bureaucracies to modernize their administrative practices, increase responsiveness and transparency, and empower citizens to shape local government actions (Noveck, 2009). In short, neogeography facilitates collective place-making rather than state-mandated designs of locales (Beyea, Geith, & McKeown, 2009).

While it is true that few cities offer e-government services beyond the most basic provision of digital forms and information (Reddick, 2004),

the idea of neogeographic-inspired municipal e-government is far from science fiction, but has begun to materialize in fact. While simple, one-way government websites have become almost universal among municipalities in the industrialized world, the shift toward transactional ones has been much slower and spatially uneven. Moon (2002) suggests that larger cities are more likely to have interactive e-government portals and to offer a broader array of applications than are small ones. A few American municipalities (e.g., Bakersfield, CA) broadcast city council meetings on the web; some (e.g., Durham, NC; Scottsdale, AZ; Fort Lauderdale, FL) offer online geographical information systems that permit location-based searches and interactive mapping (Kaylor, Deshazo, & Van Eck, 2001). In Tampere, Finland, municipal Web 2.0 sites allow citizens to provide urban planners with their views and experiences (Jaeger, 2003). In Greece, the "digital city" of Trikala was launched in 2006, giving its residents the ability to participate in telework, on-line library and school programs, emergency response systems, environmental and transportation information, and demographic data that can be utilized through publicly available geographical information systems.

NEOGEOGRAPHY IN PRACTICE: BRIÓN, GALICIA

A robust existing network of neogeographic practices can be found in Brión, located in Galicia, in northwestern Spain. Brión is a small city (population 7,000) with an unusually extensive web presence. A project to enhance its residents' input into planning circles, called SINDUR (Sociedad de la Información y Desarrollo Urbano-Regional, The Information Society and Urban-Regional Development), was started in 2003 at the initiative of faculty employed at the nearby University of Santiago de Compostela (Sexto et al., 2009). Called InfoBrión, the website (www.infobrion.

com) was developed over several years in the early 2000s as a collective effort that involved significant input from local residents, many of whom were unfamiliar with digital technologies. The project was instigated, for free, as part of a national and regional effort to overcome the limitations of Spain's digital divide and to harness the power of Web 2.0 for marginalized communities. In some respects, the community served as an experiment to understand the implications of the wider transformation into an information-based economy and society. A central purpose of the project was to allow residents to forge a local, collective geographical imagination that would be used in subsequent planning initiatives, including, for example, agricultural preservation initiatives, historical preservation, design of recreational spaces, pedestrian and bicycle transportation routes, and ordinances to control noise.

The project received enthusiastic support from the Brión municipal government and arose in conjunction with nationally-subsidized attempts to promote other uses of cyberspace such as online banking, e-commerce, distance learning, and to widen public access to information about government services. The project was greatly enabled by the implementation of free Wifi services in Brión's public spaces, including schools, parks, and libraries. As a result, local internet access became very widespread, reaching almost universal coverage. Local primary and secondary school teachers played key roles in promoting interest in the project among the town's young people. Many residents contributed using their mobile or cellular phones, while others relied on the expertise of local teachers, librarians, and government staff.

While many communities have representations on the web, InfoBrión is unusually extensive, including a plethora of: pictures and films; interviews with residents; personal biographies and life stories; samples of music; depictions of wildlife and natural landscapes; historical accounts; an online museum; paintings; architectural details; interviews with elected officials and business leaders; portraits of daily life, sports, folk culture, and emigration; and interactive opportunities for lessons and marketing for small local firms. As of 2011, its website contained more than 200 individual reports by residents, 3,000 pictures, 500 songs, and 200 home-made videos. This is not a view that attempts to represent the town coherently as a neatly packaged destination for tourists, but grapples with its people, past, and landscapes in all their contradictions and messy complexity.

Thousands of uploads to the InfoBrión website were posted by a diverse array of the town's residents over several years. Some, particularly the elderly, were unfamiliar with the internet, and a few refused to learn how to participate. Many entries are amateurish and of relatively low technical quality. Residents insisted that the site's text be in the local Gallegan language rather than Castillian Spanish. Crucially, the website's contents and organization were determined by the collective preferences of the town's residents, and their priorities often surprised the academic experts who facilitated the project. Some people published diaries of their day-to-day activities, yielding a rich trove of time-geographic information about the contours of daily life. Residents compiled a database of more than 110,000 events in the town's history. One popular application was a documentation of the town's folk culture as it evolved over the years.

Unexpectedly, an online school of horse riding emerged, complemented by myriad representations of equine festivals and contests. The local music school started online courses in music appreciation, with videos of local performances by students. The effort also gave rise to an interactive local atlas listing local residences and points of interests; maps were based on uploads of data on 16,000 locations in the town and neighboring areas. An on-line GIS allows users to query these places and make their own maps. Some residents used the site to commemorate loved ones who had died or left the town; others recorded oral histories of the very old: in a community with a disproportionately large number of elderly, this was no trivial matter. Local farmers and gardeners became enthusiastic proponents of the project as way to show off their skills with crops. One offshoot was Granxa Familiar, a network used to advertise local produce in other towns and villages. For Galician nationalists, the site became a way to celebrate the region's Celtic heritage, including, for example, the local festival of Samain. Exploits of the local *futbol* (soccer) team were described in great detail, including boasts of victories over rival teams from nearby towns. An on-line ethnography museum included photos of local handicrafts, notably shoe and hat production, as well as paintings and songs. One section contained biographies of emigrants from the town, some of whom had returned after years abroad. A virtual lost-and-found was complemented by a local version of eBay. Candidates for local political offices used it for their campaigns, and the government posted election results there. Others came to use the site as a means of keeping track of news, announcements, and lists of upcoming events or for Facebook-like personal webpages. Because the population is not homogeneous in outlook, occasionally disputes erupted over the "correct" representation of some events, particularly those with historical and political implications, and the site's chat rooms served as a public forum for airing these differences.

The InfoBrión illustrates applied neogeography in practice, and substantive differences from traditional planners. Local planners were often reduced to listening to residents' views, and were unable to enforce designs constructed in the antiseptic environment of planning offices. Rather, the town's self-image and priorities emerged organically as an emergent property, and was far more democratic as a result.

EPISTEMOLOGICAL IMPLICATIONS OF WEB 2.0 AND NEOGEOGRAPHY

Neogeography and Web 2.0 have profound philosophical implications. For example, groups utilizing neogeographic technologies are not likely to generate random samples of data, a criterion that lies at the heart of commonly accepted definitions of "the scientific method." How reliable are the results of neogeographic approaches without random sampling, the lynchpin of scientific respectability (Bruns, 2008; Sunstein, 2009)? As diverse groups of people with varying agendas harness Web 2.0 to upload their own data and interpretations, conventional views of what constitutes valid knowledge and truth come into question. What, then, is "true" when people, particularly non-experts, generate their own data and stories to interpret and make sense of the world in ways that may be markedly at odds with the rigid criteria demanded by academic experts? Furthermore, user-generated content also tends to rely on very polarizing samples – only those who either love or hate the subject matter beyond a threshold level tend to post their opinions on-line. These extremes can drown the mainstream interpretations and generate conceptual and political discord (Sunstein, 2009). In neogeography, the sharp divisions between knower and known, representations and the "real" world they portray, epistemology and ontology, are deliberately blurred. As a result, truths (for there can be more than one) are repositioned as a partial, contingent series of statements that reflect lived reality and are useful in it. This line of thought owes much to John Dewey's and particularly William James's (1907) pragmatist epistemology, in which "truth" is determined and confirmed by its utility and effectiveness in application, i.e., from its consequences; thus, "the 'true' is only the expedient in our way of thinking, just as the 'right' is only the expedient in our way of behaving" (James, 1907, p. 2). In this worldview, there is no single observable reality or one approach methodological style: rather, there are multiple realities, many different and equally viable ways of constructing knowledge, all of which require an enormous tolerance for inconsistency, incompleteness, and uncertainty.

As Jürgen Habermas (1989) famously argued, communications are central to the social process of truth construction, through which individuals and communities of interest partake in the public, discursive interpretation of reality (cf. Calhoun, 1992). Habermas's "ideal speech situation" consisting of unfettered discourse is central to the "public sphere" in which social life is reproduced and through which truth is constructed in the absence of barriers to communication. Truth in this reading is inseparable from lived experience, intent, and social practice, leading to the consensus rather than correspondence theory of truth. In this reading, all participants in a debate would theoretically have equal rights and abilities to make their views known and to challenge any other view; when all power relations have been removed from the freedom to engage in discourse, the only criteria for resolving contesting claims is their truth-value. And, importantly, "the participants in an ideal speech situation [must] be motivated solely by the desire to reach a consensus about the truth of statements and the validity of norms" (Bernstein, 1995, p. 50). If one adopts a Habermasian approach in which democracy is approximated by an "ideal speech situation" of unfettered discourse in the public sphere, neogeography provides a reasonably good approximation. Of course, access to neogeographic technologies is limited by social factors such as income, education, and often ethnicity and gender, all of which are significant determinants of the digital divide as well (Crang, Crosbie, & Graham, 2006). Nonetheless, inasmuch as anyone with simple access to web tools to upload data and download results can participate in neogeographic communities, Habermas's ideal speech situation is largely realized for a vast potential pool of participants.

FUTURE RESEARCH DIRECTIONS

Neogeography and Web 2.0 sites are useless for people without access to the internet. Accordingly, among the many areas that remain to be investigated is the role of the digital divide in shaping citizen input into urban governance. The bulk of internet users tend to be relatively well educated and economically comfortable, while those without access tend to consist of the familiar litany of the poor, elderly, ethnic minorities, and the social marginalized (e.g., the handicapped). Without input from these segments of society, the Habermasian promise of an ideal speech situation rings hollow. Consequently, much needs to be done to see how neogeographic tools can be democratized; mobile technologies would seem to hold considerable promise in this regard.

Second, almost all work on the planning implications of neogeography, volunteered geographic data, and public participatory GIS have been conducted in the economically developed world. Yet the bulk of the world's urban residents live in developing countries. In such contexts, where internet access tends to be low, cellular or mobile phone usage has grown exponentially. Thus, a second domain worthy of further consideration is how neogeographic practices may alter the contours of planning in underdeveloped nations.

CONCLUSION

Neogeographic applications of Web 2.0 technology have important implications for urban governance. Rather than accept planners as self-appointed, all-knowing experts, the ability to solicit information and views of ordinary citizens implies that planners must take seriously the views and priorities of the people for whom they plan. This idea is not new, of course, and was manifested in the form of advocacy planning in the 1960s, which acknowledged its social embeddedness and explicitly identified with the needs of the poor and socially marginalized. Similarly, Jane Jacobs (1961) famously celebrated the chaotic diversity of the street and neighborhood life, and urged planners to allow themselves to be shaped by residents' views. Yet under the neoliberal impulse to rationalize space, including privatization and public subsidies for corporate ventures, planning has become gradually detached from the interests of the public, and emphasized the physical dimensions of governance at the expense of the social and political. Neogeography offers a means to re-democratize planning, and in so doing, give up shibboleths like the pretense of objectivity, i.e., of planning as a value-free, apolitical, purely technical process (Flyvberg, 1998). Participatory planning involves incorporating the interests of multiple stakeholders, something that Web 2.0 is ideally designed to do.

The InfoBrión project gives us a glimpse of what a widespread neogeographic project can look like. With initial inspiration from academics and support by government officials, the website took on a life of its own. Far from being dominated by the views or interests of elite experts, the mass of information uploaded to the site, which is constantly in flux, reflects the needs and interests of the town's inhabitants. While most of the material was local in content, some explored the community's connections to other places, as with emigration or sports rivalries. Rather than an abstract, professional planning document, this material was intimately related to the town's residents' bodies and lives. Concerns of "accuracy" or scientific integrity here are displaced by the criteria of relevance and utility: it is in many respects an epistemological pragmatist's utopia.

Planners can no longer afford to view planning as a technical activity, but must confront its social origins and implications. This means taking seriously the views of the people for whom they plan. As Murdoch (2006, p. 144) notes, "Plan prepara-tion itself is renewed as a process of 'making story lines' so that all participants should be permitted to see their interests reflected in the final version of the plan." This mode of governance involves orchestrating an open dialogue, in Habermasian fashion, to achieve a consensus about the rules and results of planning. Such a shift means re-conceptualizing the nature of space itself, i.e., as made, not given. In so doing, planning must increasingly divorce itself from its long standing emphasis on Euclidean space and appreciate the socially constructed, relational nature of territorial relations, i.e., to approach urban governance in topological, not topographical, terms (Graham & Healey, 1999).

REFERENCES

Bernstein, J. (1995). *Recovering ethical life: Jürgen Habermas and the future of critical theory.* New York: Routledge.

Beyea, W., Geith, C., & McKeown, C. (2009). Place making through participatory planning. In Foth, M. (Ed.), *Urban informatics: The practice and promise of the real-time city* (pp. 55–67). Hershey, PA: IGI Global.

Bishr, M., & Kuhn, W. (2007). Geospatial information bottom-up: A matter of trust and semantics. In Fabrikant, S., & Wachowicz, M. (Eds.), *The European information society* (pp. 365–387). Berlin: Springer. doi:10.1007/978-3-540-72385-1_22.

Bishr, M., & Mantelas, L. (2008). A trust and reputation model for filtering and classifying knowledge about urban growth. *GeoJournal, 72,* 229–237. doi:10.1007/s10708-008-9182-4.

Bruns, A. (2008). *Blogs, Wikipedia, Second Life, and beyond: From production to produsage.* New York: Peter Lang.

Calhoun, C. (1992). *Habermas and the public sphere*. Cambridge, MA: MIT Press.

Crang, M., Crosbie, T., & Graham, S. (2006). Variable geometries of connection: Urban digital divides and the uses of information technology. *Urban Studies*, *43*(13), 2551–2570. doi:10.1080/00420980600970664.

Dodge, M., & Kitchin, R. (2005). Code and the transduction of space. *Annals of the Association of American Geographers. Association of American Geographers*, *95*, 162–180. doi:10.1111/j.1467-8306.2005.00454.x.

Dunn, C. (2007). Participatory GIS – A people's GIS? *Progress in Human Geography*, *31*(5), 616–637. doi:10.1177/0309132507081493.

Flanagin, A., & Metzger, M. (2008). The credibility of volunteered geographic information. *GeoJournal*, *72*, 137–148. doi:10.1007/s10708-008-9188-y.

Flyvberg, B. (1998). *Rationality and power: Democracy in practice*. Chicago: University of Chicago Press.

Foth, M., Bajracharya, B., Brown, R., & Hearn, G. (2009). The second life of urban planning? Using neogeography tools for community engagement. *Journal of Location Based Services*, *3*(2), 97–117. doi:10.1080/17489720903150016.

Goodchild, M. (2007). Citizens as sensors: The world of volunteered geography. *GeoJournal*, *69*, 211–221. doi:10.1007/s10708-007-9111-y.

Goodchild, M. (2009). Neogeography and the nature of geographic expertise. *Journal of Location Based Services*, *3*, 82–96. doi:10.1080/17489720902950374.

Graham, S., & Healey, P. (1999). Relational concepts of space and place: Issues for planning theory and practice. *European Planning Studies*, *7*, 623–646. doi:10.1080/09654319908720542.

Graham, S., & Marvin, S. (2001). *Splintering urbanism: Networked infrastructures, technological mobilities and the urban condition*. New York: Routledge. doi:10.4324/9780203452202.

Gurstein, M. (Ed.). (2000). *Community informatics: Enabling communities with information and communication technologies*. Hershey, PA: Idea Group.

Habermas, J. (1989). *The structural transformtion of society*. Cambridge, MA: MIT Press.

Haklay, M., Singleton, A., & Parker, C. (2008). Web mapping 2.0: The neogeography of the geoweb. *Geography Compass*, *2*, 2011–2039. doi:10.1111/j.1749-8198.2008.00167.x.

Hudson-Smith, A., Milton, R., Dearden, J., & Batty, M. (2009). The neogeography of virtual cities: Digital mirrors into a recursive world. In Foth, M. (Ed.), *Urban informatics: The practice and promise of the real-time city* (pp. 270–291). Hershey, PA: IGI Global.

Jacobs, J. (1961). *The death and life of great American cities*. New York: Random House.

Jaeger, P. (2003). The endless wire: E-government as global phenomenon. *Government Information Quarterly*, *20*(4), 323–331. doi:10.1016/j.giq.2003.08.003.

James, W. (1907;1978). *Pragmatism and the theory of truth*. Cambridge, MA: Harvard University Press.

Kaylor, C., Deshazo, R., & Van Eck, D. (2001). Gauging e-government: A report on implementing services among American cities. *Government Information Quarterly*, *18*(4), 293–307. doi:10.1016/S0740-624X(01)00089-2.

Kellerman, A. (2010). Mobile broadband services and the availability of instant access to cyberspace. *Environment & Planning A*, *42*, 2990–3005. doi:10.1068/a43283.

Kolbitsch, J., & Maurer, H. (2006). The transformation of the web: How emerging communities shape the information we consume. *Journal of Universal Computer Science, 12*(2), 187–213.

Malczewski, J. (2004). GIS-based land-use suitability analysis: A critical overview. *Progress in Planning, 62*(1), 3–65. doi:10.1016/j.progress.2003.09.002.

Moon, M. (2002). The evolution of e-government among municipalities: Rhetoric or reality? *Public Administration Review, 62*(4), 424–433. doi:10.1111/0033-3352.00196.

Murdoch, J. (2006). *Post-structuralist geography: A guide to relational space*. London: Sage.

Noveck, B. (2009). *Wiki government: How technology can make government better, democracy stronger, and citizens more powerful*. Washington, DC: Brookings Institution Press.

Rana, S., & Joliveau, T. (2009). Neogeography: An extension of mainstream geography for everyone made by everyone? *Journal of Location Based Services, 3*, 75–81. doi:10.1080/17489720903146824.

Reddick, C. (2004). A two-stage model of e-government growth: Theories and empirical evidence for U.S. cities. *Government Information Quarterly, 21*(1), 51–64. doi:10.1016/j.giq.2003.11.004.

Scharl, A. (2007). Towards the geospatial web: Media platforms for managing geotagged knowledge repositories. In Scharl, A., & Tochtermann, K. (Eds.), *The geospatial web* (pp. 3–14). London: Springer. doi:10.1007/978-1-84628-827-2_1.

Sexto, C., Arce, X., Quintá, F., & Vázquez, Y. (2009). Alfabetización digital en comunidades marginadas partir de un SIG. Estudio de caso en Galicia. *Anales de Geografía, 29*(1), 223–234.

Sieber, R. (2006). Public participation geographic information systems: A literature review and framework. *Association of American Geographers, 96*(3), 491–507. doi:10.1111/j.1467-8306.2006.00702.x.

Sui, D. (2008). The wikification of GIS and its consequences: Or Angelina Jolie's new tattoo and the future of GIS. *Computers, Environment and Urban Systems, 32*, 1–5. doi:10.1016/j.compenvurbsys.2007.12.001.

Sunstein, C. (2009). *Going to extremes: How like minds unite and divide*. New York: Oxford University Press.

Turner, A., & Forrest, B. (2008). *Where 2.0: The state of the geospatial web*. Retrieved from http://radar.oreilly.com/research/where2-report.html

Vander Wal, T. (2005). Explaining and showing broad and narrow folksonomies. *Personal InfoCloud*. Retrieved from www.vanderwal.net/random/entrysel.php?blog=1635.

Walsh, J. (2008). The beginning and end of neogeography. *Geo. Connexion, 7*, 28–30.

Wareham, J., Levy, A., & Shi, W. (2004). Wireless diffusion and mobile computing: Implications for the digital divide. *Telecommunications Policy, 28*(5-6), 439–457. doi:10.1016/j.telpol.2003.11.005.

ADDITIONAL READING

Abrams, J., & Hall, P. (2006). *Else/where: Mapping—New cartographies of networks and territories*. Minneapolis: University of Minnesota Press.

Coleman, D., Georgiadou, Y., & Labonte, J. (2009). Volunteered geographic information: The nature and motivation of producers. *International Journal of Spatial Data Infrastructures Research, GSDI-11*(Special Issue).

Dykes, J., Purves, R., Edwardes, A., & Wood, J. (2008). Exploring volunteered geographic information to describe place: Visualization of the 'Geograph British Isles' collection. In *Proceedings of GIS Research UK* (pp. 256-267). Ungis, UK: Manchester Metropolitan University Press.

Elwood, S. (2006). Critical issues in participatory GIS: Deconstructions, reconstructions, and new research directions. *Transactions in GIS, 10,* 693–708. doi:10.1111/j.1467-9671.2006.01023.x.

Elwood, S. (2008). Volunteered geographic information: Future research directions motivated by critical, participatory, and feminist GIS. *Geo-Journal, 72,* 173–183. doi:10.1007/s10708-008-9186-0.

Howe, J. (2006). The rise of crowdsourcing. *Wired Magazine, 14,* 1-4. Retrieved from http://www.wired.com/wired/archive/14.06/crowds.html

Li, F., Papagiannidis, S., & Bourlakis, M. (2010). Living in 'multiple spaces': Extending our socio-economic environment through virtual worlds. *Environment and Planning. D, Society & Space, 28,* 425–446. doi:10.1068/d14708.

Rinner, C., Keßler, C., & Andrulis, S. (2008). The use of Web 2.0 concepts to support deliberation in spatial decision-making. *Computers, Environment and Urban Systems, 32,* 386–395. doi:10.1016/j.compenvurbsys.2008.08.004.

Tapscott, D., & Williams, A. (2008). *Wikinomics: How mass collaboration changes everything.* New York: Portfolio.

Turner, A. (2006). *Introduction to neogeography.* Sebastopol, CA: O'Reilly Media.

Warf, B., & Sui, D. (2010). From GIS to neo-geography: Ontological implications and theories of truth. *Annals of GIScience, 26*(4), 197–209.

Zook, M., & Graham, M. (2007). Mapping digi-place: Geocoded internet data and the representation of place. *Environment and Planning B, 34,* 466–482. doi:10.1068/b3311.

KEY TERMS AND DEFINITIONS

E-Governance: The use of the internet to facilitate or improve the delivery of public services.

Ideal Speech Situation: A theoretical ideal proposed by Jürgen Habermas in which all constraints to debate have been removed, so that truth is obtained only through the force of argument and persuasion. It is deployed as a yardstick to assess political and pragmatic limitations to participation in public discourse.

Neogeography: The use of geographical techniques, particularly geographical information systems, by non-specialists in such a way that users may volunteer inputs and shape the collective output of a particular project.

Public Participation GIS: A type of geographical information system in which its tools are made accessible to large numbers of non-specialists, who may deploy its analytic and representational capabilities for their own purposes.

Volunteered Geographic Information: Data that has been willingly collected by non-specialists, typically by uploading the locations of particular phenomena.

Web 2.0: A subset of the World Wide Web that allows for input by users, thus facilitating interaction and collaboration. Rather than being reduced to consumers, users are thus positioned as producers of data and knowledge.

Wikification: A term inspired by the famous on-line encyclopedia Wikipedia, this refers more broadly to any process in which large numbers of people voluntarily collaborate to produce a collectively shared outcome.

Chapter 6
Tracking Public Participation in Urban Governance:
Democracy and Data Privacy

Nancy J. Obermeyer
Indiana State University, USA

ABSTRACT

This chapter examines the use of GIS, geovisualization, and other geo-locational technologies and applications, including social networking websites and mobile phones associated with Web 2.0, as a tool kit for promoting democratization or leading to loss of data privacy and freedom, focusing on the relevant historical events in 2011 and the first half of 2012. The chapter begins by presenting a brief history of the GIS and society literature, including public participation GIS, volunteered geographic information, and geoslavery. The discussion covers both the rosy view (geospatial and Web 2.0 technologies as a democratizing force) and the gloomy perspective (these same technologies as tools of control based on data capture and loss of privacy). Underlying both of these views are scale and the ability to jump scales, which are examined through the lens of Kevin Cox's (1998) "spaces of dependence and engagement." Having laid this groundwork, the chapter considers events in the recent past, focusing first on the Arab Spring movements in Tunisia and Egypt and the Occupy movement in the U.S. as examples of the optimistic perspective. It then proceeds to discuss data capture from smart phones and cell phones as examples of the pessimistic view. The chapter concludes with a discussion of how individuals may enhance the democratization potential of geotechnologies and Web 2.0 while minimizing data capture, loss of spatial data privacy, and the harm that these can bring.

INTRODUCTION

Inherent in the GIS and society literature is the role that geographic information systems and cognate technologies play in promoting or inhibiting democracy and collaborative urban governance.

DOI: 10.4018/978-1-4666-4169-3.ch006

When GIS and society first came into our lexicon in the early 1990s, GIS, GPS, and remote sensing were the technologies that came to mind. Today, mobile phones and their smartphone descendents, along with expanded internet capabilities (Web 2.0) are the most widely owned gadgets capable of collecting and storing the spatial data of private citizens. The point of concern is that these data may then be analyzed or otherwise used by public and private entities for their own purposes, often without the knowledge and to the potential detriment of the owners of the devices who supplied the information. Social media have become commonplace tools for connecting with friends, family, or colleagues, thus providing another cache of personal data that also includes a spatial component.

From the earliest days of these technologies and devices, their use and capabilities were often perceived as a double-edged sword of hope and fear (Klinkenberg, 2007). On one hand, the hope was that regular people armed with local geographic data could use their local knowledge to influence the political process and policies that affected them, thus promoting democracy and empowerment. On the other hand, it was feared that the personal data (including spatial data) gathered by public and private entities could readily be used against those who use geospatial technologies, cell phones, and social networking sites, thus harming the very people who provided their personal information.

The past couple of years have proved to be fertile ground for exploring both prognostications. The component parts of Web 2.0, including smartphones, social networking websites, and wikimaps have been important organizing tools for the "Arab Spring" as well as the "Occupy" movements. The democratizing capabilities of geospatial technologies and Web 2.0 seem to be in full bloom, in spite of the efforts of dictatorial regimes to control these technologies as a means to halt the rising tide of democracy. More ominously, what has been described as "...the most hyperbolic intrusion of privacy rights" (Derene, 2011) was perpetrated not by a government, but by a private corporation in late November of 2011, as it came to light that monitoring software by a company called "Carrier IQ" was automatically installed on the newest generation of smartphones. Then in March, 2012, a study undertaken by the American Civil Liberties Union (ACLU) of cell

phone monitoring by law enforcement agencies in the U.S. provided evidence of a rapid expansion of this practice in recent years (Lichtblau, 2012). This chapter will discuss both developments.

One element in the debate over the advantages and disadvantages of geotechnologies and spatial information that also warrants discussion is scale, and particularly, the idea of jumping scales. Whether the subject is a local movement with national (and sometimes even international) goals, or national governments (or multinational firms) keeping a closer eye on individuals, geospatial technologies and social networks made possible by Web 2.0 have made it easier to jump scales both from the top down and from the bottom up.

This chapter examines the use of GIS, geovisualization, and other geo-locational technologies and applications, including the social networking websites, cell phones, and other elements of Web 2.0 as a tool kit for promoting democratization or leading to loss of freedom, focusing on the relevant historical events in 2011 and the first half of 2012, raising issues that are highly relevant for urban governance. The chapter begins by presenting a brief history of the GIS and society literature, including a discussion of public participation GIS (PPGIS), volunteered geographic information and geoslavery. The discussion covers both the rosy view (geospatial technologies as a democratizing force) and the gloomy perspective (geospatial technologies as a tool of control based on data capture and loss of privacy), what Klinkenberg (2007) refers to as "geographies of hope and fear." A consistent theme of this discussion is the role that the evolution of technologies from expensive tools for experts to inexpensive tools for the masses has played in influencing the balance between hope and fear.

Underlying both of these views is the element of scale and the ability to jump scales, which are examined through the lens of Kevin Cox's (1998) "spaces of dependence and engagement." Having laid this groundwork, the chapter proceeds to describe events in the recent past, focusing first on the use of social networking and the tools of Web 2.0 in the Arab Spring movements in Tunisia and Egypt and the Occupy movement in the U.S. as examples of the optimistic perspective. It then proceeds to discuss data capture from smart phones and cell phones as examples of the pessimistic view. The chapter concludes with a discussion of how individuals may enhance the democratization potential of geotechnologies and Web 2.0 while minimizing data capture and loss of spatial data privacy, and the harm that may come with them.

GIS AND SOCIETY: A BRIEF HISTORY

GIS and society traces its roots to discussions in the early 1990s, when GIS was becoming more widely diffused beyond the core group of experts who had created the technology, when geographers were examining its implications for both the discipline of geography as well as for society at large. Even in these early days of discourse, Taylor (1990), Openshaw (1991), Pickles (1991), and Smith (1992) focused on the ability of GIS to serve as a means to aggregate vast quantities of information along with their spatial reference points, and the harm that could accompany this practice. Pickles (1991) warned against the rise of a "surveillant society," and described GIS as an "…extension of the monitoring and surveillant functions of the local and national state" (p. 81). A year later, Smith (1992) noted that GIS had played a significant role in the first Persian Gulf War, lending credence to early prognostications of the harm that GIS might bring with it.

Significantly, at this time, GIS was still a tool mostly for experts. It was expensive to purchase, maintain, and operate, and most base maps still awaited digitization. That most predictions were based on fear of the power of centralized control of the technology was understandable, given the stage in the GIS product life-cycle at this time. Most GIS software and data were in the hands of centralized entities, either public or private. Even as the technology began its diffusion into the larger society, later commentators including Curry (1997) and Crampton (2003) echoed the warnings of the early days of GIS. Monmonier (2002) devoted an entire book to the subject of geosurveillance technologies, describing how they work and offering his insights into spatial privacy issues.

In 1993, a "GIS and Society" workshop was organized by Tom Poiker, sponsored by the National Center for Geographic Information and Analysis (NCGIA), and held at Friday Harbor, in the state of Washington, in the U.S. This workshop led to a special issue of *Cartography and GIS* devoted to the subject of GIS and Society in January 1995, which raised mostly concerns about GIS and its implementation. A year later, in spring of 1996, the University of Minnesota hosted an NCGIA specialist meeting to develop a research agenda for GIS and society. One of the break-out groups at that meeting formed to discuss what would later be christened "Public Participation GIS" (Obermeyer, 1998).

The term, public participation GIS --- PPGIS for short --- originated in the planning profession, and was introduced to the GIS community by Xavier Lopez at a workshop on PPGIS during the summer of 1997 at the University of Maine (Schroeder, 1997). The purpose of the workshop was to develop strategies to improve access to GIS and other mapping technologies by non-governmental organizations (NGOs) and individuals in order to help them gain or amplify their voices in their communities. The evolution of PPGIS – and its rosier view --- was, at least in part, linked to changes in information technologies in general, and GIS technology in particular, that made them more accessible to non-experts through lower cost and greater ease-of-use. PPGIS was also envisioned as a means to promote the use of the technology as a tool to nurture democracy and the greater good for the larger community.

It should come as no surprise that the potential for public participation within GIS implementation (the rosy view) gained significant impetus from GIS experts in the planning profession. The planning process often requires public meetings and other avenues to solicit input from the people who are likely to be affected by changes to local infrastructure. Planners are accustomed to working both from the top down and from the grass roots up as they seek support for their projects. In fact, insights into the use of GIS provided by planners seemed to hope for and even promote the rosy view, while expressing concern (if not actual fear) about the gloomy view.

In Chicago's Pilsen neighborhood, for example, meetings that included both GIS and on-the-spot artist renderings of proposed changes enabled planners to include local knowledge of the community and thus to empower the citizens of Pilsen, a Hispanic neighborhood (Al-Kodmany, 2000). In another example, the use of GIS in Kofiase (in southern Ghana) as a framework to collect, process, and analyze data enabled villagers in the area to gain a voice in decisions regarding commercial logging in the vicinity (Kyem, 2004). However, Al-Kodmany and Kyem suggest that without this ongoing participation at all stages of the GIS - a process that Sieber (2006) describes as "coproduction of GIS" - successful resolution of any conflicts would not have been possible. Still, both Al-Kodmany's and Kyem's studies and Sieber's review of a number of other examples of PPGIS in action suggest that "... most models of PPGIS equate participation with some level of cooperation within existing government processes;" and that "the word participatory prescribes an element of top-down intercession" (Sieber, 2006, p. 500). Like Al-Kodmany, Kyem and Sieber also acknowledge that PPGIS does not guarantee empowerment, although the potential is certainly there.

WEB 2.0 AND VOLUNTEERED INFORMATION

As GIS was becoming more accessible to a wider group of users because of decreased price and greater ease-of-use, the same trends in the evolution of internet technology expanded access to the web to a vastly larger pool of information producers and consumers, enabling them both to contribute to as well as to harvest the abundant information of cyberspace. The essential foundation of Web 2.0 is the evolution of a system in which users both create and consume information in networks of friends, colleagues, and acquaintances (Allen, 2012). Allen goes on to suggest that this evolution "...was already imagined as *democratic*" (p. 4) because it was believed that the open format of cyberspace equalized the authority of all contributors. Thus, cyberspace had become a public square where diverse social groups could speak their minds (Arora, 2012).

Yet, cyberspace or Web 2.0 was not only the place where people spoke their minds and exchanged ideas in virtual space. These were spaces where individuals gave up information, often freely, to people and organizations they did not even know, or in some cases did not even know existed. For example, in the early days of the list-serve for aficionados of the Basenji (an African dog-breed), members on the list who rarely or never posted were often described as "lurkers." The term was intended to be humorous but it does hint at the dark underbelly of Web 2.0: the practice of accessing information from others who provide it freely, and the even darker notion of surveillance. Surveillance involves the deliberate and purposeful collection of data and information about individuals in order to keep track of their attributes, behaviors, location, and movements. Individuals may provide such information voluntarily, unintentionally, accidentally, by mistake, or in rarer instances, by force.

One of the key insights of ongoing discussions about surveillance is that in some instances, it "offers real benefits to those being watched" (Dobson & Fisher, 2007; 2008), thus motivating individuals to volunteer information about themselves and their location. This insight follows on Bentham's Panopticon and George Orwell's Big Brother, which suggest that security is often the primary benefit of being watched. Certainly in the years since the terrorist attacks in New York City of September 11, 2001, and the July 7, 2005 attacks on a bus in London, more people in the U.S. and Great Britain have been willing to trade their personal data privacy for security (Goss, 1995; Curry, 1997; Herbert, 2006a). While screening at U.S. airports has become more invasive since 9/11, Great Britain's estimated 4.2 million closed circuit television cameras means that this country has "...more video surveillance per capita than any other country in the world" (Landler, 2007; Nieto, 1997, p. 7).

Dobson and Fisher (2006) describe the loss of spatial data privacy as "geoslavery," acknowledging that when central authority figures know where we are, their control over us grows. William Herbert borrowed a title from a jazz tune by Rahsaan Roland Kirk and referred to this as "volunteered (geo)slavery" (2006b), as he emphasized the point that individuals often volunteer personal information on our whereabouts or at least provide sufficient information that motivated data collectors can deduce our location. In democratic societies where free speech is legal, we may not give a second thought to leaving clues to our whereabouts. On the other hand, in societies where individuals may be incarcerated or physically attacked for speaking freely, protecting speech and even saving lives can depend on keeping one's location private. The October, 2012 shooting of a 15-year-old girl who openly advocated for educating girls in Pakistan by members of the Taliban as she rode her school-bus home provides a shocking example of the worst-case scenario associated with having others know our whereabouts.

The addition of the element of volunteerism into the discussion of geospatial technologies and Web 2.0 is significant. A workshop on Volunteered Geographic Information was held in Santa Barbara, California in December 2007 to explore this development. "Volunteered Geographic Information" (VGI for short) includes websites "... such as Wikimapia and OpenStreetMap[that] are empowering citizens to create a global patchwork of geographic information, while Google Earth and other virtual globes are encouraging volunteers to develop interesting applications using their own data" (Goodchild, 2007, p. 211). Wikimapia is an open-content collaborative mapping website whose goal is to mark all objects on Earth, relying on the volunteered information of regular people. In its example of volunteered information, Wikimapia suggests providing the address and names of residents of a specific home (Wikimapia, 2012). Of course, not all information volunteered to Wikimapia will include this fine-scale level of personal spatial data, but this is the level of detail requested.

The OpenStreetMap website allows individuals who have used a global positioning system (GPS) to gather information about the location of streets, buildings, landmarks, and so on to upload that information to the website. The original motivation for the creation of OpenStreetMap was the high price of maps in the United Kingdom. Steve Coast, the creator of OpenStreetMap, organized a group of friends to take GPS devices with them on their bikes as they rode the streets on the Isle of Wight in order to record the location of these roads. They then uploaded this geographic information to their website, and invited others to do the same, thus building a map that was created by volunteers and that could be used and downloaded for free (Coast, 2007), a welcome alternative to higher-priced government and commercial map products.

The word "volunteer" may imply a situation in which that volunteer knows the costs and benefits of volunteering and thus the choice to volunteer is made freely. While it is true that some contributors to the "global patchwork of geographic information" fit this description, individuals may provide geographic (and other information) for a variety of reasons. To reiterate a point made in a previous paragraph, in some instances individuals trade private information for security (Goss, 1995; Curry, 1997; Herbert, 2006a). But information may also be traded for self-promotion (Goodchild, 2007), perhaps with the idea of enhancing one's experiences and contacts.

We may also trade information for cost savings. For example, in the summer of 2012, the Progressive Insurance company began running television commercials offering its auto insurance customers a reduced rate for installing the agency's "Snapshot" device, which captures data on their driving habits (Progressive Insurance, 2012). In this way, Progressive Insurance Company will know whether the driver it's insuring is a safe driver who obeys the rules of the road, or just a lucky driver who miraculously avoids collisions in spite of poor driving habits.

We may also exchange personal data for connectivity, as evidenced by the rise in use of Facebook, Twitter, LinkedIn, Xing, and other social and networking media. The primary lure of participating in social media is to make contact with friends and relatives more convenient (Goodchild, 2007). The amount of information that one provides to these networking sites is up to the individual. At one end of the spectrum, you might find an older person who includes only the barest of personal information and does not even include a digital image of herself, who rarely adds any updates on status, and only occasionally logs in to the site. Occasionally, she may "like" something or note that the toddler of a family member is "cute."

At the other end of the spectrum, some participants in social media such as Facebook and Twitter provide a running account of their whereabouts, illustrated with dozens of snapshots. I've noticed that many of my teenage and college-age relatives

fall in this category. Perhaps this is because of their young age and inexperience, or maybe because their generation is more comfortable with the forum than those of us who grew up in the sixties. Ironically, when you go to the Facebook Sign Up page, you will see the promise "It's free and always will be" (Facebook, 2012). Yes, it's free, unless you count the value of the private information that you are giving up, which Facebook can use for whatever purposes it chooses, including aggregating for commercial benefit. And of course, it always will be free, until Facebook changes hands and the new owners modify that policy.

In contrast, a website that attempts to caution users of Facebook, Twitter, and other social networking sites is the "Please Rob Me" website. "Please Rob Me" is dedicated to informing users of social media about the dangers of posting their geographical locations by noting that, "The danger is publicly telling people where you are. This is because it leaves one place you're definitely not... home" (2012). The point of the "Please Rob Me" website, of course, is to encourage people to protect their personal spatial data.

Many individuals who volunteer information may not even be aware of that they are doing so. Target, a discount department store chain in the U.S., tracks its customers' purchases and uses this information to send promotional coupons. Target assigns their customers a "Guest ID number" whenever they can (as do other retailers). The next step is to start gathering information based on credit card information, coupon use, survey response, web-site visits and similar contacts and then build up a data base on this unique shopper. As John Pole, a statistician for Target since 2002, said, "We want to know everything we can" (Duhigg, 2012).

Using lessons learned from psychological studies of consumer purchases, and its own baby registry, Target's statisticians were able to identify a list of specific products that a woman often purchases after she becomes pregnant. By searching their "Guest ID Number" database for female shoppers who have bought items from this list, Target can be reasonably confident that the woman is, indeed, pregnant. Target already knows the routine shopping habits of its "guests," including the day of the week they are most likely to shop. The retailer puts all these nuggets of information together with the goal of sending an appropriate coupon booklet to the mother-to-be. Target chooses this specific moment because the birth of a child, like other life-changing events, is a time when people change their buying habits and thus can be persuaded to make Target their retail destination of choice (Duhigg, 2012).

Even with this information, Target is careful about the way in which it sends these coupons, making certain to comply with all privacy laws, but also to avoid raising suspicions that they have been keeping their "guest" under surveillance. "But even if you're following the law, you can do things where people get queasy" (Pole, as quoted in Duhigg, 2012). Target addresses the queasiness quotient by including coupons offering discounts on other random products (like a flashlight or laundry detergent or dog treats) in the mailer alongside the coupons for baby products. Thus, the recipient is led to believe that she and every other Target customer received the same coupon book (Duhigg, 2012).

In one instance, the father of a teen-age Target shopper became angered when the company sent baby product coupons to his daughter and he contacted the store manager to complain. Later, after speaking to his daughter, he learned that she was, indeed, going to make him a grandfather in the near future. He later called the store manager back to apologize (Duhigg, 2012). Speaking of volunteering information, according to New York Times reporter Mr. Duhigg, Mr. Pole (the Target representative) provided an abundance of details on the retailer's marketing strategy "…while we were still speaking and before Target told him to stop" (Duhigg, 2012).

SPACES OF ENGAGEMENT

GIS, geotechnologies, and Web 2.0 have effectively enlarged what Cox calls "spaces of engagement." Cox distinguishes between what he calls "spaces of dependence" and "spaces of engagement" (Cox, 1998, p. 2). Spaces of dependence are the areas where we satisfy our basic needs based on localized relations. These basic needs constitute the elements of our material well-being, such as our families, our homes, our jobs, our schools and all that surrounds us in our day-to-day lives. But it goes beyond the material to include intangible elements such as our very sense of ourselves and of our own significance (Cox, 1998, p. 2). These are the places we depend on for our physical and emotional well-being each and every day because these are the places where we live and work. What happens in these spaces of dependence matters greatly to those who live there.

Within our spaces of dependence, we notice if our power shuts down or if our trash is not picked up. We are concerned if our spouse, our parent, or our child who shares our space of dependence is injured or becomes ill. We welcome the first snowflake of winter that falls on our place of dependence and we smile when the daffodils start bursting through the soil to let us know that spring is on its way. For some who find their spaces of dependence intolerable, emigration offers an exit. However, the high cost of emigration may make it difficult for many people to leave their original place of dependence for a different one.

In contrast, the space of engagement is defined as "…the space in which the politics of securing a space of dependence unfolds" (Cox, 1998, p. 2); the space of engagement is where we go to try to maintain or improve our situation. Our space of engagement may exist in our neighborhood, our local city hall, or our state, but it may also be at the national or international scale. Jumping scale in order to secure or enhance our home turf is a well accepted pattern. We may vote in elections at any level from the local to the national or we may write a letter to our elected official or local service providers to make positive changes. We may call our neighbors when they play their music too loud. We may choose to buy local as a way to keep our dollars (or euros) within our space of dependence. If that doesn't achieve any results, we may start or join a protest. The spaces of dependence and spaces of engagement are inextricably linked.

Although Cox makes no mention of the web and social networking sites, it is easy to make the case that the Web 2.0, with its social media, wikis and other web-based forums could easily be described as a "space of engagement" (Cox, 1998). In fact, both Allen (2012) and Arora (2012), in their discussions of Web 2.0, specifically note that cyberspace has become the virtual equivalent of a public square. In particular, Aroro notes that "chronic power inequities are embedded in our physical world, and unlike this reality, the virtual world is inherently free" (p. 604). Cyberspace, then, offers a new space of engagement. The next section speaks to this point, focusing on the protests in Tunisia and Egypt as well as the Occupy Movement, as activities in spaces of engagement that have included both the real and the virtual worlds.

THE ARAB SPRING AND OCCUPY

Arab Spring in Tunisia

The Arab Spring began in Tunisia on December 17, 2010, when Mohammed Bouazizi set himself on fire in the town center of Sid Bouzid. This 26-year-old street vendor had been fined by an inspector who challenged the legality of his stand, then confiscated his apples in a way that publicly disrespected him. This set off a scuffle between Mr. Bouazizi and the female inspector, which was joined by a pair of the inspector's colleagues,

who beat him and confiscated his electronic scale. Mr. Bouazizi went to the municipal building and demanded the return of his property, then on to the governor's office, but was rebuffed at each turn. Mr. Bouazizi's self-immolation left him with burns over ninety percent of his body. His family and friends shared digital images and videos of him as he suffered in the hospital. These shocking digital images were spread more widely as friends of friends forwarded them to their networks of friends in an ever-expanding pattern of diffusion in the virtual space of engagement. For many who saw these images, it provoked their latent feelings of distrust and dissatisfaction with Tunisia's ruling party (Howard et al., 2011; Fahim, 2011).

Tunisia's state-run media did not report on these events; moreover, the government did its best "...to ban Facebook, Twitter and video sites such as Daily Motion and YouTube" (Howard et al., 2011, p. 8), but was unsuccessful. Hackers and other activists with technical expertise who lived outside of Tunisia helped to foil the government's efforts in the interest of spreading the word about the uprising. According to Howard et al. (2011), "Less than 20 percent of the overall population actively used social-media Websites, but almost everyone had access to a mobile phone" (p. 8). As word - and pictures - spread via mobile phone and social media websites, street protests against Mr. Bouazizi's mistreatment and the authoritarian government that perpetuated this and other wrongs against its citizens grew and spread throughout the country. Al Jazeera was the first news organization to spread the word of the Tunisian protests to a wider international audience (Howard et al., 2011; Fahim, 2011; Kirkpatrick, 2011). Cleveland (1985) predicts this very phenomenon, adding that the spread of electronic information – which he describes as "leaky" – can lead to an erosion of hierarchies.

Mr. Bouazizi's life ended on January 4, 2011, but the life of the Arab Spring had only just begun. Sending a message to Tunisia's president, Zine El-Abidine Ben Ali, Facebook pages throughout the country supported the phrase, "Ben Ali, Out" (Kirkpatrick, 2011). Street protests continued and grew in size and frequency as well. To try to save his regime of twenty-three years, President Ben Ali fired his interior minister, pledged to investigate corruption, promised new freedoms and agreed to resign at the end of his term of office (in 2014), and even dismissed his entire cabinet. This was apparently too little, too late, for protests continued to gain steam until they toppled the authoritarian regime of Mr. Ben Ali, causing him to flee the country on January 14, 2011. This was "...the first time that widespread street demonstrations had overthrown an Arab leader" and raised the question of whether or not citizens in neighboring countries would follow suit (Kirkpatrick, 2011). It would not be long before the answer came: Yes.

Arab Spring in Egypt

In fact, in 2010, "Revolution 2.0" (Ghonim, 2012) was already underway in Egypt, aided, in part by Wael Ghonim, a head of Google marketing in the Middle East. As early as 2004, the Egyptian Movement for Change (a.k.a. "Kefaya," the Arabic word for "enough") opposed the extension of the presidency of Hosni Mubarak, who had served in that position for five six-year terms by that time, for a total of thirty years. Mr. Mubarak remained president into 2010 (Ghonim, 2012). As elections approached, the search for a viable alternative to Mr. Mubarak intensified. Mohamed Mostafa ElBaradei, former Director General of the International Atomic Energy Agency (IAEA) and winner (with the IAEA) of the 2005 Nobel Peace Price, was seen as a promising alternative. Mr. Ghonim determined to use his IT expertise and his weekly Google "personal work day" to help develop an online presence for Mr. AlBaradei, launching a Facebook page for his presidential pick in February 2010 and a Google e-mail group in April 2010 (Ghonim, 2012).

As in Tunisia, a galvanizing event fueled Egypt's discontent. In June of 2010, Egyptian secret police mortally beat Khaled Mohamed Said, and the image of the mortally wounded man was posted on Facebook. A group of political activists established a Facebook page, "My Name is Khaled Mohamed Said," which quickly attracted 70,000 members while a second site, "Kullena Khaled Said" ("We Are All Khaled Said") attracted 36,000 members on its first day in existence (Ghonim, 2012, p. 59). "The most difficult task remained though, which was to transfer the struggle from the virtual world to the real one" (Ghonim, 2012, p. 67). Mr. Ghonim's plan was to promote a "silent expression of disapproval" of Mr. Said's beating death symbolized by a joining of hands among interested people in both Alexandria (where the beating occurred) and Cairo (the capital city) called the Silent Stand (p. 70). Around four thousand people participated in the Alexandria protest on June 18, 2010 (Awad, 2010).

Egypt's authoritarian regime tried to remove and shut down the virtual space of engagement in hopes of squashing the rebellion. To maintain this virtual space of engagement, Mr. Ghonim turned to the Tor Project. Using their resources, he was able to "Defend ... against network surveillance and traffic analysis...Tor protects you by bouncing your communications around a distributed network of relays run by volunteers all around the world: it prevents somebody watching your Internet connection from learning what sites you visit, and it prevents the sites you visit from learning your physical location" (Tor Project, 2012).

By September, the "Kullena Khaled Said" Facebook page had 250,000 members, and "...had become a resource powerful enough to compete with official media for readership" (Ghonim, 2012, p. 113). Mr. Ghonim and his supporters decided to harness this support to organize a protest to coincide with the national elections that would be held in two stages in late November and December

2010. In his eagerness to spread the word of the upcoming "Day of Anger," as he called it, Mr. Ghonim sent the announcement from his personal account by accident, thus compromising his anonymity (p. 116). He hustled to undo the damage and was able to continue to evade the Egyptian government. He was less successful in dealing with Facebook, however, which discovered that the "Kullena Khaled Said" page was managed by "fake accounts" – a violation of Facebook policy – and shut it down. Working with compatriots living outside of Egypt, Mr. Ghonim was able to transfer administration of the page to the real account of a friend in the U.S., thus satisfying Facebook's requirement of authenticity while continuing to protect his anonymity in Egypt. Facebook re-opened the page (Ghonim, 2012).

Then in December 2010 came news from Tunisia of the self-immolation of Mohammed Bouazizi and its reverberations. A street protest already planned for January 25, 2011 was renamed "Revolution against Torture, Poverty, Corruption, and Unemployment." When news came out on January 21 that an Egyptian who had self-immolated had died, a young woman who was in Tahrir Square that day posted a video to Facebook, helping to build support and enthusiasm for the planned protest. The Egyptian government tried to sabotage the protest by setting up false accounts as its own opposition party and describing the January 25 protest as a conspiracy that would destroy Egypt. In spite of their efforts, the event in Tahrir Square "…would be marked as a historic day for Egypt's opposition movement" and Mr. Ghonim recounts that he "began tweeting like a madman on my personal account, urging everyone to come out and join the protest" (Ghonim, 2012, p. 184). Tens of thousands of Egyptians flooded Tahrir Square for the street protest.

As the protests snowballed over the next days, Egypt's President Mubarak proposed minor concessions, then greater ones (as had Tunisia's leader), until he finally stepped down on February 11, 2011 (Ghonim, 2012). Hundreds of thousands of protestors were in Tahrir Square when the news of Mr. Mubarak's resignation came. In the words of Dina Magdi, a pro-democracy campaigner there: "I have waited, I have worked all my adult life to see the power of the people come to the fore and show itself. I am speechless. The moment is not only about Mubarak stepping down, it is also about people's power to bring about the change that no-one … thought possible" (Al Jazeera, 2011). Using both virtual and actual spaces of engagement, made possible by Web 2.0, citizens of Egypt had brought an end to the country's authoritarian regime.

Occupy Wall Street and Beyond

This brings us to the Occupy movement, which found its legs on September 17, 2011 in New York City's Zuccotti Park, then spread to Atlanta, Chicago, Boston, Seattle, and more than 100 cities across the U.S. and beyond (Slaughter, 2011; Occupy Wall Street, 2012). In marking the one-month existence of the movement that began with Occupy Wall Street, Gautney (2011) writes, "Facebook is all-aflutter, and Twitter is all-atweeter, as news of 'occupations' and clashes with the powers-that-be spread like wildfire around the country." At the heart of the Occupy movement were economic concerns and disadvantages of "the 99%" of people in the U.S. "The 99%" became the euphemism-of-choice for the working- and middle-class people of the U.S., as opposed to those in the top 1% of the economic ladder, who exercise extensive control of both the central government and business. Young people who saw their opportunities for upward mobility evaporating formed the core of the Occupy movement (Gautney, 2011).

Fortunately, there were no self-immolations during the heyday of the Occupy movement, but this did not mean that there were no upsetting videos to go viral and spur new members to join and take to the streets. In September, a video showing a police officer pepper spraying a pregnant woman (Balogna, 2011) was posted on YouTube; in November in Seattle, a priest, a pregnant woman and an 84-year-old woman were pepper-sprayed by police. A report of the event by Natasha Ryan was broadcast on a local news station (Ryan, 2011) and then picked up and posted on YouTube by MoxNews (2011). Later that month, another video showing police pepper-spraying protesters at point-blank range on the campus of the University of California at Davis was posted on YouTube (Occupy Everything, 2011). These videos and many like them made the rounds of the internet, and were picked up by traditional broadcast television as well as cable TV, stirring up more outrage and fueling participation in the Occupy Movement.

Another component of the Occupy movement has been the creation of wikimaps identifying the location of street demonstrations to let others know where they could find real-world spaces of engagement. Indeed, the "Occupy Wall Street" group remains up and running with its website and announces that "The revolution continues worldwide!" (OccupyWallStreet, 2012).

Like the Arab Spring protests, Occupy is a leaderless movement that unfolded in "both a concrete and virtual space" of engagement (Gautney, 2011). Both movements were driven by "injustice and invisibility" (Slaughter, 2011). While both movements oppose greed and corruption, the ultimate goal of many of the Arab Springs protests was to push a dictator out of office, whereas the goal of the Occupy movement has been less well-defined (Gautney, 2011). Perhaps because Occupy's immediate goals are less well-articulated than those of the Arab Spring protesters, we cannot point to clear successes that match the magnitude of the toppling of authoritarian regimes. While "...the mainstream media is eager to report on Occupy's supposed demise," ... "there's a wide community of opposition being formed across many social barriers" (Vitelli, 2012). Still, one by one, the Occupy camps were taken down, some because of impending winter weather, others because they had become eyesores to their communities, and a few because they had become magnets for violence.

These examples fit the rosy prognostications of the GIS and society and debates, as both the Arab Spring and Occupy movements provide evidence of the democratizing effects of geospatial technologies and particularly of Web 2.0, in particular the use of these technologies as a means to jump scales to expand the spaces of engagement. More importantly, in some instances --- especially those related to the Arab Spring – the protesters have used the new social media as virtual spaces of engagement to help their countries make major political changes in their spaces of dependence. However, there is much work ahead in achieving a functioning, peaceful space of dependence in these and other Arab Spring countries.

SMART PHONES AND CELL PHONES: THE GLOOMY VIEW

Two news reports in 2012 have made the general public more aware of the gloomy view - the rise of surveillance - of the spread of Web 2.0 technologies. The first of these stories was reported on a video posted by a 25-year-old programmer, Trevor Eckhart, in which he exposed the presence of a software utility called Carrier IQ that is installed on millions of smartphones and collects large amounts of data from those using the phones (Eckhart, 2011). According to the Carrier IQ website, nearly 148 million handsets carrying the software have been "deployed" as of July 23, 2012 (Carrier IQ, 2012).

The Carrier IQ software is capable of collecting a great deal of information about the user's smartphone use, including keystrokes, numbers dialed, encrypted Web searches and the contents of text messages (Chen, 2011). Representatives of Carrier IQ insist that the purpose of the software is merely to identify dropped calls and errors in text messages in order to improve the performance of the devices. However, an unidentified Carrier IQ manager also admitted that the software could "probably" read text messages, although they do not record the data (Chen, 2011). Both AT&T and Sprint, which have the software loaded on their phones, say that they use the information they collect only to improve service. Apple representatives say that they are eliminating the software from their phones. Nokia's phones do not support the software (Chen, 2011). Of course, a mobile phone also automatically provides information on the location of its user, through the cell-tower technology itself.

There have been several responses to the report of this data privacy issue. U.S. Senator Al Franken quickly spoke out against the software: "Consumers need to know that their safety and privacy are being protected by the companies they trust with their sensitive information" (Franken, 2011). Several regulatory agencies in Europe recommended an investigation (Ricknäs, 2011). Shortly after the news came out, two executives of Carrier IQ met with representatives of the United States Federal Communications Commission and the Federal Trade Commission in Washington, D.C. to "educate the two agencies about the functionality of its software and answer any and all questions" (Perlroth, 2011). At the time of this writing, there was no evidence of any action having been taken against Carrier IQ or any of the cell phone providers that use it.

In March 2012, mobile phones were once again in the news, this time in reports that the tracking of cell phones by law enforcement has increased tremendously in the U.S. According to the report, Verizon stated that requests for information from law-enforcement agencies increased by 15% from 2010 to 2011, with the total number of requests from law enforcement to cell phone carriers totaling 1.3 million in that same period (Barnes, 2012).

Another report notes that some carriers offer a catalog of "surveillance fees" for providing various services to law enforcement, including determining the location of a suspect or tracing their calls and text messages (Lichtblau, 2012). This fee-for-service surveillance suggests that this practice is well entrenched and will continue. Monitoring cell phones and land lines is nothing new. During the administration of former U.S. President George W. Bush, in the wake of 9/11, phone companies were asked to assist the federal government as it monitored overseas phone calls of suspected terrorists. The former President was aided in this initiative by the U.S. Congress, which revised existing national-security surveillance statutes to make it legal for the government to wiretap electronic communications without a warrant, provided that one of the parties on the call is outside the United States (Barnes, 2012).

This development represents a major expansion of the monitoring of telephone calls of private individuals, based on 5,500 pages of records from law enforcement agencies around the U.S. that the American Civil Liberties Union (ACLU) acquired during its investigation. Local police have increased their use of cell phone tracking recently, "…with hundreds of departments, large and small, using it aggressively with little or no court oversight" (Lichtblau, 2012). Legal challenges to cell phone monitoring have been making their way through the courts in the U.S., but rulings by federal courts around the country have been inconsistent. It will likely take a ruling by the U.S. Supreme Court to bring a coherent policy defining the legal requirements for monitoring cell phones before there is a cohesive, clear cut policy for the United States.

LOOKING AHEAD: SUPPORTING DEMOCRACY, MINIMIZING SURVEILLANCE

Based on the recent evidence, both the optimists and the pessimists in the debate regarding GIS and Web 2.0 can claim victory. As Curry (1997) points out, GIS and related technologies are powerful tools in the hands of those who command them, enabling them to collect, analyze, and use information of all sorts in pursuit of their goals – however noble or insidious those goals may be. As noted, when this discussion began, these powerful tools were almost exclusively in the hands of experts, perhaps giving weight to the gloomy view that geoslavery was the more likely path. However, information technologies of all sorts – including GIS, GPS, Web 2.0 (and whatever may follow) – have become increasingly accessible to non-experts, enabling great numbers of amateurs to join the game as equals (or at least as near-equals).

In addition to the methods described above for using Web 2.0 as a space of engagement, other strategies exist, including comedy and ridicule (Monmonier, 1998). Inspired by the U.S.'s The Daily Show, a satirical news show hosted by Jon Stewart, Bassem Youssef, a heart surgeon from Cairo, Egypt began posting homemade videos in March 2011 in which he "…regularly lampoons public figures" (Hashash, 2012). This precedent-setting show is now broadcast three times each week on ONTV, an independent satellite station in Egypt. All of the country's presidential candidates appeared on the show prior to the 2012 elections, possibly to reach the young people who are especially drawn to the program (Hashash, 2012).

The gloom-and-doom view also seems to have carried with it a preconceived notion that experts would invariably be on the side of Big Brother. Instead, through capabilities of Web 2.0, and as evidenced by the Tor Project and groups like it, we have seen technical experts give freely of their time and knowledge, as well as physical and virtual resources to support democratic movements by providing sophisticated data privacy tools to the average internet user. The competition between democratization and geoslavery will most likely continue with each side winning its share of battles,

and learning from its losses. The battles will take place in a variety of spaces of engagement, both actual and virtual.

Some battles may take place in the courts, as organizations like the ACLU or individuals challenge the collection of personal data with locational references without their explicit permission. A success in the legal spaces of engagement can produce long-term change, for better or worse. The legislative branch of governments provides another venue for engagement and action. If existing laws favor those who would use their power to stifle democracy, this can be changed through elections. As citizens of Tunisia and Egypt have shown, it is possible to build democracy from the ground up, even in places where it is weak or nonexistent.

The marketplace is yet another space of engagement. The more citizens know about the data collection policies of retailers and other businesses, the more able they are to make informed choices about where to spend their money. Target is not the only discount retailer, nor is Progressive the only automobile insurance provider. As individuals, we can choose which businesses we support and vote with our dollars (or euros, yen or any other currency of choice). By organizing others to share a boycott, consumers may even be able to use the purchasing power of the group to persuade – or force – businesses to change their policies.

International spaces of engagement also represent opportunities to promote democracy. On July 5, 2012, the Human Rights Council of the United Nations "endorsed a resolution upholding the principle of freedom of expression and information on the Internet" (Bildt, 2012). The resolution was presented by Brazil, Nigeria, Sweden, Tunisia, Turkey and the United States, co-sponsored by eighty countries (Bildt, 2012) and passed by consensus (U.S. Mission, 2012). While this resolution does not carry the weight of law, it's a step in the right direction carried out in an international space of engagement. As Bildt (2012) says, "We are rapidly entering into a new world of hyperconnectivity. Mobile data traffic alone is set to increase 15-fold in the next five years. It reaches everywhere, and we see the new networks challenging the old hierarchies everywhere."

Early predictions that the power of GIS and internet technologies lies exclusively in the hands of the already powerful and expert have been upended by technical improvements that have made it possible for millions - perhaps billions - of people to own and use these technologies. Examples drawn from the Arab Spring and Occupy movements suggest that this path to empowerment will continue and will certainly be present in the urban governance context as well. Still, it is wise to understand that this is an ongoing tug-of-war that will take place in many places of engagement for years to come.

REFERENCES

Al-Kodmany, K. (2000). Public participation: Technology and democracy. *Journal of Architectural Education*, *53*(4), 220–228. doi:10.1162/104648800564635.

Allen, M. (2012). What was Web 2.0? Versions as the dominant mode of internet history. *New Media & Society*. Retrieved from http://hms.sagepub.com/content/early/2012/07/03/1461444812451567

Arora, P. (2012). Typology of Web 2.0 spheres: Understanding the cultural dimensions of social media spaces. *Current Sociology*. Retrieved from http://csi.sagepub.com/content/60/5/599

Awad, M. (2010). El Baradei leads big Egypt anti-torture protest. *Reuters*. Retrieved from http://www.reuters.com/article/2010/06/25/us-egypt-protest-elbaradei-idUSTRE65O5JC20100625

Balogna, A. (2011). NYPD police pepper spray occupy wall street protesters. *You Tube*. Retrieved from http://www.youtube.com/watch?v=TZ05rWx1pig

Barnes, J. E. (2012, July 9). Law agencies seek more data from cell carriers. *The Wall Street Journal*. Retrieved from http://online.wsj.com/article/SB1000142405270230402200457751568199885276.html?KEYWORDS=Law+agencies+seek+more+data+from+cell+carriers

Bildt, C. (2012, July 5). A victory for the internet. *New York Times*. Retrieved from http://www.nytimes.com/2012/07/06/opinion/carl-bildt-a-victory-for-the-internet.html

Carrier, I. Q. (2012). Handsets deployed. *Carrier IQ Website*. Retrieved July 22, 2012, http://www.carrieriq.com/

Chen, B. X., & Sengupta, S. (2011, December 2). Programmer raises concerns about phone-monitoring software. *New York Times*. Retrieved from http://bits.blogs.nytimes.com/2011/12/01/programmer-raises-concerns-about-phone-monitoring-software/

Cleveland, H. (1985). The twilight of hierarchy: Speculations on the global information society. *Public Administration Review*, *45*(2), 185–195. doi:10.2307/3110148.

Coast, S. (2007). OpenStreetMap. *Volunteered Geographic Information Workshop*. Retrieved from http://ncgia.ucsb.edu/projects/vgi/products.html

Cox, K. R. (1998). Spaces of dependence, spaces of engagement and the politics of scale, or: looking for local politics. *Political Geography*, *17*(1), 1–23. doi:10.1016/S0962-6298(97)00048-6.

Crampton, J. W. (2003). Cartographic rationality and the politics of geosurveillance and security. *Cartography and Geographic Information Systems, 30*(2), 135–148. doi:10.1559/152304003100011108.

Curry, M. R. (1997). The digital divide and the private realm. *Annals of the Association of American Geographers. Association of American Geographers, 87*(4), 681–699. doi:10.1111/1467-8306.00073.

Derene, G. (2011). Tracking software caught snooping on millions of smartphones. *Popular Mechanics*. Retrieved from http://www.popularmechanics.com/technology/gadgets/news/tracking-software-caught-snooping-on-millions-of-smartphone-users-6606335

Dobson, J., & Fisher, P. (2007). The panopticon's changing geography. *Geographical Review, 97*(3), 307–324.

Dobson, J. E., & Fisher, P. F. (2006). Panopticon III: Gaming the national debate over human tracking. *Chapter presented at the American Association for the Advancement of Science (AAAS)*. St. Louis, Mo.

Duhigg, C. (2012). How companies learn your secrets. *New York Times*. Retrieved from http://www.nytimes.com/2012/02/19/magazine/shopping-habits.html?_r=1&pagewanted=all

Eckhart, T. (2011). Carrier IQ Part #2. *YouTube*. Retrieved from http://www.youtube.com/watch?v=T17XQI_AYNo

Facebook. (2012). Facebook login page. *Facebook*. Retrieved from http://www.facebook.com/

Fahim, K. (2011). Slap to a man's pride set off tumult in Tunisia. *New York Times*. Retrieved from http://www.nytimes.com/2011/01/22/world/africa/22sidi.html?pagewanted=all

Franken, Al. (2011). Senator Franken demands answers from company accused of secretly logging location and private information. *Senator Al Franken website*. Retrieved from http://www.franken.senate.gov/?p=press_release&id=1868

Gautney, H. (2011). What is occupy wall street? The history of leaderless movements. *Washington Post*. Retrieved from http://www.washingtonpost.com/national/on-leadership/what-is-occupy-wall-street-the-history-of-leaderless-movements/2011/10/10/gIQAwkFjaL_story.html

Ghonim, W. (2012). *Revolution 2.0: The power of the people is greater than the people in power*. New York: Houghton Mifflin Harcourt.

Ghonim, W. (2012). *Revolution 2.0: The power of the people is greater than the people in power*. New York: Houghton Mifflin Harcourt.

Goodchild, M. F. (2007). Citizens as sensors: The world of volunteered geography. *GeoJournal, 69*(4), 211–221. doi:10.1007/s10708-007-9111-y.

Goss, J. (1995). We know who you are and we know where you live: The instrumental rationality of geodemographic systems. *Economic Geography, 71*(2), 171–198. doi:10.2307/144357.

Gupta, A. (2012). What happened to the occupy movement. *Al Jazeera*. Retrieved from http://www.aljazeera.com/indepth/opinion/2012/05/2012521151225452634.html

Gustin, S. (2011). Defiant Google Exec Wael Ghonim released from Egyptian custody. *Wired*. Retrieved from http://www.wired.com/business/2011/02/ghonim-release-reports/

Hashash, S. (2012). Egyptians tune into the programme, a 'blasphemous' TV satire. *The Guardian*. Retrieved from http://www.guardian.co.uk/world/2012/may/08/egyptians-programme-blasphemous-tv-satire

Herbert, W. A. (2006a). No direction home: Legal principles, issues, and potential solutions. *Chapter presented at the American Association for the Advancement of Science (AAAS)*. St. Louis, Mo. AAAS. (2006b). *Conversation with the author at the American Association for the Advancement of Science (AAAS) meeting*. St. Louis, Mo.

Howard, P. N., Duffy, A., Deen, F., Hussain, M., Mari, W., & Mazaid, M. (2011). *Opening closed regimes: What was the role of social media during the Arab Spring? Project on Information Technology and Political Islam*. University of Washington.

Jazeera, A. (2011). Hosni Mubarak Resigns as President. *Al Jazeera*. Retrieved from http://www.aljazeera.com/news/middleeast/2011/02/201121125158705862.html/

Kirkpatrick, D. D. (2011). Tunisia leader flees and prime minister claims power. *New York Times*. Retrieved from http://www.nytimes.com/2011/01/15/world/africa/15tunis.html/?_r=1&pagewanted=all

Klinkenberg, B. (2007). Geospatial technologies and the geographies of hope and fear. *Annals of the Association of American Geographers. Association of American Geographers*, 97(2), 350–360. doi:10.1111/j.1467-8306.2007.00541.x.

Kyem, P. A. K. (2004). Of intractable conflicts and participatory GIS applications: The search for consensus amidst competing claims and institutional demands. *Annals of the Association of American Geographers. Association of American Geographers*, 94(1), 37–57. doi:10.1111/j.1467-8306.2004.09401003.x.

Landler, M. (2007). Where little is left outside the camera's eye. *New York Times*. Retrieved from http://www.nytimes.com/2007/07/08/weekinreview/08landler.html?_r=1

Lichtblau, E. (2012). Police are using phone tracking as a routine tool. *New York Times*. Retrieved from http://bits.blogs.nytimes.com/?s=Police+are+using+phone+tracking

Monmonier, M. (1998). The three Rs of GIS-based site selection: Representation, resistance, and ridicule. In D.R. Fraser Taylor (Ed.), Policy issues in modern cartography (volume 3 of the Modern Cartography series) (pp. 233-247). Oxford: Pergamon, Elsevier Science.

Monmonier, M. (2002). *Spying with Maps*. Chicago, IL: The University of Chicago Press.

Monmonier, M. (2002). *Spying with Maps*. Chicago, IL: The University of Chicago Press.

MoxNews. (2011). Occupy – Police pepper spray priest, 84 yr old & pregnant woman. *Inside the USA*. Retrieved from http://www.youtube.com/watch?v=NnMp1e4cDj8

Moynihan, C. (2011). Wall street protest begins, with demonstrators blocked. *New York Times*. Retrieved from http://cityroom.blogs.nytimes.com/2011/09/17/wall-street-protest-begins-with-demonstrators-blocked/

Nieto, M. (1997). Public video surveillance: Is it an effective crime prevention tool? *Sacramento: California Research Bureau*. Retrieved from http://www.library.ca.gov/crb/97/05/

Obermeyer, N. J. (1998). Evolution of public participation GIS. *Cartography and Geographic Information Systems*, 25(2), 65–66. doi:10.1559/152304098782594599.

Occupy Everything. (2011). Police pepper spray students! *YouTube*. Retrieved from http://www.youtube.com/watch?v=vee1VoTZ-NY

Occupy Wall Street. (2012). Occupy wall street about and user map. *Occupy Wall Street*. Retrieved from http://occupywallst.org

Perlroth, N. (2011). Carrier IQ denies it is under investigation. *New York Times*. Retrieved from http://bits.blogs.nytimes.com/2011/12/14/carrier-iq-denies-it-is-under-investigation/

Pickles, J. (1991). Geography, GIS, and the surveillant society. *Chapters and Proceedings of Applied Geography Conferences, 14*(2), 80-91.

Please Rob Me. (2011). *Website*. Retrieved from http://pleaserobme.com/

Progressive Insurance. (2012). Over $70 million already saved with Snapshot. *Progressive Auto Insurance website*. Retrieved from http://www.progressive.com/auto/snapshot.aspx?vanity=true

Ricknäs, M. (2011). European regulators start investigating carrier IQ. *PC World*. Retrieved from http://www.pcworld.idg.com.au/article/409306/european_regulators_start_investigating_carrier_iq/

Ryan, N. (2011). Occupy Seattle protesters pepper sprayed. *King 5 News*. Retrieved from http://www.king5.com/news/local/Occupy-Seattle-protesters-pepper-sprayed-in-clash-with-officers-133930088.html

Schroeder, P. (1997). Personal e-mail communication. November 15, 1997.

Sieber, R. (2006). Public participation geographic information systems: A literature review and framework. *Annals of the Association of American Geographers. Association of American Geographers, 96*(3), 491–507. doi:10.1111/j.1467-8306.2006.00702.x.

Slaughter, A.-M. (2011). Occupied wall street, seen from abroad. *New York Times*. Retrieved from http://www.nytimes.com/2011/10/06/opinion/occupied-wall-street-seen-from-abroad.html?_r=1

Tor Project. (2012). 20 July 2012. *The Tor Project, Inc*. Retrieved from https://www.torproject.org/

United States Mission. (2012). HRC affirms that human rights must also be protected on the internet (Resolution Text). *United States Mission to the United Nations*. Retrieved from http://geneva.usmission.gov/2012/07/05/internet-resolution/

Vitelli, B. (2012). People can't seem to stop eulogizing the occupy movement. *The Guardian Media Network*. Retrieved from http://www.guardian.co.uk/media-network-partner-zone-publici/occupy-movement-eulogy

Wikimapia. (2012). Official Wikimapia FAQ. *Wikimapia*. Retrieved from http://wikimapia.org/wiki/Official_Wikimapia_FAQ

ADDITIONAL READING

Ghonim, W. (2012). Revolution 2.0: The power of the people is greater than the people in power. New York: Houghton Mifflin Harcourt.

Monmonier, M. (2002). Spying with Maps. Chicago, IL: The University of Chicago Press.

KEY TERMS AND DEFINITIONS

Geo-Location Technologies: Technologies embedded in other devices designed to provide the geographic location of that device, and the person using it.

Geoslavery: A practice in which one entity, the master, coercively or surreptitiously monitors and exerts control over the physical location of another individual (the slave).

Geospatial Technologies: The combination of hardware and software that are commonly used to collect, import, store, manipulate, analyze and display data and information with a geographical location.

Geovisualization: Short for Geographic Visualization; refers to a set of tools and techniques supporting geospatial data analysis through the use of interactive visualization.

Public Participation GIS (PPGIS): Movement within the GIS research community designed to promote the use of GIS as a tool of empowerment for local citizens and non-governmental organizations.

Social Media: Media for social interaction, using highly accessible and scalable publishing techniques. Social media use web-based technologies to transform and broadcast media monologues into social media dialogues. Examples include Facebook, Linked-In, and Twitter.

Volunteered Geographic Information (VGI): The harnessing of tools to create, assemble, and disseminate geographic data provided voluntarily by individuals (Goodchild, 2007). Some examples of this phenomenon are Wikimapia, OpenStreetMap, and Google MyMaps.

Web 2.0: Second generation of Internet-based services. These usually include tools that let people collaborate and share information online, such as social networking sites, wikis, and communication tools.

Wikimap: An open-content collaborative mapping project aimed to mark all geographical objects in the world and provide a useful description for them. It combines interactive web map with a wiki system.

Chapter 7
Volunteered Geographic Information for Disaster Management

Doris Dransch
GFZ German Research Centre for Geosciences, Germany

Joachim Fohringer
GFZ German Research Centre for Geosciences, Germany

Kathrin Poser
Water Insight BV, The Netherlands

Christian Lucas
Karlsruhe Institute of Technology (KIT), Germany

ABSTRACT

The amount of information generated and provided by citizens via the World Wide Web is constantly growing. Citizens share information, thoughts, and experiences in blogs and contribute information to web-based content sharing platforms, collaboratively created data bases that are freely usable by everybody. Disaster management as one component of urban planning to decrease a society's vulnerability can benefit from information provided by citizens. This chapter gives an overview of the application of information provided by citizens in disaster management. It points out the potential of using such information for the various phases of disaster management. Three main challenges, which affect the usefulness of information supplied by citizens, are presented in more detail: data collection, localization and quality assessment. For each of these challenges, various approaches to address them are discussed.

INTRODUCTION

Internet technology supports citizens not only to access but also to provide information. Information created by citizens, is generally called user-generated content, or - more specifically - volunteered geographic information (VGI) if it is

geographic in nature (Goodchild, 2007; Gouveia et al., 2004). Volunteered geographic information is provided by different media: text, images or video. VGI can be regarded as an extension of public participation geographic information systems (PPGIS) which intend to empower communities by improved information access and participation (Ghose, 2001; Sieber, 2006). In contrast to PPGIS, which facilitates citizens' participation, the VGI approach is predominately self-organized.

DOI: 10.4018/978-1-4666-4169-3.ch007

Extensive research in citizen science and PPGIS has proved the usefulness of involving the public in environmental monitoring (e.g. Fore et al., 2001; Engel & Voshell, 2002) and spatial planning (e.g. Weiner & Harris, 2003; Sultana et al., 2008). Recent examples have also shown the usefulness of VGI for disaster management (Goodchild & Glennon, 2010; De Longueville et al., 2010). In order to make VGI a valuable additional information source for disaster management as one component of urban planning to decrease a society's vulnerability its potential has to be examined systematically, and challenges and solutions have to be identified. This chapter gives an overview about the application of VGI in disaster management and presents existing approaches to tackle important challenges related to VGI.

APPLICATION OF VGI IN DISASTER MANAGEMENT

Potential and Challenges of Volunteered Information for Disaster Management

Natural disaster management encompasses all activities before, during and after a hazard event that aim at preventing natural disasters, reducing their impact and recovering from their losses. The disaster management process can be regarded as cycle consisting of four phases: mitigation, preparedness, response and recovery.

Disaster mitigation focuses on reducing or eliminating risk. It includes risk identification, analysis, and appraisal, as well as risk reduction. Preparedness deals with planning how to respond to hazardous events. Emergency planning, training, monitoring, forecasting, and early warning systems are proper means in this phase. In case of a disaster, response measures are necessary which maintain or re-establish public safety and provide the basic humanitarian needs of the affected population. Post-disaster recovery is the process of restoring the living conditions in the affected areas. It includes damage assessment as well as rehabilitation and reconstruction.

The varying phases of disaster management require different kinds of information which can be volunteered by the public. In the phase of risk mitigation, information about natural hazards and vulnerability parameters are of great importance to assess an area's exposure to one or more kinds of hazards. In areas where few long-term records exist, the local population's knowledge about location and extent, frequency and intensity of past natural disasters can be of high value. Mitigation also includes an open discussion of acceptable risk and mitigation options, in which the public is an important stakeholder. The main contribution the public can make in these phases via VGI is to communicate their views and perceptions about acceptable and unacceptable risk, coping strategies, possible mitigation measures, and their prioritization.

In the preparedness phase, monitoring the drivers of disasters, the hazard itself as well as vulnerability parameters is of great importance. Accurate information about vulnerability parameters, such as type of buildings, land use, or condition of protection measures are a prerequisite for risk assessment and risk reduction. Vulnerability parameters are often subject to fast changes, especially in very dynamic areas such as big cities or regions of transformation. The local public can be involved in monitoring and reporting the changes of local vulnerability parameters. This approach already exists in the context of municipal projects where people can register all kinds of deficiencies (http://www.mängelmelder.de/). Mitigation and preparedness are predominately long-term phases that require continuous information about changes in vulnerability and protection measures.

In contrast to mitigation and preparedness, the response and, to some extent, the recovery phase requires highly dynamic data, describing the extent and intensity of the hazardous event as well as resulting impacts and the current status of response activities. Citizens can provide local, detailed, and up-to-date information about the behavior of the hazard and its impact, contributing to a comprehensive picture of the actual situation. An example is the wildfire event in 2007 in California where affected people posted information about the wildfires in their own neighborhood to an internet page to inform about the expansion and behavior of the fires (Sutton et al., 2007; Goodchild & Glennon, 2010). "Did you feel it," a service established by the US Geological Survey (USGS), is a further example of VGI for disaster management. For this service, the volunteers are asked to describe the impact of an earthquake using a number of questions in a form, which is then used to derive earthquake intensity maps (Wald et al., 2011). Besides providing detailed situational information, VGI can also be used for a very first overview of a disastrous event. The increasing amount of information provided by the affected public via social media after a hazard event can be used as an indicator for an occurring event as well as for a first assessment. The spatial distribution of the posted social media news may give a fast overview about the spatial extent of the hazard event.

Volunteered geographic information offers several benefits for disaster management. VGI is highly up-to-date. Eye witnesses can document their observations directly and improve situational awareness. VGI is contextual. People have local knowledge, are aware of their surroundings, and can make sense of situations; they filter, synthesize and interpret information accordingly. VGI builds an additional information source that complements established observation systems. People may contribute information which cannot be measured by sensors since the phenomenon is not measurable or sensors are not available.

The potential of VGI to enhance disaster management activities extends to urban planning as well. One goal of urban planning is to decrease a society's vulnerability. It aims at reducing damage to population and infrastructure from natural hazards by suitable protection measures and conditions for escape and rescue. Therefore, all information concerning vulnerability issues are of avail. Volunteers can provide such information, including spatial extent and impact of former or recent hazard events, caused damage, well or bad performing emergency routes, changes in land use, or illegal dwellings. Since volunteers have local knowledge and are often eye witnesses, their information is up-to date and generated in a wider context. They can readily identify local shortcomings and deficits and thus contribute either to develop novel protection and rescue measure or to validate and improve existing ones. The broad information base required for planning activities can be fed by VGI from all phases of the disaster management cycle.

The obvious advantages of VGI however, are accompanied by some shortcomings. Unlike a sensor network, information collection from the public cannot be planned in advance so as to yield a sufficient amount of observations for the phenomenon of interest. While in-situ sensors are in general stationary at known locations, and remotely sensed data are operationally geo-referenced, human observations need to be explicitly localized in order to be useful. In-situ sensors are calibrated; the collected data is aligned to the calibration. In contrast "human sensors," as volunteers are often called, provide information that differs in type and quality.

In order to make VGI a valuable information source for disaster management despite these limitations, concepts and technology are required to alleviate the disadvantages. Firstly, proper approaches are necessary which support the collection of VGI related to the needs of disaster management. Secondly, methods have to be available that enable the accurate localization of VGI by creating spatial coordinates from all types of spatial references. Thirdly, concepts are required to assess the quality of VGI.

Various approaches regarding the mentioned requirements exist or are under development. They differ in various characteristics and thus, have benefits and drawbacks when applying them for information gathering in disaster management. In the following we introduce the most prominent approaches for data collection, localization and quality assessment of VGI and their suitability for different tasks of disaster management.

Collecting Volunteered Geographic Information

VGI can be collected via the Internet in various ways. The most prominent examples are web-based surveys, content sharing platforms and social media. The VGI collection approaches can be classified according to several characteristics: expected information volume, more or less structured data, low or high data processing effort, prompt or delayed information provision. Data provision by the various sources can be either intentional if the volunteer provides information explicitly to a given service, such as OpenStreetMap; it also can be non-intentional, if someone disseminates observations or reports within a weblog or via Twitter without the explicit intention to support a specific task, in our case disaster management. Furthermore, communication between volunteers and the entity which processes the data can be uni-directional and be restricted to simple uploading of data, or it can be bi-directional and support further information exchange, e.g. by using social networks. In the following we describe different sources for VGI, and point out their potential for disaster management.

Web-Based Surveys

Web-based (or online-) surveys are online versions of questionnaires used in many ways to receive information about a specific topic. In disaster management they can be applied to get information about a hazard event or related damages.

Volunteers are asked to answer a set of questions such as "Have you felt an earthquake?" or "Have you been affected by flooding in the last 10 years?" The answer options are mostly limited. These questionnaires are mainly static web-forms where a user-input is sent to a web-server using the Common Gateway Interface (CGI). In order to evaluate the questionnaire, custom server-side software or pre-built survey software is applied. Examples for these web-based services in the context of disaster management are questionnaires like "Have you felt an earthquake?" of the British Geological Survey, or "Did you feel it?" (http://earthquake.usgs.gov/earthquakes/dyfi/), (Wald et al., 2011) of the US Geological Survey, where volunteers can report their experiences with earthquakes (for more examples see Sbarra et al., 2010). The web-based surveys allow for obtaining a more complete description of earthquakes and damages. The acquired information is used among others for generating so called "Community Internet Intensity Maps" which are available instantly on the website showing the effects of volunteers' data submission. We developed an online questionnaire for flood damage data collection in Germany (Kreibich et al., 2008).

An advantage of web-based surveys is that VGI collected in this way is highly tailored to the needs of the data collector. Every acquired data set has the same structure and type of content which is predetermined by the design of the questionnaire. As a consequence data can be easily processed; only low effort is needed for transformation, formatting or conversion of the data. Beside this advantage, predefined questionnaires also have shortcomings; they restrict the volunteered information to the predefined questions; information not intended at time of developing the questionnaire will not be collected.

Web-based surveys are cheap, fast and simple to implement and allow for easy data processing. They are suitable for recurring questions and for the acquisition of standardized data, but are ill-suited to allow for changes or observations beyond specified questions. Using free-form text fields is possible, but this input data cannot easily be processed automatically. Online survey systems allow only unidirectional communication (volunteers submit data). They are not intended for bi-directional communication, e.g. for notifying users of events, or for alarming purpose. Comparing web-based surveys with other VGI collecting approaches, they are not the best means for prompt information provision in a hazard event. Because volunteers are mostly not immediately aware of a questionnaire in case of a hazard event, so time between occurrence of an event and data-submission could be relative long.

Prerequisites for a successful web-based survey in terms of quantity of submitted questionnaires are that volunteers know about the survey, are motivated to fill in the questionnaire and have an explicit intention to provide information for a particular task. A successful example is "Did you feel it" which has up to almost 80000 responses (Figure 1) for larger earthquakes (Wald et al., 2011).

Content Sharing Platforms

Content sharing platforms provide software tools and services which allow users to post different forms of content like text, images, or videos, and make it available to the public or restricted groups. Famous examples are Wikipedia (http://www.wikipedia.org/), Flickr (http://www.flickr.com/) or YouTube (http://www.youtube.com/). Uploaded VGI can be of different types such as comprehensive reports about crisis situations, photographs of damaged buildings, or positions of radiation spots in case of nuclear incidents. One popular example for a web-based information collection service in disaster context is "Ushahidi" (http://www.ushahidi.com/), which is a communication platform for collecting observations or reports from crisis events. Observations include eyewitness reports of violence in political crises (as the first version of the Ushahidi-website in the aftermath of Kenyas's

presidential election in 2007) as well as natural disasters like earthquakes (Haiti & Chile, 2010; Christchurch, 2011), winter storms (Washington D.C., 2010), wildfires (Russia, 2010) and floods (Queensland (McDougal, 2011), Missouri, 2011 and Thailand, 2011). Volunteers submit free-form reports in combination with date, location and optional news source link, video link, photos and contact information. In addition to data input via the World Wide Web, Ushahidi supports other communication-channels like SMS, social web sites or e-mail. Submitted reports are manually checked and verified by comparing them with other sources and reports (Okolloh, 2009). The collected and approved reports are visualized by geocoding them by means of OpenStreetMap (OSM, http://www.openstreetmap.org/) or GoogleMaps (http://maps.google.com/); additionally, they are arranged chronologically on a timeline.

Technically Ushahidi combines several web-services like GoogleMaps and OSM (Roche et al., 2011). It is built on open source software such as the server-side scripting language PHP, the relational database management system MySQL, and the SMS-platform FrontlineSMS. The hosted version of Ushahidi – Crowdmap – is also released under an open source-license and freely downloadable.

Like volunteers who take part in online surveys, users of content platforms must know the platform and they must have an intention to provide data, e.g. seeking help or providing support. Unlike VGI gathered by online surveys this data is not strictly structured, because volunteers submit free text-reports, they do not just answer explicit questions. To extract valuable information relevant to disaster management out of this unstructured data requires further processing. Automatic processing, for instance by using natural language processing or data mining-methods, is difficult and thus manual processing is almost always necessary. The volunteered data has to be parsed, transformed (e.g. location to geo-coordinates), converted (e.g. time designations), and classified (e.g. for credibility). As in online surveys a bi-directional communica-

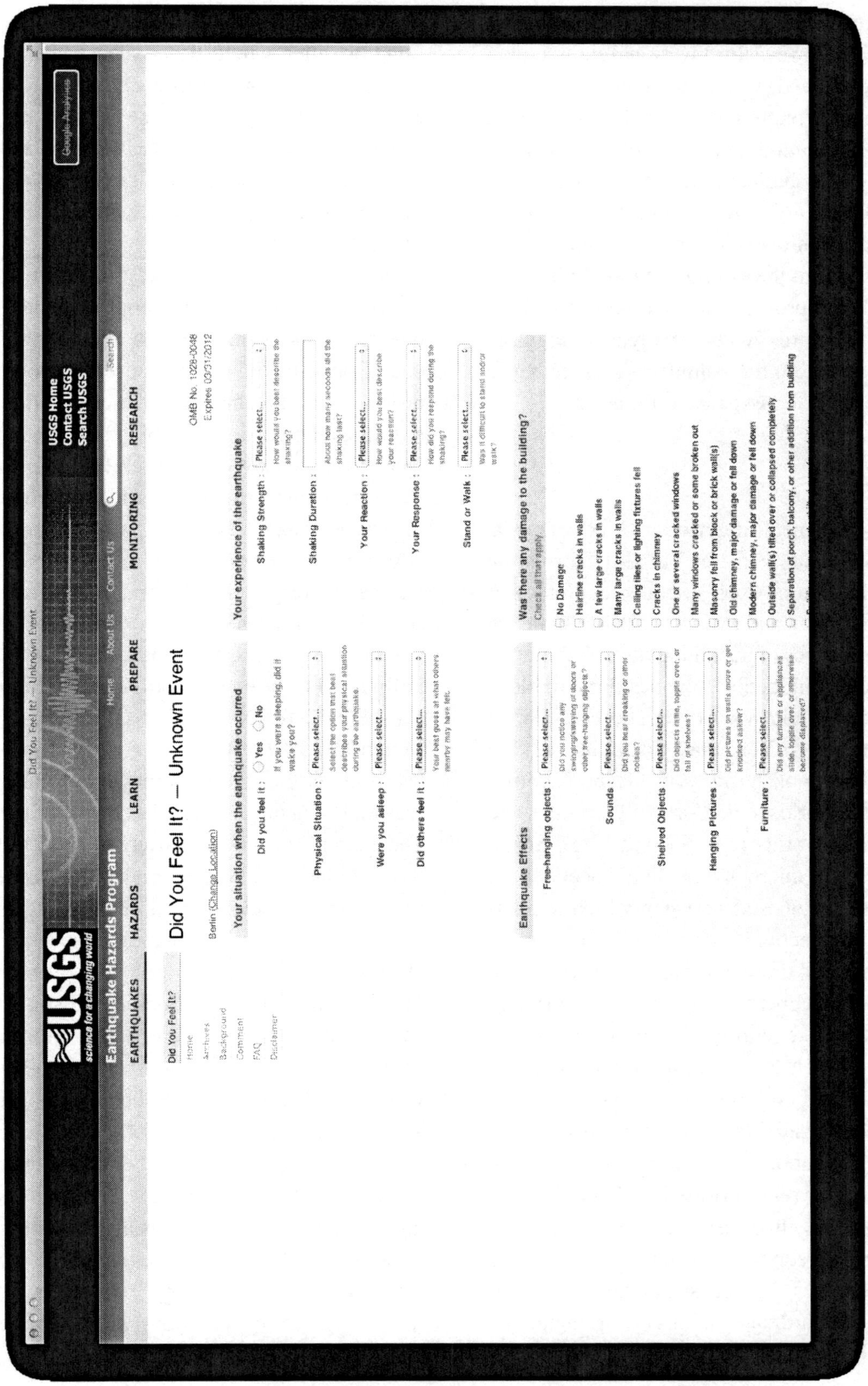

Figure 1. Screenshot of the Did you feel it?-questionnaire (© 2011, U.S. Geological Survey. Used with permission.)

tion between volunteer and the Ushahidi-service is not intended. However bi-directional communication can be realized by other channels, like e-mail, if contact information is given by volunteers. Contact information must be optional to keep anonymity of volunteers; this is essential in the case of political crisis. Regarding the amount and promptness of information provision via content sharing platforms the example of Ushahidi shows that volunteers provide information fast and extensively (Starbird, 2011). The reason might be a high intention on the volunteers' side either to get help or to offer assistance (Figure 2).

Social Media

The term social media describes all kinds of media which support interactive exchange of information and contribution of user generated content. According to Kaplan and Haenlein (2010), there are six different types of social media: collaborative projects (e.g. Wikipedia), blogs and micro blogs (e.g. Twitter, http://www.twitter.com/), content communities (e.g. YouTube), social networking sites (e.g. Facebook, http://www.facebook.com/), virtual game worlds (e.g. World of Warcraft), and virtual social worlds (e.g. Second Life). Social networks and (micro-)blogs like Facebook or Twitter are web-based services which support primarily bi-directional communication between users. Typically these services allow exchange of text-messages between members of different communities like family members, friends or colleagues. Users share information, thoughts, experiences and opinions about aspects of their lives or specific subjects. In crisis events, "social network [...] mobilize the tech community to support disaster relief efforts [...]" (Zook et al., 2010). Especially in disaster situations users provide emotional support to each other, exchange situation updates, broadcast damage reports or propose and coordinate actions (De Longueville et al., 2010; Qu et al., 2010).

Many social networks offer (micro-)blogging functionalities where users keep some kind of online diary or journal to track issues or events. Microblogging-services like Twitter support text-messages ("tweets" in Twitter) with a limited length (e.g. 140 characters). Tweets also include metadata like unique identifier, author, date, time, or location of the user.

Social media permit fastest dissemination of information. Due to their popularity and high number of users this leads to a huge volume of data. Social media can be a useful resource for near-realtime information (Doan et al., 2011). This advantage however is combined with a massive challenge: the extraction of relevant information from the text messages. Since the main intention of users of social networks is to communicate with others and not to provide specific data for disaster management, the text is relatively unspecific. Examples of tweets related to the term "earthquake" make this apparent: "Earthquake in limassol right now," "Earthquake, Magnitude 5.1 - SOUTHERN XINJIANG, CHINA - 2012 March 02, 13:40 UTC http://t.co/FxyuCmQw," or "labrinth-earthquake, if you have big speakers and play that song on, it will make a real earthquake." The examples show the variety of text messages and the related challenges. High processing effort is necessary to select appropriate messages and to extract relevant information. Data has to be ranked after retrieval, at least into relevant and irrelevant messages (Hurlock & Wilson, 2011), and classified by its content, if it is information, opinion, technology, emotion, action or other (Heverin & Zach, 2010). For further analysis, quality assessment and evaluation for a specific task is necessary (Section 4). Another challenge is the language within the messages. It differs according to the nationality and it is highly compressed or abbreviated. For instance, web-links will be automatically shortened by Twitters own URL shortening service, emotions will be enunciated by emoticons. In the worst case that leads to a

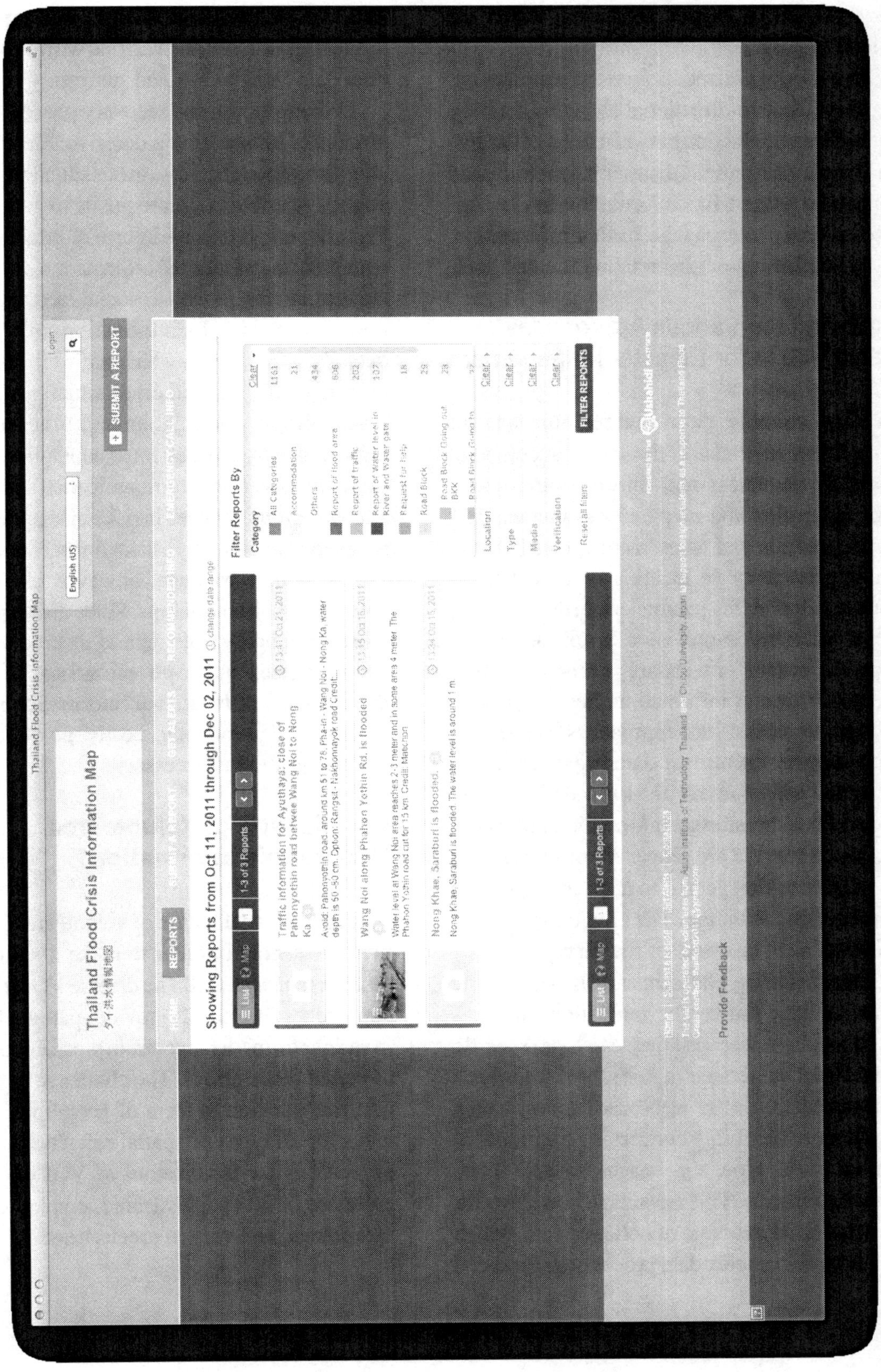

Figure 2. Screenshot of the Ushahidi Crowdmap-Website for Thailand Flood Crisis in 2011 (© 2011, Asian Institute of Technology, Thailand and Chubu University, Japan. Used with permission.)

bulky amount of cryptic messages, which are difficult to parse.

Since most social media focus on communication, they allow bi-directional channels natively, which allows interaction between users of the system. People who provide disaster information and people who process this information can be connected directly to exchange further information, e.g. by confirming or concretizing information.

Employing the Various Approaches to Collect VGI in for Disaster Management

Selecting suitable data sources for disaster management depends on the requirements with respect to timeliness and information content. In the mitigation and preparedness phases, data for risk analysis and assessment are of interest, including intensity or location of past disaster events or vulnerability parameters. In these phases, time of information-provision is not the critical factor; the crucial criteria are precision, quality and significance of information. For that reason, information collection approaches are useful which support intentional data provision, since quality and precision can be assumed higher than in case of non-intentional information provision. Web-based surveys are proper means, since they collect information geared to a specific goal and in a predefined structure. The prerequisite is that volunteers must be aware of the survey.

Content sharing platforms are also a suitable choice as data source for mitigation and preparedness phase, because they can issue specific details about vulnerable regions for risk analysis and assessment. Unlike web-based surveys, they provide more flexibility concerning user input in terms of media type, e.g. images, or data form, e.g. measurements. This advantage is achieved at the cost of strict structure of obtained data, which induces more complex data processing. Provided

data like text, images or video as well as meta data has to be processed and verified with higher effort than data from web-based surveys.

In the response and recovery phases, time and amount of information is decisive. A comprehensive picture about the disastrous situation gained as soon as possible is a prerequisite to give support. Fast and comprehensive information takes priority over precise and tailored information. In this case, content sharing as well as social media platforms are proper sources for information collecting. Especially social media which are well-known and used regularly beyond crisis situations have the potential to provide a high amount of near real-time information from the effected population. The option of bi-directional communication additionally allows persons involved in risk management to use social media to directly ask for further information. The obvious advantage, however, is combined with serious shortcomings. Since data is provided mostly implicitly, this data is unstructured, can be imprecise, and even erroneous. Moreover, the precision of locational information is highly variable. Consequently, costly post-processing and verification is necessary.

Localization of Volunteered Geographic Information

An accurate localization of volunteered information is essential in order to make it valuable for disaster management. The diverse VGI collection approaches (Section 2) provide spatial references in various forms. It ranges from precise coordinates to verbal descriptions. The challenge is to get an accurate position in form of geographic coordinates for all types of spatial references. Various approaches for localization of VGI exist. They are more or less sophisticated, employ different technology, and vary in preciseness.

Localization by Maps

A widely-used type of localization is maps. Volunteers document the spatial reference of their information in a map, the result is a coordinate related to the information. No further post-processing is required. Internet map services, such as OpenStreetMap, Google maps or Bing maps, are helpful means. The accuracy of the map-based location depends on the knowledge volunteers have about the place they refer to. Besides, the scale of the map affects accuracy; only maps with large scale enable precise positioning.

Localization by Mobile Devices

When the volunteers employ modern mobile devices, such as smartphones or tablet computers, localization is feasible by using positioning technologies included in the devices. Mobile devices allow localization either by the global positioning system (GPS) or by tracking cell tower signals of cellular networks. Since GPS requires a line-of-sight to the satellites, it is not suitable for indoor localization. Another option is to track their location on the basis of wireless internet signals from WiFi (Wireless Fidelity) access points. The WiFi solution is also suitable for indoor positioning. Drawbacks are the limitation to urban environments and the missing positional credibility in case of moving access points through relocation of their owners.

Mobile devices immediately provide coordinates that indicate the spatial position of information. The positioning accuracy varies from five meters to a hundred kilometers. It depends on the applied technology, and specific situational conditions, such as rural or urban area or availability of positioning system. A challenge in the case of localizing information by mobile devices is to make sure that the given coordinate is related to the location of the information and not to the location from where the information is sent. Both locations can be identical if the volunteer provides

the information at the same location where he/she makes the observation. If there is a delay between observing and providing information, the locations can differ. The divergence of locations can be controlled and mitigated by verifying information with other observations of the same event.

Localization by Verbal Descriptions

Often volunteers provide the location of information by verbal descriptions. This is the case especially in social media where people communicate verbally. They use either official geographical names, such as London Street, or they describe spatial relations, such as in front of the coffee shop. This type of information is not directly usable for disaster management since it cannot be used for further automatic processing such as placement on a map, or for calculating the extent of an event. For that reason, a transformation of the verbal description into coordinates is required.

In the case of official geographical names, existing gazetteer or geocoding services can be applied that link the names to spatial coordinates (Hill, 2000). Sometimes volunteers use vernacular names or vague descriptions instead of official names that do not correspond to usual gazetteers. In order to localize such information, an approach has been developed that applies additional knowledge from the World Wide Web to concretize the object and its coordinates. (Jones, Purves, Clough, & Joho, 2008).

The localization of verbal descriptions based on spatial relations is more complex and requires sophisticated approaches to transform them into coordinates. Direction, distance and other relations between objects as well as fuzziness are used to derive coordinates. A number of approaches exist (Wieczorek, Guo, & Hijmans, 2004; Guo, Liu, & Wieczorek, 2008), many are developed for handling route descriptions. We have developed a method for processing uncertain spatial references from verbal descriptions that enhances exiting ones. Our possibilistic method is a functional approach which merges spatial uncertainties and reference aspects in a combined calculation. The method is tailored to application in disaster management. Therefore domain specific influence factors, such as the credibility or timeliness, are taken into account (Lucas, 2012). First tests with the fire brigade of the city of Karlsruhe (South Germany) produced encouraging results. Figure 3 shows the localization of verbal descriptions, such as "east of the church" or "200 meters south of Kaiserstreet," in a map. The preciseness of the methodology varies from fifty to hundred meters and depends on the number of messages as well as the accuracy of the descriptions.

Ability of Localization Approaches for Disaster Management

The localization approaches are characterized by different technologies and preciseness. The technology determines to which VGI collecting approach a localization method is applicable. The preciseness identifies which tasks of disaster management are supported appropriately by localized information.

Web-based surveys collect information in a well determined and structured way. Also the spatial reference is queried in a specific type and format; usually, an address is requested or the volunteer is asked to localize all information on a map. In order to derive accurate coordinates from VGI, gazetteer- or geocoding services and map-services are required. Content sharing platforms as well as social media, in contrast, have no mandatory specifications how to describe spatial references. Spatial references could be provided by user-defined metadata, by a statement of place inside the message (e.g. the tweet) or by adding latitude and longitude from a mobile device as metadata. For that reason content sharing platforms and social media require various localization approaches to exploit all the diverse types of spatial references for disaster management. Gazetteer and geocoding services as well as approaches that can deal with vague verbal description are required for localization.

Different tasks in disaster management presume information with different spatial accuracy. For example to support search-and-rescue-missions in the response phase, information about the location of disaster victims has to be as precise as possible. Assessing the extent of a disaster event in a wider area can be based on less precise information. Spatial accuracy of VGI depends highly on localization method, technology, situational conditions, as well as knowledge of volunteers and preciseness of their observations. For that reason, no general rules can be established how to apply the various localization methods to the various phases in disaster management. Persons from disaster management should rather be aware of the varying accuracy in order to assess VGI appropriately. Verifying VGI can be supported by quality assessment methods which are a recent topic of research (Section 4).

Quality Assessment of Volunteered Geographic Information

One of the major obstacles for using VGI is its unknown quality. To tap the potential of VGI for disaster management, the data provided by anonymous and untrained people over the Internet needs to be thoroughly assessed. For operational information systems that use these data, methods for quality control need to be developed. As has been discussed in Section 2, VGI encompasses a wide range of data collection approaches, and data types; the data is collected with widely varying intentions and community structures. Therefore, it is not possible to apply the same methods for quality assessment and control to all these data. Rather, specific methods have to be developed to fit the characteristics of the data at hand.

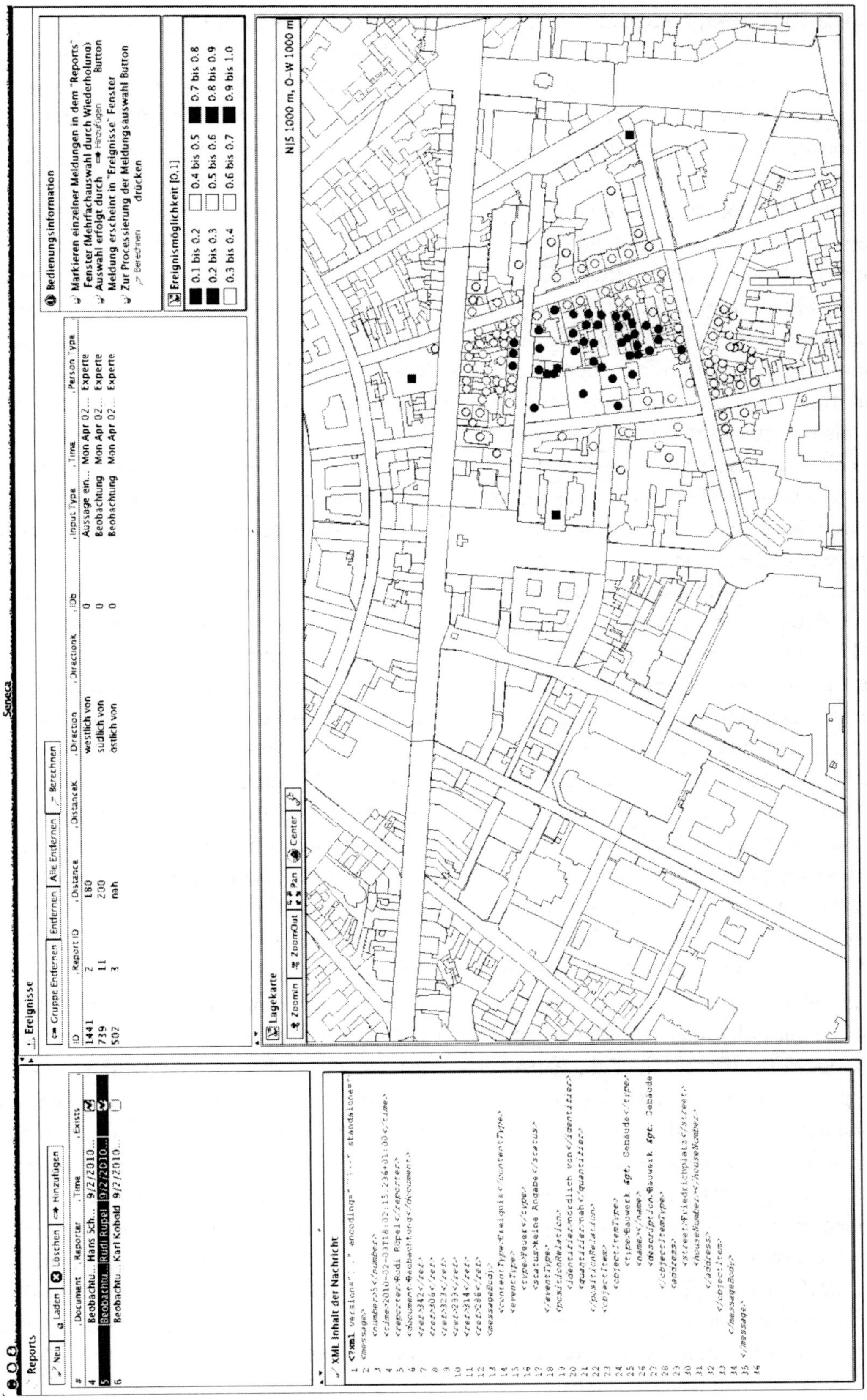

Figure 3. Screenshot of the prototype for localization verbal descriptions for the disaster management domain

Approaches for Quality Assessment

The traditional approach for data quality assessment focusses on the level of similarity between the data produced and the real-world phenomena they describe (Devillers & Jeansoulin, 2006). This approach is termed "internal data quality" by Devillers and Jeansoulin (2006) and "quality-as-accuracy" by Flanagin and Metzger (2008). Internal data quality pertains to the data themselves and is independent of their possible use. Devillers and Jeansoulin (2006) point out "external data quality" or "fitness for use" as a complementary concept, which assesses the suitability of a data set for a specific task in a specific area. External data quality assessment relies on the measures of internal data quality and explicitly stated objectives and requirements of the intended use. The requirements and the data specifications are matched to evaluate one or more data sets for their suitability for the task at hand. This concept implies that data quality is not absolute, but dependent on the intended use and the expectations of the user.

Different concepts of data quality are often applied in the Web 2.0 context with its large amounts of user-generated content: collective intelligence, credibility and aggregation. The concept of collective intelligence suggests that data assembled by large numbers of people are more likely to be accurate than data collected by single individuals because of self-policing and user data auditing within the group, i.e. it is assumed that incorrect data entered by an individual will be corrected by others (Goodchild, 2008; Hall et al., 2010).

A concept of data quality that is widely used within social networks is credibility. In contrast to accuracy, which is an objective property of information describing how well data represent the observed phenomena, credibility is a subjective perception on the part of the data user (Flanagin & Metzger, 2008). Credibility is based on trust and reputation as proxies for data quality; it relies on the users to rate the credibility of other users

and the information they contributed. Trust is in the first place an interpersonal property, i.e. between two people, whereas reputation is a collective measure of trustworthiness (in the sense of reliability) of a person by a community (Josang et al., 2007). According to Bishr and Janowicz (2010), trust exhibits people-object transitivity, i.e. interpersonal trust implies the transition of trust from the information provider to the information conveyed. This trust of a person in an information entity mediated by interpersonal trust is termed informational trust (Bishr & Janowicz, 2010). This concept can be interpreted as an implicit evaluation of external data quality: it also aims at the usefulness of data as perceived by their users. This evaluation, however, is done intuitively rather than by explicitly matching stated requirements and data specifications. This quality-as-credibility (Flanagin & Metzger, 2008) is particularly useful when individual perceptions or vague concepts are aimed at rather than objective properties. It can only be applied if there is an information community of users who collaboratively provide information and rate each other's contributions to allow for trust and reputation modeling (Bishr & Mantelas, 2008). Most Internet communities providing VGI such as Wikimapia (www.wikimapia.org) rely on such a network of registered users who contribute regularly and whose contributions can be rated and verified by other users.

Yet another approach to ensuring data quality of VGI, in particular for information extracted from content sharing communities and social networking services such as Flickr, is proposed by Mummidi and Krumm (2008) and De Longueville et al. (2010b): aggregation. This approach uses the abundance of data of unknown quality for cross-validation. It shifts the focus from the reliability of an individual piece of information to the reliability of conclusions that are drawn from the aggregation of numerous pieces of information from different sources.

Assessing the Quality of VGI for Disaster Management

While trust and reputation modeling is most often applied in web-based information communities, Flanagin and Metzger (2008) argue that it is rather the content of the data than the way they were collected that should determine which approach to data quality - quality-as-accuracy or quality-as-credibility - should be adopted. If the data is rather factual in nature, traditional internal and external quality measures can be applied, whereas information aiming at opinions or vague concepts should be assessed using trust and reputation modeling. Assessing information clusters aggregated from different sources rather than individual data items is particularly useful for large amounts of information extracted from content sharing and social networking services such as Twitter or Flickr (De Longueville et al., 2010b).

As has been pointed out, in different phases of the disaster management cycle, different kinds of information volunteered by the public can be useful. In some tasks of the mitigation and preparedness phases such as land-use planning or prioritizing of prevention measures, the public can volunteer opinions and contribute to discussions on priorities or advantages and disadvantages of measures to be taken. In these processes, which ideally consist of continued exchange of opinions and perceptions rather than facts, an information community exists. Therefore, for these processes, the quality-as-credibility approach is suitable. In the response phase, however, the affected population supplies information ad hoc, without training, and not regularly. To encourage as many people as possible to contribute information in this phase, a system for data collection should be as open as possible which includes not requiring user registration. For the mostly factual information

about hazardous events and their impacts, the quality-as-accuracy or the aggregation approaches are to be preferred.

Recently, a number of studies have explored several methods to assess different aspects of VGI data quality for disaster management. The most attention has been given to OpenStreetMap (OSM). OSM is a collaboratively created base-map of the world, which has been pivotal in the response and recovery phases of recent disasters such as the 2010 earthquake in Haiti (Coast, 2011). These quality assessments aimed at accuracy and completeness. Zielstra and Zipf (2010) have evaluated OSM data completeness by comparing it to data from TeleAtlas for the whole of Germany. They found a strong heterogeneity in data completeness, in particular between urban and rural areas, but also between larger and smaller cities. While in larger cities OSM contained even more data than Teleatlas, in rural areas coverage was found to be much lower. Haklay (2010a) evaluated OSM positional accuracy and completeness by comparing it to different data sets from the British Ordinance Survey for London. They found OSM data to be of a reasonable accuracy of about 6 meters and with an overlap of approximately 80% of motorway objects with Ordinance Survey data. However, they also noted great differences in accuracy between different areas.

For data extracted from content sharing communities, De Longueville et al. (2010b) have investigated the aggregation approach to assess the usefulness of such information. They evaluated geotagged images uploaded to Flickr that contained words such as flood or flooded in their tags in order to find a "'signal'" that would allow them to pinpoint recent flood events. They clustered the images in space and time and compared these clusters to other independent information provided by scientists and journalists. They found that VGI had been successful at detecting major flood events, but also noted the difficulty of converting the aggregated information into quantitative measurements.

A finding by Mendoza et al. (2010), who analyzed the use of Twitter during the 2010 earthquake in Chile, supports the usefulness of the aggregation approach: they could show for a small set of cases that the propagation of tweets that contain false rumors differs from tweets that contain true news in that rumors tend to be questioned more than news by the Twitter community. This finding suggests that the Twitter community works like a collaborative filter of information.

In our own research, we have evaluated the applicability of VGI for rapid loss estimation after flood events (Poser et al., 2009; Poser & Dransch, 2010). This research comprised an assessment of accuracy of observations of water level and flow velocity that were recorded in interviews with the affected population as well as a fitness-for-use analysis of these data for empirical flood loss modeling. The data were analyzed in comparison with hydraulic modeling results, measured inundation depths and gauge and terrain data. The results suggest that water level can be estimated by observers with a similar accuracy as it can be modeled with hydraulic models. Flow velocity, however, is very difficult to estimate and the results differ significantly from modeled results. It was found that despite the rather low accuracy of the observations, they can still be considered as useful for rapid damage estimation.

FUTURE RESEARCH DIRECTIONS

Utilizing information provided by citizens via World Wide Web technology is a rather novel approach. Therefore we have a lack of knowledge in many respects: We need broad experience and knowledge about the conditions that make collection and application of VGI a successful means. We need proper methods and concepts that support

extraction of suitable information from all types of VGI and that ensure good quality of VGI. And we need to evaluate the benefit of VGI for specific purpose. These questions have to be answered in the closer context of disaster management and urban planning.

Under Which Conditions does VGI become a Successful Means?

"Ushahidi" or "Did you feel it" are platforms which collect and provide a remarkable amount of VGI in case of disasters for response activities. Why are these platforms so successful? They could be used as an example to investigate the reasons for their success. Consequently, their effective concepts should be transferred and adapted to collect information relevant for planning activities in the mitigation phase of disaster management. This information could be local shortcomings or deficits in protection measures, damages caused by a hazard, well or bad performing emergency routes, or changes in land use.

Closely related to that point, the question arises how people can be convinced to contribute VGI. Several well established crowd sourcing projects exist, such as OpenStreetMap or CrisisCommons, where a defined information collection task is assigned to the crowd. Why and how do these projects successfully create suitable databases? These are essential questions that have to be answered. Knowledge about how to establish effective crowd sourcing projects is a prerequisite to ensure continuous and qualified data collection for planning activities in disaster management.

How to Extract Suitable Information from All Types of VGI and Ensure Good Quality of VGI?

VGI can be collected either directly, as it is the case in crowd sourcing projects, or it can be collected indirectly from information provided via social media such as Twitter or Facebook. In the case of a disastrous event a remarkable amount of information is provided via social media. To utilize this pool of information following research questions have to be addressed: What sort of information is useful for planning activities in disaster management? How can these messages be identified from the entirely messages? And how can suitable information automatically be extracted from the message? Proper methods and concepts that address these questions have to be developed to exploit the novel information source of social media for disaster management and related planning activities.

The internet technology, which forms the basis of VGI, allows not only providing information in a one-directional way, from the volunteer to the information collector. It also supports bi-directional communication where the information collector can contact volunteers to ask for more detailed or additional information. Open questions in this context are: How to automate the dialog and how to design the dialog system?

In order to ensure good quality of VGI, we also have to examine which information volunteers are able to provide. People mostly are not trained to determine precise measurements, like water-level in meters; they rather use proxies to describe measurements, such as "knee-deep." For that reason, it is necessary to define proper proxies that enable volunteers to provide suitable information for disaster management, especially the phases of mitigation and preparedness. Besides, existing quality assessment methods as described in chapter 4 have to be adapted and improved.

How to Evaluate the Benefit of VGI for Disaster Management and Related Urban Planning Activities?

Finally, we have to assess the benefit of VGI for disaster management and related urban planning activities. A sound judgment requires scientific investigations on the basis of well-defined criteria describing the additional value VGI is assumed to bring to disaster management. Currently, we lack such investigations and we also lack suitable criteria to evaluate VGI in the application context of disaster management. To develop proper evaluation criteria and to conduct studies that assess the benefit are also relevant topics for further research.

CONCLUSION

In general, volunteered geographic information can be judged as useful additional information source for disaster management. Various examples demonstrate the potential and benefit of VGI to provide suitable information. Although VGI is so far predominately supplied in the response phase of a hazardous event, it also offers potential to support the phases of disaster management concerned with mitigation and preparedness. Volunteers have local knowledge and are often eye witnesses; they can readily identify local changes, shortcomings and deficits. By providing this information they can support urban planning, and contribute either to develop novel protection and rescue measure, or to validate and improve existing ones. In order to extend the utilization of VGI for all phases in disaster management further research is needed. We have to investigate the conditions to efficiently collect VGI. Methods and concepts are required that support extraction of suitable information from all types of VGI, and that ensure good quality of VGI. Finally the benefit of VGI for all phases of disaster management has to be evaluated.

REFERENCES

Bishr, M., & Janowicz, K. (2010). Can we trust information? - The case of volunteered geographic information. In Devaraju, A., Llaves, A., Maué, P., & Keßler, C. (Eds.), *Towards digital earth: Search, discover and share geospatial data*. CEUR-WS.

Bishr, M., & Mantelas, L. (2008). A trust and reputation model for filtering and classifying knowledge about urban growth. *GeoJournal*, *72*(3), 229–237. doi:10.1007/s10708-008-9182-4.

Coast, S. (2011). How OpenStreetMap is changing the world. In Tanaka, K., Fröhlich, P., & Kim, K.-S. (Eds.), *Web and wireless geographical information systems* (p. 4). Berlin, Heidelberg: Springer. doi:10.1007/978-3-642-19173-2_2.

De Longueville, B., Luraschi, G., Smits, P., Peedell, S., & De Groeve, T. (2010). Citizens as sensors for natural hazards: A VGI integration workflow. *Geomatica*, *64*(1), 41–59.

Devillers, R., & Jeansoulin, R. (2006). Spatial data quality: Concepts. In Devillers, R., & Jeansoulin, R. (Eds.), *Fundamentals of spatial data quality* (pp. 31–42). London: ISTE. doi:10.1002/9780470612156.ch2.

Doan, S., Vo, B.-K. H., & Collier, N. (2011). An analysis of Twitter messages in the 2011 Tohoku Earthquake. In *Proceedings of the 4th ICST International Conference on eHealth*. Berlin/Heidelberg: Springer.

Engel, S. R., & Voshell, J. R. Jr. (2002). Volunteer biological monitoring: Can it accurately assess the ecological condition of streams? [Entomological Society of America.]. *American Entomologist*, *48*, 164–177.

Flanagin, A., & Metzger, M. (2008). The credibility of volunteered geographic information. *GeoJournal*, *72*(3), 137–148. doi:10.1007/s10708-008-9188-y.

Fore, L. S., Paulsen, K., & O'Laughlin, K. (2001). Assessing the performance of volunteers in monitoring streams. [Seattle.]. *Freshwater Biology*, *46*(1), 109–123.

Ghose, R. (2001). Use of information technology for community empowerment: Transforming geographic information systems into community information systems. *Transactions in GIS*, *5*(2), 141–163. doi:10.1111/1467-9671.00073.

Goodchild, M. F. (2007). Citizens as sensors: The world of volunteered geography. *GeoJournal*, *69*(4), 211–221. doi:10.1007/s10708-007-9111-y.

Goodchild, M. F. (2008). *Assertion and authority: The science of user-generated geographic content.* Paper presented at the Colloquium for Andrew U. Frank's 60th Birthday, Vienna.

Goodchild, M. F., & Glennon, J. A. (2010). Crowdsourcing geographic information for disaster response: A research frontier. *International Journal of Digital Earth*, *3*(3), 231–241. doi:10.1080/17538941003759255.

Gouveia, C., Fonseca, A., Câmara, A., & Ferreira, F. (2004). Promoting the use of environmental data collected by concerned citizens through information and communication technologies. *Journal of Environmental Management*, *71*(2), 135–154. doi:10.1016/j.jenvman.2004.01.009 PMID:15135948.

Guo, Q., Liu, Y., & Wieczorek, J. (2008). Georeferencing locality descriptions and computing associated uncertainty using a probabilistic approach. *International Journal of Geographical Information Science*, *22*(10), 1067–1090. doi:10.1080/13658810701851420.

Haklay, M. (2010). How good is volunteered geographical information? A comparative study of OpenStreetMap and Ordinance Survey datasets. *Environment and Planning. B, Planning & Design*, *37*(4), 682–703. doi:10.1068/b35097.

Hall, G., Chipeniuk, R., Feick, R., Leahy, M., & Deparday, V. (2010). Community-based production of geographic information using open source software and Web 2.0. *International Journal of Geographical Information Science*, *24*(5), 761–781. doi:10.1080/13658810903213288.

Harding, J. (2006). Vector data quality: A data provider's perspective. In Devillers, R., & Jeansoulin, R. (Eds.), *Fundamentals of spatial data quality* (pp. 141–159). London: ISTE. doi:10.1002/9780470612156.ch8.

Heverin, T., & Zach, L. (2010). Microblogging for crisis communication: Examination of Twitter use in response to a 2009 violent crisis in Seattle-Tacoma. Washington Area. In *Proceedings of the Seventh International Information Systems for Crisis Response and Management Conference.*

Hill, L. L. (2000). *Core elements of digital gazetteers: Placenames, categories, and footprints.* Paper presented at the Proceedings of the 4th European Conference on Research and Advanced Technology for Digital Libraries.

Hurlock, J., & Wilson, M. L. (2011). Searching twitter: Separating the tweet from the chaff. In L. A. Adamic, R. A. Baeza-Yates, & S. Counts (Eds.), *Proceedings of the Fifth International Conference on Weblogs and Social Media.* Menlo Park: The AAAI Press.

Jones, C. B., Purves, R. S., Clough, P. D., & Joho, H. (2008). Modelling vague places with knowledge from the Web. *International Journal of Geographical Information Science, 22*(10), 1045–1065. doi:10.1080/13658810701850547.

Josang, A., Ismail, R., & Boyd, C. (2007). A survey of trust and reputation systems for online service provision. *Decision Support Systems, 43*(2), 618–644. doi:10.1016/j. dss.2005.05.019.

Kaplan, A. M., & Haenlein, M. (2010). Users of the world, unite! The challenges and opportunities of Social Media. [Elsevier.]. *Business Horizons, 53*(1), 59–68. doi:10.1016/j. bushor.2009.09.003.

Kreibich, H., Poser, K., & Haubrock, S. (2008). *Web-based data acquisition of flood affected people.* Paper presented at General Assembly European Geosciences Union, Vienna.

Lucas, C. (2012). Multi-criteria modelling and clustering of spatial information. *International Journal of Geographical Information Science,* 1–19.

McDougall, K. (2011). Using volunteered information to map the Queensland Floods. In *Proceedings of the Surveying & Spatial Sciences Conference 2011.* Wellington.

Mendoza, M., Poblete, B., & Castillo, C. (2010). Twitter under crisis: Can we trust what we RT? In *1st Workshop on Social Media Analytics (SOMA '10).* New York: ACM Press.

Mummidi, L., & Krumm, J. (2008). Discovering points of interest from users' map annotations. *GeoJournal, 72*(3-4), 215–227. doi:10.1007/ s10708-008-9181-5.

Okolloh, O. (2009). Ushahidi, or "testimony": Web 2.0 tools for crowdsourcing crisis information. Participatory Learning and Action, 59(1), 65–70. London: International Institute for Environment and Development & Technical Centre for Agricultural and Rural Cooperation ACP-EU.

Poser, K., & Dransch, D. (2010). Volunteered geographic information for disaster management with application to rapid flood damage estimation. *Geomatica, 64*(1), 89–98.

Poser, K., Kreibich, H., & Dransch, D. (2009). *Assessing volunteered geographic information for rapid flood damage estimation.* Paper presented at the 12th AGILE International Conference on Geographic Information Science, Hannover.

Qu, Y., Huang, C., Zhang, P., & Zhang, J. (2011). Harnessing social media in response to major disasters. In *CSCW 2011 Workshop: Designing Social and Collaborative Systems for China.* Hangzhou.

Roche, S., Propeck-Zimmermann, E., & Merics-kay, B. (2011). GeoWeb and crisis management: Issues and perspectives of volunteered geographic information. [Springer Netherlands.]. *GeoJournal*, 1–20.

Sbarra, P., Tosi, P., & De Rubeis, V. (2010). Web-based macroseismic survey in Italy: Method validation and results. *Natural Hazards, 54*(2), 563–581. doi:10.1007/s11069-009-9488-7.

Sieber, R. (2006). Public participation geographic information systems: A literature review and framework. [Taylor & Francis Group.]. *Annals of the Association of American Geographers. Association of American Geographers, 96*(3), 491–507. doi:10.1111/j.1467-8306.2006.00702.x.

Starbird, K. (2011). *Digital volunteerism during disaster: Crowdsourcing information processing*. Paper presented at the CHI '11 Workshop on Crowdsourcing and Human Computation at the 2011 Conference on Human Factors in Computing Systems (CHI 2011). Vancouver.

Sultana, P., Thompson, P., & Green, C. (2007). Can England LEARN LESSONS from Bangladesh in introducing participatory floodplain management? *Water Resources Management, 22*(3), 357–376. doi:10.1007/s11269-007-9166-z.

Sutton, J., Palen, L., & Shklovski, I. (2008). Backchannels on the front lines: Emergent uses of social media in the 2007 southern California wildfires. Proceedings of the *5th International ISCRAM Conference* (pp. 624–632).

Wald, D., Quitoriano, V., Worden, C., Hopper, M., & Dewey, J. (2011). USGS "Did You Feel It?" Internet-based macroseismic intensity maps. *Annals of Geophysics, 54*(6).

Weiner, D., & Harris, T. M. (2003). Community-integrated GIS for land reform in South Africa. *URISA Journal, 15*(2), 61–73.

Wieczorek, J., Guo, Q., & Hijmans, R. (2004). The point-radius method for georeferencing locality descriptions and calculating associated uncertainty. *International Journal of Geographical Information Science, 18*(8), 745–767. doi:10.1080/13658810412331280211.

Zielstra, D., & Zipf, A. (2010). *A comparative study of proprietary geodata and volunteered geographic information for Germany*. Paper presented at the 13th AGILE International Conference on Geographic Information Science, Guimarães.

Zook, M., Graham, M., Shelton, T., & Gorman, S. (2010). Volunteered geographic information and crowdsourcing disaster relief: A case study of the Haitian Earthquake. *World Medical & Health Policy, 2*(2), 6–32. doi:10.2202/1948-4682.1069.

ADDITIONAL READING

Barkowsky, T. (2001). Mental processing of geographic knowledge. In D. R. Montello (Ed.), *International Conference on Spatial Information Theory: Foundations of Geographic Information Science* (pp. 371-386). London: Springer-Verlag.

Bateman, J. A., Hois, J., Ross, R., & Tenbrink, T. (2010). A linguistic ontology of space for natural language processing. *Artificial Intelligence, 174*(14), 1027–1071. doi:10.1016/j.artint.2010.05.008.

Bloch, I. (2009). *Fuzzy and bipolar mathematical morphology, applications in spatial reasoning*. Paper presented at the Proceedings of the 10th European Conference on Symbolic and Quantitative Approaches to Reasoning with Uncertainty.

De Longueville, B., Annoni, A., Schade, S., Ostlaender, N., & Whitmore, C. (2010). Digital earth's nervous system for crisis events: Real-time sensor web enablement of volunteered geographic information. *International Journal of Digital Earth, 3*(3), 242–259. doi:10.1080/17538947.2 010.484869.

De Longueville, B., Smith, R. S., & Luraschi, G. (2009). OMG, from here, I can see the flames!: A use case of mining location based social networks to acquire spatio-temporal data on forest fires. In *Proceedings of the 2009 International Workshop on Location Based Social Networks (LBSN '09)* (pp. 73–80). New York: ACM.

Dehak, S. M. R., Bloch, I., & Maitre, H. (2005). Spatial reasoning with incomplete information on relative positioning. *IEEE Transactions on Pattern Analysis and Machine Intelligence, 27*(9), 1473–1484. doi:10.1109/TPAMI.2005.186 PMID:16173189.

Dilo, A., de By, R. A., & Stein, A. (2007). A system of types and operators for handling vague spatial objects. *International Journal of Geographical Information Science, 21*(4), 397–426. doi:10.1080/13658810601037096.

Du, S., & Guo, L. (2010). Modeling and querying approximate direction relations. *ISPRS Journal of Photogrammetry and Remote Sensing, 65*(4), 328–340. doi:10.1016/j.isprsjprs.2010.03.001.

Egenhofer, M., & Mark, D. (1995). Naive geography. In Frank, A., & Kuhn, W. (Eds.), *Spatial information theory: A theoretical basis for GIS* (pp. 1–15). Springer-Verlag. doi:10.1007/3-540-60392-1_1.

Elwood, S. (2008). Volunteered geographic information: Key questions, concepts and methods to guide emerging research and practice. *GeoJournal, 72*(3-4), 133–135. doi:10.1007/s10708-008-9187-z.

Gouveia, C., & Fonseca, A. (2008). New approaches to environmental monitoring: The use of ICT to explore volunteered geographic information. *GeoJournal, 72*(3), 185–197. doi:10.1007/s10708-008-9183-3.

Gouveia, C., Fonseca, A., Camara, A., & Ferreira, F. (2004). Promoting the use of environmental data collected by concerned citizens through information and communication technologies. *Journal of Environmental Management, 71*, 135–154. doi:10.1016/j.jenvman.2004.01.009 PMID:15135948.

Guy, M., Earle, P., Ostrum, C., Gruchalla, K., & Horvath, S. (2010). Integration and dissemination of citizen reported and seismically derived earthquake information via social network technologies. In Cohen, P., Adams, N., & Berthold, M. (Eds.), *Advances in intelligent data analysis IX* (pp. 42–53). Berlin, Heidelberg: Springer. doi:10.1007/978-3-642-13062-5_6.

Hughes, A., & Palen, L. (2009). Twitter adoption and use in mass convergence and emergency events. *International Journal of Emergency Management, 6*(3), 248–260. doi:10.1504/IJEM.2009.031564.

Spinsanti, L., & Ostermann, F. (2011). Retrieve volunteered geographic information for forest fire. In *Proceedings of the 2nd Italian Information Retrieval (IIR) Workshop*. Milan.

Sun, H. (2008). Computational models for computing fuzzy cardinal directional relations between regions. *Knowledge-Based Systems, 21*(7), 599–603. doi:10.1016/j.knosys.2008.03.017.

Tenbrink, T. (2005). *Localising objects and events: Discoursal applicability conditions for spatiotemporal expressions in English and German*. University of Bremen.

Xu, W., & Zlatanova, S. (2007). Ontologies for disaster management response. In Li, Zlatanova, & Fabbri (Eds.), Geomatics solutions for disaster management (pp. 185-200). Springer Berlin/Heidelberg.

KEY TERMS AND DEFINITIONS

Content-Sharing Platform: As one form of Social media content-sharing platforms are web-based systems for sharing different kind of content, especially images, video, text or audio. Users submit their files to the platform and assign permissions for viewing to closed user groups, individual users or public. Many platforms support geotagging of uploaded content. Well known examples are YouTube for videos or Flickr for photos.

Crowd-Map: A crowd-map is an interactive map based on a crowd-sourcing approach. Volunteers provide geospatial data about a certain topic such as infrastructure facilities or incidents in case of a natural disaster. This data will be visualized in a crowd-map. Best known projects are "OpenStreetMap" and "Crowdmap."

Crowd-Sourcing: Crowd-sourcing is a concept of outsourcing a task to a distributed group of people ("the crowd"). It is used to accomplish tasks, find solutions for problems, or to gather information. In form of an open call for solutions, the problems are broadcasted to an unknown or anonymous group of solvers. Accordingly crowd-sourcing is usually web-based, respectively coordinated by using the internet. The best known projects are "Wikipedia" and "Wiktionary."

Human Sensor (also termed Citizen Sensor): A human who uses one or more of his senses to observe his environment and reports his observations in near-real time. According to Goodchild (2007), citizens form a network with over 6 billion components, which can freely move around and cannot only observe their environment, but also use their intelligence and experience to synthesize and interpret their observations.

Microblog: A type of webblog, which message size is limited. Messages are usually either private or broadcasted public visible for all users. They can consist of abbreviated text-messages, but can also include internet-links to further content. The topics of these messages ranges from simple status updates like "Earthquake right now here in LA." to complex statements e.g. about the Arab Spring. Most prominent representative for a microblog-service is Twitter.

Social Media: Internet-based platforms and services like wikis, internet forums, weblogs or social networks with focus on human communication. Social media also support creation and dissemination of user generated content in different media types like images, videos or text. Famous examples are Wikipedia, Twitter or Facebook.

Volunteered: Geographic Information (VGI): Geographic or geo-referenced information collected and made available to others through the voluntary activity of individuals or groups. VGI comes in many forms like geotagged images or microblogging messages shared on services like Flickr or Twitter. Further examples are more specific descriptions of geographic entities on content-sharing platforms such as Wikimapia or fully fledged public-domain geospatial data layers produced by volunteers such as OpenStreetMap.

Weblog/Blog: A web-based diary or journal where one or more authors publish articles about single or multiple topics either of personal subjects, or public interest. Often, readers of a weblog can leave comments for each article; this makes blogging a form of social networking. Weblogs are not limited to textual content, also allow to focus on they also include photos (photoblogs), video (so called "vlogs") or audio (podcasts).

Chapter 8
Urban Geo-Wiki:
A Crowdsourcing Tool to Improve Urban Land Cover

Linda See
International Institute for Applied Systems Analysis (IIASA), Austria

Franziska Albrecht
International Institute for Applied Systems Analysis (IIASA), Austria

Steffen Fritz
International Institute for Applied Systems Analysis (IIASA), Austria

Ian McCallum
International Institute for Applied Systems Analysis (IIASA), Austria

Christoph Perger
International Institute for Applied Systems Analysis (IIASA), Austria

Dmitry Schepaschenko
International Institute for Applied Systems Analysis (IIASA), Austria

Marijn Van der Velde
International Institute for Applied Systems Analysis (IIASA), Austria

Michael Obersteiner
International Institute for Applied Systems Analysis (IIASA), Austria

Christian Schill
University of Freiburg, Germany

ABSTRACT

Crowdsourcing is one mechanism for undertaking e-participation. This chapter considers the broader issues of crowdsourcing in the context of citizen participation and governance, illustrated with a case study in which citizens are used to validate global maps of urban extent. Urban extent is an important source of information for a range of applications related to urban planning and governance such as hazard management, food security, health and climate change. Although different products are available that map urban areas or human settlements at a global scale, they disagree in terms of both total urban extent and the spatial distribution of urban areas.

DOI: 10.4018/978-1-4666-4169-3.ch008

Samples of the urban extent from three major cities (London, Beijing and São Paulo), in areas where three recent global land cover maps disagree, are validated using data from a crowdsourcing campaign undertaken with the Geo-Wiki crowdsourcing tool. The results show that crowdsourcing has the potential to contribute to the validation of existing products of urban extent and could help users of these products to determine which map to use in a given location. More accurate information on urban extent will lead to better urban models and improved decision making, which will ultimately affect the future of a growing urban population. However, issues of sustainability, crowd retention and data quality remain challenging areas that require further research in the field of crowdsourcing.

INTRODUCTION

Urban areas contain 51% of the world's population or 3.5 billion people. This will increase to 6.3 billion by 2050 (UN, 2010). Asia and Africa have roughly 40% of urban dwellers compared to other continents but by 2050 this number will rise to more than 60% where both continents will have the highest number of urban dwellers in absolute terms, i.e. 3.4 and 1.2 billion people, respectively. These trajectories have radical implications for urban planning and sustainable resource use in the future, particularly in the developing world. Urban areas are also the largest generators of greenhouse gas (GHG) emissions where the likely future effects of climate change include millions of displaced people, shortage of water, and increased risk of flooding due to sea level rise and other climatic changes (UN-HABITAT, 2011). It is therefore necessary to know the spatial extent of urban areas in order to accurately assess GHG emissions, formulate actions for GHG reductions and promote future sustainable development.

Global urban extent is provided by remotely-sensed global land cover products. Urban land cover (or built-up or artificial surfaces) is one of the land cover classes in the GLC-2000 (Fritz et al., 2003), MODIS (Friedl et al., 2002) and GlobCover (Bicheron et al., 2008) land cover maps. When these different products are compared, significant amounts of spatial disagreement become evident (Potere & Schneider, 2009; Fritz et al., 2011c). What is needed is a much higher volume of validation data in order to truly understand how accurate

different land cover products are, not only in urban areas but for land cover more generally. This can guide the choice of which product to use in which region. The use of Google Earth for validation has already been incorporated into the validation process of both GlobCover 2009 (Bontemps et al., 2010) and a global map of rainfed agriculture (Biradar et al., 2009), which employed a small number of experts. However, due to resource implications in collecting validation data, one solution to this problem is to use crowdsourcing (Howe, 2006) or volunteered geographic information (Goodchild, 2008), which could be used as a form of citizen e-participation. The term crowdsourcing integrates the words 'crowd' and 'outsourcing,' where citizens participate by collecting information and analyzing data. Crowdsourcing actually predates the internet and includes competitions that involve the crowd in solving a problem, e.g. designing a logo or a historical example such as the Longitude Prize in which individuals were asked to design an instrument to measure longitude (Sobel, 1995). However, in the current context, crowdsourcing is generally taken to mean participation via an online or mobile environment as a result of technological advances such as Web 2.0 and the proliferation of mobile phones. Examples of successful crowdsourcing can be found in the literature (e.g. Silverton, 2009; Khatib et al., 2011) but there is not yet any large scale example of the crowdsourcing of urban extent. The aim of this chapter is to discuss crowdsourcing in the broader context of validating global urban land cover and to demonstrate how such an e-participatory approach can help determine which global land cover product to use based on a case study involving three major cities. The development towards a hybrid product is also discussed. Crowdsourcing in this context may help to improve the basic information needed for future urban planning and assessment at the global scale.

VALIDATING URBAN EXTENT THROUGH CROWDSOURCING

Background

This section provides a review of two key areas that are relevant to validating global data on urban extent. The first is a historical overview of urban mapping at the global scale and the work that has been undertaken to date in comparing products that characterize urban areas. The second review covers crowdsourcing, which can be used as a type of citizen e-participation.

History of Urban Mapping

Global mapping of urban areas via remote sensing is a relatively new development. Before remote sensing products became available for mapping land cover and other environmental parameters, the first global urban map was developed as part of the Digital Chart of the World (DCW), also referred to as the Vector Map Level Zero (Danko, 1992). Urban areas and human settlements were digitized as polygons from paper maps and integrated into this product, which was available from the 1960s until the 1990s. The DCW was also used for urban areas in the first set of global land cover maps that employed the AVHRR sensor, which was developed by the United States Geological Survey, the University of Nebraska-Lincoln and the Joint Research Centre of the European Commission (Latham et al., 2009). Since then, a range of different sensors have been used in land cover mapping. The three most recent land cover

products, i.e. the GLC-2000 (Fritz et al., 2003), MODIS v.5 (Friedl et al., 2010) and GlobCover 2005/2009 (Bicheron et al., 2008; Bontemps et al., 2010) have an urban class. A more specific urban product has also been developed from MODIS at a resolution of 1 km (Schneider et al., 2003) and 500m (Schneider et al., 2009; 2010), which uses stratification by ecoregion prior to classification.

Imhoff et al. (1997) document early attempts to map urban areas using the Meteorological Satellite Program's Operation Linescan System (DMSP-OLS) nighttime imagery, which is available to download from NOAA (2011). Nighttime lights have subsequently been used as an input to other relevant products, e.g. the LandScan global population database developed by Oak Ridge National Laboratory (ORNL) (Dobson, 2003; ORNL, 2011). Census data of average or ambient populations have been redistributed to 1km grid squares where the ambient population takes into account the movements of people through their daily travel patterns. The DMSP-OLS and Land-Scan datasets have been used together to create two further products: (i) FAO's Poverty Mapping Urban Rural (PMUR) database (FAO, 2005; 2006); and (ii) the Global Impervious Surface Area Map (IMPSA) (Elvidge et al., 2007). The Global Rural Urban Mapping Project (GRUMP) also combined a number of population and remote sensing products to create a 1 km raster population dataset (CIESIN, 2004). Finally, a historical population dataset (HYDE – History Database of the Global Environment) was created from 1700 to 2000 at a 10 km resolution (Goldewijk, 2005) to examine land use change in the past. Using thresholds, these population datasets can be used to map urban areas.

Some recent attempts have been undertaken to compare the different urban maps, e.g. Potere and Schneider (2009) compared eight global maps that contain urban areas and found that they differed by as much as an order of magnitude in their estimates of urban areas, i.e. 0.72 to 3.52 million km^2. Fritz et al. (2011c) showed that when comparing the GLC-2000, MODIS and GlobCover, agreement in the urban domain was less than 30% when comparing pairs of maps. Mapping of urban extent using remote sensing is recognized as a difficult task for a number of reasons and may explain why the differences between these products are so large. These include: the use of coarse resolution satellite imagery to capture what are often small and fragmented urban areas; the heterogeneous landscapes that comprise urban areas both spatially and spectrally; the lack of a standard definition of urban areas; geolocation errors; the rapid urbanization that diminishes the accuracy of any global data set in this domain; and differences in the methodologies and approaches used to develop these products (Herold, 2009; Potere & Schneider, 2009). An accuracy assessment of these global products is currently underway in which a larger set of validation data will be used, which will allow for a greater understanding of the accuracy on a regional basis (Potere & Schneider, 2009). Crowdsourcing provides one mechanism for increasing the volume of validation data that would aid in these types of global accuracy assessments.

Crowdsourcing

Crowdsourcing is driven by the need to perform a set of tasks, which can range from data collection and analysis to problem solving. In crowdsourcing, these tasks are undertaken by the crowd or ordinary citizens. Unlike paid employment, the crowd is technically anonymous and crowdsourcing has the potential to draw in much larger numbers of individuals than would be possible by a single company, which is why crowdsourcing is also used as one type of business model of employment. The tasks required of the crowd can be performed offline or online but crowdsourcing has generally moved into an online environment, particularly with advances in Web 2.0 technology and the proliferation of mobile telephones. The idea of crowdsourcing is based upon the 'wisdom

of the crowd' in which the collective knowledge of individuals has been shown to be better than that of a single individual. This principle has been illustrated using very simple examples such as guessing the number of jelly beans in a jar or the weight of an ox (Surowiecki, 2004).

Citizen e-participation is a much narrower field than crowdsourcing, where e-participation refers to the use of information and communication technologies to allow citizens to interact with each other and with politicians and governing bodies. A goal of e-participation is to allow citizens to influence decision making and other processes of governance. Crowdsourcing has a potential role as a type of e-participation for urban governance if the tasks are focused on providing or analyzing data related to urban decision making, and the crowdsourcing environment allows some kind of interaction with the decision maker, even if indirectly through improving key data inputs that go into the policy process.

Many examples of crowdsourcing are focused on the collection of in-situ or ground truth data, e.g. the identification of a species. The eBird project (Marris, 2010) represents a very successful application in which volunteers have contributed more than 40 million georeferenced bird sightings online, which are then used for scientific research. Such an example is successful because bird watching has long been of interest to large numbers of individuals so bringing these interests together through a single platform has resulted in a thriving online community connected through a common interest. Crowdsourcing is also used to gather large amounts of information about a particular subject, analogous to a large social survey. The difference is that information in social surveys is generally collected via a sampling strategy to obtain a representative sample of the population. Crowdsourcing, on the other hand, opens up the data collection process to a much wider, self-selecting audience. This immediately raises issues of bias in the data, depending upon how the data are subsequently used. An analysis of

OpenStreetMap in Germany, for example, showed that there are many more contributions in urban areas than rural (Neis et al., 2012). Other types of crowdsourcing include voting by the crowd when developing, for example, a new product or brand, or solving very specific problems. A good example of the latter approach is using the crowd to unravel protein structures through the FoldIt protein folding game. This application has led to significant scientific discoveries published in high level journals (e.g. Khatib et al., 2011).

A more recent innovation in crowdsourcing coupled with problem solving is through events called hackathons. These take place over a concentrated period of time, e.g. a weekend, and groups of individuals form teams to solve very specific problems both face-to-face and online. These types of events could also be considered as a type of e-participation, depending upon the nature of the problem. For example, a hackathon was held in December 2010 to analyze data from EuroStat on energy use in the EU to determine whether emissions targets were being met while future hackathons include tracking the interests and money flows of lobbyists that affect European policy and one on the analysis of EU data concerning fish subsidies. Although the participants are generally highly skilled, they are still self-selecting members of the public interested in becoming involved in issues of broader societal significance. The disadvantage of these types of events is that they require a reasonable amount of organization, funding and effort to recruit individuals. There is also no guarantee that any usable results will be generated or any evidence of whether the solutions have subsequently been adopted. However, this type of event is clearly gaining momentum as evidenced by the number of such events advertised online.

Crowdsourcing of data clearly has a real advantage in terms of the volumes of data that have and could potentially be collected in the future. There are, however, a number of disadvantages associated with this approach, namely the need to ensure both data quality and sustainability. Data quality has a fundamental impact on the subsequent use of the data for research. The quality of crowdsourced data has been questioned in the past (Flanagin & Metzger, 2008), and has only started to be addressed in the literature very recently in quantitative terms (e.g. Haklay et al., 2010; Haklay, 2010; Zielstra & Zipf, 2010). This is an issue that requires considerable attention, particularly if validation data are to be shared and used for other validation exercises in the future.

Ensuring sustainability is another non-trivial aspect of crowdsourcing. Building up a community to begin with can take considerable time and energy but ensuring long term sustainability in participation is even harder. Motivations for participation can range from having a genuine interest in the project or the internet more generally, whether the project is fun to do, the desire to make your mark upon a project or various other incentives (Goodchild, 2007b). A recent survey by Wiggins (2012) revealed which set of incentives are offered by different citizen science sites: the receipt of free training, equipment, certificates, t-shirts and other promotional materials; the presence of a ranking list so that progress against others can be monitored; provision of information about personal performance; public acknowledgement of contributions; advancement through a hierarchy of levels, e.g. from novice to expert; privileges associated with editing and moderating contributions; co-authorship on scientific publications; and the staging of events that demonstrate contributor appreciation. Thus it is clear that motivation is a key issue in crowdsourcing.

Crowdsourcing has also been criticized from an ethical point of view when it has been used as a cheap source of labor. For example, the money paid to individuals from undertaking tasks through Amazon's Mechanical Turk are not subject to any minimum wage and such a crowdsourcing system is therefore considered as an exploitation of individuals (Silberman et al., 2010). This exploitation argument is less relevant in citizen e-participation since citizens are willingly contributing their time to a cause they believe in, especially if they can see a tangible outcome from their participation. A good example is GeoPedia, which has been developed by the Slovenian company Sinergise as a crowdsourcing platform. One of their applications uses the crowd to identify waste dump sites, which then obliges the authorities to act, which has resulted in a positive and visible improvement to the landscape (Milčinski, 2011). Other ethical issues surrounding crowdsourcing include the potential for using this technology for unethical behavior such as identify theft, e.g. paying people small fees to crack passwords and bypass other mechanisms to screen out automated robots from gathering information such as CAPTCHA, or providing false reviews using an 'attack and run' technique (Harris, 2011).

Despite these shortcomings, the validation of global land cover is a prime candidate for crowdsourcing. High resolution satellite imagery is available for much of the globe but particularly in urban areas (Google, 2011). Land cover is a crucial input to many models and decision making processes, so the scientific value of improving this information is extremely high. The next section describes one branch of the Geo-Wiki crowdsourcing tools: urban geo-wiki.

USING URBAN GEO-WIKI TO VALIDATE URBAN EXTENT IN THREE CITIES

Overview of the Tool

The Urban Geo-Wiki tool can be accessed from urban.geo-wiki.org (Figure 1). Urban Geo-Wiki is one branch of a number of different Geo-Wiki crowdsourcing tools. Other branches include: agriculture, biomass, coffee, human impact and a competition branch from which the latest

Figure 1. The urban.geo-wiki.org crowdsourcing tool

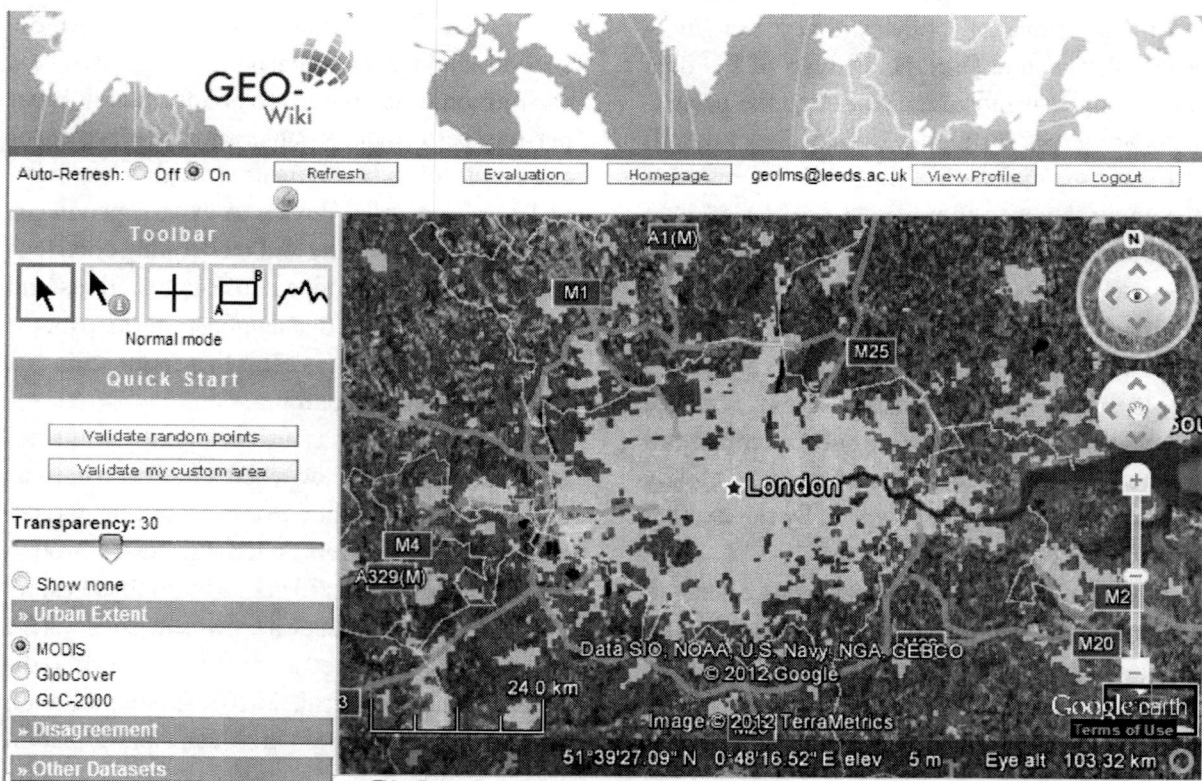

crowdsourcing campaigns are run. All of the Geo-Wiki branches including the urban one can be accessed via guest privilege but registration is recommended because validations are stored with user details. In this way users can download their own validations or the anonymous validations of others. A single registration is required and access is then provided to all the branches unless specific restrictions apply.

Once registered and logged on, Geo-Wiki will display a message if the Google Earth plug-in has not been installed. This plug-in is freely available and the user will be guided through the installation process in a seamless manner. This step will only be required the very first time that the application is launched. From then on, the user will be pre-

sented with the option to view existing maps of urban land cover or view maps of disagreement between pairs of global land cover maps draped on top of Google Earth (Figure 2).

The technical design of Geo-Wiki and a more detailed overview of the tool are provided in Fritz et al. (2012) while further information about the urban-based tool is provided in Fritz et al. (2011c).

At present there are more than 1,200 registered users of Geo-Wiki. Some initial success with increasing the amount of validations on the site was achieved by running competitions advertised during the IGARSS (International Geoscience and Remote Sensing Society) conference in 2010 and at IIASA during the Young Summer Scientists Program, with a digital camera as the incentive

Figure 2. Display of the disagreement layer in urban.geo-wiki.org, which compares urban extent in the MODIS v.5 and GLC-2000 global land cover products

for participation. It is clear that these two competitions were advertised to a very selective and skilled audience but no remote sensing skills are actually required to participate. Training materials were available with many different examples of image interpretation. The latter competition led to a database of cropland validation points for Africa at latitude-longitude intersections, which was subsequently used in the validation of an African cropland map produced by Fritz et al. (2011a). Four subsequent competitions have since generated more than 200,000 validations with a wider audience of participants. This has been achieved by advertising across a broad range of channels. Facebook has also been used as one mechanism of dissemination. Experiences with one of the data collection campaigns and a summary of the findings are documented in more detail in Perger et al. (2012). The data used in this chapter come

from a competition that was launched in February 2012 and focused on validating areas of disagreement, in particular those points where the three global land cover maps (GLC-2000, MODIS v.5 and GlobCover) completely disagree with one another. Users were automatically directed to these disagreement areas and then asked to indicate the primary, secondary and tertiary land cover types by the percentage they occupy in each pixel as applicable. This represented a large improvement over previous competitions where participants were only asked to choose the dominant land cover type. A screenshot of this competition (found at competition.geo-wiki.org) is shown in Figure 3.

As part of the data collection campaign, participants are also asked about the amount of human impact in each pixel along with the confidence in the answers provided. Since the areas of disagreement in this latter competition also included urban

Figure 3. Collection of sub-pixel land cover types in the most recent Geo-Wiki competition targeting areas where the GLC-2000, MODIS v.5 and GlobCover disagree

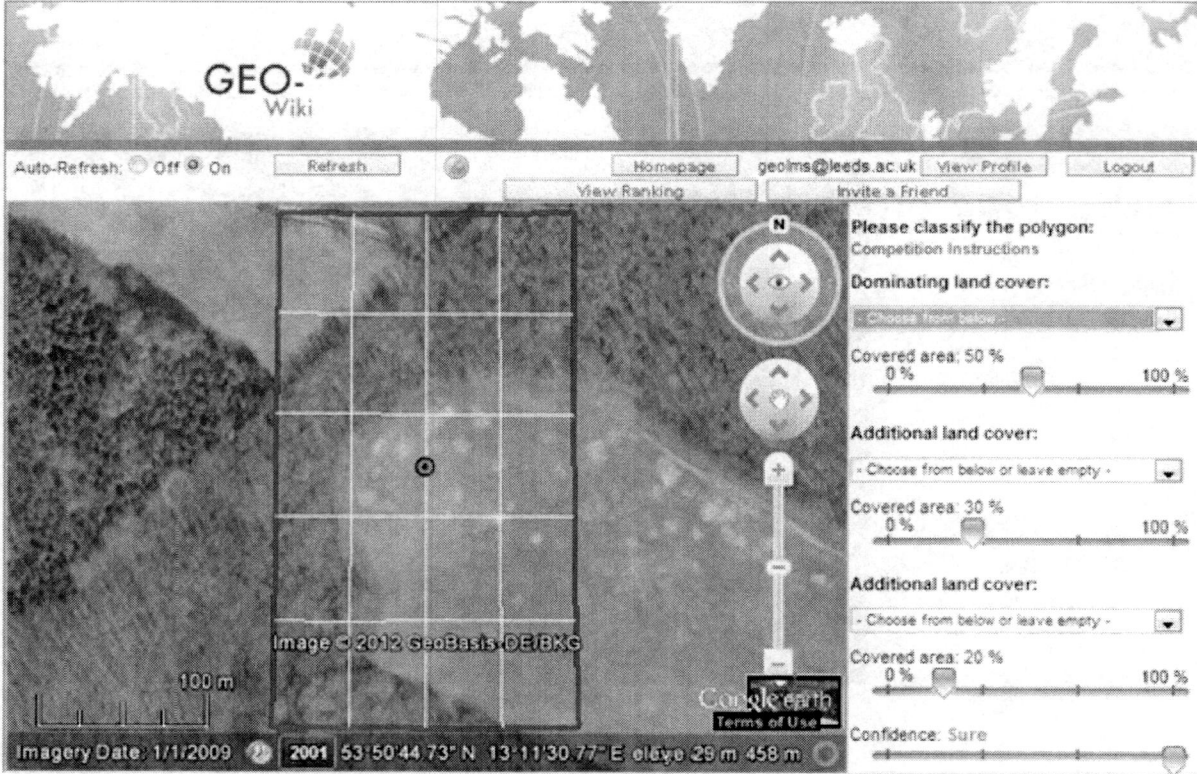

land cover, it was possible to target some of this crowdsourcing effort towards this research as described in the sections that follow.

Case Study

Samples from three cities on three different continents were chosen for validation via crowdsourcing: London, Beijing and São Paulo. The latter two are megacities, i.e. with populations greater than 10 million (Sorensen & Okata, 2011) while London currently has an estimated population of 7.8 million (ONS, 2011). As London has an urban area that continues beyond its official borders, the greater metropolitan area is estimated to have a population of 12.5 million and thus could also be considered a megacity (Marr, 2011). Despite their large size, each of these cities is very different in form and in the way that they have developed over time, providing contrasting areas for analysis. The different land cover types that comprise each city are summarized based on what appears in the three global land cover maps (GLC-2000, MODIS v.5, and GlobCover), and an examination of the spatial disagreement between these products is provided. A sample of each city is then analysed based on the validation points received from the crowdsourcing campaign.

Land Cover Types in Each City

This first analysis establishes the land cover types that comprise each city based on the three global land cover products (GLC-2000, MODIS v.5 and GlobCover), where both GLC-2000 and MODIS v.5 were first resampled to a 300m resolution to match that of GlobCover. Administrative boundaries were used as the basis to clip the land cover images. The city of London is comprised of 33 boroughs, which includes some slightly rural areas within its boundaries. However, it is the smallest of the three cities with Beijing roughly 4.5 times larger and São Paulo two magnitudes larger than London as shown in Table 1. However, this is also a function of where administrative boundaries fall. The actual amount of urban land cover, which is represented by a single class in each global land cover product, is generally similar for London but varies quite substantially for the other two cities depending upon which product is considered. In the case of Beijing, the GLC-2000 has a much lower urban extent than MODIS and GlobCover, while for São Paolo, the GLC-2000 and GlobCover are similar but a magnitude lower than that of MODIS.

Figure 4 shows the distribution of land cover types expressed as a percentage of the overall area represented by the number of pixels that comprises each city. The legends of the global land cover maps are not directly compatible so they have been remapped onto a simple legend with 10 land cover classes. For the city of London (Figure 4a), the land cover products agree that the majority of the city is urban ranging from GLC-2000 at 75% to GlobCover at 66%. Most of the remaining land cover in the city is designated as cropland or tree cover although the products disagree on which, with the GLC-2000 indicating cropland compared to tree cover as reported in GlobCover. MODIS falls somewhere in the middle, providing a mixture of both types. In addition, there are small percentages of other land

Table 1. Number of pixels contained within each city boundary and the urban extent

Land cover	London			Beijing			São Paulo		
	GLC	MODIS	GLOBC	GLC	MODIS	GLOBC	GLC	MODIS	GLOBC
Urban extent (pixels)	19960	18879	17755	5263	23933	21204	18551	112167	18963
Pixels per city	26780			124577			2818903		

Figure 4. The distribution of land cover types contained within the city boundaries of (a) London; (b) Beijing; and (c) São Paulo

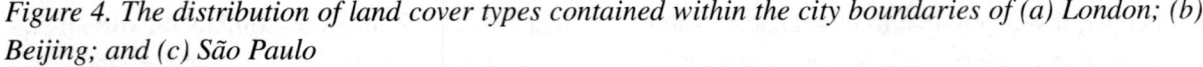

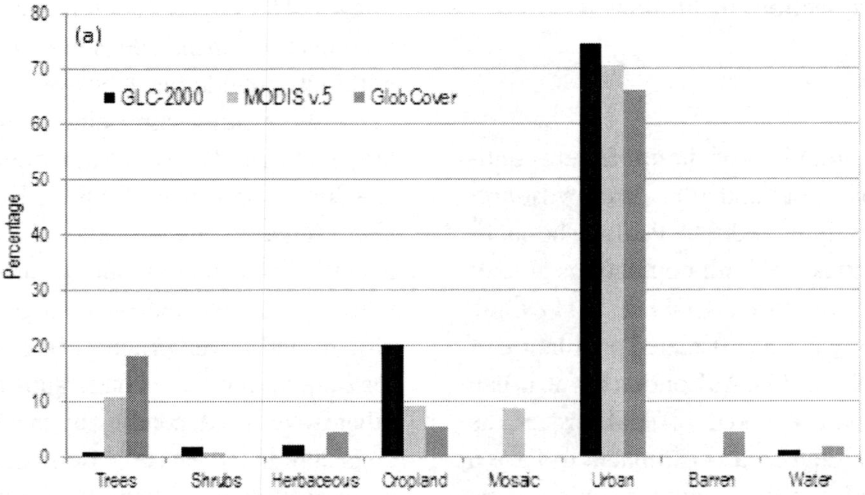

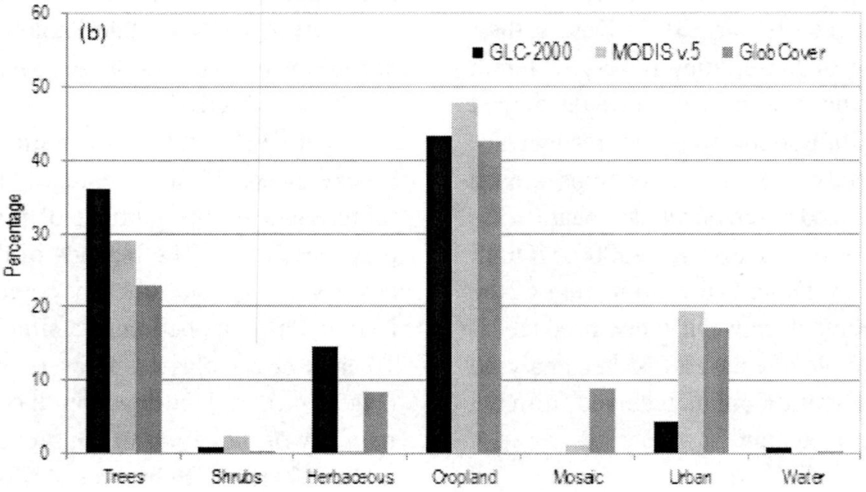

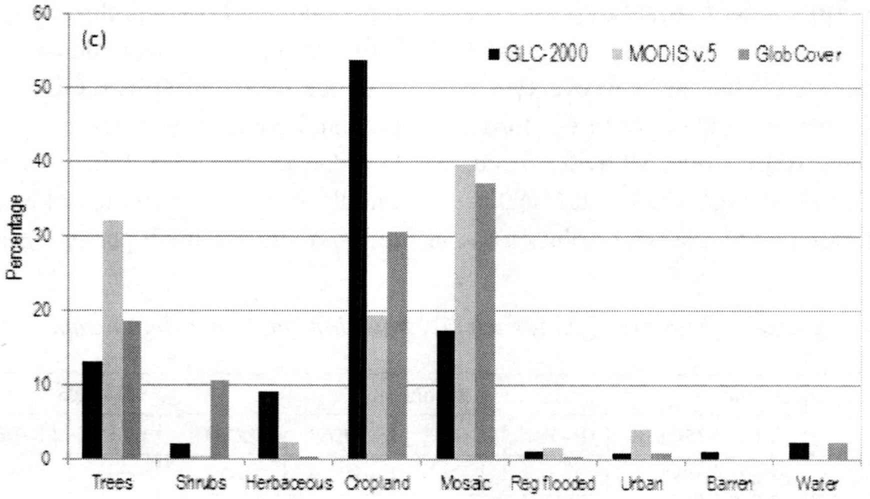

cover types that occur in the city of London. This is in contrast to Beijing and São Paulo, which show that the administrative regions of both cities are much larger than London. As a result, the actual urban core of these cities is much smaller relative to the size of the city. For Beijing (Figure 4b), the urban areas according to MODIS and GlobCover are roughly on the order of 20% of the city but only 4% according to GLC-2000. There is rough agreement that the rest of the city is cropland (43 to 48%) but less agreement on tree cover (23 to 36%) and large disparities on herbaceous, i.e. 15% for GLC-2000 but close to 0% for MODIS. Thus, not only is there disagreement on the urban core, there is also disagreement as to the combination of land covers that make up the rest of the city. For São Paulo (Figure 4c), the urban core is very small relative to the administrative boundaries for the city where the GLC-2000 and GlobCover roughly agree on 0.7% for urban extent while for MODIS it is 4%. Of the remaining land cover types, the GLC-2000 indicates that the majority is cropland (54%) (defined very generically as land cover that contains the presence of agricultural fields regardless of whether it appears in an urban landscape), where both MODIS and GlobCover are in rough agreement that the dominant land cover type is a mosaic of cropland and natural vegetation. Larger differences exist in the tree cover, shrub cover and herbaceous classes. Thus, of all three cities, São Paulo is represented with the most disparity between the three products.

Spatial Disagreement between the Three Global Land Cover Products

The previous analysis considered only the total urban area represented in each global land cover product for each city. This analysis examines the urban disagreement on a spatial basis. Each of the individual global land cover maps was first reclassified such that urban areas were given values of 1 and all other areas were given values of 0.

The maps were then summed, where a value of 3 would indicate that all three maps agree that a given pixel is urban, 2 denotes the agreement of two land cover maps and 1 indicates that only one of the global products reports urban land cover at a given pixel. Values of 0 occur where none of the maps indicate urban but another type of land cover. The results of this map overlay are shown in Figures 5, 6, and 7 for each of the three cities respectively.

Beijing (Figure 6) and São Paulo (Figure 7) show strong agreement between all three land cover maps in the core of the city. For Beijing, as you move away from this core, there is a clear concentric area where only two maps agree and then a peripheral area where only one map indicates urban. This concentric area where two maps agree is much less pronounced in São Paulo. Moreover, some of the areas on the periphery and the lines of urban area radiating away from the core of the city show the clear influence of using night time lights in the development of one of the products. London (Figure 5) shows a more mixed pattern with large continuous areas in which all three maps agree, dotted by areas of disagreement throughout the city. This could be due to the large green spaces or common areas found in London and a more complex land use structure of historical origin. The River Thames, which runs through the centre of London, is also not consistently captured by the three land cover maps and therefore shows up as an area with some disagreement.

The total disagreement in terms of the number of pixels and the percentage of the city is provided in Table 2. For London, the three land cover maps agree 66.6% of the time on urban land cover while this number is much lower for both Beijing (17.2%) and São Paulo (14.9%). Moreover, only one map indicates urban areas more than 50% of the time in both Beijing and São Paulo. Thus, for these cities, the choice of which global land cover product to use in urban-related applications is critical and may have large potential

Figure 5. Comparison of global land cover maps for urban extent in London showing the areas where one, two and three maps indicate urban land cover. The black square shows a sample of London validated by the crowd.

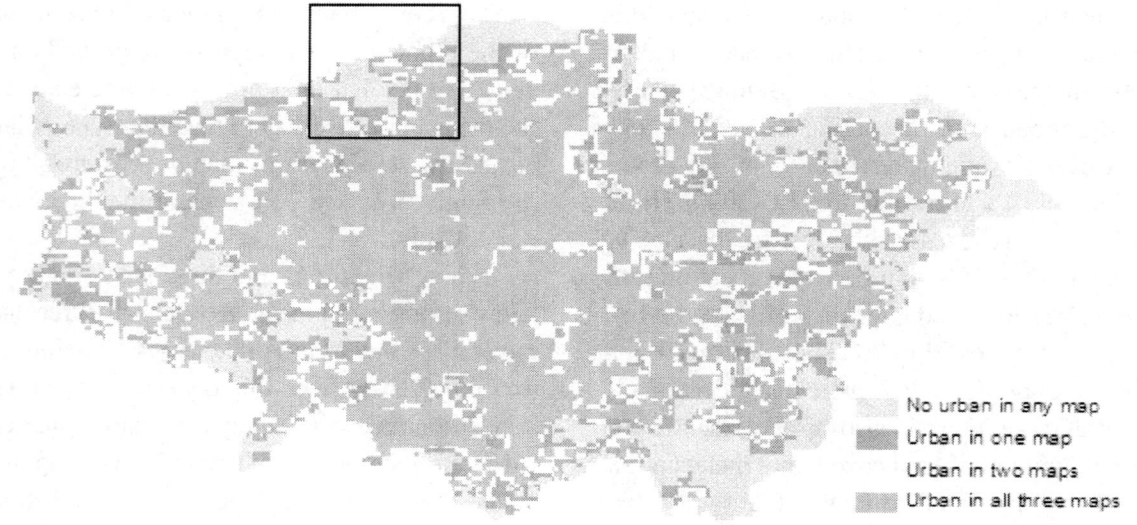

Figure 6. Comparison of global land cover maps for urban extent in Beijing showing the areas where one, two and three maps indicate urban land cover. The black square shows a sample of Beijing validated by the crowd.

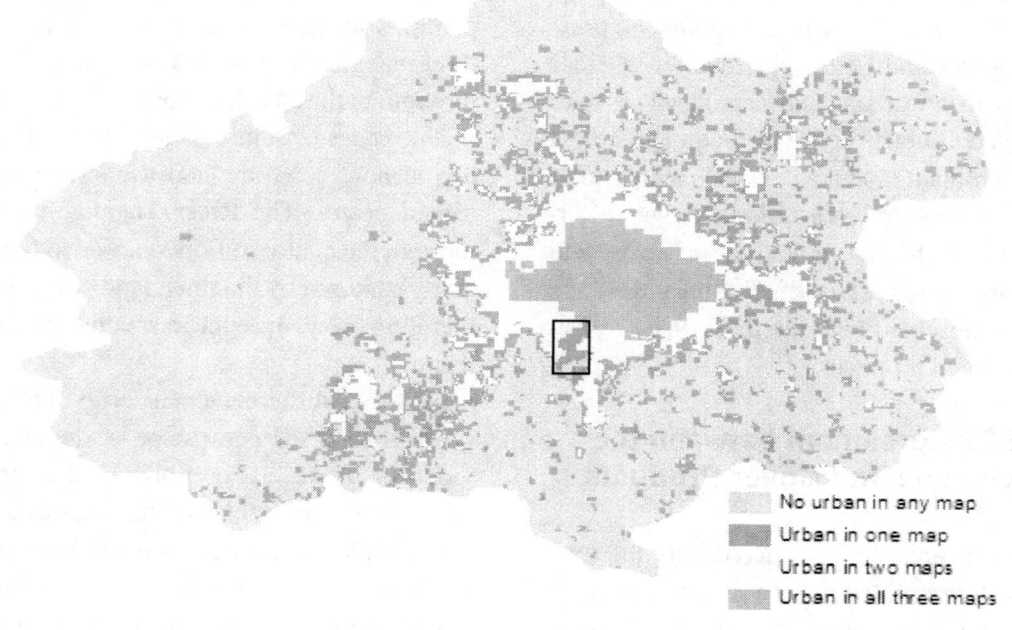

Figure 7. Comparison of global land cover maps for urban extent in São Paulo showing the areas where one, two and three maps indicate urban land cover. The black square shows a sample of São Paulo validated by the crowd.

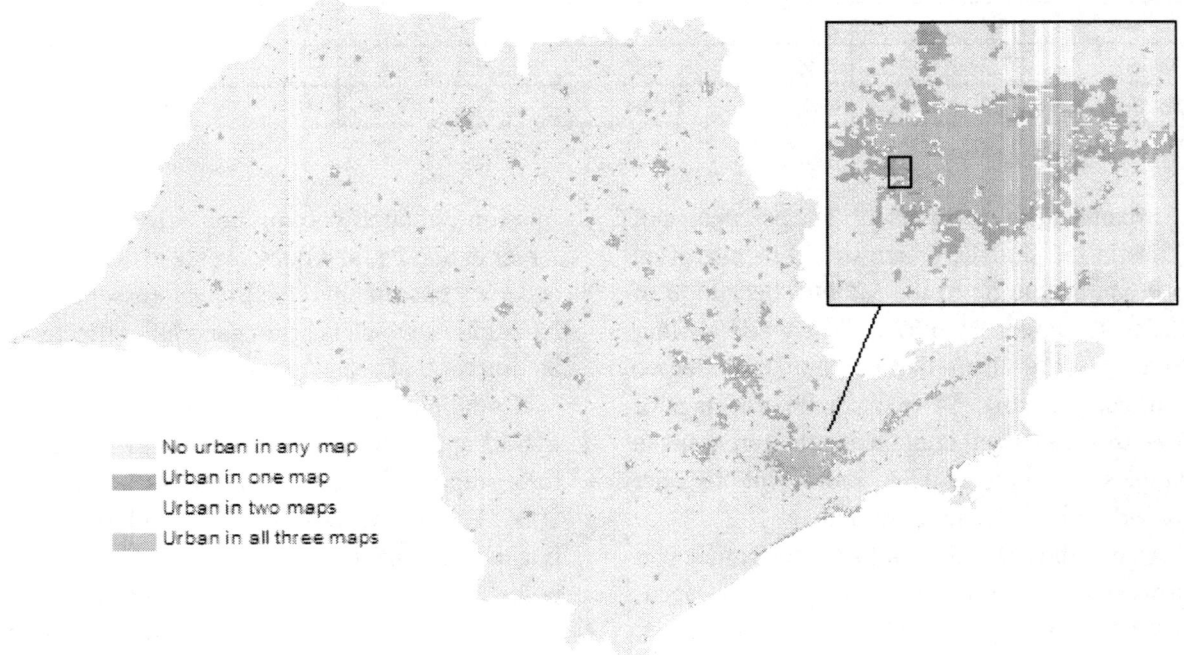

Table 2. *The amount of urban land cover based on comparing the global land cover products*

# of land cover maps with urban	London		Beijing		São Paulo	
	# of pixels	%	# of pixels	%	# of pixels	%
One map urban	3006	13.4	15256	50.5	92286	82.0
Two maps urban	4462	20.0	9757	32.3	3562	3.2
All three urban	14888	66.6	5210	17.2	16757	14.9

effects on the outcome of any data or modeling analysis. This uncertainty in global land cover has already been highlighted in the cropland and forest domains (Fritz et al., 2011b) but the message is equally relevant for urban areas.

Validation of Samples from each City

Black rectangles are displayed in Figures 5 to 7, which indicate the location of the validation samples from the crowd within each city. The samples were taken on the fringes of the urban areas where the disagreement between the maps is the largest. Validations were collected for all pixels in these three samples, where each validation contains the percentage of the dominant, secondary and tertiary land cover classes. Using the MODIS definition of urban as greater than 50% of artificial surfaces (Friedl et al., 2002) as a threshold, Table 3 summarizes the number of pixels validated by the crowd where the urban area is greater than 50%, less than 50% or where

Table 3. The crowdsourced samples of urban land cover based on crowdsourced information

City	Urban > 50%		Urban < 50%		No urban	
	# of pixels	%	# of pixels	%	# of pixels	%
London	664	57.2	345	29.7	151	13.0
Beijing	732	78.9	190	20.5	6	0.6
São Paulo	432	69.2	179	28.7	13	2.1

no urban land cover is present. The percentage of pixels in the sample, which would be classified as urban according to the MODIS definition of this class, ranges from 57 to 79% while another 20 to 30% are pixels that contain some degree of urban land cover. A very small percentage of crowdsourced pixels contain no urban areas in the samples for Beijing and São Paulo while 13% are non-urban in the London sample.

Using the 50% threshold to determine if a crowdsourced pixel was urban or not, an accuracy assessment was undertaken in which the percentage accuracy and the commission and omission errors were calculated. The results are listed in Table 4. The overall accuracy is the highest for the city of London with accuracy values similar to those found in the validation exercises of the GLC-2000 and MODIS as a whole (Mayaux et al., 2006; Friedl et al., 2010) while Glob-Cover is higher. The GLC-2000 performs much worse for Beijing and São Paulo, which is generally a result of the omission of urban areas while MODIS remains consistent relative to the performance for the sample in London. The errors in MODIS are a combination of omission and com-mission although commission errors are much larger in São Paulo. GlobCover also decreases in accuracy but remains consistent across these two latter cities, which is again generally reflected in an omission of urban areas.

Combining global land cover products in a hybrid approach has been shown to produce a better representation of land cover (See & Fritz, 2006; Fritz et al., 2011a). The simplest method is to use agreement between the maps as a starting point in the creation of such a hybrid map. Tables 5 to 7 provide further evidence for this approach, in particular when the three land cover products agree that an area is urban. For the city of London (Table 5), 93.7% of the pixels were urban according to the crowd when the three global land cover maps agree. Similarly for Beijing, 88.5% of the pixels were classified as urban by the crowd when the three land cover products agree on urban areas although the number of pixels in the sample where this was the case was small (Table 6). However, the agreement is still 84.3% when two maps agree for this particular sample in Beijing. Similar findings are in evidence in São Paulo (Table 7). Thus it is possible to gain significant

Table 4. Accuracy and commission/omission errors (in percentage) of the global land cover maps for samples validated by the crowd

Statistics	London			Beijing			SãoPaulo		
	GLC	MODIS	GLOBC	GLC	MODIS	GLOBC	GLC	MODIS	GLOBC
Accuracy	76.2	78.6	87.1	25.4	73.2	63.1	58.3	73.9	61.1
Commission	17.4	7.1	3.4	0.6	16.7	9.7	7.1	22.8	8.0
Omission	6.4	14.3	9.5	73.9	10.1	27.2	34.6	3.4	30.9

Table 5. The amount of urban land cover based on comparing the global land cover products for London

# of land cover maps with urban	Urban > 50%		Urban < 50%		No urban	
	# of pixels	%	# of pixels	%	# of pixels	%
One map urban	81	32.9	128	52.0	37	15.0
Two maps urban	116	74.8	36	23.2	3	1.9
All three urban	443	93.7	28	5.9	2	0.4
No urban	24	8.4	153	53.5	109	38.1

Table 6. The amount of urban land cover based on comparing the global land cover products for Beijing

# of land cover maps with urban	Urban > 50%		Urban < 50%		No urban	
	# of pixels	%	# of pixels	%	# of pixels	%
One map urban	234	73.4	80	25.1	5	1.6
Two maps urban	396	84.3	74	15.7	0	0.0
All three urban	46	88.5	6	11.5	0	0.0
No urban	56	64.4	27	31.0	4	4.6

Table 7. The amount of urban land cover based on comparing the global land cover products for São Paulo

# of land cover maps with urban	Urban > 50%		Urban < 50%		No urban	
	# of pixels	%	# of pixels	%	# of pixels	%
One map urban	168	64.6	83	31.9	9	3.5
Two maps urban	31	83.8	6	16.2	0	0.0
All three urban	212	82.8	42	16.4	2	0.8
No urban	21	29.6	48	67.6	2	2.8

improvements in accuracy in those areas where at least two land cover maps agree by combining the individual maps in this simple manner.

Discussion

The previous analysis demonstrated how crowdsourcing can be used to collect validation data for use in comparing global land cover maps in terms of urban extent. The results also showed that by combining global land cover maps where the majority agree, improvements in urban extent could be realized as shown in the areas where the validation samples were located. However, there

are a number of issues with using crowdsourced data in this manner including: age of the information; sustainability in terms of retaining the crowd; the quality of the data; and sample bias. Each of these issues is discussed below.

The global land cover maps used in this study relate to the years 2000 and 2005. The Google Earth imagery is from varying time periods although the high resolution imagery over cities tends to be quite recent. We are dealing with this issue by extracting the image dates from Google Earth. This temporal information layer could be used to determine which validation data to use and whether there are real issues with differences in time periods. This was not implemented in the case study but could provide added confidence in the use of the crowdsourced data in the future.

The second lesson that we have learned through using Geo-Wiki is the need to provide incentives to ensure participation. Co-authorship on a paper has proven to be an effective mechanism in attracting a crowd, resulting in a large number of validations during each competition. However, once the competition is finished, there is little further activity on the site. Although we have attempted to add more interaction via facebook, which has worked successfully during competitions, sustainability remains a serious issue for the future of Geo-Wiki. Some future developments will address this issue as discussed in the next section.

The third issue relates to the quality of the crowdsourced data and therefore the confidence or trust in this data set for use in other research applications. We have analyzed the quality of the data from one of the competitions based on a reference or expert dataset, which were provided to the participants at three different times during the competition (Comber et al., 2013). We have also examined the relative performance of users in relation to one another (Foody et al., 2013). The results showed that performance does vary by individual and by land cover type but that this information could be used to develop a set of indicators of quality. The quantity of urban areas relative to other land cover types in the sample was small but performance in identifying urban areas was 100% correct. This is because urban areas are generally covered using high resolution satellite imagery in Google Earth and they are one of the easiest land cover types to identify.

The final issue to highlight is sample bias. In each of the Geo-Wiki competitions, random samples were created based on the theme of the competition. For example, the purpose of one competition was to validate a map of land availability for biofuel production. Random samples from both inside and outside of this map of available land were presented to the crowd. However, if the full

Geo-Wiki database is to be used in validating land cover or urban extent in the future, there may be issues of under- or over-representation in urban extent or other land cover classes in general. Rather than use all the validation samples, a sampling strategy like that advocated by Olofsson et al. (2012) could be used. This would ensure that validation is undertaken using recognized sampling strategies from the remote sensing community. Sampling in the context of urban extent may also be less relevant if a more wall-to-wall approach is taken. Through the LandSpotting project, funded by the Austrian Research Promotion Agency, a series of games have been developed. Currently in a phase of beta testing, a facebook game modelled on the Civilization computer game has been developed, where the game is played on top of Google Earth. As part of building an empire, players must choose locations such as a well-known city and then use a tool to paint in the land cover types from a simple land cover legend. If this game is successful and player numbers become typical of the most popular facebook games, comprehensive crowdsourced coverage of all urban areas would theoretically be possible.

FUTURE RESEARCH DIRECTIONS

Crowdsourcing used as a form of e-participation will continue to undergo major expansion in the future as it is increasingly being recognized that citizens are both environmental and social sensors (Goodchild, 2007a; McGlade, 2010). This future trend is reflected in recent funding initiatives, e.g. through the flagship framework program of the European Union, which issued a call in 2011 for the development of citizen observatories. Interaction between citizens and decision makers was a key required component of each proposal, placing e-participation and governance firmly on the EU's agenda for research and development. One of the recently funded observatories, called CITI-SENSE (http://citi-sense.nilu.no/), focuses on urban quality, public spaces, and school indoor quality where the aim of the project is to empower citizens and citizens' groups to contribute to environmental governance, to support and influence policy priorities and decision making, and to have a say through this form of e-participation in assessing the quality and value of urban space. The citizen observatory plans to build communities in nine cities: Barcelona, Belgrade, Bilbao, Edinburgh, Haifa, Ljubljana, Oslo, Silesia and Vienna. Two EU COST actions have also been recently funded in the area of crowdsourcing: ENERGIC (European Network Exploring Research into Geospatial Information Crowdsourcing) and Mapping and the Citizen Sensor, where both will consider quality and use of the data for research. Finally, the future funding of earth observation in Europe through GMES (Global Monitoring for Environment and Security) has still not been decided, which will impact upon the availability of future remotely-sensed products including derivatives such as land cover and urban extent. European Commission officials have already warned that funding will be scaled back and in-situ observation techniques like crowdsourcing will play a much greater role than before (de Selding, 2012).

The case study illustrated the use of crowdsourcing for validation. However, an improved urban land cover product is the ultimate goal of Urban Geo-wiki. An improved product would consist of a hybrid map whereby existing products are combined, taking the most accurate pieces of each of one and merging them into a single product. The validations contributed by the crowd could also be used in the calibration process of the hybrid map whereby the determination of which product to use at a given location could be guided by the crowd. Such a product is currently being developed for global cropland but will also be undertaken for urban areas.

Our experience with Geo-Wiki so far has shown that this approach is a viable mechanism for collecting large quantities of validation data. Through a number of competitions, the database now contains almost 200,000 contributions. However, there are two main issues regarding future viability: data quality and sustainability. We are currently in the process of developing a procedure to determine the minimum number of validations required at a single pixel where the majority agrees in order to have a certain level of confidence in the validations provided by the crowd. We will also integrate user performance by land cover type into Geo-Wiki using the measures outlined in Comber et al. (2013). Together these two indicators will be used to determine a measure of quality. This is currently a key area of research being undertaken to improve Geo-Wiki.

In terms of implementation, new developments are planned. Urban Geo-Wiki is only one branch of several Geo-Wiki tools. There are other branches for validation of cropland, biomass, forest cover, coffee plantations and Australian land cover. There is also a version of Geo-Wiki that has recently been modified for use as a teaching tool in university-level physical geography courses. The development of all these different Geo-Wiki branches has required input from highly skilled programmers. A new version of Geo-Wiki will be available in the summer of 2013 which allows users to create their own Geo-Wiki branch without the need for technical or programming knowledge. This development may stimulate the uptake of Geo-Wiki type applications in other areas of e-participation and urban governance.

Geo-Wiki is not a wiki in the true sense of the word in that users cannot edit their own contributions once submitted nor can they modify the contributions of others. However, we would like to build more collaborative functionality into the system, in particular through the addition of social networking. Rather than contributing validations in isolation, users will be able to chat about individual images when encountering interesting features or discuss pixels that they found difficult to classify. They will also be able to ask questions of the experts and have an interactive experience that will be more interesting and enable learning, since users will gain more collective experience in image classification, learning from each other and from the experts. This has relevance to the issue of sustainability, where the current model relies on competitions and incentives linked to these competitions. By providing a more socially interactive environment, we hope to move to a more sustainable model. Moreover, users should be able to return to their contributions to make changes and be allowed to at least comment on the contributions of others as would be possible in a true wiki. The advantage of heading towards a wiki model is that greater collaboration between users will be possible. However, this will also have implications on time as experts will be needed that interact and provide feedback on a regular basis.

A final major development that is worth mentioning is the use of Urban Geo-Wiki to help develop the WUDAPT (World Urban Database and Access Portal Tools) in collaboration with the International Association for Urban Climate (IAUC). It is known that urban areas affect local micro-climates through the urban heat island effect (Oke, 1967) and through changing the precipitation regime of urban areas (Kaufmann et al., 2007; Russell & Hughes, 2011). However, their true effect on global climate is currently unknown as urban areas are represented in a highly simplified manner in the general circulation models (GCMs) that are used to make global climate predictions (Jin et al., 2007). The WUDAPT will use high resolution satellite imagery, Geo-Wiki and crowdsourcing to collect information on building types and land cover for all cities in the world. A mobile version of Geo-Wiki will be developed to collect more detailed information at the street level such as canyon widths, building materials and roofing types. The IAUC will call upon its membership of 8,000 individuals to help build this database. We are currently working on the development of a prototype for the city of Dublin where good reference data are available to determine the quality of the crowdsourced data. We will then

roll this out to more cities around the world. This e-participation exercise will be indirectly relevant to urban governance through the development of better climate change models and may, therefore, lead to predictions of future climate that are based on better physical representations of the urban landscape. As these predictions will form the basis of climate change mitigation and adaption strategies, the contribution of crowdsourcing in this context has huge potential.

CONCLUSION

This chapter has examined the use of crowdsourcing as one form of e-participation, illustrated via a case study to show how crowdsourcing can be used to validate urban extent from three global land cover maps.

Crowdsourced validation samples from the cities of London, Beijing and São Paulo, which were collected in a recent Geo-Wiki crowdsourcing campaign, were used to carry out an accuracy assessment on the fringes of the cities, where disagreement between the three products is the highest. Comparison of the sample areas across the different land cover products demonstrated that considerable differences exist, especially for those areas experiencing rapid change. MODIS was the most consistently accurate map across the three cities, where overall accuracies were in line with those found in Friedl et al. (2010) while both the GLC-2000 and GlobCover products were less accurate in Beijing and São Paulo based on these sample areas. Creation of a hybrid map by using areas where all three global land cover maps agree was shown to be a good starting point as the crowdsourced validation showed improved agreement relative to the accuracies of the individual products in the sample area. For Beijing and São Paulo, using areas where two of the maps agreed on urban areas also resulted in improvement. The analysis highlighted that care should be taken when deciding on which global land cover product to use in applications that require the quantification and spatial distribution of urban extent. For example, the calculation of GHG emissions or energy consumption could differ widely depending upon which product is employed as an input to these calculations. This has a potential impact on the types of policies that could be developed to curb emissions in the future. The development of a more accurate hybrid urban extent product could also greatly benefit the urban modeling and resource assessment communities. One might even argue that accurate urban mapping in the future will rely on new developments such as crowdsourcing, where there is a pressing need for more in-situ data.

However, there are still a number of issues where more research is required, e.g. how sustainable is such an approach and how can we ensure that data quality meets minimum standards in order that the data can be used with confidence in further research. Moving from a crowdsourcing system, where motivation is achieved through a competition, to a system with more sustained and continuous participation is an ongoing challenge for the Geo-Wiki team. We are working towards a system that is more socially interactive, which facilitates better exchange between the crowd and the experts and will provide an environment in which learning is a key part of the process. Such engagement may help to retain more individuals, which has proven to be a successful component of the crowdsourcing site GalaxyZoo in which galaxies are classified by the crowd. We have also developed a set of games which seamlessly integrate identification of land cover, but these are still being tested. We hope that such an approach may add a fun element to the process of validation and will thereby contribute to crowd retention. In terms of data quality, we are currently working on the development of indicators that will help us to filter the data for poor quality contributions while providing some minimum level of confidence in the rest of the data. Until such quality indicators are in place, it will be difficult to convince scientists and decision makers to use crowdsourced data. This is particularly true in the area of e-participation and urban governance where policies and future decisions may rely increasingly on this type of data in the future.

REFERENCES

Bicheron, P., Defourny, P., Brockman, C., Schouten, L., Vancutsem, C., & Huc, M. et al. (2008). *GlobCover – Products description and validation report*. Toulouse: MEDIAS-France.

Biradar, C. M., Thenkabail, P. S., Noojipady, P., Li, Y., Dheeravath, V., & Turral, H. et al. (2009). A global map of rainfed cropland areas (GMRCA) at the end of the last millennium using remote sensing. *International Journal of Applied Earth Observation and Geoinformation, 11*, 114–129. doi:10.1016/j.jag.2008.11.002.

Bontemps, S., Defourney, P., Van Bogaert, E., Arino, O., Kalogirou, V., & Perez, J. R. (2010). *GlobCover 2009 - Products description and validation report*. Toulouse: MEDIAS-France.

Center for International Earth Science Information Network (CIESIN). (2004). *Global rural-urban mapping project (GRUMP): Urban extents*. Retrieved February 21, 2011, from http://sedac.ciesin.columbia.edu/gpw

Comber, A., See, L., Fritz, S., van der Velde, M., Perger, C., & Foody, G. (in press). Using volunteered geographic information to evaluate global land cover datasets. *International Journal of Applied Earth Observation and Geoinformation*.

Danko, D. (1992). The digital chart of the world project. *Photogrammetric Engineering and Remote Sensing, 58*, 1125–1128.

de Selding, P. B. (2012). *European officials dial back GMES funding expectations.* Retrieved October 29, 2012, from http://www.spacenews.com/civil/120927-officials-gmes-funding.html

Dobson, J. E., Bright, E. A., Coleman, P. R., & Bhaduri, B. L. (2003). LandScan: A global population database for estimating populations at risk. In Mesev, V. (Ed.), *Remotely sensed cities* (pp. 267–281). London: Taylor & Francis.

Elvidge, C., Tuttle, B., Sutton, P., Baugh, K., Howard, A., & Milesi, C. et al. (2007). Global distribution and density of constructed impervious surfaces. *Sensors (Basel, Switzerland), 7,* 1962–1979. doi:10.3390/s7091962.

FAO. (2005). *Mapping global urban and rural population distributions.* Environment and Natural Resources Working Paper No. 24. Rome: FAO.

FAO. (2006). *Food insecurity, poverty and environment. Global GIS Database: DVD and atlas for the year 2000.* Environment and Natural Resources Working Paper No. 26. Rome: FAO.

Flanagin, A. J., & Metzger, M. J. (2008). The credibility of volunteered geographic information. *GeoJournal, 72,* 137–148. doi:10.1007/s10708-008-9188-y.

Foody, G., See, L., Fritz, S., Van der Velde, M., Perger, C., Schill, C., & Boyd, D. S. (in press). Assessing the accuracy of volunteered geographic information arising from multiple contributors to an internet based collaborative project. *Transactions in GIS.*

Friedl, M. A., McIver, D. K., Hodges, J. C. F., Zhang, X. Y., Muchoney, D., & Strahler, A. H. et al. (2002). Global land cover mapping from MODIS: Algorithms and early results. *Remote Sensing of Environment, 83,* 287–302. doi:10.1016/S0034-4257(02)00078-0.

Friedl, M. A., Sulla-Menashe, D., Tan, B., Schneider, A., Ramankutty, N., Sibley, A., & Huang, X. (2010). MODIS Collection 5 global land cover: Algorithm refinements and characterization of new datasets. *Remote Sensing of Environment, 114*(1), 168–182. doi:10.1016/j.rse.2009.08.016.

Fritz, S., Bartholomé, E., Belward, A., Hartley, A., Stibig, H. J., & Eva, H. et al. (2003). *Harmonisation, mosaicing and production of the Global Land Cover 2000 database (beta version).* Luxembourg: Office for Official Publications of the European Communities.

Fritz, S., McCallum, I., Schill, C., Perger, C., See, L., & Schepaschenko, D. et al. (2012). Geo-Wiki: An online platform for land cover validation and the improvement of global land cover. *Environmental Modelling & Software, 31,* 110–123. doi:10.1016/j.envsoft.2011.11.015.

Fritz, S., See, L., McCallum, I., Schill, C., Obersteiner, M., Boettcher, H., & Achard, F. (2011b). Highlighting continued uncertainty in global land cover maps. *Environmental Research Letters, 6,* 044005. doi:10.1088/1748-9326/6/4/044005.

Fritz, S., See, L., McCallum, I., Schill, C., Perger, C., & Obersteiner, M. (2011c). Building a crowdsourcing tool for the validation of urban extent and gridded population. *Lecture Notes in Computer Science, 6783,* 39–50. doi:10.1007/978-3-642-21887-3_4.

Fritz, S., You, L., Bun, A., See, L. M., McCallum, I., & Liu, J. et al. (2011a). Cropland for sub-Saharan Africa: A synergistic approach using five land cover datasets. *Geophysical Research Letters, 38,* L04404. doi:10.1029/2010GL046213.

Goldewijk, K. (2005). Three centuries of global population growth: A spatially referenced population density database for 1700-2000. *Population and Environment, 26,* 343–367. doi:10.1007/s11111-005-3346-7.

Goodchild, M. F. (2007a). Citizens as sensors: The world of volunteered geography. *GeoJournal*, *69*(4), 211–221. doi:10.1007/s10708-007-9111-y.

Goodchild, M. F. (2007b). Citizens as voluntary sensors: Spatial data infrastructure in the world of web 2.0. *International Journal of Spatial Data Infrastructure Research*, *2*, 24–32.

Goodchild, M. F. (2008). Commentary: Whither VGI? *GeoJournal*, *72*, 239–244. doi:10.1007/s10708-008-9190-4.

Haklay, M. (2010). How good is volunteered geographical information? A comparative study of OpenStreetMap and ordinance survey datasets. *Environment and Planning B*, *37*, 682–703. doi:10.1068/b35097.

Haklay, M., Basiouka, S., Antoniou, V., & Ather, A. (2010). How many volunteers does it take to map an area well? The validity of Linus' law to volunteered geographic information. *The Cartographic Journal*, *47*(4), 315–322. doi:10.1179/000870410X12911304958827.

Harris, C. G. (2011). Dirty deeds done dirt cheap: A darker side to crowdsourcing. In *Proceedings of 2011 IEEE Third International Conference on Social Computing* (pp. 1314-1317). Los Alamitos, CA: IEEE Computer Society.

Herold, M. (2009). Some recommendations for global efforts in urban monitoring and assessments from remote sensing. In Gamba, P., & Herold, M. (Eds.), *Global mapping of human settlement: Experiences, datasets and prospects* (pp. 11–23). Boca Raton, FL: CRC Press. doi:10.1201/9781420083408-c2.

Howe, J. (2006). The rise of crowdsouring. *Wired Magazine*, Issue 14.06. Retrieved May 18, 2010, from http://www.wired.com/wired/archive/14.06/crowds.html

Imhoff, M. L., Lawrence, W. T., Stutzer, D. C., & Elvidge, C. D. (1997). A technique for using composite DMSP/OLS "city lights" satellite data to map urban area. *Remote Sensing of Environment*, *61*(3), 361–370. doi:10.1016/S0034-4257(97)00046-1.

Jin, M., Shepherd, J. M., & Peters-Lidard, C. (2007). Development of a parameterization for simulating the urban temperature hazard using satellite observations in climate model. *Natural Hazards*. doi:10.1007/s11069-007-9117-2.

Kaufmann, R. K., Seto, K. C., Schneider, A., Zhou, L., & Liu, Z. (2007). Climate response to rapid urban growth: Evidence of a human-induced precipitation deficit. *Journal of Climate*, *20*, 2299–2306. doi:10.1175/JCLI4109.1.

Khatib, F., & DiMaio, F.Foldit Contenders Group, Foldit Void Crushers Group, Cooper, S., Kazmierczyk, M., Gilski, M.,…, Baker, D. (2011). Crystal structure of a monomeric retroviral protease solved by protein folding game players. *Nature Structural & Molecular Biology*, *18*, 1175–1177. doi:10.1038/nsmb.2119 PMID:21926992.

LathamJ.HuddlestonB.CumaniR.MartucciA. RosatiI.SalvatoreM., El

Marr, A. (2011). *Andrew Marr's megacities: Living in the city*. BBC.

Marris, E. (2010). Birds flock online. *Nature*. doi:10.1038/news.2010.395.

Mayaux, P., Eva, H., Gallego, J., Strahler, A. H., Herold, M., & Agrawal, S. et al. (2006). Validation of the global land cover 2000 map. *IEEE Transactions on Geoscience and Remote Sensing*, *44*(7), 1728–1737. doi:10.1109/TGRS.2006.864370.

McGlade, J. (2010). *Global citizen observatory - The role of individuals in observing and understanding our changing world*. Retrieved January 10, 2012, from http://www.eea.europa.eu/pressroom/speeches/global-citizen-observatory-the-role-of-individuals-in-observing-and-understanding-our-changing-world

Milčinski, G. (2011). *The rise of crowd-sourcing: How valuable data can we get out of VGI*. Paper presented at CAPIGI, Amsterdam.

Neis, P., Zielstra, D., & Zipf, A. (2012). The street network evolution of crowdsourced maps: OpenStreetMap in Germany 2007–2011. *Future Internet*, *4*, 1–21. doi:10.3390/fi4010001.

NOAA. (2011). *Global DMSP-OLS nighttime lights time series 1992-2009* (Version 4). Retrieved from http://www.ngdc.noaa.gov/dmsp/download.html

Office of National Statistics. (2011). *Annual mid-year population estimates, 2010*. Titchfield: Office of National Statistics UK.

Oke, T. R. (1967). City size and the urban heat island. *Atmospheric Environment*, *7*(8), 769–779. doi:10.1016/0004-6981(73)90140-6.

Olofsson, P., Stehman, S. V., Woodcock, C. E., Sulla-Menashe, D., Sibley, A. M., & Newell, J. D. et al. (2012). A global land-cover validation data set, part I: fundamental design principles. *International Journal of Remote Sensing*, *33*(18), 5768–5788. doi:10.1080/01431161.2012.674230.

ORNL. (2011). *LandScan*. Retrieved from http://www.ornl.gov/sci/landscan/

Perger, C., Fritz, S., See, L., Schill, C., Van der Velde, M., McCallum, I., & Obersteiner, M. (2012). A campaign to collect volunteered geographic information on land cover and human impact. In Jekel, T., Car, A., Strobl, J., & Griesebner, G. (Eds.), *GI_Forum 2012: Geovizualisation, society and learning* (pp. 83–91). Berlin, Offenbach: Wichmann Verlag.

Potere, D., & Schneider, A. (2009). Comparison of global urban maps. In Gamba, P., & Herold, M. (Eds.), *Global mapping of human settlement: Experiences, datasets and prospects* (pp. 269–308). Boca Raton, FL: CRC Press. doi:10.1201/9781420083408-c13.

Russell, A., & Hughes, M. (2011). Is the changing precipitation regime of Manchester, United Kingdom, driven by the development of urban areas? *International Journal of Climatology*. doi: doi:10.1002/joc.2321.

Schneider, A., Friedl, M. A., McIver, D. K., & Woodcock, C. E. (2003). Mapping urban areas by fusing multiple sources of coarse resolution remotely sensed data. *Photogrammetric Engineering and Remote Sensing*, *69*, 1377–1386.

Schneider, A., Friedl, M. A., & Potere, D. (2009). A new map of global urban extent from MODIS satellite data. *Environmental Research Letters*, *4*, 044003. doi:10.1088/1748-9326/4/4/044003.

Schneider, A., Friedl, M. A., & Potere, D. (2010). Mapping global urban areas using MODIS 500-m data: New methods and datasets based on 'urban ecoregions.'. *Remote Sensing of Environment*, *114*, 1733–1746. doi:10.1016/j.rse.2010.03.003.

See, L., & Fritz, S. (2006). Towards a global hybrid land cover map for the year 2000. *IEEE Transactions on Geoscience and Remote Sensing*, *44*(7), 1740–1746. doi:10.1109/TGRS.2006.874750.

Sidding, B. F., & El Nogoumy, N. (2009). The Africover and PMUR datasets and the challenge of human settlement mapping in Africa. In Gamba, P., & Herold, M. (Eds.), *Global mapping of human settlement: Experiences, datasets and prospects* (pp. 163–189). Boca Raton, FL: CRC Press.

Silberman, M., Irani, L., & Ross, J. (2010). Ethics and tactics of professional crowdwork. *XRDS: Crossroads. The ACM Magazine for Students*, *17*(2), 39–43. doi:10.1145/1869086.1869100.

Silvertown, J. (2009). A new dawn for citizen science. *Trends in Ecology & Evolution, 24,* 467–471. doi:10.1016/j.tree.2009.03.017 PMID:19586682.

Sobel, D. (1995). *Longitude: The true story of a lone genius who solved the greatest scientific problem of his time.* New York, NY: Walker and Company.

Sorensen, A., & Okata, J. (2011). *Megacities: Urban form, governance and sustainability.* Dordrect. Springer.

Surowiecki, J. (2004). *The wisdom of crowds: Why the many are smarter than the few and how collective wisdom shapes business, economies, societies and nations.* New York, NY: Little and Brown.

UN-HABITAT. (2011). *Global report on human settlements: Cities and climate change.* Nairobi: UN Press.

United Nations. (2010). *World urbanization prospects: The 2009 revision.* New York, NY: UN Press.

Wiggins, A. (2012, February). *Motivation by design: Technologies, experiences and incentives.* Paper presented at the 2nd Citizen Cyberscience Summit, London, UK.

Zielstra, D., & Zipf, A. A. (2010). Comparative study of proprietary geodata and volunteered geographic information for Germany. In *Proceedings of 13th AGILE International Conference on Geographic Information Science.* Guimarães, Portugal.

ADDITIONAL READING

Barr, S. L., Barnsley, M. J., & Steel, A. (2004). On the separability of urban land-use categories in fine spatial scale land-cover data using structural pattern recognition. *Environment and Planning. B, Planning & Design, 32,* 397–418. doi:10.1068/b3016.

Batty, M. (2008). The size, scale, and shape of cities. *Science, 319,* 769–771. doi:10.1126/science.1151419 PMID:18258906.

Baudot, Y. (2000). Geographical analysis of the population of fast-growing cities in the third world. In Donnay, J., Barnsley, M., & Longley, P. (Eds.), *Remote sensing and urban analysis* (pp. 229–246). London: Taylor and Francis.

Champion, T., & Hugo, G. (2004). *New forms of urbanization: Conceptualizing and measuring human settlement in the twenty-first century.* London: Ashgate Publishing Limited.

Comber, A. J., Fisher, P. F., & Wadsworth, R. A. (2005). What is land cover? *Environment and Planning B, 23,* 199–209.

Dobson, J. E., Bright, E. A., Coleman, P. R., Durfee, R. C., & Worley, B. A. (2000). A global population database for estimating populations at risk. *Photogrammetric Engineering and Remote Sensing, 66*(7), 849–857.

Gamba, P., Dell'Acqua, F., & Dasarathy, B. V. (2005). Urban remote sensing using multiple datasets: Past, present and future. *Information Fusion, 6,* 319–326. doi:10.1016/j.inffus.2005.02.007.

Henderson, M., Yeh, E. T., Gong, P., Elvidge, C., & Baugh, K. (2003). Validation of urban boundaries derived from global night-time satellite imagery. *International Journal of Remote Sensing, 24*(3), 595–609. doi:10.1080/01431160304982.

Herold, M., Goldstein, N. C., & Clarke, K. C. (2003). The spatiotemporal form of urban growth: Measurement, analysis and modeling. *Remote Sensing of Environment, 86,* 286–302. doi:10.1016/S0034-4257(03)00075-0.

Herold, M., Hemphill, J., & Clarke, K. C. (2007). Remote sensing and urban growth theory. In Weng, Q., & Quattrochi, D. (Eds.), *Urban remote sensing* (pp. 201–220). London: Taylor & Francis.

Herold, M., Scepan, J., & Clarke, K. C. (2002). The use of remote sensing and landscape metrics to describe structures and changes in urban land uses. *Environment & Planning A, 34,* 1443–1458. doi:10.1068/a3496.

Lebel, L., Thaitakoo, D., Sangawongse, S., & Huaisai, D. (2007). Views of Chiang Mai: The contributions of remote-sensing to urban governance and sustainability. In Netzband, M., Stefanov, W. L., & Redman, C. (Eds.), *Applied remote sensing for urban planning, governance and sustainability* (pp. 221–247). Berlin: Springer. doi:10.1007/978-3-540-68009-3_10.

Martin, L. R. G., Howarth, P. J., & Holder, G. (1988). Multispectral classification of land use at the rural-urban fringe using SPOT data. *Canadian Journal of Remote Sensing, 14*(2), 72–79.

Miller, R. B., & Small, C. (2003). Cities from space: Potential applications of remote sensing in urban environmental research and policy. *Environmental Science & Policy, 6*(2), 129–137. doi:10.1016/S1462-9011(03)00002-9.

Mills, G. M. (2007). Cities as agents of global change. *International Journal of Climatology, 27,* 1849–1857. doi:10.1002/joc.1604.

Montgomery, M. R. (2007). The urban transformation of the developing world. *Science, 319,* 761–764. doi:10.1126/science.1153012 PMID:18258903.

Potere, D., & Schneider, A. (2007). A critical look at representations of urban areas in global maps. *GeoJournal, 69,* 55–80. doi:10.1007/s10708-007-9102-z.

Rocchini, D., & Ricotta, C. (2007). Are landscapes as crisp as we may think? *Ecological Modelling, 204*(3-4), 535–539. doi:10.1016/j.ecolmodel.2006.12.028.

Schneider, A., & Woodcock, C. E. (2008). Compact, dispersed, fragmented, extensive? A comparison of urban expansion in twenty-five global cities using remotely sensed data, pattern metrics and census information. *Urban Studies (Edinburgh, Scotland), 45,* 659–692. doi:10.1177/0042098007087340.

Seifert, F. M. (2009). Improving urban monitoring toward a European urban atlas. In Gamba, P., & Herold, M. (Eds.), *Global mapping of human settlement: Experiences, datasets and prospects* (pp. 231–248). Boca Raton, FL: CRC Press. doi:10.1201/9781420083408-c11.

Sutton, P. C. (2003). A scale-adjusted measure of "Urban sprawl" using nighttime satellite imagery. *Remote Sensing of Environment, 86*(3), 353–369. doi:10.1016/S0034-4257(03)00078-6.

Weeks, J. R., Hill, A. G., Stow, D., Getis, A., & Fugate, D. (2007). Can you spot a neighbourhood from the air? Defining neighbourhood structure in Accra, Ghana. *GeoJournal, 69*(1-2), 9–22. doi:10.1007/s10708-007-9098-4 PMID:19478993.

Welch, R. (1980). Monitoring urban population and energy utilization patterns from satellite data. *Remote Sensing of Environment, 9,* 1–9. doi:10.1016/0034-4257(80)90043-7.

Weng, Q. (2007). *Remote sensing of impervious surfaces.* Boca Raton, FL: CRC Press. doi:10.1201/9781420043754.

Wentz, E. A., Stefanov, W. L., Gries, C., & Hope, D. (2006). Land-use and land-cover mapping from diverse data sources for an arid urban environment. *Computers, Environment and Urban Systems, 30,* 320–346. doi:10.1016/j.compenvurbsys.2004.07.002.

Wentz, E. A., Stefanov, W. L., Netzband, M., Moller, M. S., & Brazel, A. J. (2009). The urban environmental monitoring/100 cities project: Legacy of the first phase and next steps. In Gamba, P., & Herold, M. (Eds.), *Global mapping of human settlement: Experiences, datasets and prospects* (pp. 191–204). Boca Raton, FL: CRC Press. doi:10.1201/9781420083408-c9.

Zhang, J., & Foody, G. M. (1998). A fuzzy classification of sub-urban land cover from remotely sensed imagery. *International Journal of Remote Sensing*, *19*(14), 2721–2738. doi:10.1080/014311698214479.

KEY TERMS AND DEFINITIONS

Accuracy Assessment: Is used to determine the quality of a product derived through remote sensing.

Areas of Disagreement: Are those places where global land cover maps do not agree on the land cover type at a particular pixel.

Citizen Science: Is the name given to the involvement of ordinary citizens in scientific research. These are generally volunteers with a strong interest in a particular scientific subject, e.g. wildlife or astronomy. Types of activities that citizens can carry out as part of citizen science include collection of data, analysis of data, taking part in research projects, e.g. Earthwatch, building instruments, and taking part in scientific competitions.

Crowdsourcing: Denotes the process whereby individuals contribute information or undertake tasks to achieve a specific goal, generally online or via mobile phone. Reasons for involving the crowd include costs, which could be prohibitive if undertaken by a particular organization, and the need for large volumes of data or specific skills that are possessed by some individuals in the crowd.

Land Cover: Is the physical material that is found on the earth's surface. Land cover maps are created from remote sensing products and other inputs such as nighttime lights.

Land Use: Refers to how people use the land, e.g. a forest plantation for timber production. Land cover is often used as an input to land use although this information is much more difficult to characterize, especially on a global basis. One problem is the lack of a standard set of definitions of what constitutes land use.

Urban Extent: Is the spatial extent of urban areas as characterized by a number of different products, e.g. global land cover maps and population surfaces that use a threshold to define the urban extent.

Urbanization: Encompasses the set of processes and drivers that result in the growth of urban areas, in particular the movement from a more rural area to urban areas to improve economic opportunities.

Chapter 9

The Geospatial Web:
A Tool to Support the Empowerment of Citizens through E–Participation?

Karl Atzmanstorfer
Paris-Lodron University Salzburg, Austria

Thomas Blaschke
Paris-Lodron University Salzburg, Austria

ABSTRACT

This chapter introduces a spatial view to e-participation in urban governance which is based on the technological core of Geographical Information Systems (GIS) and their more recent transformation into service architectures. The chapter begins with the premise that the technological realms are available today in professional software packages and in open source software environments. It focuses on the utilization of GIS and various methodologies in participatory planning projects. The technical descriptions are limited to a degree that the reader can understand the applications envisaged. The chapter describes developments in the GIS domain which are summarized under the term 'Public Participation GIS' (PPGIS) since the 1990s. In 2005 however, the launch of Google Earth changed the situation significantly: such mapping platforms—including Microsoft Bing and others—brought mapping functionality to the computers of hundreds of millions of internet users and soon after, the term "volunteered geographic information" was created. It refers to the two-way communication possibilities using geospatial tools and to the participation of citizens in planning initiatives. The chapter highlights a few of such applications in urban planning and administration and discusses the situation in developing and emerging countries, while posing the question of whether or not such options may lead to an empowerment of citizens.

INTRODUCTION

Geospatial technologies were originally associated with the term Geographic Information Systems (GIS), which underlying principles were developed in the 1960s and 1970s. Today we can state

DOI: 10.4018/978-1-4666-4169-3.ch009

that basically all concepts which are necessary to acquire, handle, analyse and display spatial data have matured and are available in professional software solutions. Second, it is estimated that nowadays more digital maps or map-like representations are produced within one day than printed maps were produced in the history of mankind. The wide use of GPS, virtual globes, smartphones as mapping devices and other web-mapping tools has rendered possible new approaches for disseminating information and collecting crowd-sourced spatial data (Volunteered Geographic Information). These rapidly evolving technologies have brought new perspectives for redefining participatory spatial planning, e-government and urban administration, with the aim to empower citizens and communities that so far have been excluded from decision making processes. In this chapter we analyse the role of geospatial web-tools and platforms for e-participation with a particular focus on geospatial participative procedures that are triggered to support urban planning and governance, especially in developing and emerging countries where shortcomings of democratic, collaborative and integrative local and regional planning are most obvious.

FROM PUBLIC PARTICIPATION GEOGRAPHIC INFORMATION SYSTEMS (PPGIS) TO THE "GEOSPATIAL WEB"

In this section we give a brief introduction to Geographic Information Systems (GIS) as they allow the collection, processing and disseminating of spatial data, which is crucial for spatial planning. We present Public Participation GIS (PPGIS) as an approach to include citizens and communities in spatial planning and public administration, and recap the most important methods of Spatial Decision Support Systems (SDSS). Then, we analyse how the advent of Web 2.0 technologies has provided us with an increasing number of web-tools that integrate crowd-sourced data and geo-web platforms. We critically analyse whether or not these new tools increase participation of individuals and communities in spatial planning and public administration, and if they boost the empowerment of citizens in general. Furthermore we have a closer look at controversially discussed issues such as usability, privacy and quality issues that are inherent to geospatial web technologies.

A BRIEF HISTORY OF GEOGRAPHIC INFORMATION SYSTEMS (GIS)

The idea of portraying different layers of data on a series of base maps, and relating things geographically, has been around much longer than computers (Goodchild et al., 1990). One of the earliest examples of an analysis of a real-world phenomenon with an explicit spatial focus is Dr. John Snow´s map showing locations of death by cholera in central London in September, 1854 (Wienand, 2007). He used the map to track the source of the cholera outbreak to a contaminated well – an early example of spatial analysis. Indeed, the origins of spatial analysis refer to mapping of spatial events and then overlaying the information in order to see where overlapping occurred. Before the widespread availability of computers, this effect was first achieved through a base paper map and then physically overlaying transparent printouts on top.

However, the foundations of GIS as we know them today were laid in the 1960s with the first primitive computers being available for scientists. In this 'era of innovation,' Roger Tomlinson, the 'Father of GIS,' initiated the Canadian Geographic Information System (CGIS) in order to facilitate use of land inventory data in federal, provincial and regional planning – the first fully operational GIS in the world was born (Longley et al., 2001).

The 1970s saw key innovations such as the first mapping software SYMAP, mainly driven by the Harvard Laboratory for Computer Graphics and Spatial Analysis (Lembo, 2005). Furthermore, the first Earth observation satellite – Landsat 1 – was launched in 1972, which brought completely new perspectives for generating spatial data, as well as insights into processes at the Earth's surface. The 1980s brought the commercialisation of GIS, which was now recognized by an increasing number of users in academia and public administration. ArcInfo from the US-based company ESRI was the first major commercial GIS software system (Longley et al., 2001). The launch of the Global Positioning System (GPS) by the USarmy also dates back to this era – GPS and other GNSS (Global Navigation Satellite Systems) are nowadays a major source of data for navigation, surveying, and mapping (Longley et al., 2001).

The 1990s mark the breakthrough of Geographic Information Systems with numerous new software applications, data models and formats. It was then when GIS were applied to a wide field of domains, where spatial data had to be processed in order to create information that allows us to better organize our lives (ESRI, 2008): (e-) government and public administration[1], land-use planning, business, (public) health, transport, utility management, natural resource management, and disaster risk reduction, just to name some examples. Already in 1997, Clarke (1997) stated that "the growth of GIS has been a phenomenon of amazing breadth and depth and will remain so for many years to come. Clearly, GIS will integrate its way into our everyday life to such an extent that it will soon be impossible to imagine how we functioned before" (p. 6).

THE PUBLIC PARTICIPATION GIS (PPGIS) DEVELOPMENTS

The origins of PPGIS (Public Participation GIS) date back to the 1990s and early 2000s. They can retrospectively be characterized as an amalgamation of pioneer applications accompanied with a scientific debate about the role of GIS as a facilitator for empowerment or marginalisation. In the following sub-sections we give a short introduction to the origins of PPGIS, and the academic discussion that gave birth to this critical approach of using GIS. Then we analyse how the rapid technological developments in GIS have brought the foundations for a 'second wave' of PPGIS, whereby the term is less and less used by the scientific community.

Public Participation Geographic Information Systems (PPGIS)

As there is no exactly defined set of methods and tools that are used by PPGIS practitioners, there is no common and unique definition of Public Participation Geographic Information Systems within academia. Originally, PPGIS were referred to as a variety of approaches to make GIS and other spatial decision-making tools available and accessible to all those with a stake in official decisions (Schroeder, 1996), linking community participation and geographical information in a diversity of social and environmental contexts, and thus involving citizens in decision making processes (Steinmann et al., 2004; Blaschke, 2004). According to McCall and Dunn (2012), the term Public Participation Geographic Information Systems refers to a "form of participatory spatial planning which makes use of maps and other geo-information output, especially using GIS" (p. 82). Sieber (2006) states that PPGIS pertain to the "use of GIS to broaden public involvement in policy-making as well as to the value of GIS to promote the goals for non-governmental organizations (NGOs), grassroot groups, and community-based organizations" (p. 491).

Whatever definition of PPGIS we may stick to: their applications in practice are diverse and widespread. In the planning domain, PPGIS emerged in the mid-1990s, when John Pickles published his edited book 'Ground Truth – The social implications of Geographic Information Systems' - in a time, when GIS was exclusively used by a small group of experts within geography and computer science (Ghose, 2007; Kienberger, 2010; Ramasubramanian, 2010). Inspired by Pickles' book, an academic discussion evolved, where scholars such as Obermayer (1998), Schuurman (2000), Carver (2001), Craig et al. (2002) and Elwood (2006) were criticizing that the use of GIS commonly does not address non-experts and their particular spatial perspectives, and therefore are likely to perpetuate existing power-relations and marginalize vulnerable stakeholders of decision making processes. They argued how to 'socialize' GIS in a new paradigm, known as 'Critical GIS' (Corbett & Keller, 2005; Sieber, 2006; Schuurman, 2006; Pavlovskaya, 2006; Kienberger, 2010). Critical GIS may be seen as an umbrella to encompass all research on the societal effects of GIS (e.g., geo-surveillance), the social processes that should or should not be modelled by GIS (e.g., gender movement in space), or the representation, ontology, and epistemology of GIS (Ahlqvist, 2000; Agarwal, 2005; Schuurman, 2006).

Despite this still ongoing discussion about theoretical foundations and practical implications of PPGIS, they have been applied now for over a decade by practitioners of various disciplines in urban planning and community revitalization, land-use and natural resource planning, conservation and environmental management, conflict management, and many more (McCall & Dunn, 2012) - with the common goal to empower individuals and communities that so far have been excluded from spatial decision making processes. Critical discussions on how PPGIS in general, and geo-web tools in specific, lead to empowerment and/or marginalisation of citizens is given in other sections of this chapter.

GOOGLE EARTH AND VIRTUAL GLOBES: THE RAPID DEVELOPMENT SINCE 2005

Technical Developments and Standards

The recent advent of freely available Virtual Globes such as Google Earth, Microsoft Bing Maps 3D and similar applications allow users to interact with and query overhead imagery and spatial data via a three-dimensional representation of the Earth (Butler, 2006). Virtual Globes make it relatively straightforward to build spatially enabled web applications. It is simple to overlay available data layers and to visualise them (Craglia et al., 2008). Anybody can explore the high resolution imagery provided and can superimpose additional layers such as street networks, place-names, hotel information or landmarks.

Keyhole was the first company to release such an Earth-viewer in 2001 and NASA´s World Wind followed in 2003, receiving recognition in what is a relatively small community of interest. In October 2004, Google acquired Keyhole Corporation and released Google Earth in June 2005. For non-expert users, Google is associated with the notion of having created an appealing 3D browser with a 'video game-like' feeling. It is widely used and implemented by a growing variety of vendors. In June 2006, Google claimed 100 million product activations worldwide and within a year (by September 2006), about 30,000 copies of their programming interface (API) were in use worldwide (McLeod, 2006; Craglia et al., 2008), leading to an unprecedented number of applications. With KML (Keyhole Markup Language), Google created a de facto standard.

Such a pseudo-standard is not new, as there are many examples (such as VHS, ESRI´s shapefile, Adobe PDF, and so forth) where a format became standard despite the fact that it was not technically superior to its competitors. For some years, there had been friction within the standardisation community, but in 2008 KML Version 2.2 was adopted as an OGC (Open Geospatial Consortium) implementation standard (OGC, 2010).

Booming Applications

The value of scientific data increases when we can link it to the information that a user already considers important: "scientists should take this opportunity to use GIS to present their scientific results in a way that users can easily tie to other data sources" (Butler, 2006, p. 776). Online mapping services have only existed since the late 1990s, and they are mainly associated with the questions 'where is x?' and 'how do I get there?' However, recently, online map services have become much more complex and interconnected. While 2D street maps were quickly adopted by average internet users, Virtual Globes are attracting additional attention through the use of a three-dimensional representation of the Earth. Interaction with digital information is becoming much less abstract: working directly with spatial views (Google and Microsoft currently leading the way) ties the 'online domain' directly into daily individual experiences and perceptions. New consumer demand will probably turn out to be a major driver in the development of future spatial data infrastructure services (Strobl, 2005; Kiehle et al., 2007).

Another aspect is creativity and imagination. Professional GIS has its strength in spatial analysis. It is also used for visualisation and for displaying different scenarios, but it is rarely used for "playing around." By integrating tools to encourage creative imagination, we may be able to ask more innovative and socially relevant questions about the changing character of the earth's surface, especially under conditions of global environmental change. A "massification" (Blaschke et al., 2012) and the wider use of GIS is bound to potentially lead to an increasing number of applications which may not always obey standard cartographic rules such as maps which give wrong associations due to flawed colour or symbol representations based on questionable data or presumptions.

Since GIS exists as a tight coupling of spatial data, analysis, and visualisation technology, such intelligent software may create incorrect conceptual models of each of these components (Glennon, 2006). But, we should question whether the number of inappropriate uses is significant when compared to the impact of the 500+ million unique downloads of Google Earth worldwide (according to Google Press Release, 2009), and the sharply increasing number of geo-services that are being offered online and via mobile services.

Two-Way Cartography

Maps evolved as the primary method for storing and communicating knowledge of the earth's surface. They serve as repositories of both the raw data and the results of geographic inquiry, and mapmaking has always figured prominently in the skill set of geographers. Maps are thus indispensable tools in the geographers' search for understanding how human and physical processes act and interact on the earth's surface and the way the world works (Goodchild, 2004).

However, in these days Virtual Globes or other web-based mapping tools enable anyone with access to a computer and to the internet to make a map. They do not require cartographic skills what causes various challenges. For the most part, laypersons are predominantly not aware of the fact that the information they get on the screen – street maps, landmarks, 3D buildings – are models of the reality and contain various types of generalisation. As long as map-making – in a wider sense – was predominantly the domain of cartographers and GIS experts, it was in the hand of experts who were supposed to be aware of principles and limitations. Moreover, such experts presumably have skills to transform, emphasise, eliminate, summarise, exaggerate, and enlarge entities in geographic representations and to obey scaling rules (Kraak, 2003; Obermeyer, 2007). However, Virtual Globes allow any reasonably computer-literate person to make a map or other geographic representation regardless of his/her understanding of spatial concepts.

While the transition to digital mapping has taken only a few decades - with a period of time when both manual and digital techniques operated in parallel - there may be a much faster transition from the one-way communication of spatial data into a two-way, interactive geo-data publishing process. Cartography, Geography and Geoinformatics students today have to deal with Spatial Data Infrastructure (SDI) architectures, OGC standards, or the Sensor Web Enablement Initiative (SWE) in the quest for an interoperable display of real-time measurements. With the advent of Virtual Globes, the potential for making GIS functionality available to general users is dramatic: GIS as a term or abbreviation, respectively, may disappear. The range of GIS functionality – either explicit in GIS software or as services embedded in Virtual Globes – will expand.

SPATIAL DECISION SUPPORT SYSTEMS

After describing the origins and recent technological developments within Geographic Information Systems, we now may have a look at Spatial Decision Support Systems (SDSS), as they embrace some major concepts of Public Participation GIS and their implementation in spatial planning and public administration.

Decision Support Systems (DSS) in general, are specialized software products that are designed to solve non-structured problems, providing an easy-to-use user interface for experts and lay-persons. They are helping users to explore solutions by using data and models in order to generate a series of feasible alternatives for a problem by iteratively changing model parameters, and to examine the effects of these changes (Eastman et al., 1992). Whereas Decision Support Systems have been developed in operational research and management science to address business problems, Spatial Decision Support Systems (SDDS) can be viewed as their spatial analogues. They are explicitly designed to explore and structure complex spatial problems providing a framework for "integrating database management systems with analytical models, graphical display and tabular reporting capabilities, and the expert knowledge of decision makers" (Densham, 1991, p. 403; Sprague et. al., 1982). Similar to DSS, they usually consist of a database management system for spatial data, a model-based management system for analysis procedures and a user interface (Ascough et al., 2002).

SDSS help to structure decisions as described in Figure 1.

By structuring the decision making process, SDSS boost empowerment in two ways: first, the problem can be explored to increase the level of understanding and to refine the definition [of the problem]; and, second, the generation and evaluation of alternative solutions enables the decision maker to investigate the possible trade-offs between conflicting objectives and to identify unanticipated, and potentially undesirable, characteristics of solutions (Densham, 1991, p. 403).

When evaluating different scenarios by applying a decision rule to a set of alternatives in a SDSS, it is often distinguished between multi-criteria evaluation and multi-objective evaluation. The concept of multi-objective evaluation refers

Figure 1. Level of structure of problems and decisions within SDSS

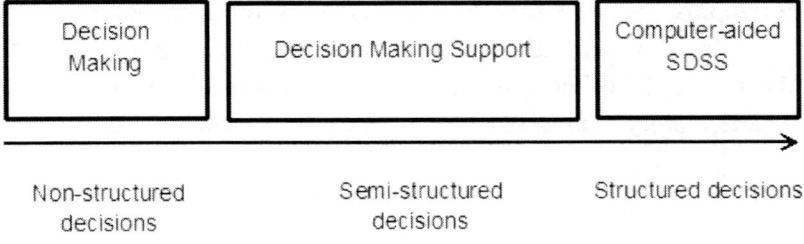

to a decision process in which several objectives must be satisfied simultaneously. In the latter, the objectives of a decision making process may be complementary, so two or more objectives are met through this decision at the same time. Or these objectives may be conflicting and cannot be met at the same time (Eastman et al., 1992). As an example, we may look at the problem of allocating scarce land to different types of land use within a city. While recreation and the protection of public green spaces are generally seen as complementary objectives, recreation and the need for construction land are usually considered as conflicting objectives. Therefore, decision rules set by the stakeholders of a decision making process determine how to settle conflicting objectives. The concept of multi-criteria evaluation in turn, describes a decision making process in which several criteria (that are parameters for decisions that can be measured and evaluated) are evaluated in order to meet one specific objective, e.g. the protection of public green spaces for recreational purposes.

In a SDSS, this is commonly achieved in a weighted linear combination of criteria that have been previously represented in spatial data models and mapped in a GIS (Malczewski, 1999; Malczewski, 2000).

If we call PPGIS for being a framework to fully integrate all stakeholders of a problem in a spatial decision making process, we should not neglect the importance and potential of Spatial Decision Support Systems. Recently, several software packages have been developed that incorporate basic and advanced methods and techniques of SDSS. CommunityViz (http://www.orton.org/tools/communityviz) is a package of software tools that allows developing scenarios for land-use planning that enable the visualisation and interpretation of the impact of different planning scenarios in a participatory matter. IDRISI

(http://www.clarklabs.org/) implements common decision making techniques in a comprehensive software package for raster analysis, just to name two common examples.

However, only a few applications have so far given access to SDSS for a broader public of non-experts (Carver, 2001; Rinner & Raubal, 2004; Li, 2006), neither are they yet implemented in geo-web solutions. Taking into consideration that the final rung of the e-participation ladder refers to online decision support systems, the integration of SDSS into geo-web applications is one of the major tasks for the future (cp. Figure 2). The advent of Web 2.0 technologies provides totally new opportunities to face this challenge. This is focused on in the next sub-sections of this chapter.

TOWARDS A NEW ERA OF PUBLIC PARTICIPATION GIS? VOLUNTEERED GEOGRAPHIC INFORMATION AND NEOGEOGRAPHY

The rapidly evolving area of geospatial data and tools, as well as recent developments in internet technologies ('Web GIS 2.0') and a subset of social networking and user-generated web content - that has been termed 'Volunteered Geographic Information' (VGI) - have disclosed so far unknown possibilities of the participation of citizens in planning initiatives and administration. The 'crowd' nowadays is able to rapidly collect data, identify problems and propose solutions for shortcomings related to their habitat on the web in a transparent way. In doing so, they increase the pressure on administrative bodies to involve citizens into a participatory planning processes and efficient governance at a local and regional scale. In this sub-section we discuss the origins of this development which were partially triggered by the development of virtual globes (e.g. Google Earth) and collaborative mapping initiatives such as http://www.openstreetmap.org.

It is important to note that geography is about understanding processes in space and time which create facts and footprints in our spatial reality. The advent of Volunteered Geographic Information (VGI) (Goodchild, 2007; 2008; Elwood, 2008) not only dramatically changes technology and its applications, but also raises a series of new basic questions for Geographic Information Science (Blaschke & Strobl, 2010). Geographic Information Science or 'GIScience' in short, increasingly deals with the effects of these changes from traditional one-way cartographic communication to a system of millions of volunteer contributors. This voluntarism certainly has the potential to relocate and redistribute productive activities from mapping agencies to networks of non-state volunteer actors. However, if we are about to design strategies and systems to maximise the advantages and minimise the risks associated with these changes, we must have a clear understanding of the people and technologies involved (Coleman, 2010).

Blaschke et al. (2012a) recently explored the role of the Geospatial Web – although they mostly refer to the term 'Virtual Globes.' They summarize recent developments from the history of Virtual Globes and the concept of a 'Digital Earth' envisioned by former US Vice-President Al Gore in a speech in 1998 (Goodchild, 2008; Elwood, 2008). The Geospatial Web, and particularly VGI, widen the user base dramatically but create some resulting challenges for GIScience and for society. Sui (2008) even speaks of a 'wikification of GIS,' Torrens (2008) speaks of 'Wifi-Geographies.' We may need to differentiate between these fast technical developments and the quest for understanding processes in space and time, which create facts and footprints in our spatial reality. These developments not only dramatically change the technology and its applications, but we may claim

that first time in history we can derive a more 'complete' picture of the behaviour of persons and groups in space and time. Blaschke et al. (2012a) conclude that geospatial web-tools and platforms will completely change the traditional mapping/ planning process which was in essence a one-way dissemination of authoritative information from mapping agencies and other authorities. Classic concepts of Geography may serve as a common denominator among and between various disciplines, acting as a facilitator for interdisciplinary research (Blaschke et al., 2012b). As a reaction to the growing demand for participatory solutions in planning and public administration, authorities such as mapping agencies, environmental protection agencies or other national or regional organisations have recently begun providing data to non-public initiatives such as OpenStreetMap, or making data generally available for participatory initiatives.

Recent literature in GIScience has provided the beginning of a new era of scientific research on fundamental issues, raised by this new two-way information channel. This approach enables bi-directional communication between the government and citizens, rather than following the traditional top-down dissemination of information (we may even claim that McLuhans law of the media may need to be revisited from this point of view). Furthermore, we may diagnose the rise of 'day to day geography' (Bissel, 2009). Some scientists – predominantly with a Geography disciplinary background - use the term 'Neogeography' (e.g. Turner, 2007; Haklay et al., 2008,; Hudson-Smith et al., 2009). This contrasts classic GIS tools, targeted techniques and applications with areas of approachable, colloquial applications. Neogeography may also be seen as an umbrella for a diverse set of practices that (mostly) fall outside the professional geographic domain. Its popularity can be credited to the ability to communicate and share data through simple, freely available tools that can be learnt quickly and effectively without immersion in professional activities (Hudson-Smith et al., 2009).

In a more personal statement we may conclude that Neogeography tends towards the intuitive, expressive, personal, absurd, and/or artistic, but they may just be idiosyncratic applications of 'real' geographic techniques. We do not favour the use of this term but acknowledge its existence when scientifically discussing the two realms which can overlap as the same problems are presented to different sets of users: experts and non-experts. In a Web 2.0 environment, geographic content and applications can be deployed and used with minimal consideration or knowledge of the underlying and fundamental principles of geodesy, cartography, and/or geography.

GEOSPATIAL WEB APPLICATIONS AND TOOLS

As it was analysed, the advent of Web 2.0 and the availability of crowd-sourced information provided the ground for the development of new applications that integrate spatial web technologies and Volunteered Geographic Information in novel and powerful tools, which aim to improve citizen participation in spatial planning and public administration, referring to the concept of good governance as a common ground of political action (Fu & Sun, 2010).

In this sub-section we provide an overview of the currently implemented asset of the Geospatial Web, which is defined as "the use of the internet to deliver geographic information and maps" (Haklay et al., 2008; 2011). As applications are very rapidly developing, this overview will not be complete or exhaustive but should provide a good representation of 'typical' applications and widely used tools.

Carver et al. (2001), Rinner and Raubal (2004), and Li (2006) report about first initiatives in order to create Collaborative Decision Support Systems (CDSS), which allowed participatory planning and decision making using web-technologies. Since then, with citizens turning from consumers to 'prosumers' of (spatial) data (Fischer, 2009), and the every-day use of collaborative functionalities in social media such as Facebook, Twitter, Youtube or Flickr, a considerable number of participatory geospatial web-platforms have been introduced in spatial planning and public administration. From an e-participation point of state, what might interest us the most is that local and regional governments are increasingly resorting to geospatial web-platforms such as FixMyStreet (http://www.fixmystreet.com/), SeeClickFix (http://en.seeclickfix.com/) or ParcScan (www.parkscan.org), where citizens can inform them about problems (potholes, graffiti, broken streetlights, etc.) that rapid and appropriate actions can be taken. Since these actions are immediately reported to the public on the platform, governmental operations become more transparent and the citizens are able to more easily monitor their outcomes (Fu & Sun, 2010; Ramasubramanian, 2010).

Besides mapping tools, geospatial web-applications integrate blogs, video blogs, RSS-feeds, twitters, social network tools, discussion forums, widgets and other applications that allow users to create their own mash-ups, combing online data from multiple sources (Ashley et al., 2009). Increasingly, these applications are accessed by mobile devices.

Crowd-sourced planning applications such as the San Jose Wiki Planning Project[2] allow users to conduct surveys, add comments and post photos about issues relevant to planning initiatives and to get involved into urban planning (e.g., http://albany2030.org/ or http://www.vanalen.org/urbanvoids/). Web 2.0 tools are used within crisis management and emergency mapping such as Sahana (http://live.osgeo.org/en/overview/sahana_overview.html), transportation (http://openplans.org), public-health management (http://westnile.ca.gov/), public safety (www.firehistory.ok.ubc.ca) and in the environmental domain where citizen observers have contributed to developing a broad understanding of critical environmental issues during the 2010 Deepwater Horizon Gulf oil spill in the Gulf of Mexico (Bednarz & Kemp, 2011), just to name some examples. Geo-wikis (e.g., http://wikimapia.org/ and http://cyclopath.org/), GeoTweets (e.g., the ArcGIS Explorer Desktop Twitter), and mash-up competitions (e.g., http://www.appsfordemocracy.org/) complete this diverse picture of tools and platforms (Fu & Sun, 2010).

Most of these applications are led by non-governmental or community-based organizations such as OpenPlans (http://openplans.org), Place-Matters (http://www.placematters.org/), Urban-Buzz (www.urbanbuzz.org) or MySociety (http://www.mysociety.org/), and resort to open-software solutions. However, recently the software industry has started to act in this domain, which proves the growing importance of these applications. In 2012, for example, one of the biggest GIS-software vendors, ESRI, launched its Community Planning web application (http://localgovtemplates2.esri.com/communityplanning/), which provides communities with a collaborative design tool to develop land use plans interactively on the web (Smith, 2012).

INCREASING PARTICIPATION LEVELS: THEORY AND APPLICATIONS

A major question remains unanswered so far. Firstly, do the technological developments that have been described in this chapter, and especially the geospatial web, really boost participation? And secondly, how should existing applications be evaluated? Let us try to answer these questions in this sub-section.

Geographic Information Systems in general, offer many benefits to facilitate participation and communication between stakeholders of a decision making process. According to Rama-subramanian (2010), these include the ability to (a) identify and clarify spatial relationships, (b) speed up information processing time to answer formal criteria-based queries in real time, (c) improve communication with and among non-specialists, and (d) create what-if scenarios that help to evaluate different planning alternatives. Geospatial web applications in specific, amplify participatory opportunities through a set of new tools and applications, as we have already seen. For evaluating whether PPGIS applications in general facilitate participation in decision making processes, Steinmann et al. (2005) propose three overall evaluation criteria:

- Interactivity, implying that some action of the users generates a response either from another user or from the application itself.
- Visualisation, as it is a powerful method for representing spatial data.
- Usability, as PPGIS applications should be easily accessible and understandable by a broad audience.

Although it is increasingly regarded as essential, public involvement in spatial decision making is not common in most countries of the world. Even in the industrialised countries it has a highly problematic history. Public scepticism about the activities and motivations of planning, design and engineering professionals remains high. Arnstein´s (1969) famous 'Ladder of Citizen Participation' is still a useful way of characterising levels of public involvement, ranging from the ideal of citizen control to creeping manipulation by officials and powerful interest.

When talking about different levels of public participation in decision making processes, we may refer to different rungs of a ladder. Arnstein (1969) used this analogy to describe the transfer of political power from traditional decision makers to citizens. This ladder was modified by Smyth (2001; found in Carver, 2003) to an 'e-participation ladder' that transfers the generic levels of participation described by Arnstein to the framework of e-participation. In Smyth's e-participation ladder, the bottom rung refers to a stage where participation entirely exists in a passive mode, and the public is informed about planning issues through data sheets and information bulletins that are delivered online. Climbing up the ladder, the level of participation and public empowerment increases, with the top rung representing full public control and responsibility for final decisions in (spatial) planning processes (Carver, 2003; Steinmann et al., 2005). The further up the ladder, the more interactive methods and tools of online-collaboration and decision making are incorporated, starting from simple online-information delivery, online discussion forums, and opinion surveys to fully adopted online decision support systems. As the level of interactivity increases, the communication between citizens and public administration transforms from being unidirectional at the bottom rung to being bidirectional on the upper rungs of the ladder (Steinmann et al., 2005). This means that information, ideas and feedback are openly and collaboratively shared between public administration and the citizens.

Figure 2 merges Arnstein's ladder of participation with Smyth's ladder of e-participation and amends those ladders with content related to Geospatial web-applications. For each rung of the participation ladder we tried to identify methods and tools of the Geospatial web that have already been applied to e-participation initiatives or might be in the future:

This metaphor of a ladder has been extensively used in literature (Carver, 2003; Blaschke, 2004; Schlossberg & Shuford, 2005; Steinmann, 2005; Baker et al., 2007; Kienberger, 2010). In a very similar approach, the International Association for Public Participation (IAP 2) links the goals of public participation with the increasing impact on decision-making in a matrix that ranges from information sharing, consultation, involvement, collaboration to empowerment (Ramasubramanian, 2010). Hennig and Vogler

(2011) amended this matrix with web-tools that refer to each stage of the participation process (cp. Table 1).

Steinmann et al. (2004), as well as Sieber (2006) carried out an extensive review of existing PPGIS applications in the mid-2000s. By then, still the majority of online PPGIS applications were limited to the stage/tool 'online discussion' and did not move further up the participation ladder towards fully involving citizens in decision making processes. Surprisingly or not, it seems that this has not changed despite the above mentioned technological advances within the last ten years. By the time of writing, the most sophisticated geospatial web-applications (e.g. FixMyStreet or SeeClickFix) referred to the second to last rung of the ladder where citizens typically report problems to the public administration. However, the highest level of participation – the complete integration of citizens into problem solving and decision making processes - has not been yet realized in any web-based software application. Referring to the matrix of Henning and Vogler (2011), empowerment of citizens is not yet fully realised in existing applications of the Geospatial web.

PRESSING ISSUES: USABILITY, PRIVACY AND DATA QUALITY

The technological developments described in this chapter, particularly the development of Virtual Globes and the geospatial web, trigger a lot of research questions in regard to data quality, privacy and usability, and how this can be asserted and verified. In this sub-section, we discuss some of these questions before we turn towards final evaluation of the geospatial web within the domain of Public Participation GIS.

Let us first discuss the issue of usability and whether or not those people that are intended to be the main beneficiaries of PPGIS can access and fully use the geospatial web. Unlike in GIS

Figure 2. Geo-web e-participation ladder, modified after Carver (2003), Smyth (2001) and Steinmann et al. (2005)

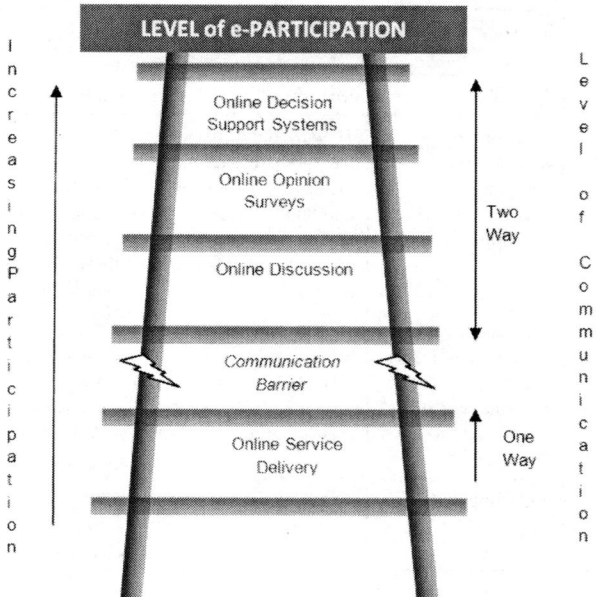

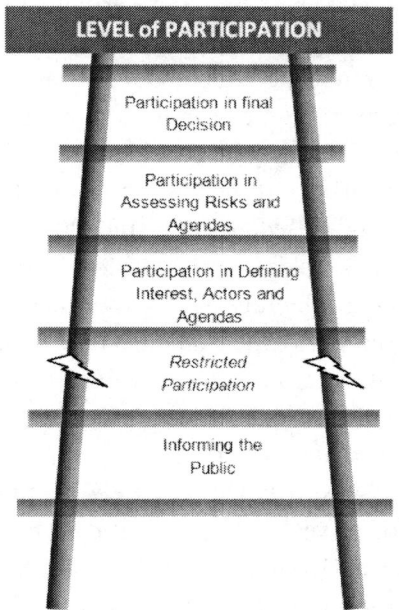

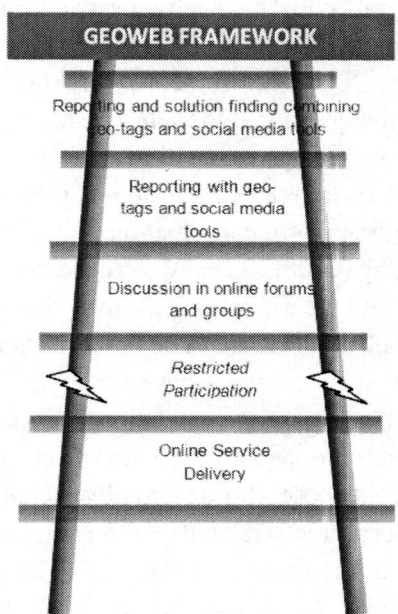

(Taylor, 1991; Pickles, 1995; Schuurman, 2000) there is basically no debate about the acceptance or rejection of Virtual Globes and the Geospatial web as a method or technology. Rather, the issue revolves around a series of open questions about how such technology will be understood relative to the practices of geography, how Virtual Globes will specifically influence representations of space, society, environment, and economy at the expense of other representations. The concept of

Table 1. Spectrum and techniques of public participation (Hennig & Vogler, 2011; adapted from IAP 2, 2007; Kingston, 2002; Milovanovic, 2003)

	One-way Communication	Two-way Communication			
	Inform	Consult	Involve	Collaborate	Empower
Objectives	To provide the public with balanced and objective information to assist them in understanding the problem, alternatives, opportunities and/or solutions.	To obtain public feedback on analysis, alternatives and/or decisions.	To work directly with the public throughout the process to ensure that public concerns and aspirations are consistently understood and considered.	To partner with the public in each aspect of the decision including the development of alternatives and the identification of the preferred solution.	To place final decision-making in the hands of the public.
Techniques	• Fact Sheets • Open houses	• Public comment • Surveys • Public meetings	• Workshops • Deliberative polling	• Citizen advisory com-mittees • Consensus-building • Participatory decision-making	• Citizens juries • Ballots • Dele-gated decision
Web-tools	• Web Sites	• On-line polls	• On-line discussion	• On-line services, forms and documents in electronic form	• On-line decision making support systems

the 'digital divide' has been extensively discussed in literature (Castells, 1996; Compaine, 2001; Elwood, 2006; Ghose, 2007; Haklay, 2012), raising the question if the selective access to ICT perpetuates exclusive social structures and hence leads to even greater exclusion of marginalized communities from participation.

Haklay (2008), states two criteria that should help PPGIS practitioners to evaluate the usability of geoweb applications: The first criterion refers to whether or not users have access to internet, discovering a strong correlation between those users who are socially excluded from decision making and those who are digitally excluded. The second criterion is related to a 'secondary digital divide' in the context of WebGIS. This 'digital skills divide' focuses on the question if the users have the skills and the knowledge required to operate geoweb tools and to handle tasks such as switching layers on and off, zooming, panning and clicking the map in order to retrieve further infor-mation about a map object, even more complex queries of information or simply understanding the concept of scale and generalization (Steinmann et

al., 2004; Haklay, 2008). Furthermore, the issue of map literacy which is defined as the "ability of the user to relate items and places on a map to the corresponding items in the real world" (Hak-lay, 2008, p. 6), may be considered as a limiting factor for efficiently using the Geospatial web (Haklay, 2008; Bednarz & Kemp, 2010; Gryl & Jekel, 2012). Taking into consideration the ever increasing availability of ICT-tools and internet all over the world, the challenge how to improve the spatial literacy of citizens will be in the focus of future discussions in this area.

The next important research topic refers to privacy issues. It is widely agreed that the pro-tection of privacy and personal data is of high importance. Geographic data becomes 'personal data,' when it is related to an identified or identifi-able natural person (Nouwt, 2008). When infor-mation about locations of people is provided we call this 'location data' or 'location information' which is commercially used in 'location based services.' Interestingly, for all applications studied in the context of this chapter we assume that the information is volunteered. If also the location as such – a coordinate or a street address – is provided, participatory Geospatial web applications are heavily concerned with this privacy issue. Nouwt distinguishes a) location data in a more narrow sense, which in general provides information about where a person or a thing is, b) 'traffic data,' which can provide information about where a person or a thing has been, and c) 'movement data' which provides information about the route a person or a thing has taken, or about the duration of a movement. Torrens (2010) even believes that developments in the precision of positioning systems and potency of contextual analysis could potentially erode locational privacy for individuals in their workplaces, homes, and recreation space. Frequently, users of Web 2.0 tools do not realize that they concede their privacy or intellectual property rights of information to online service providers when uploading content on, for example, social networks (Ashley et al., 2009). Not surprisingly geoweb-platforms such as 'RottenNeigbour' (where users have been encouraged to expose 'bad' neighbours like sex offenders, see: http://en.wikipedia.org/wiki/Rottenneighbor. com), or MyBikeLane (where citizens can report traffic violations like illegally parked cars on bike lanes; see: http://www.mybikelane.com/) have been controversially discussed in public and even raised serious legal concerns.

The third pressing issue when talking about the Geospatial web, refers to the quality of Volunteered Geographic Information. There is a legitimate concern amongst professional GIS-practitioners regarding certainty, accuracy and quality of spatial data collected by laypersons, which Crampton (2010) termed the '*GIS-wars*' of the 2000s (Fischer, 2012). Goodchild (2008) argues that cartographic products elaborated by highly qualified cartographers in traditional mapping agencies guarantee certain standards and specifications, whereas these quality standards are not necessarily inherent to crowd-sourced spatial data, so that VGI is sometimes termed "asserted geographic information, in that its content is as-serted by its creator without citation, reference, or other authority"(Goodchild, 2008, p. 220). Furthermore, VGI datasets tend to reflect the characteristics of specific online-communities of interest and do not represent the qualities of a random sample population (Fischer, 2012). Nevertheless we should not ignore the huge potential of Volunteered Geographic Information in terms of participation and empowerment of citizens, bearing in mind that VGI might not necessarily be a representative source of information or of outstanding quality.

GEOSPATIAL WEB IN DEVELOPING COUNTRIES

This section of the chapter examines the relevance of the geospatial component to the empowerment of citizens in developing countries, where shortcomings of democratic, collaborative, transparent, cross institutional and integrative local and regional planning are most obvious. In such countries it is most difficult to challenge the dominating power structures and unbalanced top-down approaches in planning and administration.

People before Technology: Characteristics of the Use of the Geospatial Web in Developing Countries

In many developing countries[3], there is a lack of health- and security-services provided by governments, transparent information policy about infrastructure projects, extraction and conservation of environmental resources, land tenure and land use management. Traditional spatial planning has been discredited as it is accounted for advocating inefficient, ineffective and even illegal projects and inadequate service provision resulting in a lack of legitimacy in the eyes of the citizens (Rakodi, 2001). The overwhelming part of society generally has little or no access to information, and political networks are likely to be excluded from non-transparent planning processes, public expenditures are often not located where they are needed most urgently or are not properly controlled by society (Resl, 2006). As a consequence, conflicts between stakeholders in local and regional planning occur, mainly in following areas: (a) territorial management and public services, (b) security, (c) public and individual transport and (d) public (eco-) health management. As in developing countries, the population in cities has grown rapidly over the last decades; problems related to spatial planning have increased especially in these urban areas and need to be addressed by an administration that uses new and innovative concepts and tools for participation (Steinberg, 2005; Fay & Morrison, 2006; Freire, 2006; Irazábal, 2009; Rodgers et al., 2011).

In the context of applying GIS in developing countries, there have been recent calls to rename Public Participation GIS (PPGIS) to Participatory GIS (PGIS) (Sieber, 2006; McCall & Dunn, 2012). While in industrialized countries of the 'Global North,' the access to spatial data and to sophisticated technologies is relatively easy, and decision making is embedded in more or less stable governance, the conditions of participatory work with GIS in developing countries are different. There, according to Kienberger (2010), PGIS is seen as "the crossing of participatory progressive development and GIScience, integrating low and high tech spatial management application [...] that should facilitate empowerment, possessing own spatial information, communication among stakeholders and as a learning process" (p. 77). Practical PGIS applications derive from community mapping and Participatory Rural Appraisal (PRA). This is a participatory map-making process which "gathers information about a community's lands and makes it visible to outsiders by using the language of cartography" (Corbert & Keller, 2005, p. 92). Nowadays, many PGIS projects in the 'Global South' are related to the conservation

and environmental domain, and especially to managing conflict over access to land and natural resources by promoting needs and rights of indigenous populations and local communities (Chapin et al., 2005; McCall & Dunn, 2012). However, PGIS applications in urban environments are rare.

The discussion of how to introduce (geo-) web 2.0 tools into the development domain basically started in September 2007, when the first international conference on 'Participatory Web 2.0 for Development' was organized by the United Nations Food and Agriculture Organization (FAO). Since then, the term 'Web2forDev' has become more and more common amongst PGIS-practitioners (for further information, please see the literature recommendations at the end of this chapter). The probably most well-known example of a Geospatial web-application in developing countries at the time of writing is Ushahidi (http://ushahidi.com/ - *Swahili for 'testimony' or 'witness'*). This is a platform that allows users to collect and upload geo-referenced information about incidents of public interest. It was created during Kenya's presidential elections in 2007 in order to provide Kenyan citizen journalists with a tool to report and map incidences of violence and peace efforts via the web and mobile phones.

The concept of digital divide that was described in the last sub-section especially refers to developing countries. However, the expanding provision of telecommunications infrastructure is helping to reduce costs and to improve access to the internet even in the 'Global South.' Furthermore, the increasing availability of mobile phones as a preferred tool for accessing and sharing information in many developing countries helps to address and overcome the digital divide (Martin & Corbett, 2011). However, especially in these countries the secondary digital divide, which refers to the skill of handling and processing spatial information (see previous sub-section), remains one of the main obstacles for using the Geospatial Web in a PGIS framework. Ashley et al. (2009) emphasise that "GIS-practitioners should not become sidetracked by a technology-driven hype, where excitement about the tools drive their usage, rather than what people can do with them" (p. 13). Furthermore, they criticise that many donor-funded projects supply equipment and tools without building community outreach services in order to build local capacity, content and acceptance. It is obvious and critically important to amend technology-driven PGIS initiatives with capacity building activities that allow users to fully access, understand, and use these tools (Sieber, 2006; Ghose, 2007; Ashely et al., 2009; McCall & Dunn, 2012). Furthermore, especially in developing countries, geoweb-tools have to resort to the social and cultural realities of the addressed citizens and communities. They have to take into consideration contextual factors such as the translation of materials into local languages (Garside, 2009), and provide a culturally and socially sensitive tool interface, data structure, data content and output design (Resl, 2006).

An evenly important factor is the organisational setting in which geoweb-tools are applied in developing countries. As GIS in general is an expert's tool, many small NGOs and community organisations are unable to use them as they cannot afford software licences and the cost of professional training (Weiner et al., 1995; Craig & Elwood, 1998; Elwood, 2006). However, the recent adoption of open source software in geoweb-tools is opening new opportunities for capacity building and outreach initiatives (Martin & Corbett, 2011). In this regard, scholars such as Resl (2006) suggest a network approach of interlinked communities, helping them to improve facilities, knowledge and capacities regarding system maintenance and management, and thus lowering undesired dependencies from other actors.

Aiming for Empowerment

Empowering marginalized communities and citizens is one of the main aims of applying the Geospatial web in developing countries. However, 'empowerment' is a widely and often casually used term. Frequently, it is referred to as both a process and an outcome of a critical reflective practice (Corbett & Keller, 2005). Carver (2001; according to Arnstein, 1969) defines empowerment "as the process by which stakeholders identify and shape their lives and the society in which they live through access to knowledge, political processes and financial, social and natural resources" (p. 62). Very interesting in the context of development countries is the definition of empowerment by Ramasubramanian (2010). She relates empowerment to the development of critical consciousness based on the theology of liberation of the Brazilian priest Paulo Freire (1970) that aims to overcome the exclusion of large parts of Latin American societies from political power since the Portuguese and Spanish colonisation of the continent. In her definition, critical consciousness "balances active engagement within a problem-solving process with a reflective analysis of the process itself and the resulting outcomes" (Ramasubramanian, 2010, p. 35). Hence, critical consciousness and thus empowerment amongst participants is achieved if,

1. The social, intellectual, and political capacity of the participants has improved.
2. The participants become more articulate and effective advocates for their own and the community's interests.
3. The Participants are more aware of the intricacies of urban governance and are better equipped to participate within these systems.
4. There is increased community cohesion.
5. There is willingness to participate, because there is increased trust in participatory processes and their outcomes (Ramasubramanian, 2010, p. 44).

We may record that the overarching goal of every P(P)GIS activity is empowerment, as P(P) GIS "can be empowering to disadvantaged groups by enabling them to use the language and tools of decision makers and so influence events that affect their lives and local geography" (Corbett

& Keller, 2005, p. 91). GIS in general and the Geospatial web in specific, are crucial for the construction of meanings of the physical environment, and allow what social geographers call the 'appropriation of space.' This refers to being empowered to challenge given meanings of space in order to achieve individual or collective aims (Gryl & Jekel, 2012). Hence, the production (and use) of spatial information through the Geospatial web allows 'actualizing citizens' for competing absolute representations of space as the Geospatial web is an instrument for hypothesis generation, democratic negotiation, and public participation in processes in a spatial domain. 'Actualizing citizens,' as opposed to 'dutiful citizens,' act through loose networks using social digital media and the Geospatial web for communication and interaction. They use digital narratives, which change their "relationships to civic knowledge and its components of authority, credibility, production-consumption, and sharing of information" (Gryl & Jekel, 2012, p. 8; according to Bennett et al., 2009, p. 108).

However, critics remain, especially when dealing with applying technology like the Geospatial web to the process of empowerment, as they introduce their own ambiguities with respect to access, equity, and digital representation of spatial knowledge (Elwood, 2006; Gryl & Jekel, 2012). Empowerment also implies the ownership and the legitimisation of the use of local knowledge with its conceptualization of space and spatial values that is generated within a participatory process. The – simplified - question 'who is the owner of the map' (Haklay, 2008), is a central element of legitimacy and empowerment and implies all stages of holding the data sources, data processing and the final information products themselves (McCall & Dunn, 2012). This is especially true for developing countries where local knowledge is of particularly high value for communities that are

likely to be excluded from information networks and decision making processes.

WHAT NEXT? FUTURE TRENDS AND DEVELOPMENTS

This chapter so far has tried to give an overview about the history, concepts and applications of the Geospatial web in the broader context of participation and empowerment. Still we are going to discuss trends and future developments that already become apparent in this last sub-section.

For a long time, collaborative mapping initiatives dominated real-world PPGIS applications (Sieber, 2006). As already mentioned in this chapter, recently available Web 2.0-techonolgies and their diffusion within society opened up new vistas for participatory planning initiatives. In this respect, Hennig et al. (2011) created the term 'social geo-communication,' referring to the participation of the public in planning processes supported by Web 2.0 platforms that allow the sharing and processing of information directly to and between the affected citizens and communities. However, the implementation of the concept of 'social geo-communication' in participatory spatial planning and public administration would demand one single web-platform that fully integrates web-mapping tools and social media in a user-friendly environment, and therefore constituting a social network for citizens and their initiatives in order to let them participate in local and regional development in an organized and structured way.

Analyzing existing geoweb-platforms that have been presented we may state that these platforms do not integrate proper tools for discussion and problem solving based on community interaction to their geo-tagging based observation and reporting frameworks. Therefore, an increasing number of scholars (Ramasubramanian, 2010;

Evans-Cowley, 2010; Fu & Sun, 2010) ask for the amplification of these platforms by adding additional functionalities which allow citizens to engage in building communities, programming activities, and in finding sound solutions rather than reporting their complaints to central (planning) offices. The availability of such spatially enabled, citizen driven and expert supported information and planning platforms would mean to finally climb the upper rung of the ladder of e-participation, what so far has not been achieved by any application. This would probably constitute a new paradigm for citizen participation in spatial planning. In an analogy to Web 2.0 we may suggest the term PPGIS 2.0 for this.

Beyond new technological developments like the ubiquitous access to the Geospatial web via smartphones or the concept of augmented reality which is about to be integrated into recent applications (Fischer, 2012), it is even more important to understand the consequences of using these tools for society, including legal issues, ethics, democracy, and equity. A respective body of knowledge specific to the geographic domain is just developing (Hudson-Smith et al., 2009). Research needs to clarify whether or not the Geospatial web can be used in order to support society to independently explore patterns from spatially 'mappable factors.' Society may then be able to utilise information about the location of phenomena and any relations between them.

However, this would presume that citizens are able to "access, read, interpret, and critically reflect of spatial information, to communicate with the aid of maps and other spatial representations, and to express location-specific opinions using geomedia" (Gryl & Jekel, 2012, p. 4). This is what Strobl (2008) refers to as a 'Spatial Citizen' that is considered as being a "growing tool for positive and productive engagement with improving and

managing society" (Bednarz & Kemp, 2011, p. 19). This 'Spatial Citizen' has appropriated the spatial domain of social life and has the "knowledge, skills, competencies, and abilities to be able to access and make sense of (geo-) information, in order to participate in democratic processes and make decisions, taking into account the situations and circumstances he encounters on a daily basis" (Gryl & Jekel, 2012, p. 8).

In the end, GIS and the Geospatial web should represent the many and convince the few that development aimed at real common wealth is a worthwhile strategy towards sustainability (Resl, 2006), and therefore help to empower citizens and communities in the quest for a better planned (urban) living environment.

CONCLUSION

In this chapter we discussed the most important concepts and tools in the domain of Geographic Information Systems (GIS) that are used to empower citizens, in order to call for their own concepts of habitat, livelihood, living conditions, infrastructure, and the access to and use of resources in the future. We have seen that regardless of the long tradition of GIS, the participatory aspect of applying GIS-tools in spatial planning and decision making is a fairly recent paradigm. However, the advent and ubiquity of Web 2.0 technologies, the availability of Virtual Globes and the increasing amount of spatial data collected by laypersons (Volunteered Geographic Information - VGI) provide so far unknown opportunities for citizen participation in the renegotiation of representations of space, especially regarding issues in urban governance. In this chapter we showed that the Geospatial web is an efficient tool in the quest for empowering citizens and altering the level of participation in decision making. This is especially true for developing countries, where the need for good governance and transparent planning is particularly high, as the overwhelming part of these countries' societies has been excluded from participation since the era of colonisation.

The increasing availability of geoweb technologies leads to new opportunities for decision-makers and ordinary citizens in order to collaborate and share information in dynamic and time-critical decision-making environments in urban planning and administration. Current projects and applications especially aim at achieving the complete integration of social media platforms and geospatial web-tools for planning initiatives and (self-) governance that are evolving at the grassroots level. Further research has to be done also regarding the societal implications of geospatial web technologies referring to usability issues, privacy and ethical implications as well as to the quality and accuracy of data that is collected in the 'crowd.' Despite an ever increasing number of Geospatial web applications that are available for citizens, communities and public administration, we may state that we are just at the beginning of a development that may completely redefine the issue of citizen participation in public administration and spatial planning in the future.

REFERENCES

Agarwal, P. (2005). Ontological considerations in GIScience. *International Journal of Geographical Information Science, 19*, 501–536. doi:10.1080/13658810500032321.

Ahlqvist, T. (2000). A quest for polygon landscapes, or GIS and the condition of epistemology. *Fennia, 178*, 97–111.

Arnstein, S. R. (1969). A ladder of citizen participation. *JAIP, 35*(4), 216–224.

Ascough, J., Rector, H. D., Hoag, D. L., McMaster, G., & Bruce, C. (2002). Multi-criteria spatial decision support systems - overview, applications, and future research directions. *Information Systems Research, 1*, 175–180.

Ashley, H., Corbet, J., Jones, D., Garside, B., & Rambaldi, G. (2009). Change at hand: Web 2.0 for development. In Holly, A., Kenton, N., & Milligan, A. (Eds.), *Participatory learning and action. London: The International Institute for Environment and Development (IIED), The Technical Centre for Agricultural and Rural Cooperation.* Wageningen: CTA.

Baker, M., Coaffee, J., & Sherriff, G. (2007). Achieving successful participation in the new UK spatial planning system. *Planning Practice and Research, 22*(1), 79–93. doi:10.1080/02697450601173371.

Bednarz, S. W., & Kemp, K. (2011). Understanding and nurturing spatial literacy. *Spatial Thinking and Geographic Information Sciences Conference 2011*. Tokyo.

Bennett, W.L., Wells, C., & Rank, A. (2009). Young citizens and civic learning: Two paradigms of citizenship in the digital age. *Citizenship Studies, 13*(2), 105–20. Retrieved March, 7, 2012 from http://dx.doi.org/10.1080/13621020902731116

Bissel, D. (2009). Visualising everyday geographies: Practices of vision through travel-time. *Transactions of the Institute of British Geographers, 32*, 42–60. doi:10.1111/j.1475-5661.2008.00326.x.

Blaschke, T. (2004). Participatory GIS for spatial decision support systems critically revisited. In Egenhofer, M., Freksa, C., & Miller, H. (Eds.), *GIScience 2004* (pp. 257–261). Adelphi, MD.

Blaschke, T., Donert, K., Gossette, F., Kienberger, S., Marani, M., Qureshi, S., & Tiede, D. (2012a). Virtual globes: Serving science and society. *Information, 3*(3), 372–390. doi:10.3390/info3030372.

Blaschke, T., & Strobl, J. (2010). Geographic information science developments. *GIS.Science - Zeitschrift für Geoinformatik, 23*(1), 9-15.

Blaschke, T., Strobl, J., Schrott, L., Marschallinger, R., Neubauer, F., & Koch, A. et al. (2012b). Geographic information science as a common cause for interdisciplinary research. In Gensel, J., Josselin, D., & Vandenbroucke, D. (Eds.), *Bridging the geographic information sciences* (pp. 411–427). Berlin, Heidelberg: Springer Lecture Notes in Geoinformation and Cartography. doi:10.1007/978-3-642-29063-3_22.

Butler, D. (2006). Virtual globes: The web-wide world. *Nature, 439,* 776–778. doi:10.1038/439776a PMID:16482123.

Caron, C., Roche, S., Goyer, D., & Jaton, A. (2008). GIScience journals ranking and evaluation: An international delphi study. *Transactions in GIS, 12*(3), 293–321. doi:10.1111/j.1467-9671.2008.01106.x.

Carver, S. (2003). *The future of participatory approaches using geographic information: Developing a research agenda for the 21st Century.* Position paper prepared for ESF-NSF Meeting on Access and Participatory Approaches in Using Geographic Information, Spoleto Italy, December 5–9, 2001.

Carver, S., Evans, A., Kingston, R., & Turton, I. (2001). Public participation, GIS, and cyberdemocracy: Evaluating on-line spatial decision support systems. *Environment and Planning. B, Planning & Design, 28,* 907–921. doi:10.1068/b2751t.

Castells, M. (1996). *The rise of the network society.* Oxford: Blackwell Publishers.

Chapin, M., Lamb, Z., & Threkeld, B. (2005). Mapping indigenous lands. *Annual Review of Anthropology, 34,* 619–638. doi:10.1146/annurev.anthro.34.081804.120429.

Clarke, K. C. (1997). *Getting started with GIS.* Upper Saddle River: Prentice Hall, Inc..

Coleman, D. J. (2010). The potential and early limitations of volunteered geographic information. *GEOMATICA, 64*(2), 209–219.

Compaine, B. M. (2001). *The digital divide. Facing a crisis or creating a myth?* Cambridge, London: MIT Press.

Corbett, J. M., & Keller, C. P. (2005). An analytical framework to examine empowerment associated with participatory geographic information systems (PGIS). *Cartographica: The International Journal for Geographic Information and Geovisualization, 40*(4), 91–102. doi:10.3138/J590-6354-P38V-4269.

Craglia, M., Goodchild, M. F., & Annoni, A. et al. (2008). Next-generation digital earth: A position paper from the Vespucci initiative for the advancement of geographic information science. *International Journal of Spatial Data Infrastructures Research, 3,* 146–167.

Craig, W., & Elwood, S. (1998). How and why community groups use maps and geographic information. *Cartography and Geographic Information Systems, 25,* 95–104. doi:10.1559/152304098782594616.

Craig, W. J., Harris, T. M., & Weiner, D. (2002). Community participation and geographic information systems. In Craig, W. J., Harris, T. M., & Weiner, D. (Eds.), *Community participation and geographic information systems* (pp. 3–16). London: Taylor and Francis.

Crampton, J. W. (2010). *Mapping: A critical introduction to cartography and GIS*. Oxford, UK: Wiley-Blackwell.

De Longueville, B. (2010). Community-based geoportals: The next generation? Concepts and methods for the geospatial Web 2.0. *Computers, Environment and Urban Systems*, *34*(4), 299–308. doi:10.1016/j.compenvurbsys.2010.04.004.

Densham, P. J. (1991). Spatial decision support systems. In D.J. Maguire, M. F. Goodchild, & D. W. Rhind (Eds.), Geographical information systems: Principles and applications, Vol.1 (pp. 403-412). Longmont, Harlow, Essex, England: Longman Scientific & Technical.

Eastman, R., Kyem, P. A., Toledano, J., & Weigen, J. (Eds.). (1992). GIS and decision making. Explorations in geographic information systems technology: A workbook series. Worcester, MA: Developed by the Clark Labs. Published by UNITAR (United Nations Institute for Training and Research).

Ellul, C., Haklay, M., & Francis, L. (2008). Empowering individuals and communities - is Web GIS the way forward? In (Proceedings) AGI GeoCommunity '08. Stratford-upon-Avon, UK.

Elwood, S. (2006). Critical issues in participatory GIS: Deconstructions, reconstructions, and new research directions. *Transactions in GIS*, *10*(5), 693–708. doi:10.1111/j.1467-9671.2006.01023.x.

Elwood, S. (2008). Volunteered geographic information: Future research directions motivated by critical, participatory, and feminist GIS. *GeoJournal*, *72*, 173–183. doi:10.1007/s10708-008-9186-0.

Environmental Systems Research Institute – ESRI. (2008). *Geography Matters*. An ESRI White Paper. Retrieved March 7, 2012, from http://www.gisday.com/cd2008/whitepaper/geography-matters.pdf

Evans-Cowley, J. S. (2010). Planning in the age of Facebook: The role of social networking in planning processes. *GeoJournal*, *75*, 407–420. doi:10.1007/s10708-010-9388-0.

Fay, M., & Morrison, M. (2006). *Infrastructure in Latin America and the Caribbean: Recent developments and key challenges*. World Bank Report.

Fischer, F. (2009). Learning in Geocommunities. An explorative view on geo-social network communities. In Jekel, T., Koller, A., & Donert, K. (Eds.), *Lernen mit Geoinformation IV* (pp. 12–21). Heidelberg: Wichman.

Fischer, F. (2012). *Geotagging and the city – Understanding the use of social location applications in urban space*. (Doctoral Thesis). Paris-Lodron University Salzburg.

Freire, M. (2006). Urban planning: Challenges in developing countries. In *Proceedings of the 1st International Congress on Human Development*. Madrid.

Garside, B. (2009). *Village voice: Towards inclusive information technologies*. IIED Briefing Papers. London: IIED. Retrieved March 7, 2012, from http://tinyurl.com/IIED-ICTbriefing

Ghose, R. (2007). Politics of scale and networks of association in public participation GIS. *Environment & Planning A*, *39*, 1961–1980. doi:10.1068/a38247.

Glennon, A. (2006). *Comments on naive geography, part 2*. Retrieved December 2, 2010, from http://geography2.blogspot.com/2006/06/comments-on-naive-geography-part-2.html

Goodchild, M. (2007). Citizens as sensors: The world of volunteered geography. *GeoJournal, 69,* 211–221. doi:10.1007/s10708-007-9111-y.

Goodchild, M. F. (2004). The validity and usefulness of laws in geographic information science and geography. *Annals of the Association of American Geographers. Association of American Geographers, 94,* 300–303. doi:10.1111/j.1467-8306.2004.09402008.x.

Goodchild, M. F. (2008). Commentary: Whither VGI? *GeoJournal, 72,* 239–244. doi:10.1007/s10708-008-9190-4.

Goodchild, M. F., & Kemp, K. K. (Eds.). (1990). *History of GIS.* NCGIA Core Curriculum 1990 Version, Unit 23. Santa Barbara: National Center of Geographic Information and Analysis, University of California, Santa Barbara. Retrieved March 12, 2012, from http://www.geog.ubc.ca/courses/klink/gis.notes/ncgia/toc.html

Google Press Release. (2009). *Introducing Google Earth 5.0.* Retrieved October 26, 2010, from http://www.google.com/intl/en/press/pressrel/20090202earthocean.html

Gryl, I., & Jekel, T. (2012). Re-centering GI in secondary education. Towards a spatial citizenship approach. *Cartographica, 47*(1), 2–12. doi:10.3138/carto.47.1.18.

Haklay, M. (2012). *'Nobody wants to do council estates' – digital divide, spatial justice and outliers.* Retrieved March 7, 2012, from http://povesham.wordpress.com/2012/03/05/nobody-wants-to-do-council-estates-digital-divide-spatial-justice-and-outliers-aag-2012/

Hakley, M., Singelton, A., & Parker, C. (2008). Web mapping 2.0: The neogeography of the GeoWeb. *Geography Compass, 2,* 2011–2039. doi:10.1111/j.1749-8198.2008.00167.x.

Harris, T. M., Rouse, L. J., & Bergeron, S. (2010). The geospatial semantic web, pareto GIS, and the humanities. In Bodenhamer, D. J., Corrigan, J., & Harris, T. M. (Eds.), *The spatial humanities: GIS and the future of humanities scholarship* (pp. 124–142). Bloomington: Indiana University Press.

Hennig, S., & Vogler, R. (2011). Participatory tool development for participatory spatial planning: The GEOKOM-PEP environment. In Jekel, T., Koller, A., Donert, K., & Vogler, R. (Eds.), *Learning with GI 2011: Implementing digital earth in education* (pp. 79–88). Berlin, Offenbach: Wichmann.

Hudson-Smith, A., Crooks, A., Gibin, M., Milton, R., & Batty, M. (2009). NeoGeography and Web 2.0: Concepts, tools and applications. *Journal of Location Based Services, 3*(2), 118–145. doi:10.1080/17489720902950366.

IAP2 - International Association of Public Participation. (2007). *Spectrum of public participation.* Retrieved March 14, 2012, from http://www.iap2.org/associations/4748/files/spectrum.pdf

Irazàbal, C. (2009). *Revisiting urban planning in Latin America and the Caribbean: Regional study prepared for revisiting urban planning: Global report on human settlements.* Retrieved January 10, 2012, from http://www.unhabitat.org/grhs/2009

Kiehle, C., Greve, K., & Heier, C. (2007). Requirements for next generation spatial data Infrastructures-standardized web based geoprocessing and web service orchestration. *Transactions in GIS, 11*(6), 819–834. doi:10.1111/j.1467-9671.2007.01076.x.

Kienberger, S. (2010). *Spatial vulnerability assessment. Methodoloy for the community and district level applied to floods in Búzi, Mozambique.* (Doctoral Thesis). Paris-Lodron University Salzburg.

Kingston, R. (2002). The role of e-government and public participation in the planning process. *XVI AESOP Congress.* July 10th – 14th 2002, Volos, Greece.

Kraak, J. M. (2003). Why maps matter in GI-Science. *The Cartographic Journal, 43*, 82–89. doi:10.1179/000870406X93526.

Lembo, A. J. (2005). *Lecture 1 – Course Objectives, Historical Perspectives of GIS, Conceptual Framework.* Cornell University. Retrieved April 12, 2012, from http://www.cornell.edu/academics/docs/Courses_of_Study_0708.pdf

Li, S. (2006). *Web-based collaborative spatial decision support systems: A technological perspective. Ryerson University.* Canada: MONOGRAFIA.

Longley, P. A., Goodchild, M. F., Maguire, D. J., & Rhind, D. W. (2001). *Geographic information systems and science.* New York: John Wiley and Sons.

MacEachren, A. M. (2000). Cartography and GIS: Facilitating collaboration. *Progress in Human Geography, 24*(3), 445–456. doi:10.1191/030913200701540528.

Malczewski, J. (1999). *GIS and multicriteria decision analysis.* New York: John Wiley and Sons.

Malczewski, J. (2000). On the use of weighted linear combination method in GIS: Common and best practice approaches. *Transactions in GIS, 4*(1), 5–22. doi:10.1111/1467-9671.00035.

Martin, M., & Corbett, J. M. (2011). *Creating the new 'new': Facilitating the growth of neo-geographers in the Global South using emergent Internet technologies.* Paper presented at GEOINFORMATIK 2011 – GEOCHANGE, June 15-17 2011, Munster, Germany.

McCall, M. K., & Dunn, C. E. (2012). Geo-information tools for participatory spatial planning: Fulfilling the criteria for 'good' governance? *Geoforum, 43*, 81–94. doi:10.1016/j.geoforum.2011.07.007.

McLead, B. (2006). *Mass-market Geo: Emerging trends and standards.* Paper presented at the CEOS WGISS-22 conference, 12 September 2006, Annapolis, MD.

Milovanovic, D. (2003). Interactive planning – use of the ICT as a support for public participation in planning urban development: Serbia and Montenegro cases. *39th ISoCaPR Congress 2003.*

Nouwt, S. (2008). *Reasonable expectations of geo-privacy?* SCRIPTed, *5*(2), 375-403. Retrieved April 6, 2012, from http://www.law.ed.ac.uk/ahrc/script-ed/vol5-2/nouwt.asp

Obermeyer, N. J. (1998). *PPGIS: The Evolution of Public Participation GIS.* Indiana State University. Retrieved March 14, 2012, from http://dusk.geo.orst.edu/ucgis/web/oregon/ppgis.pdf

Obermeyer, N. J. (2007). GIS: The maturation of a profession. *Cartography and Geographic Information Science, 34*, 129–132. doi:10.1559/152304007781002280.

OGC - Open Geospatial Consortium. (2005). *Interoperability and open architectures: An analysis of existing standardisation processes and procedures.* OGC White Paper. Retrieved July 15, 2010, from http://www.opengeospatial.org/

OGC - Open Geospatial Consortium. (2010). *KML*. Retrieved October 26, 2010, from http://www.opengeospatial.org/standards/kml/

Pavlovskaya, M. (2006). Theorizing with GIS: A tool for critical geographies? *Environment & Planning A, 38,* 2003–2020. doi:10.1068/a37326.

Pickles, J. (Ed.). (1995). *Ground truth. The social implications of geographic information systems.* New York: Guilford Press.

Pickles, J. (1997). Tool or science? GIS, technoscience and the theoretical turn. *Annals of the Association of American Geographers. Association of American Geographers, 87,* 363–372. doi:10.1111/0004-5608.00058.

Rakodi, C. (2001). Forget planning, put politics first? Priorities for urban management in developing countries. *International Journal of Applied Earth Observation, 3*(3), 209–223. doi:10.1016/S0303-2434(01)85029-7.

Ramasubramanian, L. (2010). *Geographic information science and public participation.* Berlin, Heidelberg: Springer Verlag.

Resl, R. (2006). GI for development – Can GIS challenge existing power stuructures? Working experiences from Ecuador. In Zeil, P., & Kienberger, S. (Eds.), *Geoinformation for development - Bridging the divide through partnerships* (pp. 125–136). Heidelberg: Wichmann Verlag.

Rinner, C., & Raubal, M. (2004). Personalized multi-criteria decision strategies in location-based decision support. *Journal of Geographic Information Sciences, 10*(2), 149–156.

Rodgers, D., Beall, J., & Kanbur, R. (2011). Latin American urban development into the 21st century: Towards a renewed perspective on the city. *European Journal of Development Research, 23*(4), 550–568. doi:10.1057/ejdr.2011.18.

Schlossberg, M., & Shuford, E. (2003). Delineating "Public" and "Participation" in PPGIS. *URISA Journal, 16*(2), 15–26.

Schroeder, P. (1996). Criteria for the design of a GIS/2. *Specialists' meeting for NCGIA Initiative 19: GIS and society,* Summer 1996.

Schuurman, N. (2000). Trouble in the heartland: GIS and its critics in the 1990s. *Progress in Human Geography, 24,* 569–590. doi:10.1191/030913200100189111.

Schuurman, N. (2001). Critical GIS: Theorizing an emerging discipline. *Cartographica, 36,* 1–108.

Schuurman, N. (2006). Formalization matters: Critical GIScience and ontology research. *Annals of the Association of American Geographers. Association of American Geographers, 96,* 726–739. doi:10.1111/j.1467-8306.2006.00513.x.

Sieber, R. (2006). Public participation geographic information systems: A literature review and framework. *Annals of the Association of American Geographers. Association of American Geographers, 96,* 491–507. doi:10.1111/j.1467-8306.2006.00702.x.

Smith, J. (2012, April 9th). Participation by design: Community planning…A new app for collaborative geodesign. Retrieved March 14, 2012, from http://blog.placematters.org/2012/04/09/participation-by-design-community-planning-a-new-app-for-collaborative-geodesign/

Smyth, E. (2001). *Would the Internet widen public participation?* (Master's Thesis). University of Leeds.

Sprague, R. H., & Carlson, E. D. (1982). *Building effective decision support systems.* Englewood Cliffs, NJ: Prentice-Hall, Inc..

Steinberg, F. (2005). Strategic urban planning in Latin America: Experiences of building and managing the future. *Habitat International, 29*(1), 69–93. doi:10.1016/S0197-3975(03)00063-8.

Steinmann, R., Krek, A., & Blaschke, T. (2004). Analysis of online public participatory GIS applications with respect to the differences between the US and Europe. In *UDMS 2004, 24th Urban Data Management Symposium*. Chioggia, Italy.

Steinmann, R., Krek, A., & Blaschke, T. (2005). Can online map-based applications improve citizen participation? In Böhlen, M., Gamper, J., & Polasek, W. (Eds.), *E-Government: Towards electronic democracy* (pp. 25–35). Lecture Notes in Computer Science Berlin: Springer Verlag. doi:10.1007/978-3-540-32257-3_3.

Strobl, J. (2005). GI science and technology - where next? *GIS Development, 9*, 40–43.

Strobl, J. (2008). Digital earth brainware. In Schiewe, J., & Michel, U. (Eds.), *Geoinformatics paves the highway to digital earth* (pp. 134–138). Osnabrück: University of Osnabrück.

Sui, D. Z. (2008). The wikification of GIS and its consequences: Or Angelina Jolie's new tattoo and the future of GIS. *Computers, Environment and Urban Systems, 32*, 1–5. doi:10.1016/j.compenvurbsys.2007.12.001.

Taylor, P. J. (1991). GKS. *Political Science Quarterly, 9*, 211–212.

Taylor, P. J., & Johnston, R. (1995). GIS and geography. In Pickles, J. (Ed.), *Ground truth* (pp. 68–87). New York: Guilford Press.

Torrens, P. (2008). Wi-Fi geographies. *Annals of the Association of American Geographers. Association of American Geographers, 98*(1), 59–84. doi:10.1080/00045600701734133.

Torrens, P. M. (2010). Geography and computational social science. *GeoJournal, 75*, 133–148. doi:10.1007/s10708-010-9361-y.

Turner, A. (2006). Introduction to neogeography. Sebastopol, US: O'Reilly Press.

Weiner, D., Warner, T., Harris, T., & Levin, R. (1995). Apartheid representations in a digital landscape: GIS, remote sensing, and local knowledge in Kiepersol, South Africa. *Cartography and Geographic Information Systems, 22*, 30–44. doi:10.1559/152304095782540537.

Wienand, G. (2007). Wie unterstützt geoinformation unser Gesundheitswesen. In J. Schweikart & P. Schatzl (Eds.), *GIS – Zeitschrift für Geoinformatik, (10) 2007*. Retrieved March 12, 2012, from http://www.medint.at/healthgis/motivation.htm

ADDITIONAL READING

Boulton, A. (2010). Just maps: Google's democratic map-making community? *Cartographica, 45*(1), 1–4. doi:10.3138/carto.45.1.1.

Carver, S., Evans, A., & Kingston, R. (2004). Developing and testing an online tool for teaching GIS concepts applied to spatial decision-making. *Journal of Geography in Higher Education, 28*(3), 425–438. doi:10.1080/0309826042000286983.

Chambers, R., Fox, J., McCall, M., & Rambaldi, G. (2006). Practical ethics for PGIS practitioners, facilitators, technology intermediaries, and researchers. In Ashley, H. (Ed.), *Participatory Learning and Action, 54, 106 – 113*.

Chambers, R., & Mayoux, L. (2003). Reversing the paradigm: Quantification and participatory methods. Paper submitted to the EDIAIS Conference on "New Directions in Impact Assessment for Development: Methods and Practice." University of Manchester, UK. Retrieved March 16, 2012, from http://www.iapad.org/publications/ppgis/Chambers-Mayoux.pdf

Craig, W., Harris, T., & Weiner, D. (Eds.). (2002). *Community participation and geographic information systems*. London: Taylor and Francis.

Crampton, J. (2009). Cartography: Performative, participatory, political. *Progress in Human Geography*, *33*(6), 840–848. doi:10.1177/0309132508105000.

Dennis, S. F. (2006). Prospects for qualitative GIS at the intersection of youth development and participatory urban planning. *Environment & Planning A*, *38*(11), 2039–2054. doi:10.1068/a3861.

Devas, N. (2004). Urban governance, voice and poverty in the developing world. Retrieved March 18, 2012, from http://wxy.seu.edu.cn/humanities/sociology/htmledit/uploadfile/system/20100512/20100512154247109.pdf

Dunn, C. E. (2007). Participatory GIS – a people's GIS? *Progress in Human Geography*, *31*(5), 616–637. doi:10.1177/0309132507081493.

Dunn, C. E. (2007). Participatory GIS – a people's GIS? *Progress in Human Geography*, *31*(5), 616–637. doi:10.1177/0309132507081493.

Economic Commission for Europe. (2008). *Spatial planning - Key instrument for development and effective governance with special reference to countries in transition*. Geneva, Switzerland: United Nations. Retrieved April 4, 2012, from http://www.unece.org/fileadmin/DAM/hlm/documents/Publications/spatial_planning.e.pdf

Elwood, S. (2002). Neighborhood revitalization through 'collaboration': Assessing the implications of neoliberal urban policy at the grassroots. *GeoJournal*, *58*, 121–130. doi:10.1023/B:GEJO.0000010831.73363.e3.

Elwood, S. (2006). Negotiating knowledge production: The everyday inclusions, exclusions, and contradictions of participatory GIS research. *The Professional Geographer*, *58*(2), 197–208. doi:10.1111/j.1467-9272.2006.00526.x.

Elwood, S. (2010). Geographic information science: Emerging research on the societal implications of the geospatial web. *Progress in Human Geography*, *34*(3), 349–357. doi:10.1177/0309132509340711.

Elwood, S. (2010). Geographic information science: Visualization, visual methods, and the geoweb. *Progress in Human Geography*, *35*(3), 401–408. doi:10.1177/0309132510374250.

Freire, M. (2006). *Urban planning: Challenges in developing countries*. Paper Submitted to I International congress on Human Development, Madrid, España. Retrieved January 24, 2012, from http://www.reduniversitaria.es/ficheros/Mila%20Freire(i).pdf

Ghose, R. (2001). Use of information technology for community empowerment: Transforming geographic information systems into community information systems. *Transactions in GIS*, *5*(2), 141–163. doi:10.1111/1467-9671.00073.

Ghose, R. (2005). The complexities of citizen participation through collaborative governance. *Space and Polity*, *9*(1), 61–75. doi:10.1080/13562570500078733.

Goodchild, M. F. (2007). Citizens as sensors: The world of volunteered geography. *GeoJournal*, *69*, 211–221. doi:10.1007/s10708-007-9111-y.

Kurtz, H., & Hankins, K. (2005). Guest editorial: Geographies of citizenship. *Space and Polity*, *9*(1), 1–8. doi:10.1080/14742830500078500.

Kyem, P. A., McCall, M., Rambaldi, G., & Weiner, D. (2006). Participatory spatial information management and communication in developing countries. *The Electronic Journal on Information Systems in Developing Countries, 25*(1), 1–9.

Martin, D. G. (2003). "Place-Framing" as place-making: Constituting a neighborhood for organizing and activism. *Annals of the Association of American Geographers. Association of American Geographers, 93*(3), 730–750. doi:10.1111/1467-8306.9303011.

Martin, D. G. (2004). Nonprofit foundations and grassroots organizing: Reshaping urban governance. *The Professional Geographer, 56*(3), 394–405.

McCann, E. J. (2003). Framing space and time in the city: Urban policy and the politics of spatial and temporal scale. *Journal of Urban Affairs, 25*(2), 159–178. doi:10.1111/1467-9906.t01-1-00004.

Miller, C. (2006). A beast in the field: The Google maps mashup as GIS/2. *Cartographica, 41*(3), 187–199. doi:10.3138/J0L0-5301-2262-N779.

Parks, L. (2009). Digging into Google Earth: An analysis of "Crisis in Darfur. *Geoforum, 40*, 535–545. doi:10.1016/j.geoforum.2009.04.004.

Sidlar, C. L., & Rinner, C. (2009). Utility assessment of a map-based online geo-collaboration tool. *Journal of Environmental Management, 90*, 2020–2026. doi:10.1016/j.jenvman.2007.08.030 PMID:18539381.

Sieber, R. E. (2011). *Proceedings of the 2011 Spatial Knowledge and Information Canada Conference: Vol. 1. SKI Canada*. Retrieved May 11, 2012, from http://rose.geog.mcgill.ca/ski/system/files/fm/2011/2011_Proceedings_Vol1.pdf

Tanaka, T., Abramson, D. B., & Yamazaki, Y. (2009). Using GIS in community design charrettes: Lessons from a Japan–U.S. collaboration in earthquake recovery and mitigation planning for Kobe. *Habitat International, 33*(4), 310–318. doi:10.1016/j.habitatint.2008.08.006.

Thielmann, T., Van der Velden, L., Fischer, F., & Vogler, R. (2011). *Dwelling in the Web: Towards a Googlization of Space*. Draft Paper prepared for the 1st Berlin Symposium on Internet and Society. Retrieved May 15, 2012, from http://berlinsymposium.org/sites/berlinsymposium.org/files/paper_googlizationspace-new_covertext_0.pdf

Tulloch, D. (2008). Is VGI participation? From vernal pools to video games. *GeoJournal, 72*(3-4), 161–171. doi:10.1007/s10708-008-9185-1.

KEY TERMS AND DEFINITIONS

Empowerment: A process that aims at facilitating the access to knowledge, political and financial power as well as social and natural resources to individuals and groups that have so far been excluded from decision making processes.

Geographic Information Systems (GIS): A Geographic Information System (GIS) integrates hardware, software and (spatial) data to assist in the acquisition, handling, analysis and display of geographically referenced information.

Geospatial Web: Web-applications and data infrastructures that help users find, access, and sometimes manipulate data of interest on the web dynamically and therefore provide a two-way gateway for geographic information and maps to a wide range of users.

Public Participation GIS (PPGIS): Geographic Information Systems that are applied to participatory spatial planning processes with a specific focus on non-governmental or grassroot organizations, and community-based organizations as user groups.

Spatial Decision Support Systems (SDSS): Computer-aided systems that are designed to explore and structure complex spatial problems for a more transparent and efficient decision making process.

Virtual Globes: Web-based applications that allow users to interact with and query overhead imagery and spatial data via a three-dimensional representation of the Earth.

Volunteered Geographic Information (VGI): Spatial Data collected by laypersons provided to the public for free.

ENDNOTES

[1]   According to Ellul et al. (2008), 75% of all information in local government is geographically referenced with 45 of the 122 national British e-government priorities requiring GIS (p. 2).

[2]   http://www.govtech.com/e-government/ San-Jose-Califs-Wikiplanning-Project-on. html; retrieved on March 1st, 2012.

[3]   Using the term 'developing countries' may be considered in these days as a strong generalization as it embraces complex societies. These societies may include power elites that have easy access to information and technology and are technologically sophisticated. On the contrary, there are groups of marginalized people in industrialized countries such as the United States. One can argue that at an individual level the needs of people in poor countries may be surprisingly similar to those of industrialized countries. A major difference is typically the governance and the potential to change this situation quickly – if political consensus is achieved. The authors try to avoid a political debate here and try to describe the technological developments and resulting options here in a neutral way although we are aware that there will never be a completely 'innocent' technology.

Chapter 10
Citizen Science Perspectives on E-Participation in Urban Planning

Caren Cooper
Cornell Lab of Ornithology, USA

Ashwin Balakrishnan
Southern Bronx River Watershed Alliance, USA

ABSTRACT

Citizen science is a method for an interested public to share information in order to co-create scientific knowledge, typically drawing on games and hobbies and employing electronic media such as web-based data-entry forms and online social networks. Citizen science has emerged in many fields of science (e.g., ecology, astronomy, atmospheric studies, anthropology) and advanced to produce important research findings based on high-quality, reliable data collected, and/or processed, by the public. In turn, participants have increased their interest in, and understanding of, topics related to citizen science projects, and experienced greater civic engagement and social capital. Urban planning initiatives seek to engage people in activities from data gathering to community discussions. The authors review the history of urban planning models and highlight how e-participation can overcome some of the limitations in traditional planning. The authors review how information and communication technologies (ICT) for Citizen Science methods can facilitate public participation in data collection and co-creating knowledge useful to planning decisions. The authors suggest that such efforts can ensure a collaborative rather than adversarial type of public participation and have added outcomes of increasing involvement of an informed public in other aspects of the planning process.

INTRODUCTION

With advances in Internet tools, mobile technologies, and social media, there are changes in the nature, frequency, and types of human interactions. One important change brought about by

DOI: 10.4018/978-1-4666-4169-3.ch010

information and communication technology (ICT) is the increase in the opportunity for individuals to electronically participate in activities that virtually link their real-world experiences with others. In recent decades, real-world interactions, and the social capital built upon those networks, have been declining, resulting in disengaged and civically disinclined citizens (Putnam, 2000). If this decline is attributable to the pervasiveness of technology shaping individual leisure time, then an important strategy to any endeavor that relies on participation may involve fostering virtual-world interactions and subsequent digital social capital (Mandarano et al., 2011). So far, virtual interactions have not been fully effective at replacing face-to-face communication, but consideration of their advantages and limitations can help collaborative, computer-mediated practices reach their potential (Rhoads, 2010).

Public participation in scientific research, often called Citizen Science, has emerged in many disciplines and grown in capacity and scale in recent decades. New approaches in Citizen Science have largely been in response to increased modes of e-participation (Newman et al., 2010; Goodchild, 2007; Burke et al., 2006). There are many types of communication, exchanges of information, social processes, and learning associated with participation in Citizen Science projects, but e-participation in the form of data contributions is the fundamental commonality. In urban planning, there are many types of communicative and interactive activities among public and private stakeholders and planners that can be supported by ICT, resulting in e-planning (Silva, 2010). Furthermore, urban planning processes are often ameliorated by observations and information that the public can provide. E-participation in Citizen Science has fostered greater engagement in scientific research, and e-planning can potentially increase public access and participation by increasing the avenues of engagement in the urban planning process.

In this chapter, our objective is to explore the many varieties and/or components of Citizen Science, particularly data collected and submitted electronically by the public, and how their incorporation into e-planning might lead to desired increases in public participation in urban planning processes. First, we review the history of urban planning models and, drawing on current examples

of e-planning; we highlight how e-participation can play a role in overcoming some of the limitations in traditional planning. Second, we review different models of citizen science and, drawing on examples, highlight common e-tools that assist public participation in scientific research. Third, we explore the social and learning outcomes associated with participation in Citizen Science projects and their implications for incorporating Citizen Science practices into e-participation in urban planning. Finally, we discuss challenges of e-participation common to Citizen Science and urban planning. We conclude with the suggestion that using ICT to facilitate public participation in data collection and co-creating knowledge useful to planning decisions can foster collaboration and consensus building in planning rather than conflict, and promote increased involvement of an informed public in other aspects of the planning process.

PROGRESSIONS TO E-PARTICIPATION IN URBAN PLANNING AND CITIZEN SCIENCE

Planning decisions have direct consequences for the day-to-day life of residents in cities, towns, and suburbs. In an ideal, healthy democracy, the residents of planned localities should expect to be involved in physical, social, economic, and environmental planning to ensure their communities are safe and livable. In order to build plans that are responsive to the needs of the citizens, planners must use public participation tools and processes that capture the unique knowledge and experience of residents and provide them with information about the planning process (Berry et al., 1993). When local residents are actively involved in the planning of their communities, they are more likely to be involved with and support the implementation of planning projects (Evans & Crowley, 2006; Potapchuk, 1996).

In reviewing reasons for direct citizen participation in governance, Roberts (2004) highlighted several drawbacks of public participation. Public participation in planning can be great in theory; however, it can encounter problems in practice (reviewed by Bourgoin et al., 2012). Public participation may result in stalemates when competing interest simply cannot agree on plans. Additionally, if these processes do not involve a diverse range of stakeholders, the voices of special interests may have disproportionate impacts on planning outcomes. However, new communications tools and processes that promote consensus building, information sharing, and negotiation could potentially address many of the cited problems in participation processes.

Substantive citizen participation isn't built into all planning decisions made by local, state, and federal governments, and sometimes citizens are unaware that planning decisions are being made which impact them. Often residents may be reluctant or unable to learn the procedures of planning and policymaking from planners. The technical nature of traditional planning can isolate decision making to planning and policymaking professionals (Lane, 2005). This divide is similar to the isolation and alienation of science from the public. Advances in ICT may be enlisted as tools to facilitate participation of residents in productive ways and thereby bridge the divide between participation theory and practice.

HISTORY OF PUBLIC PARTICIPATION IN URBAN PLANNING

In order to understand how the participatory practices of citizen science can help shape effective methods of e-participation in urban planning, we must first look at the general history of public participation in urban planning. Today, public participation in planning is commonly encouraged by urban planners and local governments, and often mandated by law. Arnstein's ladder of participation can serve as a guiding typology to help understand the depth of citizen participation in different planning models (Table 1, annotated version from Arnstein, 1969).

Blueprint Planning

Modern practices in urban planning are deeply rooted in planning theories of 19th Century European thinkers, such as Patrick Geddes and Ebenezer Howard (Lane, 2005). Early planners

Table 1. Guiding Typology - Arstein's Ladder of Participation

Level of Citizen Participation	Arnstien's Participation Spectrum	Planning School	Planning Model
Rung 8: Citizen Control	High Citizen Power	Pluralism	- Communicative
Rung 7: Delegated Power	Medium Citizen Power	Pluralism	- Bargaining
Rung 6: Partnership	Low Citizen Power	Pluralism	- Marxist - Advocacy - Transactive
Rung 5: Placation	Tokenism	Synoptic	- Mixed Scanning
Rung 4: Consultation	Tokenism	Synoptic	- Incrementalism - Rational -Comprehensive
Rung 3: Informing	Tokenism	Synoptic	- Synoptic
Rung 2: Therapy	Non-participation	"Blueprint" Planning	- Blueprint Planning
Rung 1: Manipulation	Non-participation	"Blueprint" Planning	

Source: Compiled by authors from Lane (2005) and Arnstein (1969)

such as Geddes and Howard, often called "blueprint" planners, viewed planning as an apolitical and technical enterprise in which planners used scientific rationality and reason to design ideal blueprints for city development that would promote the "public good" and encourage more moral societies (Lane, 2005). Blueprint planners sought to influence society mainly through the alteration of built environments, not through programmatic or policy-based means. Blueprint planners were predominantly white, privileged males and their blueprints were meant to unilaterally alter urban communities and did not aim to involve the public in the design process. In this context, the involvement of a wide range of citizens in the planning process was antithetical to blueprint planning (Lane, 2005).

Synoptic Planning

With mid-twentieth century growth of cities and suburbs, automobiles use, and travel between urban, suburban, and rural settings, a new planning paradigm was needed to understand dynamic urban systems. Planners saw the incredible mobilization efforts that occurred during World War II when administrators, analysts, and engineers worked together. In the 1950s the synoptic method (also known as systems planning and rational-comprehensive planning) emerged to more comprehensively assess the needs of cities and find policy and planning solutions that optimally addressed those needs (Lane, 2005; Silva, 2010). Extending the blueprint model, the synoptic planning model further professionalized planners as the technical experts of city function and design with heavy emphasis on scientific methods and rationality (Mandarano, 2011). During the time when synoptic planning was the dominant model, governments began to mandate public consultation into their systematic procedures of planning. Synoptic planning has a sequential methodology for data collection, analysis, and decision making (Lane, 2005). Thus, at a glance the scientific approach could make synoptic planning appear compatible with the adoption of citizen science methods. Yet, because the synoptic planning model's emphasized the planner as expert analyst of plans, citizen contributions in this paradigm were limited to token consultations on predetermined plans (Mandarano, 2011). Fortunately, some descended models of planning retained the scientific methodologies of the synoptic methods.

Plural Models of Planning

The synoptic planning model not only minimized the role of citizens in planning, but also viewed society as a homogeneous body with one "public interest" (Faludi, 1973). By neglecting to acknowledge the different communities and interest groups within cities and the various ways each utilize urban space, synoptic planning did not address the issue of equal representation (Arnstein, 1969; Lane, 2005). In the late 1960's and early 1970's, professionals and community activists began to challenge the centralized power of planners and planning commissions, and complicated the idea of a singular public interest (Hall, 1983; Lane, 2005). Acknowledging pluralism in public interest, several models of planning emerged, including those articulated by modern thinkers such as Davidoff in the 1960s (advocacy planning), Friedmann in the 1970s (transactive planning), and David Harvey in the 21st Century (transformative planning).

The advocacy planning model emerged from the involvement of urban planners in the civil rights movement. It was an organized response to the displacement of low-income communities of color by federal urban renewal schemes in cities throughout the United States. The growth of advocacy planning was bolstered by the War on Poverty, specifically the Model Cities Program. Paul Davidoff's (1965) "Advocacy and Pluralism in Planning" conveyed a vision of planning as a collaborative tool for planners and communities to address inequality in cities.

Davidoff's fundamental notions of citizen participation in planning were that 1) values are central to planning processes and the subjectivity and political motives of planners, agencies, and stakeholders should be considered; 2) there are a diversity of interests in cities, and plans and planning processes should account for this pluralism; 3) neighborhoods should have the power to create their own plans rather than simply react to the official plans created by planning professionals; 4) the planning profession should consider the social consequences linked to the physical planning of cities. Davidoff believed that a transition should be made for planners to "see physical structures and land as servants to those who use them" and consider how planners can shape urban policy to promote social and economic equity (Davidoff, 1965). As Davidoff's principles convey, advocacy planning strives to involve a diverse range of stakeholders and intimate public involvement in the creation of plans, not simply the critique of preconceived plans.

The transactive planning model, developed by Friedmann in the 1970's, encourages public participation in order for planners to learn about community needs and concerns and for the local communities to learn about planning policy and structures of power in government (Friedmann, 1973; 1994). Transactive planning comes with the expectation of face-to-face contact between planners and the residents of communities, often organized into stakeholder groups. When utilizing the transactive model, empowerment of communities are ends in themselves rather than simply the means to a planning outcome. This model envisioned planners as sensors who receive information and feedback from stakeholders and incorporate their ideas, concerns, and needs into plans.

Transformative planning, partially informed by Marxist analyses of the political economy of cities, seeks to empower marginalized communities so that the planning profession does not remain an instrument of dominant social classes (Lane, 2005). Transformative planning leverages the organizing power of community-based groups to transform traditionally excluded groups into the leaders of planning processes. The insights and knowledge of individuals in local communities are highly valued and thought of as central to planning outcomes. Transformative planning seeks to move planning from a physical design field to a politically and socially conscious discipline. In Harvey's The Right to the City, transformative urban planning and community-based leadership is a human right (Harvey, 2008). Harvey, activists, and organizers that comprise The Right to the City movement argue that residents of urban communities possess a right to transform themselves, their communities, and their cities. They call for urban residents to harness their collective power to rethink and recreate urban planning processes and the development of cities.

Limitations in Traditional Planning Practices

Despite the clear evolution of public participation and authority in planning models over the last century and a half, many elements of blueprint and synoptic planning that run counter to participatory planning have remained. Several features can limit the effectiveness of planning. First, power disparities exist: between the planner(s) and the public and among different public interest groups. Planners have technical expertise, but can't make rational decisions without information on the values and knowledge of the public. Second, planning schools typically emphasize physical design elements and neglect the facilitation skills needed to incorporate social elements, public opinions, and local knowledge. Third, planning practices remain challenged by pluralism so that planners are often idealized as the experts on serving a monolithic public interest. In reality, political complexity often creates situations where the interests of a powerful few, whether they are influential politicians, moneyed economic interests, or vocal, organized grassroots groups with narrow interests, dominate and/or create gridlock (Bourgoin et al., 2012). Fourth, the town hall model in which most planning meetings are conducted often creates a culturally inflexible space in which public participation becomes "token," temporally discontinuous, limited to responding to existing agendas, and with limited government accountability.

Irrespective of the planning paradigm, the quality of the outcome is dependent on the participation of citizens. For this reason, public participation in local land-use planning was part of Agenda 21, signed at the Rio Earth Summit in 1992 (see Bourgoin et al., 2012). The participation process should be driven by the people affected by planning decisions and who can provide knowledge that fits local context (Bourgoin et al., 2012). In order to optimize public participation, communities and planners can adopt paradigms and tools that help to democratize the planning process. For example, Bourgoin and Castella (2011) developed a role-playing game (PLUP Fiction) to train people to negotiate land zoning. The game, which includes group-building aspects and visualizations, evened power imbalances and created genuine involvement when implemented in rural Laos (Bourgin et al., 2012). Planners can be aware that political power and social plurality matter. The idea of what makes someone a technical expert or "real" planner is challenged in planning paradigms based in pluralism, and the multiple groups of stakeholders impacted by planning decisions are thought to bring valuable knowledge and experiences to the planning process (Angotti, 2007).

A Move to E-Participation

With extensive and plural involvement of the public in planning as a goal, we focus on how online tools can make planning and decision making procedures in urban planning more democratic,

engaging, and accessible. E-participation in planning encompasses a wide range of information and communications technologies (ICT), enabling the provision of open source information, the collection of data from the public, greater access to democratic processes, forums for collaboration, and communication among urban stakeholders and government. The use of online tools doesn't mean a simple shift from paper based methods to online methods. As Silva (2011) states, "This move requires a change in the methods of data collection, storage and analysis, a revision of public participation practices, new mechanisms for the control of planning scenarios, and for monitoring and evaluation of urban development processes, as well as new ethical considerations."

Several years ago, a survey of the use of e-tools by municipalities found that most use the Internet to share documents, typically zoning ordinances (Conroy & Evans-Crowley, 2006). Fewer posted the agendas of planning meetings (47%) and the minutes of these meetings (36%). About 28% of municipalities used GIS and other maps to provide information, either static or interactive. Fewer used e-mail to deliver news (18%), provide information in alternative languages (9%), or use multimedia like streaming video and/or audio (6%). None used these tools to create 'virtual meeting experiences' where citizens could interact during meetings and only 3% provided tools for online discussion groups (e.g., listservs).

Silva (2011) asserted that a sophisticated and accessible e-planning website or platform gives information about planning systems, the laws and procedures around urban planning on the local, regional and national levels. The website should include local plans in 2-D and 3-D formats, technical reports, and the ability for individuals to comment, request consultation, petition, or establish contact with planners and other stakeholders through the website (Silva, 2011). Conroy and Evans-Crowley (2006) found that the amount of ICT in local governance was positively influenced by community wealth and size, and negatively influenced by the percentage of nonwhites. These patterns are discouraging given that ICT can be leveraged to give minority groups equal access to decision-making processes in local governance.

Multiple e-tools that are important for leveraging citizen science are also important to planning. Social networks and web 2.0 platforms such as Twitter and Facebook are exciting arenas for e-participation in planning. Local governments and community based groups have initiated profiles, projects, and groups through social networks to promote citizen contributions to planning processes and communication between local government and citizens. In addition, these platforms have helped encourage citizen-to-citizen communications about urban planning processes in their neighborhoods (Conroy & Evans-Crowley, 2006).

Geographic information systems have been used as a visual platform for negotiations and to integrate stakeholder knowledge into planning, referred to as GIS-P, GIS for Participation (Cinderby, 1999). For example, in China, where there is a limited history of public participation in urban planning, and instead historically top-down, centralized, and authoritarian practices, there are uses of GIS-P in land-use planning (Wang et al., 2008). With GIS-P, capturing input and data from local people in a town-hall or forum setting does not require locals to interact independently or directly with spatial aspects of GIS (Cinderby & Forrest, 2005). More recently, planners have facilitated e-participation with GIS. Public participation geographic information systems (PPGIS) improve access to planning by making mapping and visualization technologies open to the public. PPGIS allows citizens to make location-based observations of their environment and share this data with other citizens and professionals (Haklay & Tobón, 2003). PPGIS endeavors are a form of citizen science in the sense that citizens make observations about the built environment with the hopes of informing evidence-based urban intervention.

Planners and citizens also employ e-participation to enliven the planning process through Massively Multiplayer Online Games (MMOGs). These virtual spaces allow for citizens to comprehend and explore urban plans with 3-D visualizations (Nitsche, 2009; Evans-Cowley & Hollander, 2010). The Engagement Game Lab (EGL), a research lab at Emerson College that works to produce social media and game technologies for urban planning, designed a 3-D immersive game called Participatory Chinatown to enhance participation in the master planning of Boston's Chinatown (engagementgamelab.org). In the game, participants create an avatar in order to play in the shoes of virtual residents as they look for jobs, housing, and engage in various aspects of civic life. The background of residents such as their work skill sets or language skills may influence the way they navigate the game. The comments and feedback that residents generated while using the game was included as part of the 2010 Chinatown Master Plan process. The game was successful in part because it was a strategic partnership between EGL, a local non-profit in Chinatown, a software company, and Boston's Metropolitan Area Planning Council (MAPC).

An exciting development in e-participation tools has been the ability to crowdsource, which can be defined as online open calls for data or proposals for any inquiry or problem. Planners and citizens can crowdsource information from citizens about plans, policies, the conditions of their neighborhoods, and their ideas to address urban problems. It also serves as a way to source the local knowledge of citizens to develop solutions to urban challenges (Brabham, 2009). Cell phones allow for planners and citizens to crowdsource information through SMS or social networks that are accessible through cell phones. This allows for continuous engagement and makes e-participation more accessible since more people have access to cell phones than computers (Brabham, 2009). Moreover, when used in a way that encourages citizens to be a part of planning and decision making, crowdsourcing can be a way to overcome barriers to participation, such as the inability to attend planning meetings or discrimination that citizens might experience in face-to-face settings based their appearance, background, or other factors.

These technologies have helped individual citizens, community-based organizations, and planners to improve access to planning processes, make planning more engaging, and strengthen communities through building digital social capital (Mandarano et. al., 2011). E-participation has had success in improving social inclusion, interaction between stakeholders, and ability for residents to collectively plan their neighborhoods. It has allowed for transaction of knowledge between planners and residents, visualization capabilities such as 3D immersive spaces which aren't possible on paper, and improved access to information about policymaking, laws, regulations, and planning events.

In traditional and synoptic urban planning processes, the data generated by scientific approaches tend to carry more weight than experience, opinions, perspectives, and knowledge of the lay public. Therefore, public participation in scientific aspects of planning opens a new venue for the public to participate in deliberative decision making. As such, incorporating citizen science methods into pluralistic approaches has the most promise to leverage e-participation to create a space where each citizen can make contributions that are viewed to be of equal importance and therefore carry equal weight. With e-participation in data collection providing an addition way to bring people to the table, citizen science styled participation can draw a wide spectrum of citizens into decision making, including marginalized groups such as low-income citizens, people of color, women, youth, LGBTQ individuals, immigrants, and the disabled. E-tools can help improve access to planning forums and information, and facilitate authentic involvement in planning processes such as generating ideas

for their community's future. As Brabham states, there is a lack of creative solutions in status quo planning: "[s]imply put, with so much difficulty in executing the face-to-face public participation component of a planning project, we should begin to think beyond the bounds of what might constitute public involvement in the first place." (Brabham, 2009).

CITIZEN SCIENCE

Citizen science, also termed public participation in scientific research (PPSR), is the *intentional collaborations in which members of the public engage in the process of research to generate new science-based knowledge* (Shirk et al., 2012). As a multidisciplinary endeavor, Citizen Science relies on the participation of an interested public to achieve goals attainable by the intersection of scientific and public objectives (Shirk et al., 2012). Although Citizen Science includes projects where people volunteer with face-to-face, direct supervision of scientists, such as in field-work-style vacations administered through EarthWatch, most volunteer in bits and pieces of their spare time in convenient locations, typically remote from collaborating scientists. Much of the scientific research power of Citizen Science is harbored in the widely dispersed geographic coverage of the minimal-cost observations gathered by participants (Braschler, 2009; Silvertown, 2009; Gallo & Waitt, 2011; Cooper et al., 2012) and unique access to otherwise inaccessible areas, such as lands around residences (McCaffrey, 2005; Cooper et al., 2007). As such, citizen science can span a wide spectrum of activities and designs, but frequently draws on popular interest in games and hobbies while employing electronic media such as smart phones, web-based data-entry forms, on-line geographic systems, and online social networks.

Citizen science has a foothold in many fields of science, beginning over a century ago in astronomy and ecology to more recent entrances in atmospheric studies, anthropology, and conservation. Two centuries ago, anybody who pursued science did so as a hobby, in addition to their profession, so we could say citizen science began before professional science. Science as a profession began in the late 19th century and much of early "citizen science" was carried out by the elite. There were notable large-scale citizen science projects in the 1800s that involved a cross-section of demographic groups (Cooper, 2012a; 2012b). In 1900, the National Audubon Society launched the first organized citizen science project, Christmas Bird Count, in the United States and it continues in the present day (Miller-Rushing et al., 2012). In astronomy, amateurs have been making contributions by tracking asteroids, monitoring variable stars (American Association of Variable Start Observers), and discovering comets (historically, though now they are discovered by automated tracking systems).

Citizen science has led to discoveries and important research findings based on high-quality, reliable data collected, and/or processed, by the public (Bhattacharjee, 2005). In 2006, public participants in the Lost Ladybug Project re-discovered the rare nine-spotted lady beetle, and aided scientists in subsequent discoveries in several states in the US (Losey et al., 2007). Participants and scientists in School of Ants have discovered many new species of ants and common species in unexpected places (http://schoolofants.org/discoveries). Within about three years of its launch, Galaxy Zoo has had over 200,000 participants who have classified over 100 million images of galaxies from the Sloan Digital Sky Survey (Hopkin, 2007). The images were taken by a robotic telescope so participant eyes were the first to essentially discover each galaxy. Results from Galaxy Zoo have been used in over 50 research projects, and produced over 16 peer-reviewed research articles (Raddick et al., 2010). The merits of citizen science can be seen in the peer-reviewed studies produced *and* in the social outcomes possible.

Styles of Citizen Science

Several typologies of citizen science have been developed in this emerging field (e.g., Cooper et al., 2007; Wilderman, 2007; Wiggins & Crowston, 2001; Haklay, 2012), and each can provide a different perspective in viewing citizen science. Shirk et al. (2012) divided the ways the public can participate in scientific research into five models, with the three in the middle of the spectrum describing Citizen Science:

- **Contractual Projects:** Where communities ask professional researchers to conduct a specific scientific investigation and report on the results;
- **Contributory Projects:** Which are generally designed by scientists and for which members of the public primarily contribute data;
- **Collaborative Projects:** Which are generally designed by scientists and for which members of the public contribute data but also help to refine project design, analyze data, and/or disseminate findings;
- **Co-Created Projects:** Which are designed by scientists and members of the public working together and for which at least some of the public participants are actively involved in most or all aspects of the research process; and
- **Collegial Contributions:** Where non-credentialed individuals conduct research independently with varying degrees of expected recognition by institutionalized science and/or professionals.

Although the typology describes top-down to bottom-up formation of PPSR projects, the criteria of "designed by scientists" is an over-simplification that actually means 'designed by professionals, not designed by the public.' That is, the responsibilities attributed to 'scientists' actually describes multi-disciplinary endeavors with input from scientists, educators, natural resource managers, evaluators, programmers, specialists in human-computer interactions and user-centered design: a wide variety of professionals, but not the public. The purpose of citizen science designs can be to meet multiple scientific, educational, and conservation goals: again, in all except co-created models, these goals are set by "anybody but the public." Thus, from a democratization perspective, PPSR styles represent the balance between the public and professionals in involvement, control, and expression of their authority.

Contributory projects are often large-scale, such as all the examples mentioned earlier. In such projects, communication and interactions between project scientists/staff and the public are primarily over the Internet. Participants take on the role of traditional volunteers in that they are contributing their time and efforts to a purpose (i.e., the research or conservation goals of the citizen science project) by following instructions and "doing their part." Volunteers of this nature need recognition, guidance, feedback, ongoing recruitment, nurturing, training, and evaluation. To obtain wide participation, contributory projects are often designed to leverage interest in existing hobbies, such as bird-watching, star-gazing, or beach combing (Cooper et al., 2012). The research agenda of contributory projects is controlled by the institution (e.g., government, universities, or NGOs) rather than the participants.

Collaborative and co-created projects are most likely to focus on issues of local concern and many relate to environmental justice issues. In these projects, participants get involved because the issues addressed by the research are of relevance, even though the data-collection activities may not be similar to any existing hobby activities. For example, Lena et al. (1999) documented a collaborative project involving a community-university partnership that studied disproportionately heavy truck traffic through the Hunts Point area in New York City and its effect on local asthma rates. In doing so, they uncovered an illegal use of non-designated truck routes. The data and public involvement in the project influenced public policy and supported efforts to reroute truck traffic away from residential areas. In 1999, elected officials in the Bronx, NY provided funding for a research partnership between NYU's School of Medicine and the Wagner Graduate School of Public Service with community based organizations in the South Bronx (Thurston et al., 2007). The South Bronx Environmental Health Study, a 10-year longitudinal study, aimed to determine if there was a correlation between local air quality and urban planning factors such as the number of waste-transfer stations and truck traffic. The NYU team of researchers provided the tools to measure ground-level pollution and several sites, including schools, and the community organizations enlisted their membership, mostly school students, to collect air samples with instruments attached to wheeled bookbags (Thurston et al., 2007). In the process, local residents learned valuable information about environmental quality and methods for inquiring into the environmental health of their neighborhoods. This collaborative study found a strong correlation between asthma hospitalizations rates, income, the percentage of Hispanic residents, and the number of industrial facilities that depend on trucks (Thurston et al., 2007). The community groups that were involved in this study were empowered by this research to raise awareness about respiratory health and to lobby their elected officials to enact policies and urban interventions which protect the health of South Bronx residents. In areas where school-based asthma rates are as high as 20% to 25%, the study suggested that children would particularly benefit from air conditioners or filters in the classrooms to reduce the effect of diesel fumes from nearby highways (Restrepo & Zimmerman, 2004).

This partnership allowed for more granular, street-level data to be collected. Previous air quality data collected by the Department of Environmental Conservation measured air quality from rooftop stations, whereas this study took samples at ground level where citizens live their lives. Although this study did not utilize e-participation tools, it shows the value in connecting citizens with the data-collection process. Community groups in the Bronx actively participated in the study process and execution of the research by collecting baseline environmental quality data and building a knowledge base in the community (Restrepo & Zimmerman, 2004). This research partnership resulted in 1) more detailed, ground level information was collected, 2) citizens learning about environmental health through the study process, and 3) citizens using the studies to suggest evidence-based improvements in their neighborhoods.

An example of a co-created project relates to public health and water quality where residents in Pennsylvania sought technical help from researchers at the Alliance for Aquatic Resource Monitoring (ALLARM) to jointly design and implement a long-term water quality monitoring program (Wilderman et al., 2004). Similar co-created projects have addressed monitoring urban noise (Corbett et al., 2006).

In Nepal, planners and natural resource managers facilitated villagers in the development of a community-managed livestock insurance scheme. Since the primary danger to livestock is the endangered snow leopard, the scheme includes a citizen science component to monitor snow leopards in the area (Gurung et al., 2011).

Litter clean-up on beaches by volunteers have been used in many countries to make science-based policy and management recommendations, such as in Jordan (Abu-Hilal & Al-Najjar, 2009), Chile (Bravo et al., 2009), regional projects such as the Coastwatch Europe Network (Jozwaik, 2003; http://www.Coastwatch.org/), and global project based in Japan (International PelletWatch, Ogata et al., 2009)

As the level of citizen involvement in the scientific research process increases, the participation paradigm evolves from contributory to co-created to collaborative models. In transferring concepts between Citizen Science and e-planning, we can measure degree of participation by how much people are involved in the planning process to define public issues and generate decisions. The style of Citizen Science, and to a lesser extent the technologies selected, will have major consequences that shape outcomes of the project (Shirk et al., 2012). Similarly, as Silva (2010) emphasized, "the evidence available suggests that the planning theory and the policy that guide the use of the technology is far more important than the type of tool, electronic or conventional, employed in the planning process." Note also, the enormous number of disciplines involved in the design and implementation of citizen science creates both opportunities (for leveraging public expertise in novel ways) and challenges. In similar ways, the planning arena draws upon many fields in the social sciences: transportation, economics, housing and real estate, environmental management, public health, etc.

E-Participation in Citizen Science

In citizen science, as the scale of a project increase, the need for e-participation grows. This is likely true for planning as well. As the human population grows and becomes more urban, the need for e-participation in planning will continue to grow. According to the World Health Organization, in 2010, more than half of all people live in an urban area and by 2030, 6 out of every 10 people will live in a city. Additional circumstances that increase the need for ICT in planning is when planning issues transcend municipal boundaries to encompass regions, such as watersheds. In these circumstances, shared e-platforms can help planners coordinate activities, standardize approaches, data gathering, etc, and reduce redundancy of efforts.

Like the scientific method, the citizen science method has iterative steps that lead to new insights and knowledge. The steps for contributory style projects are shown in Table 2, slightly modified from Bonney et al. (2009), along with examples of

Table 2. Steps in citizen science with examples of e-tools and projects that utilize them

		E-tools		Examples
6	Disseminate results	Blogs Online articles	E-newsletters 3rd party apps	BirdsEye App www.birdseyebirding.com
5	Display, analyze, interpret data, and disseminate results	Data visualizations Data query Data downloads Web-generated project statistics	User directed data analysis and production of charts, graphs, and maps	eBird www.ebird.org National Phenology Network www.usanpn.org
4	Accept data contributions			
	Observations	Web smartforms* Spreadsheet upload Email/SMS data entry Public kiosks	PGIS GPS Smartphones Micro blogging (mobile phone)	eBird TrailTracker Project BudBurst www.budburst.org Snow Tweets www.snowtweets.org
	Photos	Web upload w/ pick lists for controlled vocabulies*		Lost Ladybug Project www.lostladybug.org
	Physical sample	Postal mail w/ tandem web form and online GIS		School of Ants www.schoolofants.org
	Collating, cataloging, crowdsourcing	Online games w/ consensus tools* Transcription tasks		Galaxy Zoo www.galaxyzoo.org Old Weather www.oldweather.org
	Autosensing	Smart phone apps Gadgets		What's Invasive! www.whatsinvasive.com QuakeCatcher Network www.qcn.standford.edu
3	Train participants	Online training (videos, tutorials, quizzes) Demos and images Resources for K-12 teachers Online games		Invaders of Texas www.texasinvasives.org CyberTracker www.cybertracker.org BeetleBuster www.beetlebuster.info
2	Recruit and retain participants	Social networking features Certifications Digital awards Auto-generated participant statistics		Zooniverse www.zooniverse.org YardMap www.yardmap.org Stardust@home
1	Communicate goals	Website w/ embedded multimedia		xxxxx

e-tools common to each step in the process. From an e-participation perspective, PPSR styles vary greatly, and the elements directly related to data contributions (step 4 in Table 2) have advanced the most with e-tools. Of course, data contributions from the public are the one feature common to all types of citizen science. In a sense, all the stages are geared towards enabling step 4, so all the steps are relevant to efforts to bring citizen science into urban planning.

The key differences among the models are in how much participation earlier and later in the scientific process varies. Participation in the earlier stages, such as forming questions and protocols, requires a large amount of dialogue and iteration that it may always be better face-to-face. Some e-participation expands to data analysis, visualizations, and feedback on interpreting, using, and disseminating information. Contributory projects are typically large scale and the lack of face-to-face communication, and online tools as a poor substitute, may be why large-scale projects follow the contributory model. Thus, greater e-participation is currently equated with greater numbers of participants, but with an overall narrower spectrum of participation in the various steps of the citizen science process.

Citizen science projects mandate effective communication among and between participants, coordinators, and scientists (Newman et al., 2010). Thus, social networking features can be critical to the success of citizen science projects by helping to communicate goals, train people in protocols, and allow participants to communicate with each other and with the team that designed the project.

New tools, like the use of mobile phones that are capable of capturing, classifying, and transmitting image, sound, and location data, do not align with one particular type of citizen science. The spread of smart phones and mobile computing has aided Citizen Science, for example, CyberTracker, allows the (nonliterate) Khoi-San community in Southern Africa to record animal signs and create maps and inventories of species (Silvertown, 2009).

Citizen science projects are relying on online interactive mapping tools with capabilities to view and contribute geo-referenced observations at multiple spatial and temporal scales. For example, participants in eBird report the number of each species of birds seen, and not seen, at particular locations and times, thereby creating dynamic maps of the distribution of bird species, more up-to-date than printed field guides. In the wake of the 2011 Gulf Coast oil disaster, eBird provided essential baseline data and facilitated monitoring birds throughout the region. eBird's data visualization tools used bird observations, along with information from Google and the National Oceanic and Atmospheric Association (NOAA), to highlight the potential impacts of the Gulf oil spill on bird populations (Sullivan et al., 2009). In School of Ants, participants collect, freeze, and mail ants to researchers for identification, while mapping collection location with PGIS system and provided associated habitat details online. Fieldscope, a project of National Geographic, uses a web-based GIS platform to allow people to visualize and analyze their data, and to facilitate collaborative problem solving and decision making (Switzer et al., 2012).

In evaluating website design, Newman et al. (2010) emphasized the challenges to making websites that support users that vary in technological background, culture, language, system platforms, motivations, and spatial literacy. Spatial literacy is the ability to understand spatial concepts, relationships and geographic space (National Research Council et al., 2006). Newman et al. (2010) found that the "less is more" approach (Jones et al., 2009) is important with online GIS and helps designers follow the rule of thumb that users need to experience easy early success. After users have some success, then they might explore and use the platform in more depth (Newman et al., 2010). Table 3 contains guidelines for citizen-based web mapping applications from Newman et al. (2010).

Of course, when people use online tools to report what they observe (see, hear, etc) and/or contribute things they collect (e.g. photos, or air, water, noise, and light pollution samples), they are contributing data. Less obvious is when people are classifying, cataloging, or processing observations, they too are contributing data. Sometimes called 'citizen cyberscience' because participation in 100% online (Grey, 2009), or

Table 3. Guidelines for web mapping applications from Newman et al. (2010)

Communicate the purposes of the website and the roles they support
Build features for both project managers and volunteers and clearly separate them
Develop customizable data entry forms that ensure data quality, yet remain simple
Create simple map applications that visualize accuracy, precision, and uncertainty
Add fun features to foster motivation and continued involvement
Incorporate spatial literacy learning into the use of websites
Add information to help with map interpretation (improve cognitive access).
Provide a cursory understanding of spatial concepts through online help.
Allow users to formulate their own research questions and answer them (analysis).
Add features for communication between volunteers and volunteer coordinators.
Research and develop features to map attributes and visualize their accuracy.
Create transparent features that are used and explored by volunteers and volunteer coordinators; avoid limited black box systems (Merrick 2003).
Allow users to experiment, to 'fail,' and to play around by creating a test website.
Market PDAs primarily to advanced users, early adopters, and young volunteers.
Make use of web skins to target specific use cases and tasks and simplify searches.
Provide rich content even in the absence of user-contributed web content.
Clearly distinguish social networking (e.g., blogging) content from science content.
Assign volunteer coordinators a data quality role and create features for data review.
Communicate scientific rigor where appropriate.
Incorporate communication features to augment face-to-face communication through all project phases (e.g., training; data collection, entry, dissemination, and analysis; and communication from scientists back to volunteers).
Avoid advertisements and animations altogether or, if required, keep them off data entry forms, profile pages, the home page, and map pages (Nivala et al. 2008).
Create online questionnaire creation and delivery tools similar to Survey Monkey to better integrate user feedback, participation, and program evaluation.

called 'distributed intelligence' in Haklay's 2012 typology, this class of contributory projects are completely virtual and not associated with any geographic location of participants.

In designing projects with data collection components, as in citizen science, the following tradeoffs and limitations are important to consider:

1. Trade-offs typically occur between mode of participation and scale of the project with large-scale projects using e-tools to facilitate participation in data collection and maybe data exploration and small-scale projects using both face-to-face interactions and e-tools to facilitate participation in all steps of citizen science.

2. There are trade-offs among multiple project goals – science, conservation, education, community building, etc.

3. Trade-off exist between lots of participants doing "easy" or low commitment types of data collection and a fewer participants engaged in many modes of participation.

4. The digital divide limits participation.

LESSONS FROM E-PARTICIPATION IN SCIENTIFIC RESEARCH FOR E-PARTICIPATION IN URBAN PLANNING

Incorporating citizen science methods, particularly citizen data collection, into urban planning will improve planning decisions by filling critical gaps in information. Yet, citizen science outcomes extend beyond the scientific insights gained from the mass of observations of participants. The process of participating in a group scientific effort can result in transformational social and learning outcomes. For this reason, Citizen Science has gained attention from the field of Informal Science Education (ISE), which deals with learning that takes place outside of school settings. Citizen Science broadened the audience that could be actively engaged by ISE efforts, allowing those efforts to reach beyond zoos, aquaria, and nature center and into people's hobbies and leisure time (Bonney et al., 2009). Citizen science even has the potential to engage grade school students in local community governance (Mueller et al., 2012). Citizen Science projects have achieved educational goals such as increasing public understanding of science knowledge (Brossard et al., 2005), enhancing engagement or interest in the topic, increasing scientific thinking (Trumbull et al., 2000), improved natural history skills, increased awareness, and/or understanding of science, and changed attitudes and behaviors towards science (Brossard et al., 2005). Even with the caveats of potential file draw biases (not publishing studies failing to find learning outcomes) and ceiling effects (instruments too coarse to detect changes), it appears that Citizen Science can increase knowledge, awareness, and/or understanding of scientific concepts related to the study (Bonney et al., 2009).

More importantly, Citizen Science can also increase public knowledge of social and political processes, such as community structure and environmental regulation (Bonney et al., 2009), and build social capital, promote environmental action, and increase engagement in advocacy (Cornwell & Campbell, 2012). For example, in a stream monitoring project, participation did not increase learning, but did increase political participation, the size of personal networks, and feelings of community connectedness among volunteers (Overdevest & Stepenuck, 2004). A community's capacity to collectively solve local problems is related to the strength, density, and intensity of connections among people (Putnam, 2000). From an environmental justice perspective, citizens engaged in data collection for environmental monitoring can correct information and power asymmetries and enhance accountability in a regulatory process (on industry and regulatory agencies) (Overdevest & Mayer, 2008). Thus, Citizen Science can increase the civic capacity of communities and can influence the social dynamics of industry compliance (Overdevest & Mayer, 2008).

Citizen Science projects have helped to build community, increase engagement in advocacy and monitoring, and create learning opportunities. By applying the methods of Citizen Science to urban planning processes, similar benefits may also be realized in communities that are working to plan the futures of their neighborhoods. Research into public participation in urban governance shows that citizen engagement strengthens the fabric of communities, builds social capital, and creates common ground for collective action (Mandarano, 2011; Potapchuk & Crocker Jr, 1999). If citizens and other local stakeholders see that their ideas and concerns are incorporated into planning decisions, there will be more community buy-in for the implementation of plans (Evans-Cowley & Hollander, 2010). We could envision classifying contributory citizen science to urban planning as equivalent to rung 6 (partnership) in Arnstein's ladder of participation, and collaborative as rung 7 (delegated power), and co-created citizen science as rung 8 (citizen control).

By incorporating the citizen science e-tools/e-methodologies displayed in Figure 2 into urban planning participatory processes, citizens in urban planning will be empowered to be a part of the technocratic studies, which often heavily influence the planning process. Participatory processes that utilize e-tools also create opportunities to survey and capture the granular knowledge of citizens, which technocrats in city agencies or regional commissions are unable or less suited to capture since they don't have the intimate knowledge or access to the community that local citizens do. Therefore, inclusion of citizens in data collection and research can establish a new, highly valued place at the table for the public. As long as a non-token participatory model is employed, citizens can help shape study methodologies, preliminary findings, and the analysis of data that contributes to decision making. Every citizen may not become an expert on planning research, but the transparency created by this contributory process is inherently valuable because it makes planning commissions and agencies more accountable to the citizenry. Citizens will also have the opportunity to take their involvement one step further by developing research "experts" within their own communities or by contracting technical assistance to watch-dog the planning agency's research and ensure that it is scientifically sound. Citizens that are participating in urban planning will then have the capacity to produce data-based evidence to identify goals for change in their communities and make smarter planning decisions.

When the South Bronx Environmental Health Study was undertaken, e-participatory tools were less accessible, more expensive or nonexistent. Today, e-participatory tools are being used to engage a larger body of participants in the development of research and data-collection methodologies. The Common Sense Project (www.commonsensing. org), a company that develops mobile environmental sensory devices, and the West Oakland Environmental Indicators Project (WOEIP, www. woeip.org), an environmental justice participatory research organization, partnered to research the air quality of low-income neighborhoods in West Oakland.

The neighborhood of West Oakland is encircled by freeways. Since West Oakland is in close proximity to the 5th largest port in the United States, the air quality is compromised by the high volume of diesel pollution emanating from trucks and commercial ships. The rate of hospitalizations due to asthma is amongst the highest in the United States. A 2009 study by Alameda County Public health Department revealed that the cancer risk rate for West Oakland residents is double the rate for other Bay Area residents (Dutta, 2009). West Oakland is considered an environmental justice neighborhood since it is a predominantly low-income community of color that faces disproportionately high levels of air pollution.

The WOEIP and Common Sense Project saw a need to produce data on air quality and to empower West Oakland residents with the ability to form their own research inquiries, especially when they believed the findings of government agencies or planning institutions were inadequate in quality or scope. In 2010, WOEIP and Common Sense developed GIS "dust trackers" – electronic mobile devices that measure particulate matter, carbon monoxide, ozone, and nitrogen dioxide - to facilitate this research in a way that was accessible to local residents (Dutta, 2009). The dust trackers have a GPS tool that logs the location and time of each data point. The collaboration has been successful at engaging the local community by recruiting youth and adult volunteers to collect data with GIS trackers on planned routes through West Oakland. Community residents, in partnership with scientists, learn to analyze the data and monitor were air pollution is a threat in their community. WOEIP has also used the research to educate youth and local residents about urban environmental health (Dutta, 2009).

WOEIP and Common Sense continue to conduct this research with the intention of using their findings for environmental action. Current air quality readings are taken by official organization in a relatively small amount of locations. As Dutta states, these testing stations are "failing to represent the air that citizens breathe on a day-to-day basis" (Dutta, 2009). Conversely, government institutions have a strong distrust of citizen action groups that engage in scientific research because they believe the groups are biased and structure their research to exaggerate environmental health impacts. It is clear that more work needs to be done to build trust mechanisms between government planning commissions and local stakeholders and citizens (Aoki et al., 2008).

Community PlanIt, an online social platform that facilitates engagement in local planning efforts, has aimed to engage citizens by making the planning process fun, similar to the ways that citizen science has made science fun by engaging citizens in outdoor work, hobbies, and technological interests. Community Planit addresses the challenge of traditional planning processes to continuously engage citizens, rather than include citizen for short amounts of time and limited involvement in town-hall meeting formats.

Community PlanIt does this by engaging users in planning-themed online games that allow users to earn points after completing various activities or missions. At the most basic level, users are asked to simply tell planners what they think about various land use, transportation, economic, or environmental factors in their community. Community Planit further engages users through activities that allow users to step into others shoes: users are given a few character biographies and are met with challenges throughout the game.

Users are forced to think from their character's perspectives and in the process develop a stronger understanding of the lived experiences of other residents and stakeholders.

Users can also earn points by beginning campaigns and recruiting other community members. These campaigns range from park clean ups, photography missions, or assembling a meeting around a planning or policy issue. As users earn points through these mini-missions and online games, they can spend these points on the community values that are important to them, such as affordability or pedestrian mobility. The users leave the game with a sense of what users see as the most important, values, concerns, and challenges in their neighborhoods. Once this information is collected, the community convenes in a face-to-face meeting to discuss the results of the games and what the data shows about neighborhood priorities, transportation routes, and other urban information that was collected. Governmental institutions and other local stakeholders are invited to these meetings to incorporate the neighborhood concerns and ideas in future plans. Planners can take the results of the Community PlanIt games and incorporate them directly into the planning process, which has happened in Boston Public Schools, were students, teachers, and parents participated in Community PlanIt games and shared their hopes for their future of their schools and integrated their ideas into the planning process (www.communityplanit.org).

The outcomes and benefits of Community PlanIt's platform are numerous. The platform allows for users to learn more about local planning issues, to communicate with residents they would not have otherwise interacted with, to strengthen community bonds, and to enable users to send feedback and ideas directly to decision makers. As noted earlier, if a token method of engagement is used, the results of such games will not be taken seriously by planning commissions.

Some processes and frameworks for linking PPSR to citizenship practices and decision making have been developed and explored (e.g., Conrad & Daoust, 2008; Vaughan et al., 2003 – examples in Canada), but more development is needed. Some studies have found Citizen Science participants frustrated by only being able to share knowledge that fit the data forms and protocols as prepared by professionals without their input (Ellis & Waterton, 2004) or by being unable to gain the level of authority they sought (Lorimer, 2008). When participants have used their 'improved understanding' of science (that they gained from PPSR) to challenge those with scientific authority, and exploit the uncertainty in science, they have been able to balance the level of authority and co-produce conservation practices (e.g., sea turtle nest relocations, Cornwell & Campbell, 2012). The premise of the Shirk et al. (2012) framework for PPSR was that deliberative design of projects can increase likelihood of specific desired outcomes (e.g., finding the optimal solutions to community problems), always considering whose interest is being served. Deliberative design is important because interest in participation must be authentic: when interest in participation is for the sake of gaining "buy-in," the resulting participation may not enable hoped-for social transformations (Cornwall, 2008).

Common Challenges that Both Fields Face with E-Participation

The time has come for planners and local governments to take advantage of the creative and democratizing potentials of online participation tools. There has been success in citizen science to improve citizen's ability to make scientific inquiries, to increase participant learning and social networks, and to create social capital. Urban planning processes can become more accessible and give citizens more power in planning processes through adopting citizen science e-participation practices. Despite this exciting potential, there

are many shared challenges that both fields must overcome in order to achieve pluralistic participation in the physical and online arenas. Using the Internet and mobile technologies as tools to increase citizen participation raises the interrelated issues of accessibility, collaboration, and communication.

Accessibility

In urban planning processes and citizen science, there can be exclusion of communities due to lack of technological and educational access. As Internet and mobile technologies expand throughout the world, there are communities that remain excluded based on income, age, language, and other social and socioeconomic forces. Access to the Internet varies greatly between the economically developed and underdeveloped regions of the world. Even within developed nations, discrepancies in Internet access are vast in terms of wealth, gender, and race (Warf, 2001). Aside from injustices, the digital divide influences the ability to obtain needed information. In citizen science, often who participates is less important than how many people participate. But in urban planning or citizen science projects with a specific geographical focus, it matters *which* people participate. The digital divide can lead to social exclusion, especially of group without broadband internet access or advanced computer hardware (rural and/or disadvantaged urban communities –also leads to geographical inequalities). PPGIS technologies and other e-participatory tools that require fast computers and internet connections may limit lower-income communities from participating.

Access to e-participatory processes may also be influenced by the access that individuals or communities have had to education. In Citizen Science, most participants have higher education or degrees in the subject that they volunteer to do research in (Trumbull et al., 2000). Education may also play a role in urban planning citizen participation, with citizens that are more familiar with the social sciences or planning and policy arenas being more likely to participate. These groups may be savvy in finding information online about research or participation opportunities. This may lead to citizens with higher technological exposure and know-how to have a disproportionate amount of participation through online technologies (Mandarano et al., 2011). Planners need to double their efforts to reach marginalized groups (Mandarano et al., 2011).

Communication

In some cases, computer-mediated communication can be more efficient than face-to-face communication and can equalize social hierarchies (Rhoads, 2010). Nevertheless, face-to-face contact is more effective in situations that involve conflict resolution (Rhoads, 2010). When urban planning and/or citizen science projects use web tools to collect data, particularly geo-referenced data, often privacy and confidentiality become important issues. Technological advances in what is frequently termed 'participatory sensing' address data credibility and privacy issues (Burke et al., 2006).

Collaboration

Although collaborative processes are known to improve citizen science and urban planning processes, there is still a lack of willingness to adopt new models on the part of local governments and academic institutions. Planners and scientists are looked at as the experts, and the knowledge of citizens can be undervalued as a result. Relying too heavily on ICT as a venue for participation can backfire. Padgett (1993) noted that technically savvy citizens may welcome a GIS tool, but less tech-savvy may be alienated. In a California city, Innes (2005) found citizens accused planners of using more sophisticated methods in order to

manipulate the public. In part, the rate of utilization and willingness to accept new methods may be based on the demographics of a community (Conroy & Evans-Cowley, 2006; Evans-Cowley & Hollander, 2010).

CONCLUSION AND PERSPECTIVES

Urban planning involves local participation, but in a world with global problems, local decisions have a global context. Thus, the need to coordinate the creation of positive cumulative impacts requires a larger infrastructure for e-planning. Ideally, ICT can help people involved in local decisions see relevance at different scales: local, regional, national, and global.

Public participation in urban planning can be viewed as one end of the spectrum of public participation in scientific research and each can benefit from the exchange of concepts and methods. We caution looking at e-participation in planning as a silver-bullet solution to planning processes that lack engagement. Indeed, the online tools themselves could be detrimental to citizen participation if the planners and local governments don't take participation seriously. In order for e-participation to work, planners need to choose a non-tokenizing societal transformation model on Arnstein's ladder of participation. If planners adhere to the traditional planning methods, they run the risk of replicating the top-down power dynamics and limitations that prevent citizens from participating meaningfully or from influencing plans and decisions.

The highest level of participation opportunities hold that all citizens must be equally empowered and fully informed to ensure that they can exert influence on decisions that affect them (Innes, 1996). These opportunities ensure that government decisions are justifiable to each participant, regardless of their social, cultural, and economic circumstances. Programs that lack depth lead to 'token participation.' They tend to emphasize simple, one-way forms of communication that merely educate citizens to accept decisions that have already been made (Evans-Cowley & Hollander, 2010).

As e-participation evolves and more people utilize e-participatory tools, planners and citizens should closely monitor its impact. Possible ways to monitor the success of e-participation projects or platforms is to analyze 1) the demographics of who utilizes e-participation tools, 2) the amount of time users participate online, and 3) the degree to which their participation online influence planning decisions and policymaking. Lastly, as stated earlier, an analysis of the planning theories, paradigms, and practices that undergird planning processes that are undertaken by governments and commissions is core to understanding any planning process, whether it be paper-based, face-to-face, or through e-participation.

ACKNOWLEDGMENT

The authors collaborated on this chapter through the Environmental Leadership Program.

REFERENCES

Abu-Hilal, A., & Al-Najjar, T. (2009). Marine litter in coral reef areas along the Jordan Gulf of Aqaba, Red Sea. *Journal of Environmental Management*, *90*, 1043–1049. doi:10.1016/j.jenvman.2008.03.014 PMID:18490098.

Angotti, T. (2007). Advocacy and community planning: Past, present, and future. *Progressive planning: The magazine of planners network*. Retrieved November 1, 2012, from http://www.plannersnetwork.org/publications/2007_spring/angotti.htm

Aoki, P. M., Honicky, R. J., Mainwaring, A., Myers, C., Paulos, E., Subramanian, S., & Woodruff, A. (2008). Common sense: Mobile environmental sensing platforms to support community action and citizen science (demonstration). *Adjunct Proceedings Ubicomp,* Sept, 59-60.

Arnstein, S. R. (1969). Ladder of citizen participation. *Journal of the American Institute of Planners*, *35*, 216–224. doi:10.1080/01944366908977225.

Berry, J. M., Portney, K. E., & Thomson, K. (1993). *The rebirth of urban democracy*. Washington, DC: Brookings Institution.

Bhattacharjee, Y. (2005). Citizen scientists supplement work of Cornell researchers. *Science*, *308*, 1402–1403. doi:10.1126/science.308.5727.1402 PMID:15933178.

Bonney, R., Ballard, H., Jordan, R., McCallie, E., Phillips, T., Shirk, J., & Wilderman, C. C. (2009). Public participation in scientific research: Defining the field and assessing its potential for informal science education. A CAISE Inquiry Group Report. Washington, DC: Center for Advancement of Informal Science Education (CAISE).

Bourgoin, J., & Castella, J.-C. (2011). PLUP fiction: Landscape simulation for participatory land use planning in northern Lao PDR. *Mountain Research and Development*, *31*, 78–88. doi:10.1659/MRD-JOURNAL-D-10-00129.1.

Bourgoin, J., Castella, J.-C., Pullar, D., Lestrelin, G., & Bouahom, B. (2012). Toward a land zoning negotiation support platform: "Tips and tricks" for participatory land use planning in Laos. *Landscape and Urban Planning*, *104*, 270–278. doi:10.1016/j.landurbplan.2011.11.008.

Brabham, D. C. (2009). Crowdsourcing the public participation process for planning projects. *Planning Theory*, *8*, 242–262. doi:10.1177/1473095209104824.

Braschler, B. (2009). Successfully implementing a citizen-scientist approach to insect monitoring in a resource-poor country. *Bioscience*, *59*, 103–104. doi:10.1525/bio.2009.59.2.2.

Bravo, M., de los Ángeles Gallardo, M., Luna-Jorquera, G., Núñez, P., Vásquez, N., & Thiel, M. (2009). Anthropogenic debris on beaches in the SE Pacific (Chile): Results from a national survey supported by volunteers. *Marine Pollution Bulletin*, *58*, 1718–1726. doi:10.1016/j.marpolbul.2009.06.017 PMID:19665738.

Brossard, D., Lewenstein, B., & Bonney, R. (2005). Scientific knowledge and attitude change: The impact of a citizen science project. *International Journal of Science Education*, *27*, 1099–1121. doi:10.1080/09500690500069483.

Burke, J. A., Estrin, D., Hansen, M., Parker, A., Ramanathan, N., Reddy, S., & Srivastava, M. B. (2006). Participatory sensing. Papers, Center for Embedded Network Sensing, UC Los Angeles. *World Sensor Web Workshop, ACM Sensys 2006*. Boulder, Colorado.

Cinderby, S. (1999). Geographic information systems (GIS) for participation: The future of environal GIS? *International Journal of Environment and Pollution*, *11*, 304–315. doi:10.1504/IJEP.1999.002263.

Cinderyb, S., & Forrester, J. (2005). Facilitating the local governance of air pollution using GIS for participation. *Applied Geography (Sevenoaks, England)*, *2005*, 143–158. doi:10.1016/j.apgeog.2005.03.003.

Conrad, C. T., & Daoust, T. (2008). Community-based monitoring frameworks: Increasing the effectiveness of environmental stewardship. *Environmental Management*, *41*, 358–366. doi:10.1007/s00267-007-9042-x PMID:18026783.

Conroy, M. M., & Evans-Cowley, J. (2006). E-participation in planning: An analysis of cities adopting on-line citizen participation tools. *Environment and Planning. C, Government & Policy*, *24*, 371–384. doi:10.1068/c1k.

Cooper, C. B. (2012). *Retro science*. Scientific American guest blog post. Retrieved November 1, 2012, from http://blogs.scientificamerican.com/guest-blog/2012/08/23/retro-science-part-1/

Cooper, C. B. (2012). *Victorian-era citizen science: Reports of its death have been greatly exaggerated*. Scientific American guest blog post. Retrieved November 1, 2012, from http://blogs.scientificamerican.com/guest-blog/2012/08/30/victorian-era-citizen-science-reports-of-its-death-have-been-greatly-exaggerated/

Cooper, C. B., Dickinson, J., Phillips, T., & Bonney, R. (2007). Citizen science as a tool for conservation in residential ecosystems. *Ecology and Society, 12*(2), 11. Retrieved from http://www.ecologyandsociety.org/vol12/iss2/art11/

Cooper, C. B., Hochachka, W. M., & Dhondt, A. A. (2012). The opportunities and challenges of citizen science as a tool for ecological research. In Dickinson, J. L., & Bonney, R. (Eds.), *Citizen science: Public collaboration in environmental research*. Ithaca, NY: Cornell University Press.

Corbett, J., Rambaldi, G., Kyem, P., Weiner, D., Olson, R., Muchemi, J., McCall, M., & Chambers, R. (2006). Overview: Mapping for change—the emergence of a new practice. *Participatory learning and action*, 54, 13-20.

Cornwall, A. (2008). Unpacking 'participation': Models, meanings, and practices. *Community Development Journal*, *43*, 269–283. doi:10.1093/cdj/bsn010.

Cornwell, M. L., & Campbell, L. M. (2012). Co-producing conservation and knowledge: Citizen-based sea turtle monitoring in North Carolina, USA. *Social Studies of Science, 42*, 101–120. doi:10.1177/0306312711430440.

Davidoff, P. (1965). Advocacy and pluralism in planning. *Journal of the American Institute of Planners, 31*, 331–318. doi:10.1080/01944366508978187.

Dutta, P., Aoki, P. M., Kumar, N., Mainwaring, A., Myers, C., Willett, W., & Woodruff, A. (2009). Common sense: Participatory urban sensing using a network of handheld air quality monitors (demonstration). Proc. SenSys 2009. Berkeley, CA, Nov. 2009, 349-350.

Ellis, R., & Waterton, C. (2004). Environmental citizenship in the making: The participation of volunteer naturalists in UK biological recording and biodiversity policy. *Science & Public Policy, 31*, 95–105. doi:10.3152/147154304781780055.

Evans-Cowley, J. S., & Conroy, M. M. (2006). The growth of e-government in municipal planning. *Journal of Urban Technology, 12*, 81–107. doi:10.1080/10630730600752892.

Evans-Cowley, J. S., & Hollander, J. (2010). The new generation of public participation: Internet based participation tools. *Planning Research and Practice, 25*, 397–408. doi:10.1080/02697459.2010.503432.

Faludi, A. (1973). The rationale of planning theory. In Faludi, A. (Ed.), *A reader in planning theory* (pp. 35–53). Oxford, UK: Pergamon Press.

Friedmann, J. (1973). The transactive style of planning. In Friedmann, J. (Ed.), *Retracking America: A theory of transactive planning* (pp. 171–193). New York: Doubleday.

Friedmann, J. (1994). The utility of non-Euclidean planning. *Journal of the American Planning Association. American Planning Association, 60*, 377–379. doi:10.1080/01944369408975595.

Gallo, T., & Waitt, D. (2011). Creating a successful citizen science model to detect and report invasive species. *Bioscience, 61*, 459–465. doi:10.1525/bio.2011.61.6.8.

Goodchild, M. (2007). Citizens as sensors: The world of volunteered geography. *GeoJournal, 69*, 211–221. doi:10.1007/s10708-007-9111-y.

Grey, F. (2009). *The age of citizen cyberscience.* CERN Courier. Retrieved from http://cerncourier.com/cws/article/cern/38718

Gurung, G. S., Thapa, K., Kunkel, K., Thapa, G. J., Kollmair, M., & Boeker, U. M. (2011). Enhancing herder's livelihood and conserving the snow leopard in Nepal. *CATnews, 55*(Autumn), 17–21.

Haklay, M. (2012). Citizen science and volunteered geographic information – overview and typology of participation. In Sui, D. Z., Elwood, S., & Goodchild, M. F. (Eds.), *Volunteered geographic information, public participation, and crowdsourced production of geographic knowledge.* Berlin: Springer. doi:10.1007/978-94-007-4587-2_7.

Haklay, M., & Tobón, C. (2003). Usability evaluation and PPGIS: Towards a user-centred design approach. *International Journal of Geographical Information Science, 17*, 577–592. doi:10.1080/1365881031000114107.

Hall, P. (1983). The Anglo-American connection: Rival rationalities in planning theory and practice, 1955-1980. *Environment and Planning. B, Planning & Design, 10*, 41–46. doi:10.1068/b100041.

Harvey, D. (2008). The right to the city. *New Left Review*.

Hopkin, M. (2007, July 11). See new galaxies — without leaving your chair. *Nature*. doi:10.1038/news070709-7. Retrieved from http://www.nature.com/news/2007/070709/full/news070709-7.html

Innes, J. E. (1996). Planning through consensus building. *Journal of the American Planning Association. American Planning Association, 62*, 460–472. doi:10.1080/01944369608975712.

Innes, J. E. (2005). Living in the house of our predecessors: The demand for new institutions for public participation. *Planning Theory & Practice, 6*, 431–435.

Jones, C. E., Haklay, M., Griffiths, S., & Vaughan, L. (2009). A less-is-more approach to geovisualization – enhancing knowledge construction across multidisciplinary teams. *International Journal of Geographical Information Science, 23*, 1077–1093. doi:10.1080/13658810802705723.

Jóźwaik, T. (2003). Marine debris and threats to the Polish coast in 2001-sources and types. *Oceanological and Hydrogiological Studies, 32*, 73–81.

Lane, M. (2005). Public participation in planning: An intellectual history. *The Australian Geographer, 36*, 283–299. doi:10.1080/00049180500325694.

Lena, T. S., Ochieng, V., Carter, M., Holguín-Veras, J., & Kinney, P. L. (2009). Elemental carbon and $PM_{2.5}$ levels in an urban community heavily impacted by truck traffic. *Environmental Health Perspectives, 110*, 1009–1015. doi:10.1289/ehp.021101009.

Lorimer, J. (2008). Counting corncrakes: The affective science of the UK corncrake census. *Social Studies of Science, 38*, 377–405. doi:10.1177/0306312707084396.

Losey, J. E., Perlman, J. E., & Hoebeke, R. (2007). Citizen scientist rediscovers rare ninespotted lady beetle, Coccinella novemnotata, in eastern North America. *Journal of Insect Conservation, 11*, 415–417. doi:10.1007/s10841-007-9077-6.

Mandarano, L., Meenar, M., & Steins, C. (2011). Building social capital in the digital age of civic engagement. *Journal of Planning Literature, 25*, 123–135. doi:10.1177/0885412210394102.

McCaffrey, R. E. (2005). Using citizen science in urban bird studies. *Urban Habitats, 3*, 70–86.

Miller-Rushing, A., Primack, R., & Bonney, R. (2012). The history of public participation in ecological research. *Frontiers in Ecology and the Environment, 10*, 285–290. doi:10.1890/110278.

Mueller, M., Tippins, D., & Bryan, L. (2012). The future of citizen science. *Democracy & Education, 20*, 1–12.

National Research Council. Committee on the Support for Spatial Thinking: The Incorporation of Geographic Information Science Across the K-12 Curriculum, and Committee on Geography. (2006). Learning to think spatially: GIS as a support system in the K-12 curriculum. Washington, DC: National Academies Press.

Newman, G., Zimmerman, D., Crall, A., Laituri, M., Graham, J., & Stapel, L. (2010). User-friendly web mapping: Lessons from a citizen science website. *International Journal of Geographical Information Science, 24*(12), 1851–1869. doi:10.1080/13658816.2010.490532.

Nitsche, M. (2009). *Video game spaces: Image, play, and structure in 3D worlds*. Cambridge, MA: The MIT Press.

Ogata, Y., Takada, H., Mizukawa, K., Hirai, H., Iwasa, S., & Endo, S. et al. (2009).. . *Marine Pollution Bulletin*, *58*, 1437–1446. doi:10.1016/j.marpolbul.2009.06.014 PMID:19635625.

Overdevest, C., Huyck Orr, C., & Stepenuck, K. (2004). Volunteer stream monitoring and local participation in natural resource issues. *Human Ecology Review*, *11*, 177–185.

Overdevest, C., & Mayer, B. (2008). Harnessing the power of information through community monitoring: Insights from social science. *Texas Law Review*, *86*, 1493–1526.

Padgett, D. A. (1993). Technological methods for improving citizen participation in locally unacceptable land use (LULU). *Decision-Making, Computers. Environment and Urban Systems*, *17*, 513–520. doi:10.1016/0198-9715(93)90049-B.

Potapchuk, W. R. (1996). Building sustainable community politics: Synergizing participatory, institutional, and representative democracy. *National Civic Review*, *85*(3), 54–60. doi:10.1002/ncr.4100850311.

Potapchuk, W. R., & Crocker, J. P. Jr. (1999). Exploring the elements of civic capital. *National Civic Review*, *88*(3), 175–201. doi:10.1002/ncr.88303.

Putnam, R. D. (2000). *Bowling alone: The collapse and revival of American community*. New York: Simon & Schuster. doi:10.1145/358916.361990.

Raddick, M. J., Bracey, G., Gay, P. L., Lintott, C. J., Murray, P., & Schawinski, K. et al. (2010). Galaxy zoo: Exploring the motivations of citizen science volunteers. *Astronomy Education Review*, *9*, 010103–1. doi:10.3847/AER2009036.

Restrepo, C., & Zimmerman, R. (Eds.). (2004). *South Bronx environmental health and policy study: Transportation and traffic modeling, air quality, waste transfer stations, and environmental justice analyses in the South Bronx*. Final Report for Phase II & III. Retrieved November 1, 2012, from http://www.icisnyu.org/admin/files/ICISPhaseIIandIIIreport.pdf

Rhoads, M. (2010). Face-to-face and computer-mediated communication: What does theory tell us and what have we learned so far? *Journal of Planning Literature*, *25*, 111–122. doi:10.1177/0885412210382984.

Roberts, N. (2004). Public deliberation in an age of direct citizen participation. *American Review of Public Administration*, *34*, 315–353. doi:10.1177/0275074004269288.

Shirk, J. L., Ballard, H. L., Wilderman, C. C., Phillips, T., Wiggins, A., & Jordan, R. et al. (2012). *Public participation in scientific research: A framework for deliberate design. Ecology & Society*, *17*(2), 29. Retrieved from.

Silva, C. N. (2010). The e-planning paradigm – theory, methods and tools: An overview. In Silva, C. N. (Ed.), *Handbook of research on e-Planning: ICTs for urban development and monitoring* (pp. 1–14). Hershey, New York: IGI-Global. doi:10.4018/978-1-61520-929-3.ch001.

Silvertown, J. (2009). A new dawn for citizen science. *Trends in Ecology & Evolution*, *24*(9), 467–471. doi:10.1016/j.tree.2009.03.017 PMID:19586682.

Sullivan, B., Wood, C., Iliff, M., Bonney, R., Fink, D., & Kelling, S. (2009). eBird: A citizen-based bird observation network in the biological sciences. *Biological Conservation*, *142*(10), 2282–2292. doi:10.1016/j.biocon.2009.05.006.

Switzer, A., Schwille, K., Russell, E., & Edelson, D. (2012). National Geographic FieldScope: A platform for community geography. *Frontiers in Ecology and the Environment, 10*(6), 334–335. doi:10.1890/110276.

Thurston, G. D., Spira-Cohen, A., & Chi Chen, L. (2007). *South Bronx environmental health policy study (SBEHPS)*. Final Report of NYU School of Medicine Research. New York University School of Medicine. Department of Environmental Medicine. Retrieved November 1, 2012, from http://graphics8.nytimes.com/packages/pdf/nyregion/20081002_SOM.pdf

Trumbull, D. J., Bonney, R., Bascom, D., & Cabral, A. (2000). Thinking scientifically during participation in a citizen-science project. *Informal Science, 84*, 265–275.

Vaughan, H., Whitelaw, G. S., Craig, B., & Stewart, C. (2003). Linking ecological science to decision-making: Delivering environmental monitoring information as societal feedback. *Environmental Monitoring and Assessment, 88*, 399–408. doi:10.1023/A:1025593728986 PMID:14570425.

Warf, B. (2001). Segues into cyberspace: Multiple geographies of the digital divide. *Environment and Planning. B, Planning & Design, 28*, 1, 3–19. doi:10.1068/b2691.

Wiggins, A., & Crowston, K. (2011). From conservation to Crowdsourcing: A typology of citizen science. In *Proceedings of the Forty-fourth Hawaii International Conference on System Science (HICSS-44)*. Koloa, HI.

Wilderman, C. C. (2007). Models of community science: Design lessons from the field. In McEver, C., Bonney, R., Dickinson, J., Kelling, S., Rosenberg, K., & Shirk, J. L. (Eds.), *Citizen science toolkit conference*. Cornell Laboratory of Ornithology.

Wilderman, C. C., Barron, A., & Imgrund, L. (2004). Top down or bottom up? ALLARM's experience with two operational models for community science. In *Proceedings of the 4th National Water Quality Monitoring Council Conference*. Chattanooga, Tennessee, USA, May 17-20, 2004.

ADDITIONAL READING

Bonney, R., Ballard, H., Jordan, R., McCallie, E., Phillips, T., Shirk, J., & Wilderman, C. C. (2009). Public participation in scientific research: Defining the field and assessing its potential for informal science education. A CAISE Inquiry Group Report. Washington, DC: Center for Advancement of Informal Science Education (CAISE).

Dickinson, J. L., & Bonney, R. (Eds.). (2012). *Citizen science: Public collaboration in environmental research*. Ithaca, NY: Cornell University Press.

Sui, D. Z., Elwood, S., & Goodchild, M. F. (Eds.). (2012). *Volunteered geographic information, public participation, and crowdsourced production of geographic knowledge*. Berlin: Springer.

KEY TERMS AND DEFINITIONS

Citizen Cyber-Science: Public participation in science-related activities that occur completely on-line. A class of this is volunteered computing (distributing the analysis of data across a network of personal computers). Another class is crowdsourcing, which involves human cognitive input.

Citizen Science: Public participation in scientific research, typically through data collection or data processing. The term emerged in the natural science and informal education fields. Related terms are volunteer monitoring, community science, and participatory science. Other disciplines use other terms to describe public participation in science-related activities.

Community-Based Management: A bottom-up approach in which the public collaborates with other stakeholders in research and planning to manage natural resources. Other terms include community-based forestry, participatory forestry, community-based fisheries management, and even participatory action research.

DIY Science: Do-It-Yourself Science, which describes a movement of amateur scientists who carry out science-related hobbies that lead to discovery and invention, frequently used for environmental justice purposes. Related terms include Maker movement, Street science, Community science, Bucket Brigade, Open science.

Participatory Sensing: Communities using sensory equipment on mobile devices to contribute information to create knowledge.

Volunteered Geographic Information: Online systems based on user-generated content with a geographical dimension. Related terms include Volunteered GIS, Participatory GIS, Participatory photomapping, Mobile interactive GIS, Community-integrated GIS, Public participatory GIS, Community-based mapping, Participatory resource mapping, and more.

Section 3
Citizen E-Participation

Chapter 11
Mobile Participation:
Citizen Engagement in Urban Planning via Smartphones

Stefan Höffken
University of Technology Kaiserslautern, Germany

Bernd Streich
University of Technology Kaiserslautern, Germany

ABSTRACT

Smartphones and tablet computers are becoming essential in everyday life, connecting us in a powerful network through mobile web services. They open new channels of communication between citizens, institutions and administrations, offer greater access to public information, and facilitate increased participation. These new forms of collaborative social interaction revolutionize our information and knowledge society. The chapter examines the new opportunities opened up by mobile phones for mParticipation in the context of urban planning processes. After beginning with a theoretical overview about technical developments, eParticipation and the changes in communication in a networked society, it defines the concept of mParticipation. This is followed by an examination of six real-world projects. These examples are then used for the identification of best practices and for the analysis of the usefulness and effectiveness of these new participatory tools. In addition, the chapter discusses the possibilities as well as the barriers to mobile participation, and makes recommendations for the use of smartphones in urban planning. mParticipation opens new channels of communication, creates new ways of gathering local information and has the chance for creating a low-threshold gateway for citizen participation in urban planning, by improving databases and giving instant feedback.

INTRODUCTION

Nowadays, people listen to music on-the-go (first with Sony's Walkman, than mobile cd-players, later on the iPod and now on the smartphone), and instead of a desktop PC at home, they take laptops or tablet computers, which are connected to the internet, with them. More and more people use smartphones for communication (phone calls, email, and social networks), leisure (music, games), information (news on web) or financial transactions (banking), etc. They get information and access services at any time, irrespective of location; only limited by infrastructural access

DOI: 10.4018/978-1-4666-4169-3.ch011

to the mobile Internet. Banks (2008) states that mobile phones "allow citizens to engage more actively in civil society by monitoring elections and helping keep governments accountable," especially in the case of smartphones. Mobile technology is getting smaller, lighter, cheaper, more powerful, and ultimately, smarter.

This chapter is focused on mobile participation (mParticipation) and on the possibilities for citizen engagement in urban planning through the use of smartphones. Smartphones and tablet computers are becoming essential tools in our everyday life, connecting us in a powerful network through mobile web services. They open new channels of communication between citizens, institutions and administrations, offer greater access to public information and increase citizen participation in urban governance. These new forms of collaborative social interaction revolutionize our information and knowledge society and will shape the patterns of our future social life.

The chapter is focused on the latest research, new concepts and innovative projects, which are best-practice-examples for the future. The chapter doesn't focus on other important aspects: e.g. SMS-based mParticipation for empowerment and citizen engagement in third-world-countries (e.g., in African countries), where these kinds of mParticipation and ePayment via mobile phones rose in the last years (UNDP, 2012; Hellström, Karefelt, 2011; Banks, 2008; Commonwealth of Learning, 2011); neither on new forms of mobile phone based electronic payment in African countries (Streich, 2011).

Concerning urban planning, smartphones add new values to traditional methodologies and concepts. Facilitating in-situ-data collection and enabling networked cooperation they pave the way for crowdsourcing processes (see Erickson, 2010; Zeile et al., 2012). In addition to traditional media, a variety of new heterogeneous stakeholders take part in the creation and transmission of political and planning issues.

GOING MOBILE: CITIZEN ENGAGEMENT IN URBAN PLANNING VIA SMARTPHONES

Mobile Technology as Pioneer Technology

Via Smartphones all kind of information can be spread more easily and faster than ever before and from everywhere (Birkholz & Höffken, 2010). In fact, in the last years, the information and communication technologies (ICT) entered into a new important phase. Evolving in waves – from Personal Computing (1980s) to desktop internet computing (1990s and beginning of the millennium) – we entered the era of mobile communication around 2005. Before that the possibilities for mobile participation were de facto limited to SMS (Short-Message-Service). Since then mobile communication technologies have been developing continuously, based on infrastructural technologies such as GSM, UMTS, and LTE, which offer higher data rates.

As a consequence of that, mobile devices and communication became an important aspect of our daily life. While SMS still has the advantage of a wider coverage and low-threshold integration, thus offering the possibility to minimize the digital divide, in the next year's multimodal applications of smartphones will be in the focus of attention. Since the introduction of the first iPhone in 2006 the percentage of smartphones rose up to 38% in Germany (Nielsen, 2011b) and will be even more in the future, as 43% of all sold mobile phones are smart (Aquarius, 2012). In Europe, around 45% of all users now have a smartphone (Comscore, 2012) and tablet computers evolved in just 2 years (from the presentation of the first iPad) from a niche to a successful mass market product.

Therefore, the range of possible interactions and communications changed from phone calls and SMS to a much broader and internet-based infrastructure. Smartphones and tablet computers are on the market since just a few years and already shape the user's habits – mainly due to ease of use and attractive mobile internet tariffs – like no other digital instrument did before. Smartphones (plus tablet-computers) brought the mobile internet to the mainstream. In other words, the smartphone is the pioneer technology for a new era of computer applications (Mattern, 2002).

The Mobile Citizen: Pioneering Future Participation

The ability to access social networks and communicate from mobile devices is on the rise. Already, 37% of all users access social media via mobile web (Nielsen, 2011a). Yet the use of mobile internet is currently still dependent on the user's age – the biggest user group in Great Britain are youngster (16 -24 years) and young adults (25-34 years) (OfNS, 2011), which is comparable to Germany (Initiative D 21, 2012). These smart natives are always online and the mobile device defines a great part of their online activities. But also in other age groups exist so-called "power users."

These power users are a relevant player in future urban planning processes. They use the internet, Twitter, Social Media, etc. to organize and promote their interests and actively take part in their social environment. In their case the increasing importance of locality and prompt events is highly interesting (Google et al., 2012, p. 12). The globalised internet leads to a new local awareness. Some people already claim the renaissance of the public space due to the Internet (Rauterberg, 2011). Flash mobs or Smart Mobs, for example, are one indicator for this coexistence of potential spatial independence and local awareness and connected to the rise of ICT (Rheingold, 2002).

The mobile citizens are highly engaged in using the mobile web for their daily life and internalize new forms of cooperation and organisation.

Mobile communications play an important role and smartphones can be seen as pioneers for new formats of participation in the knowledge society (Streich, 2011).

Social Interaction is Getting Mobile

One important trend in this context is the merging of former separated technologies and concepts, leading to new multimedia services. Looking at the development of important technologies and tools, which were created over the last years, three main trends can be identified:

- **Online Activity and Communication is Getting Mobile:** The rise of mobile technologies is directly linked to the development of smartphones. They are a constant companion in everyday life and integrate the mobile internet with all its functionalities. Besides traditional phone calls and SMS, now status-updates on Twitter, checking and sending of emails or check-ins on Foursquare are getting common. The variety of sensors and apps allows a networked and multimodal conversation on-the-go.
- **Mobile Geoweb:** With tools like Google Maps and Openstreetmap (OSM) the field of Webmapping developed during the last years at a breathtaking pace. This so-called Geoweb got mobile during the last years. These easy-to-use web maps fundamentally changed the importance of georeferenced data and are the basis for address search and mashups (using web maps for data-visualisation). One of the greatest benefits are location-based-services (LBS), which create information about the vicinity (e.g. the nearest restaurant), but also using locational information for geotagging (the adding of spatial information).

- **Mobile Social Networks:** Social networks allow a two-way-flow of information and are now a quasi standard in the internet. From status-updates to tweets – social media tools created new form of communication. As most people are already using social media, it provides the possibility for citizen interaction (Haller, 2011). A thousand of apps are bringing former desktop-based social networks mobile; or are directly created for mobile use. The mobile version of social media widens the range from desktop-based interaction (mainly at home) to a communication on-the-go (in the public space).

Smartphones: Technological Basis

The success of smartphones is not so much based on the possibility of making phone calls – the former core business – but more and more on computing possibilities, internet-connection and variety of apps. Consequently, smartphones are expected to become the primary access to the internet in the next years. For instance in a current survey in Germany the participants ranked the internet (43%) as important as phone telephony (42%) for their daily use of smartphones (Bitkom, 2012). Following the success of mobile "hardware," former desktop-based applications like social networks, music-services, maps, etc. were supplemented with mobile versions. Furthermore, based on the multimodal functionality of smartphones, new mobile applications were developed over the last years.

From Telephony to Multifunctional Computing

In terms of functionality, smartphones can nowadays rival with simple desktop PCs. They have a multimodal functionality, connecting users in a pervasive network via web browsers or mobile applications. As "always-with-you" devices, smartphones support information processing and ubiquitous computing in everyday life. They are widely available and pervasive in use. The Smartphone penetration in developed markets (Europe, Northern America) reached more than 50% in 2011 (Techcrunch, 2011).

A similar tool, which is however not in the main focus of this chapter, is the tablet computer (e.g., iPad). Even bigger in size, tablet computers are comparable to smartphones, as they are based on the same concept: a mobile computer with a touch interface. In contrast to laptops they have a lower weight, longer running batteries, no need for booting, are easy to use on-the-go (e.g., in the metro or in a park bench). They are more mobile than laptops and therefore a device that is getting more and more relevant for mParticipation.

Context Aware Sensors

Smartphones integrate a wide array of embedded sensors, such as camera, accelerometer, gyroscope, digital compass, GPS and microphone allowing different context aware services (Lane et al., 2010). By using mobile broadband and Wi-Fi it is possible to access the internet and through the use of multi-sensor data (e.g., gyroscope) they allow the analysis and detection of the activities carried out by the user (e.g., location-detection is possible via GPS-unit, with the highest accuracy of ~ 10 m; Wi-Fi-connection with ~50 m accuracy; cell tower triangulation of ~ 100 m (Lukew, 2010); and location-based applications, like local search and navigation). Sensors like compass and gyroscope enhance more detailed location-aware information (e.g. direction and orientation of the device and the user's position).

In research projects, the integration of new sensors is explored. The NASA developed a chemical sensor for measuring CO_2 concentration, which can be connected to a smartphone (NASA, 2009), creating environmental data-sets. Another example is the Smartband, a stand-alone device connected via bluetooth to the smartphone, with integrated sensors for skin-temperature, acceleration and skin-conductance-level (Bodymonitor, 2012). Aggregated sensor data, in combination with GPS, can be used in order to carry on a psycho-physiological analysis of the urban environment (Bergner et al., 2012).

Apps

The most important factor for the success of smartphones (and tablet computers) is, in addition to innovative design and user-friendly operating systems, the extensibility of the features with the help of so-called apps (short for applications). These software applications perform specific tasks, like the integration of web-maps and GPS-information for live tracking. "They are available through application distribution platforms, which are typically operated by the owner of the mobile operating system, such as the Apple App Store, Google Play, Windows Phone Marketplace and BlackBerry App World" (Wikipedia, 2012).

Smartphones can be individually upgraded by the user via apps. Based on the hardware of the device, the spectrum reaches more than 650 000 different apps for the Apple App Store (Netzwelt, 2012). There are apps for navigation, schedule, news aggregators, instant messaging, social networking, gaming and many more. In contrast to former times, when companies were still responsible for the development of new software, users (individuals and companies) have the option of self-programming. They are able to develop new applications and add them to the application distribution platforms. Android[1] and Apple[2] encourage the users to do this, by offering tutorials and modular systems for software development.

Mobile Internet

Wireless communication and data transfer is the basic technology for all mobile devices. Different standards exist at the moment: the General Packet Radio Service (GPRS) supports flexible data transfer and constant connection up to 53,6 kbit/s (download). The Universal Mobile Telecommunication System (UMTS) was introduced in Germany in 2002 and is part of the third generation mobile cellular technology (3G). It allows transfer rates of up to 384 kbit/s. The development of high-speed downlink packet Access (HSDPA) and its improved version of HSPA allow downloads up to 42,000 kbit/s and 11,500 kbit/s upload (see Elektronikkompendium, 2012). In the future, the next standard will be Long Term Evolution (LTE), an evolution of the GSM/UMTS standard, allowing download rates up to 100 mbit/s. It's expected to cover especially rural areas, which lack high-rate internet connections.

The Success of Smartphones

The success and growing popularity of smartphones is based on following:

- **Usability:** Touchscreens and smart operating systems facilitate the handling;
- **Multi-Functionality:** Smartphones combine different features and functionalities in one medium (e.g. telephony, digital camera, personal organizer, e-mail, music);
- **Multi-Channel-Communication:** The access to mobile internet adds new channels of communication (social networks, VoIP, instant messaging);
- **Mobility:** All functionality can be used independent of location; small weight and size allow to easily take them everywhere;

- **Extensibility Via Apps:** Additional apps widen the functionality of the devices;
- **User-Driven Innovation:** The possibility to program new apps widens the functionality via collaborative innovation and creates new innovative services.

All these factors explain why smartphones are the most rapidly expanding technological innovation of all time. No other technology has ever spread so fast across the globe as mobile phones equipped with micro-computers (Streich, 2011, p. 230).

CITIZEN ENGAGEMENT IN A MOBILE SOCIETY

Participation is inherent to mobile phones (Castells et al., 2006) and they amplify participation in a spatial and temporal dimension. Furthermore smartphones amplify the variety of possible uses for public participation processes.

The internet and all related communicational channels are getting ubiquitous. "Mass communication used to be predominantly one-directional. With the diffusion of the internet a new form of communication has emerged, characterized by the capacity of sending messages from many to many, in real-time (synchronous communication) or chosen time (asynchronous communication), and with the possibility of using point-to-point communication, narrowcasting or broadcasting, depending on the purpose and characteristics of the intended communication practice" (Castells, 2009, p. 55).

With the rise of the internet in general and more recently with the emergence of Web2.0 - web applications (which facilitate interactive information sharing, interoperability, user-centred design, and collaboration on the World Wide Web) the costs of global publishing have collapsed (Shirky, 2008, p. 9). Easy-to-use communication and publishing

technologies provide low-threshold methods of communication between nearly everybody – creating a many-to-many communication. Whereas real-world communication is limited by distance and time, online tools enable many forms of instant, global, and nearly permanent communication.

Never before have people enjoyed the ability to collaboratively collect, analyse, and publish information on such a mass scale. In fact, the internet, as a multimedia communication infrastructure, allow images, sound, text, and their combination as a video, to be sent and received, created and edited. The internet is a truly interactive medium and causes a "shift from top-down, one-way communication to a vastly more participatory medium" (Höffken & Haller, 2010, p. 494). Users increasingly take part in the production of online content, publish their thoughts on blogs, share videos and photos, and connect with each other by using social networks. A many-to-many form of communication, or individual mass-communication as Castells calls it, is now possible. As Shirky (2008, p. 20 f.) argues "We are living in the middle of a remarkable increase in our ability to share, to cooperate with one another, and to take collective action, all outside the framework of traditional institutions and organizations."

Bottom-Up Participation and Collaborative Action

City planners will experience big changes and new challenges, which are directly related to the changing framework of information and knowledge. In this knowledge society, a technology-driven approach generates new social effects. The digitalization and the new patterns of organisation and cooperation, generate new modes, domains, approaches and impacts of participation in the knowledge society (see Figure 1) (Intelcities, 2008, p. 11).

The knowledge society manifests itself in new forms of production and sharing of knowledge

Figure 1. The fundamental changes in citizen participation through the use of ICT in urban governance (Source: Intelcities 2008, p. 11)

Participation Indicators	Conventional Governance Models	Digital Governance Models
Mode of Participation	Representative	Individual / Collective
Domain of Participation	In-situ	Ex-situ
Approach to Participation	Passive / Reactive	Pro-active / Interactive
Impact of Participation	Indirect / Delayed	Direct / Immediate

(Streich, 2011). This sharing is realized through networks, on one side of social actors and on the other of technical systems, interacting with each other. One characteristic feature is the "bottom-up" principle, meaning the involvement of all stakeholders. Access to information and development of knowledge are generated by potentially all actors, each with their individual contribution. Contrary to the previously standard in urban and regional planning – the "top-down" principle, as an ultimate expression of an institutional hierarchy – new forms of involvement, engagement and participation are evolving, challenging the profession of urban and regional planners (Streich, 2011, p. 52). In other words: "The days of the single, authoritative voice are coming to an end. The community has prevailed" (Reichental, 2012).

Crowdsourcing

A new trend in participation and highly related to bottom-up participation is crowdsourcing. The term is a combination of "crowd" and "outsourcing" and was created by Howe (2006). It is a phenomenon that exists since long time, but gained its importance out of the collaborative power of web-based cooperation. The web is a catalyst for this new form of collaborative action of the masses (Brabham, 2009). An integrated definition is given by Estellés Arolas and González Ladrón-de-Guevara (2012). More precise and helpful in the context of mobile

participation in the urban environment is the definition by Erickson "Crowdsourcing is the use of the perceptual and cognitive abilities of a large group of individuals to solve a problem" (Erickson, 2010).

Crowdsourcing is related to the concept of the Wisdom of the Crowds, as Surowiecki (2004) named his famous book in which he describes the high potential of the concept: "After all, think about what happens if you ask a hundred people to run a 100-meter race, and then average their times. The average time will not be better than the time of the fastest runners. It will be worse. It will be a mediocre time. But ask a hundred people to answer a question or solve a problem, and the average answer will often be at least as good as the answer of the smartest member. With most things, the average is mediocrity. With decision making, it's often excellence. You could say it's as if we've been programmed to be collectively smart."(Surowiecki, 2004, p. 11). With a wide range of examples like Wikipedia, OpenStreetMap and others, the concept of crowdsourcing and collective action moved from theory to practice, as Howard (2012) refers.

Why Smartphones Enhance mParticipation

What we see is a set of technologies and tools emerging, a communicational infrastructure that will give us the scaffolding to interact and take part in the public sphere in our cities. As shown, smartphones provide various new opportunities to improve existing participation processes. Among other advantages, the use of smart phones (and tablet computers) for mParticipation has the following ones (based on: Molinari & Ferro, 2010; Castells et al., 2006):

- **Multimodality:** It's possible to communicate via voice, text, images, video, internet.
- *In-Situ* **Communication:** Allowing components of spontaneity.
- **Real-Time-Interaction:** Unlimited around the whole world.
- **Personal Device:** Smartphones are personal devices, not shared with other persons.
- **Permanent Companion:** Smartphones are permanently carried.
- **Readiness:** Smartphones are switched on for the most of time.
- **Low Costs:** Due to flat-rate-contracts. e.g. for mobile web, SMS, etc., additional costs for participation are low.
- **Ubiquity:** It can be taken everywhere – in public and private sphere.

Users can communicate via all kinds of channels and all these channels can be used in real-time, offering short-time reactions. Therefore the mobile technologies open the ways for collaborative action. The social tools enhance exchange and spread of information and lead to new ways of engaging the citizens.

MOBILE PARTICIPATION: CONCEPT, TYPES AND LEVELS OF ENGAGEMENT

As pointed out before, the use of internet, in particular mobile internet enlarges and multiplies the forms of participation (Streich, 2011, p. 171f).

mParticipation: The Concept

mParticipation refers to the term eParticipation (electronic participation) and is the development from desktop-based participation to a participation on-the-go. To cover the variety of the concepts in theory and practice, a working definition is given:

mParticipation is the use of mobile devices (e.g., mobile phones, smart phones and tablet computers) via wireless communication technology to broaden the participation of citizens and other stakeholders by enabling them to connect with each other, generate and share information, comment and vote.

It is consequently a subset of eParticipation, which itself can be seen as a part of eGovernment and eDemocracy, and not a replacement. The term *eParticipation* includes procedures based on information and communication technology (ICT) to enable the participation of citizens and other stakeholders in political decision-making processes (Macintosh, 2004; 2006; Ifib & Zebralog, 2008; OECD, 2003). Citizen consultation and engagement of stakeholders should be more efficient and effective. It is therefore a part of *eDemocracy*, which can be defined as "the use of information and communication technologies to broaden and deepen political participation by enabling citizens to connect with one another and with their elected representatives" (Macintosh, 2004) and focuses on the fundamental possibilities for democracy in a whole. E-Government on the other hand focuses more on aspects of the decision-making process. It includes the optimization and modernization of administrative processes through ICT. The role of the citizens is more passive than in e-Participation, which, in contrast, emphasises that the citizen is an active and responsible stakeholder.

2 mParticipation: Levels of Engagement

The following table shows three levels of mobile participation – low, medium, high – with their intended use, the main technologies and the ethical claims with respect to urban planning.

mParticipation: Related Concepts

Dealing with mobile participation, the multimodality of smartphones and imbedded sensors, different concepts were developed, which are sometimes used in similar ways and overlap in many aspects.

Geocentric Crowdsourcing

Based on the concept of crowdsourcing, Erickson gives a helpful classification of different types, based on time and space. In his "four quadrant

Figure 2. Four quadrant model applied to crowdsourcing (Source: Erickson, 2010)

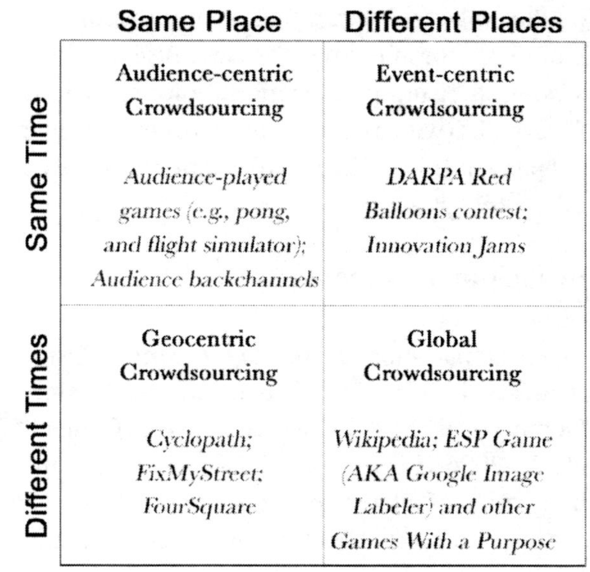

Table 1. Levels of mobile participation (Source: Streich, 2011, p. 172; own translation)

	Low-Level *(mainly Information)*	Medium-Level *(communication)*	High-Level *(real participation)*
Intended use	Presentations of data and facts	Coordination, support of planning processes	Active influencing of planning processes, free access to data, improved city-management (on new kinds of information)
Technology	Email, SMS, QR-Codes, spatial annotations Web 2.0	Social Media, (SMS) Web 2.0	Social Media, Cloud-computing, databases, Blogging, Crowdsourcing, Location-based-services Web 2.0 + Crowdsourcing
Ethical claims	Better information basis	Establish consensus between stakeholders in planning process	Equality of access to information
Interaction	One-directional (one-to-many)	Two-directional (one-to-one/one-to-many and vice versa)	Many-directional (many-to-many)

model of crowdsourcing" Erickson defines the term of geocentric crowdsourcing, as the relevant for urban topics. Here the work of the crowd is focused on a particular place or geospatial region (Erickson, 2010).

In this sense, geocentric crowdsourcing covers the main part of mParticipation (high-level mParticipation) as it defines the majority of so-called mobile participation projects. It is mainly focused on the collective acquisition of information and therefore doesn't cover process-oriented and awareness-rising participation projects, such as flash mobs (with a certain objective concern, and not just fun-oriented) or manifestations organised via mobile phones.

Participatory sensing

The term participatory sensing, or similar terms such as Citizen Sensing, Human Centered Sensing, Opportunistic Sensing, Urban Sensing (Cambell et al., 2006; Lane et al., 2008), describes the integration of citizens in the acquisition and collection of datasets about the urban environment, by using collectively gathered datasets (Abecker et al., 2012; Burke et al., 2006, 1 ff.). According to Burke et al. (2006), participatory sensing is the everyday use of "mobile devices, such as cellular

phones, to form interactive, participatory sensor networks that enable public and professional users to gather, analyse and share local knowledge." Microphones and other on-board sensors can already record environmental data, but in the future other sensors will be integrated and connected wirelessly. Participatory sensing has numerous technological and methodological similarities to mParticipation and geocentric crowdsourcing (mobile devices, use of sensors, crowdsourcing, Geoweb, etc.), but lacks the deliberative impetus and political influence, that both the other concepts share. Furthermore the user has a more passive role, as the focus lies on sensor-generated data and not on human voting or comments.

Inductive Monitoring

Based on similar technologies and comparable methodologies is the concept of inductive monitoring (Streich, 2012). It is the observation of spatial and social phenomena on the basis of the GeoWeb, location-aware social networks and mobile devices as sensors. It is different from participatory sensing in the sense that the crowd defines the range of observed topics and changes them in a dynamic process. The fundamental difference is the sovereignty of participants, defining

Table 2. mParticipation: Similarities and differences with the three related concepts (Source: own table)

	mParticipation	Geocentric Crowdsourcing	Participatory Sensing	Inductive Monitoring
Intended use	Active influencing of planning processes, free access to data, improved city-management (on new kinds of information)	Influencing of planning processes (by Collecting data, information and local knowledge)	Collecting data, information and local knowledge for experts and decision maker	Collecting data, information and local knowledge, improve database
Technology	Mobile Devices, Social Media, Cloud-computing, databases, Blogging, interactive simulations, Crowdsourcing, Location-based-services Web 2.0 & GeoWeb	Mobile Devices, Social Media, Cloud-computing, databases, Blogging, interactive simulations, Crowdsourcing, Location-based-services Web 2.0 & GeoWeb	Mobile Devices, Social Media, Cloud-computing, databases, Blogging, interactive simulations, Crowdsourcing, Location-based-services Web 2.0 & GeoWeb	Mobile Devices, Social Media, Cloud-computing, databases, Blogging, interactive simulations, Crowdsourcing, Location-based-services Web 2.0 & GeoWeb
Interaction	Many-directional (many-to-many)	Many-directional (many-to-many)	Two-directional (many-to-one and vice versa)	Two-directional (many-to-one and vice versa)

the relevance which data is worth to be obtained. The wisdom of crowds not only collects and rates data, but also defines the relevance of it.

CASE STUDIES: SIX REAL WORLD PROJECTS

In this section, the chapter presents real-world mParticipation projects directly related to urban governance. Based on internet research and literature reviews, a variety of possible examples were collected. Out of that, the six most suitable projects, in terms of the definition of mParticipation, were selected and analysed. These projects will be presented by analysis of intention (aim, topic, target group, the driving institution), participation (mode, approach, impact, possibility

of comments, activity) and technological aspects (interactivity, app-based, channels). They all are based on crowdsourcing and the use of mobile phones for asynchronous interaction.

Textizen

Textizen is a citizen feedback tool by the non-profit-organisation Code for America. "Textizen asks questions on posters in public places, then collects citizen feedback via text message. Anyone with a minute and an opinion can reply" (Textizen, 2012). As it uses SMS for communication, it is a low-threshold service for quantitative data collection, helping to improve decision-making. It actually is tested in cities in the USA like Philadelphia.

Figure 3. Using SMS for citizen Feedback (Source: http://www.textizen.com/)

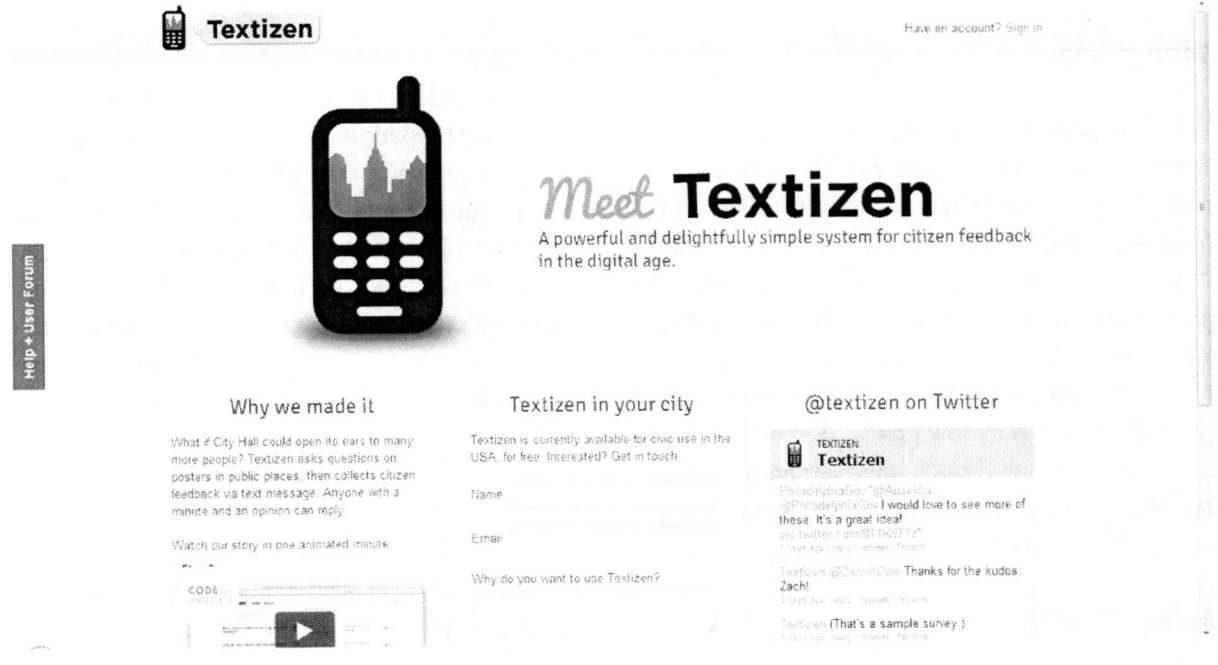

Figure 4. Wheelmap – Mapping accessibility for wheel-chairs (Source: URL: http://wheelmap.org)

Wheelmap

Wheelmap (with the subtitle "finding wheelchair-friendly places") is a project of Sozialhelden, a non-profit organization based in Berlin. The platform was founded in 2010 and its aim is the raising of public awareness of the needs of handicapped people (mainly wheelchair users, but also parents with pushchair, etc.). A staircase can be a barrier for wheelchair users and can cause the non-visit of facilities (such as town halls, doctors' offices and supermarkets). Participants can spot and mark facilities and access the information via an app (available for iOS and, Android).

Mängelmelder

Mängelmelder was initiated by a spin-off from the University of Technology of Darmstadt, which is active in the fields of eGovernment (report systems), participatory budgeting and eParticipation. Mängelmelder is a report platform to facilitate public participation and citizen engagement in German-speaking countries (Germany, Luxembourg, Austria and Switzerland). The aim is to empower citizens to report local problems (e.g. broken street lights, potholes and litter). Furthermore criticism and suggestions can be communicated to the local government. The user can use the platform via the Web, as well as via iPhone and Android App.

Cyclopath

Cyclopath is a project realised by GroupLens research lab in the Department of Computer Science and Engineering at the University of Minnesota. "Cyclopath lets you enter personal bikeability ratings for roads and trails. This unique rating system helps find the best routes for you,

Figure 5. Screenshot of the Website Mängelmelder (Source: URL: http://www.mängelmelder.de/)

Figure 6. Mapping bike lanes - Cyclopath (Source: URL: http://magic.cyclopath.org/#)

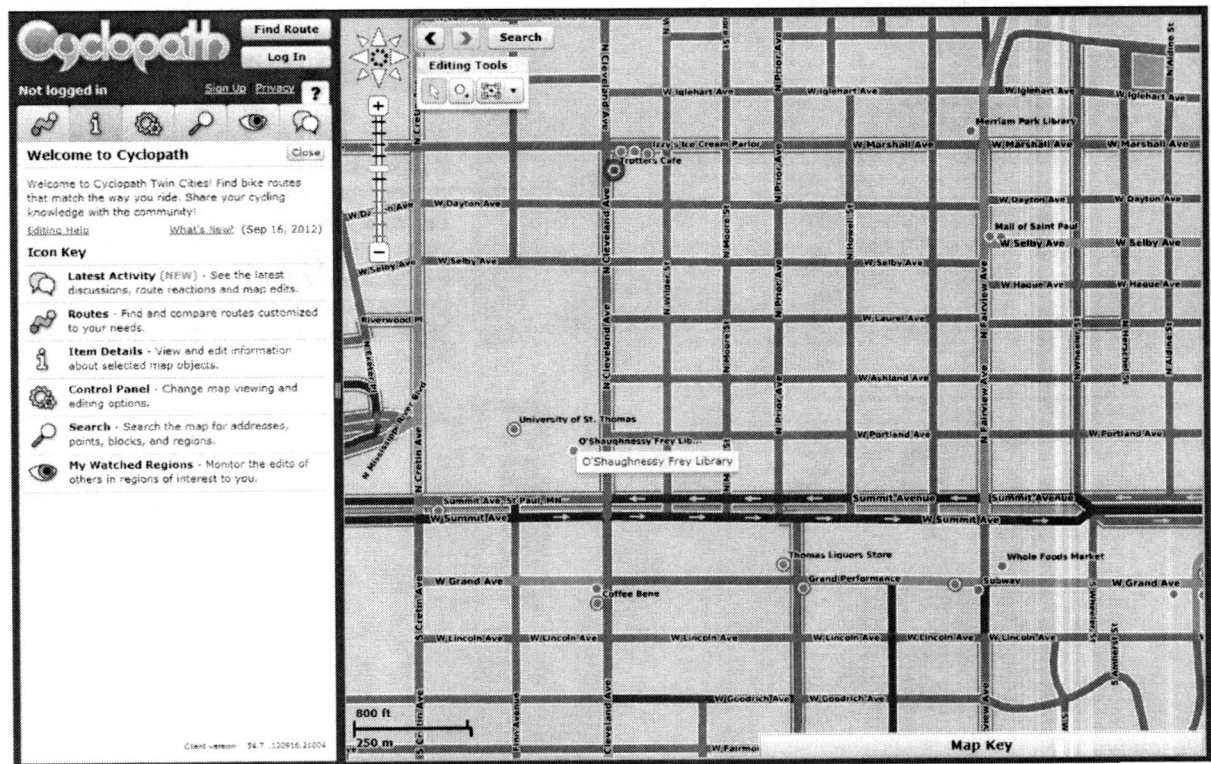

while also supporting the community with your individual knowledge." It is a report-system for problems (like potholes), but also an information-system for cyclists.

CitySourced

CitySourced calls itself "a real time mobile civic engagement platform" (CitySourced, 2012). It was released in 2009 and is a tool to facilitate public participation and governance. "CitySourced provides a free, simple, and intuitive platform empowering residents to identify civic issues (public safety, quality of life, & environmental issues, etc.) and report them to city hall for quick resolution" (CitySourced, 2012). The platform was designed for use in the United States and is hosted by the company CitySourced. The platform helps to facilitate citizen engagement and organises

feedback between citizens and administration, planning and decision-making.

Saskatoon Bike Map (Based on Ushahidi)

Saskatoon Bike Map is an application, based on the open-source-tool Ushahidi. The Bike Map is a report system for the City of Saskatoon in Canada, and operated by a group of cyclist. The project started in 2009 and had its highest activity in autumn 2010.

These six cases examined confirm the existence of similarities and differences in the apps available for mParticipation. For example:

- **Different Levels of Complexity:** The examples differ from low-complexity (low-threshold access) to a high level of complexity.

Figure 7. A smartphones-based report system – CitySourced (Source: URL: http://www.citysourced. com/default.aspx)

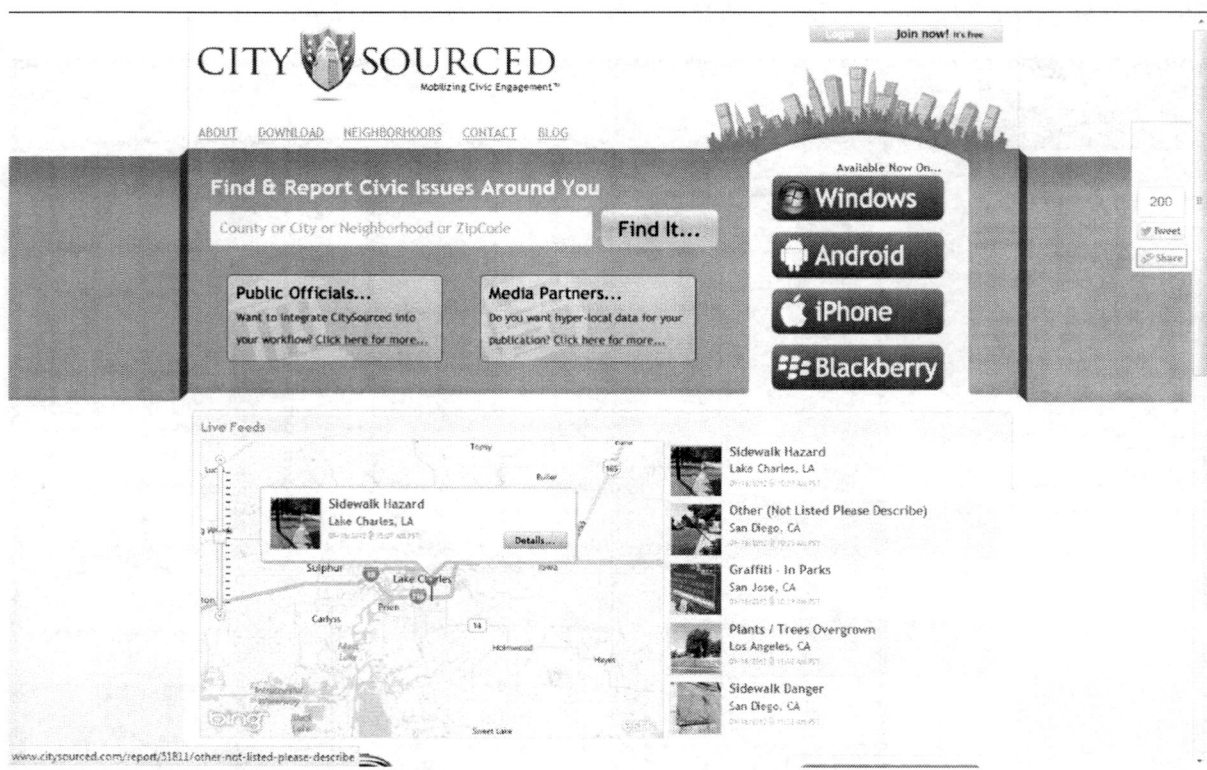

Figure 8. Mapping via Open-Source-tools – Saskatoon Bike Map (Source: URL: https://saskatoonbike-map.crowdmap.com/)

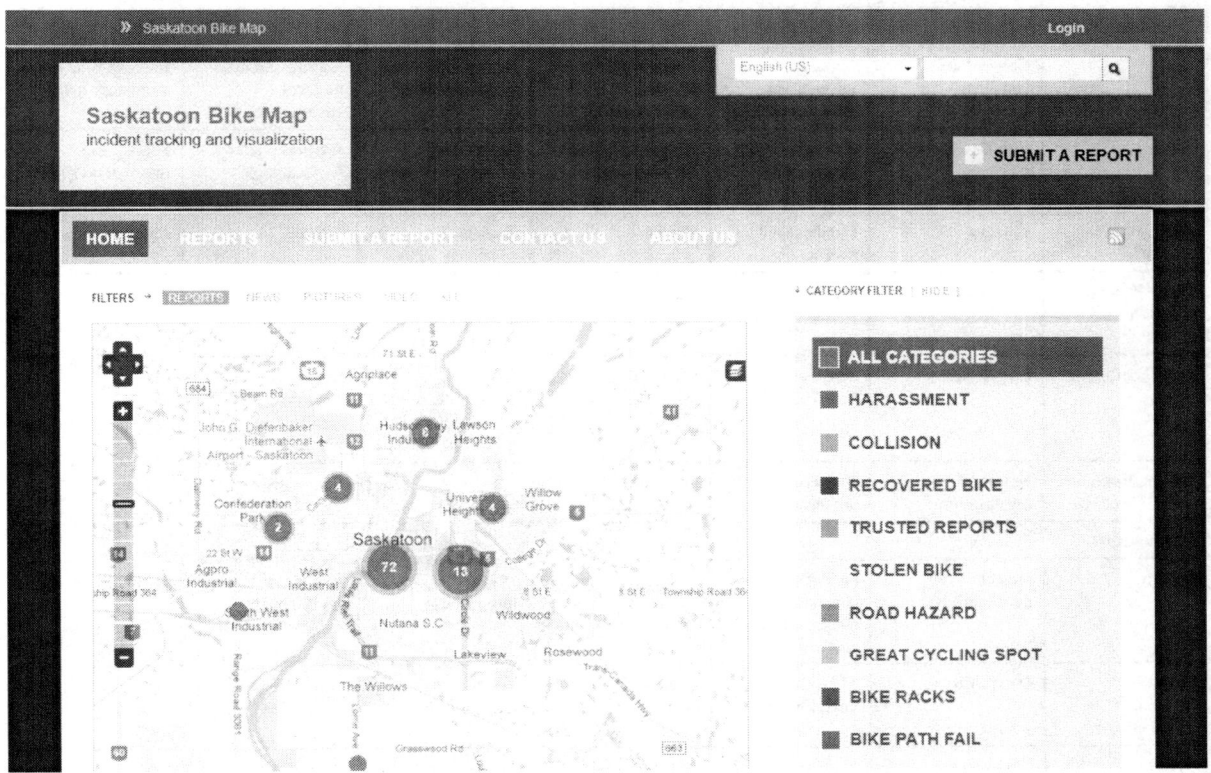

- **Using Multimodal Communication:** With the exception of one example (Textizen) all apps work on a multimodal basis, by using text, photo, and spatial annotations via the Internet. This adds additional information to the gathered (georeferenced) data (e.g., a photo proves the report about garbage in the public space).

- **SMS is a Low-Threshold Channel for Involving a Broad Community:** An unexpected result is the use of SMS in mParticipation, in the present context of high smartphone penetration. Schuler (2008, p. 144) states that a "growing number of election-monitoring organizations around the world employ SMS technology to improve the effectiveness of their monitoring efforts." But in the western world this result is surprising. With Code for America, one of the most innovative companies in the field of eGovernment in America, created a SMS-tool (Textizen). A similar approach is developed by Neighbourland (with a broad approach, in which mobile devices are just one channel among many others) with its SMS-tool (Neighbourland, 2012). The initial attempt is a platform for a broad audience, bridging problems of the digital divide, which is not any more mainly infrastructural based, due to a high penetration of (mobile) Internet in western countries; but is more and more caused by socio-eco-

Table 3. Case studies: Similarities and differences (Source: own table)

	Textizen	Wheelmap	Mängelmelder	Cyclopath	CitySourced	Bike Map
Intention						
Aim	Collect local knowledge	Improve information, awareness-rising	Improve database for local government	Improve Bike lanes, awareness-rising	Improve database for local government	Improve Bike lanes, awareness-rising
Topic	City Development	Accessibility for Handicapped people	A report platform for local topic	Report- and information system for cyclists	A report platform for local topic	Report- and information system for cyclists
Participants	Citizens	Handicapped people	Citizens	Cyclists	Citizens	Cyclists
Target group (use of information)	Administration	Handicapped people	Administration	Cyclists (planning administration)	Administration	Administration
Spatial definition	City (different)	Worldwide	Countywide (but focus on urban areas)	City (Metropolitan region of Minneapolis and St. Paul)	Countywide (but focus on urban areas)	City
Driving Institution	Non-Profit organisation	Non-Profit organisation	Company	University (Research project)	Company	Citizens
Technology						
System	project development	project development (Based on Open-source tools)	project development (Based on Open-source tools)	project development	project development	Open-source-tool
Channels	One (SMS)	Multi (Internet, Text, Photo)	Multi (Internet, Text, Photo)	Multi (Internet, Text, Photo)	Multi (Internet, Text, Photo, Video)	Multi (Internet, Text, Photo, Video, Audio)
App-Based (on mobilephone)	Yes (own app)	Yes (own app)	Yes (own app)	Yes/No (desktop-based, but no amplified by mobile app)	Yes (own app)	Yes
Participation						
Approach	Reactive	Interactive	Pro-Active	Interactive	Interactive	Pro-Active
Impact (of the information)	Direct/ Immediate	Direct/ Immediate	Direct/ Immediate	Direct/ Immediate	Direct/ Immediate	Direct/ Immediate
Ability to Comment/add data	Yes	yes	yes	yes	yes	yes
Activity	No info	High	Medium	Medium	High	Low
Other						
Costs	Low (SMS)	Low (with Internet flatrate)	Low (with Internet flatrate)	Low (with Internet flatrate)	Low (with Internet flatrate)	Low (with internet flatrate)
Barriers to Registration	No	Registration needed (Reporting)	no	Registration needed	No	No
Complexity (Learning curve)	Low	Reporting: High Use information: Medium	Medium	High	Medium	Medium/High (the URL of the channel has to be added by user, sometimes technical problems)
Level of Participation	Medium	Medium (only app) High (in combination of desktop functionality)	High	High	High	High

nomic aspects (no financial capacity for a smartphone) and different levels of media savvy (Fischer, 2012). Consequently, even in highly-connected, mobile times, the SMS is still an important channel for digital citizen participation.

- **Pass-by-Participation as a Point-of-Entry:** Low-threshold participation (e.g., like Textizen) are an important point-of-entry for the involvement of passer-bys. The aim is to get passer-bys into the process and raise awareness for the process. Automatic responses and further information (e.g., done in Textizen) are strategies to turn interested passer-bys into engaged participants.

- **Apps as a Barrier and Catalyst:** The need for the installation of apps is at first a barrier, as the app has to be installed, which is time-consuming (due to low mobile internet rates) and in some cases cost-intensive (for participants without flat rates). On the other hand, participants with an installed app are probably interested in the topic and therefore probably remain in the process. Furthermore an app can generate attention to a service and create, as a catalyst, a higher involvement.

- **User's Demands Create New Ideas:** There is no top-down (by government) creation in the six examples analyzed. Report systems are created by companies and special topics are created out of needs of the participants (e.g., Wheelmap), and research-interest (Cyclopath). It cannot be proved in this analysis, but there are indicators that user's demands create new ideas in the particular cases.

- **Time-Lag and Risk of Frustration:** Wheelmap and Cyclopath are examples in which participants are the target group. This creates higher willingness and interest of taking part, as the participants create a direct improvement for themselves (updated information). The other services have a differentiation between participants and target group.

FINDINGS

This section critically appraises these innovative methods for citizen mobile participation in urban planning, examines the effectiveness of these tools, and discusses the usefulness of mParticipation in urban planning processes. The focus is on general concepts and methodologies (e.g., multi-channel-strategies; participation on-the-go).

Minimize Excluded Groups

For minimizing exclusion and engaging a wide range of people, a multi-channel strategy is recommended, which means the integration of traditional ways of participation (e.g., meetings, brochures) and eParticipation (e.g., information, comments, animations, forums, etc.). For geocentric crowdsourcing processes the recommended multi-channel strategy is limited to the group of the so-called mobile citizens, not only by money, but also in terms of technology, as technological know-how is still required to obtain the information (e.g., use of GPS, tagging).

The expected increase in the diffusion of smartphones in the next years, the rise of the present younger generation, already embracing online tools and technology in the daily life, and a higher usability (e.g., touchscreens, smart operating systems) will probably reduce the number and size of excluded groups, but probably will never solve the problem in total. Therefore additional desktop-tools could help to enlarge the range of potential participants.

Handling of Different Platforms

As mentioned above, the need to download proprietary apps for each process is a barrier. SMS is integrated to all kinds of mobile phones and therefore offers a very low-threshold access. The tool Ushahidi is an open-source platform, adoptable to different participation tasks (with a wide range from social activism, citizen journalism and geospatial crowdsourcing). The app can be used for several projects based on Ushahidi and consequently generates a multi-use option. This kind of cross-media participation processes will be a driver for change in participatory processes but is still in its infancy.

Battery Power

The integration of sensors leads to the problem of battery power, as sensors, especially GPS, are energy consuming. Solutions can be based on software (e.g., a manual georeferenciation on a map without GPS to avoid high energy consumption), or on the hardware, improving energy efficiency (Zhuang, 2010; Sorber et al., 2005). Furthermore, improved batteries will also help to solve the problem of high energy consumption, which is sometimes an obstacle for taking part in mParticipation processes.

Privacy Concerns and Data Security

The variety of sensors and sensing technologies allows for new forms of personal data mining, directly affecting privacy. This tension between the participation's need for personal information and the individual's right to privacy is a big challenge and has to be defined in every single project. One difference to be made is between active given data and passive data collection. While active data is given voluntarily, passive data collection is not necessarily known by the user. One famous example is the case of Apple's iPhone, having included "a file on iPhone that stores location coordinates and timestamps of owner's movements" (Arthur, 2011). Awareness rising is necessary to all participants, to ensure that users have knowledge about information of location and other personal data. They should be able to determine how and when the data will be used. For better data security and privacy protection, regulations from the government are necessary.

Engaging Effectiveness

A key issue in participatory approaches is the effectiveness and intensity of the offered engagement. The mentioned surplus of mobility creates a variety of interaction, participation and collaboration. Yet the useful process depends on the activity and the involvement of the users. The technological framework is one side, but it's a different story to actually get people involved. To avoid non-participation, every project needs a strategy that outlines a project's approach to getting an audience to participate. Therefore mParticipation strategies must have a defined goal, like educating citizens about the trade-offs and alternatives of a planning project.

Low Threshold Participation

One of the major challenges regarding citizen engagement via mobile devices is the integration of citizens into the governance process. One important aspect in this case is time. Many people aren't willing to spend more than a few minutes. In this case "pass-by-participation" via low-threshold mParticipation tools can be useful and can broaden the number of participants.

FUTURE RESEARCH DIRECTIONS

Process Integration

mParticipation bridges spatial and temporal barriers and helps to integrate passer-bys. But based on previous experience it seems that mParticipation processes have a lower intensity as long-term eParticipation processes (e.g. consultations). For the purpose of crowdsourcing, smartphones offer (very) low-threshold and time-extensive access. In further research it should be examined how mParticipation can be integrated in eParticipation processes, or how it should be developed as stand-alone tools. Moreover, mParticipation should be further integrated in the process of institutional innovation (Biwer et al., 2012, p. 475), for a more efficient, transparent and effective public administration.

New Challenges for Administrations and Planners

The changes and new possibilities referred before lead to challenges, which need to be addressed by local governments and planners. The discipline of urban planning has to deal with a wide-range of different tools for citizen participation, for the collection of new data, and for the analysis of urban patterns. This means that mParticipation (and related fields) deserve further theoretical research and practical implementation. Data validation, new applications, and integration of crowdsourced data into planning processes are just some of the situations that deserve particular attention.

Administrations have to become comfortable with the shift in participation, from a top-down-approach to a more bottom-up initiated process. The networked communication leads to instant communities, which tend to become a player in the planning processes, redefining the balance of power. An example for this potential conflict is the case of Stuttgart 21 in Germany (Lösch, 2011; Althaus, 2012). This collective action and organization challenge the authorities to redefine their own role and to involve these new groups.

User-Driven-Innovation

The internet enables easy-to-use user interfaces, user-friendly interaction and generates the equality of access to information. It is on the way of even empowering people without programming skills to contribute content and use a variety of tools (e.g., weblogs, social media, open-source-tools). Web 2.0 tools function like construction sets, enabling people to create own use cases and thus lead to a democratization of technology.

The next step are homebrew apps (Economist, 2012), meaning do-it-yourself (DIY) development kits for the production of apps. As the Economist (2012) refers "App-creating software could be the machine tools of the mobile world" and will create more application-driven challenges, such as new games, new crowdsourcing platforms, new solutions for data collection, etc. This kind of Open Innovation will furthermore evolve the user's role. As Shirky (2008) points out, "The invention of a tool doesn't create change; it has to have been around long enough that most part of the society is using it. It's when a technology becomes normal, than ubiquitous, and finally so pervasive as to be invisible, that the really profound changes happen, and so for young people today, our social tools have passed normal and are heading to become ubiquitous and invisible." This is what is happening right now and more and more people will be able to contribute and shape our society through self-developed services and self-authored information.

Augmented Reality

Recent advances in mobile computing and sensor technologies enable the development of Augmented Reality (AR) applications on smartphones. Augmented reality (AR) is augmentation "of the surroundings of the user with virtual information that is registered in 3D space and seems to co-exist with the real world" (Yovcheva et al., 2012). The technology adds digital content to the existing environment, by combining virtual and real objects. This effect is called extended or enriched reality and adds new layers of information. This kind of additional information can be used for better, more intuitive and space-related information in participation projects. Focus for city development could be the use of 3D city models to present and discuss alternative planning concepts (Streich & Zeile, 2012; Broschart, 2011; Biwer et al., 2012).

More innovations in the field of mobile participation are expected. New trends as crowdsourcing, collective intelligence (Shirky, 2008), bottom-up-participation (Streich, 2011; Höffken & Kloss, 2011), citizen science (Hand, 2010), and participatory urbanism (Paulos et al., 2009) constitute some of the new and important research issues in the field of citizen participation in urban governance.

CONCLUSION

mParticipation is a dynamic field with great opportunities for citizens, urban government and urban planners. The opportunities and challenges of smartphones-based participation are diverse. Based on this technological progress, mParticipation integrates different concepts and functionalities which are connected to new developments like ubiquitous computing (Mattern, 2002; Weiser, 1991), augmented reality (Haller et al., 2006; Madden, 2011) and location based technologies (Schiller & Voisard, 2004).

The philosophy of the Web 2.0 has reached a wide part of the population (Abecker et al., 2012, p. 240). The networked organisational structure, open processes for random plug-in and plug-out of participants and an evolutionary development are common elements of new ways of participation and activism. Urban gardening projects (see Müller, 2011), tactical urbanism events (see Street Plan Collaborative, 2012) and network-based groups (see Junghans & David, 2011) are examples of these new forms of organisation and cooperation. The idea of crowdsourcing is, on one hand, based on the digital infrastructure, enabling and supporting these processes, and, on the other hand, on a new awareness about the possibilities of collaborative action. It is highly probable that citizen mParticipation, seen as part of citizen e-Participation in urban governance will seriously change the way citizens interact, cooperate and deal with each other and with local governments in the planning and management of cities and regions.

That leads to a situation that the boundaries between producers and consumers become blurred. A well informed and online public will change the exchange between representatives and interested citizens by multiplying information and communication. These new abilities of exchanging specialized information, discussing arguments and forming decisions can re-establish confidence in administrative institutions and existing procedures. The integration of citizens for providing feedback, collecting information and sharing opinions will lead to open consultation processes. mParticipation will play a relevant, innovative and dynamic part in these new forms of urban Government, by complementing and extending the existing procedures and methodologies.

ACKNOWLEDGMENT

This chapter would not have been possible without the support and inspiring discussions with our colleagues Dr.-Ing. Peter Zeile and Jan-Philipp Exner. Additionally, we would like to thank all the students working with us with so much enthusiasm and emphasis, helping to explore and research new possibilities and methodologies. The authors would like to express their gratitude to DFG – Deutsche Forschungsgemeinschaft for supporting the research project "Städtebauliche Methodenentwicklung mit GeoWeb und Mobile Computing" based in their department.

REFERENCES

Abecker, A., Kazakos, W., Melo Borges, J., & Zacharias, J. (2012). Beiträge zu einer Technologie für Anwendungen des Participatory Sensing. In: J. Strobl, T. Blaschke, & G. Griesebner (Eds.), *Angewandte Geoinformatik* 2012 (pp. 240-249). Herbert Wichmann Verlag, VDE Verlag GmbH, Berlin/Offenbach. Retrieved from http://gispoint.de/fileadmin/user_upload/paper_gis_open/537520001.pdf

Android. (n.d.). *Website*. Retrieved from http://developer.android.com/training/index.html

Apple. (n.d.). *Website*. Retrieved from http://developer.apple.com/library/ios/navigation/

Aquarius. (2012). 2012 wird zum Jahr der Smartphones. Retrieved July 17th, 2012, from http://www.aquarius.biz/de/2012/01/09/2012-wird-zum-jahr-der-smartphones/

Arthur, C. (2011, April 20). iPhone keeps record of everywhere you go. *The Guardian*. Retrieved from http://www.guardian.co.uk/technology/2011/apr/20/iphone-tracking-prompts-privacy-fears

Banks, K. (2008). *Mobile telephony and the entrepreneur: An African perspective*. Retrieved July 17th, 2012, from http://www.kiwanja.net/media/docs/Microfinance-Insights-kiwanja-2008.pdf

Bergner, B., Exner, J., Zeile, P., & Broschart, D. (2012). *Humansensorik in der räumlichen Planung*. GISPoint. Retrieved July 19th, 2012, from http://gispoint.de/fileadmin/user_upload/paper_gis_open/537520019.pdf

Birkholz, T., & Höffken, S. (2010). Reblog, RT@, FWD: Urbane Phänomene, soziale Netzwerke und vernetzte Kommunikation. *Spacemag*, *3*, 88–91.

Bitkom. (2012). *Smartphone-Funktionen: Internet wichtiger als Telefonieren*. Retrieved July 17th, 2012, from http://www.bitkom.org/de/presse/8477_72686.aspx

Biwer, J., Broschart, D., & Höffken, S. (2012). Mobile Digitalisierung von Baulücken – Baulückenerfassung mit GIS, iPad und Geoweb. In M. Schrenk, V.V. Popovich, P. Zeile, & P. Elisei (Eds.), *Proceedings REAL CORP 2012 Tagungsband*.

Bodymonitor. (2012). *Project website*. Retrieved August 19th, 2012, from http://www.bodymonitor.de/

Brabham, D. C. (2009). Crowdsourcing the public participation process for planning projects. *Planning Theory*, *8*, 242-262. Retrieved from http://plt.sagepub.com/content/8/3/242

Burke, J. A., Estrin, D., Hansen, M., Parker, A., Ramanathan, N., & Reddy, S. (2006). *Participatory sensing*. Papers, Center for Embedded Network Sensing, UC Los Angeles. Retrieved July 17th, 2012, from http://escholarship.org/uc/item/19h777qd#page-3

Castells, M. (2001). *The Internet galaxy. Reflections on the Internet, business, and society*. Oxford: Oxford University Press.

Castells, M. (2009). *Communication power*. New York: Oxford University Press.

Castells, M., Fernandez-Ardevol, M., Linchuan Qiu, J., & Sey, A. (2006). *Mobile communication and society: A global perspective*. Cambridge: MIT Press.

CitySourced. (2012). *Project website*. Retrieved July 17th, 2012, from http://www.citysourced.com/about

Commonwealth of Learning. (2011). *Designing mobile information and content strategies for grassroots participation*. Retrieved July 17th, 2012, from http://www.col.org/SiteCollectionDocuments/Watkins_Mobile%20Research_110808.pdf

ComScore. (2012). *Number of European smartphone users accessing news surges 74 percent over past year*. Retrieved July 17th, 2012, from http://www.comscore.com/Press_Events/Press_Releases/2012/3/Number_of_European_Smartphone_Users_Accessing_News_Surges_74_Percent_Over_Past_Year?piCId=66038

Economist. (2012). *Make your own Angry Birds - Homebrew apps have arrived*. Retrieved August 18th, 2012, from http://www.economist.com/node/21559366

Elektronikkompendium. (2012). *Datenübertragung im Mobilfunk*. Retrieved July 21th, 2012, from http://www.elektronik-kompendium.de/sites/kom/0910141.htm

Erickson, T. (2010). Geocentric crowdsourcing and smarter cities: Enabling urban intelligence in cities and regions. *Crowdsourcing*. Retrieved July 17th, 2012, from http://www.crowdsourcing.org/document/geocentric-crowdsourcing-and-smarter-cities/5678

Estellés Arolas, E., & González Ladrón-de-Guevara, F. (2012). Towards an integrated crowdsourcing definition. *Journal of Information Science*. Retrieved July 17th, 2012, from http://www.crowdsourcing-blog.org/wp-content/uploads/2012/02/Towards-an-integrated-crowdsourcing-definition-Estell%C3%A9s-Gonz%C3%A1lez.pdf

Fischer, S. (2012). *Minderheit vergrößert digitale Kluft*. Taz Zeitung vom 23.02.2012. Retrieved from http://www.taz.de/Internetnutzung-in-Deutschland/!88344/

Goodchild, M. F. (2007). Citizens as sensors: The world of volunteered geography. *GeoJournal*, 69, 211–221. Retrieved July 24th, 2012, from http://www.springerlink.com/content/h013jk125081j628/fulltext.pdf

Google Inc, & the Otto Group. TNS Infrastest & Trend Büro. (2012). *Go-Smart2012 – Always-in-touch – Studie zur Smartphone-Nutzung 2012*. Retrieved August 24th, 2012, from http://www.ottogroup.com/media/docs/de/studien/go_smart.pdf

Grouplens. (2012). *Project-website*. Retrieved July 24th, 2012, from http://www.grouplens.org/

Haller, C. (2011). *Micro-participation connects citizens to their governments*. Retrieved August 24th, 2012, from http://www.shareable.net/blog/micro-participation-connects-citizens-to-their-governments

Haller, M., Billinghurst, M., & Thomas, B. (Eds.). (2006). *Emerging technologies of augmented reality: Interfaces and design*. Idea Group Publishing. doi:10.4018/978-1-59904-066-0.

Hand, E. (2010). Citizen science: People power. *Nature*, *466*, 685–687. doi:10.1038/466685a PMID:20686547.

Hellström, J., & Karefelt, A. (2011). *Mobile participation? Crowdsourcing during the 2011 Uganda general elections*. Retrieved July 24th, 2012, from http://www.texttochange.org/sites/default/files/newsfiles/M4D2012_Hellstrom_Karefelt%20(1).pdf

Herring, C. (1994). An architecture of cyberspace: Spatialization of the Internet. *CiteSeer*. Retrieved July 17th, 2012, from http://citeseerx.ist.psu.edu/viewdoc/summary?doi=10.1.1.37.4604

Höffken, S. (2008). Mobile participation. *Pep-Net*. Retrieved July 17th, 2012, from http://pep-net.eu/blog/2008/06/24/mobile-participation/

Höffken, S., & Haller, C. (2010). New communication tools and eparticipation: Social media in urban planning. In M. Schrenk, V. Popovich, P. Zeile (Eds.), *RealCORP 2010, 15th International Conference, Vienna, Austria 18-20 May 2010*. Vienna: CORP – Competence Center of Urban and Regional Planning. Retrieved July 24th, 2012, from http://www.corp.at/archive/CORP2010_109.pdf

Höffken, S., & Kloss, C. (2011). Digitale Urbanisten – oder wie das Internet Stadtplanung und urbane Kultur verändert. In Forum Wohnen und Stadtentwicklung, Heft 4/2011, 198-201.

Howard, A. (2012). The emerging political force of the network of networks. *O'Reilly Radar*. Retrieved July 24th, 2012, from http://radar.oreilly.com/2012/06/12-talks-from-pdf-2012.html

Ifib, Z. (2008). *E-Partizipation – Elektronische Beteiligung von Bevölkerung und Wirtschaft am E-Government. Studie im Auftrag des Bundesministeriums des Innern, Ref. IT*. Retrieved July 17th, 2012, from http://www.ifib.de/publikationsdateien/ifib-zebralog-e-partizipation-kurz.pdf

Initiative, D. 21. (2012). *Nonliner atlas 2011 – Eine Topographie des digitalen Grabens durch Deutschland*. Retrieved September 2nd, 2012, from http://www.initiatived21.de/wp-content/uploads/2011/07/NOnliner2011.pdf

INTELCITIES. (2006). *Electronic and mobile participation in city planning and management*. Helsinki, Finland. Retrieved July 17th, 2012, from http://www.hel2.fi/tietokeskus/julkaisut/pdf/Intelcity.pdf

Junghans, A., & David, B. (2011). *Mit dem Computer in den Hosentasche entsteht ein neuer öffentlicher Zwischenraum*. Retrieved July 17th, 2012, from http://www.heise.de/tp/artikel/33/33977/1.html

Lane, N. D., Eisenman, S. B., Musolesi, M., Miluzzo, E., & Campbell, A. T. (2008). Urban sensing systems: Opportunistic or participatory? In *Proceedings of the 9th workshop on Mobile computing systems and applications, Napa Valley, California*, 11-16.

Lane, N. D., Miluzzo, E., Lu, H., Peebles, D., Choudhury, T., & Campbell, A. T. (2010). *A survey of mobile phone sensing*. Retrieved July 24th, 2012, from http://www.cs.dartmouth.edu/~campbell/papers/survey.pdf

Lösch, B. (2011). *Die Zukunftsfähigkeit der De-mokratie – Neue politische Beteiligungsformen in der Diskussion. Gesellschaft - Wirtschaft - Politik - Sozialwissenschaften für politische Bildung.* Jahrgang 61, 2012, Heft 1.

Luke, W. (2010). *Location detection technologies.* Retrieved September 14th, 2012, from http://www.lukew.com/ff/entry.asp?1089

Macintosh, A. (2004). Characterizing e-partic-ipation in policy-making. In *Proceedings of the Thirty-Seventh Annual Hawaii International Con-ference on System Sciences* (HICSS-37). January 5 – 8, 2004, Big Island, Hawaii.

Macintosh, A. (2006). eParticipation in policy making: The research and the challenges. Exploit-ing the Knowledge Economy: Issues, Applications, Case Studies. Amsterdam: IOS Press.

Madden, L. (2011). *Professional augmented real-ity browsers for Smartphones: Programming for junaio, Layar and Wikitude.* John Wiley & Sons.

Mattern, F. (2002). *Vom Handy zum allgegenwär-tigen Computer: Ubiquitous computing: Szenarien einer informatisierten Welt [Electronic ed.], Bonn.* Retrieved July 24th, 2012, from http://library.fes.de/fulltext/stabsabteilung/01183.htm

Molinari, F., & Ferro, E. (2010). *Characterising mobile participation in public decisionmaking.* Re-trieved July 24th, 2012, from http://crossroad.epu.ntua.gr/files/2010/04/02_Characterising_mobile_participation_in_public_decision-making.pdf

Müller, C. (2011). Urban Gardening – Über die Rückkehr der Gärten in die Stadt. oekom Verlag, München.

Nasa. (2009). *Ames scientist develops cell phone chemical sensor.* Retrieved July 24th, 2012, from http://www.nasa.gov/centers/ames/news/features/2009/cell_phone_sensors.html

Neighbourland. (2012). *Project-website.* Retrieved July 24th, 2012, from https://neighborland.com

Netzwelt. (2012). *WWDC 2012: Apple meldet 30 Milliarden Downloads aus dem App Store.* Retrieved July 24th, 2012, from http://www.netz-welt.de/news/92608-app-store-apple-vermeldet-30-milliarden-downloads.html

Nielsen Company. (2011a). *Social media report Q3 11.* Retrieved July 24th, 2012, from http://blog.nielsen.com/nielsenwire/social/

Nielsen Company. (2011b). *Nielsen präsentiert erste Ergebnisse aus aktuellem Smartphone Insights Report für Deutschland.* Retrieved July 24th, 2012, from http://www.nielsen.com/de/de/insights/presseseite/2011/nielsen-praesentiert-er-ste-ergebnisse-aus-aktuellem-smartphone-i.html

OfNS (Office for National Statistics). (2011). *Statistical bulletin - Internet access - households and individuals, 2011.* Retrieved September 24th, 2012, from http://www.ons.gov.uk/ons/dcp171778_227158.pdf

Paulos, E., Honicky, R., & Hooker, B. (2009). Citizen science: Enabling participatory urban-ism. In Foth, M. (Ed.), *Handbook of Research on Urban Informatics.*

Policy Brief, O. E. C. D. (2003). Engaging citi-zens online for better policy-making. *Washington OECD Observer.* Retrieved July 24th, 2012, from http://www.oecd.org/dataoecd/62/23/2501856.pdf

Rauterberg, H. (2011). Ab nach draußen! - Wie ausgerechnet das Internet eine Renaissance des öffentlichen Lebens befeuert. *Zeit Online.* Retrieved from http://www.zeit.de/2011/27/Public-Space

Reichental, J. (2012). Knowledge management in the age of social media. *O'Reilly Radar*. Retrieved July 24th, 2012, from http://radar.oreilly.com/2011/03/knowledge-management-social-media.html

Rheingold, H. (2002). *Smart mobs: The next social revolution*. Perseus Books.

Schiller, J., & Voisard, A. (Eds.). (2004). *Location-based services*. Morgan Kaufmann Publisher.

Schuler, I. (2008). SMS as a tool in election observation - Innovations case narrative: National democratic institute. In P. Auerswald and I. Quadir (Eds.), Innovations – Technology, Governance, Globalization, 3(2), 143–157. MIT Press.

Shirky, C. (2008). *Here comes everybody: The power of organizing without organizations*. New York: Penguin Press.

Sorber, J., Banerjee, N., Corner, M. D., & Rollins, S. (2005). Turducken: Hierarchical power management for mobile devices. In *Proceedings of ACM MobiSys '05, Seattle, Washington*.

Street Plan Collaborative. (2012). *Tactical urbanism 2: Short-term action, long term change*. Retrieved July 24th, 2012, from http://www.theatlanticcities.com/neighborhoods/2012/03/guide-tactical-urbanism/1387/

Streich, B. (2011). *Stadtplanung in der Wissensgesellschaft: Ein Handbuch*. Wiesbaden: VS Verlag für Sozialwissenschaften. doi:10.1007/978-3-531-93164-7.

Streich, B., & Zeile, P. (2012). *Städtebauliche Methodenentwicklung mit GeoWeb und Mobile Computing - Untersuchung über die Fortentwicklung des städtebaulichen und raumplanerischen Methodenrepertoires angestoßen durch technologische Neuerungen im Internet*. Unpublished Report on DFG Research Project. Kaiserslautern: University of Technology Kaiserslautern.

Surowiecki, J. (2004). *The wisdom of crowds*. New York: Doubleday.

Techcrunch. (2011). *It's still a feature phone world: Global smartphone penetration At 27%*. Retrieved July 24th, 2012, from http://techcrunch.com/2011/11/28/its-still-a-feature-phone-world-global-smartphone-penetration-at-27/

Textizen. (2012). *Welcome. Project-website*. Retrieved July 24th, 2012, from http://www.textizen.com/welcome

UNDP (United Nations Development Programme). (2012). *Mobile technologies and empowerment: Enhancing human development through participation and innovation*. Retrieved July 17th, 2012, from http://www.undpegov.org/sites/undpegov.org/files/undp_mobile_technology_primer.pdf

Weiser, M. (1991). The computer for the 21st Century. *Scientific American, 265*(3), 94–104. doi:10.1038/scientificamerican0991-94.

Wikipadia. (2012). *Mobile app*. Retrieved July 24th, 2012, from http://en.wikipedia.org/wiki/Mobile_app

Yovcheva, Z., Buhalis, D., & Gatzidis, C. (2012). Overview of Smartphone augmented reality applications for tourism. *e-Review of Tourism Research (eRTR), 10*(2). Retrieved July 24th, 2012, from http://eprints.bournemouth.ac.uk/20219/1/eRTR_SI_V10i2_Yovcheva_Buhalis_Gatzidis_63-66.pdf

Zeile, P., Memmel, M., & Exner, J. (2012). A new urban sensing and monitoring approach: Tagging the city with the radar sensing App. In M. Schrenk, V. Popovich, P. Zeile, P. Elisei (Eds.), *Proceedings of REAL CORP 2012. International Conference on Urban Planning, Regional Development and Information Society (REAL CORP-12)*. Re-mixing the city, May 14-16, Vienna, Austria, CORP - Competence Center of Urban and Regional Planning, Schwechat, Austria, 5/2012, pp. 17-25.

Zhuang, Z., Kim, K., & Singh, J. P. (2010). Improving energy efficiency of location sensing on Smartphones. *MobiSys '10 Proceedings of the 8th international conference on Mobile systems, applications, and services* (pp. 315-330).

ADDITIONAL READING

Batty, M., Crooks, A. T., Hudson-Smith, A., Milton, R., Anand, S., Jackson, M., & Morley, J. (2010). Data mash-ups and the future of mapping. In *Technology & Standards Watch (TechWatch)*. Retrieved http://www.jisc.ac.uk/techwatch

Bergner, B. S., & Zeile, P. (2012). Ist Barrierefreiheit messbar? In Planerin 3: 20–24.

Boulos, K., Resch, B., Crowley, D. N., Breslin, J. G., Sohn, G., & Burtner, R. et al. (2011). Crowdsourcing, citizen sensing and sensor web technologies for public and environmental health surveillance and crisis management: Trends, OGC standards and application examples. *International Journal of Health Geographics*, *10*, Retrieved from http://www.ij-healthgeographics.com/content/10/1/67 PMID:21791054.

Brückner, M. (2012). *Geocentric Crowdsourcing und Kollaborative Verwaltung – Was leisten Anliegenmanagements? Arbeitswelt der Geographie*. Retrieved July 21th, 2012, from http://arbeitsweltdergeographie.com/2012/01/11/geocentric-crowdsourcing-und-kollaborative-verwaltung-was-leisten-anliegenmanagements/

Campbell, A. T., Eisenman, S. B., Lane, N. D., Miluzzo, E., & Peterson, R. A. (2006). People-centric urban sensing. In *Proceedings of the 2nd annual international workshop on Wireless Internet* (p. 18). Boston, MA: ACM. Retrieved from http://portal.acm.org/citation.cfm?id=1234179&dl=GUIDE&coll=GUIDE&CFID=96064310&CFTOKEN=76972106

Campbell, J., & Im, T. (2012). Beyond ubiquity: Mobile government, theory and practice. *KAPA conference at Seoul National University*. Retrieved July 17th, 2012, from http://www.kapa21.or.kr/english/files/1-3-3Jesse%20Campbell.pdf

Coburn, J. (2004). Confronting the challenges in reconnecting urban planning and public health. *American Journal of Public Health*, *94*(4), 541–549. doi:10.2105/AJPH.94.4.541 PMID:15053998.

Foth, M. (2012). Urban informatics: Research and insides from libraries, cultural industries and innovative systems. *Australian Business Foundation, Sydney*. Retrieved July 20th, 2012, from http://www.abfoundation.com.au/research_project_files/56/UrbanInformaticsFinalWebversion.pdf

Höffken, S. (2011). *Die Kartierungsrevolution*. StadtBauwelt.

Lenihan, D. G. (2002). *Realigning governance: From e-government to e-democracy*. Retrieved July 17th, 2012, from http://www.kta.on.ca/KTA_site_RVSD/pdf/cg6.pdf

Teufl, P., & Zefferer, T. (2011). Opportunities and forthcoming challenges of Smartphone-based m-government services. In *European Journal of ePractice*, N° 12, March/April 201, ISSN: 1988-625X. Retrieved from http://www.epractice.eu/files/European%20Journal%20epractice%20Volume%2013%20-%2004%20-%20Megatrends%20in%20eGovernment.pdf

Trénel, M., & Märker, O. (2004). E-partizipation: Das Internet als Medium für Bürgerbeteiligung. *iPublic - Psychologie im Umweltschutz*, 8, 59-65.

KEY TERMS AND DEFINITIONS

Citizen Engagment: Is the active engagement of citizens, NGOS and other stakeholders in governmental and political processes with the ambition to improve society, encompassing formal and informal activities.

Crowdsourcing: Crowdsourcing is "the use of the perceptual and cognitive abilities of a large group of individuals to solve a problem" as Erickson (2010) defined it precisely and short.

GeoWeb: The geospatial Web (short GeoWeb) describes the combination of geospatial information and other kinds of information in the WorldWideWeb (short Web). It's the "Spatialization of the Internet" as Herring (1994) named it and can be described as the Web 3.0. The GeoWeb opens new methodological possibilities for spatial and urban planning.

Location-Based-Services: Location-Based-Services are computer programs adding value to services (e.g. address search, social media) by using locational information. These location-aware-services are an important part of the GeoWeb.

Mobile Participation: mParticipation is the use of mobile devices to broaden and deepen the participation of citizens and other stakeholders by enabling them to connect with each other, generate and share information, comment and vote. It widens eParticipation in a temporal and spatial dimension and is the basis for new crowdsourcing, bottom-up participation.

Smartphones: Smartphones are mobile phones with multimodal functionality, with a higher computing ability and integrated sensors, allowing the installation of third-party applications. With its multi-functionality, ability of personalisation and user-driven-innovation they represent a large methodological potential for urban planning and research.

ENDNOTES

[1] http://developer.android.com/training/index.html

[2] http://developer.apple.com/library/ios/navigation/

Chapter 12
Social Media for Civic Engagement:
An Exploration of Urban Governments

Thomas A. Bryer
University of Central Florida, USA

Kimberly L. Nelson
Northern Illinois University, USA

ABSTRACT

To explore the relationship between form of municipal government and deployment of social media tools for civic engagement, the authors conduct an analysis of a random set of purposively selected cities for content analysis of their social media tools. The authors use the seven forms of government identified by Nelson and Svara (2012) as the basis by which to select the sample cities. Across forms of government, there is no apparent pattern on deployment of social media tools for civic engagement. Municipalities of every form are using the tools, primarily Facebook and Twitter, and most, regardless of form, are not using the tools in a social manner. This finding is consistent with previous work by the authors and others. Important areas for future research are identified in a closing discussion.

INTRODUCTION

Civic engagement is defined as "people participating together for deliberative and collective action within an array of interests, institutions and networks, developing civic identity and involving people in the governance processes" (Cooper, 2005). In practice, however, civic engagement has

taken many forms with variable costs, and there have been ambiguous and uncertain outcomes. Designing, implementing, and facilitating "effective" participation processes is as much art as science, and as much culture/context-dependent as driven by universal values concerning citizen rights and opportunities in democratically-oriented societies. Despite these ambiguities, there is a strong chorus within academia advocating through theoretical and empirical research for the development of institutions to enhance civic engagement processes;

DOI: 10.4018/978-1-4666-4169-3.ch012

of course, there are critics as well as pragmatists equally active in the scholarly dialogues. This is perhaps no more true than within the sub-field of technology-facilitated civic engagement (e.g. e-government, social media, and social networks).

Civic engagement in urban governance has been a particularly attractive topic over the past forty years, with some interruption during the 1980s (Cooper, 2005). One instrumental writer early on was George Frederickson, who authored or edited two books: *Power, Public Opinion, and Policy in a Metropolitan Community* with Linda Schluter O'Leary, and *Neighborhood Control in the 1970s: Politics, Administration, and Citizen Participation*. These texts established a context and broad philosophical direction for the emerging interest in citizenship and civic engagement in urban communities. Preceding these writings was a work by Milton Kotler (1969), *Neighborhood Government: The Local Foundations of Public Life*, in which he argued for giving control over certain elements of public goods and common pool funding to neighborhood residents. Terry Cooper has written often about the history of civic enterprises, dating to the work of community organizer Saul Alinksy and the Industrial Areas Foundation. Alinsky worked to mobilize and empower citizens in neighborhoods, though in a more adversarial way than what Kotler suggested. Neighborhood-based governance took on more formal characteristics with the development of neighborhood councils in cities ranging from Minneapolis, MN (Berry, Portney, & Thomson, 1993), to Los Angeles (Musso, Weare, Bryer, & Cooper, 2011).

The balance of this introductory section provides a brief overview of the state of civic engagement research and writing, followed by a broad overview of literature on social media and civic engagement. Following these reviews, we focus more specifically on where these literatures interface with urban governance literatures. Website content analyses from a purposively selected sample of cities in the United States are reported

and two more in depth cases are examined in order to develop an emerging research agenda. This agenda is outlined in closing.

Civic Engagement

Public participation with government is an area of research and practice fraught with competing values claims, each legitimate, and a plethora of context-dependent findings regarding efficacy. "Successful" engagement processes are difficult to fully ascertain, though efforts to apply logical evaluation frameworks have been offered (e.g., Irvin & Stansbury, 2004; Nabatchi, 2012) and case studies claiming success are widely available (e.g., Howard, Lipsky, & Marshall, 1994; Hays & Kogl, 2007). Broadly speaking, scholars and practitioners concerned with citizenship vary in the extent to which they encourage dutiful or engaged citizenship (Dalton, 2009). Dutiful citizens are law-abiding and interested in promoting a patriotic identity; engaged citizens are law-abiding but are also concerned with acting proactively to improve community. Cooper (1991) discusses this distinction in terms of low ethical versus high ethical citizenship. Both forms of citizenship are legitimate and have been encouraged at various times and to different degrees in the history of the United States (Bryer, 2012).

The primary concern of this essay is engaged citizenship. Specifically, why is active, engaged citizenship desirable from a governmental perspective? What mechanisms are available to engage citizens in public decision-making and community enrichment? Each question is addressed in turn, before turning to existing research and practice in the use of one particular mechanism for civic engagement: social media.

Engaged Citizenship: Why and How?

A number of benefits can emerge from successful citizen engagement. The first potential benefit is for a better citizen, one who is better educated about public issues and policies. An engaged citizenry can facilitate the public policy decision-making process and improve the quality and outcomes of the decisions themselves (Stivers, 1990). Citizens who participate in the governance process are likely to be better informed and capable of understanding broader implications of a policy alternative (Sabatier, 1988; Irvin & Stansbury, 2004).

Another possible benefit of public participation is enhanced trust and belief in government responsiveness (Halvorsen, 2003). Citizens who participate in governance processes and see their ideas incorporated into policy outcomes are able to see government responsiveness firsthand. As citizens find that government officials are acting deliberately and responsibly in the participation process, they are likely to believe that officials will act diligently in other situations as well (Thomas, 1998).

However well intended a citizen engagement effort, if it is not implemented strategically and successfully, it may not only fail to achieve its expressed goals but can lead to increased mistrust on the part of citizens (Arnstein, 1969; Bryer, 2011a). Unfortunately, the literature presents evidence of both successful and unsuccessful citizen participation efforts. Successful citizen engagement programs are carefully considered and crafted to maximize the benefits for both citizens and government. Citizen panels that work together for a year or more are noted for their ability to overcome some of the weaknesses of traditional engagement strategies (Crosby, Kelly, & Schaefer, 1986; Kathlene & Martin, 1991). Unfortunately, the citizen participation techniques that are most commonly used by government have been criticized as inadequate to improve decision-making (Kweit & Kweit, 1981). The importance of strategic implementation of public participation tools is perhaps particularly apparent in regards to the use of social media (Bryer, 2011b).

Social Media and Civic Engagement

Research on the use of social media in government and for civic engagement is limited. However, the significant potential to use social media and networking tools for civic engagement is well documented. Before proceeding, we offer a definition of social media that is inclusive of a number of tools, both web-based and non-web-based. Our focus in the chapter is on web-based tools. The definition we find most fitting is: "technologies that facilitate social interaction, make possible collaboration, and enable deliberation across stakeholders" (Bryer & Zavattaro, 2011, p. 327). Web-based tools include popular platforms such as Facebook, Twitter, and YouTube, but also include wikis, blogs, and electronic commons, as they each have the potential for social interaction beyond unidirectional information sharing. Social media tools may not be intended for use by governments for civic engagement, but this is the purpose of our exploration here.

Though there are potential benefits in the use of these tools for civic engagement, there may also be potential pitfalls. Notably, Hand and Ching (2011) found that local governments in Arizona used Facebook primarily as a unidirectional communication tool; Brainard and Derrick-Mills (2011), building on work from Brainard and McNutt (2010), found that the Washington, DC Police Department used an electronic commons similarly in unidirectional fashion and in such a way that face-to-face tensions between police and community groups were merely replicated in the online environment. Bryer (2011b) described such uses of social media for civic engagement as processes that can lead to "costs of democratization," in which citizens can lose trust and decrease their efficacy if they encounter sub-optimal or non-social use of social media. Similarly, using social media to democratize governmental process without preparing citizens to make meaningful contributions can be just as harmful, as can be inferred from the quality of participation examined on the regulations.gov portal in the United States (Bryer, in press) or the assessment of a web-based participation mechanism in a local government incorporation process (Wang & Bryer, 2012).

Scholars have also found positive uses of social tools for civic engagement. For instance, Noveck (2009) described the use of wiki technology to transform the patent process in her book *Wiki Government*. Mergel (2011) described generally transformative uses of social media for engagement and practical ideas about the use of these tools across levels of government. Leighninger (2011) compels this dialogue forward by examining the transformational potential of social media for our democratic institutions, while also acknowledging the threats of a "democracy bubble" (Bryer, 2011a) preventing long-term sustainable participation by citizens.

Overall, this is an emerging area of study at the societal level (e.g., Ghonim, 2012), and across levels of government (Mossberger & Wu, 2012).

Our purpose is to focus on the use of social media for civic engagement at the municipal government level. We turn now to a brief review of civic engagement and e-government, including social media, in municipal governance.

CIVIC ENGAGEMENT, MUNICIPAL GOVERNANCE, AND SOCIAL TOOLS

Research on civic engagement and e-government adoption, two literatures related to our question, indicates that at least seven factors may be significantly related to the adoption of e-government tools by municipalities. Figure 1 presents the conceptual model for these factors, suggesting that the same factors may be significant for the social use of social media for civic engagement by cities. Links between e-government technologies and civic engagement were previously reported in earlier research findings. For example, Jennings and Zeitner (2003) used panel data from 1982 through 1997 and found that internet access was

Figure 1. Conceptual Model for Social Media Use

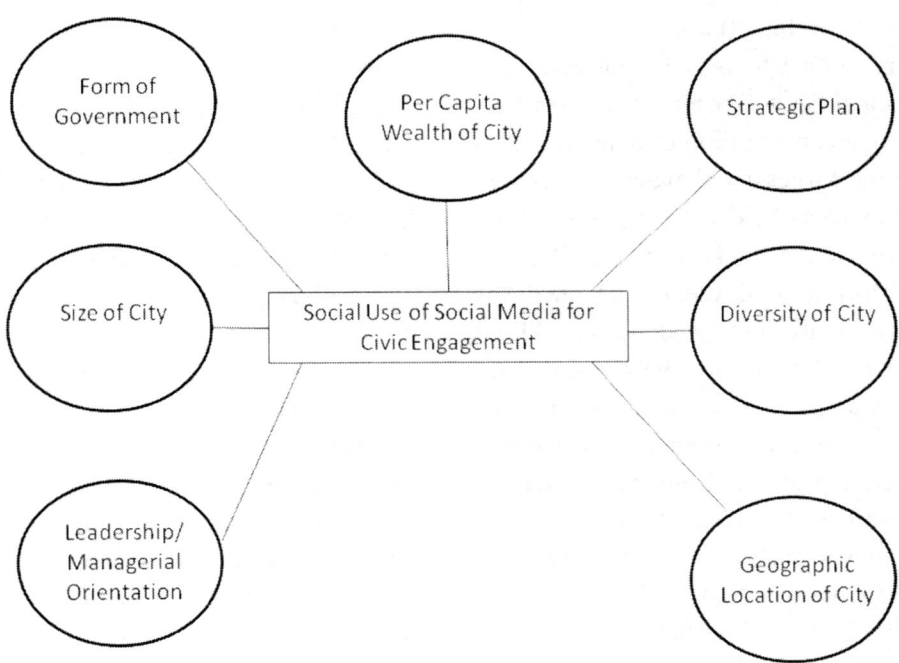

positively related to interest in public affairs and to volunteering. Citizens who were engaged prior to the introduction of the internet were likely to use the internet as an additional source of information. Reddick and Frank (2007) found that U.S. city managers also reported that e-government is a useful tool to communicate with citizens and other stakeholders. Based on these studies, we suggest the same factors are potentially significant in studying social media and civic engagement.

The two characteristics most often hypothesized as contributing to greater citizen participation in the budgeting process are size of the local government and form of government. The one nearly universal finding is that larger cities are more likely to attempt to engage citizens than their smaller counterparts (Ebdon, 2000; Wang, 2001; Franklin & Ebdon, 2005; Yang & Callahan, 2005; 2007). A number of explanations for this finding have been advanced that point to essential differences between large and small cities. Large cities tend to have greater resource capacity, a larger geographic area, more complicated policy problems and operations, and greater diversity—all of which could lead to a greater propensity to engage citizenry (Wang, 2001; Franklin & Ebdon, 2005; Ebdon & Franklin, 2006).

Researchers often hypothesize that council-manager municipalities will be more likely to institute citizen engagement efforts than municipalities using other forms. Professional managers receive training in techniques of citizen engagement that they view as management tools (Yang & Callahan, 2007) and as full-time employees can devote time to citizen engagement efforts (Ebdon & Franklin, 2006). This is consistent with the finding that greater professionalism is associated with greater interest in promoting citizen participation (Streib, 1992; Zhang & Yang, 2009). A number of studies support the hypothesis that council-manager governments have higher levels of citizen participation (Kweit & Kweit, 1981; Ebdon, 2002; Franklin & Ebdon, 2005; Yang & Callahan, 2007) while

others found no significant relationship between government form in efforts to engage citizens (Wang, 2001; Yang & Pandey, 2011).

Similar patterns are found in the use of e-government tools by cities. Nearly all local governments today have developed websites. However, the use of technologies to engage citizens is not nearly as widespread, and few local governments report positive outcomes from the implementation of e-government tools (Norris & Moon, 2005). In a longitudinal study of U.S. local governments between 2000 and 2002, Norris & Moon (2005, p. 72) conclude that local governments are making "incremental but consistent progress in adopting and deploying e-government."

Extensive research on the factors that promote the adoption of e-government tools finds that region, demographics, form of government, planning, and management orientation all may play a role in the decision about whether to promote the use of e-government at the local level. One limitation of these studies is that most rely on the ICMA E-government Surveys from 2000 and/or 2002.

As with citizen participation, the council-manager form of government (Moon, 2002; Holden, Norris, & Fletcher, 2003; Reddick, 2004) and larger local governments (Conroy & Evans-Cowley, 2004; Holden, Norris, & Fletcher, 2003; Moon, 2002; Moon & Norris, 2005) are often attributed to the adoption or early adoption of e-government tools. The form of government finding is consistent with research showing that council-manager governments are associated with a higher probability of adoption of innovative practices and technologies than other forms of government (Moon & de Leon, 2001; Nelson & Svara, 2012).

Management characteristics also seem to influence the probability that a municipality will adopt e-government practices. Reddick (2004) found that administrators who perceive e-government as holding advantages for the local government were more likely to implement e-government technologies. Moon and Norris (2005), who found no relationship between form of government and e-government implementation, did find that a greater managerial orientation towards innovation, measured through an index of innovative practices, was related to a greater use of e-government in municipalities.

Adoption of e-government in municipalities is associated with a host of other factors as well. Conroy and Evans-Cowley (2004) found that a higher median household income was associated with a greater level of e-government while the percent of non-white residents had an inverse relationship (Conroy & Evans-Cowley, 2004). Geographic variable may have some influence on adoption of e-government. Two studies found that municipalities located in the western region of the United States had a greater likelihood of adopting e-government (Conroy & Evans-Cowley, 2004; Holden, Norris, & Fletcher, 2003); Conroy and Evans-Cowley (2004) found the same relationship with southern states. A final variable that associates with greater levels of e-government adoption is the existence of a strategic plan for e-governance (Moon, 2002).

EXPLORING THE RELATIONSHIP BETEEN FORM OF GOVERNMENT AND SOCIAL MEDIA FOR CIVIC ENGAGEMENT USE

Our focus in this exploratory study is on the subject of form of government. Other factors are not studied explicitly but are discussed as appropriate in presentation of findings and implications. To explore the relationship between form of municipal government and deployment of social media tools for civic engagement, we conduct an analysis of a random set of purposively selected cities for content analysis of their social media tools. This analysis focuses on a small sample of cities representing each form of government in order to conduct an initial exploration of the question.

Future research can expand on the exploratory findings and construct survey instruments to collect the information captured in an exploratory manner here. Existing datasets, such as those kept by the International City County Managers Association, do not have adequate data to assess actual quantity and quality of social media tool usage, thus limiting the utility of those datasets. Our effort is to frame the initial questions for development in further research.

We use the seven forms of government identified by Nelson and Svara (2012) as the basis by which to select the sample cities: (1) mayor-council-manager in which the mayor is elected, (2) council (mayor) manager in which the mayor is selected by the council and from within the council, (3) empowered mayor-council-manager, in which the mayor selects the manager with consent from the council, (4) mayor and council-administrator, with Chief Administrative Officer appointed by council (5) mayor-council-administrator, with Chief Administrative Officer appointed by mayor with council consent (6) mayor-administrator-council, with Chief Administrative Officer appointed by mayor and (7) mayor-council, with no Chief Administrative Officer. Our rationale for the 7 categories is that they provide a better distinction between forms with categories 1 and 2 retaining unified executive and legislative powers present in the council-manager form, categories 5, 6, and 7 retaining the separation of powers in the mayor-council form, and categories 3 and 4 representing government that have blurred the separation/ unification of powers boundaries. Greater professionalism (categories 1 and 2) are usually associated with better performance, but this has not been examined in the context of the use of social media for civic engagement.

Cities selected for exploration of each category are randomly selected, as there is generally no demographic or economic "norm" for cities in each category. For the purpose of an initial exploratory study, this meets our need for representativeness. As discussed in the findings and in conclusion, future research can be more precise and systematic in case selection. Figure 2 shows the coding instrument used:

Findings

Across forms of government, there is no apparent pattern on deployment of social media tools for civic engagement. Municipalities of every form are using the tools, primarily Facebook and Twitter, and most, regardless of form, are not using the tools in a social manner. This finding is consistent with the conceptual work of Bryer (2011b) and analyses of specific social media tools in more limited governmental contexts (Hand & Ching, 2011; Brainard & Derrick-Mills, 2011). In other words, form of government does not appear to affect the extent to which city governments engage in two-way dialogue, as opposed to unidirectional information sharing. Even in cases where citizens respond to city posts on social media sites, local governments in our sample for the most part do not respond. Cities in each form category are discussed briefly, with special attention given to cities we found to be most innovative in engaging citizens using social media tools. It is from these cities that we draw potential lessons, and based on findings from all cities, we suggest areas for future research.

Mayor-Council-Manager

Table 1 summarizes the use of social media tools by cities with a mayor-council-manager form of government. These are cities in which the mayor is directly elected. Four cities are examined in this category: (1) Raleigh, NC, (2) Oxnard, CA, (3) Westminster, CO, and (4) Gainesville, FL, each

Figure 2. City Social Media Content Coding

City Social Media Content Coding

Instruction: Review city websites and search on Facebook and Twitter for the city.

1. Does the city maintain a social media page? Yes/No

2. If so, what social media tools are used (e.g. Facebook, Twitter)

3. If so, are the social media tools used only to share information unidirectionally with citizens? Yes/No

4. If so to #3, how often does it appear updates are posted? Multiple times per day/daily/several times a week, weekly, or less than weekly

5. If not to #3, do citizens respond to the city's posts? Yes/No

6. If so to #5, does the city respond to citizens? Yes/No

7. Is there a posted policy about the use of social media tools by the city on the website or on the social media site? Yes/No

8. What other observations do you have about the city's use of social media?

_____

_____

_____

_____

Table 1. Mayor-Council-Manager Cities

	Raleigh, NC	Oxnard, CA	Westminster, CO	Gainseville, FL
Social Media Pages?	Yes	Yes	Yes	Yes
Tools Uses	Facebook, Twitter, Flickr, YouTube	Facebook, Twitter	Facebook, Twitter	Facebook, Twitter, Flickr, YouTube
Unidirectional Communication	Yes	Yes	Mostly	Yes
Updates	Daily	Less than weekly	Less than weekly	Several times/week
Citizens Respond to City Posts?	Some	No	No	No
City Respond to Citizens' Posts?	No	No	Some	No
Social Media Posted?	Yes	No	No	Yes
Population Size	403,892	197,899	106,114	124,354

selected at random from all cities operating under this form. Each of these cities maintain a presence on social media, with all using Facebook and Twitter, two using Flickr, and one using YouTube.

Though there is variation across the examined cities with respect to the frequency of city posts on social media platforms, there is consistency in the lack of engaged interaction between city and citizen. Two of the four cities have a social media or privacy policy. Overall, it appears this form of government enables the use of social media, but

there are other factors at play within each city that may have a stronger influence than administrative structure and leadership.

Council (Mayor) Manager

Table 2 summarizes the use of social media tools by cities with a council (mayor) manager form of government. These are cities in which the mayor is selected from within the council by council members. Four cities are examined in this category:

Table 2. Council (Mayor) Manager Cities

	Temecula, CA	Thousand Oaks, CA	Cambridge, MA	Bellevue, WA
Social Media Pages?	Yes	Yes	Yes	Yes
Tools Uses	Facebook, MySpace, Flickr, Twitter	Facebook, Twitter, Google+, YouTube	Facebook, Twitter	Facebook, Twitter, YouTube, Flickr
Unidirectional Communication	Yes	Yes	Yes	Yes
Updates	Several times/week	Daily	Several times/week	u/k
Citizens Respond to City Posts?	Yes	Yes	Yes	Some
City Respond to Citizens' Posts?	Some	No	No	No
Social Media Posted?	Yes	Yes	No	Yes
Population Size	100,097	126,683	105,162	122,363

(1) Temecula, CA, (2) Thousand Oaks, CA, (3) Cambridge, MA, and (4) Bellevue, MA. Facebook is commonly used across the cities, as is Twitter. Additional platforms used by some of the cities include MySpace, Flickr, Google+, and YouTube.

Citizens in these cities appear more active in responding to city posts on social media platforms, but as with the previous category, cities are not reciprocating and engaging with citizens in two-way communication. As above, there are other factors at play within each city that may have a stronger influence than administrative structure and leadership.

Empowered Mayor-Council-Manager

Table 3 summarizes the use of social media tools by cities with an empowered mayor-council-manager form of government. These are cities in which a directly elected mayor has the power to appoint a manager with council approval. Four cities are examined in this category: (1) Kansas City, KS, (2) Kansas City, MO, (3) Cincinnati, OH, and (4) Abilene, TX. Facebook and Twitter are again commonly used platforms, as are YouTube and Flickr. Cincinnati also uses Vimeo and Linked-In.

Cincinnati uniquely lists a variety of agencies one click off their home page on the web, each using one or more social media tools. Nonetheless,

as with two of the other three cities, the quantity of tools used does not translate to two-way engagement with citizens. Kansas City, KS, however, stands out in this group, maintaining a targeted social media presence with three tools (as compared to Cincinnati's six), and they achieve daily posts on the social media, responses from citizens, and government responses in return. This is one city to which we will return for a closer examination.

Mayor-Council Administrator

Table 4 summarizes the use of social media tools by cities with a mayor and council-administrator form of government. These are cities in which there is a directly elected mayor, and an administrator appointed by the council. Two cities are examined in this category: (1) Buffalo, NY, and (2) Richmond, VA. Buffalo does not have a social media presence, and Richmond, like previous cities examined, has a Facebook and Twitter account, posts to those accounts daily but only in a unidirectional fashion.

Mayor-Council-Administrator

Table 5 summarizes the use of social media tools by cities with a mayor-council-administrator. These are cities in which there is a directly elected mayor

Table 3. Empowered Mayor-Council-Manager Cities

	Kansas City, KS	Kansas City, MO	Cincinnati, OH	Abilene, TX
Social Media Pages?	Yes	Yes	Yes	Yes
Tools Uses	Facebook, YouTube, Twitter	Facebook, Twitter	Facebook, Twitter, YouTube, Flickr, Vimeo, Linked-In	Google+, Twitter, Facebook, YouTube, Flckr
Unidirectional Communication	No	Yes	Yes	Yes
Updates	Daily	Less than weekly	Weekly	Several times/week
Citizens Respond to City Posts?	Yes	No	No	Yes
City Respond to Citizens' Posts?	Yes	No	No	No
Social Media Posted?	Yes	Yes	Yes	Yes
Population Size	145,786	459,787	296,943	131,506

Table 4. Mayor-Council Administrator Cities

	Buffalo, NY	Richmond, VA
Social Media Pages?	No	Yes
Tools Uses	n/a	Facebook, Twitter
Unidirectional Communication	n/a	Yes
Updates	n/a	Daily
Citizens Respond to City Posts?	n/a	No
City Respond to Citizens' Posts?	n/a	No
Social Media Posted?	n/a	Yes
Population Size	262,310	204,214

and council, and a chief administrative officer appointed by the mayor with council consent. Four cities are examined in this category: (1) Tampa, FL, (2) Augusta-Richmond County, GA, (3) Flint, MI, and (4) Minneapolis, MN. Postings to social media platforms are frequent across the board, using a variety tools, including again Facebook and Twitter; two Cities also use Foursquare and YouTube. Tampa also uses Flickr and Quora.

Tampa is another city that stands apart from others for its daily posting activity, and its two-way engagement between city and citizen. Tampa will be examined closer, along with Kansas City, KS for lessons and examples.

Mayor-Administrator-Council

Table 6 summarizes the use of social media tools by cities with a mayor-administrator-council form of government. These are cities in which there is a directly elected mayor and council, and the mayor appoints a chief administrative officer without council consent. Four cities are examined in this category: (1) Miami, FL, (2) Rockford, IL, (3) Jackson, MS, and (4) Pittsburgh, PA. All four cities maintain a social media presence on Facebook and Twitter; two cities also use YouTube, and Miami uses Flickr.

Unlike previously examined cities in which there were at least limited interactions where citizens respond to city posts on the social media platforms, in these four cities, there is a clear absence of citizen attentiveness to city posts. It is unclear if this may be attributable to the form of government or other factors.

Table 5. Mayor-Council-Administrator Cities

	Tampa, FL	Augusta-Richmond County, GA	Flint, MI	Minneapolis, MN
Social Media Pages?	Yes	Yes	Yes	Yes
Tools Uses	Facebook, Twitter, YouTube, Foursquare, Flickr, Quora	Facebook, Twitter	Facebook, Twitter	Facebook, Twitter, YouTube, Foursquare
Unidirectional Communication	No	Yes	Yes	Yes
Updates	Daily	Several times/week	Several times/week	No
Citizens Respond to City Posts?	Yes	No	No	No
City Respond to Citizens' Posts?	Yes	No	No	No
Social Media Posted?	Yes	No	Yes	Yes
Population Size	335,709	195,844	102,434	382,578

Table 6. Mayor-Administrator-Council Cities

	Miami, FL	Rockford, IL	Jackson, MS	Pittsburgh, PA
Social Media Pages?	Yes	Yes	Yes	Yes
Tools Uses	Facebook, Twitter, Flickr, YouTube	Facebook, Twitter	Facebook, Twitter	Facebook, Twitter, YouTube
Unidirectional Communication	Yes	Yes	Yes	Yes
Updates	Several times/week	Less than weekly	Daily	Daily
Citizens Respond to City Posts?	No	No	No	No
City Respond to Citizens' Posts?	No	No	No	No
Social Media Posted?	Yes	No	Yes	Yes
Population Size	399,457	152,871	173,514	305,704

Mayor-Council

Table 7 summarizes the use of social media tools by cities with a mayor-council form of government. These are cities in which there is a directly elected mayor and council and no chief administrative officer or manager. Four cities are examined in this category: (1) Montgomery, AL, (2) Hialeah, FL, (3) Manchester, NH, and (4) Green Bay, WI. Two of the four cities do not maintain a social media presence. The two cities that maintain a social media presence use Facebook, Twitter, and YouTube, with only one city posting at least once per week. Both cities communicate only in a unidirectional fashion. This finding is consistent with previous literature on adoption of civic engagement practices and e-government; cities without a professional administrator or manager will be less likely to adopt management innovations and civic practices.

Table 7. Mayor-Council Cities

	Montgomery, AL	Hialeah, FL	Manchester, NH	Green Bay, WI
Social Media Pages?	Yes	No	No	Yes
Tools Uses	Facebook, Twitter, YouTube	n/a	n/a	Facebook, Twitter, YouTube
Unidirectional Communication	Yes	n/a	n/a	Yes
Updates	Less than once/week	n/a	n/a	Several times/week
Citizens Respond to City Posts?	No	n/a	n/a	No
City Respond to Citizens' Posts?	No	n/a	n/a	No
Social Media Posted?	Yes	n/a	n/a	Yes
Population Size	205,764	224,669	109,565	104,057

TWO CASES EXPLORED IN DEPTH: KANSAS CITY AND TAMPA

The Kansas City, KS website (http://www.wycokck.org/) is highly interactive and accessible, with a clean image-driven look and functionality. One click in, and the visitor is taken to the Social Media Center where there is access to Facebook, Twitter, and YouTube pages for the city, as well as for individual agencies with the city. Figure 3 shows a screen shot of this access point page.

Once on the social media pages for Kansas City, visitors can find daily posts on city events, government closures, and requests for citizen input. For instance, Figure 4 shows a post advising residents of an agency closure for one week due to computer upgrades. Notably, and unique for the cities examined in this assessment, the city responded when a citizen sought clarification.

Tampa, Florida is another city that is practicing a high level of interaction with citizens using social media. Perhaps not as visually clean and image-driven as the Kansas City website, the

Tampa website still provides easy access to interactive social media tools. It is also evident that the City, and particularly the mayor, is well versed in the use of social media, tapping into not only Facebook and Twitter but Foursquare and Quora—two tools that do not appear common in local government. Figure 5 shows a screenshot from the city's website announcing the use of these two tools.

Foursquare is a social tool used to enable individuals to "check-in" to different establishments or places. The mayor uses Foursquare to do the same, allowing for transparency on what he is doing and also allowing him to promote locations around the city. Quora is a social tool that seeks to generate informed discussion and debate on substantive questions. The city is using the tool to engage is discourse on city-related issues. The final paragraph on the page screen-captured above reads: "For a few years now, we have seen elected officials engaging with citizens on Twitter and Facebook. But what's next? What will the future of government openness through social media

Figure 3. Kansas City, KS Social Media Access Page

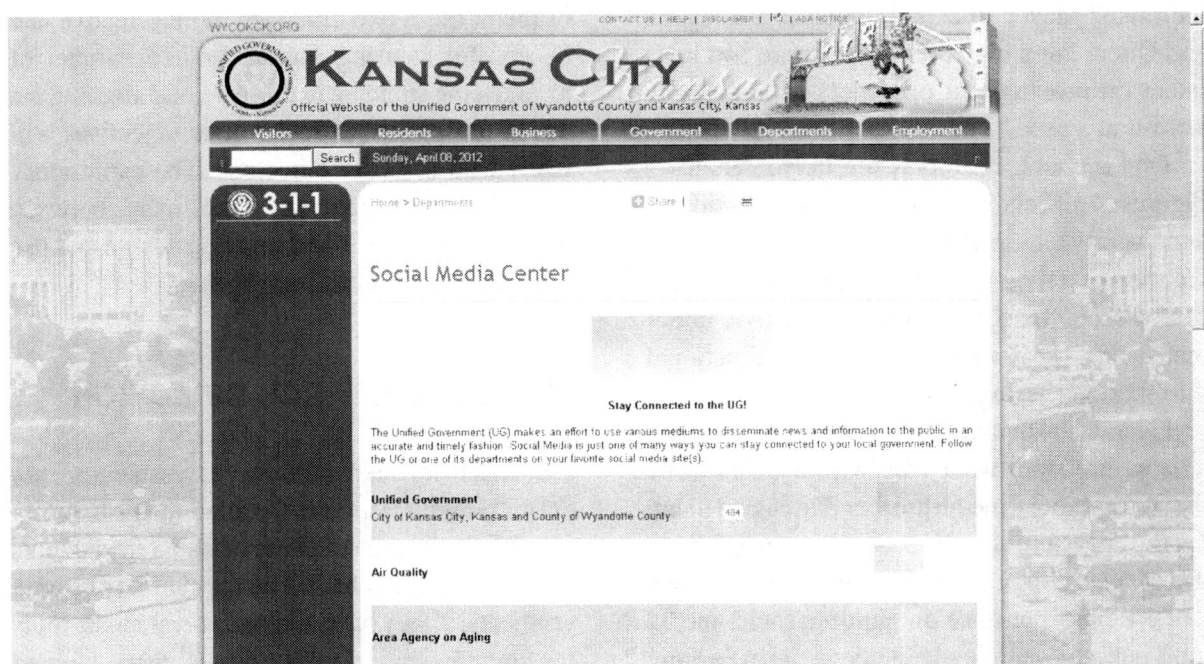

Figure 4. Kansas City, KS Sample Facebook Post

look like? Mayor Buckhorn believes foursquare and Quora are a big part of that future and he is intent on proving that one check-in and Quora answer at a time."

On Facebook, the city is similarly interactive. Figures 6 and 7 show a dialogue between residents and the city, along with an image, regarding the coloring of a river green for St. Patrick's Day. As can be seen, the city is highly interactive, rather than using the social media for unidirectional information sharing.

Overall, the two cases highlighted demonstrate a departure from what otherwise appears to be the norm of social media use for civic engagement, but the departure appears rooted in more strategic use of the technology. For instance, unlike cities that establish presence on multiple social media tools but achieve little social interaction using any

of them, these two cities are more selective and purposeful in using a more limited number of tools. Being strategic in this way, and aligning the use of tools with particular civic objectives will likely lead to better outcomes. The exploratory study does not suggest any clear linkage between form of government and strategic design and use of social tools for civic engagement.

FUTURE RESEARCH DIRECTION

Findings from this exploratory assessment are not definitive with respect to the relationship between form of government and use of social media tools for civic engagement. It does appear that city governments, if they have adopted social media tools for communicating with citizens, have adopted

Figure 5. Tampa, FL Social Media Access Page

Explore the City with Mayor Buckhorn on Foursquare

Move over Rahm Emanuel, there's a new Mayor taking foursquare by storm. Tampa Mayor Bob Buckhorn is launching the most innovative use of the application by an elected official yet. By taking advantage of features like lists and tips and personally checking-in to select venues, Buckhorn is going beyond simply setting up a branded channel.

Lists by Mayor Buckhorn include City Parks, Attractions, Dining and Shopping, Government Buildings and Public Safety. Residents of the city as well as tourists will be able to see the unique places Tampa has to offer, all recommended by the city's real-life Mayor. At many locations, Buckhorn has left his own personal tips ranging from his favorite ride at Busch Gardens to his favorite meal at the famous Columbia Restaurant.

Buckhorn has also committed to personally checking in at venues around the city. While the mayor of one of the nation's largest cities can't check in everywhere he goes, he will be sure to let citizens know when he's meeting with other city leaders, working in his office, and on occasion enjoying a night on the town. Next time you're at the theatre or dinner, you might just find that the Mayor is in the house. This means that if you check in enough at the venues he likes, you may even get to unseat the Mayor...on foursquare of course.

In addition to personally connecting with the citizens of Tampa through his foursquare check-ins, Mayor Buckhorn has also become the first elected-official in the State of Florida to engage with citizens on Quora. Quora - the question and answer service gaining users and buzz - is a logical place for politicians to engage, providing substantive answers to questions from citizens. Got a question for the Mayor that you've always been dying to ask? Here's your chance. Most people will never get a chance to talk to their Mayor face to face, but through Buckhorn's use of innovative ways to interact with the public, you'll have a chance to do the next best thing.

For a few years now, we have seen elected officials engaging with citizens on Twitter and Facebook. But what's next? What will the future of government openness through social media look like? Mayor Buckhorn believes foursquare and Quora are a big part of that future and he is intent on

them as unidirectional sharing tools, rather than tools to encourage or facilitate dialog. This raises important questions; most specifically, what are the "costs of democratization" (Bryer, 2011b) for failing to use social media in a social manner. That is, is it possible that citizens might lose trust in government if they expect that their posts on a city's social media page will be answered but find that no individual representing the government seems to be watching? Findings in this study, as well as

in empirical work by Brainard and Derrick-Mills (2011) and Hand and Ching (2011), make this a significant question to ask.

On the other hand, is it possible that city governments have it right? Are there not costs of democratization but benefits of transparency by making more information available in more accessible forms and places? Empirically, this would be a difficult question to assess. Even in cities with a Facebook page on which citizens

Figure 6. Tampa, FL Sample Facebook Post

"like" the information posted by the government, the number of "likers" relative to city population is a fraction of a percent. This poses another challenge that is akin to a falling tree in a forest. If a city government is posting information on social media platforms, but nobody is reading it, does it really matter? Is it a useful expense of resource to post information that a fraction of a percent of a population is reading and even fewer "liking" and even fewer responding?

Future research can address these questions in a deeper, more systematic way from both a government's and citizens' perspective. Research can also more deeply contextualize the use of social media in relation to a city's other online activities and civic engagement activities. Last, future research can more systematically assess the impact of form of government on social media use for civic engagement. If form of government proves not to be instrumental, a follow-up question might be, within each form, who is the person or who are the people who mostly drive social media adoption decisions? Is the driver likely to be the expert administrator or manager who received formal training in technology management and civic engagement, or is it likely to be the popularly elected mayor's intent on marketing himself along with his city? Might we find that expert administrators and managers will be more cautious in using social media in a social manner,

Figure 7. Tampa, FL Sample Facebook Post

given legal and ethical concerns—thus suggesting manager forms of government are more likely to be unidirectional? That is, what is the influence of managerial/leader orientation that was found to be significant in some studies of e-government adoption?

As suggested in the summary of the two highlighted cases, perhaps the important variable that leads to social use of social media for civic engagement is not form of government, but, as Moon (2002) found with respect to e-government adoption, is the existence of a strategic plan for the purpose. Recognizing the importance of stra-

tegic design linked to objectives (Bryer, 2011b), this may be a significant contributor. There are likely other questions that will emerge as the field digs deeper.

CONCLUSION

The use of social media by urban government administrations generally and for civic engagement in particular is an emergent issue. Research shows government agencies and offices are not using the technologies in much more than a unidirectional manner; this has potential implications for citizen engagement both in process (what do we expect of our citizens) and outcome (such as trust in government and efficacy). Use of the technologies does not appear dependent on form of government, or size of city, which is unique for literature on civic engagement and e-government in urban governments. More research is clearly needed as suggested previously. The presentation of exploratory data and discussion herein leads readers—practitioners and scholars alike—to important questions for consideration. We look forward to the research and dialog that will follow.

REFERENCES

Arnstein, S. (1969). A ladder of citizen participation. *Journal of the American Institute of Planners*, *35*, 216–224. doi:10.1080/01944366908977225.

Berry, J. M., Portney, K. E., & Thomson, K. (1993). *The rebirth of urban democracy*. Washington, DC: The Brookings Institution.

Brainard, L., & Derrick-Mills, T. (2011). Electronic commons, community policing, and communication: Online police-citizen discussion groups in Washington, DC. *Administrative Theory & Praxis*, *33*(3), 383–410. doi:10.2753/ATP1084-1806330304.

Brainard, L., & McNutt, J. (2010). Government-citizen relations: Informational, transactional, or collaborative? *Administration & Society*, *42*, 836–858. doi:10.1177/0095399710386308.

Bryer, T. A. (2011). Online public engagement in the Obama administration: Building a democracy bubble? *Policy & Internet, 3*(4), Article 3.

Bryer, T. A. (2011). The costs of democratization: Social media adaptation challenges within government agencies. *Administrative Theory & Praxis*, *33*(3), 341–361. doi:10.2753/ATP1084-1806330302.

Bryer, T. A. (2012). Encouraging citizenship in U.S. presidential administrations: An analysis of presidential records. In Schachter, H., & Yang, K. (Eds.), *The state of citizen participation in America* (pp. 55–75). Charlotte, NC: Information Age Publishing.

Bryer, T. A. (in press). Public participation in regulatory decision-making: Cases from regulations.gov. *Public Performance and Management Review*.

Bryer, T. A., & Zavattaro, S. M. (2011). Social media and public administration: Theoretical dimensions and introduction to symposium. *Administrative Theory & Praxis*, *33*(3), 325–340. doi:10.2753/ATP1084-1806330301.

Conroy, M. M., & Evans-Cowley, J. (2004). E-participation in planning: An analysis of cities adopting online citizen participation tools. *Environment and Planning. C, Government & Policy*, *24*, 371–384. doi:10.1068/c1k.

Cooper, T. L. (1991). *An ethic of citizenship for public administration*. Englewood Cliffs, NJ: Prentice Hall.

Cooper, T. L. (2005). Civic engagement in the twenty-first century: Toward a scholarly and practical agenda. *Public Administration Review*, *65*(5), 534–535. doi:10.1111/j.1540-6210.2005.00480.x.

Crosby, N., Kelly, J. M., & Schaefer, P. (1986). Citizen panels: A new approach to citizen participation. *Public Administration Review*, *46*(2), 170–178. doi:10.2307/976169.

Ebdon, C. (2000). The relationship between citizen involvement in the budget process and city structure and culture. *Public Productivity and Management Review, 23*(3), 383–393. doi:10.2307/3380726.

Ebdon, C. (2002). Beyond the public hearing: Citizen participation in the local government budget process. *Journal of Public Budgeting, Accounting, and Financial Management, 14*(2), 273–294.

Ebdon, C., & Franklin, A. L. (2004). Searching for a role for citizens in the budget process. *Public Budgeting & Finance, 24*(1), 32–49. doi:10.1111/j.0275-1100.2004.02401002.x.

Ebdon, C., & Franklin, A. L. (2006). Citizen participation in budgeting theory. *Public Administration Review, 66*(3), 437–447. doi:10.1111/j.1540-6210.2006.00600.x.

Franklin, A., & Ebdon, C. (2005). Touching the same camel?: Exploring a model of participation in budgeting. *American Review of Public Administration, 35*(2), 168–185. doi:10.1177/0275074005275621.

Frederickson, H. G. (1973). *Neighborhood control in the 1970s: Politics, administration, and citizen participation.* New York: Chandler Publishing.

Frederickson, H. G., & O'Leary, L. S. (1973). *Power, public opinion, and policy in a metropolitan community: A case study of Syracuse, New York.* New York: Praeger Publishers.

Ghonim, W. (2012). *Revolution 2.0: The power of the people is greater than the people in power: A memoir.* Boston, MA: Houghton Mifflin Harcourt.

Halvorsen, K. E. (2003). Assessing the effects of public participation. *Public Administration Review, 63*(5), 535–543. doi:10.1111/1540-6210.00317.

Hand, L. C., & Ching, B. D. (2011). You have one friend request: An exploration of power and citizen engagement in local governments' use of social media. *Administrative Theory & Praxis, 33*(3), 362–382. doi:10.2753/ATP1084-1806330303.

Hays, R. A., & Kogl, A. M. (2007). Neighborhood attachment, social capital building, and political participation: A case study of low and moderate-income residents of Waterloo, Iowa. *Journal of Urban Affairs, 29*(2), 181–205. doi:10.1111/j.1467-9906.2007.00333.x.

Holden, S. H., & Norris, D. F. et al. (2003). Electronic government at the local level: Progress to date and future issues. *Public Performance and Management Review, 26*(4), 325–344. doi:10.1177/15309576030266004002.

Howard, C., Lipsky, M., & Marshall, D. R. (1994). Citizen participation in urban politics: Rise and routinization. In Peterson, G. E. (Ed.), *Big-city politics, governance, and fiscal constraints* (pp. 153–199). Washington, DC: Urban Institute Press.

Irvin, R. A., & Stansbury, J. (2004). Citizen participation in decision making: Is it worth the effort? *Public Administration Review, 64*(1), 55–65. doi:10.1111/j.1540-6210.2004.00346.x.

Jennings, M. K., & Zeitner, V. (2003). Internet use and civic engagement: A longitudinal analysis. *Public Opinion Quarterly, 67*, 311–334. doi:10.1086/376947.

Kathlene, L., & Martin, J. A. (1991). Enhancing citizen participation: Panel designs, perspectives and policy formation. *Journal of Policy Analysis and Management, 10*(1), 46–63. doi:10.2307/3325512.

Kotler, M. (1969). *Neighborhood government: The local foundations of political life.* New York: Bobbs-Merrill.

Kweit, M. G., & Kweit, R. W. (1981). *Implementing citizen participation in a bureaucratic society.* New York: Praeger.

Leighninger, M. (2011). Citizenship and governance in a wild, wired world: How should citizens and public managers use online tools to improve democracy? *National Civic Review, 11*(2), 20–29. doi:10.1002/ncr.20056.

Mergel, I. (2011). *Using wikis in government: A guide for public managers.* Washington, DC: IBM Center for the Business of Government.

Moon, M. J. (2002). The evolution of e-government among municipalities: Rhetoric or reality? *Public Administration Review, 62*(4), 424–433. doi:10.1111/0033-3352.00196.

Moon, M. J., & Deleon, P. (2001). Municipal reinvention: Managerial values and diffusion among municipalities. *Journal of Public Administration: Research and Theory, 11,* 327–352. doi:10.1093/oxfordjournals.jpart.a003505.

Moon, M. J., & Norris, D. F. (2005). Does managerial orientation matter? The adoption of reinventing government and e-government at the municipal level. *Information Systems Journal, 15*(1), 43–60. doi:10.1111/j.1365-2575.2005.00185.x.

Mossberger, K., & Yonghong, W. (2012). *Civic engagement and local e-government: Social networking comes of age.* UIC Institute for Policy and Civic Engagement.

Musso, J., Weare, C., Bryer, T., & Cooper, T. L. (2011). Toward "strong democracy" in global cities? Social capital building, theory-driven reform, and the Los Angeles neighborhood council experience. *Public Administration Review, 71*(1), 102–111. doi:10.1111/j.1540-6210.2010.02311.x.

Nabatchi, T. (2012). *A manager's guide to evaluating citizen participation.* Wasington, DC: IBM Center for the Business of Government.

Nelson, K. L., & Svara, J. H. (2012). Form of government still matters: Fostering innovation in U.S. municipal governments. *American Review of Public Administration, 42*(3), 257–281. doi:10.1177/0275074011399898.

Norris, D. F., & Moon, M. J. (2005). Advancing e-government at the grassroots: Tortoise or hare? *Public Administration Review, 65*(1), 64–75. doi:10.1111/j.1540-6210.2005.00431.x.

Noveck, B. S. (2009). *Wiki government: How technology can make government better, democracy stronger, and citizens more powerful.* Washington, DC: Brookings Institution Press.

Reddick, C. G. (2004). Empirical models of e-government growth in local governments. *E-Service Journal, 3*(2), 59–84. doi:10.2979/ESJ.2004.3.2.59.

Reddick, C. G., & Frank, H. A. (2007). The perceived impacts of e-government on U.S. cities: A survey of Florida and Texas City managers. *Government Information Quarterly, 24*(3), 576–594. doi:10.1016/j.giq.2006.09.004.

Sabatier, P. A. (1988). An advocacy coalition framework of policy changes and the role of policy-oriented learning therein. *Policy Sciences, 21*(2–3), 129–168. doi:10.1007/BF00136406.

Stivers, C. (1990). The public agency as polis: Active citizenship in the administrative state. *Administration & Society, 22*(1), 86–105. doi:10.1177/009539979002200105.

Streib, G. (1992). Professional skill and support for democratic principles: The case of local government department heads in northern Illinois. *Administration & Society, 24*(1), 22–40. doi:10.1177/009539979202400102.

Thomas, C. W. (1998). Maintaining and restoring public trust in government agencies and their employees. *Administration & Society, 30*(2), 166–193. doi:10.1177/0095399798302003.

Wang, X. (2001). Assessing public participation in U.S. cities. *Public Performance & Management Review, 24*(4), 322–336. doi:10.2307/3381222.

Wang, X., & Bryer, T.A. (2012). Assessing the costs of public participation: A case study of two online participation mechanisms. *American Review of Public Administration*, 0275074012438727, first published on March 21, 2012 doi:10.1177/0275074012438727

Yang, K., & Callahan, K. (2005). Assessing citizen involvement efforts by local governments. *Public Performance and Management Review, 29*(2), 191–216.

Yang, K., & Callahan, K. (2007). Citizen involvement efforts and bureaucratic responsiveness: Participatory values, stakeholder pressures, and administrative practicality. *Public Administration Review, 67*(2), 249–264. doi:10.1111/j.1540-6210.2007.00711.x.

Yang, K., & Pandey, S. K. (2011). Further dissecting the black box of citizen participation: When does citizen involvement lead to good outcomes? *Public Administration Review, 71*(6), 880–892. doi:10.1111/j.1540-6210.2011.02417.x.

Zhang, Y., & Yang, K. (2009). Citizen participation in the budget process: The effect of city managers. *Journal of Public Budgeting, Accounting, and Financial Management, 21*(2), 289–317.

ADDITIONAL READING

Damodaran, L., & Olphert, W. (2006). *Informing digital futures: Strategies for citizen engagement. Dordrect.* Springer. doi:10.1007/978-1-4020-4784-8.

Goldberg, M., Pasher, E., & Levin-Sagi, M. (2006). Citizen participation in decision-making processes: Knowledge sharing in knowledge cities. *Journal of Knowledge Management, 10*(5), 92–98. doi:10.1108/13673270610691206.

Ho, A. T.-K. (2002). *Reinventing local governments and the e-government initiative. Pew Internet and American Life Project.* Washington, DC: Pew Research Center.

Holzer, M., & Kloby, K. (2005). Public performance measurement: An assessment of the state-of-the-art and models for citizen participation. *International Journal of Productivity and Performance Management, 54*(7), 517–532. doi:10.1108/17410400510622205.

Kearns, I., Bend, J., & Glem, B. (2002). *E-participation in local government.* Institute for Public Policy Research.

Manoharan, A., & Holzer, M. (2012). *Active citizen participation in e-government: A global perspective.* IGI Global Publishers. doi:10.4018/978-1-4666-0116-1.

Marlowe, J., & Portillo, S. (2006). Citizen engagement in local budgeting: Does diversity pay dividends? *Public Performance & Management Review, 30*(2), 179–202. doi:10.2753/PMR1530-9576300203.

Mergel, I. (2012). *Social media in the public sector: A guide to participation, collaboration, and transparency in the networked world.* San Francisco, CA: Jossey-Bass.

Mossberger, K., & Wu, Y. (2012). *Civic engagement and local e-government: Social networking comes of age. Research report issued February 13, 2012.* Chicago: Institute for Policy and Civic Engagement.

Moulder, E., & O'Neill, R. J. (2009). Citizen engagement and local government management. *National Civic Review*, *98*(2), 21–30. doi:10.1002/ncr.248.

Musso, J., Weare, C., Bryer, T. A., & Cooper, T. L. (2011). Toward 'strong democracy' in global cities? Social capital building, action research, and the Los Angeles neighborhood council experience. *Public Administration Review*, *71*(1), 102–111. doi:10.1111/j.1540-6210.2010.02311.x.

Noveck, B. (2009). *Wiki government: How technology can make government better, democracy stronger, and citizens more powerful*. Washington, DC: Brookings.

KEY TERMS AND DEFINITIONS

Civic Engagement: "People participating together for deliberation and collective action within an array of interests, institutions and networks, developing civic identity, and involving people in governance processes" (Cooper, 2005, p. 534).

E-Government: The use of online tools and technologies to manage government-to-government, government-to-business, or government-to-citizen interactions.

Social Media: "Technologies that facilitate social interaction, make possible collaboration, and enable deliberation across stakeholders" (Bryer & Zavattaro, 2011, p. 327).

Chapter 13
E–Participation and Citizen Relationship Management in Urban Governance:
Tools and Methods

Jim P. Huebner
University of Waterloo, Canada

ABSTRACT

Citizen relationship management (CiRM) is a combination of management approaches and information technologies for improving citizen services and citizen participation used at all levels of government. As an adaptation of private sector customer relationship management (CRM), CiRM is experiencing significant public sector adoption rates globally. However, while private sector CRM has demonstrated significant impact in the private sector, CiRM benefits are limited, and particularly lagging in the area of citizen e-participation in urban governance. This chapter provides an overview of the scope of CiRM functionality, with particular regard to the CRM origins and CiRM extensibilities, to develop a broader perspective of CiRM's capacity for addressing e-participation. Developing this perspective further, theoretical and methodological approaches to e-participation are presented and evaluated in four categories: generic CiRM participation models, e-government CiRM, democratic CiRM, and strategic CiRM. Further research opportunities are highlighted within the context of emerging organizational, technological, and societal trends.

INTRODUCTION

Citizen relationship management (CiRM) is a collection of management methods and information technologies used by governments to interact effectively with citizens (Schellong, 2008). CiRM evolved from commercial customer relationship management (CRM) technologies, and is most commonly used by municipalities as a set of information technology tools and processes to answer citizen phone enquires, route email requests, provide information via web site, and process online transactions. Increasingly, CiRM is also being used to facilitate and manage citizen online participation, or e-participation, in a variety of forms, with the potential to substantially improve

DOI: 10.4018/978-1-4666-4169-3.ch013

how citizens participate in civic affairs and how governments utilize citizens' inputs (Chang & Chen, 2007; Hildreth, 2007).

CiRM technologies are widely used to improve citizen service levels by, for example, accepting citizen enquiries and routing them to the appropriate department. This chapter discusses most common CiRM implementations that include citizen relationship tools and methods such as 911 and 311 response systems, online transaction and bill payment, information delivery and discussion portals, volunteer management, and call centre applications, among others, typically categorized as e-government CiRM. Citizen service representatives use CiRM systems to track citizen enquiries, record details of telephone conversations and outcomes throughout the steps of each enquiry, and finally note the resolution and citizen satisfaction level achieved. An underlying purpose of e-government CiRM is to enhance citizen participation through the use of Internet technologies, or e-participation. This chapter also explores other approaches to e-participation through CiRM, including several democratic and strategic approaches.

The theoretical underpinnings for CiRM-based e-participation draw from democratic governance and citizen participation, as well as organizational theory including structure, strategy and processes. An important perspective of e-participation is the relationship between government and citizens, particularly the communication patterns and transactions that form the relationship. These theories are examined in this chapter as they pertain to each of the CiRM approaches discussed.

Finally, CiRM increasingly plays a central role in developing citizen relationships. In business, CRM (customer relationship management) is used to track and analyse customer interactions to learn how to relate more effectively with customers, thereby understanding how to provide more desirable products and services, and increasing the company's value (King, 2007; Souder, 2001). Similarly, governments use CiRM to relate more effectively with citizens, for transparency and accountability (Castells & Cardoso, 2006), and to analyse what services are valued and how citizens would like them improved, and further, how citizens envision the future of their communities (Lorinc, 2006).

This chapter examines citizen-government relationships in view of democratic governance, and how e-participation is impacting those relationships in theory and in practice through CiRM tools and methods.

BACKGROUND

CiRM is described as a strategy that enables a technological focus on citizens' needs and encourages citizen participation (Reddick, 2010). Giving meaning to such a broad definition requires an examination of the background of CiRM, particularly its origins and growth in the private sector. To be clear, this chapter shall consistently distinguish between CRM as private sector *customer* relationship management and CiRM as public sector *citizen* relationship management, and CRM/CiRM where concepts apply equally to both private and public sector. Although CRM is now a powerful tool in business, it has taken a decade of trial and error to realize CRM's potential. Government has not yet arrived at a strategic understanding of how to apply CiRM effectively and maximize citizen participation. Therefore an examination of CRM is appropriate and necessary to developing a more complete understanding of the power, potential, and pitfalls of CiRM. This examination will include an overview of CRM as a strategy and management approach, CRM technological extensibility, and current trends that are significantly broadening CRM applicability in the private sector including cloud services, the expanding CRM ecosystem, and social CRM. This overview of CRM will form the basis for the examination of CiRM applications and e-participation capabilities.

CiRM Evolution

CiRM has its roots in private sector CRM. A simplistic description of CRM is a powerful contact manager that tracks information about individuals and organizations, and the many types of communications and interactions conducted with those customers. However, CRM is a much broader, complex organizational system that has been called "one of the greatest technological contributions to enterprises in the 21st century" (Chu, Yeh, & Chuang, 2008). Understanding the potential of CRM for e-participation requires a detailed review of CRM as it evolved and is currently implemented in the private sector.

CRM is an intricate collection of management methods and matching technologies that focuses the entire organization on defining, enhancing, and delivering customer value. To achieve customer value, a business has a well-defined strategy by which it competes in the marketplace. CRM therefore must first be designed around the company's strategy, and enable worker activities that achieve the strategic goals. Therefore, CRM is the combination of management approaches, organizational processes and matching technologies to enable the processes that help achieve successful strategic outcomes. These may include, in addition to the contact functions mentioned, electronic forms that facilitate transactions, workflows and knowledge resources that guide each step of a transaction process, and integrated communications and notifications that integrate all workers and departments necessary to complete the transaction. In all cases, the technology components are matched by management methods and business processes, which in turn emanate from an organization's strategic objectives.

Depending on the business, other CRM capabilities are necessary to enhance the customer value, including:

- **Sales and Marketing:** Comprehensive customer communications and marketing functions that not only push information to customers, and in some cases, automate the sales processes, but more importantly that invite customers to interact and provide feedback to the corporation, including social networking capabilities.
- **Service:** Extensive post-sales service capabilities that ensure direct customers and end-users have concerns and problems rectified.
- **Reporting and Analysis:** Tools to analyse customer preferences, service quality and satisfaction that lead to a deep understanding or a "360 degree view" of the firm's customers over time.
- Management of supplier and other relationships to ensure that upstream or feeder processes are suitably managed and optimized for the organization.
- Any other relationship functions that are necessary for achieving the strategic goals of the organization.

Some other important considerations for CRM are organizational culture, scale, and technology. CRM functions are not merely engineered processes, but are woven into organizational culture so that customer focus, or customer-centricity, is maintained and improved continuously by all employees. Second, CRM facilitates *en masse* what might be envisioned as a "close" relationship, capturing and reconstructing the essential parts of a "one-to-one relationship" and delivering these to a broad customer and market base. Third, a collection of rapid application development technologies are necessary to deliver the adaptability and flexibility required for enabling the continuously enhanced business processes in a way best suited for the individual business.

CRM is not just a technology, but is a way of doing business that relies on a holistic, customer-centric and strategic approach (Silverman, 2001). Private sector CRM has proven to be a powerful approach to achieving strategic outcomes by integrating corporate strategic goals, effective management of employee activities, communications and culture, and flexible technologies in combination unique to each corporation's strategy. Within this understanding of CRM as a business approach, the following section examines the technological factors that comprise CRM and CiRM.

CRM/CiRM Technologies

In addition to strategic approaches and business process methods, a crucial component of CRM is the underlying collection of information and communication technologies. Major software vendors, such as IBM, Microsoft, Oracle, Salesforce, and SAP offer private sector CRM software solutions that are also adapted for public sector CiRM. These are typically complete out-of-the-box (OOTB) solutions that may be used generically, or may be adapted and customized extensively depending on organizational requirements. As will be examined later, these requirements are determined by both business process needs, as well as strategic requirements. The ability to modify and extend CiRM is an important consideration in executing organizational strategy. Further, understanding the range of functional adaptability or extensibility is a key to understanding the potential of CiRM in e-participation. The following section provides a brief overview of the functional extensibility factors that comprise CRM/CiRM, including technological extensibility, cloud services, CRM ecosystem, and social CRM.

Technological Extensibility

The technological extensibility of CRM/CiRM allows the software components to be highly customized, and also to be integrated with other modules and 3rd party products or connected to existing organizational databases. The purpose of such broad extensibility is to match the technological functions of CRM to the organization's strategic and business requirements. In this way, CRM/CiRM constitutes a broad solution tightly integrating technology with strategy and management components. Some CRM systems offer user-level customization requiring little or no programming knowledge, as well as extensive programming-based customization for more extensive program modifications and inter-connectivity. CRM technological extensibility and integration provides the flexibility to quickly adapt CRM to an organization's unique requirements, and also to extend CRM's capabilities to uniquely match an organization's changing strategy and facilitate an increasing breadth of functions over time.

CRM's technological extensibility has further led to its application throughout organizations beyond customer facing functions, leading some vendors to re-label CRM as xRM. The 'x' signifies any strategic relationship, such as suppliers, agents, producers, media groups, and others in addition to customers. xRM denotes CRM technologies, management approaches, and strategic focus with a singular competitive value objective at the core that are applied to every department and function throughout an organization, not merely the sales and marketing departments. Further, xRM recognizes a "new world" of customer relationships, expanded from a traditional paradigm of direct organizational control of customer communications to a new paradigm of customers relating directly to each other for product information and evaluations (Band & Petouhoff, 2010).

Cloud-Services

Cloud services is a web-based software design model that facilitates a cloud-based, or Software as a Service (SaaS), provision of applications such as CRM. SaaS can reduce infrastructure and other up-front costs, and increases the ability to rapidly scale the software application to virtually any number of users. SaaS CRM, for example, is designed to operate securely on the external vendor's computing facilities, eliminating the time and costs normally associated with installation and maintenance of computing equipment by the client organization. Cloud-based applications offer a robust yet flexible data security model, while being openly accessible by authorized users from any Internet-accessible location. A flexible security model permits different levels of access to CRM functions and data, and is typically configurable for different types of users, including employees, managers, external organizations such as suppliers, customers, and the general public.

CRM Ecosystem

Another factor in CRM extensibility is the notion of a *CRM ecosystem*, which arises from CRM's technological extensibility and integration with customer-focused services. As such, CRM is not defined by a fixed set of technologies or organizational processes, but rather by a selected bundle of technologies and processes uniquely tailored to an organization as determined by its strategic objectives and customer focus. One example of a generic CRM ecosystem is the model by Forrester Research that outlines clusters of CRM technology functions or modules, all oriented toward the single strategic objective of achieving customer understanding (Band & Petouhoff, 2010).

Social CRM

Finally, CRM extensibility has more recently led to *social CRM,* which is the inclusion of social networking capabilities that engages customers "where and when" they communicate. Customer-generated content, such as product reviews, experiences, and product support, is often shared on public social media that lie outside a firm's control. Social CRM includes tools and methods to monitor *buzz* about the company and its products, and track growth and decline of interactions.

The Operating Model for Social CRM (Buchanan, 2010) shown in Figure 2 provides an example of the comprehensiveness of a social CRM ecosystem, beginning with the customer strategy layer on the left, the external to internal operational layers focusing on value creation, and the analytical layer on the right providing real-time insights to the total customer value experience.

Social CRM is a company's approach to listening to their customers and how they are influencing the marketplace based on their experience of value with the company's products and services. A fundamental shift is required in an organization's marketing approach, from pushing information from inside outward to attracting customers from outside inward, and recognizing "customer control of the conversation" (Greenberg, 2009) as a key dynamic in social CRM.

CRM is both powerful and complex as a result of its extensibility, and identifying real-world CRM may be very confusing if viewed only from a technological perspective. The span of possible technological capabilities and management approaches as a result of CRM extensibility precludes the possibility of a definitive technological definition of CRM. However, the addition of strategy and organizational process perspectives that center on customer value provides an integrated view of CRM as a total, customer-centric business approach incorporating organizational strategy, process methodology, and enabling technologies. This integrated view of CRM may be referred to as customer-centric CRM and represents a perspective that is transferable to the public sector as citizen-centric CiRM. The following section examines CRM and e-participation from the perspective of CRM/CiRM extensibility and citizen centricity.

CiRM APPLICATIONS AND E-PARTICIPATION

CRM in the public sector, referred to herein as CiRM, has gradually gained acceptance over the last decade, and is presently used by a large number of government organizations around the world at the national, regional or state, and local or municipal levels. CiRM adoption rates are accelerating as research is beginning to clarify benefits and best practices, while governments at all levels attempt to meet the challenges of increasing service demands, decreasing resources, and more open accountability and responsiveness to citizens.

CiRM is used to coordinate government services and help improve operational efficiencies and responsiveness to citizens. Many CiRM applications focus on citizen services, facilitating citizen transactions such as invoicing for services and account tracking. Citizens also interact extensively with government by making enquiries or requesting information about government services, submitting complaints or requests that require follow up action, and responding to government initiatives by submitting ideas. Whether citizens interact with government by telephone, email, or via Internet web forms, all of these interactions must be managed efficiently and effectively. Managing these interactions, or transactions, represents a limited application of CiRM. While transactional CiRM is a useful part of e-participation, as will be examined further in the e-government CiRM section below, the scope of CiRM and e-participation extends well beyond transactional CiRM.

CiRM Scope and Implementation

The scope of CiRM implementation is not easy to define, due both to terminology and definition. Commonly-used terminology includes government CRM, CiRM, CzRM, and more broadly, citizen-centric technologies including citizen-centric e-services, e-government, and e-participation.

E-services technologies that are custom designed by government by integrating legacy information systems with a citizen-focused interface fall within the broad scope of CiRM as defined herein, particularly where such technologies are based on management methods focussed on citizen requirements. Conversely, some CiRM implementations based on CRM vendors' offerings are not recognized by administrators as CRM due to a lack of awareness of CiRM principles (Schellong, 2008). While there is a need for much more research on CiRM, existing research is beginning to identify CiRM applications that provide a high positive impact and return on investment (ROI).

Given a broad definition of CiRM that brings together people, technology, and business processes to focus on citizen needs (Reddick, 2010), CiRM is widely adopted by all levels of government throughout the world, and its rate of adoption is accelerating. National and state (provincial or territorial) governments adopt CiRM practices to respond better to citizens in line with national or state e-citizen directives. CiRM adoption is particularly prevalent at the local government level where citizen interaction is more direct, and government services are more immediately and broadly evidenced in frequent, highly visible citizen services such as water, sewer, waste disposal, road maintenance, community planning, and recreation. The remaining challenge faced by government however is to implement CiRM strategically and effectively in order to realize the benefits of improved citizen services, satisfaction, and democratic participation. The following sections will examine the theoretical underpinnings and various approaches to the facilitation of citizen participation particularly through CiRM as they build on the organizational and functional traits of CRM presented above. The views examined in the following sections include a general overview of democratic e-participation rationale, generic frameworks, an e-government approach to CiRM, and several democratic and strategic frameworks for CiRM and e-participation.

CiRM and E-Participation

CiRM is viewed as a key enabler for e-government, with the promise of improving citizen services and government-to-citizen relationships. Imbedded in the goals of e-government is the goal toward improving levels of democratic participation of citizens (United Nations, 2010). CiRM provides many capabilities to facilitate improved citizen participation and communications in government, as implied by the relationship management focus of CiRM. Globally, municipalities are prioritizing the need for greater citizen participation, and CiRM is a key enabler in this priority. Despite some successes, the specific process of enabling e-participation through CiRM however is a strategic function that for many municipalities is still unclear and remains obstructed by numerous barriers. We will briefly review what e-participation is, and then provide an overview of different strategic approaches to e-participation through CiRM.

E-Participation Perspectives

E-participation refers to citizen involvement or engagement in the affairs of government through electronic means, typically the Internet. However, there is significant overlap in academic literature between the terms e-government, e-participation, e-services, and others. The United Nations (UN) E-Government Survey evaluates e-participation as the services and channels that facilitate inclusion and empowerment of citizens to participate in public affairs (United Nations, 2010). From the technical viewpoint of service channels, e-participation is viewed as a subset of e-government, which refers broadly to any government service or communication enabled via the Internet. However, the UN and the American Society for Public Administration also highlight the overarching social democratic goal of e-government, that is, to "improve citizen access to government information, services, and expertise, to ensure citizen participation in and satisfaction with government

processes…a permanent commitment by government to improving the relationship between the private citizen and the public sector." (Chang & Chen, 2007). Therefore from the social democratic viewpoint, citizen e-participation is recognized as an overarching or superordinate goal of e-government, rather than a subset. These two apparently dichotomous viewpoints can present challenges in applying technology to enable participation. Therefore, a theoretical grounding or framework is essential in understanding e-participation and its relational emphasis.

Generic E-Participation Frameworks

A core framework for citizen participation was proposed by Arnstein (1969), highlighting the efficacy of citizen participation as a key dimension in improved relationships, that is, that citizens realize that their participation influences government decisions in a desirable way. The different degrees of citizen influence are described by rungs on the "ladder of citizen participation" shown in Figure 3. Arnstein's topology describes eight main levels in three categories, from manipulation as non-participation, through to citizen control as the most influential degree of citizen influence. Arnstein's ladder continues to serve as a reminder that citizen participation cannot be assumed to have a desired effect, and only fulfils a democratic objective when influence is realized.

While Arnstein's topology helps describe the outcomes of various types of citizen participation, it does not attempt to prescribe effective forms of participation. It is best applied not in the prescriptive design of CiRM for e-participation, but rather as an evaluative tool for proposed or existing designs to ensure that any e-participation system achieves more than just nonparticipation or tokenism.

Simplified versions of the Arnstein's topology have been adapted by various organizations as prescriptive mechanisms. IAP2's (2008) Spectrum of Public Participation prescribes a series of citizen participation practices across five levels (inform, consult, involve, collaborate, and empower), and serves as a framework to educate community organizers and municipal practitioners about conducting and evaluating citizen participation activities that achieve influence. The OECD (2001) outlines three main levels (information, consultation, and active participation) that prescribe goals for government-citizen relations in developed and developing countries alike, around which are structured a variety of activities and resources to guide citizen participation initiatives. Figure 4 graphically summarizes these three comparative frameworks that help differentiate the degrees of influence between different forms of public participation. These frameworks represent a core dimension in e-participation, namely, the efficacy of citizen efforts to meaningfully influence decision processes.

Scope of Application

An additional factor for an e-participation framework is scope of application that includes the full range of CiRM capabilities that are possible due to CiRM extensibility. The range of CiRM functional capabilities significantly expands the scope of traditional e-participation, both extending externally beyond the government-provisioned functions, and also reaching internally to include discrete or standalone applications within the organization. First, a holistic framework for e-participation acknowledges citizen-directed or ad-hoc democratic activities that occur beyond the control or facilitation of government. E-participation theory is typically limited to technology capabilities that are provided by government to citizens, and that utilize solution frameworks oriented toward government-provided technologies. However, a social CiRM perspective includes citizen-to-citizen communications as well as citizen-initiated e-participation activities, encompassing all relevant and collaborative relationships that influence

municipal decision processes as shown in Figure 5. Citizens may self-organize into cooperative groups to collaborate and more effectively participate in and influence government affairs outside the control and facilitation of government, relying instead on popular email and independent social networking technologies to aid communication and coordination of group activities (Tapscott, 2008). Despite not being provisioned by a government body, these tools and approaches fall within the scope of CiRM technologies identified earlier, particularly social CRM. They represent relevant forms of citizen influence and can be monitored and managed as will be described later in the social CiRM section, and are therefore an important factor in a holistic CiRM e-participation framework. Further, as citizen collaboration attracts the attention of municipal officials, the municipality may seek to provide more effective collaboration tools to citizens, seeking to expand and formalize citizen participation through CiRM functions. A comprehensive e-participation framework encompasses external citizen-directed activities that influence government decisions and that may alter forms over time.

The scope of application of CiRM e-participation also extends internally to include minor or discrete citizen group activities that are facilitated by municipalities but may be considered insignificant within the comprehensive e-participation framework, and CiRM may be overlooked as an enabling technology. In a particular case, the author of this chapter interviewed a municipal worker tasked with coordinating a citizens' group. Apparently not being aware of the municipality's existing CiRM system, she approached the IT department to create a small, custom database application complete with lists, forms, email management, reports, and management functions. The IT department complied, apparently similarly unaware of their CiRM system's applicable functions. The result was a minimally adequate IT application that served only the basic information needs of the citizen coordinator, lacked numerous communications and relationship functions built into the CiRM application, segregated the citizen data from the organization, was not linked to the citizen online forums, and all at a cost to the organization higher than had the application been provisioned through CiRM.

The scope of application of an e-participation framework is significantly expanded beyond the traditional perspective by the range of CiRM capabilities, extending beyond the technology functions directly provided by the government, as well as incorporating minor, discrete functions within the organization.

Benefits and Gaps

Approaching CiRM e-participation through generic participation frameworks is beneficial and instructive to practitioners in some ways, but leaves significant gaps and challenges. A generic framework approach helps to establish a theoretical grounding for e-participation and to prescribe a variety of participation practices that would potentially be influential in municipal decision processes. It further fosters a perspective of citizen responsibility that implicitly places high value on appropriate forms of participation that advance citizen influence. A generic framework further helps to provide a general strategic focus for public sector organizations in highlighting the importance of participation, and can prescribe strategic objectives for public organizations wishing to be proactive toward citizen participation rather than merely reacting to citizen demands.

However, generic participation frameworks do not provide a comprehensive approach for designing and implementing effective e-participation. They typically do not provide a mechanism for designing and integrating various forms of participation, and are more oriented toward *point-in-time* activities or discrete issues, rather than ongoing, continuous citizen engagements. They do not ac-

commodate mass engagement, as will be examined below, being oriented instead for smaller groups or defined segments of the citizen population. Similarly, these frameworks do not adapt well for general, non-targeted participation such as general citizen satisfaction feedback or strategic planning, and fail to adequately accommodate the full scope of e-participation capabilities. They do not provision the analysis of citizen enquiries as a means to understanding citizen concerns and preferences for their community, and have no accommodation for the "participative" aspect of citizen transactions that will be examined in the next section, which is a core part of CiRM. The following sections review several approaches to CiRM e-participation that attempt to overcome these limitations while still attaining the efficacy of the core e-participation framework. The following approaches are presented in three categories or types: e-government or transactional, democratic, and strategic.

E-Government CiRM

E-government, as stated earlier, refers broadly to government-to-citizen transactions, enabled via the Internet for the purpose of serving the broad goals of improving government accountability and transparency, and enhancing democratic fundamentals of citizen participation and satisfaction. CiRM is at the core of many e-government systems.

E-Government Origins

E-government has its roots in the New Public Management movement (NPM), which emphasises improving efficiency in government business processes (Hood, 1995). CiRM is used to enable online citizen access to a full range of transactions, such as payment of taxes and utilities, application forms and requests for information, and email interactions with officials. A further application of CiRM is "311" services, whereby citizens can call a single telephone number ("311") to contact the municipality for enquiries and services. Citizen's calls are logged, tracked, routed, processed, and evaluated for resolution quality through CiRM. Ideally, 311 services are combined with online and other modes of citizen access for a full, multimodal and 24-7 citizen service suite in a single CiRM system.

In some cases, CiRM also integrates social network functions and personal transactions for a completely multi-modal holistic approach to e-government (see more below). CiRM systems and approaches almost always underlie e-government in some way, even though they may not be recognized as such. CiRM approaches may be applied to a fully customized software application, or conversely, "out-of-the-box" (OOTB) CRM software may be customized and adapted to specific requirements. One study found that internal users of CiRM in several large U.S. metropolises were completely unaware that the system was based on OOTB CRM software (Schellong, 2008).

Ultimately, the scope of CiRM in e-government is improving service quality and value to citizens within a democratic framework of transparency, accountability, and participation, thereby renewing civic engagement and creating a better quality of life for citizens (Denhardt & Denhardt, 2003). Within this scope, the focus for CIRM on improving service efficiencies is given credence by NPM, provides a realizable ROI, and can improve citizen satisfaction. The broader focus for CiRM on citizen relationships however – understanding citizen behavior through analytics and garnering influential citizen participation in substantive decision processes – is the "golden opportunity" to go beyond "self-serving" administrative processes toward citizen-centric transformation in government (Kannabiran, Xavier, & Anantharaaj, 2004). While the scope of e-government CiRM is highly citizen-centric in theory, in practice the scope is typically limited to citizen transactions.

E-Government Adoption

Under the NPM rubric, CiRM has been widely adopted and is proven to dramatically improve efficiency, thereby providing a high return on investment (ROI) for government organizations. CiRM is most widely adopted by municipal levels of government, where CiRM also finds the most varied uses and applications.

A 2009 study found that 113 of the largest 200 municipalities in the U.S. had adopted CiRM in some form (Reddick, 2010, p. 91). While most of these CiRM implementations were still in initial stages, they were found to have a positive impact on government-to-citizen communications and on citizen service quality. Some of the specific benefits of CiRM in local government are to create a more efficient, transparent and accountable government. The same study found that the most common application of CiRM was tracking citizen service requests, used by 97% of the municipalities surveyed, with 90% of them rating the application as very effective. Another common application was a citizen-searchable knowledge database, used by 85% of local governments, and judged by 60% of them to be effective. The greatest benefits, according to the survey, were to improve communications with citizens, improve consistency of service levels to citizens, prioritize citizen satisfaction in the organization, and increasingly resolve citizen requests on their first call. The study also highlights that most municipalities have implemented only the basic CiRM functions, and are lacking more advanced functionality such as wireless access, kiosks, and interactive voice systems. A fundamental omission is multichannel or multi-modal access, such that a citizen request submitted via the web channel is separate from the same citizen's contact via the telephone channel, for example, and their contact information is not updated for subsequent contact via any other channel. Some barriers to more advanced implementation were lack of funding, underutilization of available technology, identity and data security issues, and internal management and control issues. Departments found difficulty in giving up control of their customer management functions.

Many CiRM implementations are still in initial stages as governments work to update existing legacy systems, integrate disparate electronic data sources, connect segregated departments, and provide secure interfaces to citizens. The state of CiRM offerings and technological extensibility has evolved to a level of maturity that "makes the technology the easy part" (Schellong, 2008). However, CiRM adoption and effectiveness is lagging due not to technological limitations, but to the strategic complexity and priorities in local government.

E-government CiRM implementations have a tendency to over-emphasise the financial savings of efficiency improvements in business processes, and under-emphasise or overlook the more challenging citizen relationship and participatory aspects. A simplistic approach to CiRM implementation results in simply automating existing business processes and moving them online, rather than redesigning municipal processes for a citizen centric experience. In such cases, the benefits of e-government CiRM accrue essentially internally to the municipality rather than externally to the citizens (Coglianese, 2007). The emphasis on ROI and realization of cost savings overshadows an emphasis on the creation of citizen value and democratic participation (West, 2005). Alternative approaches to e-government are intended to overcome these gaps and restore a citizen focus in e-government.

Relational E-Government

While the intent of e-government is to facilitate citizen connectedness and improved participation, the relational benefits of e-government CiRM appear less quantifiable than the efficiency ben-

efits, and therefore not yet widely implemented. Several approaches to address these deficiencies are proposed. A relational perspective to CiRM in e-government (Pan, Tan, & Lim, 2006) proposes to make the relationships between government and citizens more quantifiable by considering three relational aspects:

1. **Relational Incentives:** Which are the needs and benefits to each party in the relationship.
2. **Relational Value:** The specific needs and benefits that can be satisfied through the relationship, and their relative importance or magnitude.
3. **Relational Tool:** The mechanisms to enable the identification of incentives and facilitate the realization of value, and capture a valuation of the relative magnitudes of such transactions.

Based on test cases, the relational perspective essentially views all citizen communications and interactions as strategically equivalent to direct citizen participation. Capturing and analysing relational value of all interactions between citizens and government can lead to a managerial strategy for CiRM that moves e-government beyond the limitations of NPM efficiencies and toward the democratic goals of citizen participation. Despite the merits of a relational perspective, the identification and quantification of relational factors has not been widely embraced in local government.

Collaborative E-Government

Another approach to CiRM in e-government suggests that e-government adopt a collaborative approach with citizens by the integration of Web 2.0, or social networking, technologies. Consistent with the CRM extensibilities identified earlier, the collaborative approach to CiRM integrates a participation architecture, thereby redesigning existing services to be more citizen centric and promote citizen participation (Gonzalez &

Gonzalez, 2012). Figure 6: "CRM 2.0" shows the technological topology of a relational CiRM-based e-government system. The base components include the operational and relational function of a typical CRM system and the analytical functions integral to customer-centric CRM functions, with the addition of the Web 2.0 participation architecture components to facilitate citizen collaboration.

In a review of existing literature and selected cases, Gonzalez and Gonzalez (2012) purport that integration of participation architecture components into CiRM achieves a collaborative approach in e-government with demonstrable benefits. In particular, interactions with the citizen (by municipalities) is improved across five dimensions, and collaborative governance is improved across four dimensions, including participation of citizens, and particularly online consultations and surveys (Gonzalez & Gonzalez, 2012). Many municipalities are experimenting with social networking technologies, incorporating them into their web sites and even e-participation initiatives, but largely on an ad-hoc basis and not yet in a structured manner as suggested by this collaborative approach.

E-government implementations, despite having CiRM as a core technology, are heavily skewed towards the NPM goals of attaining efficiencies and far less toward the "golden opportunity" of improving citizen participation. Where e-government implementations are evaluated solely on the financial savings, they are not extended to include relational, participatory functions. In other cases, participation improvements are incorrectly assumed to be a natural outcome of e-government implementations, but which are not realized due to lack of appropriate approaches and of suitable planning based on that faulty assumption. Explicitly collaborative and relational approaches to e-government indicate improvements to citizen participation but have not been widely adopted.

The following democratic CiRM and strategic CiRM approaches to e-participation move beyond approaching e-participation as a supplemental function of, or add-on to, e-government and instead place e-participation at the centre of the theoretical framework as a core priority.

DEMOCRATIC E-PARTICIPATION CiRM

E-participation in CiRM has foundational democratic underpinnings, as has been highlighted throughout this chapter. While e-government CiRM demonstrates gains in quality and efficiencies of administrative, transactional service delivery, it seldom achieves significant, democratic influence for citizen participation. Democratic e-participation CiRM, alternatively, is an explicit shift in emphasis from transactions to participation, based on a view of governance that is centred not on the technical aspects of service delivery but on the democratic aspects of direct citizen participation through ICTs. Several theoretical models provide insight into this perspective.

CiRM "Sophistication" Model

Democratic participation in CiRM is achieved through increasing levels of *sophistication* along two dimensions – *technology* and *need* as shown in Figure 1 (Kannabiran et al., 2004). In this theoretical model, lower levels of sophistication are centred on *automation* of existing government "business" transactions, representing a low level of sophistication of democratic needs. These needs require relatively low levels of technical sophistication, being met by core CiRM functions. A median level of need sophistication envisions the transformation of existing business transactions to a citizen-centric design, encompassing all interactions between citizen and government across

Figure 1. The extended CRM application ecosystem (Band & Petouhoff, 2010)

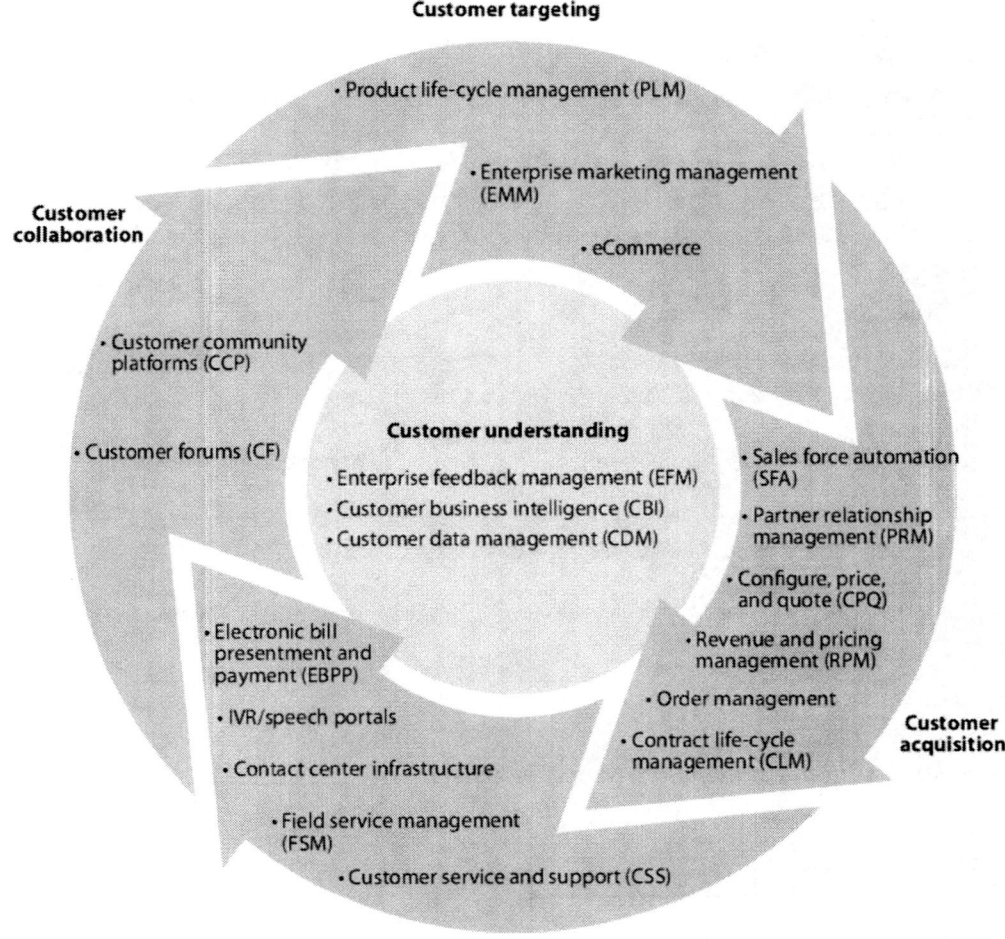

all modes or channels of interactions (Internet, telephone, written, inter-personal, etc.). Beyond achieving efficiencies and service excellence, government develops an intimate view of each citizen's requirements, provides leadership in community building, and encourages innovation (Lorinc, 2006).

Finally, a high level of democratic need sophistication proposes a "new e-government paradigm" that transforms not only business processes but citizen relationships (Kannabiran et al., 2004), wherein citizens participate in decision processes to highly influence government policy and regulation. This high level of democratic needs sophistication requires a high level of technological CiRM sophistication, including analytics, integration and extensibility, and redesigned business processes to support the needs.

CiRM may provide the golden opportunity for democratic governance transformation through e-participation, but still faces significant barriers to achieving high levels of sophistication in democratic e-participation. A review of three CiRM systems in India indicates that achieving high levels of need sophistication is subject to numerous challenges, including making a justifiable

Figure 2. Operating Model for Social CRM (Buchanan, 2010)

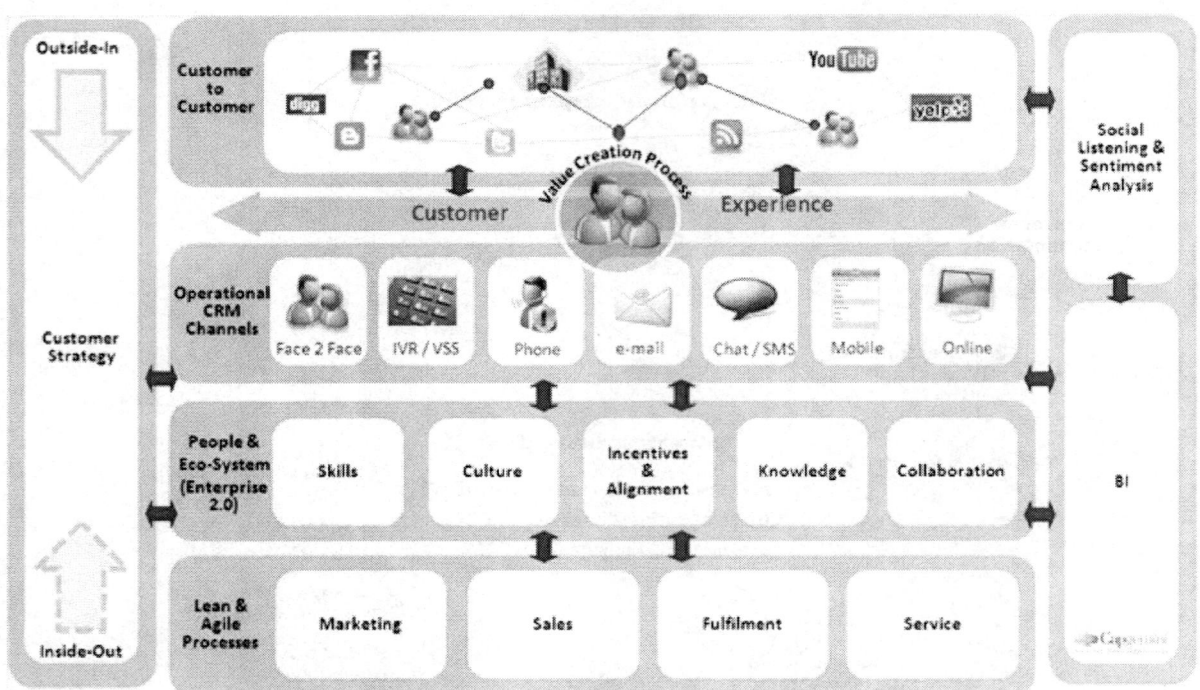

Figure 3. Ladder of Citizen Participation (Arnstein, 1969)

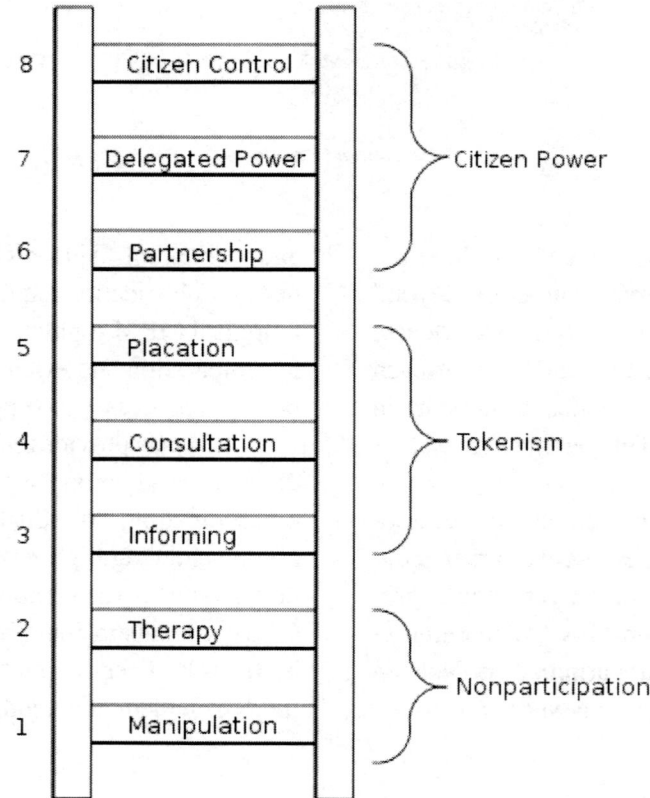

Figure 4. What is Participation (Prieto-Martin, 2009)

Figure 5. "New World" of simultaneous and collaborative relationships (Band & Petouhoff, 2010)

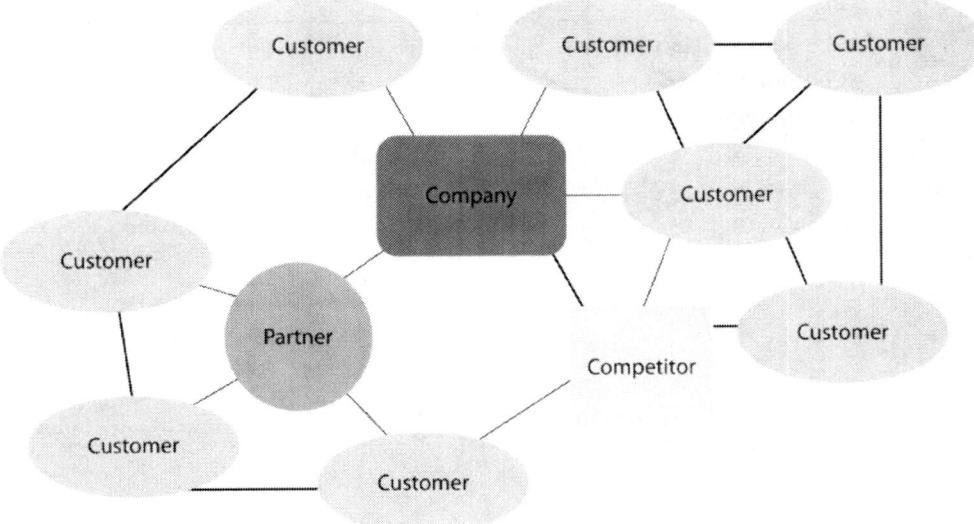

Figure 6. "CRM 2.0" (© Daniel Perez Gonzalez and Pedro Solana Gonzalez)

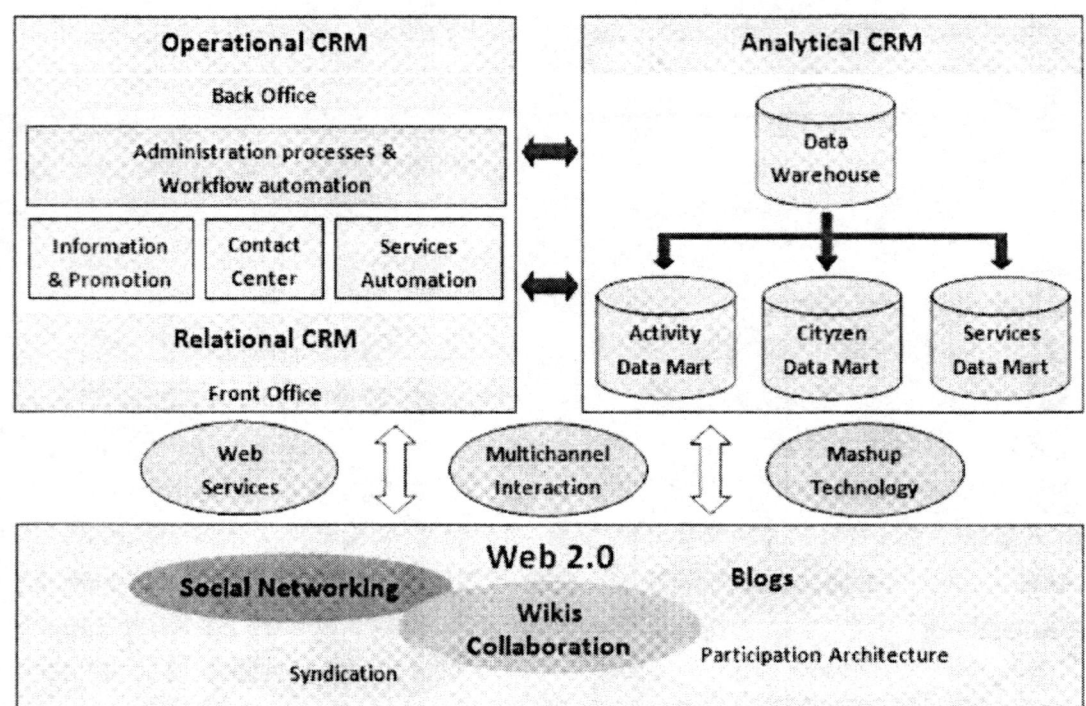

Figure 7. Evolution of government services (Kannabiran, et al., 2004)

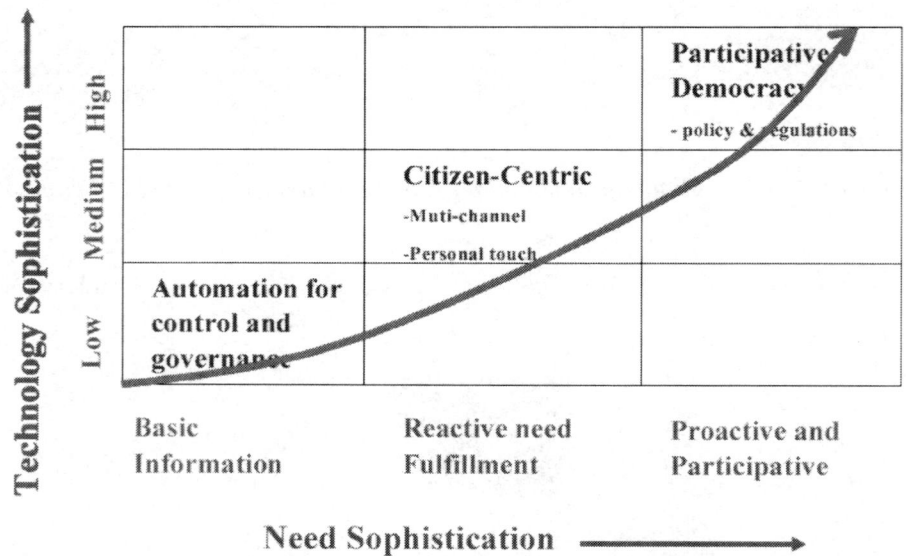

business case for investment, gaining leadership support, and overcoming the traditional mindset of government employees (Kannabiran et al., 2004).

CiRM "Insight" Model

Democratic participation in CiRM may be envisioned as a function of insight as reflected in the relationships between government and citizens. King (2007) describes three stages of relationship that account for the typical status and goals of current CiRM implementations. The informational/transactional relationship stage defines most typical CiRM implementations that, as described earlier, focus on efficient handling of transactions, including redesign of traditional business processes. The insightful relationship: council-driven stage defines the aspirations of advanced CiRM, and rests on the application of analytics and business intelligence functions to analyse current citizen transaction behaviour and understand costs and value of services delivered. These data and analyses are useful in refinement of services to specific segments of citizens according to their particular needs, and help to target and reduce the costs of public safety services (police, fire, etc.) by recognizing repetitive patterns in existing social behaviour that lead to service incidents.

This model acknowledges a barrier ("the wall") that is the inherent risk of many CiRM systems, particularly 311 and NPM-oriented transaction systems, which may simply serve to reinforce the status quo of existing governance structures and perceptions, thus essentially serving to limit citizen participation. Conceptually, as municipal decision-makers depend more on sophisticated analytical CiRM, citizens may become disengaged rather than active participants.

The third stage, the insightful relationship: citizen-driven, is described as a radical break from traditional CiRM in the public sector whereby the citizens provide guidance about their information needs. Rather than council deciding which

participation functions are provided to citizens, this CiRM stage depends on citizens providing feedback on the types of functions and analyses they need to further enhance municipal processes, provide understanding of municipal problems, and help influence future planning. This approach depends heavily on the extensibility of CRM, as well as the integration of social network functions and analytical tools for citizens to be informed about issues and communicate with the municipality and each other.

The insight approach to CiRM helps position citizen participation in CiRM as a key organizational priority, and emphasises the importance of citizen influence on the CiRM functional design. The stages are best envisioned as evaluative levels of functional acuity occurring concurrently throughout the CiRM implementation rather than sequential levels of application development. CiRM functions that facilitate citizen insight should be implemented throughout the CiRM implementation cycle across all functions. This adds a layer of complexity to OOTB implementations, necessitating a strong vision for and understanding of citizen-led participative CiRM functions.

Democratic e-participation CiRM helps focus functionality on citizen participation through intentional design and extensibility. The theoretical models for democratic e-participation emphasise citizens' democratic roles in governance theory, and the implementation of supporting functions in CiRM that fulfil a more complete vision of e-government. Democratic e-participation CiRM models impact solution design by extending the e-government functions beyond mere transaction-based CiRM to explicitly include relationship-based CiRM functions that enable effective e-participation. Further research is required to establish agreement on common methods that may be widely adopted and that demonstrate measureable benefits to citizens in order to counterbalance the attractive and quantifiable benefits of transaction-based CiRM.

Strategic CiRM

Strategic CiRM addresses the lack of commonly accepted and widely adopted practices for e-participation functions in CiRM by targeting two significant and recurring barriers, namely, lack of measurable benefits over costs, and lack of systematization. First, extending CiRM to include e-participation functions is perceived as financially costly and political risky, requiring immense effort and time to experiment with and understand various forms of e-participation. The benefits may be framed in terms of democratic ideals and are therefore of the highest order, but are difficult to quantify and demonstrate concretely. Therefore the financial, political, and social risks for e-participation are comparatively high, particularly when compared to the demonstrated ROI of NPM transactional CiRM. The alternative is to reframe the issue of e-participation as a strategic imperative rather as simply a cost/benefit decision.

Second, the systemic topology of government is such that the decision-makers within local government tend to favour benefits that accrue within the organizational scope of their mandate. Charged with managing the resources of government, decision-makers will favour transactional CiRM that demonstrates costs savings and therefore appears to fulfil their mandate, rather than favour democratic e-participation initiatives that ideally benefit citizens but do not provide clearly apparent support of decision-makers' political mandates. The result is that many forms of e-participation tend to represent an ad hoc democracy that limits citizen participation to specific issues at points in time, and to meet minimal, mandated requirements rather than supporting continuous, systemic governance processes as required by functioning democracy (Anttiroiko, 2004). The alternative is to elevate e-participation to a strategic goal.

Strategic CiRM approaches e-participation as a strategic imperative that is explicitly defined within the organizational mandate, and is therefore integrated into existing strategic decision processes, and organizational planning and business processes (Huebner, 2009). Drawing from the private sector, the primary strength of CRM to execute customer-centric strategies and processes means that CRM is regarded as far more than "just a set of software applications and IT integrations, but a business strategy that focuses on building customer service excellence" (Batista & Kawalek, 2004). Similarly, CiRM is an organizational strategy that focuses on the full range of citizen relationship interactions, including service-related transactions and democratic participation. Strategic CiRM therefore formalizes citizen participation priorities into the top-most levels of organizational planning and functioning by, for example, integrating prescriptive organizational e-participation frameworks with generally accepted strategic planning and implementation tools. Such strategic integration places responsibility for e-participation initiatives clearly within the scope of decision-makers mandates, and, as strategic objectives, above considerations solely of ROI. Thus, municipal decision-makers are no longer faced with evaluating whether e-participation provides benefits, but are rather faced with determining how to deliver on the strategic imperatives of e-participation and how to deliver benefits utilizing strategic CiRM as the strategic implementation framework. Several approaches and perspectives regarding strategic CiRM are now considered.

CRM Strategy Framework

One perspective on strategic CiRM is the framing of e-participation within a strategic value framework, or designing CiRM to deliver citizen value. Just as the delivery of customer value is a core focus of organizational strategy, so too citizen value is a core focus of government strategy. Citizen value is the realization of desired benefits as defined by citizens – a genuinely citizen-centric perspective. Each employee and organizational process is focused on delivering services that are valued by citizens, either implicitly through community values, or explicitly as recognized by citizen interaction and feedback.

A basic CRM strategy framework presented in Figure 9 identifies three levels of value delivery: improved accessibility, organizational transformation, and services innovation at the highest level. Within each level are described one or more CiRM functions necessary in achieving the value delivery targets. A UK CRM National Programme study demonstrated benefits of CiRM implementations primarily in the areas of improved customer service and citizen satisfaction, while also recognizing that progress toward a truly citizen-centric culture was limited due to barriers such as lack of workforce development planning, budget constraints, and insufficient change management (King, 2007).

This CRM strategy framework is broadly descriptive of the increasing value of e-participation delivered through ascending levels of strategic CiRM, thereby legitimizing for municipal managers the imperative of e-participation in CiRM. However, the framework lacks management controls as it is neither evaluative of specific dimensions of success nor prescriptive of methods and targets to manage the implementation of strategic CiRM goals.

CiRM Integrative Matrix

Recent research into CiRM acknowledges the difficulty of organizational transformation for the enhancement of citizen value due to the complexity of municipal governance (Reddick, 2011). Capturing the benefits of citizen-oriented e-participation in a complex environment is aided by a strategic framework that is able to capture the multiplicity of factors affecting citizen value. The Matrix of Civic Implication (Prieto-Martin, 2011) shown in Figure 10, for example, is a recent framework that aims to describe e-participation initiatives in local government comprehensively along four dimensions:

1. Intensity of collaboration.
2. Actors involved in the participatory exercise.
3. Institutionalization level.
4. Deliberativeness.

The intensity of collaboration dimension is an adaptation of Arnstein's (1969) eight-rung ladder with the addition here of two "conflict" levels, and the division of the resulting ten intensity levels into five categories.

The actor dimension differentiates the various participants, acknowledging the possible involvement of many actors across the political, corporate, and civil sectors with various roles. This dimension helps identify administrative, top-down participation directed by government as distinct from autonomous or bottom-up participation as initiated by citizens. This distinction is similar to "the wall" of council-centric CiRM versus citizen-centric CiRM as described in Figure 8.

The institutionalization level dimension describes the level of e-participation that is included or embedded into organizational processes, ranging from brief, sporadic attempts, through continuous and on toward functional and organic institutionalization. Functional institutionalization describes organizational policies or legal procedures that mandate the opportunity for citizen participation, such as mandatory hearings in urban planning or participation in municipal council. Organic institutionalization is the formation of relatively permanent or continual forms of participation, generally oriented to allow direct citizen involvement in decision processes.

Finally, the deliberative dimension describes the intensity of deliberation as a particular form of citizen participation that involves ongoing reasoned dialogue among actor groups. This dimension is indicated within the matrix by the intensity of colour or opaqueness used in mapping the participation activities onto the matrix as shown by the shaded areas in Figure 10.

Figure 8. CiRM and "the wall" (King, 2007)

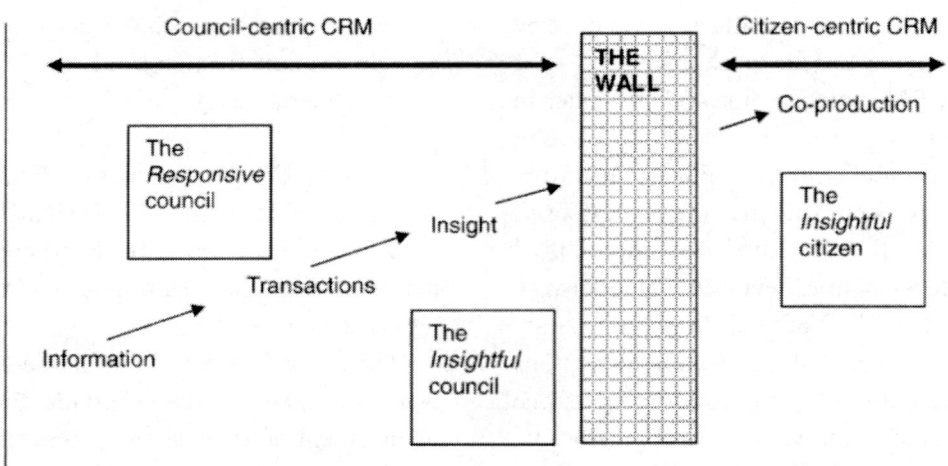

Figure 9. CRM Strategy Framework (King, 2007)

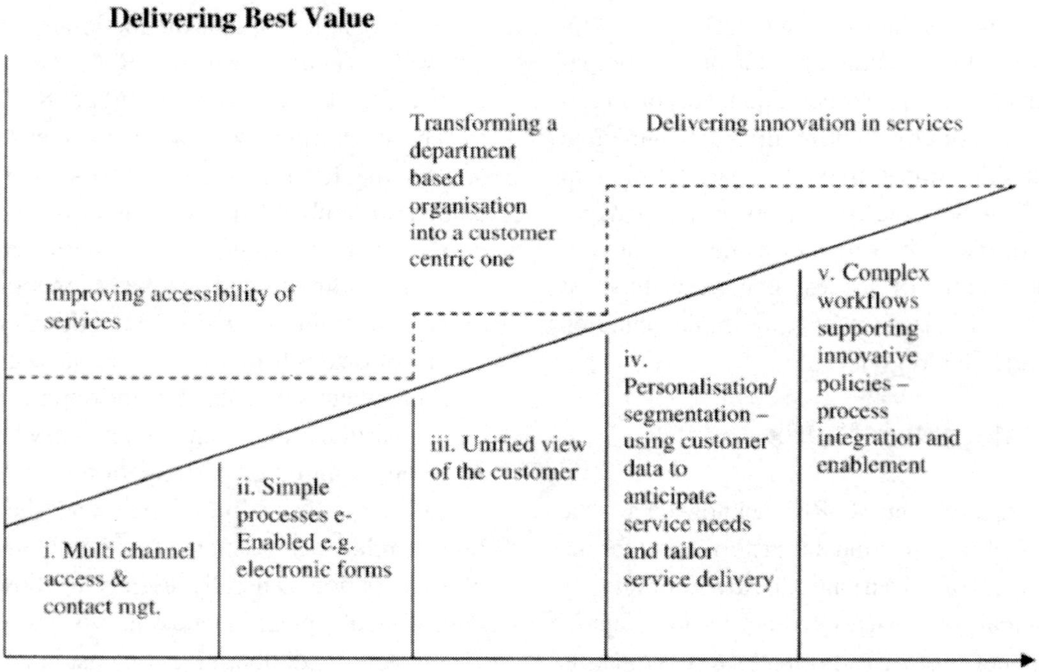

Delivering Best Value

This matrix represents a more comprehensive approach to understanding the strategic implications of e-participation by describing the deliberative impact in relation to the actors, actions and organization structure within the scope of local government. By distilling the complexity of e-participation into various dimensions within a single framework, the strategic value of e-participation may be better understood and potentially contribute to a CiRM design that targets several strategic objectives highlighted by the matrix, including: balancing the typical "ad-hoc" democratic participation with more institutionalized forms of functional and organic participation; facilitating

Figure 10. Matrix of Civic Implication (Prieto-Martin, 2011)

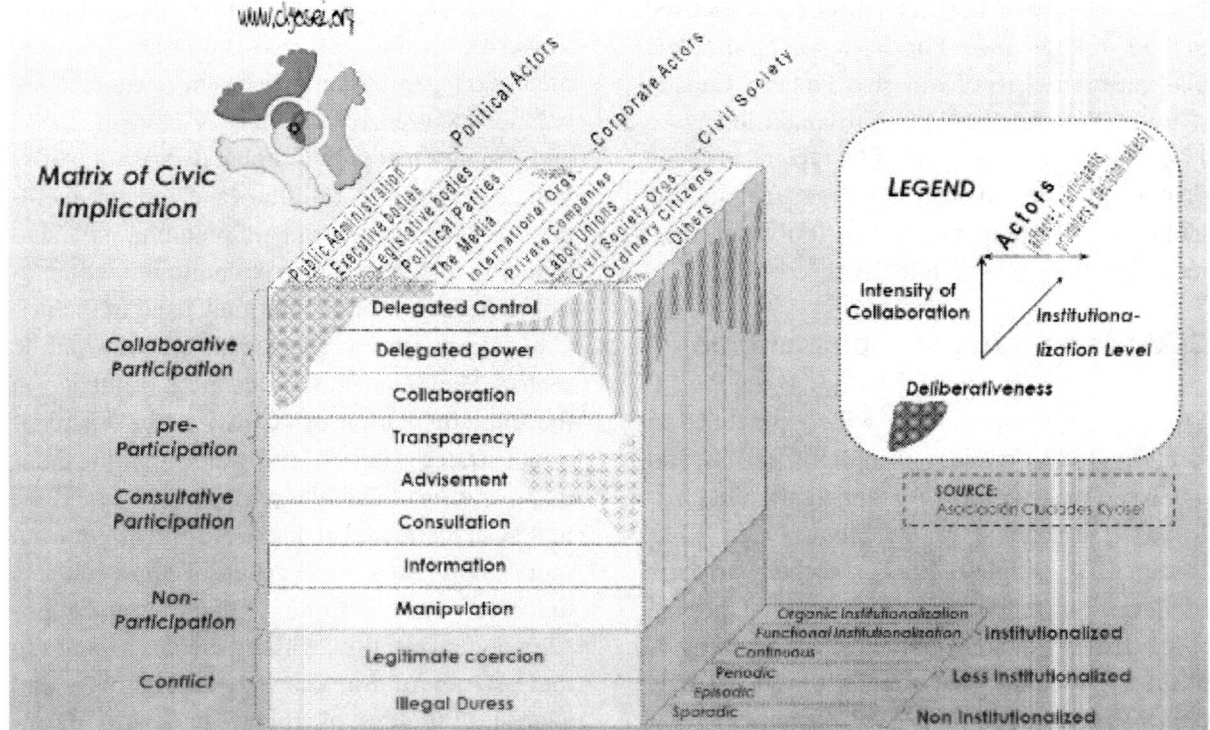

meaningful relationships and interactions across the various actors; and capturing and reporting on the various forms and intensities of collaborative activities. These CiRM design targets are well matched to the core functions of CRM identified earlier. However, the matrix is intended to be descriptive and therefore does not prescribe an "ideal" level or types of e-participation necessary for planning or evaluation. Further, the matrix does not aid in prescribing specific CiRM functions nor provide a roadmap for organizational and business process transformation that other models indicate are necessary.

CiRM and Strategic Planning

A more technical approach to strategic CiRM situates e-participation within existing municipal strategic planning and implementation frameworks by combining CiRM with strategic planning and

implementation tools. Canadian municipalities have strategic plans, typically developed with extensive citizen consultation, that define the core vision and initiatives for the organization into the near future. Strategic planning in private and public organizations is a mature area with extensive literature (Feldman, 2008; Koteen, 1989; Lightbody, 1993; T. Plant, 2009; Porter, 1990; 1991; Sagini, 2007; Seasons, 1989) and will not be dealt with in detail here. Increasingly, municipalities are including citizen participation initiatives or "pillars" in their strategic plans, making them a top-level organizational priority on parity with citizen services, municipal infrastructure, and community development initiatives. This provides the rationale and impetus for action that does not depend solely on ROI prior to acknowledging e-participation as an organizational priority. Based on the strategic planning rationale for e-participation, each municipality may plan the implementation of CiRM e-participation functions based on the broad priorities identified in their strategic plan. For example, the strategic plan outline for City of Waterloo, Ontario, Canada (City of Waterloo, 2011) represented in Figure 11 exemplifies components of a typical strategic plan, from vision to outcomes reporting, and the inclusion of participation (under "Public engagement") in the strategic initiatives.

CiRM and Strategic Implementation

While strategic planning is widely practiced in municipalities, strategic implementation and outcomes measurement remain significant challenges (Girishankar & De Silva, 1998; T. E. Plant, 2010; Shipley, 1997). Further, strategic implementation is typically based on proven value delivery models that allow for planning of business processes that align with the strategic objectives in order to deliver customer value. The lack of commonly accepted value delivery models for e-participation results in a conceptual gap between planning and implementation stages of e-participation. Strategic e-participation initiatives often lack guided implementation, and existing e-participation implementations often forge ahead with little strategic connection, creating a strategy-implementation gap in e-participation.

Some commonly accepted 'meta-models', widely accepted as strategic implementation tools, are available to fill the strategy-implementation gap. Among these in particular are balanced scorecards (Kaplan & Norton, 1996) and strategy mapping (Kaplan & Norton, 2004) which are highly rational-mechanistic methods for addressing strategic planning gaps and reducing uncertainties in strategic implementation. These tools are commonly used in the private sector with variations adapted to the public sector. They can provide detailed guidance in the implementation of "CiRM as an organizational strategy" approach by aiding in the detailed planning of CiRM e-participation functions in a systematic and sequential format. An even more highly structured group of approaches is machine readable strategy planning and reporting documentation, which provides a common meta-structure for sharing, referencing and analysis of strategic planning. The StratML (Amber, 2007), for example, is structured to enable sharing and linking of strategic plans between related government organizations, stakeholders, and community services organizations. Some governments now mandate machine-structured planning and implementation strategy documents, for example the U.S. E-Government Act, H.R. 2458 (2002).

Figure 11. Representation of 2011-2014 City of Waterloo, Strategic Plan Outline

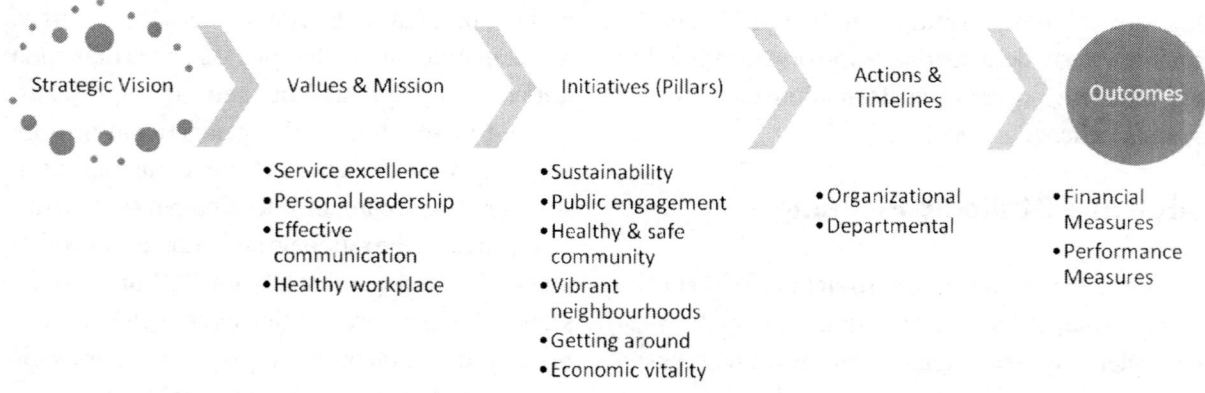

The components for strategic e-participation CiRM are established, including the widespread practice of strategic planning in local government, the availability of strategy implementation methods, the interdependence of CRM/CiRM with strategy, and the importance given to participation in strategic plans. Additional research is needed to develop common frameworks for strategic implementation as well as to demonstrate methods that link specific strategic initiatives with specific CiRM functions.

CiRM Strategic E-Participation Functions

The advantage of CiRM, to reiterate, lies in its relationship functions, and close reliance on organizational strategy. The "golden opportunity" in CiRM e-participation lies in the integration of strategy and CiRM relationship functions. Such integration may be approached from "strategic functions mapping" approach as shown in Table 1, which demonstrates how types of strategic e-participation initiatives may be mapped directly to CiRM functions. All of the CiRM functions identified are typically available "out-of-the-box", although CiRM's range of extensibility features typically allows the rapid adaptation of the CiRM system to meet specific requirements as necessary.

The strategic e-participation initiatives in Table 1 represent a range of sample citizen service perspectives from different approaches that are mapped to one or more CiRM relationship functions. For example, providing citizens with 'round the clock' (24-7) access to municipal services is citizen-centric by accommodating citizen preferences for service access, which is a common strategic goal in transactional e-government. The provision of CiRM, web-based transaction forms meets the needs for global accessibility, and integrates with other modes of citizen interaction. Issue-based participation is typical of ad-hoc democracy (Anttiroiko, 2004) mentioned earlier, represented also by the sporadic or episodic lev-

Table 1. Strategic e-participation CiRM functions map (Huebner, 2009)

Strategic e-participation initiatives	CiRM functions and characteristics
Accommodate citizen time preferences, "as & when" (24x7)	Flexible, multi-modal access and tracking; web-based, "global" accessibility
Target citizen interests	Tracking of citizen (individual, anonymous, or group) activities, history, full profile development; interest surveys
Issue-based participation	Plan "campaigns", relationships, groups, published views
Activity-based participation	Plan events, workflows, tasks
Decision-focused participation	Information broadcasting, workflows, timelines, documents & information management
Service-based engagement	Service responses, measurable, "hand-offs" with tracking
Analysis-based relationship	Use objectives measures and feedback – analysis & reports – to determine direction
Satisfaction-based relationship	Surveys to find out what people really think; track areas of positive feedback; grow capabilities, target service aspects that citizens value
Numerically-based representation	"Individual service quality accessible to all citizens"
Consistency	Workflows and templates to standardize practices and communications; knowledge-base articles with approval processes to standardize responses; complete history tracking to provide complete "view" of citizen
Automation	CiRM development platform with OOTB functionality
NAA ("not another application")	Already operational in most municipalities; integrates seamlessly with existing user data, functions, and municipal services technologies; does not add another layer of technical or administrative complexity

els of participation activity in Prieto-Martin's Matrix (2011). These are non-continuous participation activities centring on particular issues, such as a neighbourhood enhancement project or city-wide transportation initiative as examples. CiRM "campaign" functions are equivalent to initiatives with a series of promotional and/or communicative activities that are planned, tracked, communicated or broadcast, and reported in CiRM. These can range from emails or letters to phone calls, web postings, meetings, and more that may also be categorized into project milestone objectives within a campaign. Participants may be individuals – anonymous or identified – or groups as represented by discussion forums for example. Service-based engagement focuses on any municipal services, including utilities, transportation, protective services, or recreation, and targets some aspect of service level quality or citizen-value. Core CiRM functions facilitate the routing of citizen requests, automation of workflows, provisioning of documents and standard operating procedures, and "completion" and quality reporting. CiRM analytics provides reporting on specific measures or key performance indicators (KPIs) related to strategic objectives within a service area. Examples include the level of responsiveness (time-to-action, average durations of open issues), criticality to citizens (number and frequency of citizen calls; rate of repeat calls), location intensity through mapping functions (extensibility feature), and frequency of recurrences (of the same or similar issues). Satisfaction-based relationship initiatives focus on evaluating citizen-satisfaction either generally or regarding particular issues or events. Web-based or written survey forms (requiring transcription) may be integrated into CiRM forms with the results quickly tracked in reports or dashboard charts.

These examples represent types of strategic e-participation that map to specific CiRM functions that are typically OOTB CiRM functions and that may be rapidly modified to very specific requirements. This type of mapping highlights how existing and proposed public participation activities can be linked to strategic goals, or better, should arise *from* strategic goals, and further how these may be matched to specific CiRM functions.

The strategic CiRM functional mapping approach represents an alternative e-participation paradigm to both the top-down, large-scale e-participation projects that typify e-government goals and to the ad-hoc sporadic or episodic implementations that focus on discrete issues. This approach allows the rapid ad-hoc development of discrete e-participation functions as needed in the short term but are provisioned discretely within a single platform and therefore may be easily integrated strategically and systemically over time. The continual addition of discrete CiRM e-participation functions each in alignment with a strategic objective ensures that each CiRM e-participation expansion integrates into a cohesive whole. Secondly, all CiRM e-participation functions are provisioned in a single extensible software platform that shares an integrated data and security infrastructure across all functions, which as need dictates can be systemically linked through data linkages and workflows.

These strategic CiRM approaches to e-participation attempt to elevate the importance of citizen participation to the top-most levels of organizational decision-making. More than merely providing a strong democratic rationale for CiRM e-participation, these approaches aim to embed e-participation goals and methods into the continuous systemic processes of the organization, whether through complex evaluative frameworks or by integration into existing strategic methods. Additional research may help to reveal the full potential of CiRM e-participation amid changing technological and social trends. The next section will examine these trends and research directions related to CiRM e-participation.

RECENT TRENDS AND RESEARCH OPPORTUNITIES

The increasing importance of the roles of both CiRM and various forms of participation in local government highlights gaps in relevant research.

Most CRM research has focused on private sector corporations and the management of customer relationships in the cycle of value delivery and customer satisfaction. CiRM implementations currently account for a "small but healthy 6%" of the total CRM market, with a growth rate of 5.5% that exceeds private sector CRM. IDC survey results indicate that 62% of both central and local governments have CiRM implementations, an adoption rate that is similar to the private sector (Duffy, 2011). Further CiRM research is needed that looks beyond the ROI and standard business processes adapted from the private sector and toward the unique democratic participatory and citizen-centred needs of public sector.

Organizational Trends: Strategic Drivers

A key driver of CiRM research is the set of differences between private and public sector organizations, including absence of market incentives, high demands for accountability and transparency, and the multiple and complex goals of public organizations (Reddick, 2011). Further, the emergence of high-level e-participation priorities in strategic plans is a fundamental differentiator of public organizational strategy. CiRM research could help close the gap between the democratic imperative for e-participation and local government strategic planning, thus leading to a better understanding of both applicable theory and design and implementation frameworks (Huebner, 2009).

Strategic planning, as the tool that charts the path from present to future, will continue to grow in importance as global issues introduce greater complexity and challenges for local government. The growing pressure for meaningful public participation in government decision processes will require a systemic approach linking business process efficiencies with social networking opportunities for large-scale citizen participation. While CiRM may provide the "golden opportunity" to meet these challenges, local governments will be pressured to respond proactively with theoretically grounded and substantiated strategic CiRM frameworks that ensure citizens have meaningful influence on decision processes. Ad-hoc or poorly guided attempts at democratic e-participation may provide internal ROI but achieve little more than participatory tokenism, and may fail to meet citizen expectations within increasingly *social* technological trends.

Technological Trends: Functional Drivers

CRM/CiRM capabilities are continuing to evolve at a rapid pace, both to meet organizational demands for broader and deeper relationship management (xRM), and to more seamlessly incorporate emerging technological trends to strengthen strategic value delivery to customers and citizens. Trends such as social CRM, "cloud" computing, and big data analytics are rapidly taking centre stage in ICTs and will heighten citizen expectations, pressure local government, and accelerate the need for CiRM e-participation research.

Social CiRM E-Participation

Social CiRM is the inclusion of social networking capabilities in CiRM that significantly extends the capacity for direct interaction with and between citizens, as well as data collection and analysis leading to better understanding between citizens and municipalities.

Social networking technologies are already widely used in local government for numerous purposes, including: providing information targeted specifically for interested citizens; updating citizens on current events; enabling citizen deliberation on issues such as service quality, planning, finances, and development matters; and real-time mobile updates from and to citizens on road conditions or emergency responses. Figure 12 shows a "ladder" reminiscent of Arnstein's that groups participants by type of activity. The

Figure 12. The social technographics ® ladder (Band & Petouhoff, 2010)

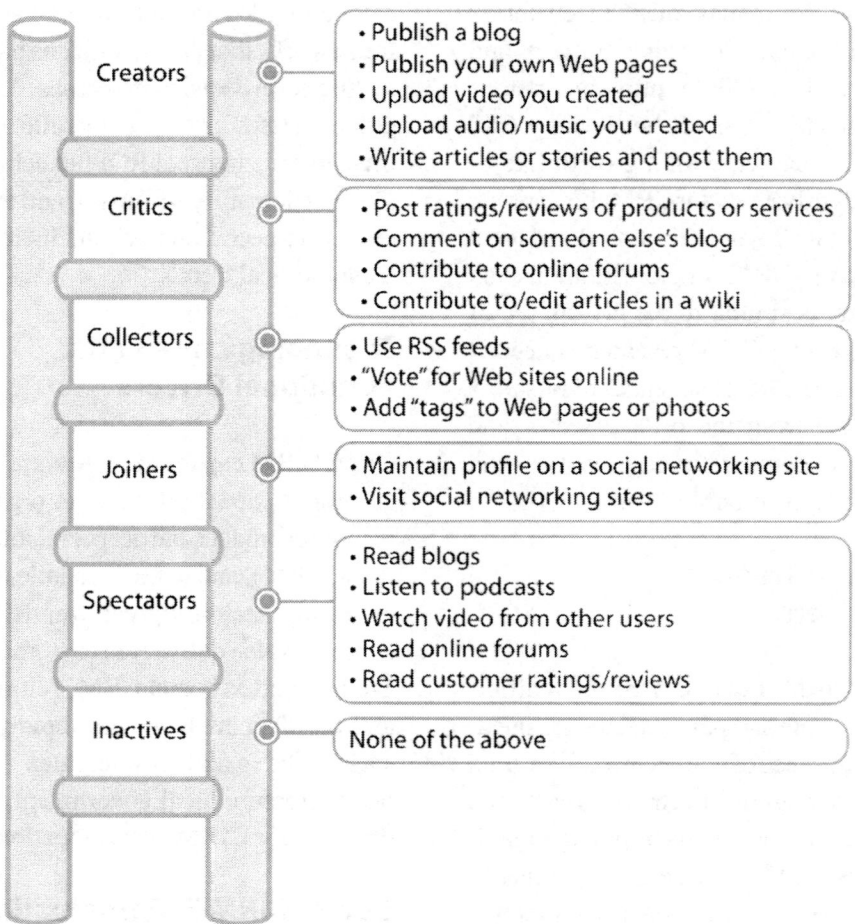

social technographics © ladder (Band & Petouhoff, 2010) categorizes types of social networking (SN) activities according to intensity of the social contribution. These SN activity types may be further associated with five social CRM objectives (listening, talking, energizing, supporting, and embracing), which are mapped directly to business functions and to CRM capabilities (Li & Bernoff, 2011). This approach, while not yet widely practiced, is one example of an integrated theoretical linkage between social network activities, business objectives, social CRM objectives, and CRM functions.

The obvious similarity between Arstein's ladder and the social technographics ® ladder should not lead to premature assumptions of valid ap-

plicability to citizen participation. Rather, the similarity may merely indicate a promising direction for CiRM e-participation research to identify, validate and refine theoretical models that attempt to correlate citizen social CiRM e-participation activities with degree of influence in local government decision-processes. Further refinement and validation through research may help to relate types of social network activities with potential for citizen influence and lead to more effective e-participation through social CiRM.

The incorporation of social CiRM with municipal e-participation potentially has several benefits. Social CiRM e-participation leads to more uniform management of social networking policy and implementation, compared to a variety of non-integrated social networking services used independently and non-uniformly by each government department. Building on the extensibility of CiRM, social CiRM e-participation would integrate with existing e-government and strategic CiRM e-participation for a more holistic view of citizen needs and desires. Social CiRM e-participation integrates with existing CiRM business processes thereby eliminating overlap and duplication of information systems and business processes, reducing development costs, and streamlining citizen services delivery and response.

Cloud Computing for CiRM E-Participation

Cloud computing is a recent trend to externalize IT infrastructure and associated hardware, software, knowledge and labour costs, and can be adopted by organizations of any size. Traditional on-premises, or "in-house," IT infrastructure may house many applications such as email, file storage, user authentication and security services, databases and mainline business applications. These all require expert support staff to ensure system reliability, data security and protection, and full operational recoverability in case of disaster, in addition to the basic hardware and software requirements. These infrastructure costs are significant and tend to limit the resources available for software and systems development. Cloud computing transfers some or all infrastructure responsibilities to an external vendor, potentially leading to large cost savings due to high scalability. All applications may be moved "to the cloud" to virtually eliminate any support staff requirements. Cloud services are accessed via Internet by the organization's users who ideally notice no difference in IT functionality.

Governments are increasingly adopting cloud computing, and CiRM for government is a leading cloud application. The U.S. government has adopted a "cloud first" policy in an attempt to reduce its $80 BB IT infrastructure costs. Salesforce, a major CRM vendor, has recently revealed a CiRM cloud service targeted exclusively for government applications (Corbin, 2012). Salesforce, like other cloud vendors, already meets the U.S. Federal Information Security Management Act (FISMA) standards, and boasts that 2/3 of federal agencies and governments in 80 percent of U.S. states already deploy Salesforce cloud services. Its government dedicated cloud service will particularly emphasise social and collaborative features, and is described as "a social revolution" in the public sector (Corbin, 2012).

CiRM cloud services, particularly those emphasizing social and collaborative features, may lead to significantly accelerated adoption of CiRM e-participation. Inherent benefits of cloud-based CiRM e-participation are reduced infrastructure costs, greater reliability and scalability of CiRM core functions, increased CiRM extensibility through rapid, agile development, and increased modularity of extended functions, leading to sharing and Internetworking of customized, extended CiRM functions. The multi-tenancy capabilities of mainline CiRM offerings allow extensibility functions to be shared across government organizations with similar systems, potentially leading to the rapid development and refinement of CiRM e-participation functions at the technical level. The costs savings associated with cloud computing for CiRM could aid in the rapid development of e-participation functions and sharing of functions among local governments.

Analytical CiRM and E-Participation

The field of data analytics aims to transform large data sets into meaningful information for organizational decision makers. "Data-directed decision-making" has always played a key role in organizations, but has significantly changed with the explosion of transactional and online data, effectively launching "the era of big data" (Economist, 2011). Analytics provides the technological infrastructure and tools for accessing vast amounts of data in non-traditional ways to gain insight to and make discoveries about the world, people, and organizations.

In the private sector, analytics are used to provide insight about customers. Social media and other sources provide organizations with vast data sets about customer needs and preferences, and dislikes, which may be harnessed to anticipate customer needs. Analytics integrated into CRM, or analytical CRM, can lead to critical customer insight and intimacy allowing, for example, the tailoring of products to meet specifically segmented customer demands thereby increasing customer satisfaction (Vizard, 2012). Most CRM offerings include some analytics functions, while extensibility features allow the addition of highly sophisticated analytical functions to CRM.

In the public sector, analytical CiRM holds equal potential to predict citizen needs and indicate citizen satisfaction, thereby aiding service delivery and planning functions to enhance citizen value. Two significant research areas are apparent in analytical CiRM. First, the government-citizen relationship is largely non-contractual, such that the relationship is not governed by a formal contract that determines the monetary exchange or timing of the relationship. While non-contractual relationship settings are more complex, potentially raising the value of analytical CiRM in helping to understand and predict citizen trends, this area remains largely unexplored (Wübben, 2008). Second, the transformation of large sets of social CiRM data into meaningful information suggests a new paradigm for e-participation, extending the scope of application of CiRM e-participation described earlier. Citizens' non-directed social networking activities may be transformed through analytics into a meaningful and systemic way of influencing municipal decision processes. Analytics functions and "big data" tools are rapidly gaining popularity and sophistication, while becoming much easier

to use for even very small organizations, possibly leading to a gateway for a new era of analytical social CiRM-based e-participation.

Societal Trends

Continually increasing rates of adoption of social networking technologies, the ubiquity of mobile computing devices, and the increasing growth of online data are among the leading technological trends that are driving societal changes and adaptations. Some of these societal trends are notable for their significant impact on e-participation.

One notable societal trend is the formation of citizen groups, such as formal Community Service Organizations (CSOs) and informal online interest groups. These are groups formed not merely around common interests but typically with organizational purpose and action exhibited through collaboration and mobilization. The dramatic global growth of such groups has been labelled the greatest movement on earth (Hawken, 2007). The growth of these groups may be a response to citizens' perceived lack of effective influence on government decision processes, or non-participation according to Arnstein's "ladder," or may be motivated by a desire to participate meaningfully in global affairs (Tapscott, 2008). Local governments that do not respond to increased citizen expectations for well-structured e-participation, as may be provisioned by CiRM, may find that citizens self-organize and collaborate against the perceived organizational barriers, and thereby ensure they effectively influence government decision processes.

Another trend is the growth of individual online activism and petitions. The growth of online petitions is showing significant influence in directing public decision processes globally, with increasing capabilities and sophistication (Prieto-Martin, 2012). While this form of participation lies beyond the traditional organizational scope of the organization, it lies within the extended social CiRM framework for e-participation, described above, as a significant influence of citizen engagement. Further, online activism in particular is noteworthy for its emergence as a significant form of global citizen influence that materialized with little or no involvement of e-participation researchers, who therefore do not have access to the very valuable information about e-participation that these systems are generating about patterns and reasons of use, users' demographics, typologies of action, success rates, etc. (Prieto-Martin, 2012).

The current organizational, technological and societal trends described carry important opportunities and challenges for e-participation research, many of which are currently being overlooked or understaffed. Growing citizen activism combined with continuing technological innovation may present significant opportunities for innovative and progressive local governments. Progressive communities that proactively empower citizens in quality of life factors, environmental challenges, and social and economic health will have a strategic advantage in attracting citizens and creating stronger, more livable communities (Lorinc, 2006).

CONCLUSION

This chapter has attempted to provide an overview of the field of CRM/CiRM and its application to e-participation. The overview of CRM highlighted its power and success in the private sector, and the growth of CiRM implementation globally, particularly in local governments. The definition of scope of CiRM is very broad given the complexity of local government, the extended range of CiRM functions, and the plethora of e-participation terms and concepts. A review of generic e-participation frameworks was provided to focus on the principle of citizen influence on government decision processes. A review of

different approaches to e-participation CiRM highlighted the capabilities, adoption, benefits, and challenges within each area. E-government CiRM is widely adopted, but has a strong transactional emphasis that focuses on efficiencies and ROI. Supplementing e-government CiRM with relational and collaborative approaches shows some promise but does not fundamentally change the transactional emphasis. Democratic e-participation CiRM models attempt to highlight the need for a new e-government paradigm and the "golden opportunity" for democratic governance transformation through e-participation. The theoretical concepts and related democratic e-participation CiRM capabilities show promise but lack significant research to establish a new baseline for e-participation practice. Strategic CiRM is a growing area that integrates e-participation goals into existing government strategic planning and implementation to counter the ROI and political barriers, and to build on the need for continuous systemic approaches to e-participation beyond the traditional discrete, periodic activities. Key challenges are proficiency with strategic planning and implementation generally, measurement of strategic outcomes, and the establishment of standard practices that map CiRM functions with strategic e-participation initiatives.

The demand for research into e-participation CiRM methods and practices will accelerate as proficiency with strategic methods improves, adoption rates and sophistication of CiRM continue to climb, and municipalities strive to meet the demands for meaningful citizen participation. In addition, research directions will be influenced by changing organizational, technological, and social trends that impact e-participation.

REFERENCES

Amber, O. (2007). *Strategy Markup Language (StratML)*. Retrieved from http://xml.gov/stratml/.

Anttiroiko, A.-V. (2004). Introduction to democratic e-governance. In Malkia, M., Anttiroiko, A.-V., & Savolainen, R. (Eds.), *eTransformation in governance: New directions in government and politics* (pp. 22–49). Hershey, PA: Idea Group Pub..

Arnstein, S. R. (1969). A ladder of citizen participation. *Journal of the American Institute of Planners, 35*(4), 216–224. doi:10.1080/01944366908977225.

Band, W., & Petouhoff, N. (2010). *Topic overview: Social CRM goes mainstream.* Cambridge, MA: Forrester Research.

Batista, L., & Kawalek, P. (2004). Translating customer-focused strategic issues into operational processes through CRM – A public sector approach. In R. Traunmüller (Ed.), Electronic Government (Vol. 3183, pp. 128-133). Springer Berlin / Heidelberg.

Buchanan, L. (2010). *A business framework and operating model for CRM and Social CRM.* Retrieved from http://www.capgemini.com/technology-blog/2010/04/a_business_framework_and_opera/.

Castells, M., & Cardoso, G. (2006). *Network society: From knowledge to policy.* Washington, DC: Center for Transatlantic Relations, Paul H. Nitze School of Advanced International Studies, Johns Hopkins University.

Chang, C.-C., & Chen, Y.-F. (2007). Designing a CRM-based e-government usability services framework: Integrating internal and external customers in public services. In Li, F. (Ed.), *Social implications and challenges of e-business* (pp. 57–77). Hershey, PA, US: Information Science Reference/IGI Global. doi:10.4018/978-1-59904-105-6.ch005.

Chu, P.-Y., Yeh, S.-C., & Chuang, M.-C. (2008). Reengineering municipality citizen electronic complaint system through citizen relationship management. *Electronic Government, 5*(3), 288–309. doi:10.1504/EG.2008.018876.

City of Waterloo. (2011). *My Future. My Say. My Waterloo.* Retrieved from www.MyFuture-Waterloo.ca.

Coglianese, G. (2007). Weak democracy, strong information: The role of information technology in the rulemaking process. In Mayer-Schonberger, V., & Lazer, D. (Eds.), *Governance and information technology: From electronic government to information government.* Cambridge, MA: MIT Press.

Corbin, K. (2012). Salesforce to launch government cloud. *CIO.* Retrieved from http://www.cio.com/article/704903/Salesforce_to_Launch_Government_Cloud

Denhardt, J. V., & Denhardt, R. B. (2003). *The new public service: Serving, not steering.* Armonk, NY: M.E. Sharpe.

Duffy, J. (2011). CRM Trends in Western Europe's Government Sector (Technology Selection, Trans.) IDC Government Insights (pp. 18): IDC.

Economist. (2011). Big data: Harnessing a game-changing asset. *Economist Intelligence Unit.*

Feldman, L. D. (2008). Strategic planning for municipalities: A users' guide [review]. *Canadian Public Administration-Administration Publique Du Canada, 51*(2), 375–376. doi:10.1111/j.1754-7121.2008.00028.x.

Girishankar, N., & De Silva, M. (1998). *Strategic management for government agencies: An institutional approach for developing and transitioning economies.* Washginton, DC: World Bank. doi:10.1596/0-8213-4234-7.

Gonzalez, D. P., & Gonzalez, P. S. (2012). CRM 2.0 and E-Government: Challenges for public administration and social effects. In Colomo-Palacios, R., Varajao, J., & Soto-Acosta, P. (Eds.), *Customer relationship management and the social and semantic web: Enabling cliens conexus*. Hershey, PA: Business Science Reference. doi:10.4018/978-1-4666-1740-7.ch062.

Greenberg, P. (2009). *Time to put a stake in the ground on social CRM*. Retrieved from http://the-56group.typepad.com/pgreenblog/2009/07/time-to-put-a-stake-in-the-ground-on-social-crm.html.

Hawken, P. (2007). *Blessed unrest: How the largest movement in the world came into being, and why no one saw it coming*. New York: Viking.

Hildreth, S. (2007). Government looks to CRM with citizen relationship management. *TechTarget, November 28*. Retrieved from http://searchcrm.techtarget.com/news/article/0,289142,sid11_gci1268193,00.html

Hood, C. (1995). The new public management in the 1980s - Variations on a theme. *Accounting, Organizations and Society*, *20*(2-3), 93–109. doi:10.1016/0361-3682(93)E0001-W.

Huebner, J. P. (2009). *CiRM for public participation: Directions for dialogue on strategic public participation technologies*. Municipal report.

IAP2. (2008). *IAP2 Spectrum of participation*. Retrieved from http://www.iap2.org/associations/4748/files/IAP2%20Spectrum_vertical.pdf

Kannabiran, G., Xavier, M. J., & Anantharaaj, A. (2004). Enabling e-governance through citizen relationship management-concept, model, and applications. *Journal of Service Research*, *4*(2), 223–240.

Kaplan, R. S., & Norton, D. P. (1996). *The balanced scorecard: Translating strategy into action*. Harvard Business School Press.

Kaplan, R. S., & Norton, D. P. (2004). *Strategy maps: Converting intangible assets into tangible outcomes*. Boston, MA: Harvard Business School Press.

King, S. F. (2007). Citizens as customer: Exploring the future of CRM in UK local government. *Government Information Quarterly*, *24*(1), 47–63. doi:10.1016/j.giq.2006.02.012.

Koteen, J. (1989). *Strategic management in public and nonprofit organizations: Thinking and acting strategically on public concerns*. New York: Praeger.

Li, C., & Bernoff, J. (2011). *Groundswell: Winning in a world transformed by social technologies* (2nd ed.). Boston: Harvard Business Press.

Lightbody, J. (1993). The strategic-planning component in the policy-making process for municipalities in Canada. *Policy Studies Journal: the Journal of the Policy Studies Organization*, *21*(1), 94–103. doi:10.1111/j.1541-0072.1993.tb01456.x.

Lorinc, J. (2006). *The new city: How the crisis in Canada's urban centres is reshaping the nation*. Toronto: Penguin Canada.

OECD. (2001). *Citzens as partners: OECD Handbook on information, consultation and public particiaption in policy-making*. Paris: OECD Publishing.

Pan, S.-L., Tan, C.-W., & Lim, E. T. K. (2006). Customer relationship management (CRM) in e-government: A relational perspective. *Decision Support Systems*, *42*(1), 237–250. doi:10.1016/j.dss.2004.12.001.

Plant, T. (2009). Strategic planning for municipalities: Ensuring progress and relevance. *Performance Improvement*, *48*(5), 26–35. doi:10.1002/pfi.20076.

Plant, T. E. (2010). *Roadmap to success: Implementing the strategic plan.* St. Thomas, Ont: Municipal World Inc.

Porter, M. E. (1990). *The competitive advantage of nations.* New York: Free Press.

Porter, M. E. (1991). *Canada at the crossroads: The reality of a new competitive environment.* Ottawa, ON: Government of Canada.

Prieto-Martin, P. (2009). *Evolution of the views on "What participation is."* Retrieved from http://pep-net.eu/blog/2009/09/09/images-for-reflection-i-evolution-of-the-views-on-%e2%80%9cwhat-participation-is%e2%80%9d/.

Prieto-Martin, P. (2011). *Presenting the "Matrix of Civic Implication."* Retrieved from http://pep-net.eu/blog/2011/11/14/presenting-the-matrix-of-civic-implication/

Prieto-Martin, P. (2012). *eParticipation is finally getting teeth...* Retrieved from http://pep-net.eu/blog/2012/05/22/eparticipation-is-finally-getting-teeth/

Reddick, C. G. (2010). Impact of citizen relationship management (CRM) on government: Evidence from U.S. local governments. *J. E-Gov., 33*(2), 88–99.

Reddick, C. G. (2011). Customer relationship management (CRM) technology and organizational change: Evidence for the bureaucratic and e-Government paradigms. *Government Information Quarterly, 28*(3), 346–353. doi:10.1016/j.giq.2010.08.005.

Sagini, M. M. (2007). *Strategic planning and management in public organizations: Behavior in organizations.* New York: University Press of America.

Schellong, A. (2008). *Citizen relationship management: A Study of CRM in government* (*Vol. 560*). Oxford: Peter Lang Publishing Group.

Seasons, M. L. (1989). *Strategic planning in local government: An application to local economic development.* University of Waterloo, Canada. Retrieved from http://proquest.umi.com/pqdweb?did=747302331&Fmt=7&clientId=16746&RQT=309&VName=PQD

Shipley, R. J. M. (1997). *Visioning in strategic planning: Theory, practice and evaluation.* University of Waterloo, Canada. Retrieved from http://proquest.umi.com/pqdweb?did=736727921&Fmt=7&clientId=16746&RQT=309&VName=PQD

Silverman, R. (2001). CRM dichotomies. *Intelligent Enterprise, 4*(8), 4.

Souder, D. (2001). CRM improves citizen service in Fairfax County. *Public Management, 83*(4), 14–21.

Tapscott, D. (2008). *Grown up digital how the net generation is changing your world.* New York: McGraw-Hill.

United Nations. (2010). *E-government survey 2010: Leveraging e-government at a time of financial and economic crisis.* 170. Retrieved from http://www2.unpan.org/egovkb/global_reports/10report.htm

United States. (2002). *E-Government Act of 2002, H.R. 2458, 107th Cong.* Retrieved from http://www.gpo.gov/fdsys/pkg/BILLS-107hr2458eh/pdf/BILLS-107hr2458eh.pdf

Vizard, M. (2012). *How analytics bring organizations closer to their customers.* King Fish Media.

West, D. M. (2005). *Digital government: Technology and public sector performance.* Princeton: Princeton University Press.

Wübben, M. (2008). *Analytical CRM: Developing and maintaining profitable customer relationships in non-contractual settings* (1st ed.). Wiesbaden: Gabler.

ADDITIONAL READING

Abbas, K., Hamed, M., & Navid, M. (2010). A process-oriented perspective on customer relationship management and organizational performance: An empirical investigation. *Industrial Marketing Management, 39*(7), 1170–1185. doi:10.1016/j. indmarman.2010.02.001.

Albrow, M., & Seckinelgin, H. (2010). Global Civil Society 2011: Globality and Absence of Justice. London School of Economics, Global Governance.

Andersen, K. N., Medaglia, R., Vatrapu, R., Henriksen, H. Z., & Gauld, R. (2011). The forgotten promise of e-government maturity: Assessing responsiveness in the digital public sector. *Government Information Quarterly, 28*(4), 439–445. doi:10.1016/j.giq.2010.12.006.

Anttiroiko, A.-V., & Malkia, M. (Eds.). (2007). *Encyclopedia of digital government.* Hershey, PA: Idea Group Reference.

Arceneaux, K., Gerber, A. S., & Green, D. P. (2010). A cautionary note on the use of matching to estimate causal effects: An empirical example comparing matching estimates to an experimental benchmark. *Sociological Methods & Research, 39*(2), 256–282. doi:10.1177/0049124110378098.

Band, W. (2009). *TechRadar™ For BP&A Professionals: The Extended CRM Application Ecosystem.* Cambridge, MA: Forrester Research.

Band, W., & Gliedman, C. (2006). *Topic overview: Customer relationship management.* Cambridge, MA: Forrester Research.

Bellamy, C., & Taylor, J. A. (1998). *Governing in the information age.* Buckingham; Bristol, PA: Open University Press.

BPIR. (2006). *Relationship management.* Retrieved Nov 28, 2008, from http://www.bpir.com/relationship-management-bpir.com/menu-id-72.html

Bucholtz, C. (2011). *CRM total cost of ownership: Fees, subscriptions, and hidden costs.* CRM Outsiders.

Carpini, M. X. D., Cook, F. L., & Jacobs, L. R. (2004). Public deliberation, discursive participation, and citizen engagement: A review of the empirical literature. *Annual Review of Political Science, 7*, 315–344. doi:10.1146/annurev.polisci.7.121003.091630.

CIVICUS. (2011). *State of Civil Society 2011.* Retrieved April 22, 2012, from https://www.civicus.org/en/news-and-resources/789-time-for-a-new-social-contract-civicus-report-suggests-a-generational-opportunity-in-the-face-of-multiple-crises.

Cochrane, K. (2009). *e-Government & Governance: Canada's experience.* Paper presented at the iGov Global Exchange, Singapore.

Cohn-Berman, B. J. (2006). Listening to the public: Adding the voices of the people to government performance measurement and reporting. New York: FCNY (Fund for the City of New York).

Cohn-Berman, B. J. (2008). Involving the public in measuring and reporting local government performance. *National Civic Review, 97*(1), 3–10. doi:10.1002/ncr.198.

Colomo-Palacios, R., Varajao, J., & Soto-Acosta, P. (2012). *Customer relationship management and the social and semantic web: Enabling cliens conexus.* Hershey, PA: Business Science Reference.

Conroy, M., & Evans-Cowley, J. (2006). E-participation in planning: An analysis of cities adopting on-line citizen participation tools. *Environment and Planning. C, Government & Policy, 24*, 371–384. doi:10.1068/c1k.

CRMguru.com. (2005). *What is CRM?* Davies, I. A., Ryals, L. J., & Holt, S. (2010). Relationship management: A sales role, or a state of mind? *Industrial Marketing Management, 39*(7), 1049–1062.

Drapeau, M. (2008). *Government 2.0: Ask what you can hack for your country*. Retrieved November 28, 2008, from http://mashable.com/2008/10/20/ask-what-you-can-hack-for-your-country/

Druke, H. (Ed.). (2005). *Local electronic government: A comparative study*. London, New York: Routledge.

Duffy, J. (2011). *CRM Trends in Western Europe's Government Sector. IDC Government Insights* (p. 18). IDC.

Flyvbjerg, B. (1998). *Rationality and power: Democracy in practice*. Chicago: University of Chicago Press.

Foucault, M. (1991). Politics and the study of discourse. In Burchell, G., Gordon, C., & Miller, P. (Eds.), *The Foucault effect: Studies in governmentality: With two lectures by and an interview with Michel Foucault*. London, Toronto: Harvester Wheatsheaf.

Freed, L. (2010). *E-government satisfaction index. American Customer Satisfaction Index*. Retrieved from http://www.foreseeresults.com/research-white-papers/thankyou-ACSI-e-gov-satisfaction-index-q1-2010.shtml

Fung, A., & Wright, E. O. (2003). *Deepening democracy: Institutional innovations in empowered participatory governance*. London, New York: Verso.

Ghose, R. (2005). The complexities of citizen participation through collaborative governance. *Space and Polity*, *9*(1), 61–75. doi:10.1080/13562570500078733.

Hansen, H., & Reinau, K. H. (2006). The citizens in e-Participation. Electronic Government. Proceedings Lecture Notes in Computer Science(4082), 70-82.

Hassan, H. S., Shehab, E., & Peppard, J. (2011). Recent advances in e-service in the public sector: State-of-the-art and future trends. *Business Process Management Journal*, *17*(3), 526–545. doi:10.1108/14637151111136405.

Industry Canada. (2010). *State of customer relationship management: The Canadian report 2010*. Ottawa: Industry Canada.

Machangana, K. (2000). *Democracy assessment tool*. PG Exchange.

Macintosh, A., & Whyte, A. (2006). *Evaluating how eparticipation changes local democracy*. Paper presented at the eGovernment Workshop '06, West London.

Malena, C. (2009). *From political won't to political will: Building support for participatory governance*. Sterling, VA: Kumarian Press.

Malkia, M., Anttiroiko, A.-V., & Savolainen, R. (Eds.). (2004). eTransformation in governance: New directions in government and politics. Hershey, PA: Idea Group Pub.

Mayer-Schonberger, V., & Lazer, D. (2007). *Governance and information technology: From electronic government to information government*. Cambridge, MA: MIT Press.

McKenzie, G., Bunio, C., Colclough, G., & Lanvin, B. (2008). *A platform for local government services: The development of the Microsoft citizen service platform*. Retrieved from https://partner.microsoft.com/download/Canada/40067623

Muehlfeit, J. (2006). *The connected government framework for local and regional government*. Retrieved from http://download.microsoft.com/download/7/f/0/7f08183b-c84f-491b-9b3f-c3d4b0521758/MS_LRG_CGF_Overview_new.pdf

Netchaeva, I. (2002). E-government and e-democracy. *The International Journal for Communication Studies, 64*, 467.

Obi, P. D. T. (Producer). (2010). *Evaluating e-government in Japan: Toward i-Japan Strategy 2015.* Mar 9, 2010.

OECD. (2003). *The e-government imperative: Main findings Policy Brief: OECD.* Washington, DC: Organization for Economic Co-operation and Development.

PTI. (2008). *Technology solutions Web & E-Government 2007-8.* Public Technology Institute.

Rui da, S., & Batista, L. (2007). Boosting government reputation through CRM. *International Journal of Public Sector Management, 20*(7), 588–560. doi:10.1108/09513550710823506.

Schellong, A. (2005). CRM in the public sector: Towards a conceptual research framework. Paper presented at the ACM International Conference Proceeding Series*; Vol. 89: Proceedings of the 2005 national conference on Digital government research*: Atlanta, Georgia; 15-18 May 2005, Inc. New York, NY.

Schellong, A. (2006). Citizen relationship management: Understanding, challenges and impact. Paper presented at the ACM International Conference Proceeding Series; *Vol. 151: Proceedings of the 2006 international conference on Digital government research.* San Diego, California; 21-24 May 2006.

Schellong, A. (2007). Crossing the boundary - Why putting the e in Government is the easy part. *PNG Working Papers, PNG07(002),* 26.

Schellong, A., & Langenberg, T. (2006). Effective citizen relationship management: Hurricane Wilma and Miami-Dade County 311. Paper presented at the ACM International Conference Proceeding Series*; Vol. 151: Proceedings of the 2006 international conference on Digital government research*: San Diego, California.

Schellong, A., & Langenberg, T. (2007). Managing citizen relationships in disasters: Hurricane Wilma, 311 and Miami-Dade County. Paper presented at the *Proceedings of the 40th Annual Hawaii International Conference on System Sciences, 3-6 Jan. 2007, Waikoloa, HI.*

Shipley, R. J. M. (2003). The sinister implications of language: The difference between a citizen and a customer. *Plan Canada, 43*(1), 28–30.

Silcock, R. (2001). What is E-government. *Parliamentary Affairs, 54*(1), 88–101. doi:10.1093/pa/54.1.88.

Silva, C. N. (2010). The e-planning paradigm - Theory, methods and tools: An overview. In Silva, C. N. (Ed.), *Handbook of research on e-planning: ICTs for urban development and monitoring.* Hershey, PA: Information Science Reference. doi:10.4018/978-1-61520-929-3.ch001.

Silva, C. N. (2010). *Handbook of research on e-planning: ICTs for urban development and monitoring.* Hershey, PA: Information Science Reference. doi:10.4018/978-1-61520-929-3.

Swift, R. S. (2001). *Accelerating customer relationships: Using CRM and relationship technologies.* Upper Saddle River, NJ: Prentice Hall PTR.

Tambouris, E., Liotas, N., Kaliviotis, D., & Tarabanis, K. (2007). A framework for scoping eParticipation. Paper presented at the ACM International Conference Proceeding Series; *Vol. 228: Proceedings of the 8th annual international conference on Digital government research: bridging disciplines & domains*; 20-23 May 2007, New York, NY.

The Economist. (2008). *EIU Democracy index: Off the march.* Economist Intelligence Unit (EIU).

United Nations. (2003). *UN global e-government survey 2003.* New York: United Nations, Department of Economic and Social Affairs.

United Nations. (2008). *Participatory governance and the millennium development goals (MDGs): Publication based on the expert group meeting on engaged governance: Citizen Participation in the Implementation of Development Goals including the Millennium Development Goals (MDGs).* New York: United Nations Department of Economic and Social Affairs.

United Nations. (2009). *What is good governance?* Retrieved from http://www.unescap.org/pdd/prs/ProjectActivities/Ongoing/gg/governance.asp

Wang, R., & Wowyang, J. (2010). *Social CRM: The new rules of relationship management.* Altimeter Group.

Williamson, I. P., & Chan, T. O. (1999). *Spatial data infrastructure management: Lessons from corporate GIS development.* Paper presented at the Proceedings of AURISA 99, Blue Mountains.

KEY TERMS AND DEFINITONS

CiRM: Citizen relationship management, that is, CRM adapted to government. See CRM.

Cloud Computing: Also cloud services or Software-as-a-service (SaaS), is the provision of some or all of an organization's computing infrastructure by an external provider, including email, database, and application servers and software. Users access the cloud services via the Internet with the potential of large cost savings due to highly scaled infrastructure.

CRM: Customer relationship management, a collection of management approaches and matching technologies that focuses an organization on defining, delivering, and enhancing customer value through effective, lasting customer relationships.

CRM Ecosystem: A view of CRM as a select bundle of technologies and management approaches that provide customer-focused applications tailored to an organization's strategic objectives.

CRM Extensibility: The adaptation of CRM to an increasingly broad range of organizational functions due to CRM's technological extensibility and integration with business processes.

CRM Technological Extensibility: The customization of CRM software components and the integration of CRM with 3rd party products or other existing organizational databases, in order to best match the technology functions of CRM to the organization's strategic and business requirements.

Customer/Citizen Centricity: In an organizational context, the view that customer or citizen preferences and needs are central to an organization's success and must guide the formation and execution of the organization's strategy. Customer/citizen centricity is achieved by organizing business and sales processes around customers'/citizens' perceptions of value, and continually measuring and adapting to outcomes.

Customer/Citizen "Value," Value Objective, or Value Proposition: In an organizational context, the central tenant of an organization's strategy which represents customers' or citizens' desires for which they will exchange money or time. The customer/citizen value may be expressed in the form of a written statement that explains to customers or citizens why they should buy or use a product or service.

E-participation: Citizen involvement or engagement in the affairs of government through electronic means, usually the Internet, via email, web pages, chat forums, and social media, and in some contexts also other ICTs such as telephone. Recent, broadly holistic usages in some contexts include traditional modes of participation, as well as analytical approaches to transactional data.

Social CRM: Tools and methods that link CRM functions to Internet social media services in order to monitor and interact with customers' postings, and follow trends on the Internet. The purpose of social CRM is to gain knowledge about customer preferences and their views of the organization and its products and services.

Strategy: In an organizational context, the collective decisions about how to best achieve the organization's central mandate, including what markets and customer desires to target, the best use of resources, achieving and sustaining success amongst competition, and satisfying stakeholder expectations.

xRM: The extension of CRM beyond customer relationships to managing all of an organization's business and relationship functions, including, as examples, suppliers, competitors, employees, stakeholders, assets, knowledge bases, market and industry conditions.

Chapter 14
Citizen Web Empowerment across Italian Cities:
A Benchmarking Approach

Elena Bellio
CERMES - Bocconi University, Italy

Luca Buccoliero
CERMES - Bocconi University, Italy

ABSTRACT

This chapter summarizes the results of a research project aimed to enlighten the issue of citizens' empowerment through municipalities' Web portals. The study was designed in order to: (a) provide some key-elements to define the content of an efficient Web strategy for municipalities, with specific focus on the issue of citizens empowerment, (b) benchmark the degree of citizen empowerment of public administrations' Websites across Italian Municipalities through the adoption of a revised version of Citizens Web Empowerment Index (CWEI) for the assessment of the official Web portals of the 104 Italian cities with over 60,000 inhabitants.

INTRODUCTION

A successful city today must offer investors security, infrastructure, and efficiency. It should recognize its natural assets, its environment and, of course, its citizens. Only through the use of ICT these goals can be reached and a city can become a "smart city." The goal is therefore the creation of a flexible administration fully able to address its territory's needs through a strong connection and interaction with its citizens.

Internet revolution worldwide has deeply affected relations on every context of exchange of goods and services. We may definitely agree that, since last decade, the major impacts on relations between 'suppliers' and 'customers' on markets consist in (Porter, 2001): low-cost availability (or availability even free of charge) to the customer of considerable amounts of information useful for purchasing decision-making, a consequent increase in the degree of transparency of markets, a significant enhancement of the empowerment of citizens/customers in many real life situations and in relations with various (public or private) suppliers.

DOI: 10.4018/978-1-4666-4169-3.ch014

Nowadays, citizens in developed countries are aware of this historic change that is taking place and they are demanding a wide scale adoption of Web channels, also within contexts such as public services (where, traditionally, exchanges of information between citizen and public administration are significantly 'asymmetric' and "formal" as for their nature).

Citizen empowerment, markedly tied in with the spread of the Internet and of technological resources as a part of our day-to-day lives (in which the Internet is now 'embedded'), represents one of the major challenges that public systems face today.

More broadly speaking, citizens are nowadays the bearers of new demand, which we may summarise as follows:

1. Access of citizens to official, customized and "on demand" information and services.
2. New opportunities for direct and informal relationships of citizens with politicians and civil servants.
3. Role as 'active player' within the network, also by sharing their own problems and complaints with others and seeking out information on the experiences of others with these same problems; Web 2.0 logic (O'Reilly, 2005) has considerably amplified this latter development.

Accordingly, public administrations' Web strategies changed their visions from a technology-centric framework to a content-centric approach and, more recently, to a citizen-centric one (King & Cotterill, 2007).

These changes bring the need to analyse the municipalities' Web strategies by answering the following question: what are the key elements of a successful municipality Web strategy in order to create "citizen empowerment"?

By focusing on the Italian context, our research tried to investigate to what extent the Italian municipalities did define a Web strategy aiming at the increase of citizens' empowerment.

The baseline research hypothesis from which the model was developed is that the information and services provided by Local Governments via the Web are capable of enhancing citizens' empowerment regarding two key dimensions: information held by citizens and control on the information with respect to his/her needs.

The first step was to develop a multidimensional indicator by using the various typologies of Web information which allow to evaluate the level of citizens' participation via the Web.

The second step was to carry out the analysis (period March-April 2012), using the indicator to assess the Websites of 104 Italian Local Governments with population over 60.000 inhabitants. The aim was to assess the current state of maturity of their Web strategy in relation to potentials for an increase in citizens' e-participation.

It is important to explain that analysis and rating of sites was based on two fundamental criteria:

- The immediacy with which information or services can be obtained while navigating the site, without impediments and time-consuming procedures coming into play when attempting to access information or services.
- Systematic (as opposed to sporadic) presence of the information or services required from the site.

CITIZEN WEB EMPOWERMENT IN WEB 2.0 AGE

Background

Over the last decade, increasing emphasis has been put on citizens and public involvement in the re-design of a citizens-focused system to help the creation of a good relationship between citizens, the administration and its politicians. So far, many administrations have introduced operational initiatives (European Commission, 2008); however, to assess the actual achievements is not easy because of the need to consider the entire network of relationships (between politicians, bureaucrats, and citizens) in order to determine if their mutual attitudes have changed.

The challenge for the Public Administration is to build over the Internet a community of participating and contributing users, rather than mere occasional visitors of Web pages.

While the objective is to really place the citizen at the center of the system, the participation of individuals in the cultural, social and political life of their own territory becomes one of the essential elements.

Government-Citizen Relationship (Citizen Trust-Satisfaction)

Citizen centric e-government should (or would) enjoy increased trust of citizens and should ensure accountability of government transactions (Gronlund, 2002). It should also provide enhanced collaboration among departments and stakeholders, thereby enabling fast decision making and consensus (Garson, 1999). Citizen centric e-government could also help avoid duplication and overhead through shared services and infrastructure, thereby helping achieve reduced service delivery cost while enhancing customer satisfaction. Business intelligence gathered via integrated service provision would also enable the government to track the effectiveness of initiatives and schemes and enhance decision making. Citizen centric e-government in its final form would provide improved transparency and consistent user interfaces and convenient channels for citizens to access e-government services (Kamarck & Nye, 2002).

Recent studies have investigated the issue whether e-government may significantly improve citizen satisfaction and trust for civil servants and political leaders. A U.S. national public opinion survey by the Council for Excellence in Govern-

ment concluded that e-government users and non-user had the same degree of trust in Government effectiveness (West, 2004). Drawing on the same data, Cohen (2006) found that the Internet may have little impact on satisfaction levels for contacts where a government official's response is required. Farrelly (2009) points out that some aspects of Area Forums may even become barriers to effective and true participation. Parent, Vandebeek, and Gemino (2005) suggested that e-government itself is not sufficient to induce trust: use of Internet in transactions with government had a positive impact only on citizens with pre-existing high levels of trust and was not able to improve neutral or negative opinions. Therefore, E-government as a mere technological solution is not a tool to improve citizen dissatisfaction in their contacts with public administrations.

Tolbert and Mossberger (2006) found a positive relationship between trust and use of a local government Website. Welch, Hinnant, and Moon (2005) found a correlation between e-government and citizens' trust in government. They showed that e-government users are in fact more likely to trust government as a result of their experiences online. However, they also found that citizens often recognize when there is a lack of interactivity in e-government services and that such perceptions correlate negatively with satisfaction. They concluded that the negative relation to interactivity might be a sign of the predominance of one-way e-government. A vision of the whole of the parts that make up the public system can also be found in Brown's (2005) and Bellio and Buccoliero's researches (Bellio, 2008; Bellio & Buccoliero, 2009; Buccoliero, 2009), which show that e-government positively affects the relationships between citizens, Public Administration and political representatives. These authors also underline that through innovative e-government activities, politicians fear a decline in the importance of their own role.

Citizen Empowerment/ Participation (Web 2.0)

To reach these objectives it is important to consider 'Web 2.0' even if it does not have a hard boundary, but rather, a gravitational core. Web 2.0 can be considered as normal developments in the Web visualized as a set of principles and practices that tie together a veritable solar system of sites that demonstrate some or all of those principles, at a varying distance from that core (Angermerier, 2005).

Tim O'Reilly has attempted to provide a clear definition: *Web 2.0 is the business revolution in the computer industry caused by the move to the Internet as a platform, and an attempt to understand the rules for success on that new platform. Chief among those rules is this: Build applications that harness network affects to get better the more people use them (O'Reilly, 2007).* The keywords are: a) Web as a platform; b) data controlled by users; c) participatory architecture.

It seems obvious that Web 2.0 is not a new version of the Web. It is therefore incorrect to see this change only from a technical point of view. The key points identified to explain what Web 2.0 refer to are: 1) User participation. The Web should be the medium that enables its users to participate and share information. The services offered are developed under the open-source paradigm, where users' interaction is a source of development and growth for the site; 2) Transformation of data ('remixability'). 'Remixability' stems from the desire of users and developers to be able to use and share information and then process them and change them by developing new concepts and ideas; 3) Design centered on the user's needs. Changes in Web design ought to be centered on the needs of the user, through the use of technology that can increase user-friendliness.

Public Administration has also begun to investigate if and how Web 2.0 could play a part in improving service delivery, democratic responsiveness and citizen participation (Fountain, 2001).

Citizens' Demand for Government Services

E-government is not just about enabling existing public services on the Internet, but rather is about a re-conceptualization of the services offered by Administrations, with citizens' expectations at the core. As public sector Web sites proliferate and expand in function, citizens who previously would visit or call government's offices, increasingly choose instead to contact Administrations online.

For most Administrations, the recent financial crisis was a wakeup call to become more transparent and efficient (Lapsley, 2010). In addition, there is also growing demand for Administrations to transform from a traditional agency and department centric model to a "Citizen-Centric" model (Abhichandani, 2008; Hewson, Jones, Hunter, & Meekings, 2004). On the other hand, it is becoming increasingly difficult to achieve these outcomes and meet the needs of the citizens with fragmented e-government initiatives. Such a situation should spur Administrations to take an integrated approach to improve the effectiveness of delivering services to their citizens (Nixon, Koutrakou, & Rawal, 2010).

It is not surprising to see Administrations making more and more use of this approach to deliver services. Recent trends include creating so called "citizen-centric Web sites" where content and services are organized around the anticipated needs of Web visitors. The adoption of this approach is widespread but there is no commonly agreed upon definition for "Web-based e-government services." McClure (2000) defined electronic government as "government's use of technology, particularly Web-based Internet applications, to enhance the access to and delivery of government information and service to citizens, business partners, employees, other agencies, and government entities." Golden et al. (Golden, 2003) argued that electronic government consists of using technology, particularly the Internet, as a means to deliver services to citizens, businesses and other entities with the purpose of providing convenient access to government information and services. In a report from the Momentum Research Group of Cunningham Communication (Shutter & de Graffenreid, 2000), "e-government" is defined as "online government services," which can be any interaction one might have with any government body or agency.

Most of the available work on Web-based service evaluation focuses on the private sector (Benbunan-Fich, 2001; Tec-Ed, 1999; Yu & Roh, 2002) and customer satisfaction (Zhang & Von Dran, 2000). Other studies that look at government agencies do not consider behavioral aspects that affect the interaction between the public and government agencies (Demchak, Friis, & La Porte, 2000; Eschenfelder, Beachboard, Mc-Clure, & Wyman, 1997; D. West, 2000). What we currently lack is adequate information about the demand for different types of Internet services. This is odd, since users will always have the last word on their value. Examining this issue from the citizen side is essential to find the right match between emerging technologies and citizen needs (Streib & Navarro, 2006).

Citizens typically ask for a specific response and use governmental Web sites as a new form of contact (Thomas & Streib, 2003). In general, citizens' activities on Administration Web sites are either looking for relevant information or completing some kind of "transaction," such as online registration, online application, database access, form downloading, online complaints process, etc.

One framework for integrating these activities is to think of these as a problem-solving process. A citizen always has a task to complete when he/she comes to an Administration Web site accessing e-services (Wilson, 1999). By definition, information reduces uncertainty; and information seeking is viewed as an action undertaken to resolve doubts and uncertainty (Wilson, 1999).

Performance of Administration Websites, in terms of facilitating citizen activities, is the core in the evaluation of Web-based e-government services.

The Internet is a powerful tool, and many authors have expressed the hope that it can transform the relationship between government and citizens (Gore, 1993; Raney, 2000; Verton, 2000). Discussions about the promise of E-government generally stress three things: easier access to information, more efficient service delivery, and improved communication.

The majority of the citizens who visit an e-government Web site have four main motives (Kutluoglu, 2010): learn about something (information services), apply for something (downloadable forms), pay for something (e-transactions), and complain about something.

The goal is to create a more dynamic government with far greater citizen involvement.

What is shown, however, is that the evolution of E-government is quite different from the expectations. Most of the existing Internet applications focus on providing information and not on developing new ways to communicate. Early research by Stowers (Stowers, 1999) found that the E-government had arrived in the form of an electronic rolodex, and Weare, Musso and Hale (1999) reached a similar conclusion. They found that local government Web sites in California served as electronic telephone books. Norris and Demeter (1999) found low levels of email and Intranet usage by cities, and concluded that there was a general reluctance to embrace these new technologies. Moon (2002) sought to compare and contrast E-government rhetoric with the reality. As an initial step, he identified five stages in the development of E-government: (1) information dissemination, (2) two way communication, (3) service and financial transaction, (4) vertical and horizontal integration, and (5) political participation. After an analysis of data collected by the

International City/County Management Association, he concluded that municipal governments were still at stage one or two. In his view, they had focused on providing information, and the two-way communication that did exist was highly structured. He described the state of e-government for many municipalities as "primitive."

Overall, there is currently a robust interest in the development of Internet applications among both Administrations and citizens, but there is a need to know far more about the demand for Internet services. There is a gap between supply and demand of eServices that calls for more understanding of the use of eServices and the characteristics of the eServices user (van Dijk, Pieterson, van Deuren, & Ebbers, 2007).

Administrations cannot continue to assume that citizens are eager to use anything that they manage to put online. The services provided must answer to citizens' need and allow them to be empowered.

Websites Content Analysis

One of the challenges in delivering e-government services is to design the Web sites to make it easier for citizens to find desired information. However, little work is found to evaluate e-government services in this sense.

In addition, current efforts on government Web site design mainly concentrate on Web site features that would enhance its usability, but few of them answers why some Web design is better than others to facilitate citizens' information seeking.

Only a few previous studies attempt to evaluate e-government provision of services through the Web. Those studies generally fall in two categories, those that borrow lessons and suggestions from the evaluation of Web based E-Commerce services for the private sector; and those that concentrate on government efforts of delivering Web-based services, but without reference to the attributes and behaviors of the citizens making use of the systems (Wang, Bretschneider, & Gant, 2005).

The work of Wood et al (Wood, 2003) is a typical study that tries to utilize lessons and experiences from evaluation of Web site performance in E-Commerce. The authors suggested use of a multidimensional Web evaluation strategy, which includes methods such as usability testing, user feedback, usage data, and Web and Internet performance, etc. that are common in the evaluation of commercial Web sites. Although this strategy could be useful, it was not adapted to the context of a government agency, which operates without competition or market considerations.

Researches by Eschenfelder et al. (1997), Demchak et al. (2000), and West (2000), represent a different approach to the evaluation of government Web sites. These works typically focused on characteristics of Web-site descriptively. In addition, although these research studies were done specifically on government applications, they did not consider characteristics of citizen or how such characteristics interact with Web characteristics to influence use. For example, the work of Eschenfelder et al. is an early attempt that explored Web site evaluation for the federal government. However, not only most of their evaluation criteria were borrowed from the private sector; these criteria also emphasized an organizational perspective of the government agency instead of one giving care to individual citizens. The work done by Demchak et al., especially their Website Attribute Evaluation System (WAES), while very systematic, is designed for evaluating the organizational openness of a government Web site solely from characteristics of the Web site itself.

Lastly, the evaluation approach used by West (2000) was developed only on the basis of characteristics found by observing Web sites (e.g. phone contact information, addresses, publications, databases, foreign language access, privacy policies, security policies, an index, disability access, services, email contact information, and search capabilities, etc). He assigned weights to these observable attributes of the Web site and used aggregate measures to evaluate e-government service delivery. This method, although is comprehensive in terms of studying Web site features, cannot reflect differences in service delivery mediated by citizens' individual variations.

Several papers have been published on the Web site quality evaluation methodology (Aladwani & Palvia, 2002; Bilsel, Büyüközkan, & Ruan, 2006; Cox & Dale, 2002; S.-E. Kim, Shaw, & Schneider, 2003; Van Iwaarden, Van der Wiele, Ball, & Millen, 2004; Van Iwaarden & Van der Wiele, 2002). Many of these publications offer frameworks containing groups of quality dimensions that are similar to the SERVQUAL (Service Quality) model proposed by Parasuraman (Parasuraman, Zeithaml, & Berry, 1988). Also some publications have been made to propose evaluation methodologies for specific Web sites such as e-government Web sites (Kaylor, Deshazo, & Eck, 2001; Smith, 2001) hotel Web sites (Chung & Law, 2003), online library Web sites (Chao, 2002; Novljan & Maja, 2004), health care Web sites (Bedell, Agrawal, & Petersen, 2004; Bilsel, et al., 2006; Buccoliero, Bellio, & Prenestini, 2010). Recently, Kuo (2004) has brought a new point of view by integrating quality function deployment aspects into the Web site quality assessment methodology.

In a number of publications, quantitative methods for Web site quality evaluation are used. Statistical methods are the most widely used assessment tool (Cox & Dale, 2002; Jeong, Oh, & Gregoire, 2003; Kim, et al., 2003; Kim & Stoel, 2004).

Through research carried out on the Websites of 35 large European cities, Torres, Pina and Acerete (2006) showed how most services offered on-line are not interactive, in terms of e-service, nor participatory in terms of e-democracy. The Internet is therefore considered a means for improving public organizations, to assure greater transparency, efficiency and customer-oriented

services (Wong & Welch, 2004); but according to the results obtained, it can be seen that it has not yet been fully exploited.

CITIZEN WEB EMPOWERMENT INDEX

Benchmarking of "Citizen Web Empowerment" in Italian Local Governments

In this study, we combine both service quality and Web site quality assessment Methodologies by adopting a revised version of an index named "Citizen Web Empowerment Index" (CWEI) (Buccoliero & Bellio, 2010), whose components are listed in Table 1.

Our study attempts to extend previous empirical research to understand and to measure the degree of citizen Web empowerment in Italian Local Governments' Portals by developing an index for benchmarking citizens' empowerment through Web portals (*Citizen Web Empowerment index*).

The Index

The index, termed Citizens Web Empowerment Index (CWEI), is given by the aggregation of 4 sub indicators, by means of which ratings could be given for the Websites of all the cities considered.

Each sub indicator is calculated on the basis of the presence of certain elements characterising the structure of the Website considered. During the stage of quantitative determination, the value 1 was ascribed to the presence of the service or of the information considered, value 0 to absence. The maximum theoretical value is 100 while each sub indicator has a different theoretical value:

CWEI = e-information + Web tools & strategies
    + e-consultation + e-decision making process

Table 1. CWEI components

CWEI	**E-information**	• Government structure; • Segmentation or life event; • Contact details; • Policies, procedures; • Budget; • Council minutes; • Newsletter and/or Web magazine.
	Web tools & strategies	• Blog and Forum; • Chat; • Social network presence; • Mobile services; • Web TV; • Open data strategy; • Web strategy evaluation EGRI (UN, 2008).
	E- consultation	• On-line polls, surveys; • On-line complaint; • Reputation systems; • Mayor's direct on-line relation with citizens.
	E-decision making process	• Evidences that the opinion of citizens is considered; • Evidence of others complaints.

The first element making up the overall index of citizen empowerment has been termed E-information. It relates to the presence on the Website of some general information regarding the city and its policies.

Assessment was conducted on a number of these characteristics: the presence of the city politicians' list, considering if there is only peoples' name and surname or a wider range of details to be able to contact the municipality officials. Clear presentation of the City Government organisational structure was also assessed since it is considered as an important way of orientation among the total amount of services provided. The on-line availability of policies, procedures and of legislation also helps. The last element considered in this sub indicator is the on-line presence of the budget and the way it is addressed.

The second component of the indicator consists in Web tools & strategies. It refers to the existence of social networking applications made for a high level of citizens' participation – empowerment. But not only the presence of the main instruments was assessed (e.g. forums, blogs, newsletters, Facebook, Twitter, Flicker, Youtube), also specific services provided through mobile were included. The presence of an "open data" and "GIS" strategy was also considered becomes they become an interesting element that makes the difference to citizens.

To construct sub-indicator E-consultation, various elements relative to the way of exchanging information with citizens were considered as reputation systems, online polls or e-surveys, online complaint. Also the direct relation between citizens and the Mayor was evaluated by searching for the presence of direct on-line involvement of citizens.

The fourth component of the indicator is termed E-decision making process. This sub-indicator assesses evidences that the municipality considers the opinion of citizens in decision making processes and gives evidence on what decisions have been taken starting from the consultation process (e.g. publication of on-line pools, e-surveys results and subsequent actions taken).

RESULTS

The evaluation task was randomly assigned to two coders (the authors). The intercoder reliability of each CWEI sub-indicator is tested on a 20-sites subset using the Krippendorff's alpha coefficient (Hayes & Krippendorff, 2007). Overall, use of CWEI rating system was found to be highly reliable as shown in Table 2.

From the analysis of the single Citizen Web Empowerment Index sub indicators we learn that, as yet, few Local Governments have developed Web-based strategies oriented toward information and user participation. It was observed that none of the local Websites surveyed had reached an overall CWEI rating approaching the maximum theoretical value of 100; in fact the average CWEI value is 37.30 over 100.

Considering the average CWEI values per sub-indicators (Table 3), it can be noticed that the higher level is given by the presence of E-information; this is not surprising since this is the only component of the index which stands in the middle between a traditional Website structure and a participatory one. On the contrary, the lowest level is registered by E-decision making process sub indicator.

Table 2. Intercoder reliability (Krippendorf's alpha values for the subindicators, yearly subset n=20)

CWEI Subindicator	α
CWEI E-information	0,9714
CWEI WEB Tools and strategies	0,9552
CWEI E-consultation	0,9509
CWEI E-decision making process	0,9009

Table 3. Average CWEI values by sub-indicators

	Average CWEI sub-indicators values
CWEI E-information	64.42/100
CWEI WEB Tools and strategies	29.29/100
CWEI E-consultation	22.12/100
CWEI E-decision making process	7.21/100

This testifies that the awareness of Local Governments on the potentials of the Web is only partial; in fact the instruments to make citizens participate in many cases exist (for example forms that allow to report problems very easily on-line, polls to evaluate certain initiatives), what is missing is something that makes citizens aware that they have been taken into account, something that gives evidence on how citizens' opinion was used in the decision making process, something that develops e-participation to empower citizens.

We notice that the maximum CWEI score obtained is 69.23 while the minimum is 7.69.

Table 4 shows the "top scores." Those Cities are very different one among the other; they are geographically distant and have different political and socio economic situations but what brings them so close is the spirit which gives birth to their portals.

The first element that has been noticed is that the top three Cities (Arezzo, Udine, Venice) represent Administrations where, before the on-line offer of services was designed, infrastructures were built. Most of those Cities have decided to

Table 4. Top CWEI scores

		CWEI value
1st	Arezzo, Udine, Venice	69.23/100
2nd	Forlì, Pisa	61.54/100
3rd	Cagliari, Modena, Turin	59.62/100

invest in optical fibers and wireless Web infrastructure, which provide easy and cheap (or even free of charge) access to the Web. The idea is to overcome the digital divide, by promoting the right to "digital citizenship." Setting the net is like creating long and safe binaries while providing tools for e-participation and citizens' empowerment is a way of putting wagons on it.

These 8 cities represent the Web portals with the best "citizen empowerment" approach in the sample. A number of other interesting and significant best practices for each sub-indicator were collected in the analysis even if just in very few cases the maximum value per sub-indicator was obtained as shown in Table 5.

Most of the Italian Cities seem not aware of the possibility of a concrete change which by now, has already been adopted in a few specific realities of the Country.

What can be noticed is that E-information maximum value is reached by the highest number of Cities in comparison with the other sub-indicators. This was possible since the presence of most of the elements considered is becoming mandatory in Italy from a legislative point of view. About E-consultation it is still very difficult to find a deep involvement of citizens in public life by the introduction of on-line polls, surveys, complaint procedures, reputation systems which are ways to reach a direct relation with citizens.

Also the E-decision making process maximum level is hard to be reached since there are many initiatives which testify the purpose to involve

Table 5. Number of cities that have obtained the maximum value per sub-indicator

	Number of Cities that have obtained the maximum value	%
E-information	8/104	7.69%
WEB Tools and strategies	0/104	0
E-consultation	1/104	0.96%
E-decision making process	3/104	2.88%

citizens in decisions but only very few cases show they've really been taken into account. A fundamental characteristic of the Web is that it is able to amplify the voices of those who previously could not be heard. Once heard, they expect to be listened to and this places an added burden on Administrations.

Not even one City obtained the maximum score in the second sub-indicator listed in Table 5 because there is still a very limited use of Web TV, and mobiles which could allow a long and interactive relation between the Administration and its citizens, plus open data strategies are still missing around Italy except in 2 Cities where the first projects have been introduced in the last twelve months.

With regard to the *E-information* component site structure was examined, including rating of sites enabling the life events model for navigation (i.e. navigation starting out from events which may characterise the life of citizens, such as "studying," "giving birth" "using public transports" or "life as a senior citizen"), or which provide clear segmentation of citizens by cluster (the elderly, women, children, foreigners etc.). Menus constructed according to these approaches may aid consultation by citizens presenting specific problems, who thus receive immediate answers targeting their specific needs.

The research reveal that around 1/3 of the sample has enabled a system for Web site use of information based on the two approaches, 1/3 uses visitor-type clusters as a means of orienting information users and 1/3 has chosen the life event logic.

The research also reveals that in most cases a list of politicians and of their personal information is offered. The presence of this information together with the introduction of the budget on-line is due to the Italian legislation requirements. While normally administrations just present a few final financial data some cities are also providing on line "program and budgeting" documents which allow citizens to understand the middle-long term strategies adopted.

Analysis of *WEB Tools and strategies* reveals that there is an increase in the use of some social networks by Local Governments but still the percentage is low (29.81% among the sample). The most used social networks are Facebook, You Tube and Twitter as shown in Tables 6 and 7, but also my Space, Flickr, G+ and Skype were considered.

It was registered that among the Cities which have an official presence on social networks there is a higher number using 3 social networks (11 cities which represent 10,58% among the total number of Cities and 35,48% among Cities using Social Networks) while none joined all the 7 that were assessed (Tables 8 and 9).

Only 10 Local Governments over 104 offer mobile services. The most significant examples are given by services for tourists which are often combined with QR codes which allow reading cultural and historical information.

The City which has registered a higher score in WEB Tools and Strategies sub-indicator is Turin where not only mobiles services are offered, but there is an intense use of blog and forums, of social networks and of videos and Web TV channels plus there are some public GIS applications which not only allow to interactively consult different cartographies but also help to personalize and share maps of the City.

Table 8. Number of social networks (SN) used by the cities and percentage among the sample

N Social Networks	N Cities	% (among total N Cities = 104)
1	8	7,69
2	6	5,77
3	11	10,58
4	5	4,81
5	1	0,96
6	-	-
7	-	-

Table 9. Number of social networks (SN) used by the cities and percentage among the ones using them

N Social Networks	N Cities	% (among Cities using SN = 31)
1	8	25.81
2	6	19.35
3	11	35.48
4	5	16.13
5	1	3.23
6	-	-
7	-	-

Table 6. Number of cities using each social network (SN) and percentage among the sample

	Facebook	Twitter	You Tube	My Space	Flickr	G+	Skype
N Cities	26	16	21	4	5	5	1
% (among total N Cities = 104)	25,00	15,38	20,19	3,85	4,81	4,81	0,96

Table 7. Number of cities using each social network (SN) and percentage among the ones using them

	Facebook	Twitter	You Tube	My Space	Flickr	G+	Skype
N Cities	26	16	21	4	5	5	1
% (among Cities using SN = 31)	83,87	51,61	67,74	12,90	16,13	16,13	3,23

The use of open data was also explored but findings show that only Florence has introduced this strategy, Rimini is starting to consider it, while none other City has even explored its applicability.

Turning to *E-consultation*, only a few portals register the presence of links which testify the direct involvement of the Mayor in on-line relations with citizens. It is hard to find tools for a true interaction between citizens and politicians.

In 60 cases, the Mayor's presence on Facebook or Twitter is shown (Table 10). It is interesting to see that 38 of the 39 Mayors which use Twitter are also using Facebook.

Being on social networks becomes a way of moving citizens from the official Web site of the City to a specific page directly linked to the politician where, through a correct use, a high level of interaction can be granted.

A wider presence of Internet pools, surveys, complaint platforms, and reputation systems is registered, even if in many cases they are just forms to fill in and send online which means that they do not completely represent the participatory way of structuring a service.

A good example regarding this sub-indicator is given by Rimini's Website which has obtained the maximum value since if offers reputation systems not only to evaluate the general agreement on the Website but also on specific areas like for example the police service plus there are online direct ways to put citizens in contact with the Administration and also ways to report the needs of a specific area, such as maintenance, repairs and removal of litter in certain districts and in public parks.

Table 10. Mayor's presence on Facebook and Twitter

	Facebook	Twitter	Both
N Mayors	59	39	38
%	56.73	37.50	36.54

In terms of *e-decision making process* there is little evidence on how decisions are taken. Even if a presence of tools which allow a participatory atmosphere is revealed, rarely the results are shown. A very efficient system has been revealed in Venice's Website where different project are running. Each of them is designed not only to allow citizens to report something but also to see what other have done or are doing and to interact with them. Furthermore people can also see what the Administration does or says, in this way it is possible to perfectly know how much people's opinion is considered in the decision making process.

Also Udine offers a range of services built with the same logic which characterizes the City of Venice. In fact, when inefficiency is reported, people can see the process which shows how they are taken into account by the Local Government. There is also an area of the Web site specifically built to collect innovative ideas coming from citizens.

In addition, correlations analysis (Pearson correlation coefficient) was evaluated using statistical package SPSS to determine if there is a link between the population of the cities and the scores of the CWEI. Results show that there is not significant correlation between the number of inhabitants and the level of the CWEI (Table 11). This testifies that on-line investments in citizen's empowerment don't depend on the dimension of the City.

FUTURE RESEARCH DIRECTIONS

CWEI index could play a role in order to understand, benchmark and monitor, also at international level, in future studies, the Web strategies of Public Administrations and it could therefore support a citizen-centred Web design of information and services. A widespread adoption of this tool could

Table 11. Correlation between population and CWEI

		POPULATION	CWEI_TOT
POPULATION	Person Correlation	1	,086
N	Significance		,388
	N	104	104
CWEI_TOT	Person Correlation	,086	1
	Significance	,388	
	N	104	104

contribute to a faster development of authoritative Web solutions aimed at citizen's empowerment, supporting both the citizen and the Administration in developing participation, transparency, and trust, which are essential to develop quality and value for money.

Benchmarking means improvement can be measured. CWEI index measures the Administration performance from the citizen's perspective rather than from the Municipality point of view.

Further research could start from the above values of CWEI and from the analysis of citizens' behaviours and attitudes when visiting the Website according with its different features. For example, the willingness to participate in the decisions regarding the City life and the level of trust in the Administration itself could be assessed.

CONCLUSION

The results of our analysis confirm the findings of other studies which show that the Web strategies of Public Administrations are still little oriented towards a provision of services designed to empower citizens.

A number of preliminary conclusions may be reached based on the CWEI:

1. The very low CWEI scores obtained by the Cities of the sample (average CWEI value is 37.30 over 100) testifies that there is still a substantial immaturity of Web strategies, which appear modulated on structures and organizational responsibilities rather than on the needs and on the demand of citizens' empowerment;

2. The assessment of the different services offered shows a lack of strategy to assume a role of active partners for citizens through the Web portals by strengthening their level of empowerment and participation. In fact very often there is a wide range of initiatives which could easily empower the citizen but they are built from the Administration perspective without being interactive and participatory. The result becomes added value only to the organization and not to citizens which appear as mere receivers of services instead of active players;

3. By creating an index made up of four sub-indicators, one of which focused on Web 2.0 tools, it was possible to understand that there is still a low penetration of this kind of tools and strategies (average sub-indicator "Web tools and strategies" value is 29.29 over 100). Tim O'Reilly (O'Reilly, 2007) believes Web 2.0 is embodied by applications that deliver richer user experiences and harness collective intelligence (two things most government Web sites do not do well). This moves an emphasis from the individual for whom information equates to power to a more collaborative, collective "group cooperation culture" that is hard to be understood and accepted by most public employees.

4. Also a weak diffusion of mobile applications was registered. This finding moves in the same direction of Web 2.0 tools adoption since also mobiles, especially smartphones,

if properly used, can turn citizens into active players in the relationship with the Administration, involving them in service co-creation, evaluation and use.

New technology and the changing expectations of citizens have introduced a new set of variables which should improve Administrations, assuring greater transparency, efficiency, and customer-oriented services but, according to the results obtained, it can be seen that it has not yet been fully exploited. Although there is theoretical and practical recognition that citizens must be more involved in public decisions, many administrators are, at best, ambivalent about public involvement or, at worst, they find it problematic. Administrators need help in addressing problems but find that the help they seek from citizens often creates new sets of problems. As a result, although many public administrators view close relationships with citizens as both necessary and desirable, most of them do not actively seek public involvement. If they do seek it, they do not use public input in making administrative decisions.

Making a move forward to better citizen engagement and governance is difficult. Historically, information technology has been seen as a controllable asset, but Web 2.0 and the associated ability to innovate on the fly threatens to take control away.

Overcoming the above mentioned highly significant limits may turn out to be a prerequisite for concrete development of the provision of services for empowered citizens (a concept for innovation, which Administrative systems are beginning to discuss).

The first thing to do here is to ensure that all planning authorities take the decision to incorporate Web strategies based on citizens needs as a new element into planning and decide upon the actions which should be undertaken to promote the achievement of citizens empowerment. For too

long now, this perspective has been missing but this is the sort of trend governments can't afford to overlook since they must create a dynamic, flexible and courageous organization that is able to meet the changing needs and expectations of local communities.

REFERENCES

Abhichandani, T. (2008). *Evaluation of e-government initiatives for citizen-centric delivery: Analysis of online public transit information services.* Berlin: VDM Verlag Publishing.

Aladwani, A., & Palvia, P. (2002). Developing and validating an instrument for measuring userperceived web quality. *Information & Management*, (39): 467–476. doi:10.1016/S0378-7206(01)00113-6.

Angermerier, M. (2005). *The huge cloud lens bubble map web 2.0.* Retrieved from http://kosmar.de/archives/2005/11/11/the-huge-cloud-lens-bubble-map-Web2.0

Bedell, S., Agrawal, A., & Petersen, L. (2004). A systematic critique of diabetes on the world wide web for patients and their physicians. *International Journal of Medical Informatics*, (73): 687–694. doi:10.1016/j.ijmedinf.2004.04.011 PMID:15325325.

Bellio, E. (2008). *Technologie web 2.0 nel rapporto pubblica amministrazione-cittadini: Un modello di valutazione.* Milan, Italy: Università Commerciale Luigi Bocconi.

Bellio, E., & Buccoliero, L. (2009). E-government and web 2.0 applications: A multi-stakeholder evaluation. In H. Jochen Scholl, M. Janssen, R. Traunmüller, & M. A. Wimmer (Eds.), *General Development Issues and Projects of EGOV 09 8th International Conference.* Linz, Austria: Trauner.

Benbunan-Fich, R. (2001). Using protocol analysis to evaluate the usability of a commercial web site. *Information & Management, 39*(2), 151–163. doi:10.1016/S0378-7206(01)00085-4.

Bilsel, R. U., Büyüközkan, G., & Ruan, D. (2006). A fuzzy preference-ranking model for a quality evaluation of hospital web sites. *International Journal of Intelligent Systems, 21*, 1181–1197. doi:10.1002/int.20177.

Brown. (2005). Electronic government and public administration. *International Review of Administrative Sciences, 71*, 241-254.

Buccoliero, L. (2009). Il governo elettronico: Modelli, strategie di innovazione ed elementi di valore per una pubblica amministrazione digitale. Milano, Italy: Tecniche Nuove.

Buccoliero, L., & Bellio, E. (2010). Citizens web empowerment in European municipalities. *Journal of E-Governance, 33*(4), 11.

Buccoliero, L., Bellio, E., & Prenestini, A. (2010). Patient web empowerment index (PWEI): A tool for the assessment of healthcare providers' web strategies: A first benchmark of Italian NHS hospitals. In C. Safran, S. Reti, & H. Marin (Eds.), *MEDINFO 2010 Proceedings of the 13th World Congress on Medical Informatics*. Amsterdam: IOS Press.

Chao, H. (2002). Assessing the quality of academic libraries on the web: The development and testing of criteria. *Library & Information Science Research*, (24): 169–194. doi:10.1016/S0740-8188(02)00111-1.

Chung, T., & Law, R. (2003). Developing a performance indicator for hotel websites. *International Journal of Hospitality Management*, (22): 119–125. doi:10.1016/S0278-4319(02)00076-2.

Cohen, J. E. (2006). Citizen satisfaction with contacting government on the internet. *Information Polity: The International Journal of Government & Democracy in the Information Age, 11*(1), 15.

Cox, J., & Dale, B. (2002). Key quality factors in web site design and use: An examination. *International Journal of Quality & Reliability Management*, (19): 862–888. doi:10.1108/02656710210434784.

Demchak, C., Friis, C., & La Porte, T. M. (2000). *Webbing governance: National differences in constructing the public face*. New York: Marcel Dekker Publishers.

Eschenfelder, K. R., Beachboard, J. C., McClure, C. R., & Wyman, S. K. (1997). Assessing U.S. federal government websites. *Government Information Quarterly, 14*(2), 16. doi:10.1016/S0740-624X(97)90018-6.

European Commission. (2008). *ICT for government and public services*. Retrieved from http://ec.europa.eu/information

Farrelly, M. (2009). Citizen participation and neighbourhood governance: Analysing democratic practice. *Local Government Studies, 35*(4), 13. doi:10.1080/03003930902992675.

Fountain, J. E. (Ed.). (2001). *Building the virtual state: Information technology and institutional change*. Washington, DC: Brookings Institution Press.

Garson, D. G. (1999). *Information technology and computer applications in public administration: Issues and trends*. New York: Idea Group Publishing. doi:10.4018/978-1-87828-952-0.

Golden, W., et al. (2003). *The role of process evolution in achieving citizen centered e-government*. Paper presented at the Ninth Americas Conference on Information Systems. New York, NY.

Gore, A. (1993). *From red tape to results: Creating a government that works better and costs less.* New York: Times Books.

Gronlund, A. (2002). *Electronic government: Design, applications and management.* Hershey, PA: Idea Group Publishing.

Hayes, A. F., & Krippendorff, K. (2007). Answering the call for a standard reliability measure for coding data. *Communication Methods and Measures, 1,* 77–89. doi:10.1080/19312450709336664.

Hewson, W., Jones, R., Hunter, D., & Meekings, A. (2004). *Towards a citizen-centric authority: Beyond CRM, e-government and the modernising agenda in the UK public sector.* Academic Press.

Jeong, M., Oh, H., & Gregoire, M. (2003). Conceptualizing web site quality and its consequences in the lodging industry. *International Journal of Hospitality Management,* (22): 161–175. doi:10.1016/S0278-4319(03)00016-1.

Kamarck, E. C., & Nye, J. S. (2002). *Governance. com: Democracy in the information age, visions of governance in the 21st century.* Washington, DC: Brookings Institution Press.

Kaylor, C., Deshazo, R., & Eck, D. (2001). Gauging e-government: A report on implementing services among American cities. *Government Information Quarterly,* (18): 293–307. doi:10.1016/S0740-624X(01)00089-2.

Kim, S., & Stoel, L. (2004). Dimensional hierarchy of retail website quality. *Information & Management,* (41): 619–633. doi:10.1016/j.im.2003.07.002.

Kim, S.-E., Shaw, T., & Schneider, H. (2003). Web site design benchmarking within industry groups. *Internet Research,* (13): 17–26. doi:10.1108/10662240310458341.

King, S., & Cotterill, S. (2007). Transformational government? The role of information technology in delivering citizen-centric local public services. *Local Government Studies, 33*(3), 21. doi:10.1080/03003930701289430.

Kuo, Y.-F. (2004). Integrating Kano's model into web-community service quality. *Total Quality Management,* (15): 925–939.

Kutluoglu, U. (2010). *What citizens want from e-government?* Retrieved from http://www.epractice.eu/en/blog/315055

Lapsley, I. (2010). *New public management in the global financial crisis-dead, alive, or born again?* London: University of Edinburgh Business School.

McClure, D. L. (2000). *Electronic government: Federal initiatives are evolving rapidly but they face significant challenges.* Academic Press.

Moon, M. J. (2002). The evolution of e-government among municipalities: Rhetoric or reality? *Public Administration Review, 62*(4), 424–433. doi:10.1111/0033-3352.00196.

Nixon, P. G., Koutrakou, V. N., & Rawal, R. (2010). *Understanding e-government in Europe: Issues and challenges.* London: Routledge.

Norris, D., & Demeter, L. (1999). Information technology and city government. In *The Municipal Yearbook.* Washington, DC: International City County Management Association.

Novljan, S., & Maja, Z. (2004). Web pages of Slovenian public libraries: Evaluation and guidelines. *The Journal of Documentation,* (60): 62–76. doi:10.1108/00220410410516653.

O'Reilly, T. (2005). *O'Reilly network: What is web 2.0.* Retrieved from http://www.oreillynet.com/lpt/a/6228

O'Reilly, T. (2007). What is web 2.0: Design patterns and business models for the next generation of software. *International Journal of Digital Economics*, *65*(1), 20.

Parasuraman, A., Zeithaml, V., & Berry, L. (1988). SERVQUAL: A multi-item scale for measuring consumer perceptions of service quality. *Journal of Retailing*, (64): 2–40.

Parent, M., Vandebeek, C. A., & Gemino, A. C. (2005). Building citizen trust through e-government. *Government Information Quarterly*, *22*, 17. doi:10.1016/j.giq.2005.10.001.

Porter, M. E. (2001). Strategy and the internet. *Harvard Business Review*, *79*(3), 63. PMID:11246925.

Raney, R. (2000, May 11). Study finds Internet of social benefit to users. *New York Times*.

Shutter, J., & de Graffenreid, E. (2000). *Benchmarking the egovernment revolution: Year 2000 report on citizen and business demand*. Academic Press.

Smith, A. (2001). Applying evaluation criteria to New Zealand government websites. *International Journal of Information Management*, *21*, 137–149. doi:10.1016/S0268-4012(01)00006-8.

Stowers, G. (1999). Becoming cyberactive: State and local governments on the world wide web. *Government Information Quarterly*, *16*(2), 111–127. doi:10.1016/S0740-624X(99)80003-3.

Streib, G., & Navarro, I. (2006). Citizen demand for interactive e-government: The case of Georgia consumer services. *American Review of Public Administration*, *36*(3), 12. doi:10.1177/0275074005283371.

Tec-Ed, I. (1999). *White paper: Assessing web site usability from server log files*. Ann Arbor, MI: Michigan.

Thomas, J. C., & Streib, G. (2003). The new face of government: Citizen-initiated contact in the era of e-government. *Journal of Public Administration Reasearch and Theory*.

Tolbert, C. J., & Mossberger, K. (2006). The effects of e-government on trust and confidence in government. *Public Administration Review*, (3): 16.

Torres, L., Pina, V., & Acerete, B. (2006). E-government developments in European union cities: Reshaping government's relationship with citizens, governance. *An International Journal of Policy. Administration and Institutions*, *19*, 277–302.

UN. (2008). *United Nations e-government survey 2008: From e-government to connected governance*. New York: Department of Economic and Social Affairs Division for Public Administration and Development Management.

van Dijk, J., Pieterson, W., van Deuren, A., & Ebbers, W. (2007). *E-services for citizens: The Dutch usage case*. Paper presented at the EGOV 2007. Berlin, Germany.

Van Iwaarden, J., Van der Wiele, T., Ball, L., & Millen, R. (2004). Perceptions about the quality of web sites: A survey amongst students at Northeastern University and Erasmus University. *Information & Management*, (41): 947–959. doi:10.1016/j.im.2003.10.002.

Van Iwaarden, J., & Van derWiele, T. (2002). *A study on the applicability of SERVQUAL dimensions for web sites*. Academic Press.

Verton, D. (2000, August 28). Electronic government. *Computerworld*.

Wang, L., Bretschneider, S., & Gant, J. (2005). *Evaluating web-based e-government services with a citizen-centric approach*. Paper presented at the 38th Hawaii International Conference on System Sciences. Hawaii, HI.

Weare, C., Musso, J., & Hale, M. (1999). Electronic democracy and the diffusion of municipal web pages in California. *Administration & Society, 31*.

Welch, E. W., Hinnant, C. C., & Moon, M. J. (2005). Linking citizen satisfactio with e-government and trust in government. *Journal of Public Administration: Research and Theory, 15*(3).

West, D. (2000). *Assessing e-government: The internet, democracy, and service delivery by state and federal governments*. Providence, RI: Brown University.

West, D. M. (2004). E-government and the transformation of service delivery and citizen attitudes. *Public Administration Review, 64*(1), 13. doi:10.1111/j.1540-6210.2004.00343.x.

Wilson, T. D. et al. (1999). *Uncertainty in information seeking*. Sheffield, UK: University of Sheffield.

Wong, W., & Welch, E. (2004). Does e-government promote accountability? A comparative analysis of website openness and government accountability. *Governance: An International Journal of Policy, Administration and Institutions, 17*(2), 275–297. doi:10.1111/j.1468-0491.2004.00246.x.

Wood, F. B. et al. (2003). A practical approach to e-government web evaluation. *IT Professional, 7*.

Yu, B., & Roh, S. (2002). The effects of menu design on information-seeking performance and user's attitude on the world wide web. *Journal of the American Society for Information Science and Technology, 53*(11), 923–933. doi:10.1002/asi.10117.

Zhang, P., & Von Dran, G. M. (2000). Satisfiers and dissatisfiers: A two-factor model for website design and evaluation. *Journal of the American Society for Information Science American Society for Information Science, 51*(14), 15. doi:10.1002/1097-4571(2000)9999:9999<::AID-ASI1039>3.0.CO;2-O.

ADDITIONAL READING

Fountain, J. E. (2001). *Building the virtual state: Information technology and institutional change*. Washington, DC: Brookings Institution Press.

Gupta, M. P., & Jana, D. (2003). E-government evaluation: A framework and case study. *Government Information Quarterly, 20*, 365–387. doi:10.1016/j.giq.2003.08.002.

O'Reilly, T. (2007). What is web 2.0: Design patterns and business models for the next generation of software. *International Journal of Digital Economics, 65*, 20.

Tolbert, C. J., & Mossberger, K. (2006). The effects of e-government on trust and confidence in government. *Public Administration Review, 66*, 354–369. doi:10.1111/j.1540-6210.2006.00594.x.

Torres, L., Pina, V., & Acerete, B. (2006). E-governance developments in European Union cities: Reshaping government's relationship with citizens. *Governance: An International Journal of Policy, Administration and Institutions, 19*, 277–302. doi:10.1111/j.1468-0491.2006.00315.x.

UNPAN. (2012). *E-government survey 2012: E-government for the people*. New York: United Nations.

Wong, W., & Welch, E. (2004). Does e-government promote accountability? *A Comparative Analysis of Website Openness and Government Accountability Governance: An International Journal of Policy. Administration and Institutions, 17*, 275–297.

KEY TERMS AND DEFINITIONS

Citizens Empowerment: Giving power to citizens. Citizens become empowered when they have the knowledge, skills, attitudes, and self-awareness necessary to influence their own behavior and that of others to improve the quality of their lives and their relationship with the Public Administration.

CWEI: Stands for "Citizen Web Empowerment Index." It is an original index made up of four sub indicators (e-information + Web tools & strategies + e-consultation + e-decision making process) created to measure the degree of citizens empowerment included into the Web strategies of local municipalities.

E-Consultation: The third CWEI sub-indicator. It includes the presence on the City Web site of on-line procedures which are designed to involve citizens asking them their opinion, making them active players in the decision making process improving significantly their empowerment.

E-Decision Making Process: The fourth CWEI sub-indicator. It shows if citizens' opinion is considered in the decision making process. This would represent a high level of citizens' empowerment.

E-Information: The first CWEI sub-indicator. It includes important information about the Administration which should be on its Web site.

E-Participation: ICT-supported citizen's participation in government processes: the processes may concern service delivery, decision making and policy making.

Web 2.0: Web concept based on user participation, "remixability" and a design centered on user's needs. It generates a new demand for citizen empowerment.

Web Tools and Strategies: The second CWEI sub-indicator. It includes the presence on the City Web site of Web tools (especially Web 2.0) which allow a continuous relation between citizens and the Administration.

Chapter 15
Policy Gadgets for Urban Governance in the Era of Social Computing:
An Italian Pilot on Telemedicine

Enrico Ferro
Istituto Superiore Mario Boella, Italy

Yannis Charalabidis
University of the Aegean, Greece

Michele Osella
Istituto Superiore Mario Boella, Italy

Euripides Loukis
University of the Aegean, Greece

ABSTRACT

The chapter introduces the concept of policy gadgets that may be expressed as the combined use of computer simulations and social media in policymaking. Such a concept is exemplified by providing the description of an Italian campaign on telemedicine, launched by the regional government of Piedmont (IT) in the context of an international research project named PADGETS (www.padgets.eu). In addition, some preliminary results are presented, which are very encouraging. The use of such instruments in urban and regional policymaking may generate significant advantages in terms of conveying society's inputs to policy makers, by providing them with a set of concise, fresh, and relevant data in a cost effective and easily understandable way.

INTRODUCTION

The soaring complexity at a social, political, and economic level that characterizes modern societies necessitates more sophisticated policy making processes. Governments are no longer in the position of having in-house sufficient resources, information or competencies to effectively respond to the complex needs and wants of an interconnected, fast-evolving and unpredictable global environment. It is thus of critical importance for policy makers to partner with society to quickly identify new emerging problems and find innovative solutions.

In such a context, the rise of social computing has recently attracted significant interest from both the academic and the professional world.

DOI: 10.4018/978-1-4666-4169-3.ch015

Web 2.0 and social media, in fact, represent a potential cornerstone in the field of public sector innovation, leading to more responsive, informed, open, transparent and collaborative forms of governance. In particular, the increased capabilities of Internet users to "organize without organizations" (Shirky, 2006), coupled with the birth of social networks, have spurred the birth of numerous virtual spaces where people express their political views, problems and needs. This provides an additional motivation for government agencies to organize their presence in the social media.

However, despite the rosy expectations and fervent impulses coming from the scientific community, government's consultations are struggling to take off due to the presence of notable difficulties in collecting, organizing, and making sense of people's opinions. In spite of the unsatisfactory results of participatory initiatives launched over the first decade of the second millennium, one ray of hope comes from the observed trend towards "government 2.0", an emerging concept which denotes a situation where canonical governmental boundaries are blurred, leaving room for opportunities to harness "prosumption", i.e., a new model of information collaborative production, where formerly passive consumers participate in an active and ongoing way. In this new paradigm, new modes of collaboration and co-creation surface and, therefore, pluralistic and networked forms of government become the dominant organizational model for service delivery and policymaking. This can be highly beneficial for urban and regional planning, taking into account its complexity, dynamism (rapid changes of context and needs) and multiple affected stakeholders.

The aim of this chapter is to present the concept of policy gadgets and their role in the process of government transformation with respect to policy making and planning towards the above directions. In particular, it is analyzed how such instruments can be used by government agencies to inform and improve the policy making cycle. In order to exemplify how policy gadgets may be adopted

in real life the chapter provides a description of an Italian pilot implementation launched by the regional government of Piedmont (Italy). The campaign focuses on a program for large scale introduction telemedicine solutions in the region of Piedmont for monitoring the health of some special patients' groups. It aims to convey information on it to interested and affected citizens of this region (e.g. patients and their families, doctors, etc.), and collect feedback from them, using social media. This campaign is conducted in the context of an international research project named PADGETS (its full title is 'Policy Gadgets Mashing Underlying Group Knowledge in Web 2.0 Media' – www. padgets.eu), partially financed as part of the ICT for governance and policy modeling objective of the seventh framework program of research of the European Commission.

Including these introductory comments, the remainder of the chapter is structured in four sections. Section two presents some background information. Section three starts with introducing the concept of policy gadgets and subsequently follows on by presenting and discussing the Italian pilot on telemedicine. Then it places the research work conducted within a number of long-term socioeconomic trends and highlights some of the future challenges and research directions. Finally, section four contains some conclusive remarks about the potential of policy gadgets to transform policy making as we know it today.

BACKGROUND INFORMATION

ICT-enabled governance has been recently explored by the European Commission's Institute for Prospective Technological Studies (IPTS), being defined as: 'the use of ICTs to comprehensively: (1) simplify and improve the internal administrative operations of government and their relations with other bodies involved in public management and service delivery; (2) facilitate public service interaction between government, citizens and other stakeholders (legislative bodies, private sector, civil society organizations, self-organised communities), thus enabling better citizen participation and overall monitoring and evaluation of decision-making processes and their implementation; and (3) ensure inclusiveness and equal opportunity for all (Misuraca *et al.*, 2011).

According to OECD (2001) the participative dimension plays a vital role in the perspective of good governance, since public participation demonstrates considerable potential to change the broader interactions between citizens and government, improving the overall quality of engagement and decision making whilst widening the involvement of all citizens (European Commission, 2009).

Nevertheless, Rittel and Webber (1973) remind us that the design of public policy in most domains is a "wicked" problem. The search for algorithmic approaches (based on the use of mathematical optimization algorithms) is bound to fail due to the very nature of these phenomena: many stakeholders with dissimilar views of the problem, values, concerns and interests; this is rendered even more complex by the paucity of opportunities to learn by trial-and-error. Owing to such peculiarities of public policy making process, several circles of deliberation are necessary to occur: stakeholders interact, raise issues concerning the problem under discussion, propose solutions and argue about advantages and disadvantages of them, finally resulting in a better understanding of the problem (Charalabidis *et al.*, 2010).

In order to reap benefits from this approach, new mechanisms are required to enable a public decision process that is more open, transparent, and participative, in which citizens' contribution is a paramount ingredient of critical importance. Taking into account dimensions such as "to what level" or "how far" citizens are engaged, three stages could be distinguished according to Macintosh's framework (Macintosh, 2004):

1. **E-Enabling:** Which is about reaching a wider audience using appropriate technologies (its main focus being accessibility and understandability of information).
2. **E-Engaging:** That is geared towards consulting a wider audience to enable deeper contributions and support deliberative debate on policy issues through top-down consultation.
3. **E-Empowering:** Which is aimed at supporting active participation and to facilitate the percolation of bottom-up ideas towards the political agenda.

Along the depicted trajectory, the rise of social computing has recently attracted significant interest: Web 2.0 *et similia*, in fact, may be considered a cornerstone in the field of public sector innovation, smoothing the way to a more responsive, informed, open, transparent and collaborative government. In particular, the increased capabilities of Internet users to create content, coupled with the birth of social networks have driven the development of more and more virtual spaces for the expression of political views, problems and needs, which may ideally move towards becoming a modern *agorae* (Boero *et al.* 2011).

Moving on to the role that social media can play in policy making, IPTS (2009) identified four key areas of potential impact: 1) enhance political participation while increasing transparency and accountability; 2) enable user-involvement and empowerment; 3) allow mass-collaboration in government and public service delivery reinforcing knowledge sharing and management; and finally, 4) contribute to support organizational, legal and regulatory changes.

According to many commentators (DiMaio et al, 2005), social computing-enabled governance mechanisms could enhance collaboration within local government agencies and interaction with stakeholders, transforming processes into more user-centric, cost-effective solutions and bringing public value to end users. The creation of more participative forms of governance represents a key pillar of the smart city initiative (European Commission, 2011) with which the European Commission has challenged the most advanced European urban areas for the years to come.

SOCIAL MEDIA IN THE POLICY DOMAIN

Policy Gadgets: Value Proposition and Novelty

Similarly to the approach of gadget applications in Web 2.0, the concept of policy gadget (or, coining a *portmanteau*, "Padget") represents a resource (content or application) created by a policy maker, which is typically instantiated within one or more social media platforms. By enabling an interaction with end users, a Padget combines the policy message with underlying group knowledge having

its *locus* in the social media milieu. In this way, Padgets aspire to play a pivotal role in conveying society's inputs to policy makers, providing them with a set of concise, fresh, and relevant data on citizens' opinions and suggestions in a cost-effective and easily understandable way.

Padgets could be compared to a "complex molecules" made up of four main components (Figure 1):

- **A Message:** That regards a policy in any of its stages and forms, i.e., a draft legal document under formulation, a law in its final stage, an EU directive under implementation, a draft policy guideline, a political article or even a campaign video. The policy message is put together adopting a modular structure (using different content types) in order to account for the heterogeneity present among end users in terms of time availability, interest in details and preference for content consumption. Typically the policy message could be structured in three parts: a

Figure 1. Padget main components

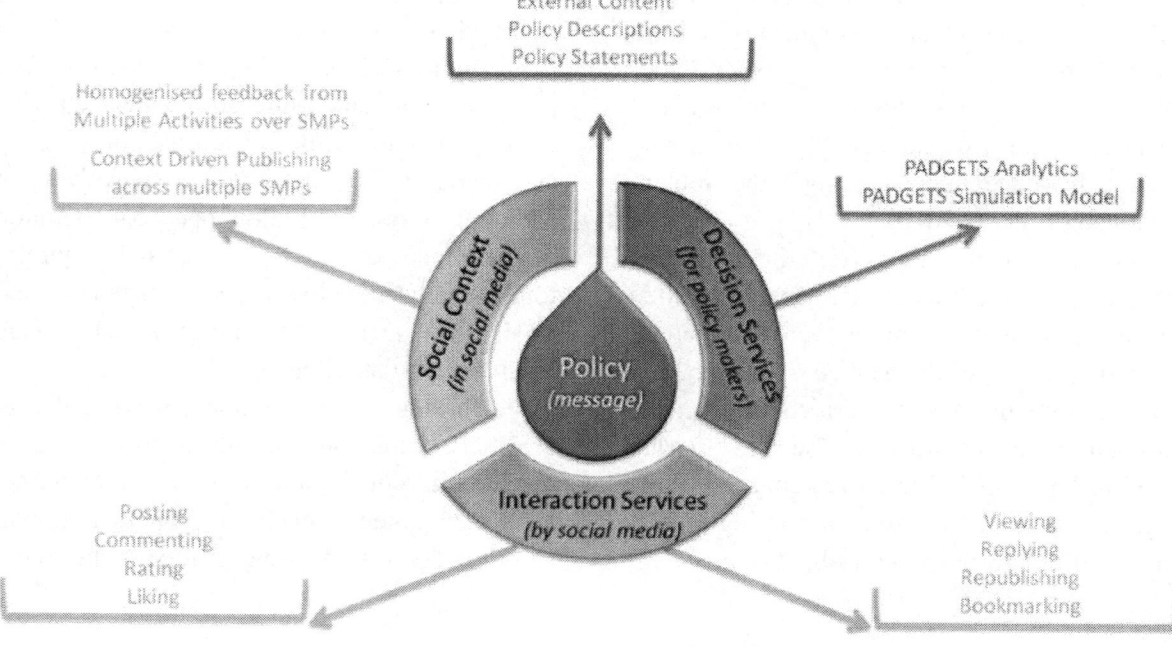

short and "catchy" policy statement, a brief policy description and a set of more extensive documentation that may be attached to the message in different guises (e.g., text, multimedia, external links).

- **A Set of Interaction Services:** That allows users to have recourse to the policy gadget (find it, access its content, share it, comment the policy message, etc.). These interfaces may be provided by either the underlying social media platforms, in which the Padget campaign has been launched, or by the Padget itself, when it takes the form of a micro application.
- **The Social Context:** That is the framework describing social activities and contents related with the policy gadget in each individual social media platform, where the policy gadget is present. As a result, this component allows the policy gadget to be a "context-aware" volume of relevant user activities and user generated contents.
- **The Decision Services:** Which are offered by two complementary modules of the PADGETS central platform. Whilst the "PADGETS analytics" module processes numeric and textual data gathered through Padget campaigns in order to calculate useful metrics and extract opinions expressed about the policy message, the "PADGETS simulation model" analyzes and projects into the near future the diffusion process of the policy message in terms of awareness (i.e., passive reception of the policy message in social media), interest (i.e., spreading or commenting the Padget announcement in social media) and acceptance (i.e., expression of positive and negative judgments about the policy idea under examination).

The value generated by policy gadgets unfolds along a number of dimensions and may vary among the different phases of the policy mak-

ing cycle. Nevertheless, in its essence it may be conceived as a reduction in the distance between policy making and society's needs, both in terms of time and tools required. In other words, the use of policy gadgets allows to better inform the policy decision process by providing a clear and dynamic picture of the disparate stakeholders' opinions and priorities.

Padgets are used in communication campaigns that may be launched by policy makers during one or more phases of the policy making cycle: agenda setting, policy analysis, policy formulation, policy implementation, and policy monitoring and evaluation (OECD, 2003). The purpose, function and - as a consequence - the value proposition of each Padget campaign may vary according to the stage of the policy cycle in which it is launched, as pointed out by Table 1.

Policy Gadgets represent an innovation in the policy making landscape. The main novelties introduced by such a tool may be briefly summarized as follows.

1. **A Relaxation of Current Constraints in Terms of Size, Frequency and Quality of Citizens' Participation:** All the different stakeholders are free to participate in any policy process they are interested in, at the time they prefer, with the effort in participation they are willing to spend, and above all

Table 1. Padget value propositions in the policy cycle

Stage in policy making cycle	Padget campaign value proposition
Agenda setting	Elicitation of needs and priorities
Analysis	Opinions gathering
Formulation	Acceptance estimation
Implementation	Assessment of awareness and interest
Evaluation	Evaluation of impact perception

using the tools with which they are already accustomed to (i.e. various social media they prefer). From the opposite perspective, policy makers can continuously access reports pertaining to stakeholders' opinion, being allowed to quickly modify and adapt the policy issues under discussion if necessary.

2. **An Integrated Management of Multiple Social Media Channels:** The presence of a Web dashboard dedicated to the policy maker decreases the complexity and heterogeneity that comes naturally while managing different social media platforms, each of which exhibits peculiarities in terms of aims, interfaces, functionalities, target audience, content types and degree of content sharing.

3. **The Creation of an "Open" Decision Support System:** Opening up the decision support process means integrate it with activities carried out over social media platforms. This allows to establishing a direct link between the decision process and the external world as well as to reason on fresh and relevant information.

4. **A Better Exploitation of Data Stemming from Interaction with the Public on Social Media:** In this respect, the decision support component provides a number of promising functionalities that generate precious knowledge to be used in order to inform the decision making process. In particular, this component allows to generate snapshots on the levels of awareness, interest and acceptance of a given policy, highlight the presence of some of the possible biases present existing in such estimations (age, gender, etc.), create possible scenarios of how such levels of awareness, interest and acceptance may vary over time (e.g., in next 12 months) and, finally, single out relevant opinions emerging from the interaction of the end users with the policy message.

Although still in its infancy, such instruments represent a promising stepping stone for the creation of a new generation of policy making, which is characterized by faster and more frequent interaction between policy makers and society. As a matter of fact, policy gadgets may promote a cultural shift within government agencies, paving the way to the creation of an "extended government" model (Raguseo & Ferro, 2011), wherein society plays a more proactively role in the policy lifecycle. Users' insightful contributions are processed through policy intelligence capabilities resident in the back-end, allowing public decision makers to anticipate and detect trends in public opinion, yielding augmented responsiveness, representativeness and efficiency to the public policy definition. Moreover, an intense use of social media coupled with further in-depth studies of network topologies may also contribute to a new approach that no longer considers individuals as isolated units of analysis, but leverages their social connections and the context in which they are immersed as a potentially useful policy tool.

Finally, peculiar traits of Policy Gadgets enable the creation of cross-sectional decision support tools easily and effectively implementable for any kind of public policy: this noticeable versatility makes them an interesting policy tool for full-fledged and frictionless participative actions also in the sphere of urban planning and governance. This can be very useful, taking into account the complexity, dynamism and multiple affected stakeholders that characterize urban planning and governance.

THE ITALIAN PILOT

In this section a description of a real life pilot implementation of the above concepts is described, which illustrates how Padgets can be applied to policy making. In particular, the pilot promoted by the regional government of Piedmont—full partner of the PADGETS project—will be presented.

Description of the Telemedicine Project

Over the last ten years Piedmont's regional government has spent, on average, 80% of its total budget for providing health services to its citizens. The increasing budget reductions currently experienced at local and at national level require regional governments to face a major challenge: significantly lower health related expenditures without deteriorating quality of service. The challenge is even more compelling if we take a long term perspective: population's average age is steadily rising and all demographic projections at our disposal show a long lasting trend of growth in health services demand.

In such a context, regional policy makers pay much attention to e-health initiatives, which seem to promise financial savings along with quality improvements in service provision. In 2008, the Piedmont Region launched a pioneering and piloting telemedicine small scale project in one of the least populated and mountainous of its provinces: Verbano-Cusio-Ossola (VCO). This telemedicine project was supported by the Local Health Authority (LHA) of VCO that serves a population of about 172,000 people, where more than 23% of people are over 65 years old.

Project's Aim

The project aimed at testing an innovative model of medical service delivery highly relying on information and communication technologies for enabling stronger communication and interaction between hospitals and the territory. In particular, the project intended to:

- Improve continuity of care and safety of patients in non-acute conditions.
- Increase quality of emergency services and outpatient care.

From an operational standpoint, the project objectives were: limiting the use of specialist outpatient services, reducing calls to emergency services and bring down the number of repeated visits to hospitals.

Target Audience and Enabling Technologies

The VCO LHA designed an innovative telemedicine service for four different categories of patients affected by heart failure disease, diabetes, chronic pulmonary occlusive disease (COPD) and cancer.

Each category of target patient followed a personalized protocol defined by the VCO LHA specialists according to the disease conditions: patients were equipped with devices able to track, store and send appropriate data to a server in a secure repository; for each disease, the medical staff of VCO LHA defined the type, the number and the frequency of the measurements to be carried out. The project enrolled about 300 patients in three years.

The technology adopted for the pilot relied on an innovative Web-based application integrated with the information system of the local health unit (LHU), a kit of medical devices for remote home care and a module for IP video communication.

Lessons Learned

From a patient's perspective, telemedicine allowed to achieve enhanced monitoring of the disease together with improved quality of life, delivering care in his/her home, thus increasing the person's ability towards self-care.

From a technological perspective, ICT technologies played a key role in the prevention of patients' isolation, connecting them with the network of LHA specialists, general practitioners, and all the other professionals involved in the health system (e.g., nursing staff, volunteers, family members).

From an organizational perspective, standard processes coupled with personalized care paths for each patient (according to his/her diseases) noticeably contributed to maintain well-being, deliver effective care to those with chronic conditions and support the most vulnerable members of society.

To summarise, the VCO telemedicine pilot may be rated among one of the most challenging experiences in the field carried out in Italy, representing a virtuous example of partnerships between administrations, private sector entities and non-profit sector. The assessment of the provision model adopted is crucial for further diffusion of telemedicine initiatives in the rest of Piedmont's regional territory.

The PADGETS Campaign

The Rationale

The replication of good practices in public policies answers the need of learning-by-doing and of finding effective solutions to complex problems, avoiding expensive and often impossible social experimentations. Furthermore, the exploitation of good practices reduces the cost and the risk of failure of public policies. However, the replication of good practices often finds several obstacles on its path, capable of jeopardizing their successful implementation. In general, replicating good practices raises issues of transferability, scalability, and relevance.

The social media campaign promoted by the regional government was aimed at exploring the possibility to implement the VCO telemedicine initiative at a large scale in the entire Piedmont region, in a context different from the initial one,

transferring the experience of a limited area to the whole region. In particular, its objective was to convey information on this extension of the telemedicine initiative in the whole Piedmont region to interested and affected citizens (e.g. patients and their families, doctors, etc.), and then collect feedback from them, using social media.

In other words, the Regional government is interested in identifying and shedding some light on a number-of issues that have to do with the extension of such a good practice from a single province with specific characteristics to the rest of the region. In particular, the regional government expected through this campaign to gain a better understanding about the levels of final users' interest in and acceptance of these telemedicine services and the technology-mediated model proposed for their provision. Also, the participation of employees from the national health system allows investigating the presence of possible internal hurdles due to organizational resistance to change as well as the presence of potential issues or improvements to consider. In particular, the data generated from the interaction between social media users and the relevant content propagated through social networks can be used as an input by the decision support component of the PADGETS platform in order to compute a series of indicators concerning this telemedicine policy (i.e., awareness, interest, acceptance) (Boero et al., 2011) as well as to detect issues and problems raised by the citizens through advanced text mining of their textual comments. Figure 2 provides a synoptic pictorial representation of the whole process that was followed in this social media campaign.

Stakeholders

Given the complexity of the debated theme, the campaign has involved a plurality of stakeholders both within and outside government's boundaries. The main stakeholders' groups are depicted in the Figure 3.

Figure 2. Overview of the social media campaign

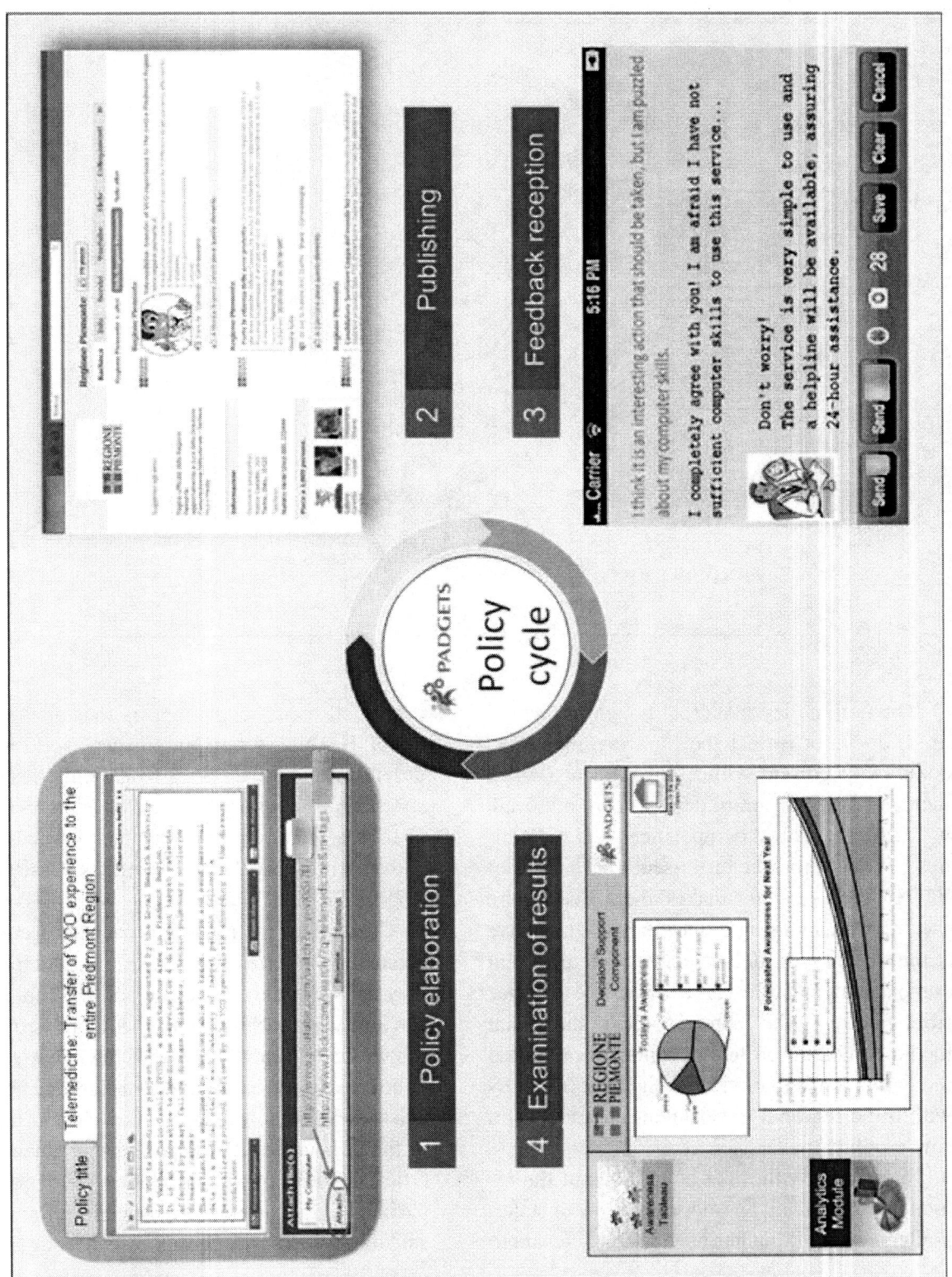

Figure 3. Stakeholder overview

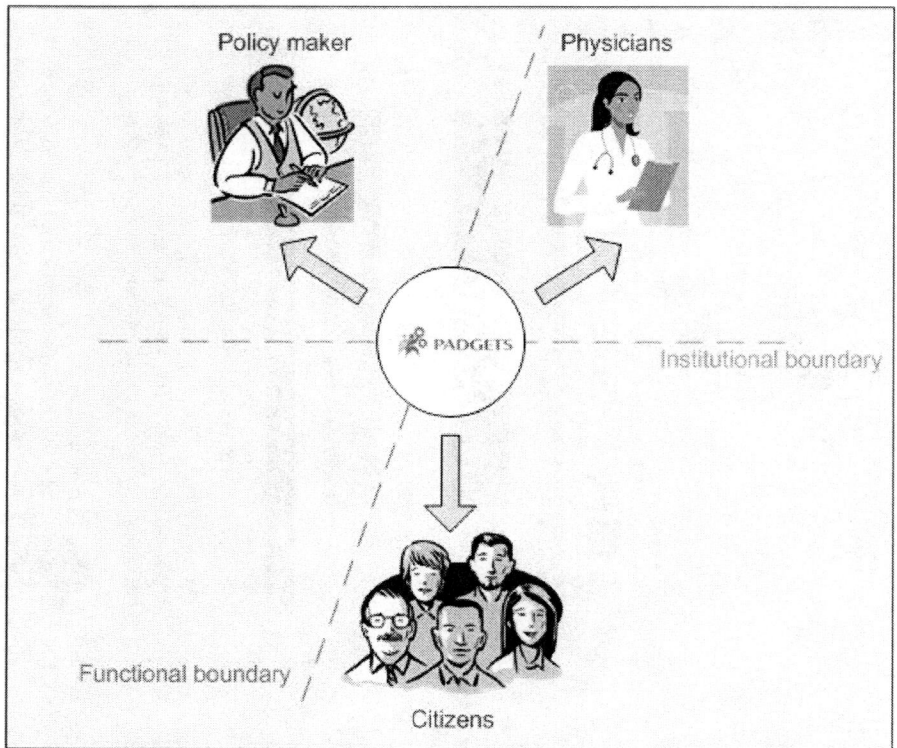

The term policy maker, although frequently used, does not reflect the high organizational complexity present within government (which includes many different departments involved, with different roles, competences and mentalities). In addition, the cross-sectional nature of ICT-enabled projects makes them even more complicated to manage, since they often involve a multiplicity of departments with different competences and roles. As it is possible to notice from Figure 4, the management of the social media campaign on telemedicine has required the active participation of a plurality of actors within the regional government and not just a single policy maker.

Remaining within the boundaries of the regional government, an important class of stakeholders, whose input has been highly relevant to the social media campaign, is that of the National Health System employees working on providing public services to patients, a broad spectrum of health care professionals involved in lifelong learning programs and associations and charities involved in patients' assistance (Figure 5).

Citizens, for their part, present heterogeneous behaviours in terms of the effort in participation they are willing to spend. In fact, the campaign has aimed at reaching at all Piedmont's citizens (about 4.5 millions), but due to the nature of the policy message to be launched during the campaign and to the different diffusion rates of social media in the population, it is expected that some specific categories of citizens will be more prone to participate to the pilot: these categories are presumably citizens with chronic diseases (e.g., heart

Figure 4. Policy maker: exemplification of stakeholder categories

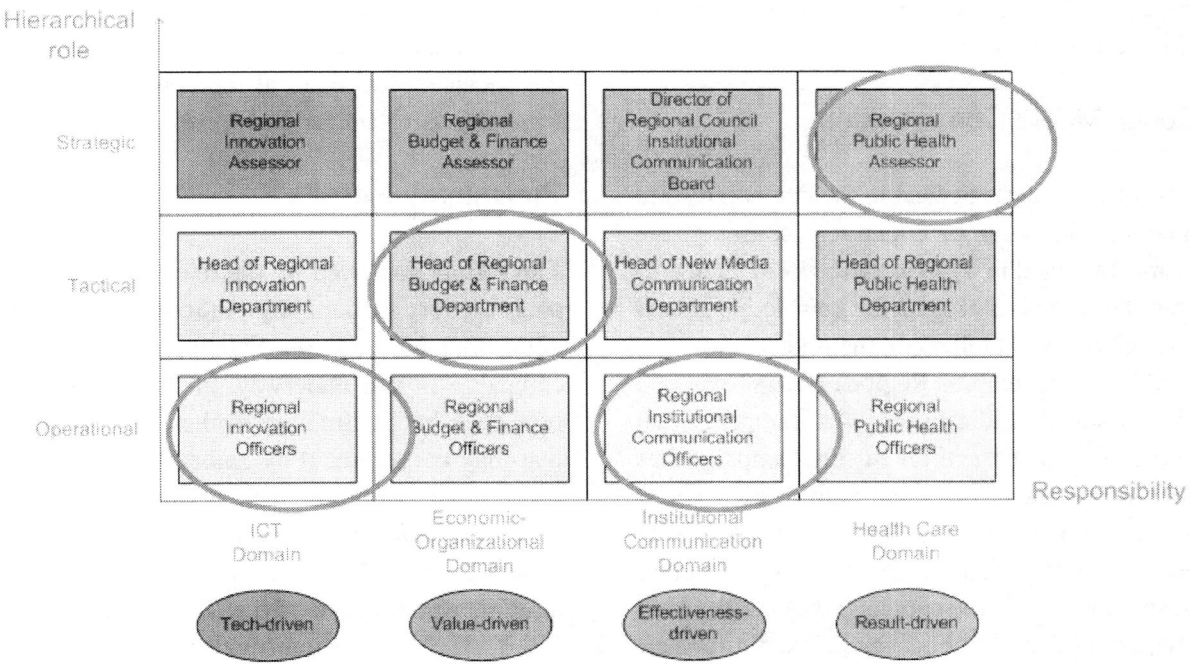

Figure 5. National health system employees: exemplification of stakeholder categories

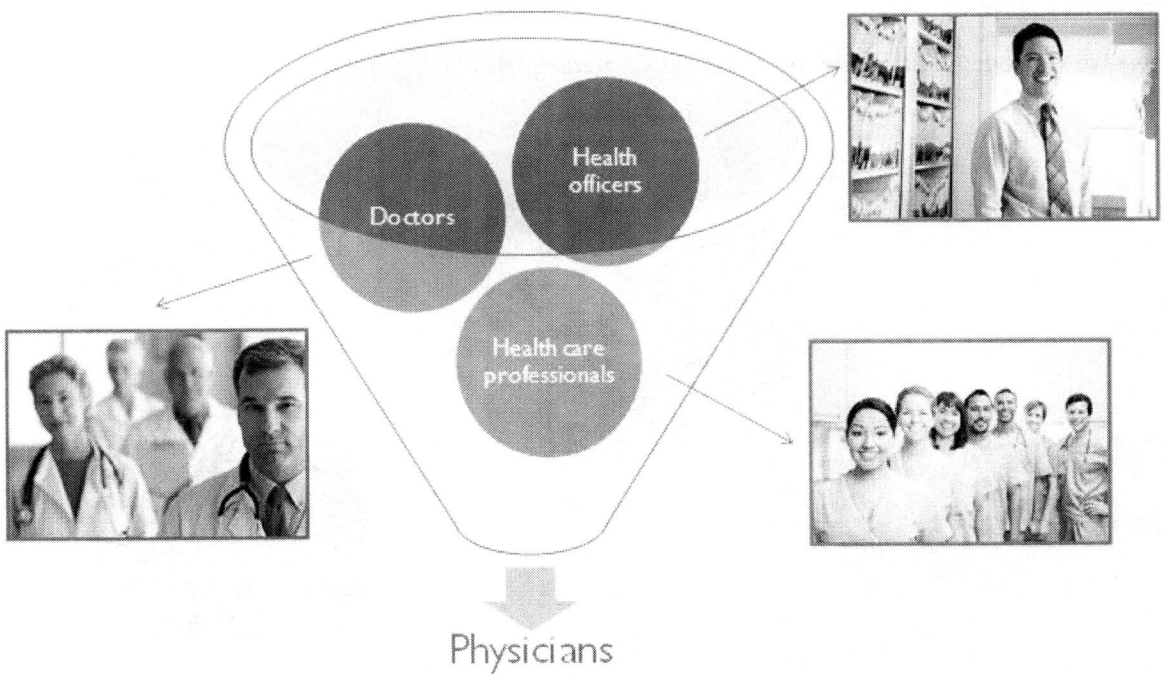

failure, diabetes, chronic pulmonary occlusive disease - COPD, and cancer) and their families (Figure 6).

Social Media Communities

Multimedia contents used in the campaign were produced in order to effectively communicate results obtained in VCO area thanks to telemedicine. They are based upon the knowledge gained through the VCO telemedicine pilot.

Although Piedmont Region officers have used several social media in the pilot campaign, the one chosen to be central in this campaign has been Facebook. This is due both to its peculiar interaction patterns as well as to the noteworthy penetration rate of it in the Piedmont's population. Beside Facebook, the campaign has made use of Twitter and YouTube. Flickr and LinkedIn, for their part, assumed an ancillary role, i.e., precious for potential virtuous synergies and viral diffusion, but not vital in order to allow and track active social engagement actions.

A glimpse of Piedmont Region's presence in the social media realm at the beginning of the campaign is visualized in Figure 7.

Preliminary Results

The results produced by the telemedicine campaign are very encouraging. Although the analysis of the abundance of information produced by the campaign is still underway, in this section we provide some preliminary evidence of the value that may be generated by embracing the use of social media for policy making purposes.

In terms of reach, the policy messages have generated over 28,000 impressions across the three main platforms used (i.e., Facebook, Twitter, and YouTube). The information for the Twitter platform has been estimated using click-throughs on bitly.com links and YouTube referrals; as a consequence, the figure represents a significant

Figure 6. Citizens: exemplification of stakeholder categories

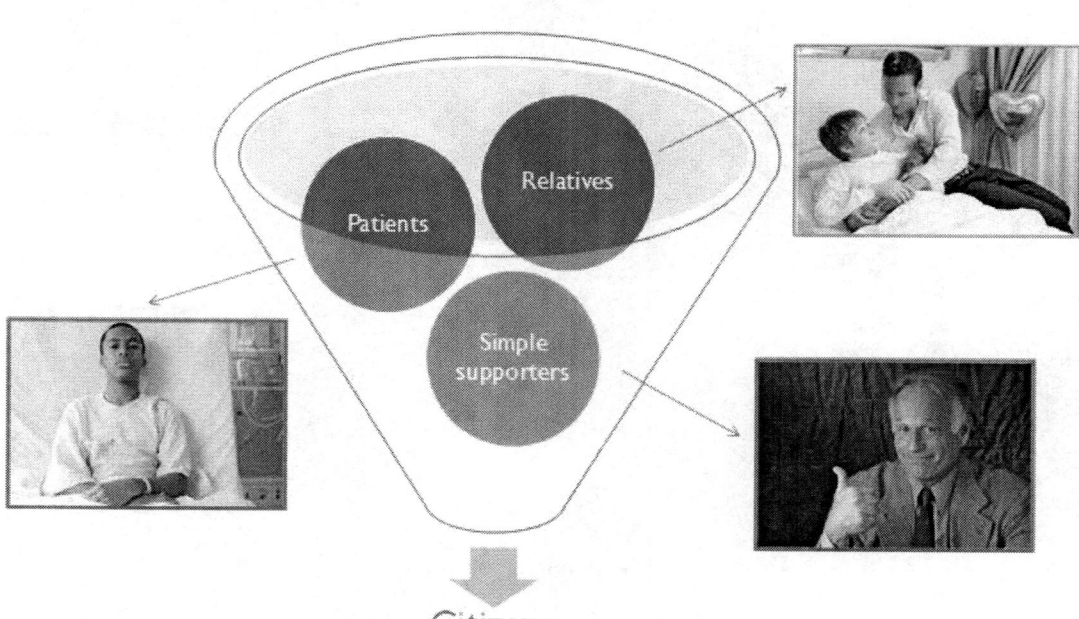

Figure 7. Piedmont region social media presence

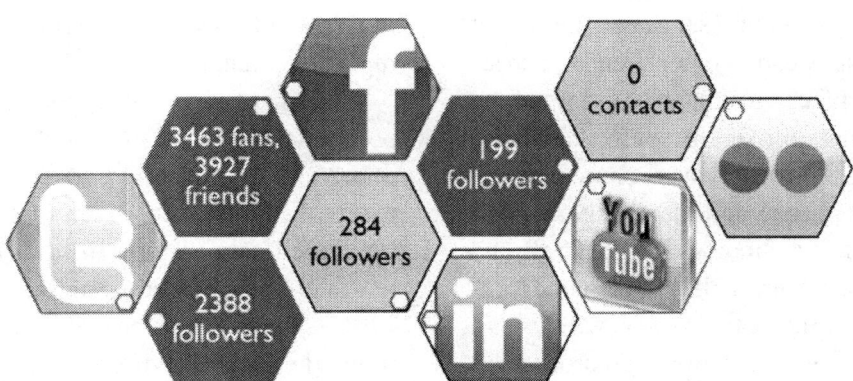

underestimation of the actual performance expressed on the specific platform. Translating impressions into unique user accounts, the data offered by the platforms' analytics show that over 11,000 accounts have been reached. It is important to stress that during the campaign the message performance of the Facebook regional government account has been multiplied by three times in terms of reach (people reached) and by twenty times in terms of engagement (number of active interactions stimulated, e.g.: shares, likes, comments, etc.).

Going beyond numbers, we are convinced that the most value has been generated in qualitative terms. As a matter of fact, the inputs received from the different stakeholder groups allowed to bring to light a number of perspectives, hopes and concerns about the implementation of telemedicine solution in the regional territory. As a result, such stimuli represent a vital input to assess and effectively manage the implementation stage of the telemedicine policy. In particular, the policy message has been received very positively by the population, who places significant expectations in terms of increase of service quality, reduction of costs for both patients (mainly in terms of time) and the regional welfare systems. At the same time, a number of concerns have been expressed (mainly by doctors) about the risk of applying a

"technocratic approach" that does not take into account the human aspects of the doctor-patient relationship. On this respect, some suggestions have been put forward about conceiving telemedicine as a complementary and not substitute solution to traditional practices.

FUTURE RESEARCH DIRECTIONS

The society and the economy in which we live and operate are becoming more and more interconnected, unstable, complex and unpredictable than they have ever been (Mureddu *et al.*, 2012). As pointed out by Taleb (2008), we live in the age of "Extremistan," a world of "tipping points" (Schelling, 1969), "cascades" and "power laws" (Barabasi, 2003), where extreme events are "the new normal" (Hinssen, 2010). The policy issues that characterize our age can be addressed only through the collaboration of all the groups of society, including the private sector and individual citizens (Goldsmith & Eggers, 2004). Nevertheless, the tools necessary to enable such collaboration are still largely unavailable. The concept of policy gadgets and the PADGETS platform represent a first attempt to provide an instrument to foster a higher level of "societal collaboration." Such an attempt may be placed within a long term trajectory in the way public policy making is going to evolve thanks to the concurrent presence of a number of socioeconomic and technological trends, such as: the widespread diffusion of Internet usage among all strata of population, a significant increase in the availability of data, a reduction in communication (and participation) costs and, finally, the rise of a social dimension in technology usage. The grand challenge for researchers, policy makers and technology vendors in the years to come will have to do with the creations of solutions and procedures capable of turning diffused competencies, contextual information and civic passion into an effective tool for increasing the ability of public policies to respond to the needs and wants of stakeholders living in urban and rural areas. Addressing such a challenge will necessitate a multidisciplinary endeavor that will require inputs from many different scientific communities, each of which offers its valuable perspective and contribution towards the construction of a data-powered collaborative form of governance. In such a scenario, big urban areas represent the perfect living labs for the development of preliminary test beds, since they are characterized by good technological infrastructures and human capital, and at the same time have such high complexity problems and needs, and many different stakeholder groups, and also they often host government agencies belonging to different administrative levels.

CONCLUSION

This chapter proposes the concept of policy gadget (Padget) as an innovative tool for leveraging the group knowledge produced over social media platforms within policymaking.

The pilot described in this document represents an important first step towards the establishment of a new style of policy making

leveraging on the opportunities offered by ICT in terms of knowledge creation as well as communities' management.

The use of ICT tools for decision support in policymaking has traditionally been a "closed door" activity, usually carried out with static external inputs in the form of codified or unstructured data coming from different sources (e.g. statistical offices). Such an approach often suffers from a number of important limitations: the lack of a direct connection with the external reality on which the policy decision has to impact, an inherent delay present in the policy response due to the lead time to collect and process the relevant data necessary for the analysis. To exemplify with a metaphor, such process could be compared to driving a car by only looking at the rear view mirror (an indirect and delayed input) rather than through the windscreen. The innovation brought by Web 2.0 consists in offering the opportunity to open up the policy making process by integrating it with the activity carried out over social media platforms. This allows to establish a direct link between the decision process and the external world as well as to reason on fresh and relevant information (going back to the metaphor, driving while looking through the windscreen and, in the near future, with the possibility to use additional on-board instrumentation).

The preliminary results of the telemedicine campaign reported in this chapter show the presence of significant potential in adopting social media for the implementation of a more participative style of policy making by local administrations in all sub-fields of urban governance. In particular, the application of a cross-platform approach seems to strengthen the reach and the engagement result of the messages posted by public administrations over social media platform. These results are expected to improve with time as society acknowledges the change in the style of communication adopted by government agencies and as the usage of such social media diffuses across urban and rural areas as well as generations of users. The approach presented in this chapter is directly transferrable to urban and regional governance, taking into account its complexity, dynamism (rapid changes of context and needs) and multiple affected stakeholders.

Concluding, a number of open issues are worth mentioning as they may represent useful food for thought for possible future research. The implementation of a meaningful cross-platform tracking still poses some challenges having to do with identity management. Furthermore, an arduous task consists in the creation and testing of an appropriate language and style of communication that government agencies have to adopt in the interaction with society. Lastly, the integration of society's voice into traditional policy making processes still presents some obstacles having to do with striking the right balance between independent and informed decision making and coherence with society's will.

REFERENCES

Barabasi, A. L. (2003). *Linked: How everything is connected to everything else and what it means for business and everyday life*. New York: Plume Books.

Boero, R., Ferro, E., Osella, M., Charalabidis, Y., & Loukis, E. (2011). Policy intelligence in the era of social computing: towards a cross-policy decision support system. In Garcia-Castro, R. et al. (Eds.), *ESWC 2011 Workshops (LNCS)* (*Vol. 7117*, pp. 217–228). Berlin: Springer-Verlag. doi:10.1007/978-3-642-25953-1_18.

Di Maio, A., Kreizman, G., Harris, R. G., Rust, B., & Rishi, S. (2005). *Government in 2020: Taking the long view*. New York: Gartner Inc..

European Commission. (2009). *European eparticipation summary report, study and supply of services on the development of eparticipation in the EU*. Brussels: European Commission.

European Commission. (2011). *Cities of tomorrow – Challenges, visions, ways forward, policy document*. Retrieved from http://bit.ly/SnJB0T

Goldsmith, S., & Eggers, W. D. (2004). *Governing by network: The new shape of the public sector*. Washington, DC: Brookings Institution.

Hinssen, P. (2010). *The new normal*. MachMedia, NV.

IPTS. (2009). *The impact of social computing on the EU information society and economy*. JRC Scientific and Technical Reports.

Macintosh, A. (2004). Characterizing e-participation in policy-making. In *Proceedings of the 37th Hawaii International Conference on System Sciences*. IEEE.

Misuraca, G., Reid, A., & Deakin, M. (2011). *Exploring emerging ICT-enabled governance models in European cities*. *JRC Technical Notes*. IPTS.

Mureddu, F., Osimo, D., Misuraca, G., & Armenia, S. (2012). *A new roadmap for next-generation policy-making*. New York: ICEGOV.

OECD. (2001). *Citizens as partners: Information, consultation and public participation in policy-making*. Paris: OECD Publishing.

OECD. (2003). *Policy brief: Engaging citizens online for better policy-making*. Paris: OECD.

Raguseo, E., & Ferro, E. (2011). E-government & organizational change: Towards an extended governance model. *Lecture Notes in Computer Science*, *6846*, 418–430. doi:10.1007/978-3-642-22878-0_35.

Rittel, H., & Webber, M. (1973). Dilemmas in a general theory of planning. *Policy Sciences, 4,* 155–169. doi:10.1007/BF01405730.

Schelling, T. (1969). Models of segregation. *The American Economic Review, 59*(2), 488–493. Retrieved from http://www.jstor.org/stable/1823701.

Shirky, C. (2009). *Here comes everybody: The power of organizing without organizations.* London: Penguin Books.

Taleb, N. (2008). *The black swan: The impact of the highly improbable.* London: Penguin Books.

ADDITIONAL READING

Dunleavy, P., & Margetts, H. Z. (2010). The second wave of digital era governance. In *Proceedings of the Annual Meeting of the American Political Science Association, 2010.* APSA.

Ferro, E., & Molinari, F. (2010). Making sense of gov 2.0 strategies: No citizens, no party. *eJournal of eDemocracy and Open Government,* 56-68.

Ferro, E., & Molinari, F. (2010). Framing web 2.0 in the process of public sector innovation: Going down the participation ladder. *European Journal of ePractice.* Retrieved from www.epracticejournal.eu

Shirky, C. (2009). *Here comes everybody: The power of organizing without organizations.* London: Penguin Books.

Tapscott, D., & Williams, A. D. (2006). *Wikinomics: How mass collaboration changes everything.* New York: Portfolio Books.

Tapscott, D., Williams, A. D., & Herman, D. (2008). *Government 2.0: Transforming government and governance for the twenty-first century.* New Paradigm.

KEY TERMS AND DEFINITIONS

Governance: The use of institutions, structures of authority and even collaboration to allocate resources and coordinate or control activity in society or the economy.

Padget: A resource (application or content), typically instantiating within a social media platform, created by a policy stakeholder, providing interactivity with citizens and other societal actors.

Padget Campaign: A Padget campaign is a set of activities covering creation, distribution (in several social media), interaction, monitoring and termination of one or more Padgets for a specific goal.

PADGETS: An EU - FP7 STREP project developing novel social media applications for policy making (its full title is 'Policy Gadgets Mashing Underlying Group Knowledge in Web 2.0 Media' – www.padgets.eu).

Smart City: A city is smart when investments in human and social capital and traditional (transport) and modern (ICT) communication infrastructure fuel sustainable economic growth and a high quality of life, with a wise management of natural resources, through participatory governance.

Social Media: Platforms used to turn communication into interactive dialogue between organizations, communities, and individuals. Andreas Kaplan and Michael Haenlein define social media as "a group of Internet-based applications that build on the ideological and technological foundations of Web 2.0, and that allow the creation and exchange of user-generated content".

Telemedicine: The use of telecommunication and information technologies in order to provide clinical health care at a distance. It helps eliminate distance barriers and can improve access to medical services that would often not be consistently available in distant rural communities. It is also used to save lives in critical care and emergency situations.

Compilation of References

Abecker, A., Kazakos, W., Melo Borges, J., & Zacharias, J. (2012). Beiträge zu einer Technologie für Anwendungen des Participatory Sensing. In: J. Strobl, T. Blaschke, & G. Griesebner (Eds.), *Angewandte Geoinformatik* 2012 (pp. 240-249). Herbert Wichmann Verlag, VDE Verlag GmbH, Berlin/Offenbach. Retrieved from http://gispoint. de/fileadmin/user_upload/paper_gis_open/537520001. pdf

Abhichandani, T. (2008). *Evaluation of e-government initiatives for citizen-centric delivery: Analysis of online public transit information services*. Berlin: VDM Verlag Publishing.

About the Government Reform for Competitiveness and Innovation Initiative. (n.d.). *U.S. White House*. Retrieved September 15, 2012, from http://www.whitehouse.gov/federalvoices/about

About the SAVE award. (n.d.). *U.S. White House*. Retrieved September 15, 2012, from http://www.whitehouse.gov/save-award/about

Abu-Hilal, A., & Al-Najjar, T. (2009). Marine litter in coral reef areas along the Jordan Gulf of Aqaba, Red Sea. *Journal of Environmental Management, 90*, 1043–1049. doi:10.1016/j.jenvman.2008.03.014 PMID:18490098.

Agarwal, P. (2005). Ontological considerations in GI-Science. *International Journal of Geographical Information Science, 19*, 501–536. doi:10.1080/13658810500032321.

Ahlqvist, T. (2000). A quest for polygon landscapes, or GIS and the condition of epistemology. *Fennia, 178*, 97–111.

Ahmed, N. (2006). *An overview of e-participation models*. New York: United Nations.

Aladwani, A., & Palvia, P. (2002). Developing and validating an instrument for measuring userperceived web quality. *Information & Management,* (39): 467–476. doi:10.1016/S0378-7206(01)00113-6.

Albrecht, S., Kohlrausch, N., Kubicek, H., Lippa, B., Marker, O., Trénel, M., Vorwek, V.,…, Wiedwald, C. (2008). *E-participation. electronic participation of citizens and the business community on egovernment*. Bremen, Germany: Institut fur Informations management.

Al-Kodmany, K. (2000). Public participation: Technology and democracy. *Journal of Architectural Education, 53*(4), 220–228. doi:10.1162/104648800564635.

Allen, M. (2012). What was Web 2.0? Versions as the dominant mode of internet history. *New Media & Society*. Retrieved from http://hms.sagepub.com/content/early/2012/07/03/1461444812451567

Amabile, T. M. (1998). How to kill creativity. *Harvard Business Review*, 77–87. PMID:10187248.

Amber, O. (2007). *Strategy Markup Language (StratML)*. Retrieved from http://xml.gov/stratml/.

Android. (n.d.). *Website*. Retrieved from http://developer. android.com/training/index.html

Angermerier, M. (2005). *The huge cloud lens bubble map web 2.0*. Retrieved from http://kosmar.de/archives/2005/11/11/the-huge-cloud-lens-bubble-map-Web2.0

Angotti, T. (2007). Advocacy and community planning: Past, present, and future. *Progressive planning: The magazine of planners network*. Retrieved November 1, 2012, from http://www.plannersnetwork.org/publications/2007_spring/angotti.htm

Anttiroiko, A.-V. (2004). Introduction to democratic e-governance. In Malkia, M., Anttiroiko, A.-V., & Savolainen, R. (Eds.), *eTransformation in governance: New directions in government and politics* (pp. 22–49). Hershey, PA: Idea Group Pub..

Anttiroiko, A.-V. (2012). Urban planning 2.0. *International Journal of E-Planning Research, 1*(1), 16–30. doi:10.4018/ijepr.2012010103.

Aoki, P. M., Honicky, R. J., Mainwaring, A., Myers, C., Paulos, E., Subramanian, S., & Woodruff, A. (2008). Common sense: Mobile environmental sensing platforms to support community action and citizen science (demonstration). *Adjunct Proceedings Ubicomp,* Sept, 59-60.

Apple. (n.d.). *Website.* Retrieved from http://developer.apple.com/library/ios/navigation/

Aquarius. (2012). 2012 wird zum Jahr der Smartphones. Retrieved July 17th, 2012, from http://www.aquarius.biz/de/2012/01/09/2012-wird-zum-jahr-der-smartphones/

Arnstein, S. R. (1969). A ladder of citizen participation. *Journal of the American Institute of Planners, 35*(4), 216–224. doi:10.1080/01944366908977225.

Arora, P. (2012). Typology of Web 2.0 spheres: Understanding the cultural dimensions of social media spaces. *Current Sociology.* Retrieved from http://csi.sagepub.com/content/60/5/599

Arrow, K. J. (1951). *Social choice and individual values.* New York: Wiley.

Arthur, C. (2011, April 20). iPhone keeps record of everywhere you go. *The Guardian.* Retrieved from http://www.guardian.co.uk/technology/2011/apr/20/iphone-tracking-prompts-privacy-fears

Ascough, J., Rector, H. D., Hoag, D. L., McMaster, G., & Bruce, C. (2002). Multi-criteria spatial decision support systems - overview, applications, and future research directions. *Information Systems Research, 1,* 175–180.

Ashley, H., Corbet, J., Jones, D., Garside, B., & Rambaldi, G. (2009). Change at hand: Web 2.0 for development. In Holly, A., Kenton, N., & Milligan, A. (Eds.), *Participatory learning and action.* London: The International Institute for Environment and Development (IIED), The Technical Centre for Agricultural and Rural Cooperation. Wageningen: CTA.

Atkinson, G. M., & Wald, D. J. (2007). "Did You Feel It?" intensity data: A surprisingly good measure of earthquake ground motion. *Seismological Research Letters, 78*(3), 362–368. doi:10.1785/gssrl.78.3.362.

Awad, M. (2010). El Baradei leads big Egypt anti-torture protest. *Reuters.* Retrieved from http://www.reuters.com/article/2010/06/25/us-egypt-protest-elbaradei-idUSTRE65O5JC20100625

Ayanso, A., & Moyers, D. (2012). The role of social media in the public sector: Opportunities and challenges. In Kloby, K., & D'Agostinho, M. J. (Eds.), *Citizen 2.0: Public and governmental interaction through Web 2.0 technologies* (pp. 1–22). Hershey: IGI-Global. doi:10.4018/978-1-4666-0318-9.ch001.

Baker, M., Coaffee, J., & Sherriff, G. (2007). Achieving successful participation in the new UK spatial planning system. *Planning Practice and Research, 22*(1), 79–93. doi:10.1080/02697450601173371.

Balogna, A. (2011). NYPD police pepper spray occupy wall street protesters. *You Tube.* Retrieved from http://www.youtube.com/watch?v=TZ05rWx1pig

Band, W., & Petouhoff, N. (2010). *Topic overview: Social CRM goes mainstream.* Cambridge, MA: Forrester Research.

Banks, K. (2008). *Mobile telephony and the entrepreneur: An African perspective.* Retrieved July 17th, 2012, from http://www.kiwanja.net/media/docs/Microfinance-Insights-kiwanja-2008.pdf

Barabasi, A. L. (2003). *Linked: How everything is connected to everything else and what it means for business and everyday life.* New York: Plume Books.

Barnes, J. E. (2012, July 9). Law agencies seek more data from cell carriers. *The Wall Street Journal.* Retrieved from http://online.wsj.com/article/SB10001424052702304022004577515681998852676.html?KEYWORDS=Law+agencies+seek+more+data+from+cell+carriers

Barr, J., & Cabrera, L. F. (2006). AI gets a brain: New technology allows software to tap real human intelligence. *ACM Queue; Tomorrow's Computing Today, 4*(4), 24–29. doi:10.1145/1142055.1142067.

Batista, L., & Kawalek, P. (2004). Translating customer-focused strategic issues into operational processes through CRM – A public sector approach. In R. Traunmüller (Ed.), Electronic Government (Vol. 3183, pp. 128-133). Springer Berlin / Heidelberg.

Baumgarten, J., & Chui, M. (2009). E-government 2.0. *McKinsey Quarterly*. Retrieved from http://www.mckinseyquarterly.com/E-government_20_2408

Beath, C. M., & Orlikowski, W. J. (1994). The contradictory structure of systems development methodologies: Deconstructing the IS-user relationship in information engineering. *Information Systems Research*, 5(4), 350–377. doi:10.1287/isre.5.4.350.

Bedell, S., Agrawal, A., & Petersen, L. (2004). A systematic critique of diabetes on the world wide web for patients and their physicians. *International Journal of Medical Informatics*, (73): 687–694. doi:10.1016/j.ijmedinf.2004.04.011 PMID:15325325.

Bednarz, S. W., & Kemp, K. (2011). Understanding and nurturing spatial literacy. *Spatial Thinking and Geographic Information Sciences Conference 2011*. Tokyo.

Behrouzi, M. (2005). *Democracy as the political empowerment of the citizen: Direct - deliberative e-democracy*. Lanham, MD: Lexington Books.

Bélanger, F., & Carter, L. (2009). The impact of the digital divide on e-government use. *Communications of the ACM*, 52(4), 132–135. doi:10.1145/1498765.1498801.

Bellio, E., & Buccoliero, L. (2009). E-government and web 2.0 applications: A multi-stakeholder evaluation. In H. Jochen Scholl, M. Janssen, R. Traunmüller, & M. A. Wimmer (Eds.), *General Development Issues and Projects of EGOV 09 8th International Conference*. Linz, Austria: Trauner.

Bellio, E. (2008). *Technologie web 2.0 nel rapporto pubblica amministrazione-cittadini: Un modello di valutazione*. Milan, Italy: Università Commerciale Luigi Bocconi.

Benbunan-Fich, R. (2001). Using protocol analysis to evaluate the usability of a commercial web site. *Information & Management*, 39(2), 151–163. doi:10.1016/S0378-7206(01)00085-4.

Benkler, Y. (2002). Coase's penguin, or, Linux and The nature of the firm. *The Yale Law Journal*, 112(3), 369–446. doi:10.2307/1562247.

Bennett, W.L., Wells, C., & Rank, A. (2009). Young citizens and civic learning: Two paradigms of citizenship in the digital age. *Citizenship Studies, 13* (2), 105–20. Retrieved March, 7, 2012 from http://dx.doi.org/10.1080/13621020902731116

Bergner, B., Exner, J., Zeile, P., & Broschart, D. (2012). *Humansensorik in der räumlichen Planung*. GISPoint. Retrieved July 19th, 2012, from http://gispoint.de/fileadmin/user_upload/paper_gis_open/537520019.pdf

Bernstein, J. (1995). *Recovering ethical life: Jürgen Habermas and the future of critical theory*. New York: Routledge.

Berry, J. M., Portney, K. E., & Thomson, K. (1993). *The rebirth of urban democracy*. Washington, DC: Brookings Institution.

Bertot, J. C., Jaeger, P. T., Munson, S., & Glaisyer, T. (2010). Engaging the public in open government: Social media technology and policy for government transparency. *IEEE Computer*, 43(11), 60–67. doi:10.1109/MC.2010.325.

Beyea, W., Geith, C., & McKeown, C. (2009). Place making through participatory planning. In Foth, M. (Ed.), *Urban informatics: The practice and promise of the real-time city* (pp. 55–67). Hershey, PA: IGI Global.

Bhattacharjee, Y. (2005). Citizen scientists supplement work of Cornell researchers. *Science, 308*, 1402–1403. doi:10.1126/science.308.5727.1402 PMID:15933178.

Bicheron, P., Defourny, P., Brockman, C., Schouten, L., Vancutsem, C., & Huc, M. et al. (2008). *GlobCover – Products description and validation report*. Toulouse: MEDIAS-France.

Bildt, C. (2012, July 5). A victory for the internet. *New York Times*. Retrieved from http://www.nytimes.com/2012/07/06/opinion/carl-bildt-a-victory-for-the-internet.html

Bilsel, R. U., Büyüközkan, G., & Ruan, D. (2006). A fuzzy preference-ranking model for a quality evaluation of hospital web sites. *International Journal of Intelligent Systems, 21*, 1181–1197. doi:10.1002/int.20177.

Biradar, C. M., Thenkabail, P. S., Noojipady, P., Li, Y., Dheeravath, V., & Turral, H. et al. (2009). A global map of rainfed cropland areas (GMRCA) at the end of the last millennium using remote sensing. *International Journal of Applied Earth Observation and Geoinformation, 11,* 114–129. doi:10.1016/j.jag.2008.11.002.

Birkholz, T., & Höffken, S. (2010). Reblog, RT@, FWD: Urbane Phänomene, soziale Netzwerke und vernetzte Kommunikation. *Spacemag, 3,* 88–91.

Bishr, M., & Janowicz, K. (2010). Can we trust information? - The case of volunteered geographic information. In Devaraju, A., Llaves, A., Maué, P., & Keßler, C. (Eds.), *Towards digital earth: Search, discover and share geospatial data.* CEUR-WS.

Bishr, M., & Kuhn, W. (2007). Geospatial information bottom-up: A matter of trust and semantics. In Fabrikant, S., & Wachowicz, M. (Eds.), *The European information society* (pp. 365–387). Berlin: Springer. doi:10.1007/978-3-540-72385-1_22.

Bishr, M., & Mantelas, L. (2008). A trust and reputation model for filtering and classifying knowledge about urban growth. *GeoJournal, 72*(3), 229–237. doi:10.1007/s10708-008-9182-4.

Bissel, D. (2009). Visualising everyday geographies: Practices of vision through travel-time. *Transactions of the Institute of British Geographers, 32,* 42–60. doi:10.1111/j.1475-5661.2008.00326.x.

Bitkom. (2012). *Smartphone-Funktionen: Internet wichtiger als Telefonieren.* Retrieved July 17th, 2012, from http://www.bitkom.org/de/presse/8477_72686.aspx

Biwer, J., Broschart, D., & Höffken, S. (2012). Mobile Digitalisierung von Baulücken – Baulückenerfassung mit GIS, iPad und Geoweb. In M. Schrenk, V.V. Popovich, P. Zeile, & P. Elisei (Eds.), *Proceedings REAL CORP 2012 Tagungsband.*

Blaschke, T., & Strobl, J. (2010). Geographic information science developments. *GIS.Science - Zeitschrift für Geoinformatik, 23*(1), 9-15.

Blaschke, T. (2004). Participatory GIS for spatial decision support systems critically revisited. In Egenhofer, M., Freksa, C., & Miller, H. (Eds.), *GIScience 2004* (pp. 257–261). Adelphi, MD.

Blaschke, T., Donert, K., Gossette, F., Kienberger, S., Marani, M., Qureshi, S., & Tiede, D. (2012). Virtual globes: Serving science and society. *Information, 3*(3), 372–390. doi:10.3390/info3030372.

Blaschke, T., Strobl, J., Schrott, L., Marschallinger, R., Neubauer, F., & Koch, A. et al. (2012). Geographic information science as a common cause for interdisciplinary research. In Gensel, J., Josselin, D., & Vandenbroucke, D. (Eds.), *Bridging the geographic information sciences* (pp. 411–427). Berlin, Heidelberg: Springer Lecture Notes in Geoinformation and Cartography. doi:10.1007/978-3-642-29063-3_22.

Bluestein, F. (2009, August 5). Limited public forum analysis revisited. *Coates' canons: NC local government law blog* [Weblog]. Retrieved September 15, 2012, from http://canons.sog.unc.edu/?p=139

Bluestein, F. (2010a, March 3). Free speech rights in government social media sites. *Coates' canons: NC local government law blog* [Weblog]. Retrieved September 15, 2012, from http://canons.sog.unc.edu/?p=1970

Bluestein, F. (2010b, April 14). Citizen participation information as public record. *Coates' canons: NC local government law blog* [Weblog]. Retrieved September 15, 2012, from http://canons.sog.unc.edu/?p=2238

Bodymonitor. (2012). *Project website.* Retrieved August 19th, 2012, from http://www.bodymonitor.de/

Boero, R., Ferro, E., Osella, M., Charalabidis, Y., & Loukis, E. (2011). Policy intelligence in the era of social computing: towards a cross-policy decision support system. In Garcia-Castro, R. et al. (Eds.), *ESWC 2011 Workshops (LNCS)* (Vol. 7117, pp. 217–228). Berlin: Springer-Verlag. doi:10.1007/978-3-642-25953-1_18.

Bongard, J. C., Hines, P. D. H., Conger, D., Hurd, P., & Lu, Z. (in press). Crowdsourcing predictors of behavioral outcomes. *IEEE Transactions on Systems, Man, and Cybernetics. Part A, Systems and Humans.*

Bonney, R., Ballard, H., Jordan, R., McCallie, E., Phillips, T., Shirk, J., & Wilderman, C. C. (2009). Public participation in scientific research: Defining the field and assessing its potential for informal science education. A CAISE Inquiry Group Report. Washington, DC: Center for Advancement of Informal Science Education (CAISE).

Bontemps, S., Defourney, P., Van Bogaert, E., Arino, O., Kalogirou, V., & Perez, J. R. (2010). *GlobCover 2009 - Products description and validation report*. Toulouse: MEDIAS-France.

Bottger, P. C., & Yetton, P. W. (1988). An integration of process and decision scheme explanations of group problem solving performance. *Organizational Behavior and Human Decision Processes, 42*(2), 234–249. doi:10.1016/0749-5978(88)90014-3.

Boulianne, S. (2009). Does Internet use affect engagement? A meta-analysis of research. *Political Communication, 26*(2), 193–211. doi:10.1080/10584600902854363.

Bourgoin, J., & Castella, J.-C. (2011). PLUP fiction: Landscape simulation for participatory land use planning in northern Lao PDR. *Mountain Research and Development, 31*, 78–88. doi:10.1659/MRD-JOURNAL-D-10-00129.1.

Bourgoin, J., Castella, J.-C., Pullar, D., Lestrelin, G., & Bouahom, B. (2012). Toward a land zoning negotiation support platform: "Tips and tricks" for participatory land use planning in Laos. *Landscape and Urban Planning, 104*, 270–278. doi:10.1016/j.landurbplan.2011.11.008.

Brabham, D. C. (2008). Moving the crowd at iStockphoto: The composition of the crowd and motivations for participation in a crowdsourcing application. *First Monday, 13*(6). Retrieved September 15, 2012, from http://firstmonday.org/htbin/cgiwrap/bin/ojs/index.php/fm/article/view/2159/1969

Brabham, D. C. (2009). Crowdsourcing the public participation process for planning projects. *Planning Theory, 8*, 242-262. Retrieved from http://plt.sagepub.com/content/8/3/242

Brabham, D. C. (2009). Crowdsourced advertising: How we outperform Madison Avenue. *Flow: A Critical Forum on Television and Media Culture, 9*(10). Retrieved September 15, 2012, from http://flowtv.org/?p=3221

Brabham, D. C., Sanchez, T. W., & Bartholomew, K. (2010). *Crowdsourcing public participation in transit planning: Preliminary results from the Next Stop Design case*. Presented at the annual meeting of the Transportation Research Board of the National Academies, Washington, DC.

Brabham, D. C. (2008). Crowdsourcing as a model for problem solving: An introduction and cases. *Convergence. The International Journal of Research into New Media Technologies, 14*(1). doi:10.1177/1354856507084420.

Brabham, D. C. (2009). Crowdsourcing the public participation process for planning projects. *Planning Theory, 8*(3), 242–262. doi:10.1177/1473095209104824.

Brabham, D. C. (2010). Moving the crowd at Threadless: Motivations for participation in a crowdsourcing application. *Information Communication and Society, 13*(8), 1122–1145. doi:10.1080/13691181003624090.

Brabham, D. C. (2012). Crowdsourcing: A model for leveraging online communities. In Delwiche, A., & Henderson, J. J. (Eds.), *The participatory cultures handbook* (pp. 120–129). New York: Routledge.

Brainard, L., & Derrick-Mills, T. (2011). Electronic commons, community policing, and communication: Online police-citizen discussion groups in Washington, DC. *Administrative Theory & Praxis, 33*(3), 383–410. doi:10.2753/ATP1084-1806330304.

Brainard, L., & McNutt, J. (2010). Government-citizen relations: Informational, transactional, or collaborative? *Administration & Society, 42*, 836–858. doi:10.1177/0095399710386308.

Braschler, B. (2009). Successfully implementing a citizen-scientist approach to insect monitoring in a resource-poor country. *Bioscience, 59*, 103–104. doi:10.1525/bio.2009.59.2.2.

Bravo, M., de los Ángeles Gallardo, M., Luna-Jorquera, G., Núñez, P., Vásquez, N., & Thiel, M. (2009). Anthropogenic debris on beaches in the SE Pacific (Chile): Results from a national survey supported by volunteers. *Marine Pollution Bulletin, 58*, 1718–1726. doi:10.1016/j.marpolbul.2009.06.017 PMID:19665738.

Brossard, D., Lewenstein, B., & Bonney, R. (2005). Scientific knowledge and attitude change: The impact of a citizen science project. *International Journal of Science Education, 27*, 1099–1121. doi:10.1080/09500690500069483.

Brown. (2005). Electronic government and public administration. *International Review of Administrative Sciences, 71*, 241-254.

Bruns, A. (2008). *Blogs, Wikipedia, Second Life, and beyond: From production to produsage.* New York: Peter Lang.

Bryer, T. A. (2011). Online public engagement in the Obama administration: Building a democracy bubble? *Policy & Internet, 3*(4), Article 3.

Bryer, T. A. (2011). The costs of democratization: Social media adaptation challenges within government agencies. *Administrative Theory & Praxis, 33*(3), 341–361. doi:10.2753/ATP1084-1806330302.

Bryer, T. A. (2012). Encouraging citizenship in U.S. presidential administrations: An analysis of presidential records. In Schachter, H., & Yang, K. (Eds.), *The state of citizen participation in America* (pp. 55–75). Charlotte, NC: Information Age Publishing.

Bryer, T. A. (in press). Public participation in regulatory decision-making: Cases from regulations.gov. *Public Performance and Management Review.*

Bryer, T. A., & Zavattaro, S. M. (2011). Social media and public administration: Theoretical dimensions and introduction to symposium. *Administrative Theory & Praxis, 33*(3), 325–340. doi:10.2753/ATP1084-1806330301.

Buccoliero, L. (2009). Il governo elettronico: Modelli, strategie di innovazione ed elementi di valore per una pubblica amministrazione digitale. Milano, Italy: Tecniche Nuove.

Buccoliero, L., Bellio, E., & Prenestini, A. (2010). Patient web empowerment index (PWEI): A tool for the assessment of healthcare providers' web strategies: A first benchmark of Italian NHS hospitals. In C. Safran, S. Reti, & H. Marin (Eds.), *MEDINFO 2010 Proceedings of the 13th World Congress on Medical Informatics.* Amsterdam: IOS Press.

Buccoliero, L., & Bellio, E. (2010). Citizens web empowerment in European municipalities. *Journal of E-Governance, 33*(4), 11.

Buchanan, L. (2010). *A business framework and operating model for CRM and Social CRM.* Retrieved from http://www.capgemini.com/technology-blog/2010/04/a_business_framework_and_opera/.

Buchanan, E. A. (2012). E-research ethics and e-planning: Emerging considerations for transformative research. *International Journal of E-Planning Research, 1*(1), 5–15. doi:10.4018/ijepr.2012010102.

Buhrmester, M., Kwang, T., & Gosling, S. D. (2011). Amazon's mechanical Turk: A new source of inexpensive, yet high-quality, data? *Perspectives on Psychological Science, 6*(1), 3–5. doi:10.1177/1745691610393980.

Burby, R. J. (2003). Making plans that matter: Citizen involvement and government action. *Journal of the American Planning Association. American Planning Association, 69*(1), 33–49. doi:10.1080/01944360308976292.

Burke, J. A., Estrin, D., Hansen, M., Parker, A., Ramanathan, N., Reddy, S., & Srivastava, M. B. (2006). Participatory sensing. Papers, Center for Embedded Network Sensing, UC Los Angeles. *World Sensor Web Workshop, ACM Sensys 2006.* Boulder, Colorado.

Butler, D. (2006). Virtual globes: The web-wide world. *Nature, 439*, 776–778. doi:10.1038/439776a PMID:16482123.

Calhoun, C. (1992). *Habermas and the public sphere.* Cambridge, MA: MIT Press.

Callison-Burch, C. (2009). Fast, cheap, and creative: Evaluating translation quality using Amazon's mechanical Turk. *Proceedings of the 2009 conference on empirical methods in natural language processing* (pp. 286–295). Stroudsburg, PA: Association for Computational Linguistics.

Cammaerts, B. (2008). Critiques on the participatory potentials of Web 2.0. *Communication, Culture & Critique, 1*(4), 358–377. doi:10.1111/j.1753-9137.2008.00028.x.

Caron, C., Roche, S., Goyer, D., & Jaton, A. (2008). GIScience journals ranking and evaluation: An international delphi study. *Transactions in GIS, 12*(3), 293–321. doi:10.1111/j.1467-9671.2008.01106.x.

Carrier, I. Q. (2012). Handsets deployed. *Carrier IQ Website.* Retrieved July 22, 2012, http://www.carrieriq.com/

Carver, S. (2003). *The future of participatory approaches using geographic information: Developing a research agenda for the 21st Century*. Position paper prepared for ESF-NSF Meeting on Access and Participatory Approaches in Using Geographic Information, Spoleto Italy, December 5–9, 2001.

Carver, S., Evans, A., Kingston, R., & Turton, I. (2001). Public participation, GIS, and cyberdemocracy: Evaluating on-line spatial decision support systems. *Environment and Planning. B, Planning & Design, 28*, 907–921. doi:10.1068/b2751t.

Casey, C., & Li, J. (2012). Web 2.0 technologies and authentic public participation: Engaging citizens in decision making processes. In Kloby, K., & D'Agostinho, M. J. (Eds.), *Citizen 2.0: Public and governmental interaction through Web 2.0 technologies* (pp. 197–223). Hershey: IGI-Global. doi:10.4018/978-1-4666-0318-9.ch011.

Castells, M. (1996). *The rise of the network society*. Oxford: Blackwell Publishers.

Castells, M. (2001). *The Internet galaxy. Reflections on the Internet, business, and society*. Oxford: Oxford University Press.

Castells, M. (2009). *Communication power*. New York: Oxford University Press.

Castells, M., & Cardoso, G. (2006). *Network society: From knowledge to policy*. Washington, DC: Center for Transatlantic Relations, Paul H. Nitze School of Advanced International Studies, Johns Hopkins University.

Castells, M., Fernandez-Ardevol, M., Linchuan Qiu, J., & Sey, A. (2006). *Mobile communication and society: A global perspective*. Cambridge: MIT Press.

Center for International Earth Science Information Network (CIESIN). (2004). *Global rural-urban mapping project (GRUMP): Urban extents*. Retrieved February 21, 2011, from http://sedac.ciesin.columbia.edu/gpw

Chang, C.-C., & Chen, Y.-F. (2007). Designing a CRM-based e-government usability services framework: Integrating internal and external customers in public services. In Li, F. (Ed.), *Social implications and challenges of e-business* (pp. 57–77). Hershey, PA, US: Information Science Reference/IGI Global. doi:10.4018/978-1-59904-105-6.ch005.

Chao, H. (2002). Assessing the quality of academic libraries on the web: The development and testing of criteria. *Library & Information Science Research, (24)*: 169–194. doi:10.1016/S0740-8188(02)00111-1.

Chapin, M., Lamb, Z., & Threkeld, B. (2005). Mapping indigenous lands. *Annual Review of Anthropology, 34*, 619–638. doi:10.1146/annurev.anthro.34.081804.120429.

Chen, B. X., & Sengupta, S. (2011, December 2). Programmer raises concerns about phone-monitoring software. *New York Times*. Retrieved from http://bits.blogs.nytimes.com/2011/12/01/programmer-raises-concerns-about-phone-monitoring-software/

Chesbrough, H. (2003). *Open innovation: The new imperative for creating and profiting from technology*. Boston, MA: Harvard Business Press.

Chopra, A., & Metzenbaum, S. (2010, December 8). Designing for democracy. *U.S. White House Open Government Initiative* [Weblog]. Retrieved September 15, 2012, from http://www.whitehouse.gov/blog/2010/12/08/designing-democracy-0

Chung, T., & Law, R. (2003). Developing a performance indicator for hotel websites. *International Journal of Hospitality Management, (22)*: 119–125. doi:10.1016/S0278-4319(02)00076-2.

Chun, S. A., & Artigas, F. (2012). Sensors and crowdsourcing for environmental awareness and emergency planning. *International Journal of E-Planning Research, 1*(1), 56–74. doi:10.4018/ijepr.2012010106.

Chu, P.-Y., Yeh, S.-C., & Chuang, M.-C. (2008). Reengineering municipality citizen electronic complaint system through citizen relationship management. *Electronic Government, 5*(3), 288–309. doi:10.1504/EG.2008.018876.

Cinderby, S. (1999). Geographic information systems (GIS) for participation: The future of environal GIS? *International Journal of Environment and Pollution, 11*, 304–315. doi:10.1504/IJEP.1999.002263.

Cinderyb, S., & Forrester, J. (2005). Facilitating the local governance of air pollution using GIS for participation. *Applied Geography (Sevenoaks, England), 2005*, 143–158. doi:10.1016/j.apgeog.2005.03.003.

City of Waterloo. (2011). *My Future. My Say. My Waterloo.* Retrieved from www.MyFutureWaterloo.ca.

CitySourced. (2012). *Project website.* Retrieved July 17th, 2012, from http://www.citysourced.com/about

Clarke, K. C. (1997). *Getting started with GIS.* Upper Saddle River: Prentice Hall, Inc..

Cleveland, H. (1985). The twilight of hierarchy: Speculations on the global information society. *Public Administration Review, 45*(2), 185–195. doi:10.2307/3110148.

Coast, S. (2007). OpenStreetMap. *Volunteered Geographic Information Workshop.* Retrieved from http://ncgia.ucsb.edu/projects/vgi/products.html

Coast, S. (2011). How OpenStreetMap is changing the world. In Tanaka, K., Fröhlich, P., & Kim, K.-S. (Eds.), *Web and wireless geographical information systems* (p. 4). Berlin, Heidelberg: Springer. doi:10.1007/978-3-642-19173-2_2.

Coglianese, G. (2007). Weak democracy, strong information: The role of information technology in the rulemaking process. In Mayer-Schonberger, V., & Lazer, D. (Eds.), *Governance and information technology: From electronic government to information government.* Cambridge, MA: MIT Press.

Cohen, J. E. (2006). Citizen satisfaction with contacting government on the internet. *Information Polity: The International Journal of Government & Democracy in the Information Age, 11*(1), 15.

Coleman, S., & Gotze, J. (n.d.). *Bowling together: Online public engagement in policy deliberation.* London: Hansard Society – London School of Economics.

Coleman, D. J. (2010). The potential and early limitations of volunteered geographic information. *GEOMATICA, 64*(2), 209–219.

Coleman, S., & Gøtze, J. (2001). *Bowling together: Online public engagement in policy deliberation online public engagement in policy deliberation.* London, UK: Hansard Society.

Comber, A., See, L., Fritz, S., van der Velde, M., Perger, C., & Foody, G. (in press). Using volunteered geographic information to evaluate global land cover datasets. *International Journal of Applied Earth Observation and Geoinformation.*

Commonwealth of Learning. (2011). *Designing mobile information and content strategies for grassroots participation.* Retrieved July 17th, 2012, from http://www.col.org/SiteCollectionDocuments/Watkins_Mobile%20Research_110808.pdf

Compaine, B. M. (2001). *The digital divide. Facing a crisis or creating a myth?* Cambridge, London: MIT Press.

ComScore. (2012). *Number of European smartphone users accessing news surges 74 percent over past year.* Retrieved July 17th, 2012, from http://www.comscore.com/Press_Events/Press_Releases/2012/3/Number_of_European_Smartphone_Users_Accessing_News_Surges_74_Percent_Over_Past_Year?piCId=66038

Conrad, C. T., & Daoust, T. (2008). Community-based monitoring frameworks: Increasing the effectiveness of environmental stewardship. *Environmental Management, 41*, 358–366. doi:10.1007/s00267-007-9042-x PMID:18026783.

Conroy, M. M., & Evans-Cowley, J. (2004). E-participation in planning: An analysis of cities adopting online citizen participation tools. *Environment and Planning. C, Government & Policy, 24*, 371–384. doi:10.1068/c1k.

Conroy, M. M., & Evans-Cowley, J. (2006). E-participation in planning: An analysis of cities adopting on-line citizen participation tools. *Environment and Planning. C, Government & Policy, 24*, 371–384. doi:10.1068/c1k.

Cooke, B., & Kothari, U. (2001). *Participation: The new tyranny?* London, UK: Zed Books.

Cooper, C. B. (2012). *Retro science.* Scientific American guest blog post. Retrieved November 1, 2012, from http://blogs.scientificamerican.com/guest-blog/2012/08/23/retro-science-part-1/

Cooper, C. B. (2012). *Victorian-era citizen science: Reports of its death have been greatly exaggerated.* Scientific American guest blog post. Retrieved November 1, 2012, from http://blogs.scientificamerican.com/guestblog/2012/08/30/victorian-era-citizen-science-reports-of-its-death-have-been-greatly-exaggerated/

Cooper, C. B., Dickinson, J., Phillips, T., & Bonney, R. (2007). Citizen science as a tool for conservation in residential ecosystems. *Ecology and Society, 12*(2), 11. Retrieved from http://www.ecologyandsociety.org/vol12/iss2/art11/

Cooper, C. B., Dickinson, J., Phillips, T., & Bonney, R. (2007). Citizen science as a tool for conservation in residential ecosystems. *Ecology and Society, 12*(2), 11.

Cooper, C. B., Hochachka, W. M., & Dhondt, A. A. (2012). The opportunities and challenges of citizen science as a tool for ecological research. In Dickinson, J. L., & Bonney, R. (Eds.), *Citizen science: Public collaboration in environmental research.* Ithaca, NY: Cornell University Press.

Cooper, T. L. (1991). *An ethic of citizenship for public administration.* Englewood Cliffs, NJ: Prentice Hall.

Cooper, T. L. (2005). Civic engagement in the twenty-first century: Toward a scholarly and practical agenda. *Public Administration Review, 65*(5), 534–535. doi:10.1111/j.1540-6210.2005.00480.x.

Corbett, J., Rambaldi, G., Kyem, P., Weiner, D., Olson, R., Muchemi, J., McCall, M., & Chambers, R. (2006). Overview: Mapping for change—the emergence of a new practice. *Participatory learning and action,* 54, 13-20.

Corbett, J. M., & Keller, C. P. (2005). An analytical framework to examine empowerment associated with participatory geographic information systems (PGIS). *Cartographica: The International Journal for Geographic Information and Geovisualization, 40*(4), 91–102. doi:10.3138/J590-6354-P38V-4269.

Corbin, K. (2012). Salesforce to launch government cloud. *CIO.* Retrieved from http://www.cio.com/article/704903/Salesforce_to_Launch_Government_Cloud

Cornwall, A. (2008). Unpacking 'participation': Models, meanings, and practices. *Community Development Journal, 43,* 269–283. doi:10.1093/cdj/bsn010.

Cornwell, M. L., & Campbell, L. M. (2012). Co-producing conservation and knowledge: Citizen-based sea turtle monitoring in North Carolina, USA. *Social Studies of Science, 42,* 101–120. doi:10.1177/0306312711430440.

Cox, J., & Dale, B. (2002). Key quality factors in web site design and use: An examination. *International Journal of Quality & Reliability Management,* (19): 862–888. doi:10.1108/02656710210434784.

Cox, K. R. (1998). Spaces of dependence, spaces of engagement and the politics of scale, or: looking for local politics. *Political Geography, 17*(1), 1–23. doi:10.1016/S0962-6298(97)00048-6.

Craglia, M., Goodchild, M. F., & Annoni, A. et al. (2008). Next-generation digital earth: A position paper from the Vespucci initiative for the advancement of geographic information science. *International Journal of Spatial Data Infrastructures Research, 3,* 146–167.

Craig, W. J., Harris, T. M., & Weiner, D. (2002). Community participation and geographic information systems. In Craig, W. J., Harris, T. M., & Weiner, D. (Eds.), *Community participation and geographic information systems* (pp. 3–16). London: Taylor and Francis.

Craig, W., & Elwood, S. (1998). How and why community groups use maps and geographic information. *Cartography and Geographic Information Systems, 25,* 95–104. doi:10.1559/152304098782594616.

Crampton, J. W. (2003). Cartographic rationality and the politics of geosurveillance and security. *Cartography and Geographic Information Systems, 30*(2), 135–148. doi:10.1559/152304003100011108.

Crampton, J. W. (2010). *Mapping: A critical introduction to cartography and GIS.* Oxford, UK: Wiley-Blackwell.

Crang, M., Crosbie, T., & Graham, S. (2006). Variable geometries of connection: Urban digital divides and the uses of information technology. *Urban Studies (Edinburgh, Scotland), 43*(13), 2551–2570. doi:10.1080/00420980600970664.

Crosby, N., Kelly, J. M., & Schaefer, P. (1986). Citizen panels: A new approach to citizen participation. *Public Administration Review, 46*(2), 170–178. doi:10.2307/976169.

Curry, M. R. (1997). The digital divide and the private realm. *Annals of the Association of American Geographers. Association of American Geographers*, 87(4), 681–699. doi:10.1111/1467-8306.00073.

Dai, X., & Norton, P. (2008). *The Internet and parliamentary democracy in Europe: A comparative study of the ethics of political communication in the digital age.* New York, NY: Routledge.

Damurski, Ł. (2012). E-participation in urban planning: Online tools for citizen engagement in Poland and in Germany. *International Journal of E-Planning Research*, 1(3), 40–67. doi:10.4018/ijepr.2012070103.

Danko, D. (1992). The digital chart of the world project. *Photogrammetric Engineering and Remote Sensing*, 58, 1125–1128.

Davidoff, P. (1965). Advocacy and pluralism in planning. *Journal of the American Institute of Planners*, 31, 331–318. doi:10.1080/01944366508978187.

De Longueville, B. (2010). Community-based geoportals: The next generation? Concepts and methods for the geospatial Web 2.0. *Computers, Environment and Urban Systems*, 34(4), 299–308. doi:10.1016/j.compenvurbsys.2010.04.004.

De Longueville, B., Luraschi, G., Smits, P., Peedell, S., & De Groeve, T. (2010). Citizens as sensors for natural hazards: A VGI integration workflow. *Geomatica*, 64(1), 41–59.

de Selding, P. B. (2012). *European officials dial back GMES funding expectations.* Retrieved October 29, 2012, from http://www.spacenews.com/civil/120927-officials-gmes-funding.html

Demchak, C., Friis, C., & La Porte, T. M. (2000). *Webbing governance: National differences in constructing the public face.* New York: Marcel Dekker Publishers.

Denhardt, J. V., & Denhardt, R. B. (2003). *The new public service: Serving, not steering.* Armonk, NY: M.E. Sharpe.

Dennis, A. R., & Reinicke, B. A. (2004). BETA versus VHS and the acceptance of electronic brainstorming technology. *Management Information Systems Quarterly*, 28(1), 1–20.

Dennis, A. R., Tyran, C. K., Vogel, D. R., & Nunamaker, J. F. (1997). Group support systems planning strategic. *Journal of Management Information Systems*, 14(1), 155–184.

Dennis, A. R., Wixom, B. H., & Vandenberg, R. J. (2001). Understanding fit and appropriation effects in group support systems via meta-analysis. *Management Information Systems Quarterly*, 25(2), 167–193. doi:10.2307/3250928.

Densham, P. J. (1991). Spatial decision support systems. In D.J. Maguire, M. F. Goodchild, & D. W. Rhind (Eds.), Geographical information systems: Principles and applications, Vol.1 (pp. 403–412). Longmont, Harlow, Essex, England: Longman Scientific & Technical.

Derene, G. (2011). Tracking software caught snooping on millions of smartphones. *Popular Mechanics*. Retrieved from http://www.popularmechanics.com/technology/gadgets/news/tracking-software-caught-snooping-on-millions-of-smartphone-users-6606335

Devillers, R., & Jeansoulin, R. (2006). Spatial data quality: Concepts. In Devillers, R., & Jeansoulin, R. (Eds.), *Fundamentals of spatial data quality* (pp. 31–42). London: ISTE. doi:10.1002/9780470612156.ch2.

Di Maio, A., Kreizman, G., Harris, R. G., Rust, B., & Rishi, S. (2005). *Government in 2020: Taking the long view.* New York: Gartner Inc..

Dijk, J. (2000). Models of democracy and concepts of communication. In Hacker, K., & van Dijk, J. (Eds.), *Digital democracy, issues of theory and practice*. London: Sage.

Doan, S., Vo, B.-K. H., & Collier, N. (2011). An analysis of Twitter messages in the 2011 Tohoku Earthquake. In *Proceedings of the 4th ICST International Conference on eHealth*. Berlin/Heidelberg: Springer.

Dobson, J. E., & Fisher, P. F. (2006). Panopticon III: Gaming the national debate over human tracking. *Chapter presented at the American Association for the Advancement of Science (AAAS)*. St. Louis, Mo.

Dobson, J. E., Bright, E. A., Coleman, P. R., & Bhaduri, B. L. (2003). LandScan: A global population database for estimating populations at risk. In Mesev, V. (Ed.), *Remotely sensed cities* (pp. 267–281). London: Taylor & Francis.

Dobson, J., & Fisher, P. (2007). The panopticon's changing geography. *Geographical Review*, *97*(3), 307–324.

Dodge, M., & Kitchin, R. (2005). Code and the transduction of space. *Annals of the Association of American Geographers. Association of American Geographers*, *95*, 162–180. doi:10.1111/j.1467-8306.2005.00454.x.

Drucker, S., & Gumpert, G. (1995). Freedom and liability in cyberspace: Media, metaphors and paths of regulation. *Free Speech Yearbook*, *33*, 49–64. doi:10.1080/08997225.1995.10556182.

Duffy, J. (2011). CRM Trends in Western Europe's Government Sector (Technology Selection, Trans.) IDC Government Insights (pp. 18): IDC.

Duhigg, C. (2012). How companies learn your secrets. *New York Times*. Retrieved from http://www.nytimes.com/2012/02/19/magazine/shopping-habits.html?_r=1&pagewanted=all

Dunn, C. (2007). Participatory GIS – A people's GIS? *Progress in Human Geography*, *31*(5), 616–637. doi:10.1177/0309132507081493.

Dunn, C. E. (2007). Participatory GIS – A people's GIS? *Progress in Human Geography*, *31*(5), 616–637. doi:10.1177/0309132507081493.

Dutta, P., Aoki, P. M., Kumar, N., Mainwaring, A., Myers, C., Willett, W., & Woodruff, A. (2009). Common sense: Participatory urban sensing using a network of handheld air quality monitors (demonstration). Proc. SenSys 2009. Berkeley, CA, Nov. 2009, 349-350.

Dutton, W. H. (1996). Network rules of order: Regulating speech in public electronic fora. *Media Culture & Society*, *18*(2), 269–290. doi:10.1177/016344396018002006.

Eastman, R., Kyem, P. A., Toledano, J., & Weigen, J. (Eds.). (1992). GIS and decision making. Explorations in geographic information systems technology: A workbook series. Worcester, MA: Developed by the Clark Labs. Published by UNITAR (United Nations Institute for Training and Research).

Ebdon, C. (2000). The relationship between citizen involvement in the budget process and city structure and culture. *Public Productivity and Management Review*, *23*(3), 383–393. doi:10.2307/3380726.

Ebdon, C. (2002). Beyond the public hearing: Citizen participation in the local government budget process. *Journal of Public Budgeting, Accounting, and Financial Management*, *14*(2), 273–294.

Ebdon, C., & Franklin, A. L. (2004). Searching for a role for citizens in the budget process. *Public Budgeting & Finance*, *24*(1), 32–49. doi:10.1111/j.0275-1100.2004.02401002.x.

Ebdon, C., & Franklin, A. L. (2006). Citizen participation in budgeting theory. *Public Administration Review*, *66*(3), 437–447. doi:10.1111/j.1540-6210.2006.00600.x.

EC. (2009). *European e-participation. Summary Report*. Brussels: European Commission.

Eckhart, T. (2011). Carrier IQ Part #2. *YouTube*. Retrieved from http://www.youtube.com/watch?v=T17XQI_AYNo

Economist. (2011). Big data: Harnessing a game-changing asset. *Economist Intelligence Unit*.

Economist. (2012). *Make your own Angry Birds - Homebrew apps have arrived*. Retrieved August 18th, 2012, from http://www.economist.com/node/21559366

Elektronikkompendium. (2012). *Datenübertragung im Mobilfunk*. Retrieved July 21th, 2012, from http://www.elektronik-kompendium.de/sites/kom/0910141.htm

Ellis, R., & Waterton, C. (2004). Environmental citizenship in the making: The participation of volunteer naturalists in UK biological recording and biodiversity policy. *Science & Public Policy*, *31*, 95–105. doi:10.3152/147154304781780055.

Ellul, C., Haklay, M., & Francis, L. (2008). Empowering individuals and communities - is Web GIS the way forward? In (Proceedings) AGI GeoCommunity '08. Stratford-upon-Avon, UK.

Elvidge, C., Tuttle, B., Sutton, P., Baugh, K., Howard, A., & Milesi, C. et al. (2007). Global distribution and density of constructed impervious surfaces. *Sensors (Basel, Switzerland)*, *7*, 1962–1979. doi:10.3390/s7091962.

Elwood, S. (2006). Critical issues in participatory GIS: Deconstructions, reconstructions, and new research directions. *Transactions in GIS*, *10*(5), 693–708. doi:10.1111/j.1467-9671.2006.01023.x.

Elwood, S. (2008). Volunteered geographic information: Future research directions motivated by critical, participatory, and feminist GIS. *GeoJournal, 72*, 173–183. doi:10.1007/s10708-008-9186-0.

Engel, S. R., & Voshell, J. R. Jr. (2002). Volunteer biological monitoring: Can it accurately assess the ecological condition of streams?[Entomological Society of America.]. *American Entomologist, 48*, 164–177.

Environmental Systems Research Institute – ESRI. (2008). *Geography Matters*. An ESRI White Paper. Retrieved March 7, 2012, from http://www.gisday.com/cd2008/whitepaper/geography-matters.pdf

Erickson, T. (2010). Geocentric crowdsourcing and smarter cities: Enabling urban intelligence in cities and regions. *Crowdsourcing*. Retrieved July 17th, 2012, from http://www.crowdsourcing.org/document/geocentric-crowdsourcing-and-smarter-cities/5678

Eschenfelder, K. R., Beachboard, J. C., McClure, C. R., & Wyman, S. K. (1997). Assessing U.S. federal government websites. *Government Information Quarterly, 14*(2), 16. doi:10.1016/S0740-624X(97)90018-6.

Estellés Arolas, E., & González Ladrón-de-Guevara, F. (2012). Towards an integrated crowdsourcing definition. *Journal of Information Science*. Retrieved July 17th, 2012, from http://www.crowdsourcing-blog.org/wp-content/uploads/2012/02/Towards-an-integrated-crowdsourcing-definition-Estell%C3%A9s-Gonz%C3%A1lez.pdf

European Commission. (2007). *Communicating about Europe via the Internet - engaging the citizens*. Retrieved from http://ec.europa.eu/dgs/communication/pdf/internet-strategy_en.pdf

European Commission. (2008). *ICT for government and public services*. Retrieved from http://ec.europa.eu/information

European Commission. (2009). *European eparticipation summary report, study and supply of services on the development of eparticipation in the EU*. Brussels: European Commission.

European Commission. (2011). *Cities of tomorrow – Challenges, visions, ways forward, policy document*. Retrieved from http://bit.ly/SnJB0T

Evans-Cowley, J. S. (2010). Planning in the age of Facebook: The role of social networking in planning processes. *GeoJournal, 75*, 407–420. doi:10.1007/s10708-010-9388-0.

Evans-Cowley, J. S. (2012). There's an app for that: Mobile applications for urban planning. *International Journal of E-Planning Research, 1*(2), 79–87. doi:10.4018/ijepr.2012040105.

Evans-Cowley, J. S., & Conroy, M. M. (2006). The growth of e-government in municipal planning. *Journal of Urban Technology, 12*, 81–107. doi:10.1080/10630730600752892.

Evans-Cowley, J. S., & Hollander, J. (2010). The new generation of public participation: Internet based participation tools. *Planning Research and Practice, 25*, 397–408. doi:10.1080/02697459.2010.503432.

Evans-Cowley, J., & Hollander, J. (2010). The new generation of public participation: Internet-based participation tools. *Planning Practice and Research, 25*(3), 397–408. doi:10.1080/02697459.2010.503432.

Facebook. (2012). Facebook login page. *Facebook*. Retrieved from http://www.facebook.com/

Fahim, K. (2011). Slap to a man's pride set off tumult in Tunisia. *New York Times*. Retrieved from http://www.nytimes.com/2011/01/22/world/africa/22sidi.html?pagewanted=all

Faludi, A. (1973). The rationale of planning theory. In Faludi, A. (Ed.), *A reader in planning theory* (pp. 35–53). Oxford, UK: Pergamon Press.

FAO. (2005). *Mapping global urban and rural population distributions*. Environment and Natural Resources Working Paper No. 24. Rome: FAO.

FAO. (2006). *Food insecurity, poverty and environment. Global GIS Database: DVD and atlas for the year 2000*. Environment and Natural Resources Working Paper No. 26. Rome: FAO.

Farrelly, M. (2009). Citizen participation and neighbourhood governance: Analysing democratic practice. *Local Government Studies, 35*(4), 13. doi:10.1080/03003930902992675.

Fay, M., & Morrison, M. (2006). *Infrastructure in Latin America and the Caribbean: Recent developments and key challenges.* World Bank Report.

Feldman, L. D. (2008). Strategic planning for municipalities: A users' guide[review]. *Canadian Public Administration-Administration Publique Du Canada, 51*(2), 375–376. doi:10.1111/j.1754-7121.2008.00028.x.

Felt, U., & Fochler, M. (2008). The bottom-up meanings of the concept of public participation in science and technology. *Science & Public Policy, 35*(7), 489–499. doi:10.3152/030234208X329086.

Fischer, F. (2012). *Geotagging and the city – Understanding the use of social location applications in urban space.* (Doctoral Thesis). Paris-Lodron University Salzburg.

Fischer, S. (2012). *Minderheit vergrößert digitale Kluft.* Taz Zeitung vom 23.02.2012. Retrieved from http://www.taz.de/Internetnutzung-in-Deutschland/!88344/

Fischer, F. (2009). Learning in Geocommunities. An explorative view on geo-social network communities. In Jekel, T., Koller, A., & Donert, K. (Eds.), *Lernen mit Geoinformation IV* (pp. 12–21). Heidelberg: Wichman.

Fisher, E. (1999). Low literacy levels in adults: Implications for patient education. *Journal of Continuing Education in Nursing, 30*(2), 56–61. PMID:10382455.

Flanagin, A. J., & Metzger, M. J. (2008). The credibility of volunteered geographic information. *GeoJournal, 72,* 137–148. doi:10.1007/s10708-008-9188-y.

Flanagin, A., & Metzger, M. (2008). The credibility of volunteered geographic information. *GeoJournal, 72*(3), 137–148. doi:10.1007/s10708-008-9188-y.

Fletcher, A. (2006). *Do consumers want to design unique products on the Internet?: A study of the online virtual community of Threadless.com and their attitudes to mass customisation, mass production and collaborative design.* (Unpublished bachelor's thesis). Nottingham Trent University.

Flyvberg, B. (1998). *Rationality and power: Democracy in practice.* Chicago: University of Chicago Press.

Foody, G., See, L., Fritz, S., Van der Velde, M., Perger, C., Schill, C., & Boyd, D. S. (in press). Assessing the accuracy of volunteered geographic information arising from multiple contributors to an internet based collaborative project. *Transactions in GIS.*

Fore, L. S., Paulsen, K., & O'Laughlin, K. (2001). Assessing the performance of volunteers in monitoring streams.[Seattle.]. *Freshwater Biology, 46*(1), 109–123.

Foth, M., Bajracharya, B., Brown, R. A., & Hearn, G. N. (2009). The second life of urban planning? Using neogeography tools for community engagement. *Journal of Location Based Services, 3*(2), 97–117. doi:10.1080/17489720903150016.

Foth, M., Bajracharya, B., Brown, R., & Hearn, G. (2009). The second life of urban planning? Using neogeography tools for community engagement. *Journal of Location Based Services, 3*(2), 97–117. doi:10.1080/17489720903150016.

Fountain, J. E. (Ed.). (2001). *Building the virtual state: Information technology and institutional change.* Washington, DC: Brookings Institution Press.

Franken, Al. (2011). Senator Franken demands answers from company accused of secretly logging location and private information. *Senator Al Franken website.* Retrieved from http://www.franken.senate.gov/?p=press_release&id=1868

Franklin, A., & Ebdon, C. (2005). Touching the same camel?: Exploring a model of participation in budgeting. *American Review of Public Administration, 35*(2), 168–185. doi:10.1177/0275074005275621.

Frederickson, H. G. (1973). *Neighborhood control in the 1970s: Politics, administration, and citizen participation.* New York: Chandler Publishing.

Frederickson, H. G., & O'Leary, L. S. (1973). *Power, public opinion, and policy in a metropolitan community: A case study of Syracuse, New York.* New York: Praeger Publishers.

Freire, M. (2006). Urban planning: Challenges in developing countries. In *Proceedings of the 1ˢᵗ International Congress on Human Development.* Madrid.

French, S., Insua, D. R., & Ruggeri, F. (2007). E-participation and decision analysis. *Decision Analysis, 4*(4), 211–226. doi:10.1287/deca.1070.0098.

Friedl, M. A., McIver, D. K., Hodges, J. C. F., Zhang, X. Y., Muchoney, D., & Strahler, A. H. et al. (2002). Global land cover mapping from MODIS: Algorithms and early results. *Remote Sensing of Environment, 83*, 287–302. doi:10.1016/S0034-4257(02)00078-0.

Friedl, M. A., Sulla-Menashe, D., Tan, B., Schneider, A., Ramankutty, N., Sibley, A., & Huang, X. (2010). MODIS Collection 5 global land cover: Algorithm refinements and characterization of new datasets. *Remote Sensing of Environment, 114*(1), 168–182. doi:10.1016/j.rse.2009.08.016.

Friedmann, J. (1973). The transactive style of planning. In Friedmann, J. (Ed.), *Retracking America: A theory of transactive planning* (pp. 171–193). New York: Doubleday.

Friedmann, J. (1994). The utility of non-Euclidean planning. *Journal of the American Planning Association. American Planning Association, 60*, 377–379. doi:10.1080/01944369408975595.

Fritz, S., Bartholomé, E., Belward, A., Hartley, A., Stibig, H. J., & Eva, H. et al. (2003). *Harmonisation, mosaicing and production of the Global Land Cover 2000 database (beta version)*. Luxembourg: Office for Official Publications of the European Communities.

Fritz, S., McCallum, I., Schill, C., Perger, C., See, L., & Schepaschenko, D. et al. (2012). Geo-Wiki: An online platform for land cover validation and the improvement of global land cover. *Environmental Modelling & Software, 31*, 110–123. doi:10.1016/j.envsoft.2011.11.015.

Fritz, S., See, L., McCallum, I., Schill, C., Obersteiner, M., Boettcher, H., & Achard, F. (2011). Highlighting continued uncertainty in global land cover maps. *Environmental Research Letters, 6*, 044005. doi:10.1088/1748-9326/6/4/044005.

Fritz, S., See, L., McCallum, I., Schill, C., Perger, C., & Obersteiner, M. (2011). Building a crowd-sourcing tool for the validation of urban extent and gridded population. *Lecture Notes in Computer Science, 6783*, 39–50. doi:10.1007/978-3-642-21887-3_4.

Fritz, S., You, L., Bun, A., See, L. M., McCallum, I., & Liu, J. et al. (2011). Cropland for sub-Saharan Africa: A synergistic approach using five land cover datasets. *Geophysical Research Letters, 38*, L04404. doi:10.1029/2010GL046213.

Fung, A. (2006). Varieties of participation in complex governance. Public Administration Review, Vol. 66, suplement: 66-75.

Gallo, T., & Waitt, D. (2011). Creating a successful citizen science model to detect and report invasive species. *Bioscience, 61*, 459–465. doi:10.1525/bio.2011.61.6.8.

Garside, B. (2009). *Village voice: Towards inclusive information technologies*. IIED Briefing Papers. London: IIED. Retrieved March 7, 2012, from http://tinyurl.com/IIED-ICTbriefing

Garson, D. G. (1999). *Information technology and computer applications in public administration: Issues and trends*. New York: Idea Group Publishing. doi:10.4018/978-1-87828-952-0.

Gascó, M. (2003). New technologies and institutional change in public administration. *Social Science Computer Review, 21*(1), 6–14. doi:10.1177/0894439302238967.

Gautney, H. (2011). What is occupy wall street? The history of leaderless movements. *Washington Post*. Retrieved from http://www.washingtonpost.com/national/on-leadership/what-is-occupy-wall-street-the-history-of-leaderless-movements/2011/10/10/gIQAwkFjaL_story.html

Ghonim, W. (2012). *Revolution 2.0: The power of the people is greater than the people in power*. New York: Houghton Mifflin Harcourt.

Ghose, R. (2001). Use of information technology for community empowerment: Transforming geographic information systems into community information systems. *Transactions in GIS, 5*(2), 141–163. doi:10.1111/1467-9671.00073.

Ghose, R. (2007). Politics of scale and networks of association in public participation GIS. *Environment & Planning A, 39*, 1961–1980. doi:10.1068/a38247.

Gibson, R. K., Lusoli, W., & Ward, S. (2005). Online participation in the UK: Testing a 'Contextualised' model of Internet effects. *British Journal of Politics and International Relations*, 7(4), 561–583. doi:10.1111/j.1467-856X.2005.00209.x.

Gill, K. (n.d.). *What is the fairness doctrine?* Retrieved from http://uspolitics.about.com/od/electionissues/a/fcc_fairness.htm

Giridharadas, A. (2009, September 12). "Athens" on the net. *New York Times*. Retrieved September 15, 2012, from http://www.nytimes.com/2009/09/13/weekinreview/13giridharadas.html?_r=3

Girishankar, N., & De Silva, M. (1998). *Strategic management for government agencies: An institutional approach for developing and transitioning economies.* Washginton, DC: World Bank. doi:10.1596/0-8213-4234-7.

Glennon, A. (2006). *Comments on naive geography, part 2.* Retrieved December 2, 2010, from http://geography2.blogspot.com/2006/06/comments-on-naive-geography-part-2.html

Golden, W., et al. (2003). *The role of process evolution in achieving citizen centered e-government.* Paper presented at the Ninth Americas Conference on Information Systems. New York, NY.

Goldewijk, K. (2005). Three centuries of global population growth: A spatially referenced population density database for 1700-2000. *Population and Environment*, 26, 343–367. doi:10.1007/s11111-005-3346-7.

Goldsmith, S., & Eggers, W. D. (2004). *Governing by network: The new shape of the public sector.* Washington, DC: Brookings Institution.

Gonzalez, D. P., & Gonzalez, P. S. (2012). CRM 2.0 and E-Government: Challenges for public administration and social effects. In Colomo-Palacios, R., Varajao, J., & Soto-Acosta, P. (Eds.), *Customer relationship management and the social and semantic web: Enabling cliens conexus.* Hershey, PA: Business Science Reference. doi:10.4018/978-1-4666-1740-7.ch062.

Goodchild, M. F. (2007). Citizens as sensors: The world of volunteered geography. *GeoJournal*, 69, 211–221. Retrieved July 24th, 2012, from http://www.springerlink.com/content/h013jk125081j628/fulltext.pdf

Goodchild, M. F. (2008). *Assertion and authority: The science of user-generated geographic content.* Paper presented at the Colloquium for Andrew U. Frank's 60th Birthday, Vienna.

Goodchild, M. F., & Kemp, K. K. (Eds.). (1990). *History of GIS.* NCGIA Core Curriculum 1990 Version, Unit 23. Santa Barbara: National Center of Geographic Information and Analysis, University of California, Santa Barbara. Retrieved March 12, 2012, from http://www.geog.ubc.ca/courses/klink/gis.notes/ncgia/toc.html

Goodchild, M. (2007). Citizens as sensors: The world of volunteered geography. *GeoJournal*, 69, 211–221. doi:10.1007/s10708-007-9111-y.

Goodchild, M. (2009). Neogeography and the nature of geographic expertise. *Journal of Location Based Services*, 3, 82–96. doi:10.1080/17489720902950374.

Goodchild, M. F. (2004). The validity and usefulness of laws in geographic information science and geography. *Annals of the Association of American Geographers. Association of American Geographers*, 94, 300–303. doi:10.1111/j.1467-8306.2004.09402008.x.

Goodchild, M. F. (2007). Citizens as sensors: The world of volunteered geography. *GeoJournal*, 69(4), 211–221. doi:10.1007/s10708-007-9111-y.

Goodchild, M. F. (2007). Citizens as voluntary sensors: Spatial data infrastructure in the world of web 2.0. *International Journal of Spatial Data Infrastructure Research*, 2, 24–32.

Goodchild, M. F. (2008). Commentary: Whither VGI? *GeoJournal*, 72, 239–244. doi:10.1007/s10708-008-9190-4.

Goodchild, M. F. (2009). NeoGeography and the nature of geographic expertise. *Journal of Location Based Services*, 3(2), 82–96. doi:10.1080/17489720902950374.

Goodchild, M. F., & Glennon, J. A. (2010). Crowdsourcing geographic information for disaster response: A research frontier. *International Journal of Digital Earth*, 3(3), 231–241. doi:10.1080/17538941003759255.

Google Inc, & the Otto Group. TNS Infrastest & Trend Büro. (2012). *Go-Smart2012 – Always-in-touch – Studie zur Smartphone-Nutzung 2012*. Retrieved August 24th, 2012, from http://www.ottogroup.com/media/docs/de/studien/go_smart.pdf

Google Press Release. (2009). *Introducing Google Earth 5.0*. Retrieved October 26, 2010, from http://www.google.com/intl/en/press/pressrel/20090202earthocean.html

Gore, A. (1993). *From red tape to results: Creating a government that works better and costs less*. New York: Times Books.

Goss, J. (1995). We know who you are and we know where you live: The instrumental rationality of geodemographic systems. *Economic Geography*, *71*(2), 171–198. doi:10.2307/144357.

Gouveia, C., Fonseca, A., Câmara, A., & Ferreira, F. (2004). Promoting the use of environmental data collected by concerned citizens through information and communication technologies. *Journal of Environmental Management*, *71*(2), 135–154. doi:10.1016/j.jenvman.2004.01.009 PMID:15135948.

Graham, S., & Healey, P. (1999). Relational concepts of space and place: Issues for planning theory and practice. *European Planning Studies*, *7*, 623–646. doi:10.1080/09654319908720542.

Graham, S., & Marvin, S. (2001). *Splintering urbanism: Networked infrastructures, technological mobilities and the urban condition*. New York: Routledge. doi:10.4324/9780203452202.

Grant, R. A., & Stothers, M. (2007). iStockphoto.com: Turning community in commerce (Harvard Business School Case No. 907-E13). Cambridge, MA: Harvard Business School.

Greenberg, P. (2009). *Time to put a stake in the ground on social CRM*. Retrieved from http://the56group.typepad.com/pgreenblog/2009/07/time-to-put-a-stake-in-the-ground-on-social-crm.html.

Grey, F. (2009). *The age of citizen cyberscience*. CERN Courier. Retrieved from http://cerncourier.com/cws/article/cern/38718

Gronlund, A. (2002). *Electronic government: Design, applications and management*. Hershey, PA: Idea Group Publishing.

Gronlund, Å. (2003). Emerging electronic infrastructures: Exploring democratic components. *Social Science Computer Review*, *21*(1), 55–72. doi:10.1177/0894439302238971.

Grouplens. (2012). *Project-website*. Retrieved July 24th, 2012, from http://www.grouplens.org/

Gryl, I., & Jekel, T. (2012). Re-centering GI in secondary education. Towards a spatial citizenship approach. *Cartographica*, *47*(1), 2–12. doi:10.3138/carto.47.1.18.

Guo, Q., Liu, Y., & Wieczorek, J. (2008). Georeferencing locality descriptions and computing associated uncertainty using a probabilistic approach. *International Journal of Geographical Information Science*, *22*(10), 1067–1090. doi:10.1080/13658810701851420.

Gupta, A. (2012). What happened to the occupy movement. *Al Jazeera*. Retrieved from http://www.aljazeera.com/indepth/opinion/2012/05/2012521151225452634.html

Gurstein, M. (Ed.). (2000). *Community informatics: Enabling communities with information and communication technologies*. Hershey, PA: Idea Group.

Gurung, G. S., Thapa, K., Kunkel, K., Thapa, G. J., Kollmair, M., & Boeker, U. M. (2011). Enhancing herder's livelihood and conserving the snow leopard in Nepal. *CATnews*, *55*(Autumn), 17–21.

Gustin, S. (2011). Defiant Google Exec Wael Ghonim released from Egyptian custody. *Wired*. Retrieved from http://www.wired.com/business/2011/02/ghonim-release-reports/

Habermas, J. (1985). *The theory of communicative action* (*Vol. 1*). Boston: Beacon Press.

Habermas, J. (1989). *The structural transformtion of society*. Cambridge, MA: MIT Press.

Habermas, J. (1999). Three normative models of democracy: Liberal, republican, procedural. In Kearney, R., & Dooley, M. (Eds.), *Questioning ethics: Contemporary debates in philosophy*. New York, NY: Routledge.

Haklay, M. (2012). *'Nobody wants to do council estates' – digital divide, spatial justice and outliers.* Retrieved March 7, 2012, from http://povesham.wordpress.com/2012/03/05/nobody-wants-to-do-council-estates-digital-divide-spatial-justice-and-outliers-aag-2012/

Haklay, M. (2010). How good is volunteered geographical information? A comparative study of OpenStreetMap and ordinance survey datasets. *Environment and Planning B, 37,* 682–703. doi:10.1068/b35097.

Haklay, M. (2012). Citizen science and volunteered geographic information – overview and typology of participation. In Sui, D. Z., Elwood, S., & Goodchild, M. F. (Eds.), *Volunteered geographic information, public participation, and crowdsourced production of geographic knowledge.* Berlin: Springer. doi:10.1007/978-94-007-4587-2_7.

Haklay, M., Basiouka, S., Antoniou, V., & Ather, A. (2010). How many volunteers does it take to map an area well? The validity of Linus' law to volunteered geographic information. *The Cartographic Journal, 47*(4), 315–322. doi:10.1179/000870410X12911304958827.

Haklay, M., Singleton, A., & Parker, C. (2008). Web mapping 2.0: The neogeography of the GeoWeb. *Geography Compass, 2*(6), 2011–2039. doi:10.1111/j.1749-8198.2008.00167.x.

Haklay, M., & Tobón, C. (2003). Usability evaluation and PPGIS: Towards a user-centred design approach. *International Journal of Geographical Information Science, 17,* 577–592. doi:10.1080/13658103100114107.

Hakley, M., Singelton, A., & Parker, C. (2008). Web mapping 2.0: The neogeography of the GeoWeb. *Geography Compass, 2,* 2011–2039. doi:10.1111/j.1749-8198.2008.00167.x.

Haller, C. (2011). *Micro-participation connects citizens to their governments.* Retrieved August 24th, 2012, from http://www.shareable.net/blog/micro-participation-connects-citizens-to-their-governments

Haller, M., Billinghurst, M., & Thomas, B. (Eds.). (2006). *Emerging technologies of augmented reality: Interfaces and design.* Idea Group Publishing. doi:10.4018/978-1-59904-066-0.

Hall, G., Chipeniuk, R., Feick, R., Leahy, M., & Deparday, V. (2010). Community-based production of geographic information using open source software and Web 2.0. *International Journal of Geographical Information Science, 24*(5), 761–781. doi:10.1080/13658810903213288.

Hall, P. (1983). The Anglo-American connection: Rival rationalities in planning theory and practice, 1955-1980. *Environment and Planning. B, Planning & Design, 10,* 41–46. doi:10.1068/b100041.

Halvorsen, K. E. (2003). Assessing the effects of public participation. *Public Administration Review, 63*(5), 535–543. doi:10.1111/1540-6210.00317.

Hand, E. (2010). Citizen science: People power. *Nature, 466,* 685–687. doi:10.1038/466685a PMID:20686547.

Hand, L. C., & Ching, B. D. (2011). You have one friend request: An exploration of power and citizen engagement in local governments' use of social media. *Administrative Theory & Praxis, 33*(3), 362–382. doi:10.2753/ATP1084-1806330303.

Harding, J. (2006). Vector data quality: A data provider's perspective. In Devillers, R., & Jeansoulin, R. (Eds.), *Fundamentals of spatial data quality* (pp. 141–159). London: ISTE. doi:10.1002/9780470612156.ch8.

Hargittai, E. (2003). The digital divide and what to do about it. In Jones, D. C. (Ed.), *New economy handbook* (pp. 821–839). San Diego, CA: Academic Press.

Harris, C. G. (2011). Dirty deeds done dirt cheap: A darker side to crowdsourcing. In *Proceedings of 2011 IEEE Third International Conference on Social Computing* (pp. 1314-1317). Los Alamitos, CA: IEEE Computer Society.

Harris, T. M., Rouse, L. J., & Bergeron, S. (2010). The geospatial semantic web, pareto GIS, and the humanities. In Bodenhamer, D. J., Corrigan, J., & Harris, T. M. (Eds.), *The spatial humanities: GIS and the future of humanities scholarship* (pp. 124–142). Bloomington: Indiana University Press.

Harvey, D. (2008). The right to the city. *New Left Review.*

Hashash, S. (2012). Egyptians tune into the programme, a 'blasphemous' TV satire. *The Guardian.* Retrieved from http://www.guardian.co.uk/world/2012/may/08/egyptians-programme-blasphemous-tv-satire

Hawken, P. (2007). *Blessed unrest: How the largest movement in the world came into being, and why no one saw it coming*. New York: Viking.

Hayes, A. F., & Krippendorff, K. (2007). Answering the call for a standard reliability measure for coding data. *Communication Methods and Measures, 1*, 77–89. doi:10.1080/19312450709336664.

Hays, R. A., & Kogl, A. M. (2007). Neighborhood attachment, social capital building, and political participation: A case study of low and moderate-income residents of Waterloo, Iowa. *Journal of Urban Affairs, 29*(2), 181–205. doi:10.1111/j.1467-9906.2007.00333.x.

Hellström, J., & Karefelt, A. (2011). *Mobile participation? Crowdsourcing during the 2011 Uganda general elections*. Retrieved July 24th, 2012, from http://www.texttochange.org/sites/default/files/newsfiles/M4D2012_Hellstrom_Karefelt%20(1).pdf

Hennig, S., & Vogler, R. (2011). Participatory tool development for participatory spatial planning: The GEOKOM-PEP environment. In Jekel, T., Koller, A., Donert, K., & Vogler, R. (Eds.), *Learning with GI 2011: Implementing digital earth in education* (pp. 79–88). Berlin, Offenbach: Wichmann.

Herbert, W. A. (2006). No direction home: Legal principles, issues, and potential solutions. *Chapter presented at the American Association for the Advancement of Science (AAAS)*. St. Louis, Mo. AAAS. (2006). *Conversation with the author at the American Association for the Advancement of Science (AAAS) meeting*. St. Louis, Mo.

Hercheui, M. D. (2009). Virtual communities and democratic debates: A case study on institutional influences. *International Conference on Information Systems (ICIS) Proceedings*. Phoenix.

Herold, M. (2009). Some recommendations for global efforts in urban monitoring and assessments from remote sensing. In Gamba, P., & Herold, M. (Eds.), *Global mapping of human settlement: Experiences, datasets and prospects* (pp. 11–23). Boca Raton, FL: CRC Press. doi:10.1201/9781420083408-c2.

Herring, C. (1994). An architecture of cyberspace: Spatialization of the Internet. *CiteSeer*. Retrieved July 17th, 2012, from http://citeseerx.ist.psu.edu/viewdoc/summary?doi=10.1.1.37.4604

Heverin, T., & Zach, L. (2010). Microblogging for crisis communication: Examination of Twitter use in response to a 2009 violent crisis in Seattle-Tacoma. Washington Area. In *Proceedings of the Seventh International Information Systems for Crisis Response and Management Conference*.

Hewson, W., Jones, R., Hunter, D., & Meekings, A. (2004). *Towards a citizen-centric authority: Beyond CRM, e-government and the modernising agenda in the UK public sector*. Academic Press.

Hildreth, S. (2007). Government looks to CRM with citizen relationship management. *TechTarget, November 28*. Retrieved from http://searchcrm.techtarget.com/news/article/0,289142,sid11_gci1268193,00.html

Hill, L. L. (2000). *Core elements of digital gazetteers: Placenames, categories, and footprints*. Paper presented at the Proceedings of the 4th European Conference on Research and Advanced Technology for Digital Libraries.

Hinssen, P. (2010). *The new normal*. MachMedia, NV.

Hirschheim, R. A., Klein, H. K., & Lyytinen, K. (1995). *Information systems development and data modeling: Conceptual and philosophical foundations*. Cambridge University Press. doi:10.1017/CBO9780511895425.

Hirst, P. (1990). *Representative democracy and its limits*. Cambridge: Polity Press.

Hoch, C., Dalton, L. C., & So, F. S. (2000). *The practice of local government planning*. Washington, DC: International City/County Management Association.

Höffken, S. (2008). Mobile participation. *Pep-Net*. Retrieved July 17th, 2012, from http://pep-net.eu/blog/2008/06/24/mobile-participation/

Höffken, S., & Haller, C. (2010). New communication tools and eparticipation: Social media in urban planning. In M. Schrenk, V. Popovich, P. Zeile (Eds.), *RealCORP 2010, 15th International Conference, Vienna, Austria 18-20 May 2010*. Vienna: CORP – Competence Center of Urban and Regional Planning. Retrieved July 24th, 2012, from http://www.corp.at/archive/CORP2010_109.pdf

Höffken, S., & Kloss, C. (2011). Digitale Urbanisten – oder wie das Internet Stadtplanung und urbane Kultur verändert. In Forum Wohnen und Stadtentwicklung, Heft 4/2011, 198-201.

Höffken, S., & Streich, B. (2011). Engaging the mobile citizens – How mobile devices offer new ways of civil engagement. In M. Schrenk, V. V. Popovich, and P. Zeile (Eds.), *Proceedings REAL CORP 2011*. 18-20 May.

Holden, S. H., & Norris, D. F. et al. (2003). Electronic government at the local level: Progress to date and future issues. *Public Performance and Management Review, 26*(4), 325–344. doi:10.1177/15309576030266004002.

Holzer, M., & Kim, S.-T. (2008). *Digital governance in municipalities worldwide. A longitudinal assessment of municipal Websites throughout the world*. Newark: National Center for Public Performance, Rutgers University.

Holzer, M., Manoharan, A., & Ryzin, G. V. (2010). Global cities on the Web: An empirical typology of municipal Websites. *International Public Management Review, 11*(3), 104–121.

Hood, C. (1995). The new public management in the 1980s - Variations on a theme. *Accounting, Organizations and Society, 20*(2-3), 93–109. doi:10.1016/0361-3682(93) E0001-W.

Hopkin, M. (2007, July 11). See new galaxies — without leaving your chair. *Nature*. doi:10.1038/news070709-7. Retrieved from http://www.nature.com/news/2007/070709/full/news070709-7.html

Howard, A. (2012). The emerging political force of the network of networks. *O'Reilly Radar*. Retrieved July 24th, 2012, from http://radar.oreilly.com/2012/06/12-talks-from-pdf-2012.html

Howard, C., Lipsky, M., & Marshall, D. R. (1994). Citizen participation in urban politics: Rise and routinization. In Peterson, G. E. (Ed.), *Big-city politics, governance, and fiscal constraints* (pp. 153–199). Washington, DC: Urban Institute Press.

Howard, P. N., Duffy, A., Deen, F., Hussain, M., Mari, W., & Mazaid, M. (2011). *Opening closed regimes: What was the role of social media during the Arab Spring? Project on Information Technology and Political Islam*. University of Washington.

Howe, J. (2006). The rise of crowdsouring. *Wired Magazine*, Issue 14.06. Retrieved May 18, 2010, from http://www.wired.com/wired/archive/14.06/crowds.html

Howe, J. (2006a, June). The rise of crowdsourcing. *Wired, 14*(6). Retrieved September 15, 2012, from http://www.wired.com/wired/archive/14.06/crowds.html

Howe, J. (2006b, June 16). Neo neologisms. *Crowdsourcing: Tracking the rise of the amateur* [Weblog]. Retrieved September 15, 2012, from http://www.crowdsourcing.com/cs/2006/06/neo_neologisms.html

Howe, J. (2008). *Crowdsourcing: Why the power of the crowd is driving the future of business*. New York: Crown.

http://adage.com/article/agency-news/pepsi-dewmocracy-push-threatens-crowd-shops/140120/

Hudson-Smith, A., Crooks, A., Gibin, M., Milton, R., & Batty, M. (2009). NeoGeography and Web 2.0: Concepts, tools and applications. *Journal of Location Based Services, 3*(2), 118–145. doi:10.1080/17489720902950366.

Hudson-Smith, A., Milton, R., Dearden, J., & Batty, M. (2009). The neogeography of virtual cities: Digital mirrors into a recursive world. In Foth, M. (Ed.), *Urban informatics: The practice and promise of the real-time city* (pp. 270–291). Hershey, PA: IGI Global.

Huebner, J. P. (2009). *CiRM for public participation: Directions for dialogue on strategic public participation technologies*. Municipal report.

Hurlock, J., & Wilson, M. L. (2011). Searching twitter: Separating the tweet from the chaff. In L. A. Adamic, R. A. Baeza-Yates, & S. Counts (Eds.), *Proceedings of the Fifth International Conference on Weblogs and Social Media*. Menlo Park: The AAAI Press.

IAP2 - International Association of Public Participation. (2007). *Spectrum of public participation*. Retrieved March 14, 2012, from http://www.iap2.org/associations/4748/files/spectrum.pdf

IAP2. (2008). *IAP2 Spectrum of participation*. Retrieved from http://www.iap2.org/associations/4748/files/IAP2%20Spectrum_vertical.pdf

iceland-crowdsourcing-constitution-facebook?CMP=twt_gu

Ifib, Z. (2008). *E-Partizipation – Elektronische Beteiligung von Bevölkerung und Wirtschaft am E-Government. Studie im Auftrag des Bundesministeriums des Innern, Ref. IT*. Retrieved July 17th, 2012, from http://www.ifib.de/publikationsdateien/ifib-zebralog-e-partizipation-kurz.pdf

Imhoff, M. L., Lawrence, W. T., Stutzer, D. C., & Elvidge, C. D. (1997). A technique for using composite DMSP/OLS "city lights" satellite data to map urban area. *Remote Sensing of Environment, 61*(3), 361–370. doi:10.1016/S0034-4257(97)00046-1.

Initiative, D. 21. (2012). *Nonliner atlas 2011 – Eine Topographie des digitalen Grabens durch Deutschland.* Retrieved September 2nd, 2012, from http://www.initiatived21.de/wp-content/uploads/2011/07/NOnliner2011.pdf

Innes, J. E. (1996). Planning through consensus building. *Journal of the American Planning Association. American Planning Association, 62*, 460–472. doi:10.1080/01944369608975712.

Innes, J. E. (2005). Living in the house of our predecessors: The demand for new institutions for public participation. *Planning Theory & Practice, 6*, 431–435.

INTELCITIES. (2006). *Electronic and mobile participation in city planning and management.* Helsinki, Finland. Retrieved July 17th, 2012, from http://www.hel2.fi/tietokeskus/julkaisut/pdf/Intelcity.pdf

Ipeirotis, P. G., Provost, F., & Wang, J. (2010). Quality management on Amazon mechanical Turk. In R. Chandrasekar, E. Chi, M. Chickering, P. G. Ipeirotis, W. Mason, F. Provost, J. Tam et al. (Eds.), *Proceedings of the ACM SIGKDD Workshop on Human Computation* (pp. 64–67). New York: Association for Computing Machinery.

Ipeirotis, P. G. (2010). Analyzing the Amazon mechanical Turk marketplace. *XRDS: Crossroads. The ACM Magazine for Students, 17*(2), 16–21. doi:10.1145/1869086.1869094.

IPTS. (2009). *The impact of social computing on the EU information society and economy.* JRC Scientific and Technical Reports.

Irazàbal, C. (2009). *Revisiting urban planning in Latin America and the Caribbean: Regional study prepared for revisiting urban planning: Global report on human settlements.* Retrieved January 10, 2012, from http://www.unhabitat.org/grhs/2009

Irvin, R. A., & Stansbury, J. (2004). Citizen participation in decision making: Is it worth the effort? *Public Administration Review, 64*(1), 55–65. doi:10.1111/j.1540-6210.2004.00346.x.

Jacobs, J. (1961). *The death and life of great American cities.* New York: Random House.

Jaeger, P. (2003). The endless wire: E-government as global phenomenon. *Government Information Quarterly, 20*(4), 323–331. doi:10.1016/j.giq.2003.08.003.

Jain, A., & Patnayakuni, R. (2003). Public expectations and public scrutiny: An agenda for research in the context of e-government. *American Conference on Information Systems (AMCIS) Proceedings.* Tampa.

James, P., Fernando, T., Hamilton, A., & Curwell, S. (2004). *Enhancing the decision-making process in urban spatial planning using advanced ICT.* University of Salford, Issues Paper, April 2004.

James, W. (1907;1978). Pragmatism and the theory of truth. Cambridge, MA: Harvard University Press.

Jazeera, A. (2011). Hosni Mubarak Resigns as President. *Al Jazeera.* Retrieved from http://www.aljazeera.com/news/middleeast/2011/02/201121125158705862.html/

Jennings, M. K., & Zeitner, V. (2003). Internet use and civic engagement: A longitudinal analysis. *Public Opinion Quarterly, 67*, 311–334. doi:10.1086/376947.

Jeong, M., Oh, H., & Gregoire, M. (2003). Conceptualizing web site quality and its consequences in the lodging industry. *International Journal of Hospitality Management,* (22): 161–175. doi:10.1016/S0278-4319(03)00016-1.

Jeppesen, L. B., & Lakhani, K. R. (2010). Marginality and problem-solving effectiveness in broadcast search. *Organization Science, 21*(5), 1016–1033. doi:10.1287/orsc.1090.0491.

Jin, M., Shepherd, J. M., & Peters-Lidard, C. (2007). Development of a parameterization for simulating the urban temperature hazard using satellite observations in climate model. *Natural Hazards.* doi:10.1007/s11069-007-9117-2.

Johnson, A. (2011, February 17). City: SeeClickFix has good first month. *WRAL.com.* Retrieved September 15, 2012, from http://www.wral.com/news/news_briefs/story/9128944

Johnson, N. B. (2010, August 30). How agencies are crowd-sourcing their way out of problems. *Federal Times.* Retrieved September 15, 2012, from http://www.federaltimes.com/article/20100830/AGENCY03/8300301/1001

Jones, C. B., Purves, R. S., Clough, P. D., & Joho, H. (2008). Modelling vague places with knowledge from the Web. *International Journal of Geographical Information Science*, *22*(10), 1045–1065. doi:10.1080/13658810701850547.

Jones, C. E., Haklay, M., Griffiths, S., & Vaughan, L. (2009). A less-is-more approach to geovisualization – enhancing knowledge construction across multidisciplinary teams. *International Journal of Geographical Information Science*, *23*, 1077–1093. doi:10.1080/13658810802705723.

Josang, A., Ismail, R., & Boyd, C. (2007). A survey of trust and reputation systems for online service provision. *Decision Support Systems*, *43*(2), 618–644. doi:10.1016/j.dss.2005.05.019.

Joutsen, A., Nieminen, V., Vuorensola, T., & Lekman, L. (2008). Wreck a movie: Empowering the masses for film productions. In A. Lugmayr, F. Mäyrä, H. Franssila, & K. Lietsala (Eds.), *12th international MindTrek conference: Entertainment and media in the ubiquitous era* (pp. 141–144). New York: Association for Computing Machinery.

Jóźwiak, T. (2003). Marine debris and threats to the Polish coast in 2001-sources and types. *Oceanological and Hydrogiological Studies*, *32*, 73–81.

Junghans, A., & David, B. (2011). *Mit dem Computer in den Hosentasche entsteht ein neuer öffentlicher Zwischenraum*. Retrieved July 17th, 2012, from http://www.heise.de/tp/artikel/33/33977/1.html

Kaiser, E. J., Godschalk, D. R., & Chapin, F. S. Jr. (1995). *Urban land use planning* (4th ed.). Urbana: University of Illinois Press.

Kamarck, E. C., & Nye, J. S. (2002). *Governance.com: Democracy in the information age, visions of governance in the 21st century*. Washington, DC: Brookings Institution Press.

Kang, D. J., & Dyson, L. E. (2007). Internet politics in South Korea: The case of Rohsamo and Ohmynews Internet politics in South Korea. *18th Australasian Conference on Information Systems Proceedings* (pp. 1027-1034). Toowoomba.

Kannabiran, G., Xavier, M. J., & Anantharaaj, A. (2004). Enabling e-governance through citizen relationship management-concept, model, and applications. *Journal of Service Research*, *4*(2), 223–240.

Kaplan, A. M., & Haenlein, M. (2010). Users of the world, unite! The challenges and opportunities of Social Media.[Elsevier.]. *Business Horizons*, *53*(1), 59–68. doi:10.1016/j.bushor.2009.09.003.

Kaplan, R. S., & Norton, D. P. (1996). *The balanced scorecard: Translating strategy into action*. Harvard Business School Press.

Kaplan, R. S., & Norton, D. P. (2004). *Strategy maps: Converting intangible assets into tangible outcomes*. Boston, MA: Harvard Business School Press.

Kathlene, L., & Martin, J. A. (1991). Enhancing citizen participation: Panel designs, perspectives and policy formation. *Journal of Policy Analysis and Management*, *10*(1), 46–63. doi:10.2307/3325512.

Kaufmann, R. K., Seto, K. C., Schneider, A., Zhou, L., & Liu, Z. (2007). Climate response to rapid urban growth: Evidence of a human-induced precipitation deficit. *Journal of Climate*, *20*, 2299–2306. doi:10.1175/JCLI4109.1.

Kaylor, C., Deshazo, R., & Van Eck, D. (2001). Gauging e-government: A report on implementing services among American cities. *Government Information Quarterly*, *18*(4), 293–307. doi:10.1016/S0740-624X(01)00089-2.

Kellerman, A. (2010). Mobile broadband services and the availability of instant access to cyberspace. *Environment & Planning A*, *42*, 2990–3005. doi:10.1068/a43283.

Khatib, F., & DiMaio, F.Foldit Contenders Group, Foldit Void Crushers Group, Cooper, S., Kazmierczyk, M., Gilski, M.,…, Baker, D. (2011). Crystal structure of a monomeric retroviral protease solved by protein folding game players. *Nature Structural & Molecular Biology*, *18*, 1175–1177. doi:10.1038/nsmb.2119 PMID:21926992.

Kiehle, C., Greve, K., & Heier, C. (2007). Requirements for next generation spatial data Infrastructures-standardized web based geoprocessing and web service orchestration. *Transactions in GIS*, *11*(6), 819–834. doi:10.1111/j.1467-9671.2007.01076.x.

Kienberger, S. (2010). *Spatial vulnerability assessment. Methodoloy for the community and district level applied to floods in Búzi, Mozambique.* (Doctoral Thesis). Paris-Lodron University Salzburg.

Kim, S., & Lee, J. (2012). Citizen participation and transparency in local government: An empirical analysis. *2nd Global Conference on Transparency.* Utrecht University, Netherlands.

Kim, S.-E., Shaw, T., & Schneider, H. (2003). Web site design benchmarking within industry groups. *Internet Research*, (13): 17–26. doi:10.1108/10662240310458341.

Kim, S., & Stoel, L. (2004). Dimensional hierarchy of retail website quality. *Information & Management*, (41): 619–633. doi:10.1016/j.im.2003.07.002.

King, S. F. (2007). Citizens as customer: Exploring the future of CRM in UK local government. *Government Information Quarterly*, 24(1), 47–63. doi:10.1016/j.giq.2006.02.012.

King, S., & Cotterill, S. (2007). Transformational government? The role of information technology in delivering citizen-centric local public services. *Local Government Studies*, 33(3), 21. doi:10.1080/03003930701289430.

Kingston, R. (2002). *The role of e-government and public participation in the planning process XVI AESOP Congress.* Volos, Greece, July 10th –14th 2002.

Kingston, R. (2002). The role of e-government and public participation in the planning process. *XVI AESOP Congress.* July 10th – 14th 2002, Volos, Greece.

Kirkpatrick, D. D. (2011). Tunisia leader flees and prime minister claims power. *New York Times.* Retrieved from http://www.nytimes.com/2011/01/15/world/africa/15tunis.html/?_r=1&pagewanted=all

Kleeman, F., Voss, G. G., & Rieder, K. (2008). Un(der) paid innovators: The commercial utilization of consumer work through crowdsourcing. *Science. Technology and Innovation Studies*, 4(1), 5–26.

Klinkenberg, B. (2007). Geospatial technologies and the geographies of hope and fear. *Annals of the Association of American Geographers. Association of American Geographers*, 97(2), 350–360. doi:10.1111/j.1467-8306.2007.00541.x.

Klosterman, R. E. (2012). E-planning in retrospect and prospect. *International Journal of E-Planning Research*, 1(1), 1–4. doi:10.4018/ijepr.2012010101.

Kolbitsch, J., & Maurer, H. (2006). The transformation of the web: How emerging communities shape the information we consume. *Journal of Universal Computer Science*, 12(2), 187–213.

Koteen, J. (1989). *Strategic management in public and nonprofit organizations: Thinking and acting strategically on public concerns.* New York: Praeger.

Kotler, M. (1969). *Neighborhood government: The local foundations of political life.* New York: Bobbs-Merrill.

Kraak, J. M. (2003). Why maps matter in GIScience. *The Cartographic Journal*, 43, 82–89. doi:10.1179/000870406X93526.

Kreibich, H., Poser, K., & Haubrock, S. (2008). *Web-based data acquisition of flood affected people.* Paper presented at General Assembly European Geosciences Union, Vienna.

Kubicek, H. (2010). The potential of e-participation in urban planning: A European perspective. In Silva, C. N. (Ed.), *Handbook of research on e-planning: ICTs for urban development and monitoring.* Hershey: IGI-Global. doi:10.4018/978-1-61520-929-3.ch009.

Kuo, Y.-F. (2004). Integrating Kano's model into web-community service quality. *Total Quality Management*, (15): 925–939.

Kutluoglu, U. (2010). *What citizens want from e-government?* Retrieved from http://www.epractice.eu/en/blog/315055

Kweit, M. G., & Kweit, R. W. (1981). *Implementing citizen participation in a bureaucratic society.* New York: Praeger.

Kyem, P. A. K. (2004). Of intractable conflicts and participatory GIS applications: The search for consensus amidst competing claims and institutional demands. *Annals of the Association of American Geographers. Association of American Geographers*, 94(1), 37–57. doi:10.1111/j.1467-8306.2004.09401003.x.

Lakhani, K. R., & Kanji, Z. (2008). Threadless: The business of community (Harvard Business School Multimedia/Video Case No. 608-707). Cambridge, MA: Harvard Business School.

Lakhani, K. R. (2008). *InnoCentive.com (A) (Harvard Business School Case No. 608-170)*. Cambridge, MA: Harvard Business School.

Landler, M. (2007). Where little is left outside the camera's eye. *New York Times*. Retrieved from http://www.nytimes.com/2007/07/08/weekinreview/08landler.html?_r=1

Lane, N. D., Eisenman, S. B., Musolesi, M., Miluzzo, E., & Campbell, A. T. (2008). Urban sensing systems: Opportunistic or participatory? In *Proceedings of the 9th workshop on Mobile computing systems and applications, Napa Valley, California*, 11-16.

Lane, N. D., Miluzzo, E., Lu, H., Peebles, D., Choudhury, T., & Campbell, A. T. (2010). *A survey of mobile phone sensing*. Retrieved July 24th, 2012, from http://www.cs.dartmouth.edu/~campbell/papers/survey.pdf

Lane, M. (2005). Public participation in planning: An intellectual history. *The Australian Geographer, 36*, 283–299. doi:10.1080/00049180500325694.

Lang, A. S. I. D., & Rio-Ross, J. (2011). Using Amazon mechanical Turk to transcribe historical handwritten documents. *Code4Lib Journal, 15*. Retrieved September 15, 2012, from http://journal.code4lib.org/articles/6004

Lange, P. G. (2006). What is your claim to flame? *First Monday, 11*(9). Retrieved September 15, 2012, from http://firstmonday.org/htbin/cgiwrap/bin/ojs/index.php/fm/article/view/1393/1311

Lanza, V., & Prosperi, D. C. (2009). Collaborative e-governance: Describing and pre-calibrating the digital milieu in urban and regional planning. In Krek, A., Rumor, M., Zlatanova, S., & Fendel, E. M. (Eds.), *Urban and regional data management: UDMS annual 2009* (pp. 373–383). Leiden, The Netherlands: CRC Press/Balkema.

Lapsley, I. (2010). *New public management in the global financial crisis-dead, alive, or born again?* London: University of Edinburgh Business School.

Lara, S., & Naval, C. (2012). Social networks, civic engagement, and young people. In Manoharan, A., & Holzer, M. (Eds.), *Active citizen participation in e-government. A global perspective* (pp. 187–205). Hershey: IGI-Global. doi:10.4018/978-1-4666-0116-1.ch010.

Latham J. Huddleston B. Cumani R. Martucci A. Rosati I. Salvatore M. , El

Lazarus, W., & Mora, F. (2000). *Online content for low-income and underserved Americans: The digital divide's new frontier*. Santa Monica, CA: The Children's Partnership. Retrieved from http://www.policyarchive.org/handle/10207/bitstreams/6881.pdf

Leighninger, M. (2011). Citizenship and governance in a wild, wired world: How should citizens and public managers use online tools to improve democracy? *National Civic Review, 11*(2), 20–29. doi:10.1002/ncr.20056.

Lembo, A. J. (2005). *Lecture 1 – Course Objectives, Historical Perspectives of GIS, Conceptual Framework*. Cornell University. Retrieved April 12, 2012, from http://www.cornell.edu/academics/docs/Courses_of_Study_0708.pdf

Lena, T. S., Ochieng, V., Carter, M., Holguín-Veras, J., & Kinney, P. L. (2009). Elemental carbon and $PM_{2.5}$ levels in an urban community heavily impacted by truck traffic. *Environmental Health Perspectives, 110*, 1009–1015. doi:10.1289/ehp.021101009.

Lessig, L. (1999). *Code: And other laws of cyberspace*. New York: Basic Books.

Lessig, L. (2004). *Free culture: How big media uses technology and the law to lock down culture and control creativity*. New York: Penguin Press.

Lévy, P. (1997). *Collective intelligence: Mankind's emerging world in cyberspace* (Bononno, R., Trans.). New York: Plenum.

Li, C., & Bernoff, J. (2011). *Groundswell: Winning in a world transformed by social technologies* (2nd ed.). Boston: Harvard Business Press.

Lichtblau, E. (2012). Police are using phone tracking as a routine tool. *New York Times*. Retrieved from http://bits.blogs.nytimes.com/?s=Police+are+using+phone+tracking

Lietsala, K., & Joutsen, A. (2007). Hang-a-rounds and true believers: A case analysis of the roles and motivational factors of the Star Wreck fans. In A. Lugmayr, K. Lietsala, & J. Kallenbach (Eds.), *MindTrek 2007 Conference Proceedings* (pp. 25–30). Tampere, Finland: Tampere University of Technology.

Lightbody, J. (1993). The strategic-planning component in the policy-making process for municipalities in Canada. *Policy Studies Journal: the Journal of the Policy Studies Organization, 21*(1), 94–103. doi:10.1111/j.1541-0072.1993.tb01456.x.

Lips, M., & Rapson, A. (2010). Exploring public record-keeping behaviors in wiki-supported public consultation activities in the New Zealand public sector. In R. H. Sprague Jr. (Ed.), *Proceedings of the 43rd Hawaii International Conference on System Sciences*. Los Alamitos, CA: IEEE Computer Society.

Li, S. (2006). *Web-based collaborative spatial decision support systems: A technological perspective. Ryerson University*. Canada: MONOGRAFIA.

Locke, J. (2005). *The second treatise of government. Keystones of democracy*. New York, NY: Barnes and Noble.

Long, E. (2009, December 7). Administration announces finalists in cost-cutting contest. *GovernmentExecutive.com*. Retrieved September 15, 2012, from http://www.govexec.com/story_page.cfm?filepath=/dailyfed/1209/12070911.htm

Longley, P. A., Goodchild, M. F., Maguire, D. J., & Rhind, D. W. (2001). *Geographic information systems and science*. New York: John Wiley and Sons.

Lorimer, J. (2008). Counting corncrakes: The affective science of the UK corncrake census. *Social Studies of Science, 38*, 377–405. doi:10.1177/0306312707084396.

Lorinc, J. (2006). *The new city: How the crisis in Canada's urban centres is reshaping the nation*. Toronto: Penguin Canada.

Lösch, B. (2011). *Die Zukunftsfähigkeit der Demokratie – Neue politische Beteiligungsformen in der Diskussion. Gesellschaft - Wirtschaft - Politik - Sozialwissenschaften für politische Bildung*. Jahrgang 61, 2012, Heft 1.

Losey, J. E., Perlman, J. E., & Hoebeke, R. (2007). Citizen scientist rediscovers rare ninespotted lady beetle, Coccinella novemnotata, in eastern North America. *Journal of Insect Conservation, 11*, 415–417. doi:10.1007/s10841-007-9077-6.

Lucas, C. (2012). Multi-criteria modelling and clustering of spatial information. *International Journal of Geographical Information Science*, 1–19.

Luke, W. (2010). *Location detection technologies*. Retrieved September 14th, 2012, from http://www.lukew.com/ff/entry.asp?1089

Lyons, W., & Alexander, R. (2000). A tale of two electorates: Generational replacement and the decline of voting in presidential elections. *The Journal of Politics, 26*(4), 1014–1034.

M&M lovers pick purple. (2002, June 20). *CNN Money*. Retrieved September 15, 2012, from http://money.cnn.com/2002/06/20/news/companies/mandms/

MacEachren, A. M. (2000). Cartography and GIS: Facilitating collaboration. *Progress in Human Geography, 24*(3), 445–456. doi:10.1191/030913200701540528.

Macintosh, A. (2004). Characterizing e-participation in policy-making. In *Proceedings of the 37th Hawaii International Conference on System Sciences*. IEEE.

Macintosh, A. (2006). eParticipation in policy making: The research and the challenges. Exploiting the Knowledge Economy: Issues, Applications, Case Studies. Amsterdam: IOS Press.

Macintosh, A., Robson, E., Smith, E., & Whyte, A. (2003). Electronic democracy and young people. *Social Science Computer Review, 21*(1), 43–54. doi:10.1177/0894439302238970.

Macintosh, A., & Whyte, A. (2006). *Evaluating how e-participation changes local democracy. E-Government Workshop '06 (eGov 06)*. London: Brunel University.

Macintosh, A., Whyte, A., & Renton, A. (2005). *From the top down. An evaluation of e-Democracy activities initiated by councils and governments*. Bristol: Bristol City Council.

Macpherson, C. B. (1977). *The life and times of liberal democracy*. Oxford: Oxford University Press.

Madden, L. (2011). *Professional augmented reality browsers for Smartphones: Programming for junaio, Layar and Wikitude*. John Wiley & Sons.

Maher, K., & Belkin, D. (2011, February 16). State plans anger unions. *The Wall Street Journal*. Retrieved from http://online.wsj.com/article/SB100014240527487033 12904576146554263530400.html

Malczewski, J. (1999). *GIS and multicriteria decision analysis*. New York: John Wiley and Sons.

Malczewski, J. (2000). On the use of weighted linear combination method in GIS: Common and best practice approaches. *Transactions in GIS, 4*(1), 5–22. doi:10.1111/1467-9671.00035.

Malczewski, J. (2004). GIS-based land-use suitability analysis: A critical overview. *Progress in Planning, 62*(1), 3–65. doi:10.1016/j.progress.2003.09.002.

Mandarano, L., Meenar, M., & Steins, C. (2011). Building social capital in the digital age of civic engagement. *Journal of Planning Literature, 25*, 123–135. doi:10.1177/0885412210394102.

Markus, M. L. (2004). Technochange management: Using IT to drive organizational change. *Journal of Information Technology, 19*(1), 4–20. doi:10.1057/palgrave.jit.2000002.

Markus, M. L., & Robey, D. (1988). Information technology and organizational change: Causal structure in theory and research. *Management Science, 34*(5), 583–598. doi:10.1287/mnsc.34.5.583.

Marr, A. (2011). *Andrew Marr's megacities: Living in the city*. BBC.

Marris, E. (2010). Birds flock online. *Nature*. doi:10.1038/news.2010.395.

Martin, M., & Corbett, J. M. (2011). *Creating the new 'new': Facilitating the growth of neo-geographers in the Global South using emergent Internet technologies*. Paper presented at GEOINFORMATIK 2011 – GEOCHANGE, June 15-17 2011, Munster, Germany.

Mattern, F. (2002). *Vom Handy zum allgegenwärtigen Computer: Ubiquitous computing: Szenarien einer informatisierten Welt [Electronic ed.], Bonn*. Retrieved July 24th, 2012, from http://library.fes.de/fulltext/stabsabteilung/01183.htm

Mayaux, P., Eva, H., Gallego, J., Strahler, A. H., Herold, M., & Agrawal, S. et al. (2006). Validation of the global land cover 2000 map. *IEEE Transactions on Geoscience and Remote Sensing, 44*(7), 1728–1737. doi:10.1109/TGRS.2006.864370.

McCaffrey, R. E. (2005). Using citizen science in urban bird studies. *Urban Habitats, 3*(1).

McCall, M. K., & Dunn, C. E. (2012). Geo-information tools for participatory spatial planning: Fulfilling the criteria for 'good' governance? *Geoforum, 43*, 81–94. doi:10.1016/j.geoforum.2011.07.007.

McClure, D. L. (2000). *Electronic government: Federal initiatives are evolving rapidly but they face significant challenges*. Academic Press.

McDougall, K. (2011). Using volunteered information to map the Queensland Floods. In *Proceedings of the Surveying & Spatial Sciences Conference 2011*. Wellington.

McGlade, J. (2010). *Global citizen observatory - The role of individuals in observing and understanding our changing world*. Retrieved January 10, 2012, from http://www.eea.europa.eu/pressroom/speeches/global-citizen-observatory-the-role-of-individuals-in-observing-and-understanding-our-changing-world

McHenry, K., Marini, L., Kejriwal, M., Kooper, R., & Bajcsy, P. (2011, September 22). Toward free and searchable historical census images. *SPIE Newsroom*. Retrieved September 15, 2012, from http://spie.org/x57241.xml

McLead, B. (2006). *Mass-market Geo: Emerging trends and standards*. Paper presented at the CEOS WGISS-22 conference, 12 September 2006, Annapolis, MD.

Mehra, B., Merkel, C., & Bishop, A. P. (2004). The Internet for empowerment of minority and marginalized users. *New Media & Society, 6*(6), 781–802. doi:10.1177/146144804047513.

Mendoza, M., Poblete, B., & Castillo, C. (2010). Twitter under crisis: Can we trust what we RT? In *1st Workshop on Social Media Analytics (SOMA '10)*. New York: ACM Press.

Mergel, I. (2011). *Using wikis in government: A guide for public managers*. Washington, DC: IBM Center for the Business of Government.

Messina, M. J. (2012). *Crowdsourcing for transit-oriented planning projects: A case study of "inTeractive Somerville."* (Unpublished M.A. thesis). Tufts University.

Milčinski, G. (2011). *The rise of crowd-sourcing: How valuable data can we get out of VGI*. Paper presented at CAPIGI, Amsterdam.

Miller-Rushing, A., Primack, R., & Bonney, R. (2012). The history of public participation in ecological research. *Frontiers in Ecology and the Environment, 10*, 285–290. doi:10.1890/110278.

Mill, J. S. (1985). *On liberty*. New York: Penguin Press.

Milovanovic, D. (2003). Interactive planning – use of the ICT as a support for public participation in planning urban development: Serbia and Montenegro cases. *39th ISoCaRP Congress 2003*.

Misuraca, G., Reid, A., & Deakin, M. (2011). *Exploring emerging ICT-enabled governance models in European cities. JRC Technical Notes*. IPTS.

Molinari, F., & Ferro, E. (2010). *Characterising mobile participation in public decisionmaking*. Retrieved July 24th, 2012, from http://crossroad.epu.ntua.gr/files/2010/04/02_Characterising_mobile_participation_in_public_decision-making.pdf

Monmonier, M. (1998). The three Rs of GIS-based site selection: Representation, resistance, and ridicule. In D.R. Fraser Taylor (Ed.), Policy issues in modern cartography (volume 3 of the Modern Cartography series) (pp. 233-247). Oxford: Pergamon, Elsevier Science.

Monmonier, M. (2002). *Spying with Maps*. Chicago, IL: The University of Chicago Press.

Moody, R. (2007). Assessing the role of GIS in e-government: A tale of e-participation in two cities. In Wimmer, M. A., Scholl, H. J., & Grönlund, A. (Eds.), *EGOV 2007, LNCS 4656* (pp. 354–365). doi:10.1007/978-3-540-74444-3_30.

Moon, M. J. (2000). The evolution of e-government among municipalities: Rhetoric or reality? *Public Administration Review, 62*(4), 424–433. doi:10.1111/0033-3352.00196.

Moon, M. J. (2002). The evolution of e-government among municipalities: Rhetoric or reality? *Public Administration Review, 62*(4), 424–433. doi:10.1111/0033-3352.00196.

Moon, M. J., & Deleon, P. (2001). Municipal reinvention: Managerial values and diffusion among municipalities. *Journal of Public Administration: Research and Theory, 11*, 327–352. doi:10.1093/oxfordjournals.jpart.a003505.

Moon, M. J., & Norris, D. F. (2005). Does managerial orientation matter? The adoption of reinventing government and e-government at the municipal level. *Information Systems Journal, 15*(1), 43–60. doi:10.1111/j.1365-2575.2005.00185.x.

Mossberger, K., & Yonghong, W. (2012). *Civic engagement and local e-government: Social networking comes of age*. UIC Institute for Policy and Civic Engagement.

MoxNews. (2011). Occupy – Police pepper spray priest, 84 yr old & pregnant woman. *Inside the USA*. Retrieved from http://www.youtube.com/watch?v=NnMp1e4cDj8

Moynihan, C. (2011). Wall street protest begins, with demonstrators blocked. *New York Times*. Retrieved from http://cityroom.blogs.nytimes.com/2011/09/17/wall-street-protest-begins-with-demonstrators-blocked/

Mueller, M., Tippins, D., & Bryan, L. (2012). The future of citizen science. *Democracy & Education, 20*, 1–12.

Müller, C. (2011). Urban Gardening – Über die Rückkehr der Gärten in die Stadt. oekom Verlag, München.

Mummidi, L., & Krumm, J. (2008). Discovering points of interest from users' map annotations. *GeoJournal, 72*(3-4), 215–227. doi:10.1007/s10708-008-9181-5.

Murdoch, J. (2006). *Post-structuralist geography: A guide to relational space*. London: Sage.

Mureddu, F., Osimo, D., Misuraca, G., & Armenia, S. (2012). *A new roadmap for next-generation policy-making*. New York: ICEGOV.

Musso, J., Weare, C., Bryer, T., & Cooper, T. L. (2011). Toward "strong democracy" in global cities? Social capital building, theory-driven reform, and the Los Angeles neighborhood council experience. *Public Administration Review, 71*(1), 102–111. doi:10.1111/j.1540-6210.2010.02311.x.

Nabatchi, T. (2012). *A manager's guide to evaluating citizen participation*. Wasington, DC: IBM Center for the Business of Government.

Nasa. (2009). *Ames scientist develops cell phone chemical sensor*. Retrieved July 24th, 2012, from http://www.nasa.gov/centers/ames/news/features/2009/cell_phone_sensors.html

NASCIO. (2010). *Friends, followers, and feeds: A national survey of social media use in state government*. Lexington, KY: Author. Retrieved from http://www.nascio.org/publications/documents/NASCIO-SocialMedia.pdf

National Research Council. Committee on the Support for Spatial Thinking: The Incorporation of Geographic Information Science Across the K-12 Curriculum, and Committee on Geography. (2006). Learning to think spatially: GIS as a support system in the K-12 curriculum. Washington, DC: National Academies Press.

Neighbourland. (2012). *Project-website*. Retrieved July 24th, 2012, from https://neighborland.com

Neis, P., Zielstra, D., & Zipf, A. (2012). The street network evolution of crowdsourced maps: OpenStreetMap in Germany 2007–2011. *Future Internet, 4*, 1–21. doi:10.3390/fi4010001.

Nelson, K. L., & Svara, J. H. (2012). Form of government still matters: Fostering innovation in U.S. municipal governments. *American Review of Public Administration, 42*(3), 257–281. doi:10.1177/0275074011399898.

Netzwelt. (2012). *WWDC 2012: Apple meldet 30 Milliarden Downloads aus dem App Store*. Retrieved July 24th, 2012, from http://www.netzwelt.de/news/92608-app-store-apple-vermeldet-30-milliarden-downloads.html

Newman, G., Zimmerman, D., Crall, A., Laituri, M., Graham, J., & Stapel, L. (2010). User-friendly web mapping: Lessons from a citizen science website. *International Journal of Geographical Information Science, 24*(12), 1851–1869. doi:10.1080/13658816.2010.490532.

Nielsen Company. (2011). *Social media report Q3 11*. Retrieved July 24th, 2012, from http://blog.nielsen.com/nielsenwire/social/

Nielsen Company. (2011). *Nielsen präsentiert erste Ergebnisse aus aktuellem Smartphone Insights Report für Deutschland*. Retrieved July 24th, 2012, from http://www.nielsen.com/de/de/insights/presseseite/2011/nielsen-praesentiert-erste-ergebnisse-aus-aktuellem-smartphone-i.html

Nieto, M. (1997). Public video surveillance: Is it an effective crime prevention tool? *Sacramento: California Research Bureau*. Retrieved from http://www.library.ca.gov/crb/97/05/

Nitsche, M. (2009). *Video game spaces: Image, play, and structure in 3D worlds*. Cambridge, MA: The MIT Press.

Nixon, P. G., Koutrakou, V. N., & Rawal, R. (2010). *Understanding e-government in Europe: Issues and challenges*. London: Routledge.

NOAA. (2011). *Global DMSP-OLS nighttime lights time series 1992-2009* (Version 4). Retrieved from http://www.ngdc.noaa.gov/dmsp/download.html

Norris, P. (2004). *Deepening democracy via e-governance (Draft chapter for the UN World Public Sector Report)*. Retrieved from http://www.hks.harvard.edu/fs/pnorris/Acrobat/World%20Public%20Sector%20Report.pdf

Norris, D. F., & Moon, M. J. (2005). Advancing e-government at the grassroots: Tortoise or hare? *Public Administration Review, 65*(1), 64–75. doi:10.1111/j.1540-6210.2005.00431.x.

Norris, D., & Demeter, L. (1999). Information technology and city government. In *The Municipal Yearbook*. Washington, DC: International City County Management Association.

Nouwt, S. (2008). *Reasonable expectations of geo-privacy?* SCRIPTed, *5*(2), 375-403. Retrieved April 6, 2012, from http://www.law.ed.ac.uk/ahrc/script-ed/vol5-2/nouwt.asp

Noveck, B. (2009). *Wiki government: How technology can make government better, democracy stronger, and citizens more powerful.* Washington, DC: Brookings Institution Press.

Noveck, B. S. (2003). Designing deliberative democracy in cyberspace: The role of the cyber-lawyer. *Boston University Journal of Science and Technology Law, 9*(1), 1–91.

Noveck, B. S. (2006). "Peer to Patent": Collective intelligence, open review, and patent reform. *Harvard Journal of Law & Technology, 20*(1), 123–262.

Noveck, B. S. (2009). *Wiki government. How technology can make government better, democracy stronger, and citizens more powerful.* Washington: Brookings Institution Press.

Novljan, S., & Maja, Z. (2004). Web pages of Slovenian public libraries: Evaluation and guidelines. *The Journal of Documentation,* (60): 62–76. doi:10.1108/00220410410516653.

Obama, B. (n.d.). *Transparency and open government* [Presidential memorandum]. Retrieved September 15, 2012, from http://www.whitehouse.gov/the_press_office/Transparency_and_Open_Government

Obermeyer, N. J. (1998). *PPGIS: The Evolution of Public Participation GIS.* Indiana State University. Retrieved March 14, 2012, from http://dusk.geo.orst.edu/ucgis/web/oregon/ppgis.pdf

Obermeyer, N. J. (1998). The evolution of public participation GIS. *Cartography and GIS, special issue on Public Participation GIS, 25*(2), 65-66.

Obermeyer, N. J. (1998). Evolution of public participation GIS. *Cartography and Geographic Information Systems, 25*(2), 65–66. doi:10.1559/152304098782594599.

Obermeyer, N. J. (2007). GIS: The maturation of a profession. *Cartography and Geographic Information Science, 34*, 129–132. doi:10.1559/152304007781002280.

Occupy Everything. (2011). Police pepper spray students! *YouTube.* Retrieved from http://www.youtube.com/watch?v=vee1VoTZ-NY

Occupy Wall Street. (2012). Occupy wall street about and user map. *Occupy Wall Street.* Retrieved from http://occupywallst.org

OECD. (2001). *Citizens as partners: Information, consultation and public participation in policy-making.* Paris: OECD Publishing.

OECD. (2001). *Citzens as partners: OECD Handbook on information, consultation and public particiaption in policy-making.* Paris: OECD Publishing.

OECD. (2003). *Policy brief: Engaging citizens online for better policy-making.* Paris: OECD.

OECD. (2003). *Promises and problems of e-democracy: Challenges of citizen on-line engagement.* Paris: OECD.

Office of National Statistics. (2011). *Annual mid-year population estimates, 2010.* Titchfield: Office of National Statistics UK.

OfNS (Office for National Statistics). (2011). *Statistical bulletin - Internet access - households and individuals, 2011.* Retrieved September 24th, 2012, from http://www.ons.gov.uk/ons/dcp171778_227158.pdf

Ogata, Y., Takada, H., Mizukawa, K., Hirai, H., Iwasa, S., & Endo, S. et al. (2009)... *Marine Pollution Bulletin, 58,* 1437–1446. doi:10.1016/j.marpolbul.2009.06.014 PMID:19635625.

OGC - Open Geospatial Consortium. (2005). *Interoperability and open architectures: An analysis of existing standardisation processes and procedures.* OGC White Paper. Retrieved July 15, 2010, from http://www.opengeospatial.org/

OGC - Open Geospatial Consortium. (2010). *KML.* Retrieved October 26, 2010, from http://www.opengeospatial.org/standards/kml/

Oke, T. R. (1967). City size and the urban heat island. *Atmospheric Environment, 7*(8), 769–779. doi:10.1016/0004-6981(73)90140-6.

Okolloh, O. (2009). Ushahidi, or "testimony": Web 2.0 tools for crowdsourcing crisis information. *Participatory Learning and Action, 59*(1), 65–70. London: International Institute for Environment and Development & Technical Centre for Agricultural and Rural Cooperation ACP-EU.

Olofsson, P., Stehman, S. V., Woodcock, C. E., Sulla-Menashe, D., Sibley, A. M., & Newell, J. D. et al. (2012). A global land-cover validation data set, part I: fundamental design principles. *International Journal of Remote Sensing, 33*(18), 5768–5788. doi:10.1080/0143 1161.2012.674230.

Olson, M. (1965). *The logic of collective action: Public goods and the theory of groups.* Cambridge, MA: Harvard University Press.

O'Reilly, T. (2005). *O'Reilly network: What is web 2.0.* Retrieved from http://www.oreillynet.com/lpt/a/6228

O'Reilly, T. (2007). What is web 2.0: Design patterns and business models for the next generation of software. *International Journal of Digital Economics, 65*(1), 20.

ORNL. (2011). *LandScan.* Retrieved from http://www.ornl.gov/sci/landscan/

Osimo, D. (2008). *Web 2.0 in government: Why and how?* Luxembourg: JRC Scientific and Technical Reports. Office of Official Publications of the European Communities, European Communities.

Overdevest, C., Huyck Orr, C., & Stepenuck, K. (2004). Volunteer stream monitoring and local participation in natural resource issues. *Human Ecology Review, 11*, 177–185.

Overdevest, C., & Mayer, B. (2008). Harnessing the power of information through community monitoring: Insights from social science. *Texas Law Review, 86*(7), 1493–1526.

Padgett, D. A. (1993). Technological methods for improving citizen participation in locally unacceptable land use (LULU). *Decision-Making, Computers. Environment and Urban Systems, 17*, 513–520. doi:10.1016/0198-9715(93)90049-B.

Päivärinta, T., & Sæbø, Ø. (2006). Models of e-democracy. *Communications of the Association for Information Systems, 17*(1), 818–840.

Pan, S.-L., Tan, C.-W., & Lim, E. T. K. (2006). Customer relationship management (CRM) in e-government: A relational perspective. *Decision Support Systems, 42*(1), 237–250. doi:10.1016/j.dss.2004.12.001.

Parameswaran, M., & Whinston, A. B. (2007). Social computing: An overview. *Communications of the Association for Information Systems, 19*, 762–780.

Parasuraman, A., Zeithaml, V., & Berry, L. (1988). SERVQUAL: A multi-item scale for measuring consumer perceptions of service quality. *Journal of Retailing,* (64): 2–40.

Parent, M., Vandebeek, C. A., & Gemino, A. C. (2005). Building citizen trust through e-government. *Government Information Quarterly, 22*, 17. doi:10.1016/j.giq.2005.10.001.

Parry, G., Moyser, G., & Day, N. (1992). *Political participation and democracy in Britain.* New York, NY: Cambridge University Press. doi:10.1017/CBO9780511558726.

Paulos, E., Honicky, R., & Hooker, B. (2009). Citizen science: Enabling participatory urbanism. In Foth, M. (Ed.), *Handbook of Research on Urban Informatics.*

Pavlovskaya, M. (2006). Theorizing with GIS: A tool for critical geographies? *Environment & Planning A, 38*, 2003–2020. doi:10.1068/a37326.

Peart, M. N., & Diaz, J. R. (2007). *Comparative project on local e-democracy initiatives in Europe and North America.* Geneve: University of Geneve and European Science Foundation.

Peng, Z.-R. (2001). Internet GIS for public participation. *Environment and Planning. B, Planning & Design, 28*, 889–905. doi:10.1068/b2750t.

Perger, C., Fritz, S., See, L., Schill, C., Van der Velde, M., McCallum, I., & Obersteiner, M. (2012). A campaign to collect volunteered geographic information on land cover and human impact. In Jekel, T., Car, A., Strobl, J., & Griesebner, G. (Eds.), *GI_Forum 2012: Geovizualisation, society and learning* (pp. 83–91). Berlin, Offenbach: Wichmann Verlag.

Perlroth, N. (2011). Carrier IQ denies it is under investigation. *New York Times*. Retrieved from http://bits.blogs.nytimes.com/2011/12/14/carrier-iq-denies-it-is-under-investigation/

Phang, C. W., & Kankanhalli, A. (2005). A research framework for citizen participation via eConsultation. *Americas Conference on Information Systems (AMCIS) Proceedings*. Omaha, NE.

Phang, C. W., Kankanhalli, A., Chua, Z., & Goh, K.-Y. (2007). Investigating participation in online policy discussion forums over time: Does network structure matter? *International Conference on Information Systems (ICIS) Proceedings*. Montreal, Canada.

Phang, C. W., & Kankanhalli, A. (2008). A framework of ICT exploitation for e-participation initiatives. *Communications of the ACM*, *51*(12), 128–132. doi:10.1145/1409360.1409385.

Phang, C. W., Sutanto, J., Kankanhalli, A., Li, Y., Tan, B. C. Y., & Teo, H.-H. (2006). Senior citizens' acceptance of information systems: A study in the context of e-government services. *IEEE Transactions on Engineering Management*, *53*(4), 555–569. doi:10.1109/TEM.2006.883710.

Pickles, J. (1991). Geography, GIS, and the surveillant society. *Chapters and Proceedings of Applied Geography Conferences*, *14*(2), 80-91.

Pickles, J. (1997). Tool or science? GIS, technoscience and the theoretical turn. *Annals of the Association of American Geographers. Association of American Geographers*, *87*, 363–372. doi:10.1111/0004-5608.00058.

Pickles, J. (Ed.). (1995). *Ground truth. The social implications of geographic information systems*. New York: Guilford Press.

Plant, T. E. (2010). *Roadmap to success: Implementing the strategic plan*. St. Thomas, Ont: Municipal World Inc.

Plant, T. (2009). Strategic planning for municipalities: Ensuring progress and relevance. *Performance Improvement*, *48*(5), 26–35. doi:10.1002/pfi.20076.

Please Rob Me. (2011). *Website*. Retrieved from http://pleaserobme.com/

Policy Brief, O. E. C. D. (2003). Engaging citizens online for better policy-making. *Washington OECD Observer*. Retrieved July 24th, 2012, from http://www.oecd.org/dataoecd/62/23/2501856.pdf

Porter, M. E. (1990). *The competitive advantage of nations*. New York: Free Press.

Porter, M. E. (1991). *Canada at the crossroads: The reality of a new competitive environment*. Ottawa, ON: Government of Canada.

Porter, M. E. (2001). Strategy and the internet. *Harvard Business Review*, *79*(3), 63. PMID:11246925.

Poser, K., Kreibich, H., & Dransch, D. (2009). *Assessing volunteered geographic information for rapid flood damage estimation*. Paper presented at the 12th AGILE International Conference on Geographic Information Science, Hannover.

Poser, K., & Dransch, D. (2010). Volunteered geographic information for disaster management with application to rapid flood damage estimation. *Geomatica*, *64*(1), 89–98.

Post, R. C. (1995). *Constitutional domains: Democracy, community, management*. Cambridge, MA: Harvard University Press.

Potapchuk, W. R. (1996). Building sustainable community politics: Synergizing participatory, institutional, and representative democracy. *National Civic Review*, *85*(3), 54–60. doi:10.1002/ncr.4100850311.

Potapchuk, W. R., & Crocker, J. P. Jr. (1999). Exploring the elements of civic capital. *National Civic Review*, *88*(3), 175–201. doi:10.1002/ncr.88303.

Potere, D., & Schneider, A. (2009). Comparison of global urban maps. In Gamba, P., & Herold, M. (Eds.), *Global mapping of human settlement: Experiences, datasets and prospects* (pp. 269–308). Boca Raton, FL: CRC Press. doi:10.1201/9781420083408-c13.

Prieto-Martin, P. (2009). *Evolution of the views on "What participation is."* Retrieved from http://pep-net.eu/blog/2009/09/09/images-for-reflection-i-evolution-of-the-views-on-%e2%80%9cwhat-participation-is%e2%80%9d/.

Prieto-Martin, P. (2011). *Presenting the "Matrix of Civic Implication."* Retrieved from http://pep-net. eu/blog/2011/11/14/presenting-the-matrix-of-civic-implication/

Prieto-Martin, P. (2012). *eParticipation is finally getting teeth...* Retrieved from http://pep-net.eu/blog/2012/05/22/eparticipation-is-finally-getting-teeth/

prodandref/WaldEtAlECEESDYFI.pdf

Progressive Insurance. (2012). Over $70 million already saved with Snapshot. *Progressive Auto Insurance website.* Retrieved from http://www.progressive.com/auto/snapshot.aspx?vanity=true

Putnam, R. D. (2000). *Bowling alone: The collapse and revival of American community.* New York: Simon & Schuster. doi:10.1145/358916.361990.

Qu, Y., Huang, C., Zhang, P., & Zhang, J. (2011). Harnessing social media in response to major disasters. In *CSCW 2011 Workshop: Designing Social and Collaborative Systems for China.* Hangzhou.

Raddick, M. J., Bracey, G., Gay, P. L., Lintott, C. J., Murray, P., & Schawinski, K. et al. (2010). Galaxy zoo: Exploring the motivations of citizen science volunteers. *Astronomy Education Review, 9,* 010103–1. doi:10.3847/AER2009036.

Raguseo, E., & Ferro, E. (2011). E-government & organizational change: Towards an extended governance model. *Lecture Notes in Computer Science, 6846,* 418–430. doi:10.1007/978-3-642-22878-0_35.

Rainie, L. (2010). *Internet, broadband, and cell phone statistics.* Washington, DC: Pew Internet & American Life Project.

Rakodi, C. (2001). Forget planning, put politics first? Priorities for urban management in developing countries. *International Journal of Applied Earth Observation, 3*(3), 209–223. doi:10.1016/S0303-2434(01)85029-7.

Ramasubramanian, L. (2010). *Geographic information science and public participation.* Berlin, Heidelberg: Springer Verlag.

Rana, S., & Joliveau, T. (2009). Neogeography: An extension of mainstream geography for everyone made by everyone? *Journal of Location Based Services, 3,* 75–81. doi:10.1080/17489720903146824.

Raney, R. (2000, May 11). Study finds Internet of social benefit to users. *New York Times.*

Rauterberg, H. (2011). Ab nach draußen! - Wie ausgerechnet das Internet eine Renaissance des öffentlichen Lebens befeuert. *Zeit Online.* Retrieved from http://www.zeit.de/2011/27/Public-Space

Reddick, C. (2004). A two-stage model of e-government growth: Theories and empirical evidence for U.S. cities. *Government Information Quarterly, 21*(1), 51–64. doi:10.1016/j.giq.2003.11.004.

Reddick, C. G. (2004). Empirical models of e-government growth in local governments. *E-Service Journal, 3*(2), 59–84. doi:10.2979/ESJ.2004.3.2.59.

Reddick, C. G. (2010). Impact of citizen relationship management (CRM) on government: Evidence from U.S. local governments. *J. E-Gov., 33*(2), 88–99.

Reddick, C. G. (2011). Customer relationship management (CRM) technology and organizational change: Evidence for the bureaucratic and e-Government paradigms. *Government Information Quarterly, 28*(3), 346–353. doi:10.1016/j.giq.2010.08.005.

Reddick, C. G., & Frank, H. A. (2007). The perceived impacts of e-government on U.S. cities: A survey of Florida and Texas City managers. *Government Information Quarterly, 24*(3), 576–594. doi:10.1016/j.giq.2006.09.004.

Reichental, J. (2012). Knowledge management in the age of social media. *O'Reilly Radar.* Retrieved July 24th, 2012, from http://radar.oreilly.com/2011/03/knowledge-management-social-media.html

Resl, R. (2006). GI for development – Can GIS challenge existing power stuructures? Working experiences from Ecuador. In Zeil, P., & Kienberger, S. (Eds.), *Geoinformation for development - Bridging the divide through partnerships* (pp. 125–136). Heidelberg: Wichmann Verlag.

Restrepo, C., & Zimmerman, R. (Eds.). (2004). *South Bronx environmental health and policy study: Transportation and traffic modeling, air quality, waste transfer stations, and environmental justice analyses in the South Bronx*. Final Report for Phase II & III. Retrieved November 1, 2012, from http://www.icisnyu.org/admin/files/ICISPhaseIIandIIIreport.pdf

Rheingold, H. (2002). *Smart mobs: The next social revolution*. Perseus Books.

Rhoads, M. (2010). Face-to-face and computer-mediated communication: What does theory tell us and what have we learned so far? *Journal of Planning Literature, 25*, 111–122. doi:10.1177/0885412210382984.

Ricknäs, M. (2011). European regulators start investigating carrier IQ. *PC World*. Retrieved from http://www.pcworld.idg.com.au/article/409306/european_regulators_start_investigating_carrier_iq/

Rinner, C., & Raubal, M. (2004). Personalized multi-criteria decision strategies in location-based decision support. *Journal of Geographic Information Sciences, 10*(2), 149–156.

Rittel, H., & Webber, M. (1973). Dilemmas in a general theory of planning. *Policy Sciences, 4*, 155–169. doi:10.1007/BF01405730.

Roberts, N. (2004). Public deliberation in an age of direct citizen participation. *American Review of Public Administration, 34*, 315–353. doi:10.1177/0275074004269288.

Roche, S., Propeck-Zimmermann, E., & Mericskay, B. (2011). GeoWeb and crisis management: Issues and perspectives of volunteered geographic information.[Springer Netherlands.]. *GeoJournal*, 1–20.

Rodgers, D., Beall, J., & Kanbur, R. (2011). Latin American urban development into the 21st century: Towards a renewed perspective on the city. *European Journal of Development Research, 23*(4), 550–568. doi:10.1057/ejdr.2011.18.

Rosa, P., & Pereira, Â. G. (2008). *E-participation. Promoting dialog and deliberation between institutions and civil society*. Luxembourg: European Commission Joint Research Center.

Rousseau, J.-J. (2005). *The social contract. Keystones of democracy*. New York, NY: Barnes and Noble.

Russell, A., & Hughes, M. (2011). Is the changing precipitation regime of Manchester, United Kingdom, driven by the development of urban areas? *International Journal of Climatology*. doi: doi:10.1002/joc.2321.

Ryan, N. (2011). Occupy Seattle protesters pepper sprayed. *King 5 News*. Retrieved from http://www.king5.com/news/local/Occupy-Seattle-protesters-pepper-sprayed-in-clash-with-officers-133930088.html

Saad-Sulonen, J. (2012). The role of the creation and sharing of digital media content in participatory e-planning. *International Journal of E-Planning Research, 1*(2), 1–22. doi:10.4018/ijepr.2012040101.

Sabatier, P. A. (1988). An advocacy coalition framework of policy changes and the role of policy-oriented learning therein. *Policy Sciences, 21*(2–3), 129–168. doi:10.1007/BF00136406.

Sæbø, Ø. (2006). A process for identifying objectives and technological forms in e-democracy initiatives. *Americas Conference on Information Systems (AMCIS) Proceedings*. Acapulco.

Sæbø, Ø., & Päivärinta, T. (2005). Autopoietic cybergenres for e-democracy? Genre analysis of a web-based discussion board. *Proceedings of the 38th Hawaii International Conference on System Sciences*.

Sagini, M. M. (2007). *Strategic planning and management in public organizations: Behavior in organizations*. New York: University Press of America.

Sahu, G. P., Dwivedi, Y. K., & Weerakkody, V. (2009). *E-Government development and diffusion: Inhibitors and facilitators of digital democracy*. Hershey, PA: IGI Global. doi:10.4018/978-1-60566-713-3.

Sartori, G. (1987). *The theory of democracy revisited*. Chatham, NJ: Chatham House.

Sbarra, P., Tosi, P., & De Rubeis, V. (2010). Web-based macroseismic survey in Italy: Method validation and results. *Natural Hazards, 54*(2), 563–581. doi:10.1007/s11069-009-9488-7.

Scharl, A. (2007). Towards the geospatial web: Media platforms for managing geotagged knowledge repositories. In Scharl, A., & Tochtermann, K. (Eds.), *The geospatial web* (pp. 3–14). London: Springer. doi:10.1007/978-1-84628-827-2_1.

Schatteman, A., Mohammed-Spigner, D., & Poluse, G. (2012). Citizen participation through municipal Websites: A global scorecard. In Manoharan, A., & Holzer, M. (Eds.), *Active citizen participation in e-government. A global perspective* (pp. 403–414). Hershey: IGI-Global. doi:10.4018/978-1-4666-0116-1.ch020.

Schelling, T. (1969). Models of segregation. *The American Economic Review, 59*(2), 488–493. Retrieved from http://www.jstor.org/stable/1823701.

Schellong, A. (2008). *Citizen relationship management: A Study of CRM in government (Vol. 560)*. Oxford: Peter Lang Publishing Group.

Schiller, J., & Voisard, A. (Eds.). (2004). *Location-based services*. Morgan Kaufmann Publisher.

Schlossberg, M., & Shuford, E. (2003). Delineating "Public" and "Participation" in PPGIS. *URISA Journal, 16*(2), 15–26.

Schneider, A., Friedl, M. A., McIver, D. K., & Woodcock, C. E. (2003). Mapping urban areas by fusing multiple sources of coarse resolution remotely sensed data. *Photogrammetric Engineering and Remote Sensing, 69*, 1377–1386.

Schneider, A., Friedl, M. A., & Potere, D. (2009). A new map of global urban extent from MODIS satellite data. *Environmental Research Letters, 4*, 044003. doi:10.1088/1748-9326/4/4/044003.

Schneider, A., Friedl, M. A., & Potere, D. (2010). Mapping global urban areas using MODIS 500-m data: New methods and datasets based on 'urban ecoregions.'. *Remote Sensing of Environment, 114*, 1733–1746. doi:10.1016/j.rse.2010.03.003.

Schroeder, P. (1996). Criteria for the design of a GIS/2. *Specialists' meeting for NCGIA Initiative 19: GIS and society*, Summer 1996.

Schroeder, P. (1997). Personal e-mail communication. November 15, 1997.

Schuler, I. (2008). SMS as a tool in election observation - Innovations case narrative: National democratic institute. In P. Auerswald and I. Quadir (Eds.), Innovations – Technology, Governance, Globalization, 3(2), 143–157. MIT Press.

Schuurman, N. (2000). Trouble in the heartland: GIS and its critics in the 1990s. *Progress in Human Geography, 24*, 569–590. doi:10.1191/030913200100189111.

Schuurman, N. (2001). Critical GIS: Theorizing an emerging discipline. *Cartographica, 36*, 1–108.

Schuurman, N. (2006). Formalization matters: Critical GIScience and ontology research. *Annals of the Association of American Geographers. Association of American Geographers, 96*, 726–739. doi:10.1111/j.1467-8306.2006.00513.x.

Seasons, M. L. (1989). *Strategic planning in local government: An application to local economic development*. University of Waterloo, Canada. Retrieved from http://proquest.umi.com/pqdweb?did=747302331&Fmt=7&clientId=16746&RQT=309&VName=PQD

See, L., & Fritz, S. (2006). Towards a global hybrid land cover map for the year 2000. *IEEE Transactions on Geoscience and Remote Sensing, 44*(7), 1740–1746. doi:10.1109/TGRS.2006.874750.

Sen, A. K. (1999). Democracy as a universal value. *Journal of Democracy, 10*(3), 3–17. doi:10.1353/jod.1999.0055.

Servon, L. J. (2002). *Bridging the digital divide: Technology, community, and public policy*. Malden, MA: Blackwell. doi:10.1002/9780470773529.

Servon, L. J., & Nelson, M. K. (2001). Community technology centers: Narrowing the digital divide in low-income, urban communities. *Journal of Urban Affairs, 23*(3/4), 279–290. doi:10.1111/0735-2166.00089.

Sexto, C., Arce, X., Quintá, F., & Vázquez, Y. (2009). Alfabetización digital en comunidades marginadas a partir de un SIG. Estudio de caso en Galicia. *Anales de Geografía, 29*(1), 223–234.

Sharma, R. (2011). Investigating the effect of participation-limiting structures on outcomes of e-democracy systems. *Pacific Asia Conference on Information Systems (PACIS) Proceedings*. Brisbane, Paper 174.

Shipley, R. J. M. (1997). *Visioning in strategic planning: Theory, practice and evaluation.* University of Waterloo, Canada. Retrieved from http://proquest.umi.com/pqdweb?did=736727921&Fmt=7&clientId=16746&RQT=309&VName=PQD

Shirk, J. L., Ballard, H. L., Wilderman, C. C., Phillips, T., Wiggins, A., & Jordan, R. et al. (2012). *Public participation in scientific research: A framework for deliberate design. Ecology & Society, 17(2), 29.* Retrieved from.

Shirky, C. (2008). *Here comes everybody: The power of organizing without organizations.* New York: Penguin Press.

Shutter, J., & de Graffenreid, E. (2000). *Benchmarking the egovernment revolution: Year 2000 report on citizen and business demand.* Academic Press.

Sidding, B. F., & El Nogoumy, N. (2009). The Africover and PMUR datasets and the challenge of human settlement mapping in Africa. In Gamba, P., & Herold, M. (Eds.), *Global mapping of human settlement: Experiences, datasets and prospects* (pp. 163–189). Boca Raton, FL: CRC Press.

Siddique, H. (2011, June 9). Mob rule: Iceland crowdsources its next constitution: Country recovering from collapse of its banks and government is using social media to get citizens to share their ideas. *The Guardian.* Retrieved September 15, 2012, from http://www.guardian.co.uk/world/2011/jun/09/

Sieber, R. (2006). Public participation geographic information systems: A literature review and framework.[Taylor & Francis Group.]. *Annals of the Association of American Geographers. Association of American Geographers, 96*(3), 491–507. doi:10.1111/j.1467-8306.2006.00702.x.

Sifry, M. (2004). The rise of open-source politics. *Nation (New York, N.Y.),* 4.

Silberman, M., Irani, L., & Ross, J. (2010). Ethics and tactics of professional crowdwork. *XRDS: Crossroads. The ACM Magazine for Students, 17*(2), 39–43. doi:10.1145/1869086.1869100.

Silva, C. N. (2010). *Handbook of research on e-planning: ICTs for urban development and monitoring.* Hershey: IGI-Global. doi:10.4018/978-1-61520-929-3.

Silva, C. N. (2010). The e-planning paradigm. Theory, Methods and Tools: An overview. In Silva, C. N. (Ed.), *Handbook of research on e-planning: ICTs for urban development and monitoring.* Hershey: IGI-Global. doi:10.4018/978-1-61520-929-3.ch001.

Silva, C. N. (2012). *Online research methods in urban and planning studies: Design and outcomes.* Hershey: IGI-Global.

Silva, C. N. (2012). Research methods for urban planning in the digital age. In Silva, C. N. (Ed.), *Online research methods in urban and planning studies: Design and outcomes* (pp. 1–16). Hershey: IGI-Global. doi:10.4018/978-1-4666-0074-4.ch001.

Silverman, R. (2001). CRM dichotomies. *Intelligent Enterprise, 4*(8), 4.

Silvertown, J. (2009). A new dawn for citizen science. *Trends in Ecology & Evolution, 24*(9), 467–471. doi:10.1016/j.tree.2009.03.017 PMID:19586682.

Slaughter, A.-M. (2011). Occupied wall street, seen from abroad. *New York Times.* Retrieved from http://www.nytimes.com/2011/10/06/opinion/occupied-wall-street-seen-from-abroad.html?_r=1

Smith, A. (2010, August 7). SeeClickFix celebrates 50G issues reported. *New Haven Register.* Retrieved September 15, 2012, from http://www.nhregister.com/articles/2010/08/07/news/aa3_neseeclickfix080710.txt

Smith, J. (2012, April 9th). Participation by design: Community planning…A new app for collaborative geodesign. Retrieved March 14, 2012, from http://blog.placematters.org/2012/04/09/participation-by-design-community-planning-a-new-app-for-collaborative-geodesign/

Smith, A. (2001). Applying evaluation criteria to New Zealand government websites. *International Journal of Information Management, 21,* 137–149. doi:10.1016/S0268-4012(01)00006-8.

Smith, A., Schlozman, K. L., Verba, S., & Brady, H. (2009). *The Internet and civic engagement.* Washington: Pew Internet & American Life Project.

Smyth, E. (2001). *Would the Internet widen public participation?* (Master's Thesis). University of Leeds.

Sobel, D. (1995). *Longitude: The true story of a lone genius who solved the greatest scientific problem of his time.* New York, NY: Walker and Company.

Sorber, J., Banerjee, N., Corner, M. D., & Rollins, S. (2005). Turducken: Hierarchical power management for mobile devices. In *Proceedings of ACM MobiSys '05, Seattle, Washington.*

Sorensen, A., & Okata, J. (2011). *Megacities: Urban form, governance and sustainability. Dordrect.* Springer.

Souder, D. (2001). CRM improves citizen service in Fairfax County. *Public Management, 83*(4), 14–21.

Sprague, R. H., & Carlson, E. D. (1982). *Building effective decision support systems.* Englewood Cliffs, NJ: Prentice-Hall, Inc..

Srivastava, S. C., & Teo, T. S. H. (2009). Citizen trust development for e-government adoption and usage: Insights from young adults in Singapore. *Communications of the Association for Information Systems, 25*(1), 359–378.

Starbird, K. (2011). Digital volunteerism during disaster: Crowdsourcing information processing. CHI 2011. May 7-12. Vancouver, BC, Canada.

Steinberg, F. (2005). Strategic urban planning in Latin America: Experiences of building and managing the future. *Habitat International, 29*(1), 69–93. doi:10.1016/S0197-3975(03)00063-8.

Steinmann, R., Krek, A., & Blaschke, T. (2004). Analysis of online public participatory GIS applications with respect to the differences between the US and Europe. In *UDMS 2004, 24th Urban Data Management Symposium.* Chioggia, Italy.

Steinmann, R., Krek, A., & Blaschke, T. (2005). Can online map-based applications improve citizen participation? In Böhlen, M., Gamper, J., & Polasek, W. (Eds.), *E-Government: Towards electronic democracy* (pp. 25–35). Lecture Notes in Computer ScienceBerlin: Springer Verlag. doi:10.1007/978-3-540-32257-3_3.

Stivers, C. (1990). The public agency as polis: Active citizenship in the administrative state. *Administration & Society, 22*(1), 86–105. doi:10.1177/009539979002200105.

Stowers, G. (1999). Becoming cyberactive: State and local governments on the world wide web. *Government Information Quarterly, 16*(2), 111–127. doi:10.1016/S0740-624X(99)80003-3.

Street Plan Collaborative. (2012). *Tactical urbanism 2: Short-term action, long term change.* Retrieved July 24th, 2012, from http://www.theatlanticcities.com/neighborhoods/2012/03/guide-tactical-urbanism/1387/

Streib, G. (1992). Professional skill and support for democratic principles: The case of local government department heads in northern Illinois. *Administration & Society, 24*(1), 22–40. doi:10.1177/009539979202400102.

Streib, G., & Navarro, I. (2006). Citizen demand for interactive e-government: The case of Georgia consumer services. *American Review of Public Administration, 36*(3), 12. doi:10.1177/0275074005283371.

Streich, B., & Zeile, P. (2012). *Städtebauliche Methodenentwicklung mit GeoWeb und Mobile Computing - Untersuchung über die Fortentwicklung des städtebaulichen und raumplanerischen Methodenrepertoires angestoßen durch technologische Neuerungen im Internet.* Unpublished Report on DFG Research Project. Kaiserslautern: University of Technology Kaiserslautern.

Streich, B. (2011). *Stadtplanung in der Wissensgesellschaft: Ein Handbuch.* Wiesbaden: VS Verlag für Sozialwissenschaften. doi:10.1007/978-3-531-93164-7.

Strobl, J. (2005). GI science and technology - where next? *GIS Development, 9*, 40–43.

Strobl, J. (2008). Digital earth brainware. In Schiewe, J., & Michel, U. (Eds.), *Geoinformatics paves the highway to digital earth* (pp. 134–138). Osnabrück: University of Osnabrück.

Sui, D. (2008). The wikification of GIS and its consequences: Or Angelina Jolie's new tattoo and the future of GIS. *Computers, Environment and Urban Systems, 32*, 1–5. doi:10.1016/j.compenvurbsys.2007.12.001.

Sui, D. Z. (2008). The wikification of GIS and its consequences: Or Angelina Jolie's new tattoo and the future of GIS. *Computers, Environment and Urban Systems, 32*, 1–5. doi:10.1016/j.compenvurbsys.2007.12.001.

Suler, J. R. (2004). The online disinhibition effect. *Cyberpsychology & Behavior, 7*, 321–326. doi:10.1089/1094931041291295 PMID:15257832.

Sullivan, B., Wood, C., Iliff, M., Bonney, R., Fink, D., & Kelling, S. (2009). eBird: A citizen-based bird observation network in the biological sciences. *Biological Conservation, 142*(10), 2282–2292. doi:10.1016/j.biocon.2009.05.006.

Sultana, P., Thompson, P., & Green, C. (2007). Can England LEARN LESSONS from Bangladesh in introducing participatory floodplain management? *Water Resources Management, 22*(3), 357–376. doi:10.1007/s11269-007-9166-z.

Sundstrom, L.-M. (2012). I-Government: Interactive government enabling civic engagement and a new volunteerism. In Kloby, K., & D'Agostinho, M. J. (Eds.), *Citizen 2.0: Public and governmental interaction through Web 2.0 technologies* (pp. 297–308). Hershey, PA: IGI-Global. doi:10.4018/978-1-4666-0318-9.ch015.

Sunstein, C. (2009). *Going to extremes: How like minds unite and divide.* New York: Oxford University Press.

Surowiecki, J. (2004). *The wisdom of crowds: Why the many are smarter than the few and how collective wisdom shapes business, economies, societies and nations.* New York, NY: Little and Brown.

Sutton, J., Palen, L., & Shklovski, I. (2008). Backchannels on the front lines: Emergent uses of social media in the 2007 southern California wildfires. Proceedings of the *5th International ISCRAM Conference* (pp. 624–632).

Suzumura, K. (2005). An interview with Paul Samuelson: Welfare economics, "old" and "new," and social choice theory. *Social Choice and Welfare, 25*, 327–356. doi:10.1007/s00355-005-0007-9.

Switzer, A., Schwille, K., Russell, E., & Edelson, D. (2012). National Geographic FieldScope: A platform for community geography. *Frontiers in Ecology and the Environment, 10*(6), 334–335. doi:10.1890/110276.

Tait, E. (2012). Web 2.0 for eParticipation: Transformational Tweeting or devaluation of democracy? In Kloby, K., & D'Agostinho, M. J. (Eds.), *Citizen 2.0: Public and governmental interaction through Web 2.0 technologies* (pp. 224–249). Hershey: IGI-Global. doi:10.4018/978-1-4666-0318-9.ch012.

Taleb, N. (2008). *The black swan: The impact of the highly improbable.* London: Penguin Books.

Tapscott, D. (2008). *Grown up digital how the net generation is changing your world.* New York: McGraw-Hill.

Taylor, P. J. (1991). GKS. *Political Science Quarterly, 9*, 211–212.

Taylor, P. J., & Johnston, R. (1995). GIS and geography. In Pickles, J. (Ed.), *Ground truth* (pp. 68–87). New York: Guilford Press.

Tec-Ed, I. (1999). *White paper: Assessing web site usability from server log files.* Ann Arbor, MI: Michigan.

Techcrunch. (2011). *It's still a feature phone world: Global smartphone penetration At 27%.* Retrieved July 24th, 2012, from http://techcrunch.com/2011/11/28/its-still-a-feature-phone-world-global-smartphone-penetration-at-27/

Textizen. (2012). *Welcome. Project-website.* Retrieved July 24th, 2012, from http://www.textizen.com/welcome

Thomas, J. C., & Streib, G. (2003). The new face of government: Citizen-initiated contact in the era of e-government. *Journal of Public Administration Reasearch and Theory.*

Thomas, C. W. (1998). Maintaining and restoring public trust in government agencies and their employees. *Administration & Society, 30*(2), 166–193. doi:10.1177/0095399798302003.

Thurston, G. D., Spira-Cohen, A., & Chi Chen, L. (2007). *South Bronx environmental health policy study (SBEHPS).* Final Report of NYU School of Medicine Research. New York University School of Medicine. Department of Environmental Medicine. Retrieved November 1, 2012, from http://graphics8.nytimes.com/packages/pdf/nyregion/20081002_SOM.pdf

Tolbert, C. J., & Mossberger, K. (2006). The effects of e-government on trust and confidence in government. *Public Administration Review,* (3): 16.

Tor Project. (2012). 20 July 2012. *The Tor Project, Inc.* Retrieved from https://www.torproject.org/

Torrens, P. (2008). Wi-Fi geographies. *Annals of the Association of American Geographers. Association of American Geographers, 98*(1), 59–84. doi:10.1080/00045600701734133.

Torrens, P. M. (2010). Geography and computational social science. *GeoJournal, 75,* 133–148. doi:10.1007/s10708-010-9361-y.

Torres, L., Pina, V., & Acerete, B. (2006). E-government developments in European union cities: Reshaping government's relationship with citizens, governance. *An International Journal of Policy. Administration and Institutions, 19,* 277–302.

Trumbull, D. J., Bonney, R., Bascom, D., & Cabral, A. (2000). Thinking scientifically during participation in a citizen-science project. *Informal Science, 84,* 265–275.

Turner, A. (2006). Introduction to neogeography. Sebastopol, US: O'Reilly Press.

Turner, A., & Forrest, B. (2008). *Where 2.0: The state of the geospatial web.* Retrieved from http://radar.oreilly.com/research/where2-report.html

UN. (2006). *Compendium of innovative e-government practices (Vol. II).* New York: United Nations, Department of Economic and Social Affairs.

UN. (2008). *United Nations e-government survey 2008: From e-government to connected governance.* New York: Department of Economic and Social Affairs Division for Public Administration and Development Management.

UN. (2009). *Compendium of innovative e-government practices (Vol. III).* New York: United Nations, Department of Economic and Social Affairs.

UN. (2011). *World urbanization prospects, the 2011 revision.* Retrieved from http://esa.un.org/unup/Documentation/final-report.htm

UNDP (United Nations Development Programme). (2012). *Mobile technologies and empowerment: Enhancing human development through participation and innovation.* Retrieved July 17th, 2012, from http://www.undpegov.org/sites/undpegov.org/files/undp_mobile_technology_primer.pdf

UN-HABITAT. (2011). *Global report on human settlements: Cities and climate change.* Nairobi: UN Press.

United Nations. (2010). *E-government survey 2010: Leveraging e-government at a time of financial and economic crisis.* 170. Retrieved from http://www2.unpan.org/egovkb/global_reports/10report.htm

United Nations. (2010). *World urbanization prospects: The 2009 revision.* New York, NY: UN Press.

United States Mission. (2012). HRC affirms that human rights must also be protected on the internet (Resolution Text). *United States Mission to the United Nations.* Retrieved from http://geneva.usmission.gov/2012/07/05/internet-resolution/

United States. (2002). *E-Government Act of 2002, H.R. 2458, 107th Cong.* Retrieved from http://www.gpo.gov/fdsys/pkg/BILLS-107hr2458eh/pdf/BILLS-107hr2458eh.pdf

Urquhart, E. S. (2012). *Listening to the crowd: A content analysis of social media chatter about a crowdsourcing contest.* (Unpublished B.A. Honors thesis). University of North Carolina at Chapel Hill.

van Dijk, J., Pieterson, W., van Deuren, A., & Ebbers, W. (2007). *E-services for citizens: The Dutch usage case.* Paper presented at the EGOV 2007. Berlin, Germany.

Van Iwaarden, J., Van der Wiele, T., Ball, L., & Millen, R. (2004). Perceptions about the quality of web sites: A survey amongst students at Northeastern University and Erasmus University. *Information & Management,* (41): 947–959. doi:10.1016/j.im.2003.10.002.

Van Iwaarden, J., & Van derWiele, T. (2002). *A study on the applicability of SERVQUAL dimensions for web sites.* Academic Press.

Van Laer, J., & Van Aelst, P. (2010). Internet and social movement action repertoires. Opportunities and limitations. *Information Communication and Society, 2010,* 1–26.

van Mill, D. (2006). *Deliberation, social choice and absolutist democracy.* New York, NY: Routledge.

Vander Wal, T. (2005). Explaining and showing broad and narrow folksonomies. *Personal InfoCloud.* Retrieved from www.vanderwal.net/random/entrysel.php?blog=1635.

Vaughan, H., Whitelaw, G. S., Craig, B., & Stewart, C. (2003). Linking ecological science to decision-making: Delivering environmental monitoring information as societal feedback. *Environmental Monitoring and Assessment, 88,* 399–408. doi:10.1023/A:1025593728986 PMID:14570425.

Verba, S., & Nie, N. (1972). *Participation in America: Political democracy and social equality.* New York, NY: Harper and Row.

Verba, S., Schlozman, K., & Brady, H. (1995). *Voice and equality: Civic voluntarism in American politics.* Cambridge, MA: Harvard University Press.

Verton, D. (2000, August 28). Electronic government. *Computerworld.*

Vicente, M. R., & López, A. J. (2010). A multidimensional analysis of the disability digital divide: Some evidence for internet use. *The Information Society, 26*(1), 48–64. doi:10.1080/01615440903423245.

Villarroel, J. A., & Reis, F. (2010). *Intra-corporate crowdsourcing (ICC): Leveraging upon rank and site marginality for innovation.* Presented at the Crowd-Conf2010, San Francisco, CA. Retrieved September 15, 2012, from http://www.crowdconf2010.com/images/finalpapers/villarroel.pdf

Vitelli, B. (2012). People can't seem to stop eulogizing the occupy movement. *The Guardian Media Network.* Retrieved from http://www.guardian.co.uk/media-network-partner-zone-publici/occupy-movement-eulogy

Vizard, M. (2012). *How analytics bring organizations closer to their customers.* King Fish Media.

von Ahn, L., Maurer, B., McMillen, C., Abraham, D., & Blum, M. (2008). reCAPTCHA: Human-based character recognition via Web security measures. *Science, 321*(5895), 1465–1468. doi:10.1126/science.1160379 PMID:18703711.

Von Hippel, E. (2005). *Democratizing innovation.* Cambridge, MA: MIT Press.

Vukovic, M., & Bartolini, C. (2010). Towards a research agenda for enterprise crowdsourcing. *Lecture Notes in Computer Science, 6415,* 425–434. doi:10.1007/978-3-642-16558-0_36.

Wald, D. J., Quitoriano, V., & Dewey, J. W. (2006). *USGS "Did You Feel It?" community Internet intensity maps: Macroseismic data collection via the Internet.* Presented at the First European conference on earthquake engineering and seismology, Geneva, Switzerland. Retrieved September 15, 2012, from http://ehp2-earthquake.wr.usgs.gov/earthquakes/pager/

Wald, D., Quitoriano, V., Worden, C., Hopper, M., & Dewey, J. (2011). USGS "Did You Feel It?" Internet-based macroseismic intensity maps. *Annals of Geophysics, 54*(6).

Walsh, J. (2008). The beginning and end of neogeography. *Geo. Connexion, 7,* 28–30.

Wang, L., Bretschneider, S., & Gant, J. (2005). *Evaluating web-based e-government services with a citizen-centric approach.* Paper presented at the 38th Hawaii International Conference on System Sciences. Hawaii, HI.

Wang, X., & Bryer, T. A. (2012). Assessing the costs of public participation: A case study of two online participation mechanisms. *American Review of Public Administration,* 0275074012438727, first published on March 21, 2012 doi:10.1177/0275074012438727

Wang, X. (2001). Assessing public participation in U.S. cities. *Public Performance & Management Review, 24*(4), 322–336. doi:10.2307/3381222.

Wareham, J., Levy, A., & Shi, W. (2004). Wireless diffusion and mobile computing: Implications for the digital divide. *Telecommunications Policy, 28*(5-6), 439–457. doi:10.1016/j.telpol.2003.11.005.

Warf, B. (2001). Segues into cyberspace: Multiple geographies of the digital divide. *Environment and Planning. B, Planning & Design, 28,* 1, 3–19. doi:10.1068/b2691.

Warf, B., & Sui, D. (2010). From GIS to neogeography: Ontological implications and theories of truth. *Annals of GIScience, 26*(4), 197–209.

Warren, M. E., & Pearse, H. (2008). *Designing deliberative democracy: The British Columbia citizens' assembly.* Cambridge, UK: Cambridge University Press. doi:10.1017/CBO9780511491177.

Warschauer, M., & Matuchniak, T. (2010). New technology and digital worlds: Analyzing evidence of equity in access, use, and outcomes. *Review of Research in Education, 34*(1), 179–225. doi:10.3102/0091732X09349791.

Weare, C., Musso, J., & Hale, M. (1999). Electronic democracy and the diffusion of municipal web pages in California. *Administration & Society, 31.*

Weber, L., Loumakis, A., & Bergman, J. (2003). Who participates and why? An analysis of citizens on the Internet and the mass public. *Social Science Computer Review, 21*(1), 25–32. doi:10.1177/0894439302238969.

Weerakkody, V., Janssen, M., & Dwivedi, Y. K. (2009). *Handbook of research on ICT-enabled transformational government: A global perspective.* IGI Global. doi:10.4018/978-1-60566-390-6.

Weiner, D., & Harris, T. M. (2003). Community-integrated GIS for land reform in South Africa. *URISA Journal, 15*(2), 61–73.

Weiner, D., Warner, T., Harris, T., & Levin, R. (1995). Apartheid representations in a digital landscape: GIS, remote sensing, and local knowledge in Kiepersol, South Africa. *Cartography and Geographic Information Systems, 22,* 30–44. doi:10.1559/152304095782540537.

Weiser, M. (1991). The computer for the 21st Century. *Scientific American, 265*(3), 94–104. doi:10.1038/scientificamerican0991-94.

Welch, E. W., Hinnant, C. C., & Moon, M. J. (2005). Linking citizen satisfactio with e-government and trust in government. *Journal of Public Administration: Research and Theory, 15*(3).

West, D. (2000). *Assessing e-government: The internet, democracy, and service delivery by state and federal governments.* Providence, RI: Brown University.

West, D. M. (2004). E-government and the transformation of service delivery and citizen attitudes. *Public Administration Review, 64*(1), 13. doi:10.1111/j.1540-6210.2004.00343.x.

West, D. M. (2005). *Digital government: Technology and public sector performance.* Princeton: Princeton University Press.

Whitla, P. (2009). Crowdsourcing and its application in marketing activities. *Contemporary Management Research, 5*(1), 15–28.

Wieczorek, J., Guo, Q., & Hijmans, R. (2004). The point-radius method for georeferencing locality descriptions and calculating associated uncertainty. *International Journal of Geographical Information Science, 18*(8), 745–767. doi:10.1080/13658810412331280211.

Wienand, G. (2007). Wie unterstützt geoinformation unser Gesundheitswesen. In J. Schweikart & P. Schatzl (Eds.), *GIS – Zeitschrift für Geoinformatik, (10) 2007.* Retrieved March 12, 2012, from http://www.medint.at/healthgis/motivation.htm

Wiggins, A. (2012, February). *Motivation by design: Technologies, experiences and incentives.* Paper presented at the 2nd Citizen Cyberscience Summit, London, UK.

Wiggins, A., & Crowston, K. (2010). Distributed scientific collaboration: Research opportunities in citizen science. In *The Changing Dynamics of Scientific Collaboration, CSCW 2010 Workshop.* Savannah, GA.

Wiggins, A., & Crowston, K. (2011). From conservation to crowdsourcing: A typology of citizen science. *44th Hawai International Conference on system Sciences (HICSS).*

Wikimapia. (2012). Official Wikimapia FAQ. *Wikimapia.* Retrieved from http://wikimapia.org/wiki/Official_Wikimapia_FAQ

Wikipadia. (2012). *Mobile app.* Retrieved July 24th, 2012, from http://en.wikipedia.org/wiki/Mobile_app

Wilderman, C. C., Barron, A., & Imgrund, L. (2004). Top down or bottom up? ALLARM's experience with two operational models for community science. In *Proceedings of the 4th National Water Quality Monitoring Council Conference.* Chattanooga, Tennessee, USA, May 17-20, 2004.

Wilderman, C. C. (2007). Models of community science: Design lessons from the field. In McEver, C., Bonney, R., Dickinson, J., Kelling, S., Rosenberg, K., & Shirk, J. L. (Eds.), *Citizen science toolkit conference.* Cornell Laboratory of Ornithology.

Wilson, D. B. (2009). Weaving the Navajo.Net. *Journal on Telecommunications & High Technology Law, 7*(2), 425–461.

Wilson, T. D. et al. (1999). *Uncertainty in information seeking.* Sheffield, UK: University of Sheffield.

Wong, W., & Welch, E. (2004). Does e-government promote accountability? A comparative analysis of website openness and government accountability. *Governance: An International Journal of Policy, Administration and Institutions, 17*(2), 275–297. doi:10.1111/j.1468-0491.2004.00246.x.

Wood, F. B. et al. (2003). A practical approach to e-government web evaluation. *IT Professional, 7.*

Wübben, M. (2008). *Analytical CRM: Developing and maintaining profitable customer relationships in non-contractual settings* (1st ed.). Wiesbaden: Gabler.

Yancey, A. K., Ory, M. G., & Davis, S. M. (2006). Dissemination of physical activity promotion interventions in underserved populations. *American Journal of Preventive Medicine, 31*(4), 82–91. doi:10.1016/j.amepre.2006.06.020 PMID:16979472.

Yang, K., & Callahan, K. (2005). Assessing citizen involvement efforts by local governments. *Public Performance and Management Review, 29*(2), 191–216.

Yang, K., & Callahan, K. (2007). Citizen involvement efforts and bureaucratic responsiveness: Participatory values, stakeholder pressures, and administrative practicality. *Public Administration Review, 67*(2), 249–264. doi:10.1111/j.1540-6210.2007.00711.x.

Yang, K., & Pandey, S. K. (2011). Further dissecting the black box of citizen participation: When does citizen involvement lead to good outcomes? *Public Administration Review, 71*(6), 880–892. doi:10.1111/j.1540-6210.2011.02417.x.

Yetton, P. W., & Vroom, V. H. (1973). *Leadership and decision-making*. University of Pittsburgh Press.

Yovcheva, Z., Buhalis, D., & Gatzidis, C. (2012). Overview of Smartphone augmented reality applications for tourism. *e-Review of Tourism Research (eRTR), 10*(2). Retrieved July 24th, 2012, from http://eprints.bournemouth.ac.uk/20219/1/eRTR_SI_V10i2_Yovcheva_Buhalis_Gatzidis_63-66.pdf

Yu, B., & Roh, S. (2002). The effects of menu design on information-seeking performance and user's attitude on the world wide web. *Journal of the American Society for Information Science and Technology, 53*(11), 923–933. doi:10.1002/asi.10117.

Zavattaro, S. M. (2012). Records management, privacy, and social media: An overview. In Kloby, K., & D'Agostinho, M. J. (Eds.), *Citizen 2.0: Public and governmental interaction through Web 2.0 technologies* (pp. 41–64). Hershey: IGI-Global. doi:10.4018/978-1-4666-0318-9.ch003.

Zeile, P., Memmel, M., & Exner, J. (2012). A new urban sensing and monitoring approach: Tagging the city with the radar sensing App. In M. Schrenk, V. Popovich, P. Zeile, P. Elisei (Eds.), *Proceedings of REAL CORP 2012. International Conference on Urban Planning, Regional Development and Information Society (REAL CORP-12)*. Re-mixing the city, May 14-16, Vienna, Austria, CORP - Competence Center of Urban and Regional Planning, Schwechat, Austria, 5/2012, pp. 17-25.

Zhang, P., & Von Dran, G. M. (2000). Satisfiers and dissatisfiers: A two-factor model for website design and evaluation. *Journal of the American Society for Information Science American Society for Information Science, 51*(14), 15. doi:10.1002/1097-4571(2000)9999:9999<::AID-ASI1039>3.0.CO;2-O.

Zhang, Y., & Yang, K. (2009). Citizen participation in the budget process: The effect of city managers. *Journal of Public Budgeting, Accounting, and Financial Management, 21*(2), 289–317.

Zhuang, Z., Kim, K., & Singh, J. P. (2010). Improving energy efficiency of location sensing on Smartphones. *MobiSys '10 Proceedings of the 8th international conference on Mobile systems, applications, and services* (pp. 315-330).

Zielstra, D., & Zipf, A. (2010). *A comparative study of proprietary geodata and volunteered geographic information for Germany*. Paper presented at the 13th AGILE International Conference on Geographic Information Science, Guimarães.

Zmuda, N. (2009, November 2). New Pepsi "Dewmocracy" push threatens to crowd out shops. *AdAge.com*. Retrieved September 15, 2012, from

Zook, M., Graham, M., Shelton, T., & Gorman, S. (2010). Volunteered geographic information and crowdsourcing disaster relief: A case study of the Haitian Earthquake. *World Medical & Health Policy, 2*(2), 6–32. doi:10.2202/1948-4682.1069.

About the Contributors

Carlos Nunes Silva, PhD, is Professor Auxiliar at the Institute of Geography and Spatial Planning, University of Lisbon, Portugal. His research interests are mainly focused on local government policies, history and theory of urban planning, urban and metropolitan governance, urban planning ethics, urban planning in Africa, research methods, e-government, and e-planning. His recent publications include the *Handbook of Research on E-Planning: ICT for Urban Development and Monitoring* (2010) and *Online Research Methods in Urban and Planning Studies: Design and Outcomes* (2012). He is the Editor-in-Chief of the *International Journal of E-Planning Research* (IJEPR).

* * *

Franziska Albrecht has been a Research Assistant at the International Institute for Applied Systems Analysis in the Ecosystems Services and Management Program since September 2011. From 2005 to 2008, she studied international forest ecosystem management at the University of Applied Sciences Eberswalde, Germany. In December 2011, she graduated with a Masters degree in forestry from the University of Natural Resources and Life Sciences in Vienna. Her research interests include ecosystem services, ecology and global information science, as well as remote sensing and land cover mapping.

Karl Atzmanstorfer is a Research Associate in the Paris-Lodron University Salzburg, Austria, and Academic Coordinator of UNIGIS in Latin America, University San Francisco de Quito (USFQ), Ecuador. Karl Atzmanstorfer holds an MSc in Applied Geoinformatics and an MSc in Geography, History, and Political/Social Sciences from Salzburg University. His scientific interests focus on the use of GIS in Latin America. He worked on the application of GIS in Public Health Planning at UNAN Leon, Nicaragua and on the development of a GIS-model for environmental niche detection that was designed to support the diversification of tropical smallholder agriculture with high-value crops (master thesis at the International Center of Tropical Agriculture, CIAT, Colombia). Since 2009, he is coordinating the postgraduate distance learning program UNIGIS in Latin America (www.unigis.net/quito). Furthermore, he is giving support to the participatory capacity building initiative AmazonGISnet, an indigenous-lead initiative for the local and regional planning of the Ecuadorian Amazon Provinces, and other community based (GIS-) projects in Ecuador.

Ashwin Balakrishnan is currently a candidate for a Masters in City Planning degree at the Massachusetts Institute of Technology in Cambridge, Massachusetts. He is focusing on urban health and economic development, and how planners can use technology to improve public participation in urban planning processes. His previous experience includes working as a campaign coordinator for the Southern Bronx River Watershed Alliance – a collaboration of Bronx-based community organizations and city-wide advocacy organizations working primarily to remove the Sheridan Expressway and replace it with housing, open space, and economic opportunities for the South Bronx. Ashwin graduated from Pomona College in 2009 with a degree in Environmental Analysis, Biology. He has researched and worked on environmental justice and health projects in California, Louisiana, and India.

Elena Bellio, M.sc., Research fellow at CERMES - Department of Marketing of Bocconi University, Milan, Italy. Her research activities are focused on the following areas: Social and public service Marketing, E-government, E-Health, Innovation and marketing of public services, Citizen Relationship Management. She has several published papers and articles on national and international reviews.

Thomas Blaschke is Full Professor at the Paris-Lodron University Salzburg, Austria, Deputy Chair, Department of Geoinformatics, Head of Research Studio iSPACE, and Director of Doctoral College GIScience. His research interests include methodological issues of the integration of GIS, remote sensing and image processing also with aspects of participation and human-environment interaction. Prior positions comprise several lecturer, senior lecturer, and professor positions in Germany, Austria and the UK as well as temporary affiliations as guest professor and visiting scientist in Germany and the US including a Fulbright professorship at California State University. His academic record yields 280+ scientific publications including 60 journal publications. He is author, co-author or editor of 17 books and received several academic prices and awards including the Christian-Doppler Prize 1995. He has been and is project leader in various international and national research projects and serves on various editing boards of international journals, conference committees and for a dozen National research councils.

Daren C. Brabham is an assistant professor in the School of Journalism & Mass Communication at the University of North Carolina at Chapel Hill. He is also a faculty fellow in the Center for Urban and Regional Studies and an executive education instructor for the Kenan-Flagler Business School at UNC-Chapel Hill. Among the first to publish research on crowdsourcing, his work has appeared in *Convergence; First Monday; Information, Communication & Society; Planning Theory*; and *The Participatory Cultures Handbook*; and his research has been funded by the U.S. Federal Transit Administration and the IBM Center for the Business of Government. His first book, *Crowdsourcing*, will be published in spring 2013 with MIT Press. He earned a B.A. at Trinity University and an M.S. and Ph.D. in communication at the University of Utah.

Marc Brenman was Executive Director, Washington Human Rights Commission, and Senior Policy Advisor for Civil Rights, U.S. Dept. of Transportation. His work focuses on race, limited English proficiency, disability, sex discrimination, LGBT rights, culturally appropriate ADR, corporate social responsibility, international human rights, and other social justice issues. He co-authored, *The Right to Transportation* and *Planning as if People Matter: Governing for Social Equity* with Tom Sanchez. He has taught civil rights history, human rights, public policy development, and advocacy at Evergreen College. In 2010, he assisted Public Advocates in winning the first civil rights case under the federal stimulus law, for $70 million. In 2012, he won first prize in the Americans for Democratic Action essay contest, on what Martin Luther King would say to President Obama.

Thomas A. Bryer is assistant professor and director of the Center for Public and Nonprofit Management in the School of Public Administration at the University of Central Florida. His research and teaching focuses on public participation, cross-sector collaboration, and citizenship. He has published widely in top ranked journals including *Public Administration Review, Journal of Public Administration Research and Theory, American Review of Public Administration*, and *Public Performance and Management Review*. He has presented his research on social media for public participation in the United States and Europe.

Luca Buccoliero, PhD in Public Management, is Professor at Bocconi University (Department of Marketing), Milan, Italy, senior Professor at SDA Bocconi School of Management and coordinator of "Citizen Customer" research lab at CERMES Bocconi (Centre for Research on Marketing & Services). He was visiting researcher at Waseda University Tokyo. His fields of research and teaching include the following: Information and Communication Technologies in the Public Sector, E-health, E-government. He has several articles published on national and international journals.

Yannis Charalabidis is Assistant Professor in the University of Aegean, in the area of e-Governance Information Systems, coordinating policymaking, research, and pilot application projects for governments and enterprises worldwide. A computer engineer with a PhD in complex information systems, he has been employed for several years as an Executive Director in Singular IT Group, a leading software development and company expansion in Eastern Europe, India and the US. During the last 20 years he has been the coordinator or technical leader in numerous FP6, FP7 and National research projects in the areas of e-Business and e-Governance (PRAXIS, GENESIS, WEB.DEP, LEXIS, MOMENTUM, FEED, Greek e-GIF, Greek Interoperability Centre, PADGETS, CROSSROAD, ENSEMBLE, ENGAGE). He has published more the 100 papers in international journals and conferences. He is Best Paper Award winner of the EGOV 2008 Conference, Best e-Government Paper Nominee in the 42nd HICSS Conference and 1st Prize Nominee in the 2009 European e-Government Awards.

Caren Cooper is a scientist at the Cornell Lab of Ornithology, Cornell University, USA. Cooper carries out research on birds almost exclusively with data collected by willing and able hobbyists. Research via citizen science permits her to study ecological patterns and processes at continental-scales, in natural areas and around residences. Cooper has a PhD in Biology from Virginia Tech, a Masters in Zoology & Physiology from the University of Wyoming, and a Bachelor of Science in Zoology from North Carolina State University. Cooper is co-editor of an upcoming special feature about citizen science for the online journal *Ecology & Society*. Also, Cooper is a Senior Fellow in the Environmental Leadership Program, writing a book exploring the social and scientific impacts of citizen science, highlighting stories of the co-production of knowledge around the globe. Cooper is a guest blogger for *Scientific American* and blogger for *Citizen Sci* in the PLoS blog network.

Doris Dransch is Professor for Geoinformation Management and Visualization at Helmholtz Centre Potsdam, German Research Centre for Geosciences, and Humboldt-University at Berlin. She studied Geography, Geology and Cartography at Free University Berlin and received her Ph.D. in Geography. She is member of the Center for Disaster and Risk Reduction Technology (CEDIM) and member of the Advisory Board of the German Committee for Disaster Reduction. Her research area is Geoinformation Science. One focus is on the application of volunteered geographic information VGI in disaster management. Another research field is visual analytics which facilitates data exploration by interactive visual means.

Enrico Ferro is the Head of the Business Model and Policy Innovation Unit at Mario Boella Institute (ISMB), a research team studying the economic, social and policy implications of information and communication technologies. Over the last ten years Dr. Ferro has worked in many projects financed by the European Commission with roles ranging from scientific supervisor to senior expert (Regional-IST, UNDERSTAND, B3Regions, IDEAL-EU, PADGETS, CROSSROAD, ENGAGE). Dr. Ferro also holds an Adjunct Professor position at the Polytechnic of Turin and at the International Labour Bureau of the United Nations where he regularly lectures on information management and strategies in both the public and the private sector. His research work has produced over forty academic publications, one handbook of research and over fifty research reports.

Joachim Fohringer is a scientist at the Centre for Disaster Management and Risk Reduction Technology, a research association of the German Research Centre for Geosciences (GFZ) and the Karlsruhe Institute of Technology (KIT). He received a Diploma in Computer Science from the Free University Berlin. His research work is related to Web-based information systems and social media. One focus is on the application of Volunteered Geographic Information (VGI) in disaster management. He investigates localization and evaluation of messages from micro-blogging-services like Twitter for rapid damage assessment after hazard events such as floods, earthquakes, or hurricanes.

Steffen Fritz is a Research Scholar in the Ecosystem Services and Management Programme at the International Institute for Applied Systems Analysis (IIASA). He is the driving force behind Geo-Wiki, a global land cover validation tool based on crowdsourcing. He is currently the principal investigator of several projects funded by the Austrian Agency for the Promotion of Science, the European Space Agency, and the European Union. Dr Fritz studied physics and geography at the University of Tübingen, received his MSc from the University of Durham in 1996 and a PhD from the University of Leeds in 2001. He worked as a post-doc at the Joint Research Centre in 2002 where his tasks were to mosaic, harmonize, and produce the Global Land Cover 2000 database, and to carry out the validation of the regional GLC-2000 contributions within the tropics.

Stefan Höffken is scientific researcher at the University of Kaiserslautern (Germany), department of Prof. Dr.-Ing. Bernd Streich, since 2009. He was lecturer for Cartography, Webmapping, and GIS 2010/2011 and research assistant for Emotional Webmapping in 2009 at the University of Technology of Berlin. He worked at Zebralog (eParticipation, Online Moderation) from 2007 - 2009, and as a freelancer in different Planning Offices in Berlin. He is a founder and member of Urbanophil - Netzwerk für urbane Kultur e.V (www.urbanophil.net), member of the Editorial staff for the journal *PLANERIN* (www.srl.de/planerin), and author for BAUWELT (www.bauweltde).

Jim Huebner is a senior management and information technology professional, having held chief executive positions in business, government, and non-profit sectors. He specializes in strategic planning and technology, and has designed and managed customer relationship management projects for multinational companies since the early 1990s. He reports and lectures on project management, marketing, and finance, as well as cultural psychology, sustainability, and social innovation. His PhD research at University of Waterloo examines the role of ICT and specifically CiRM in municipal public engagement. He holds an MBA from Wilfrid Laurier University, BA from University of Waterloo, BEd from University of Manitoba, professional certification in municipal finance, is a certified technology professional, a Certified Management Accountant, and a Senior Member of the American Society for Quality. He is founder of the Strategic Participatory Applications Research Cluster (SPARC) at University of Waterloo, has a passion for philanthropy, and is a member of the Order of Arctic Adventurers.

Atreyi Kankanhalli is Associate Professor in the Department of Information Systems and Assistant Dean (Undergraduate Studies) in the School of Computing at the National University of Singapore (NUS). She serves as the Coordinator of the Service Systems Innovation Research Laboratory at NUS. Dr. Kankanhalli conducts research in the areas of knowledge management, IT innovation adoption and change management, and IT-enabled innovation in service sectors (e.g., Government, Healthcare) with a wide range of organizations sponsored by government and industry grants. Her work has appeared in a number of journals including *MIS Quarterly, Information Systems Research*, and *Journal of Management Information Systems*. Dr. Kankanhalli serves on the editorial boards of *MIS Quarterly, Information Systems Research*, and *IEEE Transactions on Engineering Management*. She is a recipient of the IBM Faculty Award and the IBM Smarter Planet Industry Skills Innovation Award among others. She has been listed among the leading IS researchers globally.

Euripidis Loukis is Associate Professor of Information Systems & Decision Support Systems at the Department of Information and Communication Systems Engineering, University of the Aegean. Previously he has been Information Systems Advisor at the Ministry to the Presidency of the Government of Greece (1991-2002), and National Representative of Greece in the programs 'Telematics' and 'IDA' (Interchange of Data between Administrations) of the European Union. He has extensive research activity in the areas of e-government, e-participation, ICT-induced structural change of firms and innovation, and has participated in numerous national and international research projects. Dr Euripidis Loukis is the author of more than 100 scientific publications in international journals and conferences in the above areas. One of his publications has been honored with the International Award of the American Society of Mechanical Engineers (ASME), while another one has been honored with the best paper award of the European Mediterranean Conference on Information Systems (EMCIS).

Christian Lucas is a post-doc researcher at the Institute of Photogrammetry and Remote Sensing at Karlsruhe Institute of Technology (KIT). At the same time, Dr. Lucas is member of the Center for Disaster Management and Risk Reduction Technology (CEDIM), a research association of the German Research Centre for Geosciences (GFZ) and the KIT. He studied Geodaesie and Geoinformatics at the Leibniz University of Hanover and obtained in 2010 a PhD in the field of spatial information science from KIT. His research interests are on spatial information theory with a focus on methods and algorithms for modeling uncertain and fuzzy spatial information. Currently, he investigates the field of crowdsourcing in the context of disaster management.

Ian McCallum is a researcher in the Ecosystem Services and Management (ESM) Program at the International Institute for Applied Systems Analysis (IIASA) in Austria. He holds a graduate degree in Forest Science from Lakehead University in Canada, where he specialized in the application of geographic information systems and remote sensing. He has contributed to numerous research projects at IIASA applying geo-spatial analysis to global environmental problems ranging including biomass estimation, carbon accounting and modelling, and global land cover validation. He is an active member of the Geo-Wiki team and co-leads the GEO Task ID-03, which focuses on the incentives needed to join the Global Earth Observation System of Systems (GEOSS).

Kimberly L. Nelson is an assistant professor in the Division of Public Administration at Northern Illinois University. She holds a bachelor's degree from Virginia Tech and a Ph.D. from North Carolina State University. Her research and teaching focuses on local government management with emphases on form of government, council relations, and local government innovation. She has published a number of book chapters and her work has appeared in academic journals including *The American Review of Public Administration, Urban Affairs Review*, and *State and Local Government Review*. In addition, Dr. Nelson has served as a local government consultant for strategic planning and facilitating board relationships.

Nancy J. Obermeyer is an Associate Professor of Geography at Indiana State University, USA. Her research interests have emphasized the institutional and societal ramifications of implementing geographic information systems. She has also been involved with the development of certification for GIS professionals, and is co-author (with Jeffrey Pinto) of Managing GIS (Guilford 1994, 2004). In an earlier career in public service, Nancy held professional assignments with the State of Illinois in the areas of Planning, Transportation, and Energy. Nancy earned her Ph.D. at the University of Chicago in 1987 and did a Post-Doc at the National Center for Geographic Information and Analysis at the University of Maine from 1988-1990. She is currently a member of the board of directors of the Urban and Regional Information Systems Association.

Michael Obersteiner is leader of the Ecosystems Services and Management (ESM) Program at the International Institute for Applied Systems Analysis (IIASA) in Laxenburg, Austria. He joined IIASA's Forestry Program (FOR) in 1993 and has been leading the Group on Global Land-Use Modeling and Environmental Economics since 2001. His background includes the fields of global terrestrial ecosystems and economics, having completed graduate studies both in Austria and abroad. Dr Obersteiner's research experience stretches from plant physiology and biophysical modeling in the areas of ecosystems, forestry, and agriculture to environmental economics, bioenergy engineering, and climate change sciences. Dr Obersteiner has been a consultant to a number of national and international organizations, including inter alia the European Commission, WWF, OECD, and other national and international institutions.

Michele Osella holds a Researcher position at Istituto Superiore Mario Boella in Turin, Italy. He works in the Business Model & Policy Innovation Unit, supporting policy makers and managers in using ICTs as leverage to favor socioeconomic development and competitiveness. In the academic sphere, he is PhD Candidate and Adjunct Lecturer at the Polytechnic of Turin. Prominent strands of research on which he is focused are social computing, open innovation, as well as Internet economics, with a keen interest on groundbreaking business models. Taking into account afore-said scientific areas, Michele is currently involved in a number of national and international projects developed both in private and public sectors.

Christoph Perger received his MSc degree from the University of Applied Sciences in Wiener Neustadt (FHWN) in 2009 in Information Technology and Geographic Information Science. He worked there from 2005 to 2009 as a research and project assistant and, during an internship at the International Institute for Applied Systems Analysis (IIASA), began the development of Geo-Wiki.org, a global land cover validation tool based on crowdsourcing. Since 2009, he has worked as a research and teaching assistant in the field of GIS applications, data modelling, and application and Web programming at the FHWN. He rejoined IIASA as a Research Scholar in 2011 where he continues the work on Geo-Wiki and related land cover and remote sensing topics.

Kathrin Poser studied Geoecology at the University of Potsdam and also holds an M.Sc. degree in Photogrammetry and Geoinformatics from the Hochschule für Technik Stuttgart - University of Applied Sciences. Her research experience includes hydrological modelling, flood damage estimation and geographical data analysis and management. She is currently working as a Marie Curie Experienced Researcher at Water Insight BV in Wageningen, where she is responsible for spatial data management and analysis as well as the design and implementation of Web-based information systems. In parallel, she is finishing up her doctoral thesis on "Humans as Sensors - Integration and Assessment of Information from the Affected Population for Flood Disaster Management" at the Humboldt-University in Berlin.

Tom W. Sanchez earned his PhD in City Planning from Georgia Tech in 1996 and has since taught at Iowa State University, Portland State University, the University of Utah, and is currently professor of Urban Affairs and Planning at Virginia Tech. Sanchez conducts research in the areas of environmental justice, technology, and the social aspects of planning and policy. He also serves as editor of *Housing Policy Debate* and is a nonresident senior fellow of the Brookings Institution. In 2012, he co-authored *Planning as if People Matter: Governing for Social Equity* (Island Press) with Marc Brenman. In 2007, they co-authored *The Right to Transportation: Moving to Equity* (American Planning Association). In 2013, he will co-teach with Jennifer Evans-Cowley (Ohio State University), a Massive Open Online Course (MOOC) on technology and cities.

Dmitry Schepashchenko has been a Research Scholar at the International Institute of Applied Systems Analysis (IIASA) since 2007 and is a professor in the Department of Pedology at Moscow State Forest University (MSFU), where he graduated in forestry with a specialization in soil science. He received a PhD degree in soil science in 1993 from the Dokuchaev Soil Science Institute in Moscow. His recent projects have included full carbon accounting of Northern Eurasia and the development of biomass. geo-wiki.org, which is a branch of the Geo-Wiki crowdsourcing tool for visualization and improvement of global and regional biomass datasets.

Christian Schill received his diploma in physics in 1997 from the Albert-Ludwig-University of Freiburg, Germany, and joined the Department of Remote Sensing and Landscape Information Systems (FELIS) as a research scholar in 2001. His main interests are geodata infrastructures, the European INSPIRE directive and related activities, ISO- and OGC-Standards (Web services like WFS, WMS metadata [ISO 19115/ISO 19139], GML) as well as geodatabases, namely PostGIS on postgresql. He joined the Geo-Wiki team in 2009 to work on the backend of this crowdsourcing platform.

Linda See is a Research Scholar at the International Institute for Applied Systems Analysis (IIASA) in the Ecosystems Services and Management Programme. She has a PhD in spatial applications of fuzzy logic from the School of Geography, University of Leeds, where she taught for 11 years as a Senior Lecturer in Computational Geography and GIS. She has an MSc in physical geography form McMaster University and a BSc in physical geography and environmental management from the University of Toronto. In between her MSc and PhD, she spent one year working at the Max Planck Institut für Aeronomie near Göttingen followed by four years at the Food and Agriculture Organization of the United Nations in Rome. She is now working on Geo-Wiki, land cover validation, and crowdsourcing.

Rajeev Sharma is Associate Professor in the School of Information Systems and Technology at the University of Wollongong, Australia. His research interests include the implementation of IS innovations, the management of IS projects, and the strategic management of IS. His research has been published in *MIS Quarterly, Information and Organization, Information Systems Journal*, and *Journal of Information Technology*, as well as proceedings of the International Conference on Information Systems, European Conference on Information Systems, Pacific Asia Conference on Information Systems, and presented at the Academy of Management Meetings. Rajeev serves on the editorial boards of the *Journal of Information Technology* and *Journal of Strategic Information Systems*. He has over seven years' experience in industry, including executive teaching and consulting to large corporations. He is a graduate of the Australian Graduate School of Management, the Indian Institute of Management Bangalore, and the University of Delhi.

Bernd Streich is Professor in Kaiserslautern at the Department for Computer Aided Design in Urban Planning and Architecture. He received his Doctoral degree in 1983 (Dissertation: "Simulation of Urban Form/Design by Using Computer Techniques") and his Habilitation in 1987 ("Foundations of a Theory on General Leading Concepts in Urban Planning"). From 1997-2001 he was substitute of the professorship for urban planning at the University of Bonn. Bernd Streich is member of the German Academy for Urban Development and Regional Planning (DASL), Academy for Spatial Research and Planning (ARL), and Higher Expert Committee for Land Valuation and Real Property of Rheinland-Pfalz.

Mahdieh Taher is a research assistant in the Department of Information Systems, School of Computing at the National University of Singapore (NUS). Her research interests include strategic information systems, enterprise systems implementation, and qualitative research methods. Her research has been published in the proceedings of the International Conference on Information Systems (ICIS) and Pacific Asia Conference on Information Systems (PACIS).

Marijn Van der Velde is a Research Scholar with IIASA's Ecosystems Services and Management (ESM) Program. He obtained his MSc in Physical Geography from the University of Amsterdam and his PhD in Environmental Sciences from the University of Louvain. Marijn continued with a NOAA Climate & Global Change Postdoctoral Fellowship at the Earth Institute of Columbia University in the USA. Prior to joining IIASA, he was a Research Scientist at the Joint Research Centre of the European Commission. His research focuses on large-scale assessments of the management and interactions of agriculture and natural resources under increasing societal demands and climate change combining insights from models and experimental data, including the analysis of Web search data for environmental applications. For further information see www.marijnvandervelde.org.

Barney Warf is a professor of Geography at the University of Kansas. His research and teaching interests lie within the broad domain of human geography. Much of his research concerns economic geography, emphasizing services and telecommunications. His work straddles contemporary political economy and social theory on the one hand and traditional quantitative, empirical approaches on the other. He has studied a range of topics that fall under the umbrella of globalization, including New York as a global city, telecommunications, offshore banking, international networks of financial and producer services, and the geographies of the Internet. He has also written on military spending, voting technologies, the U.S. Electoral College, and religious diversity. He has authored, co-authored, or co-edited seven books, two encyclopedias, 32 book chapters, and roughly 100 refereed journal articles.

Index

A

ad-hoc democracy 264, 269
advocacy planning model 175
Alliance for Aquatic Resource Monitoring (AL-LARM) 182
American Civil Liberties Union (ACLU) 81, 91
Application Programming Interfaces (API) 70
Arab Spring 39, 80-82, 87-88, 90, 93, 95, 118
Asynchronous Javascript and XML (AJAX) 70
Augmented Reality (AR) 217

B

balanced scorecards 268
baseline research hypothesis 285
Bay Area Rapid Transit 38-39
Broadcast Search Approach (BS) 54

C

Canadian Geographic Information System (CGIS) 145
Carrier IQ 81, 90-91, 93-94, 96
Chief Administrative Officer 231, 235-236
chronic pulmonary occlusive disease (COPD) 309
citizen-centric CiRM 251, 265
Citizen centric e-government 286
citizen empowerment 284-285, 287, 291, 293, 302
Citizen relationship management (CiRM) 247
Citizen Science 1, 3-4, 9, 11, 13, 15, 99, 123, 141, 143, 172-175, 178-196, 218, 220, 222
Citizens Web Empowerment Index (CWEI) 284, 290, 292, 302
citizen value 257, 264-265, 274, 282
civic engagement 13-14, 44-45, 72, 172, 194, 210, 226-232, 236, 238, 240-246, 256
Cloud services 248, 250, 273, 282
collaborative approach 257-258
Collaborative Decision Support Systems (CDSS) 152

collaborative governance 169, 258, 280
Common Gateway Interface (CGI) 101
Community PlanIt 188
Community Service Organizations (CSOs) 274
Context Aware Sensors 202
cracking 58
crowd resistance 57-58
crowdslapping 57-58, 68
customer-centric CRM 251, 258
customer facing 250
customer focus 249, 251
customer relationship management (CRM) 247, 277-278
customer understanding 251
Cyclopath 153, 210-211, 215

D

data quality 98, 110-111, 114, 120, 123, 135, 137, 154
Decision Support Systems (DSS) 149
deliberative dimension 265
destructive crowdslapping 57-58
Digital Chart of the World (DCW) 121
direct democracy 22-23, 25-26, 33, 36
disaster management 17, 98-102, 105-109, 111-113, 115, 118
discourse theories 24-25, 33
disinhibition effect 58, 65
disruptive crowdslapping 57-58
Distributed Human Intelligence Tasking Approach (DHIT) 56
do-it-yourself (DIY) 217

E

E-consultation 2, 290-291, 293, 295, 302
E-decision making process 290-293, 295, 302
e-democracy 1-2, 4, 8, 13, 16, 19-21, 23-29, 31-40, 44-45, 224, 281, 290

e-democratization 20-21, 26, 29
e-government 36-40, 44-45, 278
engaged citizenship 227
Engagement Game Lab (EGL) 178
e-tools 1, 5-8, 173, 177-179, 183, 185, 187
European Network Exploring Research into Geospatial
     Information Crowdsourcing (ENERGIC) 135
extensibility 203-204, 248, 250-251, 254, 257, 259,
     263, 269-270, 273-274, 282

F

face-to-face human interactions 40
Food and Agriculture Organization (FAO) 158
Foursquare 201, 235, 237-238
free speech 50-51, 56-58, 61-62, 84

G

general circulation models (GCMs) 136
General Packet Radio Service (GPRS) 203
Geographic Information Science (GIScience) 15, 79,
     151, 158, 162-163, 165, 167
geographic information systems (GIS) 36, 144-145,
     161, 170, 192
geoslavery 80-81, 84, 92, 96
geovisualization 80-81, 96, 163, 194
Geo-Wiki 11, 16, 66, 119-120, 124-126, 134-138
Global Navigation Satellite Systems (GNSS) 146
global positioning system (GPS) 84, 107, 145
Global Rural Urban Mapping Project (GRUMP) 121
Google Earth 17, 70-71, 84, 120, 125, 133-134, 144,
     147-148, 151, 165, 169
government crowdsourcing application 59
greenhouse gas (GHG) 120

H

hackathon 123
high-speed downlink packet Access (HSDPA) 203
human sensors 100

I

ideal speech situation 69-70, 75, 79
InfoBrión 72-74, 76
Informal Science Education (ISE) 186
informational/transactional relationship 263
information systems (IS) 19, 29
InnoCentive 52, 54, 63
Institute for Prospective Technological Studies
     (IPTS) 304

institutionalization level 265
intensity of collaboration 265
internal data quality 110
International Association for Urban Climate (IAUC)
     136
International Atomic Energy Agency (IAEA) 88
International Geoscience and Remote Sensing Soci-
     ety (IGARSS) 125
Internetworking 273

K

key performance indicators (KPIs) 270
Knowledge Discovery and Management Approach
     (KDM) 53

L

learning regions 71
Local Health Authority (LHA) 309
local health unit (LHU) 309
localization 98, 100-101, 106-109
location-based-services (LBS) 201
Long Term Evolution (LTE) 203

M

MapQuest 71
Massively Multiplayer Online Games (MMOGs)
     178
Matrix of Civic Implication 265, 267, 278
Metropolitan Area Planning Council (MAPC) 178
Microblogging 115, 118
micro-crowdsourcing 40
minority rights 26, 34
mParticipation 199-200, 202, 205-209, 212, 215-
     218, 224
multi-modal access 256
multi-tenancy 273

N

National Center for Geographic Information and
     Analysis (NCGIA) 82
National Oceanic and Atmospheric Association
     (NOAA) 184
neogeography 1, 3-4, 9, 11-12, 14-15, 69-72, 74-79,
     150-152, 165, 168
New Public Management movement (NPM) 255
non-contractual 274, 278
non-governmental organizations (NGOs) 82, 146

O

Oak Ridge National Laboratory (ORNL) 121
Occupy Movement 80, 82, 87, 89-90, 94, 96
Open Geospatial Consortium (OGC) 147
Open Source Politics 2
Open Source Urbanism 2
OpenStreetMaps (OSM) 70, 84, 93, 97, 101-102,
    107, 111-112, 114, 118, 123, 139-140, 151,
    201, 205
Operation Linescan System 121
out-of-the-box (OOTB) 250

P

Padget campaign 307, 318
Padgets 303-304, 306-310, 315-316, 318
participation architecture 257-258
Participatory GIS (PGIS) 158
Participatory Rural Appraisal (PRA) 158
participatory sensing 190, 192, 197, 208, 219
Peer-Vetted Creative Production Approach (PVCP) 55
Pew Internet & American Life Project 14, 40, 42-43, 46
planning process 12, 36, 83, 151, 165, 172-173, 175,
    177-178, 182, 187-188, 191
policy-advisory spectrum 50-51, 60-61
prosumption 304
public interest 21, 47, 118, 158, 175-176
public participation GIS (PPGIS) 81, 96, 145-146,
    158, 170
public participation in scientific research (PPSR) 179

Q

Quora 235, 237-238

R

rational choice theories 25-26, 34
relational perspective 257, 277
return on investment (ROI) 252, 256

S

scientific research process 182
scope of application 254-255, 274
Securing Americans' Value and Efficiency (SAVE) 54
Service Quality (SERVQUAL) 290
smart city 284, 306, 318
Social choice theories 24-25, 34

social embeddedness 75
social equity 35-36, 45
socio-economic theories 24-26, 34
Software as a Service (SaaS) 250
Spatial Data Infrastructure (SDI) 149
Spatial Decision Support Systems (SDSS) 144-145,
    149, 170
strategy-implementation gap 268
strategy mapping 268
supply-side approach 39

T

technological extensibility 248, 250-251, 257, 282
telemedicine 303-304, 309-310, 312, 314-316, 318
Textizen 209, 212-213, 215, 223
Sensor Web Enablement Initiative (SWE) 149
third generation mobile cellular technology (3G)
    203
transactive planning model 176

U

United Nations (UN) 253
Universal Mobile Telecommunication System
    (UMTS) 203
US Geological Survey (USGS) 53, 100
U.S. Patent and Trademark Office (USPTO) 53
Utah Transit Authority (UTA) 55

V

value delivery 265, 268, 271
value objective 250, 282
Verbano-Cusio-Ossola (VCO) 309
Virtual Globes 7, 84, 144, 147-149, 151, 154-155,
    161, 163, 170

W

Web portals 284, 290, 293, 296
Website Attribute Evaluation System (WAES) 289
Wheelmap 209-210, 215
wikification 69, 71, 78-79, 151, 167
Wiki Government 2, 13, 67, 78, 229, 244, 246
Wikimapia 84, 96-97, 110, 118, 153
Wireless Fidelity (WiFi) 73, 107
World Urban Database and Access Portal Tools
    (WUDAPT) 136

Lightning Source UK Ltd.
Milton Keynes UK
UKOW01n0101050614

232884UK00009B/48/P